((speak my name))

((speak my name))

BLACK MEN ON MASCULINITY AND THE AMERICAN DREAM

EDITED BY
DON BELTON

BEACON PRESS
BOSTON

Beacon Press
25 Beacon Street
Boston, Massachusetts 02108-2892

Beacon Press books
are published under the auspices of
the Unitarian Universalist Association of Congregations.

99 98 97   8 7 6 5 4 3 2

Text design by John Kane
Composition by Wilsted & Taylor

Library of Congress Cataloging-in-Publication Data

Speak my name: Black men on masculinity and the American dream /
    edited with an introduction by Don Belton; with a foreword by
    August Wilson.
        p.   cm.
    Includes bibliographical references.
    ISBN 0-8070-0936-9 (cloth)
    ISBN 0-8070-0937-7 (paper)
        1. Afro-American men.   2. Masculinity (Psychology)—United States.
    I. Belton, Don.
    E185.86.S685   1995
    155.8'496073'0081—dc20   95-22316
                                                        CIP

Our father's thoughts come shining down.
—Traditional

This book is dedicated to the Spirit.
In the name of Papa Legba,
James Baldwin,
Jack Johnson, Kid Thompson, Countee Cullen,
Langston Hughes, Sidney Bechet, Thomas Dorsey,
John Coltrane, Romare Bearden, Ralph Ellison, Duke Ellington,
Larry Young, Melvin Dixon, Jackie Wilson, Bruce Nugent, Alvin Ailey,
Frankie Lymon, Huey Newton, David Walker, Sun Ra, Sam Cooke,
Dexter Gordon, Prophet Jones, Harold Jackman, Eddie Kendricks,
Joseph Beam, Marvin Gaye, Oscar Micheaux, Beauford Delaney,
Marlon Riggs, Richard Wright, Frederick Douglass,
Thelonious Monk, Staggerlee, Arthur H. Fauset,
Will Marion Cook, Prophet Cherry, Reverend James Cleveland,
and Reverend Doctor Gates.
In the name of mercy,
ancestors, mysteries, and friends.

Father, I stretch my hand to Thee
No other help I know . . .
—Traditional

Contents

Foreword

August Wilson

The first male image that I carry is not of my father but of a family friend and neighbor, Charlie Burley, the brilliant Hall of Fame prizefighter. A combination of intelligence, the handsome yet bruised face, the swollen knuckles embodying the speed and power and grace of his rough trade, the starched white shirt, the embossed silk tie, the cashmere coat, the exquisite felt fur of the broad-brimmed quintessential hundred-dollar Stetson (the kind Staggerlee wore), and the highly polished yam-colored Florsheim shoes that completed his Friday night regalia. It was style with a capital S. But it was more than being a connoisseur of fine haberdashery; it was attitude and presentation. The men on the corner with their big hats and polished shoes carried and lent weight to a world that was beholden to their casual elegance as they mocked the condition of their life and paraded through the streets like warrior kings.

If men are warriors, then as black men we are warriors of a subject people whose history and relationship with the society in which we live has been a long and troubled one, involving, among other things, murder and mayhem. Reduced to its most fundamental truth, black men are a commodity of flesh and muscle which has lost its value in the marketplace. We are left over from history.

Out of the historical rubble of slavery, fired in the kiln of evolution and survival, black men like Charlie Burley forged and honed new disciplines and elevated their presence into an art. They were bad. If only in an abstract of style. A language of aesthetics that created its own rules and knew no limits. They styled because that is who they were. The style was not a comment. It was not how they saw themselves. It was who they were, and it was symphonic in its breadth and complexity. The style became all. It was the reason for being. And if they stumbled on their way to victory, the occasion had presented them with the possibility, however brief, that in one brilliant blaze of style and substance they might transform and forever enlarge the possibilities of what might exist. They might, by the sheer power of their presence, enlarge the universe.

It is clear that the idea we have of ourselves is drastically different from the images propagated and promoted by nineteenth-century Europe and twentieth-century America. What we lack is the ability to give the ideas and images we have of ourselves a widespread presence, to give them legitimacy and credence in the same manner in which the debasing and denigrating images that provide other Americans with a basis for their fear and dislike of us are legitimized by constant repetition through myriad avenues of broadcast and dissemination. That those images remain consistently unchallenged is one of our greatest failures as men charged with the defense of the body politic. Our ignorance of the value and the power of image as a contributing and determining factor in our condition—and most importantly in our future—is most telling in the cruel flowering of self-hate as evidenced by the suicidal bullets of misplaced rage and mock anarchy.

As men, we are charged with the defense of the race, of the ethnic tribes of our genetic marrow. We are charged with propagation and we are charged with the advancement of prosperity. But where as men do we find sustenance? In what place of our fathers, when from our father's house issues the prodigal who squanders the body's abilities? If our fathers faltered on the stairs to self-determination, we did not falter on the stairs to honor. Their courage has never been lacking. Our understanding of the processes that usurped and bludgeoned their identities, that deprived them of continuity, of their sense of history and well-being, has not been full and comprehensive. Depriving us of our language not only deprived us of a tool necessary for organizing and communicating ideas about the self and the world, it also deprived us of our understanding of our duty and the celebration of heroics.

Our duty as black men is to alter the relationship of power and responsibility. To move from the hull of a ship, so to speak, to a self-determining, self-respecting, and self-defending people. It is black men who bear the burden of the political reality of our powerlessness. To the extent that our powerlessness lessens our ability to defend and develop ourselves, that burden becomes intolerable. The heft we carry on the basketball courts and the football fields, the brawn and boldness in the boxing rings, does not translate into political heft. For too long we have been victims of political circumstance, and our failures of political will have left us standing at the levee, beholden to the roustabouts and pontificating on the virtues of poverty and victimization.

Our traverse of the continent in search of jobs and security in our homes and our persons has not met with welcome or success. We have borne the brunt of America's paranoia. Our brace of songs, our faithful hearts, and fruitful penises have enabled our survival despite the rampant hostilities we encounter. If the atlas of our geography is muted, it is not lacking the boldness of our imagination and our invention. We have traversed the soil of North America, bringing advantage to it as farmer, mule trainer, singer, shaper of wood and iron. We have picked cotton and shined shoes, we have bludgeoned the malleable parts of ourselves into new and brash identities that are shattered and bruised by the gun and the bullet. And now the only duty our young men seem ready to imagine is to their maleness with its reckless display of braggadocio, its bright intelligence, its bold and foolish embrace of hate and happenstance. If we are not our brother's keeper then we are still our brother's witness. We are co-conspirator in his story and in his future.

This is the breach into which the writers of the present volume boldly step. They bear witness. They bring testimony. They give voice and vent to our history. They recall those occasions when we did speak our names in the clandestine confines of the slave quarters where our music and manners were our own property and our names defined our character and our culture. Where our speech and remark of each other's names was a political act. They are proof that if we do not squander our inheritance, if we maintain the fervor of the acolyte and the fierce intelligence of the zealot, we can all speak our names on and on, into the last night of a universe already suspect and falling.

Finally, this book was brought to port by steady hands, an accurate compass and the furious rejection of anything resembling compromise. I salute the editor.

Acknowledgments

I wish to thank everyone who supported the completion of this book. I am deeply grateful to *Speak My Name*'s authors, each of whom I consider a brother and a benefactor. I thank every writer who responded to the call for submissions for this anthology. Unfortunately, neither the limitations of space nor the book's thematic progression permitted me to use all the fine contributions I received. To those who provided their support and solidarity throughout this journey, I say thank you: Patrice Gaines, David Leeming, Florence Ladd, James Campbell, Glenn Ligon, Shay Youngblood, Eve Kosofsky Sedgwick, Michele Wallace, Eleanor Wilner, Charles Johnson, Gloria Wade-Gayles, Joseph Brochin, Philip Patrick, Elaine Shelly, and Patricia Bell-Scott. David Bradley, Gloria Naylor, Rashidah Ismaili, Michael Thelwell, Marita Golden, and the late Doris Jean Austin provided invaluable introductions to writers. Thank you, Deborah Chasman, Tisha Hooks, and Jonathon Aubry: I could not have done this without you.

Introduction: Speak My Name

Don Belton

At the 1992 Republican National Convention, presidential candidate Pat Buchanan announced there is a cultural war going on in America. Buchanan's dispatch had all the sweep and dimension of news that remains news. Indeed, America has been the site of cultural warfare for a very long time. The essential truth in Buchanan's announcement can be excavated all the way back to our nation's inception, when we were not yet even a nation but a colony.

The incredible burst of industry and imagination that created America during the seventeenth and eighteenth centuries gave birth to a nation paradoxically poised both to fulfill a potential as ancient as humanity itself and quite possibly to destroy all traces of humanity as it had previously been known.

It has now become a fairly well-accepted fact that the making of America demanded the murder of millions of Indians. Nationally, we mythologize this violence as an event occurring somewhere in the remote past, but the true legacy of our past requires our nation to re-enact those murders every day in order to perpetuate the mythic basis for America. As Americans, we, each of us as citizens, daily collect our measure of material privilege and psychic pain from this enduring violence. Still, it is perhaps our incorruptability as humans, if not our real heroism, that makes us continue to believe in the possibility of redemption. The consuming project of America went on to turn African children, women, and men into slaves, and turned those slaves into citizens, even prototypical or quintessential *Americans*.

The violence that gave birth to our nation is not especially unique in the annals of nation-making. The entire created world is either the result of warfare in heaven or the result of a riotous "big bang," depending on your preference for religious or scientific lore. According to the biblical writer Matthew, even the kingdom of heaven "allows violence, and the violent bear it away." The nature of the cultural warfare at the heart of the ongoing American experiment is the spiritual violence of a nation at war with its own soul, daily reproducing its own destruction and redemption. Though our national print, TV, and movie industries keep us entertained and terrorized with a vision of a world rent with senseless violent acts, there is actually evidence to support a belief that, on the whole, Americans live unprecedentedly long, safe, and materially rich lives. Yet, as Americans, we live in a virtual atmosphere of violence and the fear of violence.

Historically, the black male body has been scapegoated in the cultural imagination to represent the violence we fear as a nation. The irony in this, of course, is that the black male body has perhaps endured the most sustained and brutal punishment of all in the building of our nation, and all for the existential crime of being black instead of white. During the first quarter of this century, the public hanging, castration, and burning of black men was not only a regular event in the South and the Midwest but a public rite and form of civic entertainment. As Louis Armstrong sang, "What did I do to be so black and blue?" Indeed. As this century ends, black men have already been named an "endangered species" in popular and academic discussion. The national discussion about black men's lives is very often one in which the voices of black men are marginalized or silenced—one in which the only authorized voices are those of the "experts" such as journalists, sociologists, undertakers, policemen, and politicians.

In the early eighteenth century something amazing occurred, a seemingly simple thing that in reality was every bit as dramatic as the shift occurring around 10,000 B.C., when humanity went from a simpler agricultural base to the kind of civilization that could produce the Pyramids. That amazing thing was this: by the eighteenth century, within Christianity there was a new tradition in the depiction of the warrior angel Michael subduing Satan; around this time, Satan, who previously had been portrayed alternately as a dragon or as a white man twisting in chains beneath the blond Michael's feet, acquired a black face. This change coincided with the rise of America and the consolidation of the American myth of whiteness. It also parallels the white domination of Africa. Historically, there is no notion of racial whiteness before the appearance of this image of a black man chained and writhing beneath a white man's feet.

To consider, then, Buchanan's cultural war for what it is, consider this: I am a black man born into what was, in the late 1950s, Philadelphia's premier integrated neighborhood. I was a toddler lying in my mother's lap when John Kennedy's motorcade rode down our block carrying Kennedy to the presidency, trailing hope. That same neighborhood now lies stunned and vanquished, surrounded by abandoned factory buildings. I was born the third son of a man who worked himself to death, a man from whom I inherited a legacy of masculine silence about one's own pain going back seven generations. My father fought in the Second World War and daily faced both humiliation and physical torture by his white comrades in order to defend his nation. My father was not a political man, but shortly after the assassination of Martin Luther King, Jr., my father called my elementary school to have me officially excused for the day and took me to the remnant of Dr. King's Poor People's March when it passed through Philadelphia.

Despite the legacy of slavery, an institution that destroyed not only the agency of the father but also his name, I still can follow my male lineage back to a triple great-grandfather in Virginia in the early nineteenth century. What I know of this man is that he rode like a god and taught three generations of white men horsemanship and hunting, as well as the general deportment of a gentleman. I know that what dignity those white men acquired, whoever they were, they learned from the tutelage of a black man who could teach dignity because his race had lost everything and still had the heroism to recreate itself in a lost new world.

I know that it is a corrupt and meretricious lie that America is built mostly on the work and ingenuity of white men. It is also a lie that black men for the first centuries of this nation's life only picked cotton and led mules, though certainly you don't have an America without the plain labor and love of black men. I know that black men like my great-great-great-grandfather Albert Stone authored the myth of whiteness as much as did their white "masters," long before the waves of German, then Irish, then Jewish immigrants achieved the American shore to become "white" by learning to pronounce the stinging epithet "nigger."

I am one man. While I speak from a position of black and American masculinity, I am not a representative for these positions. The black man is not a monolith. There is no *the* black man. There could not be, anymore than there could be any such person as *the* white man. These are cultural myths, and yet these myths are important metaphors for power in a country still poised for either fulfilling a momentous human potential or destroying the world.

This current anthology, *Speak My Name*, grew out of my own impetus to experience a richer sense of community and communion among other black male writers and to share and apply that experience in a larger context. During the process of developing, collecting, and editing the material for this anthology I have traveled a lot. While issuing from Saint Paul, Minnesota, where I have lived and taught literature and fiction writing at a small liberal arts college, this project has also traveled with me on my first trips to Africa, Brazil, Italy, Ireland, England, France, and the Netherlands. Though I have called myself an American since I could speak, the first time I can remember being called an American *first* was in France. Africa is the only place I have been so far where being black and male is a normative experience. There, I experienced an enormous sense of relief to find that the combination of my race and gender was not enough in itself to victimize or vilify me. My work on the anthology also formed the basis of a literature course I taught, called "Black Masculinity," using race and masculinity to generate new readings of Western texts from Shakespeare's *Tempest* to Defoe's *Robinson Crusoe*. During the early stages of work on this book, my father died suddenly. The morning after I completed writing *Voodoo for Charles* for this anthology, my eldest brother shot himself to death more than a thousand miles from my writing room. I have been sustained in large measure by the fellowship that produced the book you now hold. In a way not fully understood, this book is imprinted with my life over the past few years.

When I began working on *Speak My Name*, to my best knowledge there had not been an anthology to take on the specificity and diversity of black men's lives. I edited this anthology because I personally required it in order to better understand how black men have changed since the 1960s, to better understand how those three intervening decades have *required* change of black men. At this critical hour, no one seems to know who black men are beyond a narrow mainstream representation in which it seems they can only be superathletes, superentertainers, or supercriminals. I needed to help expand and humanize that range, not only for the sake of a generation of young black men who are now making their dangerous passage into manhood, but for an entire nation and a world more intimately connected and interdependent than ever before.

Speak My Name is the first mainstream anthology of contemporary black men's writing. Most of the stories, essays, and personal narratives collected here were written specifically in response to my call for contributions; others are anthologized here for the first time. As for the title, within black American culture from the time of slavery, telling someone to "speak my name" has held a challenge to tell the truth about the interlocutor's deepest attributes. Names exist to counteract confusion of identity or location. The phrase also enacts a request to be held in remembrance during a time of crisis. It is a means of saying we are people with proper names and distinctive faces and familial pasts.

In structuring the book, I thought of jazz music's compositional model of theme and variation, giving my contributors a series of extended solos that develop toward visions of masculinity as a struggle for hope. Their narrative performances move through attempts to come to terms with stereotypes and vested notions of masculinity to pieces about specific relationships, to broader connections with community, and, finally, to celebration. Here is a replete ensemble of well-known authors, often in uncharacteristic voice. You will also hear some new voices along the way, illuminated by the pure pleasure of new writers reaching, hitting, and holding their notes.

Speak My Name does not culminate in a definitive statement about black men or America. Rather it deals with a complex set of questions from which I trust will spring dialogue and even healing. Neither is *Speak My Name* a protest. It counts the mercurial wages and gifts of laughter, love, and rage. It is an assessment of the intense beauty and dread of physical and spiritual landscapes. It is a broadcast of personal witness and triumph, and, for me personally, a true instance of grace.

((part one))

HOW DOES IT FEEL TO BE A PROBLEM?

How Does It Feel
to Be a Problem?

Trey Ellis

How does it feel to be a problem?
—W. E. B. Du Bois

Du Bois was putting words into the mouth of a white questioner. No one ever actually came out and asked him to answer them. No one has ever actually come out and asked me, either, yet I know that many are itching to. I know I would be. Black men are this nation's outlaw celebrities. It doesn't matter what other modifiers also describe our individual essences—mechanic, police officer, left-handed, Virginian, kind, gangbanger, tall—"black man" overrides them all and makes us all, equally, desperadoes. My friends and I sometimes take perverse pride in the fear the combination of our sex and skin instills in everyone else—the taxis that bolt past us as our arms wave high over our meticulously coiffed heads, the receptionists who mistake us for suit-wearing bike messengers, the cops who clutch their .45s when they see us saunter out of Häagen-Dazs. Imagine the weird power you'd feel if you were a bank teller, a postal worker, or a postmodern novelist who is able to make a cop quake with fear and call for backup. Unfortunately, these expectations can get to us after a while. Listen to black comedian Franklin

Ajaye: "I was walking down the street last night and this old white couple kept looking back at me like I was going to rob them. . . . So I did."

Don't get me wrong. I know that black men commit a disproportionate number of America's crimes. In fact, I need to know that, since murder at the hands of another black man is the leading cause of death in my age group. Ironically, black men have more right than anyone else to run and hide when other black men head our way on the sidewalk. Yet we don't (most of us, anyway), because we bother to separate the few bad from the legion of good.

American society as a whole, however tars us all with the same brush. We have become the international symbol for rape, murder, robbery, and uncontrolled libido. Our faces on the news have become synonymous with anger, ignorance, and poverty.

Increasingly, America seems to be painting us into two corners. In one, we're the monsters they've always said we were. In the other corner, we're fine but all those other black men are monsters; we are anointed honorary whites so long as we abandon every trace of our ethnicity.

Black conservatives such as Shelby Steele espouse individual liberation through assimilation. In one way, he is absolutely correct. It is irrefutable that if we African Americans abandoned our culture, stopped griping, and joined the melting pot, we would be better off. The catch is the very real limit to our ambition. If we play by Steele's rules—work hard, scrimp, save, and study—then one day one of us just might become vice president of the United States. Therein lies the rub. In this land of opportunity we can be promised riches, a degree of respect, and respectability, but we know we are still barred from the highest corridors of power. It's a crippling message. How can you expect someone to dedicate his entire life to training for the Olympics if all he can hope for is a silver medal?

Drug dealing and other criminal activities are the only pursuits that offer us unlimited possibilities. Since we are already vilified anyway, goes the twisted logic, at least the sky's the limit in that arena. I'm not making excuses for the black criminal—I despise him for poisoning and shooting more of my people than the cowardly Klan ever did. But we need to understand him as a human being if we're ever going to save him, or at least save his younger brother or his son.

When black folks mention slavery the rest of America yawns. But our country, with its history as the home of the slave, has yet to reconcile that legacy with its reputation as the land of the free. Slavery was as evil an act as ever committed by anyone on the planet. Nazis, the Khmer

Rouge—that's not the sort of company Americans like to keep. Slavery may seem like ancient history to whites, but it doesn't to blacks. Today's problems have deep roots, and until we understand the dark side of our history, our nation will never pull itself out of its current racial morass.

If, in American popular culture, black signifies poor, ignorant, and angry, then white signifies upper-middle-class, educated, and moderate. From "Ozzie & Harriet" to "Home Improvement," upper-middle-class white households are passed off as average white families. The lives of white folks are cleaned up and idealized. Popular culture assumes you will attend some sort of college, own a home, and marry the mother of your child. You are defined by the richest, handsomest, smartest, and kindest among you. We are defined by our worst. Although seventy-five percent of black men never have anything to do with the criminal justice system, we are looked on as anomalies, freaks of nature, or, worse, thugs-in-waiting.

Sadly, black people are starting to believe the bad press. If we string two sentences together, other black folks say, "Oh my, how well-spoken he is." If we are married to the mothers of our children, Delores Williams, a black activist in Los Angeles, hands us a certificate and invites us to an awards banquet. So little is expected of us that even our half-efforts are wildly and inappropriately praised.

Finally, and curiously, some of the stereotypes that make us seem the least human—and the most animalistic—also make us seem the most male. We are famous around the world for our physical and sexual potency. And what is more at the essence of stereotypical machismo than bulging muscles and big dangling balls? Although we hate being America's villains, it's not always all bad—in America, villains have always been perversely revered.

Confessions of a Nice Negro, or Why I Shaved My Head

Robin D. G. Kelley

It happened just the other day—two days into the new year, to be exact. I had dashed into the deserted lobby of an Ann Arbor movie theater, pulling the door behind me to escape the freezing winter winds Michigan residents have come to know so well. Behind the counter knelt a young white teenager filling the popcorn bin with bags of that awful pre-popped stuff. Hardly the enthusiastic employee; from a distance it looked like she was lost in deep thought. The generous display of body piercing suggested an X-generation flowerchild—perhaps an anthropology major into acid jazz and environmentalism, I thought. Sporting a black New York Yankees baseball cap and a black-and-beige scarf over my nose and mouth, I must have looked like I had stepped out of a John Singleton film. And because I was already late, I rushed madly toward the ticket counter.

The flower child was startled: "I don't have anything in the cash register," she blurted as she pulled the bag of popcorn in front of her for protection.

"Huh? I just want one ticket for *Little Women*, please—the two-fifteen show. My wife and daughter should already be in there." I slowly gestured to the theater door and gave her one of those innocent childlike glances I used to give my mom when I wanted to sit on her lap.

"Oh god . . . I'm so sorry. A reflex. Just one ticket? You only missed the first twenty minutes. Enjoy the show."

Enjoy the show? Barely 1995 and here we go again. Another bout with racism in a so-called liberal college town; another racial drama in which I play the prime suspect. And yet I have to confess the situation was pretty funny. Just two hours earlier I couldn't persuade Elleza, my four-year-old daughter, to put her toys away; time-out did nothing, yelling had no effect, and the evil stare made no impact whatsoever. Thoroughly frustrated, I had only one option left: "Okay, I'm gonna tell Mommy!" Of course it worked.

So those five seconds as a media-made black man felt kind of good. I know it's a product of racism. I know that the myth of black male violence has resulted in the deaths of many innocent boys and men of darker hue. I know that the power to scare is not real power. I know all that—after all, I study this stuff for a living! For the moment, though, it felt good. (Besides, the ability to scare with your body can come in handy, especially when you're trying to get a good seat in a theater or avoid long lines.)

I shouldn't admit this, but I take particular pleasure in putting fear into people on the lookout for black male criminality mainly because those moments are so rare for me. Indeed, my *inability* to employ black-maleness as a weapon is the story of my life. Why I don't possess it, or rather possess so little of it, escapes me. I grew up poor in Harlem and Afrodena (the Negro West Side of Pasadena/Altadena, California). My mom was single during my formative preadolescent years, and for a brief moment she even received a welfare check. A hard life makes a hard nigga, so I've been told.

Never an egghead or a dork, as a teenager I was pretty cool. I did the house-party circuit on Friday and Saturday nights and used to stroll down the block toting the serious Radio Raheem boombox. Why, I even invaded movie theaters in the company of ten or fifteen hooded and high-topped black bodies, colonizing the balconies and occupying two seats per person. Armed with popcorn and Raisinettes as our missiles of choice, we dared any usher to ask us to leave. Those of us who had cars (we called them hoopties or rides back in that day) spent our lunch hours and precious class time hanging out in the school parking lot, running down our Die Hards to pump up Cameo, Funkadelic, Grandmaster Flash from our car stereos. I sported dickies and Levis, picked up that gangsta stroll, and when the shag came in style I was with it—always armed with a silk scarf to ensure that my hair was laid. Granted, I vomited after drinking malt liquor for the first time and my only hit of a joint ended abruptly in an asthma attack. But I was cool.

Sure, I was cool, but nobody feared me. That I'm relatively short with dimples and curly hair, speak softly in a rather medium to high-pitched voice, and have a "girl's name" doesn't help matters. And everyone knows that light skin is less threatening to white people than blue-black or midnight brown. Besides, growing up with a soft-spoken, uncharacteristically passive West Indian mother deep into East Indian religions, a mother who sometimes walked barefoot in the streets of Harlem, a mother who insisted on proper diction and never, ever, ever used a swear word, screwed me up royally. I could never curse right. My mouth had trouble forming the words—"fuck" always came out as "fock" and "goddamn" always sounded like it's spelled, not "gotdayum," the way my Pasadena homies pronounced it in their Calabama twang. I don't even recall saying the word "bitch" unless I was quoting somebody or some authorless vernacular rhyme. For some unknown reason, that word scared me.

Moms dressed me up in the coolest mod outfits—short pant suits with matching hats, Nehru jackets, those sixties British-looking turtlenecks. Sure, she got some of that stuff from John's Bargain Store or Goodwill, but I always looked "cute." More stylish than roguish. Kinda like W. E. B. Du Bois as a toddler, or those turn-of-the-century photos of middle-class West Indian boys who grow up to become prime ministers or poets. Ghetto ethnographers back in the late sixties and early seventies would not have found me or my family very "authentic," especially if they had discovered that one of my middle names is Gibran, after the Lebanese poet Kahlil Gibran.

Everybody seemed to like me. Teachers liked me, kids liked me; I even fell in with some notorious teenage criminals at Pasadena High School because *they* liked me. I remember one memorable night in the ninth grade when I went down to the Pasadena Boys' Club to take photos of some of my partners on the basketball team. On my way home some big kids, eleventh-graders to be exact, tried to take my camera. The ringleader pulled out a knife and gently poked it against my chest. I told them it was my stepfather's camera and if I came home without it he'd kick my ass for a week. Miraculously, this launched a whole conversation about stepfathers and how messed up they are, which must have made them feel sorry for me. Within minutes we were cool; they let me go unmolested and I had made another friend.

In affairs of the heart, however, "being liked" had the opposite effect. I can only recall having had four fights in my entire life, all of which were with girls who supposedly liked me but thoroughly beat my behind. Sadly, my record in the boxing ring of puppy love is still 0–4. By the time I graduated to serious dating, being a nice guy seemed like the root of all my romantic problems. I resisted jealously, tried to be understanding, brought flowers and balloons, opened doors, wrote poems and songs, and seemed to always be on my knees for one reason or another. If you've ever watched "Love Connection" or read *Cosmopolitan*, you know the rest of the story: I practically never had sex and most of the women I dated left me in the cold for roughnecks. My last girlfriend in high school, the woman I took to my prom, the woman I once thought I'd die for, tried to show me the light: "Why do you always ask me what I want? Why don't you just *tell* me what you want me to do? Why don't you take charge and *be a man*? If you want to be a real man you can't be nice all the time!"

I always thought she was wrong; being nice has nothing to do with being a man. While I still think she's wrong, it's an established fact that our culture links manhood to terror and power, and that black men are frequently imaged as the ultimate in hypermasculinity. But the black man as the prototype of violent hypermasculinity is as much a fiction as the happy Sambo. No matter what critics and stand-up comics might say, I know from experience that not all black men—and here I'm only speaking of well-lighted or daytime situations—generate fear. Who scares and who doesn't has a lot to do with the body in question; it is dependent on factors such as age, skin color, size, clothes, hairstyle, and even the sound of one's voice. The cops who beat Rodney King and the jury who acquitted King's assailants openly admitted that the size, shape, and color of his body automatically made him a threat to the officers' safety.

On the other hand, the threatening black male body can take the most incongruous forms. Some of the hardest brothas on my block in West Pasadena kept their perms in pink rollers and hairnets. It was not unusual to see young black men in public with curlers, tank-top undershirts, sweatpants, black mid-calf dress socks, and Stacey Adams shoes, hanging out on the corner or on the basketball court. And we all knew that these brothas were not to be messed with. (The rest of the world probably knows it by now, too, since black males in curlers are occasionally featured on "Cops" and "America's Most Wanted" as notorious drug dealers or heartless pimps.)

Whatever the source of this ineffable terror, my body simply lacked it. Indeed, the older I got and the more ensconced I became in the world of academia, the less threatening I seemed. Marrying and having a child also reduced the threat factor. By the time I hit my late twenties, my wife,

Diedra, and I found ourselves in the awkward position of being everyone's favorite Negroes. I don't know how many times we've attended dinner parties where we were the only African Americans in the room. Occasionally there were others, but we seemed to have a monopoly on the dinner party invitations. This not only happened in Ann Arbor, where there is a small but substantial black population to choose from, but in the Negro mecca of Atlanta, Georgia. Our hosts always felt comfortable asking us "sensitive" questions about race that they would not dare ask other black colleagues and friends: What do African Americans think about Farrakahn? Ben Chavis? Nelson Mandela? Most of my black students are very conservative and career-oriented—why is that? How can we mend the relations between blacks and Jews? Do you celebrate Kwanzaa? Do you put anything in your hair to make it that way? What are the starting salaries for young black faculty nowadays?

Of course, these sorts of exchanges appear regularly in most black autobiographies. As soon as they're comfortable, it is not uncommon for white people to take the opportunity to find out everything they've always wanted to know about "us" (which also applies to other people of color, I'm sure) but were afraid to ask. That they feel perfectly at ease asking dumb or unanswerable questions is not simply a case of (mis)perceived racelessness. Being a "nice Negro" has a lot to do with gender, and my peculiar form of "left-feminist-funny-guy" masculinity—a little Kevin Hooks, some Bobby McFerrin, a dash of Woody Allen—is regarded as less threatening than that of most other black men.

Not that I mind the soft-sensitive masculine persona—after all, it is the genuine me, a product of my mother's heroic and revolutionary child-rearing style. But there are moments when I wish I could invoke the intimidation factor of blackmaleness on demand. If I only had that look—that Malcolm X / Mike Tyson / Ice Cube / Larry Fishburne / Bigger Thomas / Fruit of Islam look—I could keep the stupid questions at bay, make college administrators tremble, and scare editors into submission. Subconsciously, I decided that I had to do something about my image. Then, as if by magic, my wish was fulfilled.

Actually, it began as an accident involving a pair of electric clippers and sleep deprivation—a bad auto-cut gone awry. With my lowtop fade on the verge of a Sly Stone afro, I was in desperate need of a trim. Diedra didn't have the time to do it, and as it was February (Black History Month), I was on the chitlin' lecture circuit and couldn't spare forty-five minutes at a barber shop, so I elected to do it myself. Standing in a well-lighted bathroom, armed with two mirrors, I started trimming. Despite a steady hand and what I've always believed was a good eye, my hair turned out lopsided. I kept trimming and trimming to correct my error, but as my flattop sank lower, a yellow patch of scalp began to rise above the surrounding hair, like one of those big granite mounds dotting the grassy knolls of Central Park. A nice yarmulke could have covered it, but that would have been more difficult to explain than a bald spot. So, bearing in mind role models like Michael Jordan, Charles Barkley, Stanley Crouch, and Onyx (then the hip-hop group of the hour), I decided to take it all off.

I didn't think much of it at first, but the new style accomplished what years of evil stares and carefully crafted sartorial statements could not: I began to scare people. The effect was immediate and dramatic. Passing strangers avoided me and smiled less frequently. Those who did smile or make eye contact seemed to be deliberately trying to disarm me—a common strategy taught in campus rape-prevention centers. Scaring people was fun for a while, but I especially enjoyed standing in line at the supermarket with my bald head, baggy pants, high-top Reeboks, and long black hooded down coat, humming old standards like "Darn That Dream," "A Foggy Day," and "I Could Write a Book." Now *that* brought some stares. I must have been convincing, since I adore those songs and have been humming them ever since I can remember. No simple case of cultural hybridity here, just your average menace to society with a deep appreciation for Gershwin, Rodgers and Hart, Van Heusen, Cole Porter, and Jerome Kern.

Among my colleagues, my bald head became the lead subject of every conversation. "You look older, more mature." "With that new cut you come across as much more serious than usual." "You really look quite rugged and masculine with a bald head." My close friends dispensed with the euphemisms and went straight to the point: "Damn. You look scary!" The most painful comment was that I looked like a "B-Boy wannabe" and was "too old for that shit." I had to remind my friend that I'm an OBB (Original B-Boy), that I was in the eleventh grade in 1979 when the Sugar Hill Gang dropped "Rapper's Delight," and that *his* tired behind was in graduate school at the time. Besides, B-Boy was not the intent.

In the end, however, I got more questions than comments. Was I in crisis? Did I want to talk? What was I trying to say by shaving my head? What was the political point of my actions? Once the novelty passed, I began getting those "speak for the race" questions that irritated the hell out of me when I had hair. Why have *black men* begun to shave their heads in greater numbers? Why have so many black athletes decided to shave their heads? Does this new trend have some kind of phallic meaning? Against my better judgment, I found myself coming up with answers to these questions—call it an academician's reflex. I don't remember exactly what I said, but it usually began with black prizefighter Jack Johnson, America's real life "baaad nigger" of the early twentieth century, whose head was always shaved and greased, and ended with the hip-hop community's embrace of an outlaw status. Whatever it was, it made sense at the time.

The publicity photo for my recent book, *Race Rebels*, clearly generated the most controversy among my colleagues. It diverged dramatically from the photo on my first book, where I look particularly innocent, almost angelic. In that first photo I smiled just enough to make my dimples visible; my eyes gazed away from the camera in sort of a dreamy, contemplative pose; my haircut was nondescript and the natural sunlight had a kind of halo effect. The Izod shirt was the icing on the cake. By contrast, the photograph for *Race Rebels* (which Diedra set up and shot, by the way) has me looking directly into the camera, arms folded, bald head glistening from baby oil and rear window light, with a grimace that could give Snoop Doggy Dogg a run for his money. The lens made my arms appear much larger than they really are, creating a kind of Popeye effect. Soon after the book came out, I received several e-mail messages about the photo. A particularly memorable one came from a friend and fellow historian in Australia. In the course of explaining to me how he had corrected one of his students who had read an essay of mine and presumed I was a woman, he wrote: "Mind you, the photo in your book should make things clear—the angle and foreshortening of the arms, and the hairstyle make it one of the more masculine author photos I've seen recently????!!!!!!"

My publisher really milked this photo, which actually fit well with the book's title. For the American Studies Association meeting in Nashville, Tennessee, which took place the week the book came out, my publisher bought a full-page ad on the back cover of an ASA handout, with my mug staring dead at you. Everywhere I turned—in hotel elevators, hallways, lobbies, meeting rooms—I saw myself, and it was not exactly a pretty sight. The quality of the reproduction (essentially a high-contrast xerox) made me appear harder, meaner, and crazier than the original photograph.

The situation became even stranger since I had decided to abandon the skinhead look and grow my hair back. In fact, by the time of the ASA meeting I was on the road (since abandoned) toward a big Black Power Afro—a retro style that at the time seemed to be making a comeback. Worse still, I had come to participate in a round-table discussion on black hair! My paper, titled "Nap Time: Historicizing the Afro," explored the political implications of competing narratives of the Afro's origins and meaning. Overall, it was a terrific session; the room was packed and the discussion was stimulating. But inevitably the question came up: "Although this isn't directly related to his paper, I'd like to find out from Professor Kelley why he shaved his head. Professor Kelley, given the panel's topic and in light of the current ads floating about with your picture on them, can you shed some light on what is attractive to black men about baldness?" The question was posed by a very distinguished and widely read African-American literary scholar. Hardly the naif, he knew the answers as well as I did, but wanted to generate a public discussion. And he succeeded. For ten minutes the audience ran the gamut of issues revolving around race, gender, sexuality, and the politics of style. Even the issue of bald heads as phallic symbols came up. "It's probably true," I said, "but when I was cutting my hair at three-o'clock in the morning I wasn't thinking 'penis.'" Eventually the discussion drifted from black masculinity to the tremendous workloads of minority scholars, which, in all honesty, was the source of my baldness in the first place. Unlike the golden old days, when doing hair was highly ritualized and completely integrated into daily life, we're so busy mentoring and publishing and speaking and fighting that we have very little time to attend to our heads.

Beyond the session itself, that ad continued to haunt me during the entire conference. Every ten minutes, or so it seemed, someone came up to me and offered unsolicited commentary on the photo. One person slyly suggested that in order to make the picture complete I should have posed with an Uzi. When I approached a very good friend of mine, a historian who is partly my Jewish mother and partly my confidante and *always* looking out for my best interests, the first words out of her mouth were, "Robin, I hate that picture! It's the worst picture of you I've ever seen. It doesn't do you justice. Why did you let them use it?"

"It's not that bad," I replied. "Diedra likes it—she took the picture. You just don't like my bald head."

"No, that's not it. I like the bald look on some men, and you have a very nice head. The problem is the photo and the fact that I know what kind of person you are. None of your gentleness and lovability comes out in that picture. Now, don't get a swelled head when I say this, but you have a delightful face and expression that makes people feel good, even when you're talking about serious stuff. The way you smile, there's something unbelievably safe about you."

It was a painful compliment. And yet I knew deep down that she was telling the truth. I've always been unbelievably safe, not just because of my look but because of my actions. Not that I consciously try to put people at ease, to erase conflict and difference, to remain silent on sensitive issues. I can't quite put my finger on it. Perhaps it's my mother's politeness drills? Perhaps it's a manifestation of my continuing bout with shyness? Maybe it has something to do with the sense of joy I get from stimulating conversations? Or maybe it's linked to the fact that my mom refused to raise me in a manner boys are accustomed to? Most likely it is a product of cultural capital—the fact that I *can* speak the language, (re)cite the texts, exhibit the manners and mannerisms that are inherent to bourgeois academic culture. My colleagues identify with me because I can talk intelligently about their scholarship on their terms, which invariably has the effect of creating an illusion of brilliance. As Frantz Fanon said in *Black Skin, White Masks*, the mere fact that he was an articulate *black* man who read a lot rendered him a stunning specimen of erudition in the eyes of his fellow intellectuals in Paris.

Whatever the source of my ineffable lovability, I've learned that it's not entirely a bad thing. In fact, if the rest of the world could look a little deeper, beyond the hardcore exterior—the wide bodies, the carefully constructed grimaces, the performance of terror—they would find many, many brothas much nicer and smarter than myself. The problem lies in a racist culture, a highly gendered racist culture, that is so deeply enmeshed in the fabric of daily life that it's practically invisible. The very existence of the "nice Negro," like the model-minority myth pinned on Asian Americans, renders the war on those "other," hardcore niggas justifiable and even palatable. In a little-known essay on the public image of world champion boxer Joe Louis, the radical Trinidadian writer C. L. R. James put it best: "This attempt to hold up Louis as a model Negro has strong overtones of condescension and race prejudice. It implies: 'See! When a Negro knows how to conduct himself, he gets on very well and we all love him.' From there the next step is: 'If only all Negroes behaved like Joe, the race problem would be solved.'"[1]

Of course we all know this is a bunch of fiction. Behaving "like Joe"

---

1. C. L. R. James, "Joe Louis and Jack Johnson," *Labor Action*, 1 July 1946.

was merely a code for deference and patience, which is all the more remarkable given his vocation. Unlike his predecessor Jack Johnson—the bald-headed prize fighter who transgressed racial boundaries by sleeping with and even marrying white women, who refused to apologize for his "outrageous" behavior, who boasted of his prowess in every facet of life (he even wrapped gauze around his penis to make it appear bigger under his boxing shorts)—Joe Louis was America's hero. As James put it, he was a credit to his race, "I mean the human race."[2] (Re)presented as a humble Alabama boy, God-fearing and devoid of hatred, Louis was constructed in the press as a raceless man whose masculinity was put to good, patriotic use. To many of his white fans, he was a man in the ring and a boy—a good boy—outside of it. To many black folks, he was a hero because he had the license to kick white men's butts and yet maintain the admiration and respect of a nation. Thus, despite similarities in race, class, and vocation, and their common iconization, Louis and Johnson exhibited public behavior that reflected radically different masculinities.

Here, then, is a lesson we cannot ignore. There is some truth in the implication that race (or gender) conflict is partly linked to behavior and how certain behavior is perceived. If our society, for example, could dispense with rigid, archaic notions of appropriate masculine and feminine behavior, perhaps we might create a world that nurtures, encourages, and even rewards nice guys. If violence were not so central to American culture—to the way manhood is defined, to the way in which the state keeps African-American men in check, to the way men interact with women, to the way oppressed peoples interact with one another—perhaps we might see the withering away of white fears of black men. Perhaps young black men wouldn't feel the need to adopt hardened, threatening postures merely to survive in a Doggy-Dogg world. Not that black men ought to become colored equivalents of Alan Alda. Rather, black men ought to be whomever or whatever they want to be, without unwarranted criticism or societal pressures to conform to a particular definition of manhood. They could finally dress down without suspicion, talk loudly without surveillance, and love each other without sanction. Fortunately, such a transformation would also mean the long-awaited death of the "nice Negro."

Not in my lifetime. Any fool can look around and see that the situation for race and gender relations in general, and for black males in particular,

---

2. Ibid.

has taken a turn for the worse—and relief is nowhere in sight. In the meantime, I will make the most of my "nice Negro" status." When it's all said and done, there is nothing romantic or interesting about playing Bigger Thomas. Maybe I can't persuade a well-dressed white couple to give up their box seats, but at least they'll listen to me. For now. . . .

The Night I Was Nobody

John Edgar Wideman

On July 4th, the fireworks day, the day for picnics and patriotic speeches, I was in Clovis, New Mexico, to watch my daughter, Jamila, and her team, the Central Massachusetts Cougars, compete in the Junior Olympics Basketball national tourney. During our ten-day visit to Clovis the weather had been bizarre. Hailstones large as golf balls. Torrents of rain flooding streets hubcap deep. Running through pelting rain from their van to a gym, Jamila and several teammates cramming through a doorway had looked back just in time to see a funnel cloud touch down a few blocks away. Continuous sheet lightning had shattered the horizon, crackling for hours night and day. Spectacular, off-the-charts weather flexing its muscles, reminding people what little control they have over their lives.

Hail rat-tat-tatting against our windshield our first day in town wasn't exactly a warm welcome, but things got better fast. Clovis people were glad to see us and the mini-spike we triggered in the local economy. Hospitable, generous, our hosts lavished upon us the same kind of hands-on affection and attention to detail that had transformed an unpromising place in the middle of nowhere into a very livable community.

On top of all that, the Cougars were kicking butt, so the night of July

3rd I wanted to celebrate with a frozen margarita. I couldn't pry anybody else away from "Bubba's," the movable feast of beer, chips, and chatter the adults traveling with the Cougars improvised nightly in the King's Inn Motel parking lot, so I drove off alone to find one perfect margarita.

Inside the door of Kelley's Bar and Lounge I was flagged by a guy collecting a cover charge and told I couldn't enter wearing my Malcolm X hat. I asked why; the guy hesitated, conferred a moment with his partner, then declared that Malcolm X hats were against the dress code. For a split second I thought it might be that *no* caps were allowed in Kelley's. But the door crew and two or three others hanging around the entranceway all wore the billed caps ubiquitous in New Mexico, duplicates of mine, except theirs sported the logos of feedstores and truck stops instead of a silver *X*.

What careened through my mind in the next couple of minutes is essentially unsayable but included scenes from my own half-century of life as a black man, clips from five hundred years of black/white meetings on slave ships, auction blocks, plantations, basketball courts, in the Supreme Court's marble halls, in beds, back alleys and back rooms, kisses and lynch ropes and contracts for millions of dollars so a black face will grace a cereal box. To tease away my anger I tried joking with folks in other places. Hey, Spike Lee. That hat you gave me on the set of the Malcolm movie in Cairo ain't legal in Clovis.

But nothing about these white guys barring my way was really funny. Part of me wanted to get down and dirty. Curse the suckers. Were they prepared to do battle to keep me and my cap out? Another voice said, Be cool. Don't sully your hands. Walk away and call the cops or a lawyer. Forget these chumps. Sue the owner. Or should I win hearts and minds? Look, fellas, I understand why the *X* on my cap might offend or scare you. You probably don't know much about Malcolm. The incredible metamorphoses of his thinking, his soul. By the time he was assassinated he wasn't a racist, didn't advocate violence. He was trying to make sense of America's impossible history, free himself, free us from the crippling legacy of race hate and oppression.

While all of the above occupied my mind, my body, on its own, had assumed a gunfighter's vigilance, hands ready at sides, head cocked, weight poised, eyes tight and hard on the doorkeeper yet alert to anything stirring on the periphery. Many other eyes, all in white faces, were checking out the entranceway, recognizing the ingredients of a racial incident. Hadn't they witnessed Los Angeles going berserk on their TV screens just a couple months ago? That truck driver beaten nearly to death in the street, those packs of black hoodlums burning and looting? Invisible lines were being drawn in the air, in the sand, invisible chips bristled on shoulders.

The weather again. Our American racial weather, turbulent, unchanging in its changeability, its power to rock us and stun us and smack us from our routines and tear us apart as if none of our cities, our pieties, our promises, our dreams, ever stood a chance of holding on. The racial weather. Outside us, then suddenly, unforgettably, unforgivingly inside, reminding us of what we've only pretended to have forgotten. Our limits, our flaws. The lies and compromises we practice to avoid dealing honestly with the contradictions of race. How dependent we are on luck to survive—*when* we survive—the racial weather.

One minute you're a person, the next moment somebody starts treating you as if you're not. Often it happens just that way, just that suddenly. Particularly if you are a black man in America. Race and racism are a force larger than individuals, more powerful than law or education or government or the church, a force able to wipe these institutions away in the charged moments, minuscule or mountainous, when black and white come face to face. In Watts in 1965, or a few less-than-glorious minutes in Clovis, New Mexico, on the eve of the day that commemorates our country's freedom, our inalienable right as a nation, as citizens, to life, liberty, equality, the pursuit of happiness, those precepts and principles that still look good on paper but are often as worthless as a sheet of newspaper to protect you in a storm if you're a black man at the wrong time in the wrong place.

None of this is news, is it? Not July 3rd in Clovis, when a tiny misfire occurred, or yesterday in your town or tomorrow in mine? But haven't we made progress? Aren't things much better than they used to be? Hasn't enough been done?

•

We ask the wrong questions when we look around and see a handful of fabulously wealthy black people, a few others entering the middle classes. Far more striking than the positive changes are the abiding patterns and assumptions that have not changed. Not all black people are mired in social pathology, but the bottom rung of the ladder of opportunity (and the space *beneath* the bottom rung) is still defined by the color of the people trapped there—and many *are* still trapped there, no doubt about it, because their status was inherited, determined generation after generation by blood, by color. Once, all black people were legally excluded from full participation in the mainstream. Then fewer. Now only some. But the mechanisms of disenfranchisement that originally separated African Americans from other Americans persist, if not legally, then in the apartheid mind-set, convictions and practices of the majority. The seeds sleep but don't die. Ten who suffer from exclusion today can become ten thousand tomorrow. Racial weather can change that quickly.

How would the bouncer have responded if I'd calmly declared, "This is a free country, I can wear any hat I choose"? Would he thank me for standing up for our shared birthright? Or would he have to admit, if pushed, that American rights belong only to *some* Americans, white Americans?

We didn't get that far in our conversation. We usually don't. The girls' faces pulled me from the edge—girls of all colors, sizes, shapes, gritty kids bonding through hard clean competition. Weren't these guys who didn't like my X cap kids too? Who did they think I was? What did they think they were protecting? I backed out, backed down, climbed in my car and drove away from Kelley's. After all, I didn't want Kelley's. I wanted a frozen margarita and a mellow celebration. So I bought plenty of ice and the ingredients for a margarita and rejoined the festivities at Bubba's. Everybody there volunteered to go back with me to Kelley's, but I didn't want to spoil the victory party, taint our daughters' accomplishments, erase the high marks Clovis had earned hosting us.

But I haven't forgotten what happened in Kelley's. I write about it now because this is my country, the country where my sons and daughter are growing up, and your daughters and sons, and the crisis, the affliction, the same ole, same ole waste of life continues across the land, the nightmarish weather of racism, starbursts of misery in the dark.

The statistics of inequality don't demonstrate a "black crisis"—that perspective confuses cause and victim, solutions and responsibility. When the rain falls, it falls on us all. The bad news about black men— that they die sooner and more violently than white men, are more ravaged by unemployment and lack of opportunity, are more exposed to drugs, disease, broken families, and police brutality, more likely to go to jail than college, more cheated by the inertia and callousness of a government that represents and protects the most needy the least—this is not a "black problem," but a *national* shame affecting us all. Wrenching ourselves free from the long nightmare of racism will require collective determination, countless individual acts of will, gutsy, informed, unselfish. To imagine the terrible cost of not healing ourselves, we must first imagine how good it would feel to be healed.

On Violence

David Nicholson

Maybe things would have been different if instead of only being born to the culture I'd grown up in it as well. But I spent much of my childhood in Jamaica, and when my parents separated and my mother returned to America with her four children, this middle-class boy, whose dentist father and high school teacher mother had sent him to the Queen's Preparatory School in Kingston, was completely unprepared for what he found on the predatory streets and playgrounds of black Washington, D.C.

I had no sense of rhythm and I couldn't dance. I couldn't (and still can't) dribble well enough to play basketball. For years the purpose and the verbal agility of "the dozens" (which we called joneing) eluded me.

The worst, though, was the casual violence—everybody seemed to want to fight. Someone pushed someone else in line waiting to go out to the playground. Someone said something about someone else's mother. Someone *said* someone had said something about a third someone else's mother. Sex didn't matter (some girls terrified all but the most fearless boys) and neither did the pretext. If a serious enough offense had been committed, or even merely alleged, push soon came to shove as books were dropped and fists raised and the aggrieved parties—surrounded by a crowd gleefully chanting "Fight! Fight!"—circled each other with murder in their eyes.

Raised to believe gentlemen obeyed two essential commandments—they did not hit girls, and they did not hit anyone who wore glasses—I would have been fixed in an insoluble moral quandary if a glasses-wearing girl had dared me to fight. But somehow it was arranged that I would fight another boy in the fifth-grade class of Mrs. Omega P. Millen (so named, she'd told us, because her mother had forsworn more children after her birth). I don't remember how it happened, but someone probably offered the usual reasons—Furman had said something about my mother or I'd said something about his. The truth, though, was that Furman, fair-skinned and freckled, with curly, ginger-colored hair, was as much of an outsider because of his color as I was because of my accent. A fight would decide which of us belonged.

We met in an alley near school. When it was over, the spectators who'd gathered, jamming the mouth of the alley so that Furman and I had to be escorted in, must have been as disappointed as ticketholders who'd mortgaged their homes for ringside seats at the Tyson-Spinks title fight. Furman and I circled each other warily until he pushed me or I pushed him or someone in the crowd pushed us into each other. After a moment or two of wrestling on the dirty brick paving, rolling around on the trash and broken glass, I shoved Furman away and stood.

Memory plays tricks, of course, but I don't think I was afraid. Not as afraid as I would be later, when, coming home from the High's Dairy Store on Rhode Island Avenue with a quart of ice cream on Sunday, some bigger boy, backed by two or three of his cronies, demanded a nickel. If I said I didn't have one, they'd leave me to choose between two humiliations—having my pockets searched or fighting all three, one after the other. And I certainly wasn't as afraid as I would be when, as I walked home alone, four or five boys jumped me because I'd strayed into a neighborhood where outsiders had to be ready to fight just to walk down the street.

So what I remember feeling in the alley was not fear but puzzlement. The fight with Furman had seemed like a joke right up to the moment we'd squared off against one another. I hadn't taken it seriously, and now it felt like a piece of foolishness that had gone too far. No one else seemed to have enough sense to call a halt, so it was up to me. I found my glasses, put them on, and announced I wasn't going to fight. I'd done nothing to Furman. He'd done nothing to me. And, besides, one of us might get hurt.

There was a moment of silence and then a low grumbling of disappointment as the boys and girls who'd come expecting to see a fight realized there wasn't going to be one. I went home, one or two friends walking with me, assuring me that it was all right, I didn't have to fight if I didn't want to.

But I knew they were wrong. And I knew they knew it too.

It is a terrible thing to be condemned by others as a coward, but it is even worse to condemn yourself as one. For that reason, I brood about that time in the alley more often than is probably healthy, even given that I'm a writer and my stock in trade is memories and the past. Lately, however, I've been thinking about it as I read, or read about, the new violence-laden autobiographies by black men—Nathan McCall's *Makes Me Wanna Holler*, Kody Scott's *Monster*. I don't listen to rap music (the phrase has always struck me as an oxymoron), but I'm aware that the genre has become one of art-imitating-life-imitating-art as entertainers like Tupac Shakur are arrested and charged with crimes ranging from sexual assault to murder. And then, if all that wasn't enough, there were the T-shirts and sweatshirts featuring Mike Tyson's face and the ominous legend "I'll be back," and those bearing the legend "Shut Up Bitch, or I'll O.J. You."

More and more it's begun to seem, as we enter the middle of the 1990s, that violence and black men go together as well as the fingers of the hand make up the fist. What's most troubling is that not only has the media seized on America's enduring bogeyman, the bad nigger, as an object of fear and pity, but that black men (and women) have also gleefully embraced that image. It's as if a generation, soured by disappointment in the post–civil rights era, has given up all hope of achievement and decided that it's almost as good to be feared as it is to be respected.

And so where does that leave me, who long ago eschewed violence, whether from fear or cowardice or simply because I couldn't see the point of it? Feeling at forty-three much the same as I'd felt facing Furman in the alley—that I'd been given a choice that really wasn't a choice. If I fought, I'd become like the rest of the boys. If I didn't, I'd be a sissy. What I really wanted was just to be me.

●

Perhaps I'm making too much out of all this. Perhaps that afternoon in the alley was part of some perfectly normal rite of passage. Perhaps all boys test each other to find out who will fight and who will not. And perhaps by not fighting Furman or, later, any of a number of bullies and thugs, I threw away the opportunity to earn their respect. Perhaps.

All I knew then was that the rules were different from those I'd learned growing up in Jamaica, and that while almost all of the children I'd known there were also black, violence was of mystifying importance to the black boys of Washington, D.C. One reason for the difference, I see now, was poverty. My school chums in Jamaica were all middle-class, but most of us in Mrs. Millen's (and later Miss Garner's) classroom were poor enough to relish our mid-morning snack of government-issue oatmeal cookies, soft and sweet at their centers, and half-pints of warm, slightly sour milk. On winter days, windows closed and the radiators steaming, the stale air in the classroom smelled faintly of sweat and dust and urine and un-washed clothes. I remember it as the smell of poverty and of crippling apathy.

Small wonder, then, that because so many of the boys had precious little except their bodies with which to celebrate life, violence became part of that celebration. It offered them a way of feeling masculine as well as the chance to be feared, to feel important.

But I never understood the tribal nature of the violence, the random-ness and the gratuitousness of it, until I saw how they'd probably been introduced to it before they were aware of what was happening, before they were old enough to understand there might be other choices. I was driving past a public housing project one gray winter afternoon when I saw two boys facing each other on the brown lawn. Each boy howled, runny-nosed in fear, as the man towering over them directed their tiny fists at each other.

They couldn't have been much older than three.

•

Years after my abortive fight with Furman in the alley, I had a summer job downtown in the District Build-ing, working for an agency of the city government. Five of us, all high school or college students, were summer help. We spent the day sorting building plans and building permits in a narrow, dusty back room lined with filing cabinets and ceiling-high wooden shelves. Sometimes we had to deal with citizens seeking copies of plans or permits, but most of the time we were left alone to work by ourselves, only nominally supervised.

One of the other boys (I'll call him Earl) was a freshman or sophomore at Howard. Under other circumstances—if we'd met, say, in one of the integrated church coffee houses or drama groups I'd begun to frequent because they allowed me the freedom to be black and myself in ways segregated situations did not—perhaps Earl and I might have been friends. Skinny and bespectacled, we looked enough alike to be brothers. We read books and valued them. We spoke standard English. All of that, of course, set us apart from the other boys. For that reason, instead of becoming friends with Earl, I decided to hate him.

The other boys encouraged me, aiding and abetting, but they were only accomplices, because I had made up my own mind. We goaded Earl. We taunted him. Finally, one of the other boys told me Earl had dropped some of my files and picked them up without putting them back in order. Earl hadn't, of course, and I knew it. But I also knew my choice was to fight him or become identified with him. And Earl, with his suspiciously effeminate air of striving for refinement, was not someone I wanted to be identified with.

What happened was worse than if I had beaten him, worse than if he had fought back and beaten me. Earl simply refused to fight. He crumpled, stood crying, holding his glasses, begging me to leave him alone. I didn't hit him, but I joined with the others in making him do my work as well as his own while the rest of us sat drinking sodas or coffee, watching and making jokes.

I wish now I'd done something else. That I'd refused to fight Earl. That I'd suggested we join forces to resist the others. That I'd gone, on his behalf, to complain to our supervisor. But I didn't. And, sickened, I learned a lesson—it felt no better to threaten violence against someone incapable of resisting than it had been to be the one threatened and equally incapable of resistance.

.

What's missing here is the kind of Ellisonian epiphany—I am who I am, and no one else—that might have long ago allowed me to let go of all this. Instead, I've had to make do with patchwork realizations and small comforts.

One evening a few years ago I was standing on the street I grew up on, talking with a man I'd known since we were both children. He is younger than I am, so I hadn't known him well. Still, I knew him well enough to know he'd been comfortable on that street in ways I had not. So I was surprised when all of a sudden he told me he had always admired me. Puzzled but curious, I asked why, and he said it was because I hadn't stayed in the neighborhood; I'd left it to live other places and see other things.

For a moment I was speechless. I knew, of course, that there were qualities—the apparent cool and the readiness to deal that we call an ability to hang—that he possessed and I lacked. I envied him those. But it was inconceivable he might also envy me.

Hard on the heels of that realization came another. Life was a series of stages and I'd passed through one, but precisely because I'd long ago left that street I hadn't known it: violence was a function of age, even for black men (like the one I was talking to) who weren't middle-class and who lacked intellectual pretensions. A wishful capacity for it might remain one of the ways we defined ourselves, and were defined, however, the truth was that after a certain point even the bad boys were forced to realize they were no longer boys and that suddenly but almost imperceptibly they'd become one step too slow to continue in the game. It's then that, for all but the most stubborn, violence becomes a matter of ritual and voyeurism: football on Sundays, heated arguments in the barbershop, the heavyweight championship on pay-per-view.

•

During that same sojourn in the old neighborhood, I was walking to church one winter Sunday morning. I was almost there when I heard them, and then I rounded the corner and saw a man and a woman screaming at each other beside the iron fence in front of the churchyard while a little boy watched. A few late parishioners walked past, conscientiously ignoring them.

It's been long enough now so that the details are hazy. But I remember that he pushed her, and then she pushed him, and that they were screaming at each other. And I remember their faces, his young and still beardless, adorned with that practiced air of aggrievement I remembered from my childhood after one boy had sucker-punched another and gotten caught by Mrs. Millen or Miss Garner, an insolent glare that said, "Why you lookin' at me for? I ain't did shit." The girl's face would have been pretty except that it was twisted with tears and anger. The little boy stood a little away, looking at them, and what was terrifying about it was that his face showed no expression at all.

I stepped into it, right between them, begging them to calm down, circling with them, hands out to keep them apart. He was bigger than I am, and younger. He may have pushed me once, trying to reach past to get at her. She bent to pick up a brick and lunged after him. I held her back.

Finally the police came.

An hour or so later, when I was finally home, I started to shake, thinking about what I'd done, thinking about what could have happened if he'd had a gun or a knife, or if the two of them had turned on me. Mostly, though, I thought about the little boy, looking up at me from under the hood of his parka when I stooped to ask if he was all right. He'd nodded, almost diffidently, nothing in his eyes at all that I could read. And I had thought, as I patted him on the shoulder and said, "Everything's going to be okay," that I was lying, that it wasn't going to be okay at all.

Because in that moment I could see the past—and the futures—of so many of the boys I'd first encountered on the streets and playgrounds around First Street and Rhode Island Avenue. They'd all had the same look in their eyes, the same distancing of themselves from what was happening around them. In time, I thought, this boy, too, would go on to acquire the same wariness, a quality of disguised hurt, a quality of removal and disavowal. In some important way he, like them, would cease to care. It wasn't just that these boys had come to expect to be blamed when they really had done nothing, although that was part of it. No, what was really important was that they'd made it so that it didn't matter any more. Because they'd long ago discovered that the way to survive was to hide their real selves from the world. And no matter what happened, they would never, ever, let anything touch them.

I write this now for the boy I once was who almost had his love of books and poetry beaten out of him. I write it for Earl, wherever and whoever he is, as a way of asking his forgiveness for having humiliated him in a vain attempt to avenge my own humiliations. I write it for the boy whose parents fought in front of the church that winter morning, hoping he made it whole into manhood despite the odds against him. And I write it for the boys whose names I never knew or can't remember, the ones whose eyes in elementary school were deader than any child's should ever be. Now I understand, I feel the pain they could not admit. In this way perhaps I can also one day forgive them.

Why Must a Black Writer Write About Sex?

Dany Laferriere
Translated by David Homel

I Am a Black Writer

A girl came up to me in the street.

"Are you the writer?"

"Sometimes."

"Can I ask you a question?"

"Of course."

"Is the book *your* story?"

"What do you mean by that?"

"I saw you on TV the other day, and I was wondering whether all those things really happened to you."

"Yes and no."

She wasn't surprised or confused, she just wanted a straight explanation.

"Is that it?"

"I don't know what to tell you . . . No one can tell a story exactly the way it happened. You fix it up. You try to find the key emotion. You fall into the trap of nostalgia. And there's nothing further from the truth than nostalgia."

"So it really isn't your story."

"May I ask *you* a question?"

"Why would you do that?" She blushed. "I never wrote a book."

"But you read books."

"I like to read."

"Why is it so important to know if the story really happened to the author?"

She thought about that one.

"You just want to know."

"I see . . . Why?"

"I don't know," she said with a pained smile. "You feel closer to him that way."

"What if he was lying to you?"

"What do you mean?"

"What if he told you it was his story, even if it really wasn't?"

"I'd be disappointed." She laughed, a little embarrassed. "I suppose we never know the truth."

"So why bother?"

"It's just a fantasy."

She laughed.

"Are you keeping something from me?"

"Maybe, but I don't know what."

She smiled again.

"Where do you like to read?" I asked her.

"Anywhere."

"In the subway?"

"There, too."

Nothing fascinates me more than a girl reading in the subway. I don't know why, but Tolstoy wins it hands down underground. With *Anna Karenina*, naturally.

"Some people read anywhere, but not just anything," I said, without really knowing what that meant.

She gave me a penetrating look.

"I read anything."

"Which means you're the perfect reader."

A car swept by. She leapt aside to safety.

"I'm sure you don't finish every book."

"Sorry, I didn't catch that," she said, getting over her fright.

"When you start a book, do you always finish it?"

"Always."

By now she had recovered her wits.

"There's something here that doesn't add up," I told her.

"Maybe because I never remember anything." She chuckled.

"How can that be?"

"I don't remember the author's name . . ."

My heart sank.

". . . Or even the title of the book."

"I suppose that really isn't important. The book's the only thing that matters."

She sighed.

"I never remember the subject either. Sometimes I think I've never read a single book in my life."

"That's incredible! You read something, and a minute later it's gone?"

"I'm afraid so."

A long pause.

"Then why read?"

"It passes the time."

"I see . . . Does it bother you when you forget?"

"Oh, yes!"

She seemed hurt that I would ask her such a question.

"I imagine your forgetfulness causes trouble in the rest of your life."

"No. It only happens with books. Do you think I'm disturbed? Sorry—not at all. I work in an office not far from here, and believe it or not, you need a good memory in my line of work. I'm a legal secretary."

"Why did you come up to me in the street? You seem like the shy type to me."

A peal of fine laughter burst from her throat.

"I am shy, you're right. I don't know why. I guess because I saw you on TV."

"Maybe you've read one of my books . . ."

"No. At least, I don't think so."

A moment's hesitation.

"Well, maybe yes. I might have read one of your books."

"There's no way of being vain around you."

She laughed her shy laugh.

"I'm sorry."

"I'd like to ask you something."

"Yes," she breathed, turning her head to one side.

"Are you in love?"

This time her laughter was harsh.

"You're a strange one . . . But why not? You're a writer."

"A black writer," I pointed out.

"What's that mean? Is it better?"

"Unfortunately not."

"So?"

"That's the way it is."

"Is it?"

"Yes."

"Too bad."

"There are certain advantages, you know."

"For example?"

"There are fewer of us. It's easier to become the greatest living black writer."

"Then what?" she asked slyly.

"Then you die, of course."

My eye was briefly captured by a girl walking on the other side of the street. A girl with an enormously short green skirt, a veritable handkerchief, and legs that must be worth more than a brooch from Tiffany's. When I turned back to continue the conversation, the reader had gone. Where did she come from? Where was she going? What did she want from me? No sense asking those questions in America.

America, We Are Here

Back then, I was trying to write a book and survive in America at the same time. (I'll never figure out how that ambition wormed its way into me.) One of those two pursuits had to go. Time to choose, man. But a problem arose: I wanted everything. That's the way drowning men are. I wanted a novel, girls (fascinating girls, the products of modernity, weight-loss diets, the mad longings of older men), alcohol, and laughter. My due—that's all. That which America had promised me. I know America has made a lot of promises to a very large number of people, but I was intent on making her keep her word. I was furious at her, and I don't like to be double-crossed. At the time, I'm sure you'll remember, at the beginning of the 1980s (so long ago!) the bars in any North American city were chock-full of confused, aging hippies—they were confused before they became hippies—empty-eyed Africans who always had a drum within easy striking distance—the type never changes, no matter the location or the decade—Caribbeans in search of their identity, starving white poetesses who lived off alfalfa sprouts and Hindu mythology, aggressive young black girls who knew they didn't stand a chance in this insane game of roulette because the black men were only into white women, and the white guys into money and power. Late in the evening, I wandered through these lunar landscapes where sensations had long since replaced sentiment. I took notes. I scribbled away in the washrooms of crummy bars. I carried on endless conversations until dawn with starving intellectuals, out-of-work actresses, philosophers without influence, tubercular poetesses, the bottomest of the bottom dogs. I jumped into that pool once in a while and found myself in a strange bed with a girl I didn't remember having courted. (I left the bar last light with the black-haired girl, I'm sure I did, so what's this bottle-blonde with the green fingernails doing here?) But I never took drugs. God had given me the gift of loud, powerful, happy, contagious laughter, a child's laugh that drove girls wild. They wanted to laugh so badly, and there wasn't much to laugh about back then. When I immigrated to North America, I made sure I brought that laughter in my battered metal suitcase, an ancestral legacy. We always laughed a lot around my house. My grandfather's deep laughter would shake the walls. I laughed, I drank wine, I made love with the energy of a child who's been locked inside a candy shop, and I wrote it all down. As soon as the girl scampered off to the bathroom, I would start scribbling down notes. The edge of a bed or the corner of a table was my desk. I'd note down a good line, a sensual walk, a pained smile, all the details of life. Everything fascinated me. I wrote down everything that moved, and things never stopped moving, believe me. All around me, the world (the girl, the dress on the floor, my underwear lost in the sheets, that long naked back moving towards the stereo, then Bob Marley's music), the elements of my universe turned at top speed. How could words halt the flight of time, girls wheeling away, desire burning anew? Often I would fall asleep with my head against my old Remington, asking myself those unanswerable questions. Am I the troubadour of low-rent America, always on the edge of an overdose, up against the wall, handcuffs slapped on, with two cops breathing down my neck? America discounting her life, counting her pennies, the America of immigrants, blacks and poor white girls who've lost their way? America of empty eyes and pallid dawn. In the end, I wrote that damned novel, and America was forced, at least as far as I was concerned, to come through on a few of her promises. I know she gives more to some than they need; with others, she swipes the hunk of stale bread from their clenched fists. But I made her pay at least a third of her debt. I'm naive, I know. I can see the audience smiling, but my mental system needs to believe in this victory, as tiny as it may be. A third of a victory. For others, not a penny of the debt has been paid. America owes an enormous amount to Third World youth. I'm not just talking about historical debt (slavery, the rape of natural resources, the balance of payments, etc.); there's a sexual debt, too. Everything we've been promised by magazines, posters, the movies, television. America is a happy hunting ground, that's what gets beaten into our heads every day, come and stalk the most delicious morsels (young American beauties with long legs, pink mouths, superior smiles), come and pick the wild fruit of this new Promised Land. For you, young men of the Third World, America will be a doe quivering under the buckshot of your caresses. The call went out around the world, and we heard it, even the blue men of the desert heard it. Remember the global village? They've got American TV in the middle of the Sahara. Westward, ho! It was a new gold rush. And when each new arrival showed up, he was told, "Sorry, the party's over." I can still picture the sad smile of that Bedouin, old in years but still vigorous (remember, brother, those horny old goats from the Old Testament), who had sold his camel to attend the party. I met up with all of them in a tiny bar on Park Avenue. While you're waiting for the next fiesta, the manpower counselor told us, you have to work. There's work for everyone in America (the old carrot and stick, brother). We've got you coming and going. What? Work? Our Bedouin didn't come here to work. He crossed the desert and sailed the seas because he'd been told that in America the girls were free and easy. Oh no, you didn't quite understand! What didn't we understand? All the songs and novels and films from America ever since the end of the 1950s talk about sex and sex alone, and now you're telling us we didn't understand? Didn't understand what? What were we supposed to have understood from that showy sexuality, that profusion of naked bodies, that total disclosure, that Hollywood heat? You should know we have some very sophisticated devices in the desert; we can tune in America. The resolution is exceptional, and there's no interference in the Sahara. In the evening we gather in our tents lit by the cathode screen and watch you. Watching how you do what you do is a great pleasure for us. Some pretty girl is always laughing on a beach somewhere. The next minute, a big blond guy shows up and jumps her. She slips between his fingers, and he chases her into the surf. She fights, but he holds her tight and both of them sink to the bottom. Every evening it's the same menu, with slight variations. The sea is bluer, the girl blonder, the guy more muscled. All our dreams revolve around this life of ease. That's what we want: the easy life. Those breasts and asses and teeth and laughter—after a while it started affecting our libido. What could be more natural? And now here we are in America and you dare tell us that we didn't understand? Understand what? I ask the question again. What were we supposed to have understood? You made us mad with desire. Today we stand before you, a long chain of men (in our country, adventure is the realm of men), penises erect, appetites insatiable, ready for the battle of the sexes and the races. We'll fight to the finish, America.

Albert Murray on Stage:
An Interview

Louis Edwards

Albert Murray, born in 1916, is a grand
surviving griot from a prodigious generation that includes writers Ralph Ellison, John
A. Williams, and Ernest Gaines. He is a cultural critic (*The Omni-Americans* [1970],
The Hero and the Blues [1973], *Stomping the Blues* [1976]) and a fiction writer (*Train
Whistle Guitar* [1974], *The Spyglass Tree* [1990]). Louis Edwards is as gifted a young
writer as can be drawn from a new generation of writers re-creating the story of
black male witness in America. His first novel, *Ten Seconds* (1991), was hailed by
critics and fellow writers alike. Edwards, born in 1962, has already won the
prestigious Whiting Writer's Award and is completing a new novel. The following
conversation, in part inscribing the living ritual of black, male mentorship, took place
on July 13, 1994, in Murray's Harlem apartment, where he lives with his wife and
daughter. [Ed.]

EDWARDS: I'd like to begin with a discussion of *The Omni-Americans*, not
just because it's the beginning of your publishing history, but because it's
such a beginning and such a way to hear your voice for the first time. So
how did that book come about? Talk about the political and literary cli-
mates at the time—late sixties, early seventies—and about how the book
was received.

MURRAY: Well, it was obviously a book that was stimulated by the civil rights movement. And it had to do with what I thought was basic—that is, the question of identity and who these people were and how they saw themselves in the actions that they were participating in. To me it's always a matter of context and a matter of the broadest possible human context. So I wanted to define what it meant to be an American, and how we fit into it, and I came up with the idea that we're *fundamental* to it—that you can't be an American unless you're part *us*, just as you can't be an American unless you're part *them*. I came up with the concept of a culture that as a context makes for, literally and figuratively speaking, a mulatto culture. I was thinking the whole time I was writing *The Omni-Americans* about "all-American," but I couldn't use that term because I didn't want to get confused with that term as it's used in athletics. But it means "all-American." "Omni-Americans" means "all-Americans." America is interwoven with all these different strains. The subtitle of that section of the book is "E Pluribus Unum"—one out of many. Whether you want to get all tangled up in "melting pot" or "glorious mosaic" or any of those phrases is another thing. It just means that people are interwoven, and they represent what Constance Rourke calls a composite. Then you can start defining individuals in their variations, but they're in that context and they can only define themselves in that context. They're in a position where they're the heirs of all the culture of all the ages. Because of innovations in communication and transportation, the ideas of people all over the world and people of different epochs impinge upon us, on part of our consciousness.

EDWARDS: Then the term "omni-Americans" applies not just to African-Americans, but to all Americans, and to—well, maybe not to all people, but perhaps we're discussing "omni-humanity."

MURRAY: Yes. Absolutely. We're looking for universality. We're looking for the common ground of man. And what you're doing when you separate the American from all of that, is you're talking about *idiomatic* identity. You see? And if you go from culture, instead of the impossibility of race . . . because you can't *define* race. It doesn't meet our intellectual standard with a scientific observation and definition and whatever. It won't meet it! You see, race is an ideological concept. It has to do with manipulating people, and with power, and with controlling people in a certain way. It has no reality, no basis in reality. Because, see, if you try to make a genetic definition—"has this gene, has that gene"—how many of this gene or these genes or those genes would it take to make you white or black or yellow or brown or red, if you use this crude ratio? Now how do you determine who has that many, and where's the line of demarcation? It's an *impossible* situation. So what you enter into to make sense of things are patterns and variations in culture. What you find are variations we can call idiomatic—idiomatic variations. People do the same things, have the same basic human impulses, but they come out differently. The language changes because of the environment and so forth. Now, you can get the environment, you can get the cultural elements, and from those things you can predict the behavior of people fairly well. But if you look at such racial characteristics as may be used—whether it's the shape of certain body parts, the texture of the hair, the lips, and all—you cannot get a scientific correlation between how the guy looks and how he behaves. If you find a large number of people who look like each other and behave like each other, it's because of the culture. Because there are too many other variations. If you've got guys from stovepipe black to snow blond, you're going to find all the variations in mankind, even though idiomatically they might speak the same, they might *sound* the same.

EDWARDS: The ideas that you espoused in *The Omni-Americans*, were they considered radical? I mean, there are those who would say this is wrong even today. The social scientists would still argue with you.

MURRAY: But they're segregationists. I make the point in *The Omni-Americans* that nobody is more dependent upon segregation than the social scientist.

EDWARDS: It's his work.

MURRAY: That's why I call social science as used in America a folklore of white supremacy and a *fake*lore of black pathology. Anything that black people do is abnormal. If it's good, it's still abnormal. So if you're well conditioned, like superstar basketball players, it's because there's something wrong with you. Any other time when you're discussing such matters, if you've got these things together, if you're discharging the emotional thing that your system is healthier, if you're laughing and you're making jokes and you're playing around, then you're automatically, by any other definition of psychiatry and so forth, you're happier and you're on better terms with life. But then somebody will say something is wrong with you if you're not angry enough—which is a pathological condition.

Even if you're in the face of danger, you're still in an abnormal functioning of the body because you're confronted with danger, but it's not the
most desired state of human existence. You've got that balance between a
perception of jeopardy and a technology for coping with it *and* a sense of
the ridiculousness and a sense of the futility or the emptiness, after all, of
it. Because once you get to be good enough at science, you're linked up
with particles and waves! [Laughter.]

So then all you've got left are metaphors, and those metaphors had better be adequate. And they're adequate if they add up to the possibility of
dynamic equilibrium which brings a sense of fulfillment and therefore
happiness.

EDWARDS: Well, many of your metaphors have, I think, serious political
implications and resonance, but they do not read that way. They don't
read as politics. They read more as philosophy.

MURRAY: Well, it's a human thing.

EDWARDS: Back to the search for universal humanity.

MURRAY: Let me give you an analogy, a rough Murray analogy. If you
went to the athletic department of a college . . . you have one guy who is
a coach of the basketball team, the track team, and another guy who is a
physical director. He teaches physical education, he conditions the body
for all those other things. If you do well enough, if you can pass all of that,
then you might be a basketball player, you might be a track guy—the application of the conditioning. In other words, if our humanities, if our
metaphors, if our arts are adequate, then our ideals and aspirations will
be adequate. It wouldn't be just a matter of food, clothing, and shelter.
It would be a human transcendence that goes beyond that, that takes you
beyond our conception of what human or plant life is. It's those ideas or
those images of human possibility that make for aspiration, that make for
a sense of achievement—and a sense of failure. So you've got literature
right there. If you get a wrong definition of what the objectives are, if you
go for material things—just go for money, or just for power—you will
then cause a lot of confusion and it won't be adding toward the thing that
you really want, which is that dynamic equilibrium, which is always pre-

carious, but which makes for what we call happiness, which is very, very delicate at all times. It has to be watched at all times because it changes. But it's what we want. We know it when we get it.

EDWARDS: The requirements to bring about happiness change.

MURRAY: You've got to have a sense of actual achievement. One of the things about my writing that I want to make people conscious of is the underlying ritual that's there. That's what keeps them informed that I'm going to be applying this to politics, I'm going to be applying this to this type of administration. But you've got a vision of life which is adequate, so that it enriches your political program, your political position, or what you *want*.

Count Basie and I were working on his book, and when we got near the end we started looking through collections of pictures. At one point there—I guess just before he was leaving Kansas City to come to New York—there's a picture of him and he has a gold tooth in the front of his mouth. And when I saw this picture I said, "Hey, Count. What happened to that gold tooth?" He looked at the picture and he said, "I didn't know what to want." Isn't that terrific? "I didn't know what to want." When he got more hip, he took that thing out; he had beautiful teeth that went so well with his complexion and all.

EDWARDS: That's a great story.

MURRAY: We're talking about the political implications of what I was doing. . . . It was a matter of laying an adequate foundation, so that whatever you do on top of it would be adequate.

EDWARDS: Now, one of the most complex works that you've written would be *South to a Very Old Place*—in my opinion—which, I'll admit, I had a hard time fully comprehending. I realize that there is a very intricate pattern that is at work there. Could you discuss what you were up to? I think it might help people approach that work.

MURRAY: *The Omni-Americans* would be a discussion where I'm wearing the hat of the intellectual, where I'm trying to set up the issues and address basic questions. *South to a Very Old Place* tries to be a work of art, where the actions and the pictures have their own application. If you give people a legend, they want a picture. If you give them a picture, they want a legend. If you wear two hats, as a novelist and an intellectual, you do them both. As a college teacher, I could do them both. I wanted to be an artist. I tried my best to make *South to a Very Old Place* a work of art.

EDWARDS: It's clearly that.

MURRAY: I wanted it to be read for the pleasure of how it is written, and then all of that stuff is all loaded. You can say all kinds of things that mean all kinds of things, and it's all in focus if you get the art working for you. With the hocus-pocus you make it swing, and then you get all that other stuff. You want to make the ineffable articulate. So you're in an interesting area there, and when you get to *Train Whistle*, there's an attempt to give you the clue . . . "the also and the also" of this or that; you should get the whole. "Also and also" is the ultimate implication, the personal, the local, the worldwide implications. The also and the also: *etcetera*. It's endless.

That's like music again. I start with real fundamentals. Entropy. So when I'm writing about the blues, it's the whole philosophical system right there. What's the blues? Entropy. The tendency of all phenomena to become random, to fall apart. It's chaos. That's what so devastating about the blues. So what you've got to do is superimpose a form on that. That's why I can make jazz and the jazz musician central to my whole literary, philosophical system of American identity, because we simply are the stars of [that system], the touchstone of it. I can take a Lester Young take-off on Jefferson. I could take a Cootie Williams and Louis Armstrong thing on Lincoln. I can do all this. You can play with all that stuff and make it feel right even if you can't articulate it yet. It's that type of thing. And nobody's come up with an image of the American that I think is richer in possibility and more consistent with the assumptions underlying the social contract that we live in terms of.

EDWARDS: Are you saying or implying that the order in which you've published your work is part of an overall plan or scheme? Because from *The Omni-Americans* to *South to a Very Old Place* to *Train Whistle Guitar*— I think *The Hero and the Blues* may be in between the two latter works— the works all flow into one another. Or is that serendipity?

MURRAY: Well, in a sense. . . . When I got into the pieces that add up to *The Omni-Americans*, I realized I was writing on a theme, the theme of identity. The title of the book has to do with identity. We're the all-

Americans. We symbolize that more than anything else. It's a mulatto culture. Boom! You can just play all kinds of changes. You can write fifteen-hundred-page books on that stuff. But what I'd been doing was thinking through the whole thing and I had really written *The Hero and the Blues* first. That's what I was working on when the assignments that would become *The Omni-Americans* started coming in, so I had the context. I had the intellectual frame of reference. I was working it out, working on an aesthetic. So when I started writing these pieces, I knew I was writing a book, because it was inside a context. I wanted to deal with the richest possible context, and what came out was all I knew about literature, all this stuff on my shelves. When I was ready to open up, there I was writing a book! You know, "Thomas Mann, who said this and this . . ." I was gone! I knew where I was going on that. Then I get that *e pluribus unum*, how far back you go . . . .

If I were not so realistic and didn't have to face the tragic dimension of life—as well as life's farcical dimension—I would be very much depressed. Too many of the black intellectuals have been unable to address the first fifteen pages of *The Omni-Americans*. I enter history at the middle point in the Middle Passage. My work sets up a cultural and intellectual context in which we can define ourselves as Americans—second to none. Any African who jumped overboard en route to the New World is not my ancestor, because what we do has to do with survival in this state. You don't have a better prototype for the self-created American than Harriet Tubman, Fredrick Douglass, or Louis Armstrong picking up that horn. My work establishes the basis of our American identity. . . . And that's where the necessity of swing begins. Eternal resilience. Perpetual creativity. . . . So by the time I got into *The Omni-Americans*, I was going. It *had* to be a book. Then you feed in these other things which I was dealing with at the time—jazz, literature, style. I would just bounce them against a frame of reference. That's how *The Omni-Americans* came to be.

But when you get to *South to a Very Old Place*, that started out as an assignment for a series that Willie Morris was running at *Harper's* magazine, called "Going Home in America." Some people would go to the Midwest; some people would go to this place, that place. He asked me to do one and I decided to go south. Then I started playing with irony immediately. Go north. Go north this way, go north that way. Go north and south. Then to be sure you get it, you've got Joyce, you've got Mann, you've got all these people to help you. So you put Christopher Columbus there and say, "He went east by going west; I'm going south by going north." You're playing with all these things if you're a contemporary writer. You've got to write as if all these people exist.

EDWARDS [laughing]: That leads to another question I have. I want you to talk about some of the very significant relationships you've had with some of the great black male artists of this century.

MURRAY: What do all these guys have in common? What do Ellison, Ellington, Basie, Marsalis, and Bearden have in common? Me. [Laughter.]

EDWARDS: I know! It's interesting. I guess we can talk about some of them individually. I guess I'm most curious about your relationship with Ralph Ellison. How many years older was he?

MURRAY: Two. I'm seventy-eight, and he died at eighty. He was two years ahead of me at school. May have been more than that, but he had been there two years when I got there—Tuskegee. So we were contemporaries. I was there looking for—you know, it's like in *South to a Very Old Place*: "I'm the one determines what the value is." I would say, "Well, this is a pretty good book to read." I was doing that with upperclassmen. "This guy ain't shit. This guy is pretty good. This guy is a hustler." I was making all those judgments. But I think they stand up. I was looking for people who were serious about all this stuff, about the ancestral imperatives. Who was really shucking and who was doing the other stuff. I was looking. And he [Ellison] impressed me more than any other upperclassman. Some other guys, they looked good, they dressed well. They were taking Mr. Sprague's course in the novel. They were reading all these novels. *Clarissa Harlowe*, *Tom Jones*. Ellison and all these guys were reading these books. So I watched this stuff happening, and I noticed Ralph doing some other stuff. I knew he was trying to sculpt. I noticed that he would be at the other end of the library with his music paper spread out, doing copy work. And he was in the band, so he wasn't a cadet. I was a cadet. You had to be a cadet at Tuskegee. ROTC. It was like a Big Ten school, like a farm and technical school. See, Booker T. Washington wanted *everything*. [Laughter.]

EDWARDS: Which is not what you usually hear. The concept in [my] mind is something else. Something more limited.

MURRAY: Right. We had the damndest library. So the two hardest guys to read, black writers, because of all the literary background and references, are Ellison and Murray. All the other guys from Howard . . . you can read Sterling Brown and all these guys easily. But so far as the kinds of references you have to know: Ellison and Murray.

So I was watching Ralph. And then I was reading these books, and I would see his name in the books. They had that little slip in the books when you used to borrow them from the library. There was a place where you had to sign for it, and then they would stamp it. When you checked out a book, you could open the back of the book, and you could see the last time it was read and who had read it. Then I got to know his signature, and he was reading the books I was going to have to read; he had read them. So that was a real upperclassman for you. But he was always a loner-type guy, watchful-eyed, so I didn't venture to introduce myself to him. He worked in the library, a part-time student job.

The first exchange we ever had was . . . I had read Sinclair Lewis's *Arrowsmith* in a Modern Library edition, which was a flexible edition at that time. A green suede binding. I had read André Maurois's book *Ariel: The Life of Shelley.* I was reading about Byron, Shelley, and Keats and what those guys were reading. I was reading about reading and all that. I was a real college student. Everybody figured I should have gone to Yale or Harvard—to Brown, to an Ivy League school. But I was going to Tuskegee, and I was not going to let anybody at Harvard, Yale, and whatnot get a better education than was available to me there. So I was reading these books and what these guys were doing. And they'd talk about how Shelley would be reading all the time. He would fold the book and stick it in his pocket, his back pocket. So I had a flexible book, Sinclair Lewis's *Arrowsmith*, and I'd fold it up and stick it in my pocket, wherever I stopped reading. I wouldn't put a bookmark in it. Just fold it and stick it in my hip pocket, like Shelley. I was probably wearing a tam and a goatee too at that time. *Benvenuto Cellini.* I probably had seen that movie with Frederick March or something like that. All this bohemian stuff that was part of being collegiate, if you were serious. So I go to the library to turn this book in or to get it renewed, and Ralph is at the desk. And Ralph looks at the book and says, "What do you think this is? A pocket edition?" [Laughter.] That's the first exchange.

But I would see him, and I would notice him, and I would see books. . . . When I went to read T. S. Eliot, his name was there. When I went to read Robinson Jeffers, all those things, his name was in there.

In many of the books, he was the only guy. Then Hamilton and I were reading different books.

But I really didn't meet Ralph until about 1942. I knew he was in New York. I knew he had started writing. He had majored in music, but it didn't surprise me that he was writing reviews in magazines, because I knew he was a great reader and he was one of the favorites of Mr. Sprague's, who was my English teacher, too. We used to talk about Ralph. I was reading all of the magazines. I'd pick up one and say, "Hey, this guy reviewed a book by Waters Turpin called *These Low Grounds*." I can remember this. "Oh, I saw that phrase that Ellison said the other day, 'Malraux pointed out the other day that we are returning to fundamentals.'" I'd say, "Damn, boy! He's up there!" He was into the life. So when I came to New York in '42, another Tuskegian named Mike Rabb was up here on a fellowship going to Columbia, taking hospital administration because he was being moved into the position of administrative director of the Tuskegee Institute Hospital. He was staying over here at the Y. He and I were talking about other Tuskegians who were staying in New York, and he mentioned Ellison, whom he had known. He had a nickname for Ellison. he always referred to Ellison as Sousa, as in John Philip, because he was the student concert master. If you'd see the band in the stands, Ellison would be the guy conducting it. So Mike called him Sousa. So we went to see Ralph. He was living right up on the hill there where CCNY was. He was married to a nightclub singer named Rose Poindexter. When we walked into his place, the first thing I saw when he sat back in his chair, the first thing I saw was the Malraux over his shoulder. Then, having been introduced to him, I kept in touch with him on my own. It didn't take him long to find out that I was one of the few guys who read the same kinds of books. So it was automatic. Like that.

EDWARDS: So the two of you had a relationship from then on?

MURRAY: Mmm hmm. We were writing letters and so forth. You know about the stuff that I read at the funeral, the memorial?

EDWARDS: Yes. I was there. They're wonderful letters.

MURRAY: There's a whole collection of those things, which I'll show you one day.

That was '42. In '48 or '47, after I got converted to the reserves from the Air Force at the end of the war, I came to NYU to go to graduate school. And Ralph was by this time out of the merchant marines and into *Invisible Man*. I got back in touch with him. That fall when I came to grad school at NYU, he had published the first excerpt, the prologue from *Invisible Man*, in *Horizon* magazine. Then *Partisan* bought [the] "Battle Royal" [section]. But meanwhile we were in touch, you see, and I'd come up to see him. This is during the [cultural] heyday of 52nd Street.

EDWARDS: Right. So you're busy. [Laughter.]

MURRAY: You know, catching Duke at the Paramount, catching those shows. But my hangout was the 42nd Street Library, because graduate school was at night at NYU at that time. So Ralph was working on *Invisible Man* across the street from Rockefeller Center, across 49th Street, right across from Saks. Eight floors up there was a jewelry store that was run by some friends of Francis Steegmuller, author of *Flaubert and Madame Bovary* and *Maupassant: A Lion in the Path*. In the back of the jewelry store there was an office which they didn't use. Francis had used it, but he was in Europe at that time. So Ralph would get up in the morning and pack his attaché case, dress up, and go to work. Sometimes he would come down to the library and we would talk. Or we would stop at Gotham Book Mart.

EDWARDS: Were you writing at this time?

MURRAY: Yeah, I was trying to. But I was reading and figuring out what I was going to do. I had tried to write plays and stuff like that. By this time I was into Mann, Hemingway, and all that. Because it was out of Mann, out of Thomas Mann, that I got the idea that you could find a basis, an aesthetic model in your [own] idiom for literature. So when he started talking about dialectic orchestration and leitmotifs and things like that, I started thinking about riffs, breaks, and things like that. And then as I started studying, it all made for *The Hero and the Blues*—more for *The Hero and the Blues* than for *Stomping the Blues*. In *Stomping the Blues*, I just go back and clarify the whole notion of organizing literature around musical composition. If I could find the literary equivalent of Ellington, I could out-trump Melville, Twain, and Whitman.

EDWARDS: What do you see as the relationship between your work and Ellison's? *Is* there a relationship? There's certainly not, I don't think, a *simple* relationship.

MURRAY: Well, they're two different things. His is more—well, the political implications are more obvious. Whereas my aesthetic preoccupation and my sense of the total human context—although I work as hard as I can to get the local color and idomatic particulars right, but that to me is what the writer always does. But you want the political, the social to seem incidental. You get that, and you don't even know you've got it. So he's more—I've been thinking about that. I was thinking about the differences in the sensibility. There's a certain amount of explanation of black folk stuff for white folks, which I refuse to do. See, he would do that. He would say certain things which I wouldn't say.

EDWARDS: Because of your different sensibility.

MURRAY: Yeah. It's just that you take it all, and you do it. See, you do it, and it's like "C-Jam Blues." You know, you swing it. And that's it. And then the guy himself says, "Geez, I wish I was brown-skinned." That's what you try to do.

My work doesn't ever stick to ethnicity and yet I don't want anyone ever to be thought of as a greater authority on ethnicity. They should say, "Ask him, he *knows*." Or, "He's got the voice. He's got the this, he's got the that." But the whole thing is—like Duke, you see . . . I want to say that Negroes never looked or sounded better than in Murray and Duke. With everybody else, they've got to go through a certain amount of mud. But they sump'm else, Murray and Duke. That's an *ambition*. You see what I'm saying? So the guy says, "I wanna be like that." See, I don't have any problem with teaching at an exclusive school, a white school, like Washington and Lee. When all the kids run after me it's because they're my boys. "I wanna be like him." It's that type of thing that you want to do. And you want to cut across that. Why is Stan Getz playing like that? Why are those guys running around looking like Miles? What's Gerry Mulligan *doing?* Every time he picks up his horn he wants you to feel that he was in Kansas City. He was hanging out with that. He wants to say, "I have as much authority dealing with these nuances as these guys. I don't want you to say that mine is different. I don't want you to say that I'm playing with an accent." Like the guy says, "Don't bother Stan Kenton, he thinks he's swinging." [Laughter.]

So the difference between me and Ralph Ellison is the difference between emphasis and the difference in literary strategy. But we have much of the same information and there's no conflict at all in our ultimate goals.

But I could not write *Invisible Man*. Look, look, with all the stuff and all the talk and so forth, Invisible Man is a victim. He's got the possibilities, but he's in a *hole*.

EDWARDS: But he doesn't submit. He's ultimately committed to the struggle of life.

MURRAY: He's a tragic hero with the possibility of redemption. Not really redemption, but rejuvenation, metamorphosis, all those things. But basically all the stuff that's happening to him is closer to a sense of tragedy.

EDWARDS: But a universal sense of tragedy.

MURRAY: Of course. We're not talking about disaster. We're talking about the nobility of tragedy. I'm interested in epics. It's another literary strategy altogether. I write about heroic possibility. I'm one of the few Americans to write about heroism. If you take me somewhere and the guy says, "We gotta get together because we gon' do this and them people did this to us and they did that to us, so we mad as hell," I'm going to say, "We gon' get up in the morning and we gon' do this and we gon' do that, and then we gon' *zap* the motherfuckers!" You see, that's the difference, and that's what they're not ready for. They're wallowing around being victims. I can't *stand* that! Because there is none of that in jazz. You triumph over that.

EDWARDS: Stomp it.

MURRAY: You see what I mean? And all these people know that. They go home. They play some low-down dirty blues. What did they want to do? Go out and fight white people, or go fuck? They want to get some pussy. They don't want to go out there and talk about no damn injustice and taxes and no money. The only time they talk about money is when they don't have enough money to get a gal, so she went off with another guy. So they're talking about art as fertility ritual.

EDWARDS: Which is what the blues is about.

MURRAY: You stomp the blues—that's a purification ritual. Why do you purify it? You have these two universal rituals—one to purify the environment of that which menaces human life, the other is the fertility ritual to ensure the continuation of the species. To revitalize existence. The union of lovers ensures the continuation of life. That's why we have the copulating blues. *So I can get in her pants.* [Laughter.] *If I don't get in her pants, ain't gon' be no tomorrow*—for me or nobody else! We got all these children out of wedlock because we still stomp the blues every Saturday night. This goes back not only to Storyville but also to Sophocles.

And I keep hoping against hope that I'm gonna win, you know, that people will see that our foreparents had respect for themselves, that they believed in their own humanity and integrity. They could not be torn apart. They weren't putting on a front. They were for real. In *Gone With the Wind*, when Mammy is fitting Scarlett O'Hara's corset and she tells her mistress, "You done had a baby, you ain't never gon' be no eighteen-and-a-half inches again," it's because Mammy knows what is behind the façade of the plantation mistress. *She* made Scarlett into a lady. Our foreparents knew what was behind the myth of whiteness, because they helped create it. Later, Scarlett O'Hara sees the devastation of the South, and still she keeps her dignity. Who taught her that? Aunt Jemima. Uncle Ben.

EDWARDS: Let's talk a little bit about Romare Bearden.

MURRAY: Yeah, Romy.

EDWARDS: And your relationship to him.

MURRAY: I had known about Bearden on my own, but I also knew of Bearden's work through Ralph. In fact, in [my daughter's] room there's a painting which Bearden originally gave to Ralph. Ralph gave it to me because he ran out of space, and then I was instrumental in his getting a *bigger* Bearden painting when I got him to do [his essay] on Bearden for the Albany exhibition. Then he was supposed to do another and he copped out on it and I had to do it. But by this time I was Bearden's chief literary advisor. We [Bearden and I] collaborated on most of his stuff.

EDWARDS: When you say collaborate, what do you mean?

MURRAY: He'd say, "Well, *we're* gonna do a one-man show." And then I'd say, "We oughta do something on jazz." And Bearden would say, "What should I do?" Now, we spent more time with each other than either of us spent with any other guys. Looking at paintings together, going to exhibitions. Doing things like that. So we could talk painting. We could talk music.

I met him in Paris in 1950. . . . Then, when I retired, we became buddies. We saw each other on an even more regular basis than Ellison and I did, although Ellison and I talked on the phone a lot. Romy and I would get together and we would go and look at all these paintings. That would have started in 1963, when I moved to New York and got back in touch with him. We were always doing things together—looking at paintings, buying books. And when he started making a lot of money with his painting, he would buy books. He would buy two of them, you know. And we used to meet at Books & Company, because a friend of ours had started it. We would meet over there every Saturday and we would hold court. People would find us over there. Meanwhile, I'd be setting up the outline and naming the paintings. He would say, "What should I do now?" You know contemporary painting, the major painters, right?

EDWARDS: Sure.

MURRAY: See, Romy can't stand up without Pieter de Hooch, Vermeer, the Dutch on this side—he [even] looked like a Dutchman—and Matisse on the other. To get to modern art, you can't go back through [the] Middle Passage and get there that way. Because they don't get into modern art. You go through the Musee de L'Homme. Romy and I would communicate just like that. All painting concepts and stuff like that. So he'd say, "What can I do?" And so I'd say, "What about Storyville Odalisque?" You know, Matisse. Bing! He's off. You know, you've got twelve numbers on that. So what has he got? You can see it right off. You can see the design. I would think in terms of design, but in poetic and metaphorical terms. So I would say, "Well, you've got a professor." See the piano player. You got an ornate mirror. You got a room. You've got a woman partly dressed. This guy sitting over here. So you've got the stylization of the keys. It's like Matisse's odalisques. You know, they're very busy. A long way from the cut-outs. It's boogie-woogie. It comes right out of pointillism. So you can give these things the illusion of busyness.

All these are visual statements with a literary overtone. So that, as abstract as the paintings were, they come back with a representational type of thing. But what saved it, how *we*, in a sense, saved it, was—he was moving in a direction to make it known—I came up with the concept of "The Prevalence of Ritual." He was doing a bunch of conjure women, playing around with that. This was when I came on board of collaboration. We were doing lots of other things, but then I started visiting his studio a lot, and he liked my phrases. And he was a big reader of mine. All you've got to do is look at the paintings and see how many trains there are. Trains! I saw these conjure women. And there was a bestseller a few years before that was called *The Prevalence of Witches*, and that phrase stuck with me. I gave it to him, and mine stuck—"The Prevalence of Ritual." Wham! It hit him. And that, I submit, saved his painting from genre painting. You know what I mean by that?

MURRAY: If you look at a painter like Jacob Lawrence, his painting is genre—what Negroes look like, how they live, the way their neighborhood looks. These are the peasants represented as art, like the wonderful peasant life of France. Painting critics call that genre.

EDWARDS: So how did "The Prevalence of Ritual" elevate or save Bearden from genre?

MURRAY: The stylization overshadows the report. So Romy could do a series on anything and it wouldn't be genre. See all of this jazz we did? Well, it's not just illustrating jazz. [Murray is pointing to a large Romare Bearden painting hanging in the apartment.] That's just a painting on it's own right. See, that's Duke Ellington. Look at that painting. Look at the variation. Look at these rectangles; they're different colors. Look at these rectangles on the piano legs. Look at this! Look at the glistening on the top of the piano. That's a half-moon. So you see how these figures are in there. Look how the white is played with. Now, instead of the keyboard, it's that little fence between the ringside and the others. But you've still got the same type of strokes in the painting.

EDWARDS: So it's the stylization—

MURRAY: It's swinging! That sonofabitch is *swinging*, man. But if you just get the report. . . . This is not quirky twist on a report; that's another thing. But it's the *painting* that does it. Art is a process by which raw experience is stylized into aesthetic statement. So what we have on the wall is not a report, but an aesthetic statement. When you deal with those fundamentals like that, you can keep it in focus. You can learn to appreciate what the guy's doing. You can see how he's playing with these things. This becomes not white but *light*. So the drumheads are light. They're reflecting light. So, too, with the shine on Duke's knee.

EDWARDS: What's this painting called?

MURRAY: *Duke Ellington on Stage*. Oh, I named a lot of them, and I set the context for a lot of them. Romy would call my wife and say, "Well, I've been pretty busy. Tell Al, tell Al I got to see him. I've got all these orphans over here that need names." [Laughter.] There was no sense of competition. Bearden loved writing and I loved painting. We had extremely close and shared aesthetic insights.

EDWARDS: You've written books and essays about music and literature. Do you think you'll ever write a book about art?

MURRAY: Not really. You know the Bearden piece? That's about it.

EDWARDS: You obviously have a lot to offer on the subject.

MURRAY: I might. You never know what'll happen. . . . Little articles might just happen if I find I want to say this, want to say that. Just like you want to come by and talk to me about something—

EDWARDS: Might stimulate something?

MURRAY: Mmm hmm.

((part two))

PLAYING HARDBALL

Mr. Brown and the Sweet Science

Randall Kenan

He stood no more than five foot eleven or perhaps even five foot ten when I first met him, though his presence made him seem seven feet tall. His face was broad, his nose—once broken in a boxing match—commanded his face, and his eyes were concentrated, fierce. He often joked that Jamaicans and Haitians and other island people often assumed him to be a kinsmen, though he was from New York, such was the darkness and ur-African nature of his features and color. He often said his hue held tones of copper: a man made of metal. He always wore his hair extremely close-cropped, and as his neck was thick and his shoulders broad, his being seemed to fill up a room—not simply by the sheer power of his body, I am convinced, but by the power and strength of his soul.

When I first met him he had given up the boxing ring itself and was now a trainer, though his physique was still that of a fighter. He told me that boxing had been called the Sweet Science, that it was an art, not mere brawling, a matter of brain more than body, a craft of intelligence and discipline. Above all, discipline. At less than five years of age I had never met a man quite like him—an athlete, an urbane, dapper gentleman. His wit was sharp, quick and humane; his learning was vast and his mind ever inquisitive.

To me his will seemed palpable, a tangible thing. Though he was gentle and genteel, he also inspired something akin to fear in those who did not know him, a dread understanding that if he were crossed in the wrong way, hell might be unleashed—his a righteous fire, that of a warrior, a shaman, a bard, and an artisan. It has been said of Pope Gregory XII that his will was so great that for him to make up his mind was for the thing to be done, that his concentration was so awesome that sparks flew up from the heels of his sandals as he paced the garden.

To me, Mr. John W. Brown is such a man. Mr. Brown.

•

I came into this world virtually fatherless and motherless. Illegitimate. Left, figuratively, on the doorstep of my paternal grandfather, a benevolent businessman, and in turn given to his sister, my great-aunt. For my first three years her husband was an early source of affection and guidance and male presence. Nearly thirty years later I still remember his image: the large face, the light coloring, the sparkling eyes, the tall carriage with the straw fedora, the expansive smile and hearty laugh.

This was in Chinquapin, North Carolina, in the late sixties and early seventies, rural to a fault, with farms and tractors and hogs and chickens and fields of corn and tobacco. The church still occupied a place of omnipresence and order in the lives of the country folk—Chinquapin being the sort of community that ideological conservatives wax idyllic over in our present age of obsession with crime and anxiety about technology.

One day during September when I was three, outside a packhouse wherein women graded cured leaves of tobacco, lying next to me, my great-uncle died.

I remember most powerfully not so much a feeling of loss, but a sense of bewilderment. The distraught and grief-stricken look on my great-aunt's face, the confusion, the sudden absence of male touch and mirth.

Bewildered I would remain, little did I know, for many, many years to come.

•

Mr. Brown loved to talk. His interests were broad, from politics to science, from history to horticulture, always centering around human nature—he was first and foremost a student of man. He knew more songs and song lyrics than I will probably ever know, and could and would sing entire songs for eras I could never know, giving me a way into seeing the thirties, forties, fifties: "Just give me flyjalapa on the side." Mr. Brown loved to laugh, and his laugh was belly-hard and soul-deep. I remember laughing so hard with him that it physically hurt me. He knew more jokes than the comedians on TV: "The other day it was so hot . . ." "How hot was it, Mr. B.?" "It was so hot I saw a man in a corn field with a mule, the corn started popping, the mule saw it, thought it was snow, and froze to death." Humor to him was a balm and a salve, a way to teach and transform the world, a way to gain distance and immediacy. Humor was weapon and medicine—with it he could do almost anything.

But behind the laughter I could almost see his brain zipping and darting and crackling, taking in, analyzing. To this day I marvel at the speed of his mind—always several steps ahead, always working. Mr. Brown was the first man I knew who was composed of many parts—parts not at war, but in congress.

Make no mistake: men had been around. My grandfather, who lived in a nearby town, stopped by my great-aunt's farm several times a week, and his interest in me was genuine, but the demands of his business severely limited his time. Across the road from us lived my cousin Norman, who to me was very old when I was born, who ran his large farm with a wizard's mysterious majesty. His son, Roma, a high-school teacher—large, deep-voiced, capacious, avuncular, sometimes farmer, always deacon and trustee of the church—was certainly a frequent presence in our house. To be sure, cousins and uncles and men in this farm community were known to me, and me to them. Hard-working, often God-fearing, decent, good men. Yet for one reason or another their presence was somewhat distant; they had families of their own; their time—and rightly so—was devoted to their own sons. For many years my most important lessons were taught to me by the ever-present, seemingly all-encompassing, loving miracle of women. Aunts, grandmothers, cousins.

Especially my great-aunt Mary, who was a lioness and a grand vizier and a sorceress. To me she had magic powers and superhuman strength; to me she held the world together with her very fingers—and still does. I never felt neglected, in truth, or deficient; and in truth I never was. Yet beneath the surface, where changes were beginning that would later be made outwardly manifest, I had no way of knowing I had much to learn about that construct, that myth, that burden, that terrible reality of being a man, a black man in America.

•

Of course he stood out from the very beginning. Clearly he was a Yankee, which is not a disparaging term among Southern black folk, as it is among Southern white folk, but it is assuredly a mark of difference. Everything about him—his clothes, his walk, his clipped way of talking, his manners—bespoke New York City. Our good country people were at once charmed, beguiled, curious, suspicious, defensive, transfixed. Largely he was a mystery—they knew not his people, they knew not his history—for Southerners dwell within the tumult and continuity of history as do no other creatures. John W. Brown was a bright dark anomaly among them. To me he was a continuing amazement.

Early memories. At five, visiting my great-aunt's daughter in New York. Mr. Brown taking me to a gym in Harlem. The smell of sweat and the leather of boxing gloves. Watching Mr. Brown skipping rope with the speed of lightning, punching the speed bag, sparring. Visiting the Bronx zoo: the chimps, the tigers, the giraffe, seals, gorillas, polar bears, pythons. I remember most vividly the pythons. Chinatown. My first attempt to use chopsticks. Summer vacation. Waiting for Mr. Brown and my cousin to arrive down home. His vocal amazement at the remoteness and the space of the country. Everyone still chuckles at the memory of his mistaking tobacco plants for huge collard greens. His fascination with the quotidian elements of country life, those everyday miracles which a country boy finds hopelessly boring: cucumber patches, dirt roads, mockingbirds, deer, dogs, apple trees. Over time I gradually began to see his fascination with the commonplace, learning to take little for granted, gaining a new sight.

I remember one summer day him pointing out on the front page of the newspaper that Duke Ellington had died. Duke who? And my education and abiding fascination with jazz commenced. Sarah Vaughan, Count Basie, Tito Puente, and Lady Day—all suddenly became lifelong gifts. Music was no longer just music; it had a history, a form, a style, a meaning. My ears became instruments and I learned how to listen.

Nowadays we wail and gnash our teeth at our "wayward young black men," a seemingly "lost generation" given to violence, to lawlessness, to low self-esteem. I often ask, Are we truly lost? Are we truly wayward? But does anyone ever ask, Who is teaching them to listen? Who is teaching them to see?

.

I had been a dreamy kid, aloft in fantasy and make-believe. Comic books, fairy stories, tales of the amazing and especially of the fantastic were my real world. Paying little attention to the outside world, I lived for Star Trek and Spiderman and the vampires, werewolves, and bigfoots of horror novels, though I was frightened unto death of the dark.

Out on my great-aunt's farm, literally miles away from other boys my age, I made my own world in my head, peopled with elves and space aliens and wizards and whatever else I saw fit. Reality was not real, and without intervention who knows where time would have taken me? Who knows where I would have learned those lessons a young black man sorely needs to learn in order to become a man?

I did not know, as I know now, that for a young black man—struggling for some sense of himself in this world with the added pressures of his dark skin and his relegated rung on the ladder of society—the imperative is that he understand himself via his maleness, via his history, via his soul, and how that insight is of the utmost importance, the difference in some cases between life and death, for if a young African-American male does not come to terms with the myths the world holds about him and the realities of what lies in wait outside the gates of his home, then his ignorance may well rise up in the middle of the night and slay him like a thief.

.

In 1972, Mr. Brown and his wife—my cousin—and their less-than-a-year-old daughter moved down from New York to build a house in Chinquapin. They all lived with us for the year that their house was being completed. The lot on which it was to be built had been bulldozed, and in the rear of the property lurked this monstrous and forbidding mountain of earth and timber and tree stumps which had to be done away with.

Offers came from certain men in the community to dynamite the stumps; people made bids for great sums of money to take care of this onerous business. Mr. Brown was having none of it. In mid-January he struck out with a pickax, a shovel, an ax, and a few other tools, and single-handedly attacked what the family had begun to call the Pile.

This became his daily occupation, his goal—to decimate the Pile by the beginning of spring when the snakes came out, and to recover the land as the site for a garden.

Needless to say, folk in the community began to gossip behind his back about that uppity Yankee thinking he could actually take on that huge job alone and without heavy equipment, about how he'd give up in a few weeks and hire someone to do it for him. People would stop by and look, give specious advice, and go back and gossip some more. Mr. Brown would often ruefully note that for all the advice he received he never received any offers of help.

So he went on without help, except for my pitiful attempts after school and those of two other cousins on rare occasions—digging up stumps, cutting down brush, chopping wood, redistributing soil, burning debris. He once almost lost his vision when a thorn snagged his eye. He was soon back to work.

Each day after school I'd visit the site and he would show me the day's progress and give me a task. He would talk to me, debriefing me on my studies ("How did you do on that English test? Tell me what you learned about the Aztecs"), filling in gaps of history ("Ah, so you've never heard of the Black Panther Party? Well . . ."), admonishing me to take my studies and my life seriously, taking me, a ten-year-old boy with comic books and toys on the brain, seriously, seeing more of my future than I could even have imagined, recognizing about me strengths and weaknesses it would take decades for me to discover. Teaching me by example and by presence.

I say by example for in seeing in him take on the Pile alone I saw one of humankind's most awesome displays: a man sets himself a huge project, applies himself to it day by day, hour by hour, one task at a time, religiously, and by using time and discipline he accomplishes that goal. A simple lesson, in truth, but one that needs to be witnessed to be fully comprehended.

I say by presence for by being there each day, by physically being at hand and taking an active interest in my well-being and development, an unspoken bond had emerged between Mr. Brown and me which I could actually count on. Not that the women around me took no interest in me, far from it, but Mr. Brown brought another understanding, a man's understanding of how I would have to exist in the world, a knowledge of what I, as a male, a black male, would face, which a woman could not so readily foresee nor understand from personal experience.

Eventually spring came, as it is wont to do, and as Mr. Brown had decreed the Pile was a thing of the past. In its place lay a manageable piece of earth ready for tilling. He set out to plant his first garden—just as he had begun to plant a forest of ideas in my brain.

Oddly enough, folk in the community were not so quick to refer to Mr. Brown as that crazy Yankee after that.

•

Mr. Brown believed that a sound body promotes a sound mind. He would cajole me to come running with him early in the morning (he spat upon the word "jog"). I never matched his number of miles or his endurance, but he pushed me to go my limit.

I would watch boxing matches with him on television and he demystified the sport for me, teaching me the difference between a jab and an uppercut, between when a fighter was fighting smart and when a fighter was fighting dumb, sending orders through the television screen.

Once he tried to teach me to box. In his garage he put me through the paces, the muscle-wrenching exercises, the breathing exercises, the skipping rope. Only when we sparred did it become apparent that I had no aptitude—or desire—to hit or be hit. I remember beginning to sob, at eleven or twelve, as much as from embarrassment as from the sting of a few light raps to the noggin. Mr. Brown simply stopped and helped me off with my gloves—the Golden Gloves he had been awarded as a youth—the tears slipping down my cheeks. He said to me that day, as he looked me square in the face with no hint of either judgment or disappointment, "Remember, tears are not a sign of weakness."

Though I never put on a pair of boxing gloves again in my life, I never felt like a weakling.

•

When Mr. Brown said he was going to join the Chinquapin Volunteer Fire Squad, I didn't give it much thought. When he said later that he was going to join the rescue squad, my interest was piqued.

Being a small, unincorporated community, all of Chinquapin's services were strictly volunteer. Mr. Brown thought it only reasonable that if he, being a homeowner, was going to depend upon the goodness of his fellow neighbors for the safety of his home, then he should participate in the process for them. He also noted how few black men in the community actually belonged to the fire and rescue squads and who took active roles, and he felt—especially since many of the community's so-called leaders were not members—that this negligence sent out not only a message of hypocrisy, but also a generally negative message about the response of African-American males to their own responsibilities.

He quickly became an officer in the fire squad, took a course at the local community college to become a certified emergency medical technician, and joined the rescue squad.

Those nights he was on call, sleeping over at the station, he sometimes allowed me to stay over with him—on non-school nights, of course. For a kid who had to go to bed after the eleven o'clock news, the prospect of sitting up all night at the fire station in the company of men waiting to "come to the rescue" was a predictably heart-pumping experience. Imagine the glee of an already too-fertile imagination at being One of the Men for a night, at the exciting prospect of being in the Action, as if awaiting a call from the Batphone! Often on Friday nights someone would be out back roasting a hog for the weekly Saturday barbecue sale to benefit the Fire and Rescue volunteers, and Mr. Brown and I would bring a chicken which we would season and place on the coals. To date that's the best chicken I can ever remember having—so succulent, so tender—me munching that good and hot chicken over tales of Mr. Brown's exploits as a youth in New York not as rough-and-tumble as it would become, but tougher and angrier than a country boy could truly imagine. Wide-eared, I gobbled up the stories with the chicken, not realizing that in truth Mr. Brown was feeding me cautionary tales as well, tales of survival and ingenuity, tales of growing up.

There were fires and rescues during "my watch," and though I was not allowed to go out, later I would be there, wide-eyed and expectant, to hear the sad tales of demise or the happy tales of success, and I would see how Mr. Brown, either stoic in reflection or jubilant in victory, would examine the event—the squad's work, his work, the mistakes, the cause for the accident—in effect teaching me some of life's harshest and most practical of lessons, giving me a firm sense of reality: Beware, be aware, be wise.

On two distinct occasions, I remember Mr. Brown and his partner being called to fatal accidents involving classmates of mine. Any illusions about my own immortality were duly snuffed out. Though I did not actually see the car wreck or the shooting accident, I saw the blood in the ambulance afterward and no greater cautionary message exists—especially if you know where the blood came from. We spoke of death, Mr. Brown and I, of how it came when it came and of how we should be, could only be, prepared. Such intense lessons about reality are indeed rare, and only years later am I beginning to see the depth and the clarity of those moments, and how at such an early age I came to an appreciation of the brevity and frailty of our lives upon this earth.

Being there with Mr. Brown, though great fun, also affixed in my head the idea of a black man sharing in responsibility and involving himself in altruistic causes. Any time I hear disparaging nonsense about the selfishness and irresponsibility and inconsistency of African American men, I remember Mr. Brown and think, No, I know a hero. He is a black man.

•

Mr. Brown taught me how to squeeze water from a knife, how to separate my thumb from my hand and make it glide across my palm—illusions. He also taught me how to tell the difference between illusion and reality.

It was my twelfth birthday. Mr. Brown asked me if I would like all the hamburgers and french fries and hot dogs I could eat. My eyes grew big. My mouth watered. Sure! He took me down to the local Tastee Freeze, where I greedily ordered something like four hamburgers, four hot dogs, several orders of fries, a coke. O what gustatory bliss! Imagine a newly twelve-year-old boy with carte blanche to eat unlimited amounts of junk food. Mr. Brown sat next to me calmly, with a devilish grin planted on his face which I was too absorbed to note, egging me on. "Have another, why don't you? Oh, you can eat another. Sure. Come on. Knock yourself out. It's your birthday! Another hot dog, please. You want another hamburger? Give him two more. There you go . . ."

I have no recollection of how much I actually ate that day, but needless to say I vividly remember the ensuing night and day—the first day of my school career that I was forced to stay home with profound stomach pains. Mr. Brown came by to visit. "Would you like another hamburger?"

I got the message. Literally years passed by before I could look at a hamburger or a hot dog without feeling sick to my stomach. I had never been a greedy child, but to this day the brilliance of that lesson is not lost on me, the crystalline wisdom of teaching a young boy a lifelong lesson about gluttony he'd never forget, a lesson no amount of preaching and punishing could accomplish. Diabolical, to be sure, but frightfully wise nonetheless. And effective.

•

Life lessons don't come easily, nor the wisdom to concoct them. Mr. Brown in many ways remained a mystery to me throughout my growing up, even as we grew closer. Much of the mystery was intertwined with how he came to be so wise, so resolute, so independent, and at base so kind and so loving—as when I saw his fierce love for his wife and two daughters. He would tell tales of working for the City of New York and of his earliest jobs, of the difficulties and the determination involved in his own "making it," of how his discipline and caginess were born out of necessity. He would tell me I had one thing he did not have—him, someone to teach me the lessons he had had to figure out on his own. So when he lectured me on the evils of drugs and alcohol and crime and violence, these conversations never felt like lectures but like messages from some other side, guideposts left by a wanderer who had safely made a journey.

•

Many lessons, much wisdom. Even after I went away to college he continued to teach me by word and by example—when he told me to follow my heart and head in writing, when he supported my move to New York and bolstered my courage and calmed my fears, when he himself began a new career as a special education teacher and basketball coach for "challenged" youngsters and demonstrated how mirth and honesty and genuine concern can turn people around. When I would come home to visit he would talk for hours about these kids and their problems and about how, beneath the surface, they just needed someone to take time with them, to be real with them and dole out a little glee, understanding, and caring.

Undoubtedly the most painful lesson came in the late eighties, when Mr. Brown had reached his late fifties and out of the blue was stricken with a rare blood disease. His health, his energy waned. He was hospitalized. I was called home from New York.

I remember the scene in the hospital: the fear and anguish of his two daughters and his wife, and of my great-aunt, his mother-in-law, who had become, over the years, his best buddy. And Mr. Brown himself, hitched up to all manner of blipping, blurping, blinking machines—the jungle of IV tubes, the respirator down his throat. I remember standing by and feeling absolutely helpless. Helpless for him, helpless for my family, helpless for me. Remembering all those lessons, remembering his admonition. Beware, be aware, be prepared. I wasn't. He was pronounced dead. But he didn't stay dead.

His recovery was full, though he lost a thumb, and I do believe he even gained something in the process—something grand and not easily uttered. I could see it in his eyes, hear it in his voice. Especially in those quiet moments when I would catch him peering into the evening sun. Certainly I and my family gained something, something more than time, more than hope. I attributed his resurrection to his indomitable will, to those sparks that flew from his heels when he thought and walked. He simply said it just wasn't his time, that God had further use for him on this plane. In any case, seeing him literally on his deathbed and coming back to life, going back to gardening and fishing, taught me something more. As before, implicitly and explicitly he had shown me a lesson that Batman and the Lone Ranger and Rambo never could, for in seeing him battle with death and the imponderable mystery, in seeing him contemplate his mortality and his loved ones, I never once saw him lose his dignity or his courage or his grand humor or his unshakeable sense of self and what was most important and valuable to him. Here was a new profile in courage and will and strength, something undreamt of in fantasies of musclebound warriors and gun-toting action heroes.

What is courage? I had seen it firsthand. The only times I saw him cry were when he was faced with the outpouring of concern and love from his former students and friends—a note of prayer scribbled on a greeting card by a nine-year-old or a visit from members of the basketball team he had coached made him mist up, made his voice crack, and he'd pause, look at his wife, and shake his head in a sign like gratitude, like acceptance, like affirmation of these demonstrations that he was held not only in high esteem but in love and affection.

Though there was a cornucopia of lessons, the most abiding lesson learned from Mr. Brown is this: Yes, one man can make a supreme difference. Do not merely try—do. If you fail—and you might—no one can fault you, especially and most importantly, not you yourself.

We are none of us mistakes, but rather the simple and complex merging and parting of events and genetics, the coincidences and absences and doubts which surround and make up the human heart. The mysteries that we are—so naked to ourselves, but seen only through a glass darkly even by our closest friends and kin, if at all—are but the sum of these life particles. Or, to paraphrase the poet Tennyson, I am a part of all the people and places I have met. None are more important to my being who I am than Mr. Brown.

Such words as "father" and "mentor" pale next to the devotion and gratitude I feel toward this one man, a man made of dust and water, just like the rest of us, no more or less, another mortal being, simply. But in this life, in this country, in this black America, I count myself as one of the more fortunate among black men. I had Mr. Brown, who taught me the Sweet Science of Life.

(from *Colored People*)

Playing Hardball

Henry Louis Gates, Jr.

Daddy worked all the time, every day but Sunday. Two jobs—twice a day, in and out, eat and work, work and eat. Evenings, we watched television together, all of us, I'd done my homework and Daddy had devoured the newspaper or a book. He was always reading, it seemed, especially detective stories. He was a charter subscriber to *Alfred Hitchcock's Magazine* and loved detective movies on TV.

My brother Rocky was the one he was close to. Rocky worshiped sports, while I worshiped Rocky. I chased after him like a lapdog. I wanted to be just like him. But the five years between us loomed like Kilimanjaro. We were always out of phase. And he felt crowded by my adoring gaze.

Rocky and I didn't exactly start off on the right foot. When I was born, my parents moved my brother to Big Mom's house, to live with her and Little Jim, who was our first cousin and Nemo's son and the firstborn male of our generation in the Coleman family. It was not an uncommon arrangement to shift an older child to his or her grandparents', because of crowding. Since we had only three rooms, plus a tiny room with a toilet, my parents thought the move was for the best. And Big Mom's house was only a couple hundred yards straight up the hill. Still, it's difficult to gauge the trauma of that displacement, all these years later. Five years of bliss, ended by my big head popping out.

But Rocky was compensated: he was Daddy's boy. Like the rest of Piedmont, they were baseball fanatics. They knew who had done what and when, how much everyone had hit, in what inning, who had scored the most runs in 1922, who the most rbi's. They could sit in front of a TV for hours at a time, watching inning after tedious inning of baseball, baseball, baseball. Or sit at Forbes Field in Pittsburgh through a double-header without getting tired or longing to go home. One night when I was seven, we saw Sandy Koufax of the Dodgers pitch one game, then his teammate Don Drysdale pitch another. It was the most boring night of my life, though later I came to realize what a feat I had witnessed—two of baseball's greatest pitchers back-to-back.

I enjoyed *going* to the games in Pittsburgh because even then I loved to travel. One of Daddy's friends would drive me. I was fascinated with geography. And since I was even more fascinated with food, a keen and abiding interest of mine, I liked the games for that reason too. We would stop to eat at Howard Johnson's, going and coming. And there'd be hot dogs and sodas at the games, as well as popcorn and candy, to pass the eternity of successive innings in the July heat. Howard Johnson's was a five-star restaurant in Piedmont.

I used to get up early to have breakfast with Daddy, eating from his plate. I'll still spear a heavily peppered fried potato or a bit of egg off his plate today. My food didn't taste as good as his. Still doesn't. I used to drink coffee, too, in order to be just like Daddy. Coffee will make you black, he'd tell me, with the intention of putting me off. From the beginning I used a lot of pepper, because he did, and he did because his father did. I remember reading James Agee's *A Death in the Family* and being moved by a description of the extra pepper that the father's wife puts on his eggs the very morning that he is killed in the car. "Why are you frying eggs *this* time of day?" Mama asked me that evening. "Have you seen the pepper, Mama?" I replied.

An unathletic child with too great an interest in food—no wonder I was fat, and therefore compelled to wear "husky" clothes.

My Skippy's not *fat*, Mama would lie. He's husky.

But I *was* fat, and felt fatter every time Mama repeated her lie. My mama loved me like life itself. Maybe she didn't see me as fat. But I was. And whoever thought of the euphemism "husky" should be shot. I was short and round—not obese, mind you, but *fat*. Still, I was clean and energetic, and most of the time I was cheerful. And I liked to play with other kids, not so much because I enjoyed the things we did together but because I could watch them be happy.

But sports created a bond between Rocky and my father that excluded me, and though my father had no known athletic talent himself, my own unathletc bearing compounded my problems. For not only was I overweight, I had been born with flat feet and wore "corrective shoes." They were the bane of my existence, those shoes. While Rocky would be wearing long, pointy-toed, cool leather "gentlemen," I'd be shod in blunt-ended, round toed, fat-footed shoes that nobody but your mother could love.

And Mama *did* love those shoes. Elegant, she'd say. They're Stride-Rite. Stride-*wrong*, I'd think. Mama, I want some nice shoes, I'd beg, like Rocky's.

Still, I guess they did what they were meant to do, because I have good arches now. Even today I look at the imprint of my wet foot at a swimming pool, just to make certain that my foot is still arched. I don't ever again want to wear those dull brown or black corrective shoes.

What made it all the more poignant was that Rocky—tall, lean, and handsome, blessed with my father's metabolism—was a true athlete. He would be the first Negro captain of the basketball team in high school and receive "the watch" at graduation. (He was the first colored to do that, too.)

Maybe Mama thought I was husky, but Daddy knew better, and he made no secret of it. Two-Ton Tony Galento, he and Rocky would say, or they'd call me Chicken Flinsterwall or Fletcher Bissett, after Milton Berle's and Jack Benny's characters in a made-for-TV movie about two complete cowards. I hated Daddy for doing that and yielded him as unconquerable terrain to my brother, clinging desperately to my mother for protection.

Ironically, I had Daddy's athletic ability, or lack thereof, just as I have his body. (We were the same size ring, gloves, shoes, shirt, suits, and hat.) And, like him, I love to hear a good story. But during my first twelve or so years we were alienated from each other. I despised sports because I was overweight and scared to death. Especially of baseball—hardball, we called it. Yet I felt I had no choice but to try out for Little League. Everyone my age did Little League, after all. They made me a Giant, decided I was a catcher because I was "stout, like Roy Campanella," dressed me in a chest protector and a mask, and squatted me behind a batter.

It's hard to catch a baseball with your eyes closed. Each time a ball came over the plate, I thanked the Good Lord that the batter hadn't confused my nappy head with the baseball that had popped its way into my mitt. My one time at bat was an experience in blindness; miraculously, I wasn't hit in the head. With a 3 and 2 count, I got a ball, so I walked. They put in a runner for me. Everybody patted me on the back like I had just won the World Series. And everybody said nice things about my "eye." Yeah, I thought. My tightly closed eye.

Afterward, Pop and I stopped at the Cut-Rate to get a caramel ice cream cone, then began the long walk up the hill to Pearl Street. I was exhausted, so we walked easy. He was biding his time, taking smaller steps than usual so that I could keep up. "You know that you don't have to play baseball, don't you, boy?" All of a sudden I knew how Moses had felt on Mount Sinai. His voice was a bolt out of the blue. Oh, I want to play, I responded in a squeaky voice. "But you know that you don't *have* to play. I never was a good player. Always afraid of the ball. Uncoordinated, too. I can't even run straight." We laughed. "I became the manager of the team," he said. That caramel ice cream sure tasted good. I held Daddy's hand almost all the way home.

In my one time at bat I had got on base. I had confronted the dragon and he was mine. I had, I had . . . been absurdly lucky . . . and I couldn't *wait* to give them back their baseball suit. It was about that time that Daddy stopped teasing me about being fat. That day he knew me, and he seemed to care.

Yes, Pop and I had some hard times. He thought that I didn't love him and I thought he didn't love me. At times we both were right. "I didn't think you wanted me around," he told me much later. "I thought that I embarrassed you." He did embarrass me, but not like you might think, not the usual way parents embarrass children in front of their friends, for example. He had a habit of correcting me in front of strangers or white people, especially if they were settling an argument between me and Pop by something they had just said, by a question they had answered. See, I *told* you so, he'd say loudly, embarrassing the hell out of me with a deliberateness that puzzled and vexed me. I hated him when he did that.

And despite my efforts to keep up, he and my brother had somehow made me feel as if I were an android, something not quite a person. I used to dream about going away to military school, and wrote to our congressman, Harley Staggers, for a list of names. I used to devour *McKeever and the Colonel* on Sunday nights and dream about the freedom of starting over at a high-powered, regimented school away from home. Daddy and Rocky would make heavy-handed jokes about queers and sissies. I wasn't their direct target, but I guess it was another form of masculine camaraderie that marked me as less manly than my brother.

And while I didn't fantasize about boys, I did love the companionship of boys and men, loved hearing them talk and watching their rituals, loved the warmth that their company could bring. I even loved being with the Coleman boys at one of their shrimp or squirrel feeds, when they would play cards. Generally, though, I just enjoyed being on the edge of the circle, watching and listening and laughing, basking in the warmth, memorizing the stories, trying to strip away illusions, getting at what was really coming down.

On the Distinction of "Jr."

Houston A. Baker, Jr.

I am eleven years old, giddy with the joy of fire and awed by the seeming invulnerability of my father. He is removing dead coals from the glowing bed of the furnace. He is risking the peril of flames. We are sharing, I think, the heroism of taking care of the family. We are together. He is intense, sweating slightly across the brow. He still wears the shirt and tie from another long day's work. For some reason I am prompted to move with the pure spirit of being. I begin dancing around the furnace room with light abandon. My voice slides up the scale to a high falsetto. I am possessed by some primitive god of fire; I feel joyful and secure. I am supremely happy, high-voiced, fluid.

Then I am suddenly flattened against a limestone wall, bolts of lightning and bright stars flashing in my head. I have been hard and viciously slapped in the mouth as a thunderous voice shouts, "Damnit! Houston, Jr.! Stop acting like a sissy!" (sissy, *n.* 1. an effeminate boy or man; a milksop 2. a timid or cowardly person 3 [informal]. sister). Having heard my falsetto chant, my father had turned from the furnace with the quick instinct of an exorcist. He had hit me with the fury of a man seeing a ghost. The smell of woodsmoke is what I recall as I ran up the basement stairs and out into the Louisville night, astonished at how much I had angered my sacred and invulnerable father, whose moods of manhood were as predictable as the San Andreas Fault.

My name contains the sign of ownership and descent appropriate to the bourgeoisie. I am not a "second" or "II." I am a "junior" (junior, *adj.* 1. younger: used to distinguish the son from the father of the same name, and written, *Jr.* after the full name). The inheritance that passes to me from "Sr."—the man at the furnace—remains a mystery seasoned by small details.

He was born in Louisville, Kentucky, to a mother whose entire life was spent as a domestic for white families. His great-grandmother had escaped, or so the story was told, from a Mississippi slaveholder. She made her way to Kentucky with her owner in hot pursuit. His father, my paternal grandfather, was so light-complexioned that he might easily have been mistaken for the white slaveholder from whom my great-great-grandmother escaped. Harry was my paternal grandfather's name, and his greatest talent, or so I was led to believe, was fishing.

The cryptic unreadability of my father's life appears before me with the strange attraction and repulsion of a keloid. (keloid, *n.* a mass of hyperplastic, fibrous connective tissue, usually at the site of a scar). I want to turn away from his wounds, the scars, the disorder that I believe ripped his consciousness and shredded his boyhood days. But I cannot turn away. With each new revelation or additional detail supplied by my mother, who is in her mid-eighties, or by my older brother, in his mid-fifties, my attention is more firmly riveted. My head and gaze are fixed like Winston's in Orwell's *1984.* I see the pain coming, but am never certain where it will fall.

Prostitutes were a successful and shame-free business for my father's grandmother. From my father's boyhood perspective, his grandmother's "girls" must have seemed like uncanny citizens of a bizarre extended family. I vaguely remember his telling me one day, in a faraway voice, that his first sexual encounter was with one of his grandmother's girls, who in effect "raped" him.

So much is difficult to turn away from in what I perceive to be the scarring of my father's life. There is his mother urging him to stay forever her own "good Negro Christian boy," yet regaling, tempting, titillating him with tales of the glory of white success. Tales of the spartanly clean windows, shining cars, and infinite spaces of white opportunity in America. His boozy father, hunkered down in an old leather chair with the radio playing schmaltzy popular songs, dozing in the middle of some urgent question his son was trying to ask. Reverend Shepherd, a white Anglo-Saxon messiah of a boxing coach, urging those black Presbyterian boys of Grace Church to self-extermination for the glory of God and the good health of a "Negro race" that white American insurance companies would not even consider as clients.

Houston, Sr.'s answer to the aching incoherence of his boyhood was summed up in an exhortation that he barked at my brothers and me whenever we came close to tears or were on the brink of a child's response to pain. This exhortation—an admonishment that was his Rosetta stone for surviving chaos—was "Be a man!" There was nothing, mind you, ethnic or racial in this injunction. Just "Be a man!"

Since I remember no stories from my father's lips about being comforted by the arms of his mother or told fuzzy bedtime stories by Harry, I have to assume Houston, Sr., was like the children of the Dickens character Mrs. Jelleby, who just "tumbled up." This process translates in Afro-American terms as "jes' grew."

Houston, Sr., was left on his own to formulate commandments for his life. There were no tender revelations from his parents or burning-bush epiphanies from the mountaintop. "Be a man!" was therefore his resonant admission that only the most tightly self-controlled and unbelievably balanced postures could ensure a journey from *can't* to *can* in America. There was no time or space for sentimentality, tears, flabby biceps, fear, or illness in the stark image of American conquest my father set before himself. His notion of success was as deadpan and puritanical as the resolutions scripted by F. Scott Fitzgerald's Great Gatsby. Houston Sr.'s manhood code was every bit as full as Gatsby's of cowboy morality, gutsy goodwill, and trembling guilt about treating one's parents better. Mental control was like sexual control in my father's vision; it was a kind of *coitus interruptus* expressed in maxims like "illness and pain are all in the mind," "a woman should never make a man lose control," "race has nothing to do with merit in the United States," "the successful man keeps himself mentally, physically, and spiritually fit." Manhood was a fearless, controlled, purposeful, responsible achievement. And its stoutest testimony was a redoubtably athletic body combined with a basso profundo for speaking one's name—especially to white folks. "Hello," he would growl in his deepest bass, "my name is **Baker—Houston A. Baker!**" I often step back and watch, and hear myself in the presence of whites—especially those who overpopulate the American academy—growling like my father: "Hello, I'm **Houston A. Baker, Jr.!**"

If Houston, Sr., had a notion of heaven, I suspect he saw it as a brightly modern building where his own well-lit and comfortably furnished office was situated right next to the executive suite of Booker T. Washington. Washington's manly singleness of purpose and institutional achievements were taught to my father. He absorbed them into his very bones while putting himself through West Virginia State College under the mentorship of the great John W. Davis. Houston, Sr., and Booker T., building a world of American manhood, service, progress, and control; Houston, Sr., and Booker T., in their lives of service becoming swarthy replicas of ideal white businessmen like Carnegie or Vanderbilt the Elder.

And, like Booker T.'s paradise at Tuskegee, Houston, Sr.'s ideal heaven would surely have housed wives tending children who if they were male would be vigorously instructed to "Be a man!" When not tending children, these wives would be satellites of manly Negro enterprise, raising funds and devoting themselves to the institutional growth of a world designed by and pleasing principally to men. In my father's heaven there would certainly be no confusion between love and sex, race and achievement, adults and children, men and not-men.

•

With the household furnace billowing smoke and ash on that evening long ago, my father must have suffered the fright of his life when he heard my falsetto and turned to see my lithe dance, accentuated by the whitewashed walls and the glow of the fire. Houston, Sr., could only, I think, have grasped this scene as a perverse return of his arduously repressed boyhood. His boyhood had been marked by a Louisville East End of commercial sexuality and muscular Christianity. The West End had been colored by a mother's ambivalent love for her light-skinned prodigy. He struck out in a flash against what he must have heard and seen as my demonic possession by the haunting fiends of unmanliness. What, after all, could God be thinking if he had somehow bequeathed to Houston, Sr., a sissy instead of a son? And so he hit me very hard. Walking in the woodsmoke air that autumn evening (actually just around the block and through the back alley, since I didn't dare stay out too long), I could not get a handle on what precisely I had done to make Houston, Sr., so angry.

Many years after the event, I learned the term "homophobia" and labelled my father's actions accordingly. As I think now about that moment long ago, I realize that my father was indeed afraid, yet his fear was not nearly so simple or clearly-defined as an aversion to physical, emotional, intense and romantic love between men. There is a strong part of me that knows my father was fascinated by and even attracted at a level of deep admiration to what he believed, with great earnestness, to be the intellectual superiority and discipline of what he called the homosexual lifestyle. I think what terrified him on that evening years ago was not homosexuality as he ideally conceived it. Rather, he was afraid on that autumn evening that I was fast approaching adolescence and had not found what he deemed to be the controlling voice of American manhood. Clearly, then, it was time for Houston, Sr.—he knew this with both fierce dismay and instinctive terror—to busy himself with the disciplining of Jr.

The tragic emotional shortcoming of that evening was that my father did not realize that the letters at the end of my name were not meant to confirm his ownership or responsibility with respect to my name. "Jr."— as its formal definition makes abundantly clear—is meant to distinguish a younger self from the woundings of "Sr." It is sad that my father failed to realize that it was precisely those feelings of assurance, security, and protection which he had bestowed on me that overwhelmed me, that made me want somehow to dance for him.

It has required many hours of painful thought since that violent moment in which my father branded me a sissy to extract and shape for myself a reasonable definition of my life in relation to my father's. For decades I have sought patterns to fulfill a Jr.'s life. Mercifully, I have found some. They include much that my father was forced to ignore, deny, reject, or misunderstand. He could never, for example, have given approving voice to the informal definition of "sissy" that is sisterhood. Tragically, he never envisioned a successful man's life as one measured and defined by its intimate, if always incomplete, understanding and sharing of a woman's joys, dangers, voice, and solacing touch—shaped definitively, that is to say, by sisterhood.

Unlike the "Sr." produced by ordeals I have yet fully to comprehend, it is impossible for me to imagine "Jr." without a strong woman's touch. I am now the middle-aged father of a quite remarkable son. And at this moment I imagine that with God's grace I shall be able to live up to the standard of distinction the concluding marks of my name are meant to signify. If I do achieve such distinction, perhaps in some far-off fall twilight my son will dance for me. Speaking through rhythmic motion and with the very voice of possession, he will pronounce his own name in the world.

A Mighty Good Man

Dennis A. Williams

He was Confectioner's, the old candy-and-drug store where I bought my first copy of *Fantastic Four* while he had a beer next door. And Proctor Park, where I learned to chase a frisbee while the women dished potato salad and other people's business. And the transistor radio that brought the Yankees to life while we barbecued chicken in the back yard. And the best toy on Christmas, and a ride on the ferris wheel. He was my past and also my future: he never told me about women and never had children, but he showed me how to be a husband and a father. It's not his fault that I'm not as good at either as he was; without him I might never have bothered at all.

Orphaned at a young age, Willis Hall was raised by an older sister and her husband in the Italian-accented, semi-industrial confines of Utica, on the Mohawk River in upstate New York. He grew to be an easy-going, gentle man, tall and handsome in the 1940s style that never left him, with a pencil-thin mustache and stocking-cap wavy hair. One summer, while he worked as a hotel waiter, a local hairdresser introduced him to a girl from North Carolina who was working in the service of a white family. Milia—he called her Mally—was a bold beauty, as outspoken as he was reserved, and maybe that was what got his attention: she was the rest of him and brought out the best of him. He knew it right away, but she went back home a few times before he won her heart. And then, in the first year of their marriage, he was called to three years' service in World War II.

After he came home he never left her again, not until the day he died in his sleep five months after he'd asked her to help him up and drive him to the store so he could buy her a Valentine's Day card, unable to bear the thought of missing the occasion. That was four months after she had somehow wangled a ride to join him in the hospital during the East Coast's worst storm in decades (the doctors sent her home before she was snowed in for several days, which would have been fine with her). He died only, in fact, after she had finally told him, as he lay asleep in the hospital bed in their home, that it was all right for him to go. They'd hung on as long as they could, for fifty-two years. A few days later, he ran his last errand—he went on ahead to hold a table for them on the other side.

While Willis was away at war, Milia befriended a precocious teenager who had moved up from Mississippi with her mother, the niece of the husband of Willis's sister. Milia and the teenager decided to simplify the relationship by calling themselves cousins, and fifty years later it was she—my mother—whom Willis asked to stay with Milia when he made his final trip. By the time I was able to untangle the actual familial relationships (I was well into adulthood), they hardly mattered. It was enough to know that I belonged to Willis—that we all belonged to one another—in a way that biology could never account for. Willis and Milia never had children of their own. With her family still in North Carolina and his scattered, our family—my mother, grandmother, older brother, and I—living fifty miles away in Syracuse, became next of kin. For some reason it was I, the second child, who was named their godson, even though it was understood that they were the surrogate parents for both of us. That was a particular blessing because they were the only married parents I had; my mother and father had separated when I was a year old and later divorced.

Significantly, Willis knew my father and never attempted to take his place. It would have been easy to do. My father lived farther away and communicated regularly but saw me less often. He was a sometimes mysterious and fearsome figure, a writer and bachelor living a strange life in the Oz of Manhattan. Though never mean and often generous, he presumably felt compelled to assert his authority in order to make up for lost time and to mold my brother and me, as was his obligation. In many ways, being with my father was work; being with Willis was uncomplicated fun. He always seemed willing to let us do whatever we wanted to do, but that never turned out to be anything bad. I can only now begin to appreciate how much effort and genius that requires—to guide without commands, to correct without rebuke, to set limits without saying no. I took this apparently effortless form of implicit parenting for granted. I knew always how much my brother and I meant to Willis, but I didn't know and shouldn't have known how much he might have wanted to claim us. Unlike the women in my life—my mother, grandmother, and godmother—Willis never said a word or made a gesture to criticize my father or diminish his authority, though arguably he would have had the most to gain from doing so. Instead, he became his own special kind of father figure. He drew his authority from kindness and earned my love by loving me as if I were his own while never pretending that I was.

Willis was something of a square, though he never seemed so to me because the residual hipness of his adult world clung to him in his casually natty appearance, the rarely played (when I was around, anyway) Joe Williams and Dinah Washington records in the living room, the passing references to this club and that pool hall. When he did party, it seemed more out of a desire to escort Milia and my young mother on a fun outing. That, of course, was the telling difference. I knew even then without being told that to be truly hip, to be that kind of manly man, one had to enjoy a life without women. Willis was the opposite kind of ladies' man, the kind considered by women to be "a good man." He had no friends with whom he would rather keep company than his wife. He was also a man of the church, and in that peculiarly female atmosphere, only the pastor gets to be "the real man," the sultan of the harem. All the others, the deacons and trustees and ushers and Sunday school teachers, admired as they are as civic-minded role models, in the end are doing women's work. Willis filled the role cheerfully. At his funeral, I learned that he had been known as the Minister of Kindness among his congregation, a description that fit his relationship with the rest of the world as well, and one that demonstrated his dignity and pleasure in being uncool.

For my childish purposes, however, he was just as cool as he needed to be. He played tonk and crazy eights with my brother and me, bought us suction-cup bow-and-arrow sets and didn't mind when we lost all the arrows on the roof, took us up to the park to launch frisbees and water-powered rockets. It didn't take much out of him, because he supervised our more active play without actually taking part, often getting us going and then laying back to dig it. My brother, not the most lively of characters, would eventually join him, perhaps stretching out under a shade tree in the park, while I dashed around like a puppy, retrieving a variety of projectiles, and the womenfolk chided them both for running me ragged. I can't say I didn't mind; at some point I usually began to feel ganged-up on and taken advantage of. But any frustration or anger I felt was always directed at my brother, who was getting his own brand of manhood training by aligning himself with the big guy at my expense.

Though he was a big man, six-foot and farm-solid, Willis believed in taking it easy. He worked hard, but I never saw him in that role, and in fact my only personal confirmation that he was a working man at all was the lunchbox on the kitchen counter that Milia would pack for him on Sunday nights, after we had gone. (She worked as well, as a nursing-home dietician; two-earner families were the norm among working-class black folks of my acquaintance, and so the notion of a working wife as threatening to one's manhood has always seemed silly to me.) For me, Willis was entirely a creature of leisure—weekends, holidays, vacations—and primarily the sort now scorned as "couch potatoes." He watched baseball and football on TV and drank beer; he drove to outings and tended the barbecue at gatherings, and ran domestic errands with us in tow. He did what needed to be done with unfailing good spirits that made any request, especially from Milia, seem urgent. But he didn't go looking for action. One of my earliest memories of him is washing the car, a two-tone green '57 Chevy, and maybe I remember that precisely because he wasn't the sort who was always waxing or crawling underneath. When automated car washes became more available, he had no qualms about giving up that duty, either.

My father, on the other hand, preferred to move. With him we were always doing—and learning. A much-anticipated vacation in New York might turn into a camping trip in the then wilds of Easthampton, with target shooting and no toilets. Even now, I never know when I'll have to hold a ladder or some power tool before I get to sit down and hold a scotch. That's not all bad; it has become a part of our ritual. Such activity, however, always carries expectations. It's not just getting it done or even doing it together, but also about the responsibility to get it done right, and the pending judgement of dissatisfaction if (when) I've screwed it up (still). Even at rest, my father was always teaching, cramming us with lessons that often had the short-term effect of taking the fun out of things he invariably judged racist, corrupt, or just plain stupid.

Being with Willis was relaxing in more ways than one. His laid-back demeanor helped cool my brother and me out without replacing our youthful activity with chores. When there was work to be done we joined him because we wanted to—the fellas hanging together—and helped when we could without any performance pressure. When he accompanied me on my one and only Cub Scout camping trip, I knew he was there only for me and wouldn't care if I couldn't catch a fish. But most of the time it was okay just to sit around, play cards, look at TV, and talk that noncommital man-talk, occasionally filling gaps in the silence that buffered us from the girl-talk in the next room. And in doing so my brother and I absorbed a different lesson than the ones my father so diligently conveyed: that we were equals, and could act like (literally mimic) a grown man without seeming to audition for the part; that this was our birthright, who we already were though yet to become; that we didn't have to put a bullet through a beer can, start a proper fire, or pass a current events quiz to belong.

As a father, I've never quite gotten the knack of Willis's more benign approach, which may have something to do with the difference between being a father and being a father figure. I still can't dependably make a decent fire, but I'm always conscious of showing my children how to do things properly. (Somehow I still feel I'm the one with the performance pressure, though.) The quizzes I'm good at; I constantly find myself delivering mini-lectures to a daughter and son who have far fewer qualms than I ever had about rolling their eyes in impatience and changing the subject—or even warning me that I'm starting to sound like Grandpa, which I take as a compliment. Yet as much as I know that these things are a father's duty, my lazy afternoons with Willis remind me always that there must be more. And so I catch myself and stop teaching and preaching and try to let them share my space uncritically, to offer the easy companionship—the security of being—that I finally settled into with my father and that Willis could afford to give me all along.

Like the occasional sip of Utica Club or Genesee beer. It seemed to me that he drank a lot of it, but he didn't; it was just one of those man-things I didn't see often in a house run by women. At our place, he drank from tall, slender glasses, otherwise unused, embossed with a spiral of dalmatians pursuing a bright red fox. (Highballs, on the other hand, were a unisex, special occasion treat; in either case, I was left with ginger ale.) Being more a regular guy than my father, Willis also became the primary target of traditional man's gifts: cigarette lighters (though he rarely smoked), cheap cologne, shaving supplies. I had no idea about what things men really used or wanted, other than what the drugstores told me on Father's Day and Christmas. Willis was no help, of course, because he never wanted anything from us except to be around.

Timing was everything. While they came to our house for Christmas—Santa and Mrs. Claus in a Chevrolet—we always went to Utica on the weekend nearest my birthday, which is usually also Father's Day. I have always related the two in my mind, and the transference has been remarkably completed; the celebration of my status takes precedence over the marking of my birth, and I want nothing more—really—than to be with my children.

When I was six, my mother took me on a train trip to St. Louis, a grand adventure for which I still don't know why I was selected. We returned home on a Sunday afternoon, and I was thoroughly prepared to rub my brother's face in the triumph of my special status as our mother's chosen escort. But he wasn't home. Willis and Milia, with their unfailing sense of justice, had appeared to whisk him off to the local amusement park. They brought him back hours later full of junk food and thrills, and my deflated—no, outraged—reaction only confirmed that they had done their duty and evened the scales. Of course they would have done the same for me, as I knew perfectly well. They were *my* godparents but *our* guardian angels.

One September Saturday when I was eleven, Willis and Milia came to spend the weekend. As usual, "the boys" hung out together, which meant toys and comics, games and TV, while "the girls" went shopping. The difference this time was that both groups were mobile, because my mother had bought our first car a few months before. But that mobility brought a new risk, and late in the afternoon, after we had finished our rounds, Willis answered the phone and learned that there had been an accident. All my mothers—my mother, grandmother, and godmother— were in the hospital, and for a short, scary time I was forced to confront the possibility that the boys might be all that was left of the family. The thought was scary only because of the potential loss, not because I was concerned for an instant about what would become of me. I knew we were in the right place, and in the right hands. In retrospect, I'm sure that had the worst happened, my brother and I would have gone to live with our father; Willis would have insisted, no matter how much he may have wanted, in that moment especially, to embrace us as his sole and rightful heirs.

As it turned out, the panic, at least the worst of it, was momentary. My grandmother, whose head had shattered the windshield, was hurt the worst but not badly. Willis was perfectly calm throughout, as he conveyed the news, took us to the hospital, and waited with us through several hours until everybody came home in one piece. It was a typically bravura performance, without fear or bluster or any hint of the over-emotionalism that might have undone us. Just as he would do thirty years later, when he sought to hold off death as he hadn't been able to hold off Uncle Sam, he simply asserted that everything was going to be okay. In fact, it didn't occur to me *until* thirty years later, when I realized how desperately he wanted not to be separated from Milia, how fearfully great the prospect of his own loss must have been for him then.

By rights, my experiences with Willis should have left me eager to re-create them with a son of my own. But that was not the case. I always wanted a daughter. Maybe I just never believed that Willis's kindly approach could really work with anyone whose maleness hadn't already been dampened by relentless matriarchy. Luckily, because my wife favored boys as much as I did girls, I had no qualms about entering parenthood. When our daughter was born, my wife's first words, delivered without any obvious bitterness, were, You got what you wanted. She never gave up hope for a boy, although it was fully seven years later before I was able to believe that I was ready for a male child. When our son arrived, it wasn't long before all the matriarchs pronounced him, with equal parts admiration and dread, "a real boy." He was physical and intuitive, completely and stereotypically unlike our willful and obsessively organized daughter, who commanded more attention and energy simply by being there than our son did by literally climbing walls. The pronouncement of the women triggered all my deepest insecurities. If "real boyness" was a good thing, why hadn't they sought to promote it in me? If it was a bad thing, was I being implicitly challenged to train him as if he were a German shepherd? And how was I supposed to do that when I had been, in a sense, so effectively neutered as a boy-child myself that I had hardly ever pulled at the leash?

My father offered one model, which remains useful. One move in particular ranks in memory with anything I ever saw from any commanding figure, from Jim Brown to Patrick Ewing. Sitting on the floor of our apartment with my brother, helping him set up an electric train, my father once became extremely annoyed. In a single movement he snatched my brother up by the collar, unfastened and withdrew his belt, and delivered a series of lashes with the speed of Ali's jabs. I was thoroughly impressed and intimidated—no way was I ever going to mess with *this* guy. My grandmother, who was home at the time, was apparently impressed as well. For all her sideways criticism of the man who had left her daughter, she did nothing to intervene. I suspect now that she was gratified in the way women are when a man takes charge of a situation they *want* him to take charge of. It was the sort of performance my wife may have in mind when she tells me I need to do something about *my* son.

But Dad was a visitor. Kicking ass becomes much less complicated when you know you're leaving town the next day. Watching his day-to-day dealing with my younger brother by a second marriage yielded few comparable moments of righteous clarity. Alternately tough and conspiratorial, he often seemed just as confused and frustrated as everybody else.

It took me a long time to figure it out, but Willis was the answer. At least half the answer, because it was impossible to know for certain how he would have acted if he had had to deal with me *all* the time. Somehow, though, I suspect he could never have resorted to even the kind of physical punishment usually applied to children in general and to boys in particular. Firm when necessary, he never became angry enough to raise a hand. It probably helped that he was a master at the secret warning that is far more common than the wait-till-your-father-gets-home cliché. Your mother wouldn't like that, he would say, or, Milia might get upset if you do that. That he himself might disapprove—that I might let *him* down—was too horrible a prospect to contemplate, and therein lay his power.

It doesn't always work, but it helps. It would be wrong to suggest that my mother and grandmother ever gave me anything but unconditional love. Willis, however, added the irreplaceable ingredient of friendship, a luxury the women never felt, justifiably, that they could provide. For most men, including myself, it is nearly impossible to pull off this man-to-boy solidarity without at the same time conveying a sense of disrespect for the woman involved—it usually comes across as, I don't know why she's so pissed off and in fact I think she's crazy, but you know she's going to go off on you and make my life miserable, too, so just do what she wants and forget about it. Willis's absolute devotion to my godmother made it work, because his deflection of anger never translated into the notion that Milia was unjust or unreasonable. How could she be? He adored her, and he himself would never do anything to make her unhappy. As a result, his warnings reaffirmed rather than undermined her authority, developed within me a healthy respect for her, and had the benefit (in addition to getting me to do right) of teaching me how to love a woman.

I haven't lived up to his standard. Who could? However, as I grew into his kind of ladies' man, often wondering whether my eagerness to please others, especially women, was the perverse accomplishment of some matriarchal conspiracy, his example fortified me. It's easy enough to know that a man's greatest pleasure should come from the happiness of the woman he loves, but it's hard not to feel like the world's last fool when trying to live by that rule. Nearing the end of a second decade of marriage (not even halfway to Willis's record), I become increasingly conscious of his unselfconscious legacy.

But it is with my children, my son in particular, that I feel his influence most strongly. Playing ball in the back yard with him, making a run to the comics shop, or watching the Knicks on TV, I am eerily aware of the parallels—and of my desire for such moments to mean as much to him as they once did to me. Not long ago, as we were walking somewhere, my son tried to position himself so that his shadow could disappear completely into mine. It was an innocent, spontaneous gesture, typical of his fascination with natural phenomena. And it filled me with awe. Instinctively, I began to puff myself up, to make myself big enough to contain him, to assure myself that I was equal to the task. It worked. He felt satisfied, I felt blessed.

The last time I saw Willis I carried with me a secret. A few days before, I had discovered what I believed to be a tumor and I was convinced it was malignant. It later turned out to be neither, but the hypochondria served a purpose. Instead of coming to Willis with the mournful pity of a scheduled (and unacknowledged) farewell, I came for a final lesson in dignity and strength, more amazed than ever that he could be so fearlessly tranquil in the face of losing what he loved so fiercely—not life itself, but his life with Milia.

As it happened, my actual birthday fell on Father's Day that year, and I knew I had to be there with him. Reality intervened; Milia suggested we come two weeks earlier, because at that point you could never be sure. He was dressed and sitting up for the occasion, though confined to his bedroom. "Getting stronger every day," he said as he had before, although by then he must have known it wasn't true. Having finally found a physical activity worthy of his mightiest efforts, he had spent much of his bulk wrestling death to a standstill long after the doctors had expected him to succumb.

We sat together for a while pretending it wasn't the bedroom, and watched the New York Mets play the Houston Astros, and traded knowing comments about how dreadful an exercise that was. I was ready for him to falter, to show a hint of despair so that I could comfort him for a change. I had steeled myself to be ready to do that for him. He never needed it, or if he did he never let me know, just as he had never let Milia know. It wasn't in him. Milia brought him a plate of lunch on a tray, which he barely touched—said he wasn't hungry but that the food, as usual, was good. My son joined us for a bit before urging me to play a game of nerf-catch in the back yard. I was reluctant to go, but Milia said Willis needed a nap anyway. So we went and played, while my wife and daughter followed the script by becoming the girls who chatted with Milia in the kitchen. Everything was as it was. Finally, we brought the kids upstairs to say good-bye (for now, ostensibly), and I embraced him. And we went home.

I had imagined that at that point I would have been consumed by grief. Instead, despite my imagined tumor and his all-too-real one, I felt wonderful. Because I had left Willis knowing with absolute certainty two things I had not known before. One was that the only reason I had to fear dying was that I would leave my wife and children alone, and as long as I realized that—and lived as if I believed it—I could face death, paradoxically, with no fear at all.

The next day my doctor exposed my tumor as a fantasy. A month later Willis was dead. I tried to be sad, but he had left me nothing to be sad about, except in the most self-pitying way, which he himself would have found pointless. I felt proud of him, not so much for his yearlong struggle with death as for his seventy-eight-year conquest of life, which proved that good men *aren't* hard to find. What's hard for us is accepting that it's okay to be one—to purge ourselves of ego and to find satisfaction, even joy, in a generosity that invites the scorn of those who will always see weakness in unselfish strength. Our friends will think we have grown soft. Our children will seize upon any indecision or resentment as evidence that our indulgence is artificial. And even our women will suspect our motives. The only way to achieve that heightened level of manhood and retain the barest measure of respect is to let go the notion of manhood itself almost entirely, at least as it's commonly understood, as a role that obliges us to bury part of ourselves prematurely, just because. Willis avoided that trap by finding his manhood in his humanity. And in the example of his living he left me a map so that I might do the same—if I'm man enough to try.

Shades

William Henry Lewis

I was fourteen that summer. August brought a heat I had never known, and during the dreamlike drought of those days I saw my father for the first time in my life.

The tulip poplars faded to yellow before September came that year. There had been no rain for weeks and the people's faces along Eleventh Street wore a longing for something cool and wet, something distant, like the promise of a balmy October. Talk of weather was of the heat and the dry taste in their mouths, and they were frustrated at having to notice something other than the weather in their daily pleasantries. Sometimes, in the haven of afternoon porch shade or in the still and cooler places of late night, they drank and laughed, content because they had managed to make it through the day.

What I noticed was the way the skin of my neighbors glistened as they toiled in their back yards, trying to save their gardens or working a few more miles into their cars. My own skin surprised me each morning in the mirror, becoming darker and darker, my hair lightening, dispelling my assumption that it had always been a curly black, the whole of me a new and stranger blend of browns from day after day of basketball on asphalt courts or racing the other boys down the street after the Icee truck each afternoon.

I came to believe that it was the heat that made things happen. It was a summer of empty sidewalks, people I knew drifting in and out of the alleyways where trees gave more shade, the dirt there cooler to walk on than any paved surface. Strangers would walk through the neighborhood seemingly lost, the dust and the sun's glare making that place look like somewhere else they were trying to go. Sitting on our porch, I watched people I'd never seen before walk by seemingly drawn to those rippling pools of heat glistening above the asphalt, as if something must be happening just beyond where that warmth quivered down the street. And at night I'd look out from the porch of our house a few blocks off Eleventh and scan the neighborhood, wanting to see some change, something besides the nearby rumble of freight trains and the monotony of heat, something refreshing and new. In heat like that, everyone sat on their porches looking out into the night and hoping for something better to come up with the sun.

It was during such a summer, my mother told me, that my father got home from the third shift at the bottling plant, woke her with his naked body already on top of her, entered her before she was able to say no, sweat on her through moments of whiskey breath and indolent thrusting, came without saying a word, and walked back out of our house forever. He never uttered a word, she said, for it was not his way to speak much when it was hot. My mother was a wise woman and spoke almost as beautifully as she sang. She told me he'd left with the rumble of the trains. She told me this with a smooth, distant voice, as if it were the story of someone else, and it was strange to me that she might have wanted to cry at something like that but didn't, as if there were no need anymore.

She said she lay still after he left, certain only of his sweat, the workshirt he'd left behind, and her body calming itself from the silent insistence of his thrusts. She lay still for at least an hour, aware of two things: feeling the semen her body wouldn't hold slowly leaving her and dripping onto the sheets, and knowing that some part of what her body did hold would fight and form itself into what became me nine months later.

I was ten years old when she told me this. After she sat me down and said, This is how you came to me, I knew that I would never feel like I was ten for the rest of that year. She told me what it was to love someone, what it was to make love to someone, and what it took to make someone. Sometimes, she said, all three don't happen at once. When she said that I didn't quite know what it meant, but I felt her need to tell me. She seemed determined not to hold it from me. It seemed as if somehow she was pushing me ahead of my growing. And I felt uncomfortable with it, the way second-hand shoes are at first comfortless. Soon the pain wasn't as great, just hard to place.

After that she filled my home life with lessons, stories, and observations that had a tone of insistence in them, each one told in a way that dared me to let it drift from my mind. By the end of my eleventh year I learned of her sister Alva, who cut two of her husband's fingers off, one for each of his mistresses. At twelve, I had no misunderstanding of why, someday soon, for nothing more than a few dollars, I might be stabbed by one of the same boys that I played basketball with at the rec center. At thirteen I came to know that my cousin Dexter hadn't become sick and been hospitalized in St. Louis, but had gotten a young white girl pregnant and was rumored to be someone's yardman in Hyde Park. And when I was fourteen, through the tree-withering heat of August, during the Watertown Blues Festival, in throngs of sweaty, wide-smiling people, my mother pointed out to me my father.

For the annual festival they closed off Eleventh Street from the downtown square all the way up to where the freight railway cuts through the city, where our neighborhood ends and the land rises up to the surrounding hills dotted with houses the wealthy built to avoid flooding and neighbors with low incomes. Amidst the summer heat were the sizzle of barbecue at every corner, steamy blues from performance stages erected in the many empty lots up and down the street, and of course the scores of people, crammed together, wearing the lightest clothing they could without looking loose. By early evening the street would be completely filled with people and the blues would have dominion over the crowd.

The sad, slow blues songs my mother loved the most. The Watertown Festival was her favorite social event of the year. She had a tight-skinned sort of pride through most days of the year, countered by the softer, bare-shouldered self of the blues festival, where she wore yellow or orange-red outfits and deep, brownish-red lipstick against the chestnut shine of her cheeks. More men took the time to risk getting to know her and every year it was a different man; the summer suitors from past years learned quickly that although she wore that lipstick and although an orange-red skirt never looked better on another pair of hips, never again would she have a man leave his workshirt hanging on her bedpost. With that kind of poise she swayed through the crowds of people, smiling at many, hugging some, and stopping at times to dance with no one in particular.

When I was younger than fourteen, I had no choice but to go. Early in the afternoon she'd make me shower and put on a fresh cotton shirt. You need to hear the blues, boy, a body needs something to tell itself what's good and what's not. At fourteen, my mother approached me differently. She simply came out to the yard where I was watering her garden and said, You going? and waited for me to turn to her and say yes. I didn't know if I liked the blues or not.

We started at the top of Eleventh Street and worked our way downtown over the few hours of the festival. We passed neighbors and friends from church, my mother's boss from Belk's Dry Goods, and Reverend Riggins, who was drinking beer from a paper cup instead of a can. Midway down Eleventh, in front of Macky's Mellow Tone Grill, I bumped into my cousin Wilbert, who had sneaked a tall-boy of Miller High-Life from a cooler somewhere up the street. A zydeco band was warming up for Etta James. We stood as still as we could in the intense heat and shared sips of that beer while we watched my mother—with her own beer—swaying with a man twice her age to the zip and smack of the washboard.

Etta James had already captured the crowd when Wilbert brought back a large plate of ribs and another beer. My mother came over to share our ribs and Wilbert was silent after deftly dropping the can of beer behind his back. I stood there listening, taking in the heat, the music, the hint of beer on my mother's breath. The crowd had a pulse to it, still moving up and down the street but stopping to hear the growl of Etta James's voice. The sense of closeness was almost too much. My mother was swaying back and forth on her heels, giving a little dip to her pelvis every so often and mouthing the words to the songs. At any given moment, one or two men would be looking at her, she seemingly oblivious and lost in the music.

But she too must have felt the closeness of the people. She was looking away from the stage, focusing on a commotion of laughter in front of Macky's, where voices were hooting above the music. She took hold of my shoulders and turned me towards the bar. In a circle of loud men, all holding beer, all howling in laughter—some shirtless and others in work clothes—stood a large man in a worn gray suit, tugging his tie jokingly like a noose, pushing the men into new waves of laughter each moment. His hair was nappy, like he had just risen from bed. But he smiled as if that was never his main concern anyway, and he held a presence in that circle of people which made me think he had worn that suit for just such an appearance. My mother held my shoulders tightly for a moment, not tense or angry or anxious, just firm, and then let go.

"There's your father," she said, and turned away, drifting back into the music and dancing people. Watching her glide towards the stage, I felt obligated not to follow. When I could see her no longer I looked back to the circle of men and the man that my mother had pointed out. From the way he was laughing he looked like a man who didn't care who he might have bothered with his noise. Certainly his friends didn't seem to mind. Their group commanded a large space of sidewalk in front of the bar. People made looping detours into the crowd instead of walking straight through that wide open circle of drunken activity. The men stamped their feet, hit each other in the arms, and howled as if this afternoon was their own party. I turned to tell Wilbert, but he had gone. I watched the man who was my father slapping his friends' hands, bent over in laughter, sweat soaking his shirt under that suit.

He was a very passionate-looking man, full in his voice, expressively confident in his gestures, and as I watched him I was thinking of that night fourteen years ago and the lazy thrust of his that my mother told me had no passion in it at all. I wondered where he must have been all those years and realized how shocked I was to see the real man to fill the image my mother had made. She had made him up for me, but never whole, never fully graspable. I was thinking of his silence, the voice I'd never heard. And wanting nothing else at that moment but to be closer, I walked towards that circle of men. I walked as if I were headed into Macky's Mellow Tone and they stopped laughing as I split their gathering. The smell of liquor, cheap cologne, and musky sweat hit my nostrils and I was immediately aware not only that I had no reason for going or chance of getting into Macky's, but also that I was passing through a circle of strange people. I stopped a few feet from the entrance and focused on the quilted fake leather covering the door's surface. It was red, faded fabric and I looked at that for what seemed a long time because I was afraid to turn back into the laughter. The men had started talking again, slowly working themselves back into their own good time. But they weren't laughing at me. I turned to face them and they seemed to have forgotten that I was there.

I looked up at my father, who was turned slightly away from me. His mouth was open and primed to laugh, but no sound was coming out. His teeth were large and I could see where sometime before he had lost two of them. Watching him from the street, I had only seen his mouth move and had to imagine what he was saying. Now, so close to him, close enough to smell him, to touch him, I could hear nothing. But I could feel the closeness of the crowd, those unfamiliar men, my father. Then he looked down at me. His mouth closed and suddenly he wasn't grinning.

He reached out his hand and I straightened up as my mother might have told me to do. I arced my hand out to slide across his palm, but he pulled his hand back, smiling, a jokester, like he was too slick for my eagerness.

He reached into his suit jacket and pulled out a pair of sunglasses. Watertown is a small town, and when he put those glasses on he looked like he had come from somewhere else. I knew I hadn't seen him before that day. I wondered when in the past few days he must have drifted into town. On what wave of early morning heat had he arrived?

I looked at myself in the reflection of the mirrored lenses and thought, So this is me.

"Them's slick basketball sneakers you got," he said. "You a bad brother on the court?"

I could only see the edge of one eye behind those glasses, but I decided that he was interested.

"Yeah, I am! I'm gonna be like George Gervin, you just watch." And I was sure we'd go inside to Macky's and talk after that. We'd talk about basketball in its entirety and then he'd ask me if I was doing well in school and I'd say, Not too hot, and he'd get on me about that as if he'd always been keeping tabs on me. Then we would toast to something big, something we could share in the loving of it, like Bill Russell's fingerroll lay-up or the pulled pork sandwich at Ray's Round Belly Ribs or the fact that I had grown two inches that year, even though he wouldn't have known that. We might pause for a moment, both of us quiet, both of us knowing what that silence was about, and he'd look real serious and anxious at the same time, a man like him having too hard a face to explain anything that had happened or hadn't happened. But he'd by trying. He'd say, Hey, brother, cut me the slack, you know how it goes . . . And I might say, It's cool, or I might say nothing at all but know that sometime later on we would spend hours shooting hoop together up at the rec center and when I'd beaten him two out of three at twenty-one, he'd hug me like he'd always known what it was like to love me.

My father took off his sunglasses and looked down at me for a long, silent moment. He was a large man with a square jaw and a wide, shiny forehead, but his skin looked soft, a gentle light brown. My mother must have believed in his eyes. They were gray-blue, calm and yet fierce, like the eyes of kinfolk down in Baton Rouge. His mouth was slightly open; he was going to speak and I noticed that his teeth were yellow when I saw him face to face. He wouldn't stop smiling. A thought struck me right then that he might not know who I was.

One of his friends grabbed at his jacket. "Let's roll, bro. Tyree's leavin'!"

He jerked free and threw that man a look that made me stiffen.

The man read his face and then laughed nervously. "Be cool, nigger, break bad someplace else. We got ladies waitin'."

"I'm cool, brother. I'm cool . . ." My father looked back at me. In the mix of the music and the crowd, which I'd almost forgotten about, I could barely hear him. "I'm cold solid." He crouched down, wiped his sunglasses on a shirttail and put them in my pocket. His crouch was close. Close enough for me to smell the liquor on his breath. For him to hug me. Close enough for me to know that he wouldn't. But I didn't turn away. I told myself I didn't care that he was not perfect.

He rose without saying anything else, turned from me, and walked to the corner of Eleventh Street and the alleyway, where his friends were waiting. They were insistent on him hurrying, and once they were sure he was going to join them they turned down the alley. I didn't cry, although I wouldn't have been embarrassed if I had. I watched them leave and the only thing I felt was a wish that my father, on this one day, had never known those men. He started to follow them, but before he left he stopped to look over the scene there on Eleventh Street. He looked way up the street, to where the crowd thinned out and then beyond that, maybe to where the city was split by the train tracks running on a loose curve around our neighborhood to the river, or maybe not as far as that, to just a few blocks before the tracks and two streets off Eleventh, where sometime earlier than fourteen years ago he might have heard the train's early morning rumble when he stepped from our back porch.

A Turn for the Worse

Bruce Morrow

[My father] is kind and gentle, and has
worked hard for me so that I am able to write these words. We are not friends: he is
my father, and I am his son. We are silent when alone together . . . Our love for each
other, though great, may never be spoken. It is the often unspoken love that Black
men give to other Black men in a world where we are forced to cup our hands over
our mouths or suffer under the lash of imprisonment, unemployment, or even death.
But these words, which fail, are precisely the words that are life-giving and
continuing. They must be given voice. What legacy is to be found in our silence?
—Joseph Beam, "Brother to Brother:
Words from the Heart"

Things have taken a turn for the
worse. My mother, upon returning from my brother's house outside Atlanta for a one-week Christmas vacation, has found a crack addict in her
own home again. Things have taken a turn for the worse, my mother said.
She was so happy that I'd called, and I might as well know that Rufus
was back on his drugs again. After a short pause she said she was tired,
she'd just finished bringing the laundry up from the basement and that
was the reason she was out of breath, from climbing those stairs, and now
she had to go get Rufus's rent-a-car out of the pound. He'd gone and given

it away, she said, just let somebody have it. After an absence of four days he'd arrived home on foot. I asked her why he had rented a car in the first place, what had happened to his car. He gave that away, too, she said, or someone took it. I don't know, she said, and tried to catch her breath, to think it through again, to make sure it all made sense. Maybe somebody did steal it. That's what he told her when he got home: someone had stolen his car and he was scared, and she *had* to take him to the police station to report it. I told my mother—half joking, half speaking my mind—that she should report him, too.

Since she found out last summer that my stepfather of twenty-six years is a pipehead my mother has tried everything she can think of to help him. But things only get worse. She's tried pleading, then crying, yelling and crying, begging while crying. She's tried outpatient care, inpatient care, God's care—all to no avail. I say now is the time for my mother to change the locks on the doors, pack up his things, and set herself free. Get rid of him. Kick him out and keep him out. Don't let him back in ever again.

And yes, I know. I know these aren't easy things for my mother to do. I know it's easier said than done. I know something, anything, everything could go wrong. *I know. I know.* But something has to be done. These things have to be said. He might end up taking my mother down with him, that's what scares me. He already goes away for days and days without calling. He's now given away his car and a rent-a-car for drugs. What's he going to do—give the house away, turn the basement or the garage into a little drug den? When's he going to start stealing (if he hasn't already) from my mother's wallet? Her jewelry box? Her bank account? Has he already taken things from the house? Has he given his body away for drugs? Has someone given him sex so he can buy *them* drugs? Does he know about safe sex? It's too close, too close, even if I live in New York and they live in Ohio, and all I can do is call every day and make sure everything is all right.

These aren't easy things for me to say. Rufus, my stepfather, is the only father I know. He married my mother, an unwed mother of two, when she was twenty-six and he thirty. I was four, my brother three. And, like the scar on my face, an upside down check-mark above and to the right of my lips, he has been in my life ever since. (Mind you, he didn't give me that scar; his whippings never left permanent marks. The two incidents, the corner of a schoolbook slicing my face open and Rufus marrying my mother, just happened at about the same time.) My brother and I never called him Father or Daddy and he never adopted us. We have different last names but he's my father nonetheless. When someone asks me about my father, it's him that I talk about, him that I think of. When I fill out official papers, forms and applications, I fill in the blank "Father's Name" with his.

•

He's got brown, brown skin that always seems to have a brilliance, like a piece of hardwood furniture waxed and polished to a high, satiny glow. He's got a square face, a firm face with dark eyes you hardly see because what you really notice, even after that first look, is his forehead covered in brown shiny skin curving over the top of his balding head. The hair he does have is short, curly, and black and is usually hidden under a baseball cap, the kind truckers like to wear, the kind made of foamlike material with ventilating mesh sections on the sides and the brand names of auto parts written on the front—Champion, Firestone, Motorcraft, Delco.

He's a big man, not tall, but thick like a tree trunk, wide through the chest, broad across the shoulders from years of hard work. The thickness of his neck and arms always makes it hard for my mother to find shirts that fit him without being too long in the sleeves. When they first married, Rufus could flex his melon-sized biceps and lift me on one side and my brother on the other. Like a large crane or an amusement park ride at Geagua Lake, he'd lift us up off the ground and swing us around until we fell to the floor dizzy with delight and laughter and asked him to do it again. He always said funny things like "What's up, Zeek?" or "Slide me some skin" or "Holy mackerel, Andy" or "Save the bones for Henry Jones 'cause Henry Jones don't eat no meat." After everyone finished dinner he'd take the bones off of all the plates and stack them on his; he'd put a whole bone in his mouth, lick it clean, then break it in half and suck out the marrow. "That's right," he'd say when he was finished and there were nothing but chewed up shards of bones on his plate, "Henry Jones don't eat no meat."

He always boasted about the foods he liked to eat, how much he liked to eat, the way he liked to eat. Crispy fried frog legs. Buckets of chitlins with hot sauce. Plates of greens, turnips, and mustards and collards, with cornbread to soak up the puddles of green juice—"lickah," as he called it. He ate second and third plates of dinner, with loaves of bread and six-packs of beer—all in one sitting. He liked good scotch (Chivas, Johnny Walker, Glenlivet). He liked good cognac (Courvosier V.S.O.P.), good gin (Tanqueray, Bombay), any kind of whiskey, bourbon, but never rum. He liked Budweiser, Old English 800 Malt Liquor, Rolling Rock, and some Red Bud every once in a while.

He was never drunk, sloppy, or out of control, as I remember it. I didn't consider him an alcoholic or a person with a drinking problem. He just liked to consume mass quantities out of pure braggadocio; he had to have the best and most of everything he wanted in life. Ever since I moved to New York City almost ten years ago, Rufus's ongoing joke with me has been, "When you gonna send that?" which means, When you gonna send me that gold Rolex with diamonds around the dial? He's asked this question so often he doesn't even have to say "Rolex" anymore—or even "watch." Whenever I call or visit for Christmas he asks about "that." "That" is all he has to say. "So, Bruce, when you gonna send me *that*?"

Rufus is like that. He repeats things, says the same things over and over again. "Save the bones for Henry Jones 'cause Henry Jones don't eat no meat." He tells the same jokes, the same stories over and over again. Like how when he was growing up in West Memphis, Arkansas, he had to lift washing machines and bathtubs all by himself and put them on his father's pickup truck; poor, black and undereducated (he didn't finish high school), Rufus had to contribute to his family's income by working lots of odd jobs. "That's right," he would say, "that's right, I had to fix those machines and lift them too." And it seemed he'd get madder and madder every time he said it. "That's right," he'd say as he pulled his belt off.

He never punched us or hit us with his big thick hands, scarred and callused from working the night shift in an aluminum stamping plant for years and years. He always used the closest belt, the one around his waist; or he'd use a switch, a strong green vine he'd found in the yard and kept in the basement just in case; or he'd use an extension cord, a telephone wire, the old rubber fanbelt he'd just taken out of his good car. He would beat us until the welts ran together on our arms and it looked like we were stained the color of mashed grapes, fruit pulp ready for making wine. He turned like that, without notice, with little or no provocation. That's the way Rufus was. You never questioned his authority or you wouldn't hear the end of it—or you'd wish hearing was all there was.

He was an American success, of a certain kind, who'd risen above his humble beginnings to the middle class. He had a high-paying blue-collar job, a loving family, and a suburban house. He was a doer, always fixing things, changing the oil in his bronze-colored showboat of a Buick, waxing his car to a satiny finish with Turtle Wax car polish, painting the front porch and the trim on the house (the rest of the house was aluminum-sided), cleaning the gutters, cutting the grass, trying to get rid of the tree in the front yard because he thought it was ruining the grass. To have the perfect yard, a suburban American dream, he resodded twice, rolled the ground flat then planted a special blend of grass seeds that were supposed to grow well in dark, damp areas with lots of gnarly tree roots. He cut branches off of trees that blocked the sunlight and dropped too many leaves in the yard and the gutter.

He finally decided that the tree in the front yard had to go if his lawn was ever going to look as good as our neighbor's across the street, so he tried killing it by pouring acid down a hole he'd bored deep into the trunk. But that tree wouldn't die, didn't die until he had it cut down by a well-paid team of professionals equipped with heavy-duty saws, hooks, pulleys, and hydraulic lifting cranes. We watched from the front porch as the men, in regulation red plaid lumberjack shirts, yellow hardhats, tan utility belts, faded blue dungarees, and greased brown hiking boots, started from the top, sixty feet high, and worked their way down to the withered tree trunk, taking every precaution necessary to avoid any damage to our fine house or that of our neighbors.

Now, my mother says, Rufus won't even fix himself a sandwich. He hardly ever eats. He doesn't sleep or rest much, either. He's just wasting away. He's almost scrawny, she says. But I can't imagine it. A two-hundred-thirty-pound, five-foot-ten-inch man who had his shirts custom made or special ordered from a "big-and-tall" men's fashion catalogue. How much does he weigh now? I can't imagine him not making sure the driveway's shoveled when needed and the garbage is bagged for pickup every week and his hair's cut short and neat every month even though he wears a baseball cap most of the time. I can't imagine my stepfather a crack addict, a dope fiend, a pipehead. My mother says he's down to a thirty-two-inch waist. His skin doesn't shine anymore, it's gray, my mother tells me. He works a few days a week, afraid someone's going to ask for a urine sample, or, worse, a blood sample. Ain't no way around that one, my mother says, ain't no Chinese tea gonna clean you out *that* good. All he want's the pay, get some money and call in sick the rest of the week. He gives his whole check away so he can smoke for days and days straight. He doesn't do much else. He doesn't come home, my mother says, he doesn't worry about where he sleeps or where he shits. He lifts his pipe to his mouth, puts the pipe to his lips, lights, relights, and lights again. I imagine all around him tiny lights flickering in the dark. He's a firefly caught in a mayonnaise jar. He's a crackhead caught in a crack house burning his fingers trying to light his "shit." But he don't drop it, not even after inhaling it all into his lungs, not even after holding it, clutching it oh so near and dear to him. He holds onto his pipe while everything else dwindles away.

•

I walk home from the subway with my head held low and my shoulders hunched over to fight the cold. It's been the worst winter I've ever experienced in New York. The temperature hasn't gone above freezing in weeks. All I want to do is get home, stay home, be home. I want to go visit my mother but I can't afford it. Maybe I could talk some sense into Rufus, stay there with him, watch him, make sure he doesn't slip or fall. I could shovel the driveway, throw salt down, organize my parent's bills, protect them.

Until recently I'd never worried about my parents facing "the problems of today"—drugs, crime, AIDS. I thought of them simply growing old together, retiring, getting pensions and social security, getting high cholesterol, arthritis. Cancer and Alzheimer's were my biggest worries. Not drugs. I never thought about drugs—crack—really affecting my life. Those nightmare stories of "the chronic" were just that, stories, cautionary tales. For me the drug problem in America was the problem of others—the poor, the undereducated, the underachievers, the overachievers. Or at least that's the way the drug problem in America is portrayed. It's them over there, the blacks who've taken over and destroyed our cities, the minorities who've never finished high school, the ones on welfare; or it's those white corporate megalomaniacs, or those white suburban teenagers turned into bad seeds.

(On my way home this frigid cold winter night, I see many black and Latino male youths just hanging out on street corners, and I see at least five cars filled with white male youths driving through the narrow side streets of Washington Heights, then heading back to Jersey. I don't know for sure that drug transactions are occurring all around me, but it's definitely suspect.)

When I was in high school I used to pinch from the brown paper grocery bag of weed that Rufus kept in the back of his closet. I'd take a whole handful, sell some at school, and smoke the rest with friends. I did it to spite him. I always made sure I didn't take too much at one time. But he knew. He'd ask me for a cigarette and then ask if I had anything else, something stronger. I'd laugh knowingly but never answer.

Like all our other missed conversations, our chances to get to know one another, we never talked about getting high. We never shared a joint. I took and he accepted. It was our secret.

•

I've spoken to Rufus twice since I found out he was a drug abuser, an addict, a crackhead. The first time I spoke to him was to return the Christmas greeting he left on my answering machine. His voice sounded giddy and light when I listened to his message, and for a moment, for a bit of a quick second, I thought he was as high as a kite. He laughed—giggled—as he wished me a merry Christmas. I knew he was alone in Cleveland and my mother away in Atlanta visiting my brother. It didn't sound like a good idea to me for him to be left alone on a holiday two weeks after getting out of rehab, but as my mother told me, "He's going to do what he wants to do. He's going to do drugs if I'm there or if I'm not there. It's up to him. I can't be responsible for him doing drugs. You want to go watch him?" I didn't. But I was more than happy to get a Christmas message from Rufus and I refused to consider for any amount of time that he was fucked up and filled with more than holiday cheer.

I called him back the day after Christmas and we had a nice conversation. He immediately asked, "When you gonna send me that?" He asked it six or seven times in our ten-minute conversation. "I guess it's in the mail," he joked, and I asked him about the record amount of snow in Cleveland and if it really looked like the picture in the *Times.* "Yeah, I had to dig my way out the house," he said. "Over two feet of snow and it's still snowing." He said he'd spent Christmas with his daughter (the stepsister I didn't meet until I was in college), her husband, and their two children. He said it was real nice and I made up some lame excuse about getting off the phone and going to bed early. I just didn't have much to say to Rufus and I didn't want to reveal my suspicions about his state. He'd been out of his four-week rehab for less than two weeks.

The next time I spoke to Rufus was a surprise. I hadn't expected him to answer the phone when I called home. He's seldom home when I call. He used to always be at work. And now that my mother was sure Rufus had spent over a thousand dollars between Christmas and New Year's and had also given his car away, I was so surprised he was home that I hung up the phone. A drug addict had answered the phone; I'd called long distance and a crackhead in Cleveland Heights, Ohio, had answered. I figured I'd better wait awhile so he wouldn't suspect me of hanging up on him. I called back ten minutes later.

"Hello," he said in his normal, sleepy voice.

"Hey Rufus," I said, "so you decided to come back." I couldn't stop myself from saying what was on my mind.

"Yeah, I'm back. I know, I guess I didn't make it long."

"Well, why'd you come back? You should have just stayed away." I couldn't stop myself. I had to just ask and get it out of the way.

"What, Bruce? Just who do you think you are?"

I hadn't expected him to react, but he was already as angry and mad as I was. My mother had told me it was no use arguing with him because it didn't faze him, it just added fuel to his anger. I thought I could be smarter than that. But I wasn't.

"Just who do you think you are telling me I shouldn't come here? I live here, you don't."

"Well, then, why'd you go away for so many days? Why don't you just go live there?" I asked, raising my voice to match his. I couldn't help myself.

"Who do you think you are?" he asked again and again. "I'm not ready. I guess I'm not ready to stop. And I can't stop until *I* want to." He had learned twelve-step-speak during his rehab. "That's right. Until *I* want to. I don't need you telling me what I should and shouldn't be doing. Shit, this is my house. Where else am I going to go?"

"You can just go back where you've been. Smoking crack. Doing drugs. Just go back there."

"Well, I can't quit until I want to. I can't do it 'cause you say so. I can't do it 'cause your momma say so. I need to quit when I'm ready, that's the only time. Where the hell do you get off telling me not to come to my own house, my home?"

I didn't think that was what I had said, but he did. I couldn't say a word. I didn't want to get him mad—at me, at my brother, at my mother. He just kept right on anyway.

"This is *my* house," he said, "and I can be here if I want to. Who are you to judge me? I ain't judging you. That's right. I ain't judging the way you living."

That pretty much knocked me over. I'd played right into it. I sat down and stopped listening to what he was saying. I thought, Here I am arguing with Rufus, with my stepfather, with this man who'll do anything to justify his big mistake, even make some crazed equation about my life with my lover of five years to his smoking crack. I refused to let it play out that way.

"How *am* I living, Rufus?" I asked. "You're the drug addict. I'm gay, and maybe you think that's illegal, but it's not. You're the one addicted to crack. You're the crackhead. You should be in jail. I'm not doing anything illegal. I'm not doing illegal drugs."

"Why you want to judge me that way, Bruce?" he asked in a hurt voice. "I ain't never said anything about the way you live over there. I ain't."

"Rufus, you don't seem to understand. You're the drug addict."

"Why you calling here telling me I got to go back, I got to go? This is my home. I ain't moving no fucking place. That's right. Who do you think you are? Who do you think you're talking to? Why are you saying these things?"

"Because I care about you."

"Well, why didn't you say that sooner? Why didn't you say that a long time ago?"

I didn't have an answer for that. I couldn't speak of love. My anger had blurred my vision.

"I called to talk to my mother," I said. I wanted out of this conversation. "Where is she? Where's my mother?"

"She's not here."

"Well, I'll call back."

"You better," he said, knowing he was victorious. The stakes were love, unspoken, understood love between a father and a son, and if I couldn't put up I better shut up.

"You must be out of your mind," he said after a brief pause. "This is my home and I'm not leaving."

And that was exactly what I was afraid of. I still am. That's what I fear the most—my mother being held hostage in her own home by her husband of twenty-six years.

My mother walked in the house right then and he gave her the phone. She told me she was all right, that she had to take it a step at a time, she got too scared if she thought it all had to be over with at once. I agreed, but it sounded like something a facilitator would say at an AlAnon meeting. Why couldn't she just give him the boot, kick him out and be over and done with it? I wanted it to be that simple but I knew it wouldn't be. Rufus had just proved that. I didn't know shit. There was no room in his life for my reality as a gay man content and happy in a long-term relationship, just like there was no room in my life for a drug abuser. I just wanted him to ask me, "So when you going to send me that? I hope you put that Rolex in the mail first-class." Why didn't he ask?

I've always thought the reason Rufus wanted me to get him a gold Rolex was because he thought things like gold watches and designer clothing were cheaper in New York, or he thought everyone in New York had expensive things, lived the high life, so why didn't I send him a nice watch? But now that I'm writing about this running joke with Rufus, I'm beginning to think there's even more implied and embedded in that question. Maybe in his roundabout way Rufus was also asking me when I'm going to make it big in New York, be the success "that" he knows I'm going to be, and send him "that" gold Rolex with diamonds around the dial. He knows I'm going to be a success. He's encouraging me in that secret code we speak, that secret we share. Our love for one another.

When I was young and determined to get away from this man who is my father, I thought of nothing but getting away. I was scared of him then and I hid in my room reading, watching TV, listening to the radio, and planning my escape. I didn't know I was going to New York, I didn't know I was going to become a writer, but I knew I was going to get away, to make it. Now I want him back.

((part three))

GO HOME TO YOUR WIFE

Go Home to Your Wife

Cecil Brown

"Speakin' of marriage," Uncle Elmo announced. He took a swig from the mason jar and smacked his lips while he screwed the lid back on the jar tightly, as if he was never going to drink another drop from it, then placed the jar along beside his boot. "If I'm a happily married man today—and I am!—I owe it to my sistuh Amanda!"

"Sho' you do!" Essau Nealey, the old man sitting next to him chanted. "That's right! Uh-huh!"

Uncle Elmo took the mason jar up again, unscrewed the lid, took another swig, screwed the lid back again tightly and placed it in the exact same spot near his clay-crusted boot.

"Yup, you sho' right about that!" Gordon Tuggles, sitting across from them, agreed. "That woman's always got her nose in somebody else's business!" The other man, Isham Hinson, pulled on his long red beard and chuckled to himself.

"Just to give ya some idea of how she gets into people's business, I was in love with a gal and Amanda knowed it before I did!" He glared at us incredulously. "That's right! She did!" Uncle Elmo said. "Now of course that was many years ago. That man sittin' right there," he said, pointing a finger at me, "wasn't nothin' but a baby then. Now look at 'im. He's a man now." The men looked at me as if I had suddenly grown from a baby to full maturity in a few seconds.

"Now, the way she figured out I was in love," he went on, "was she had cooked this big meal—an' my sistuh could really cook up some grub—and that man right there"—he pointed again at me—"looked down at my plate and said, 'Elmo ain't ate nothin' yet.' And my sistuh seed this and said, 'He ain't ate nothin' yet 'cause he's in love!' See, in them days when folks fell in love they lost they appetite for food. And me bein' a young feller that liked to eat, when my sistuh seed that I hadn't touch my food, figured I was in love. And she was right. I was in love with this gal and didn't even know it. That's why I said Amanda was so nosey that she would know somethin' about you before you knowed it about yo'self."

I sat there and tried to remember that particular incident, but I couldn't. It had been many years since I had left home, and even these old faces staring at me were only vague in memory. I had come home to the wedding of a childhood friend. The wedding was to take place at Lee's Chapel church, and this was the night before, the night when all the men got together with the bridegroom for a bachelor party.

We had gathered at my Aunt Amanda's house, probably because she, with the biggest brick house in the town, had the most available space, but also because she had the biggest heart in town and whenever there was a social function everybody assumed it would take place at her house. This living room we sat in was the very one I was forbidden to enter when I was growing up in her house as a child.

When I was about four or five I came to live with this aunt because my father was "in trouble" and couldn't support his wife and two children. I was too young to know what this "trouble" meant, but Aunt Amanda raised us like her own children, and it was because of her that I had a happy childhood, went to the university, and became a normal human being.

Each year she would pile my brother and me into her big Buick and take us to visit my father, who lived in a huge gray building at the foot of the green Shannadoh Valley mountains, and on each visit my father would take me on a walk alone and call me his "little man," and tell me to be a good boy, to obey his sister, and that when he came home we would have us a "real good time." I was exceedingly proud of these private talks and loved my father very much.

When I was twelve my father came out of prison, and of course by this time I knew much more about his trouble. I also knew a great deal about how hard his sister had worked to bring up my brother and me to be unscathed by my father's tragedy. I knew how hard she had worked to save money to pay for his lawyers—how she, working beside men, had cut down timber, had farmed the land, had dug roots out of the ground, had picked cotton, had cooked for white people to get the money to bring us up with.

When my father was reunited with our mother, Aunt Amanda, without a murmuring word, simply handed us over to our parents even though she had grown to love us, had sent us off to our first days at school, had comforted us at night when we were afraid of the dark, had told us our first ghost stories, had ironed our clothes and packed our lunchboxes. I'd often felt the desire to put something down on paper about her, but it wasn't until I heard my Uncle Elmo tell the story about how she had influenced his life that I began to gather an idea about how to do it.

It was at this bachelor party that my uncle told this story about his sister, the indefatigable woman who'd raised us. Picture, then, a group of ten Southern men, some of them still in their teens, others in their sixties, but all of them the products of a small town. The older men, with names like Essau Nealey, Isham Hinson, George Russia, and Gordon Tuggles, sit around my Uncle Elmo swapping lies, just as they have been doing for the past forty years, with their legs crossed at the knee, their long, wrinkled hands in easy reach of a mason jar of clear-colored corn whiskey.

The younger men are dressed in gabardine slacks of bright blues and reds. The older men are still in their overalls, which are frayed and thread-bare; huge boots are laced to their feet. The story they are going to hear the older men have heard many times before. It is a story in which they themselves have played a major part, and yet they each follow its unfolding with the interest of someone hearing it for the first time. They will laugh or grimace to the expression of it according to their own individual remembrances, and will nod at each other occasionally as if they are reacting to the same impressions.

My Uncle Elmo is a long, thin black man, with a thin face and small, inscrutable eyes that seem to glow with an inner light. He speaks in a voice which is neither old nor young but young when he is speaking of his youth and old when he means to draw a conclusion from his youthful experiences. He is wearing a plaid sports jacket over his overalls, a jacket he wears on special occasions to suggest that he has "dressed up." We are sitting in Aunt Amanda's living room, on plastic-covered sofas (the sofas were new when I was a child and the plastic covers have turned yellow in their duty to protect the material beneath). Also in the room are a piano, a table upon which a gold-gilt edition of the King James Bible lies, and a statue of Jesus Christ that stands on a whatnot table in the corner.

My Uncle Elmo has a curious way of telling the story. Sometimes he looks off into the distance, training his eyes on the corner of the room and addressing the statue, and then suddenly, without notice, he looks right into the eyes of his auditors. When he speaks of the sound of an animal, he makes the sound by slapping his open hand against his leg. It's strange for me to witness this master storyteller because I still remember him when he was a young man who was always at odds with the family because he spent most of his time hanging around the alley, drinking and living a life without aim. The story he is telling, however, is about the time he fell in love, got married, and became an upstanding member of the community—and how it all came about because of the peculiar character of his sister.

•

"My sistuh said, 'He ain't ate nothin' 'cause he in love with Kathleen Smith.' And at the mention of the gal's name my heart come jes' a-jumpin', see—'cause she was right! 'Him and that gal bein' courtin' each other on the sly,' she says, and she was right! You know what we called courtin' back in them days. You took a gal out for some ice cream a couple times and she smiled at you and you *grinned* at her and you was courtin'. Now this Kathleen was a light brown-skinned gal, and had this here little tiny waist and a pair of great big hips, and the purtiest smile in the world. And when Amanda let the cat out the bag, I realized I was in love and so I come jest to talkin' about how much I liked Kathleen.

"Next thing I knowed, Lofton—that's my sistuh's husband, y'all know 'im—asked me, said, 'Boy, when you gettin' married?' jest like that. Now I was puzzled 'cause I jes' done found out I was in love, so how am I gonna know when I'm gonna get married? So I says, 'I donno,' and my sistuh says, 'Do you want to marry Kathleen?' And I didn't even think about it, I says, 'Yes.' And my sistuh says, 'When you gonna tell Kathleen?' and I says, 'Right now,' and jumps up from the table, see. But 'fore I can get out the door, Amanda says to me, 'When you gets married, where you gonna live?' and I says, 'I donno,' and she says to me, 'When you gets married you can have Pappa's house.'

"Now Pappa hadn't been dead more'n a year and I always liked Pappa's house, but he left the house to Amanda, see? But she says to me, 'Mamma and Pappa would want you to have that house,' and so she give me the house.

"So I run over to Kathleen's house to ask her if she'll marry me and she said she would and so we gets married right down the road here in Lee's Chapel, where that boy over there gonna get married tomorra, see. And everybody come to the weddin', and I mean everybody—even a few white people come. Now we move into Pappa's house with all the gifts my sistuh and our friends give to us. A new frigidaire, dishes and spoons, and blankets for the bed, and jes' about everything you can imagine. And so we're jes' as happy as a newly married couple could be, see.

"Now here comes the mean part of the story, and the reason why I'm tellin' it in the first place. Marriage is a mean business for a young man if he don't watch his step. Now I tell you why I say this. A lot of married men start tipping out on they wives, see. They look at these young gals and next thing they know, they done forgot about the vow of faithfulness they make to God and their wives. See my point? So one of these married men—I ain't callin' no names—said to me, 'Now that you married, you oughta be gettin' some of the benefits of married life!' said 'Yeah, these young gals in this town loves married men,' said, 'These young gals like the married men 'cause they know what to do.' Yeah, they kept sayin' things like this to me, see, but I would go on about my business, not payin' them any attention 'cause I was happy with what I had at home, see.

"Now I had me a good job at Reiglewood Paper Company, mixin' chemicals, makin' good money, and buyin' my young wife anything her heart desires. And when I come home she be waitin' for me in a new negli-jay and we put on some of this here rock 'n' roll music, not none of this here loud rock 'n' roll but the slow kind, see, and we pull down them shades just when the sun goin' down and turn on this red light we had and we'd have ourselves a good time! So what these wicked married men would tell me in one ear would go out the other ear.

"But you know if you keep hearin' wickedness, one day you gonna start thinkin' wicked too. So I start noticing the way these young gals would be so free with me, see. But I wouldn't give 'em no real opportunity to tempt me. Now I don't know how she knew it, but my sistuh Amanda come by the house one day when Kathleen was out in the garden and she said to me, she said, 'Elmo, you married a good woman.' And I said, 'That's right.' And she said, 'Now I'm yo' sistuh and I wants you to remember—if you get any more wicked thoughts about these young gals, come talk to me about it.'

I said to myself, She must be readin' my mind. Then she goes on, 'If you can't stop listenin' to these married men, I'll have the pastor talk to you. Would you like for me to have the pastor talk to you on Sunday?' I told her I didn't mind talkin' to the pastor, jest to pacify her, see. But you know what? Come next Sunday, I had clean forgot all about it. Here come Reverend Ezell Banister saying he want to have a little chat with me, so I says okay and we walks over to the sycamore tree, jest me and him, see.

"Now as y'all know, this Ezell Banister is a curious fellow. He's thin as a rail despite the fact that all week he eats chicken and cakes at the houses of the women while their husbands are workin'. Before he was a preacher he was livin' up in Harlem shinnin' shoes, I heard. And he got this part down the middle of his head, which is sign of either a con artist or a number runner. I still ain't made up my mind about that feller! Anyway, he come home a'askin' me a whole lot of questions about my wife, see. But I figure since he's a man of God, I'd go along wit him. He ask me, 'Brother Elmo, have you been tempted by women other than yo' wife?' I didn't want to have this talk with him any longer, now that's a fact! And I'm thinkin' Amanda done gone too far now! So I tells him, 'Naw, Reverend, I ain't tempted,' and he shake his head, like he do, and says, 'Uh-huh,' like he don't believe me.

"Now, by this time I'm pretty disgusted by the whole thing and can't wait to get away. 'Now you know you oughtta do somethin' for the Lord,' he says, 'to get this wickedness out of yo' heart!' And then he tells me I should go chop wood for Lucille Green. Y'all know she'd been sick for a long time, bless her soul—she's dead now. So I says okay, I'll do it, mostly just to get away from 'im. I go home and I tells this to Kathleen, and she says it's a good thing to do.

"So later on that week I go by the old woman's house, down in the alley. Lucille lived right in the middle of a busy neighborhood, and so I goes on out the back to the woodpile, chop up some wood and take it in the back door. A young gal is in the kitchen but I didn't see it was Rosina, the gal that Lucille's daughter Rose had. She was then nearly seventeen years old.

"'Hello,' she says, 'how you doin', Elmo?' I says, 'Ain't you Rose's chile?' She says, 'Yeah, that's right,' and I says, 'Well, you certainly have grown up some!' Now she's followin' me with her eyes and a big grin on her pretty little face, see. I dumped the wood in back of the stove, in the woodbox, said, 'How's yo' grandma?' 'She's asleep,' she says, smilin' again, and give out a sort of chuckle that had a dark mysterious meanin' to it. 'She won't be up for a long while.' 'In that case, I'll be goin'. You tell her I chopped the wood for her. An' I hope she gets better. We miss her over at the church.'

"Rosina ran around me quick and stood with her back at the door. 'Don't go so soon, Elmo,' she said, 'I want somebody to talk to!' 'Somebody to talk to? Talk to yo' friends!' I told her. 'I don't have any,' she said. 'At school,' I said. 'That's just the problem,' she said, moaning with her head downcasted, 'I done finished school. When Gramma gets better, I can go up to Philly and get a job. But right now I ain't got nobody to talk to. Most of my friends done left.'

"I felt a little sorry for her, 'cause she was right. These kids nowadays, soon as they get out of high school they shoot up North. This poor girl had to sit home with her grandma. I stood there thinkin' about loneliness.

" 'What's yo' sign?' she asked me all of a sudden. I guess I'd been standing there starin' at her like a fool. 'What astrological sign were you born under?'

"When I told her my birthday she said I was a double sagittaris and I felt like sayin' that my wife was waitin' for me, which, incidently was the truth, but like a fool I didn't say a word. And why I didn't, I'll never know. Anyway, Rosina asked me if I'd help her with somethin'. I says 'What?' and she says she bought a new dress and she wanted to get my opinion on how it looked, and I says, 'Okay,' and the next thing I know I'm in her bedroom watchin' her put on this dress and take it off. And let me tell you now, she was a very attractive girl under those clothes!

" 'How you like this dress?' Rosina asked me, pullin' that dress up over her brown thighs. She gave me another invitin' smile. She was a curious girl, this Rosina. 'I like it fine,' I told her, and got up from the chair. I couldn't help but think all this had been arranged by my sistuh and that slick-headed preacher. They thought I'd be tempted by Rosina to go after her stuff, but I felt good I hadn't been tempted.

"I turned towards the door an' Rosina ran after me like a hungry dog bein' cheated out of a piece of juicy meat. 'Elmo, don't go!' she moaned. I just let her go on. She pressed her hot body up against my leg and put her arms around my waist and buried her head in my chest.

" 'I love married men,' she told me, and that's when I knowed she musta been put up to this by my sistuh. They were tryin' to tempt me! To see if I'd betray my wife! 'You're wicked, chile!' I told her, an' I pushed her away from me and hurried out the door.

"I got on in my truck and drove down to the swamp. Took my new shotgun with me an' walked along the edge of the cornfield. It was gettin' dark now and the jackrabbits were out nibblin' on that green corn. I kilt two and headed on to the house. Now, all the time I'm feelin' pretty good about the business with Rosina, see. I'm figurin' real proud 'cause I didn't fall into my sistuh's trap.

"I seed a kerosene lamp in the window and I knowed Kathleen done lighted it, waitin' up for me. When I get in the door I smells turnip greens and I sees Kathleen sittin' at the dinner table with the plates turned down, but she's lookin' down in the mouth. 'I kilt a couple rabbits,' I says and take 'em in the kitchen, but she don't say nothin'. I don't say nothin' but I know somethin' is wrong. I sit down at the table and pretty soon she looks up at me and her face is wet. She been crying, see.

"'Where you been?' she asked me, looking like she about to cry again.

"'Honey, you know I had to go cut wood for Miz Lucille Green, then I went down into the swamp to try out my new gun.' I had jest bought that new pump gun not more'n a week before and I hadn't had time to try it out.

"'Naw you ain't! You been with that Rosina!' she blurted out and started just a'cryin' like crazy. Now who could've told her that but my sistuh? I did my best to tell her it wasn't true, but I knowed I was already lyin'. She wouldn't listen and we had our first fight. In bed she turned her back to me and wouldn't say a word to me even the next mornin'. Doubt had already cast his shadow between me and my wife, see.

"I went on to work next day feelin' pretty disgusted with my sistuh. When I got off, I drove right over to her house. I took my gun with me, meanin' to show Lofton how it worked. When I come into the livin' room I hear the piano just a'goin'. Amanda had bought her a piano and at fifty-three she decided to learn to play it. She couldn't play but two songs after workin' at it a whole year and one of those was 'Nearer My God to Thee,' and that was what she was playin' when I walked in. I sat the gun down in the corner, and she finally turned to me and closed the lid to the piano.

"'Amanda, I don't like the way you been puttin' your nose into my business,' I said right off. Her smile showed me the gold in her back teeth. 'If the shoe fit,' she said pushin' her heavy weight off the piano stool, 'wear it.' And she headed towards the kitchen, 'I don't like to see you abuse Kathleen like that.'

"'What you talkin' about? You and that damn preacher got me to go over to that woman's house in the first place! I love my wife, and I ain't interested in that damn Rosina! I'da never been over to that woman's house if you hadn't got that man to have me chop her wood.'

"'You was tempted and don't you deny it! I know you men,' she said, and started stirrin' a pot of rice on the stove. 'I wasn't tempted!' I yelled back. 'That's the whole point. I was gettin' along good with my wife. Why did you have to go spoil it?! Ain't nothin' between me and Rosina.'

" 'Just like Pappa.'

" 'What you mean by that?!' I asked her. But I already knowed what she was gettin' at. She always believed Pappa had been mean to Mamma, that he had women while she was still livin'.

" 'You men ain't no damn good. All you want to do is whoremonger with these young gals. And you married a good woman, but look how you treatin' her. Layin' up with that trashy thing, Rosina. Kathleen is a saint, and if you keep on with that Rosina you gonna lose her!'

" 'Well, *you* ain't no saint!' When I said that, Amanda turned on me like a tiger. It's hard to get her angry but I know how to do it, boy. By the way I said what I said she knowed what I was talkin' about. See, I know things about my sistuh that nobody in this town knows. But I'm not a tattletale like she is. Everybody has some secret they don't want nobody to know that she had a child, but being an unwedded mother, she gave it to the lady next door an' the boy grew up without hardly ever layin' eyes on her. I was at her house one day when the boy came by to see her. He was a man then, twenty years old or so, had on an Army uniform. Lucky Amanda's husband wasn't there, 'cause she's always been embarrassed by that boy's comin' into the world the way he did. She gave him some money and told him never to come see her again. I believe it's the shame about this boy that made her so generous to children.

"She stood there, holdin' the spoon at me. 'After all I done for you, boy, you gonna talk to me like that?!' She was barkin' at me.

" 'Just stay out of my damn business,' I told her, 'and whatever I do with Rosina is my own business.'

" 'You better go on to your wife, Elmo,' she said an' she swung that spoon at me. I went through the livin' room, but she picked up the broom and came behind me with it. 'Stay out of my damn business,' I yelled, 'or I'll tell Lofton somethin' he don't even know about you!'

"When I got to the front porch, I turned around and I saw her standin' under the front porch light, holdin' the broom at her side and cryin' like a baby. I never seen my sistuh cry before. I got in the truck and started down the road. It really made me feel bad that I'd said what I said to her like that. I didn't mean to hurt her feelings, but she really got on my nerves. Stickin' her nose into other people's business.

"When I got to the highway I realized I left my gun at her house. I started to turn the truck around and go back for it, but I decided against the idea. With her havin' hurt feelin's I didn't feel like facin' her. Not now,

I thought, maybe later. Maybe I'll go by Rosina's house. Why not? My sistuh thinks I'm sleepin' with her anyway! But I really had no interest in goin' to bed with that gal. I figured I'd get her to make me some coffee or I'd jest sit there and talk with her. Get this confusion off my mind.

"When I walked in Rosina's house I asked about her grandma. She winked at me and said her grandma was asleep, jest like before. I followed her to the kitchen. Well, I thought, since Amanda knows everythin' about my life, I wonder if she knows *when* I'm gonna sleep with Rosina. Can she find out I'm gonna sleep with her *now*? I made up my mind to go all the way with Rosina if she tempted me again. Let Amanda go tell my wife *that*! After all the temptation I had to put up with, nobody believed me, an' was I to blame if I did it? No, 'course not. An' who put me up to do it? The damn preacher himself and my nosy sistuh!

"While Rosina fixed me somethin' to eat, all I could hear ringin' in my head was my damn sistuh's voice—'Go home to your wife, go home to your wife'—and it really got me goin', I tell you!

"As soon's I finished eatin' the cabbage and pig tails she fixed for me, Rosina took me by the hand and led me to her bedroom. We sat down on the bed. 'Is there somethin' wrong, Sweet Daddy,' she asked me. I liked it when she called me Sweet Daddy. See, that evilness was already workin' its magic in my heart. 'Amanda told me I should go home to my wife,' I told her.

"'Go home to your wife?! That's an old idea. Sweet Daddy, if you go home to your wife, you'll miss this present I have for you.' She stood up and walked over to the middle of the room and started untyin' the knot that held her dress together. I sat there watchin' as that knot came a'loose in long, slender brown fingers. When she finished the dress fell open.

"'I loves you, Rosina,' I heard myself sayin'. She slipped part of the dress over her shoulder. Before, when she undressed for me she was just showin' off. Now she was for real.

"'What you say, Sweet Daddy?'

"I told her again. 'As much as your wife?' she asked me. She dropped the dress from the other shoulder.

"'More than my wife,' I muttered. My tongue done got swollen up in my mouth from seein' her buck naked and shameless before me.

"'Prove it, Sweet Daddy,' she said, and she came and sat on the bed near me. I reached for her, but she pulled back. 'What you mean?' I axed her.

"'Take off your clothes, too,' she said. Now, just to show you how the devil can slip into ya' heart without you knowin' it, I jumped up—done forgot about my wife, see—and got outta my clothes. I stood there buck naked. I started for the bed where she was, but she held me off with her hand.

"'Cool down, Pappa,' she said, 'or you gonna blow yo' stack.' Anyway, we was jest gettin' in bed when I heard a loud explosion. Jumpin' up, I ran to the window.

"*Kaaapow! Yaaawrr! Kaaapow! Yaaawrr!*

"'What in the name of God is that?!' I exclaimed to Rosina. She lept up. 'An earthquake!' the poor gal cried out, an' before we could move another inch a second one come. The windows of the bedroom shook. I could hear the voices of the neighbors risin' like an ocean of concern. The sound of windows goin' up and people yellin' out.

"'What the hell's goin' on out there?!' I grabbed for my pants but couldn't find 'em. Instead, I pulled the sheet around me just as another explosion went off.

"*Kaaapow!* I rushed to the window where Rosina was, but all we seen was George Russian's big black head stickin' out the window next door. I didn't want him to see me, naturally, so I stuck my head back in quickly. Whatever was goin' on out there I wasn't goin' to go out because somebody would see me. And that was the thing I couldn't afford.

"Rosina was already in the kitchen, peepin' out the back window.

"*Kaaapow! Kaaapow!* Rosina pushed me down. 'Everybody's out there! Don't let 'em see you!' she warned me, and she took me by the hand quick. But I managed to pull away from her and take a peep myself.

"From the window all I seen was Esau Nealey standin' on his back porch in his overalls. Isham Hinson was also standin' on his porch. Then I looked to the left and saw George Tuggles and his wife standin' on *their* porch. They all lookin' down at somebody or somethin' I couldn't see.

"'What is it?' I ask Rosina. I could tell from the look on her face—a guilty look—she's seen what I ain't.

"'What you gotta do,' she said, quiet, 'is go out the front door.'

"'Me? Go out the front door? With all those people, the whole damn town practically out there? You crazy!'

"She shook her head. 'No, you got to—quick,' she said and grabbed my arm.

"'I ain't goin' nowhere!' I screamed in a whisper.

"*Kaaapow! Kaaapow!* The explosion went off again. Rosina said, 'Come on. You better go now!'

"Again I resisted. If it was an earthquake I'd a rather die in the rubbish than let these people catch me. 'Why should I go out there?' I asked her.

"'I'll show you why,' she said, an' she took me to the kitchen window again. She pulled back the curtain. Standin' there in the yard under a chinnyberry tree was my sistuh Amanda, holdin' my automatic shotgun, which she was pointin' up in the air. And while I watched she let off a shot.

"'*Kaaapow! Kaaapow!*' the gun went, and then my sistuh yelled out, 'Go home to your wife!'

"I thrusted the curtain back and turned to Rosina. 'Jesus almighty! How can I get outta here?'

"'I told you. Out the front!'

"I suddenly remembered I'd parked my truck in front of George Russian's house, so I could pretend I was visitin' him. Now all I had to do was make it to the truck. If everybody was in the back, I figured I had a good chance.

"'My pants! Where's my pants?' I searched the room, but I couldn't find 'em. 'Here, take this,' Rosina said, and put somethin' in my hand. I didn't care, long as it covered my nakedness. She led me to the front door and I went out with the cloth she gave me to cover myself. Outside I didn't see a soul.

"Great! Then I came down the steps. Dan Creek pulled up in his Ford pickup. Now Dan Creek is a white boy and he don't live in the alley but sometimes he comes down here to buy liquor. 'Why, Elmo,' he's grinnin' out the window, 'What the hell you doin' standin' there with a dress on?'

"'Eh? What? Dress?' I look down at myself and realize Rosina done handed me one of her old dresses and I'm holdin' it up against my chest for protectin' against my nakedness.

"'Oh, this jest a joke . . . Eh? 'scuse me, Dan, but I must be goin'. See ya later!' I turned and started off jest as natural as I could, see. But jest as I turned, somebody called my name. 'Elmo! Elmo!' I looked up and saw Leon Lord leanin' off the bannister of his porch. 'Whatcha been doin'? Getting a little bit of tail? Ha, ha, ha.' And I seen everybody who been starin' out their windows in the backyard was now gatherin' around me in the *front* yard. Gordon Tuggles started laughin' with Leon Lord, and Esau Nealey joined in wit 'em. Then Isham Hinson, pullin' on his beard, grinned wit 'em. Mary Pierce came around the house with Amanda, still holdin' my shotgun.

"She fired another shot, '*Kaaapow yaawr!* Go home to your wife!'

"'Please,' I heard myself sayin', 'please don't tell my wife! Please don't tell my wife!'

"They laughed together and some of 'em took up the chant from my sistuh. 'Go home to your wife,' Mary Pierce jeered at me, 'You whore-monger!'

"I started to my truck, but I kept sayin' to 'em, 'Jest don't tell my wife! Jest don't tell my wife! Thank you!'

"When I pulled Rosina's dress up to my neck they all laughed. My sistuh laughed harder'n anybody. I ran to the truck and jumped in. Just when I'd got in gear I turned and seen Rosina on the porch, laughin' with the rest of 'em, and my heart jest about sunk to the bottom of my feet.

"When I drove up into the yard, I saw the kerosene lamp burning its yellow glow. I figured Kathleen would leave me for sure then. The best I could do, I thought, was to tell her the truth and then pack my bags and get up North, maybe to Harlem. Then I realize there's somethin' sittin' beside me in the truck seat. I saw somebody'd put a bundle of clothes in the seat next to me. I threw the dress off and put on my work clothes and went on in the house.

"Kathleen was sittin' at the dinner table. And when she saw me she jumped up and ran into my arms.

" 'Elmo, I'm sorry I ever doubted you,' she said, coverin' my face with kisses. 'I'll never doubt you again. Amanda came over this mornin' and told me I was wrong to suspect you. She told me you loved me and wasn't studin' that Rosina. Amanda's right! Forgive me, baby?'

"I realized then I was safe.

" 'Rosina? Honey, you gotta be jokin',' I told her, holdin' her tight in my arms. 'I never thought about that gal once! I love you and I'll always be faithful to you.'

" 'Supper's on the table,' she told me and then led me to the dinner table.

"This is a curious town. I've lived with my wife for the last ten years and not one person's ever mentioned this incident to Kathleen. If they did, she never let me know about it. But sometimes one of these fellows, like old George Russia, will tease me about it. We maybe huntin' in the woods or just playin' checkers and somebody'll say, 'Go home to your wife,' and we have a good laugh, and then it's over with.

"Now, as far as my sistuh goes, I understand why she has her nose in everybody's business. If she don't have her nose in yo' business, how can she know when you need help? She helped me see how close I came to losin' my love for my wife. And Rosina? Well, I never talked to her about that 'cause not long afterwards Amanda helped her get the money for a bus ticket to the North, but my own suspicion is she was in on the whole thing from the start. Like I said before, she was a strange gal.

"I told you this story to show you how I come to be a happily married man and how I live with a clear conscience with my Kathleen all these years because of my busybody sistuh. An' even now, whenever I get the urge to do somethin' like that again, I hear my sistuh's voice sayin', 'Go home to your wife!' I tells all the young fellers gettin' married they oughtta have a sistuh like Amanda."

My Mother and Mitch

Clarence Major

He was just somebody who had
dialed the wrong number. This is how it started and I wasn't concerned
about it. Not at first. I don't even remember if I was there when he first
called, but I do, all these many years later, remember my mother on the
phone speaking to him in her best quiet voice, trying to sound as ladylike
as she knew how.

She had these different voices for talking to different people on different occasions. I could tell by my mother's proper voice that this man was
somebody she wanted to make a good impression on, a man she thought
she might like to know. This was back when my mother was still a young
woman, divorced but still young enough to believe that she was not completely finished with men. She was a skeptic from the beginning, I knew
that even then. But some part of her thought the right man might come
along some day.

I don't know exactly what it was about him that attracted her, though.
People are too mysterious to know that well. I know that now and I must
have been smart enough not to wonder too hard about it back then.

Since I remember hearing her tell him her name, she must not have
given it out right off the bat when he first called. She was a city woman
with a child and had developed a certain alertness to danger. One thing

you didn't do was give your name to a stranger on the phone. You never knew who to trust in a city like Chicago. The place was full of crazy people and criminals.

She said, "My name is *Mrs*. Jayne Anderson." I can still hear her laying the emphasis on the "Mrs." although she had been separated from my father for twelve years by 1951, when this man dialed her number by accident.

Mitch Kibbs was the name he gave her. I guess he must have told her who he was the very first time, just after he apologized for calling her by mistake. I can't remember who he was trying to call. He must have told her and she must have told me, but it's gone now. I think they must have talked a pretty good while that first time. The first thing that I remember about him was that he lived with his sister who was older than he. The next thing was that he was very old. He must have been fifty, and to me at fifteen that was deep into age. If my mother was old at thirty, fifty was ancient. Then the other thing about him was that he was white.

They'd talked five or six times, I think, before he came out and said he was white, but she knew it before he told her. I think he made this claim only after he started suspecting he might not be talking to another white person. But the thing was he didn't know for sure she was black. I was at home lying on the couch pretending to read a magazine when I heard her say, "I am a colored lady." Those were her words exactly. She placed her emphasis on the word "lady."

I had never known my mother to date any white men. She would hang up from talking with him and she and I would sit at the kitchen table and she'd tell me what he'd said. They were telling each other the bits and pieces of their lives, listening to each other, feeling their way as they talked. She spoke slowly, remembering all the details. I watched her scowl and the way her eyes narrowed as she puzzled over his confessions as she told me in her own words about him. She was especially puzzled about his reaction to her confession about being colored.

That night she looked across to me with that fearful look that was hers alone and said, "Tommy, I doubt if he will ever call back. Not after tonight. He didn't know. You know that."

Feeling grown up because she was treating me that way, I said, "I wouldn't be so sure."

But he called back soon after that.

I was curious about her interest in this particular old white man, so I always listened carefully. I was a little bit scared, too, because I suspected he might be some kind of maniac or pervert. I had no good reason to fear such a thing except that I thought it strange that anybody could spend as much time as he and my mother did talking on the phone without any desire for human contact. She had never had a telephone relationship before and at that time all I knew about telephone relationships was that they were insane and conducted by people who probably needed to be put away. This meant that I also had the sad feeling that my mother was a bit crazy too. But more important than these fearful fantasies, I thought I was witnessing a change in my mother. It seemed important and I didn't want to misunderstand it or miss the point of it. I tried to look on the bright side, which was what my mother always said I should try to do.

He certainly didn't sound dangerous. Two or three times I myself answered the phone when he called and he always said, "Hello, Tommy, this is Mitch. May I speak to your mother?" and I always said, "Sure, just a minute." He never asked me how I was doing or anything like that and I never had anything special to say to him.

•

After he'd been calling for over a month I sort of lost interest in hearing about their talk. But she went right on telling me what he said. I was a polite boy, so I listened despite the fact that I had decided that Mitch Kibbs and his ancient sister, Temple Erikson, were crazy but harmless. My poor mother was lonely, that was all. I had it all figured out. He wasn't an ax murderer who was going to sneak up on her one evening when she was coming home from her job at the factory and split her open from the top down. (We were always hearing about things like this, so I knew it wasn't impossible.)

My interest would pick up occasionally. I was especially interested in what happened the first time my mother herself made the call to his house. She told me that Temple Erikson answered the phone. Mother and I were eating dinner when she started talking about Temple Erikson.

"She's a little off in the head."

I didn't say anything, but it confirmed my suspicion. What surprised me was my mother's ability to recognize it. "What'd she say?"

"She rattled on about the Wild West and the Indians and having to hide in a barrel or something like that. Said the Indians were shooting arrows at them and she was just a little girl who hid in a barrel."

I thought about this. "Maybe she lived out West when she was young. You know? She must be a hundred by now. That would make her the right age."

"Oh, come on, now. What she said was she married when she was fourteen, married this Erikson fellow. As near as I could figure out he must have been a leather tanner but seems he also hunted fur and sold it to make a living. She never had a child."

"None of that sounds crazy." I was disappointed.

"She was talking crazy, though."

"How so?"

"She thinks the Indians are coming back to attack the house any day now. She says things like Erikson was still living, like he was just off there in the next room, taking a nap. One of the first things Mitch told me was his sister and he moved in together after her husband died, and that was twenty years ago."

"How did the husband die?"

"Huh?"

"How did he die?"

She finished chewing her peas first. "Kicked in the head by a horse. Bled to death."

I burst out laughing because the image was so bright in my mind and I couldn't help myself. My pretty mother had a sense of humor even when she didn't mean to show it.

She chewed her peas in a ladylike manner. This was long before she lost her teeth. Sitting there across the table from her, I knew I loved her and needed her and I knew she loved and needed me. I was not yet fearing that she needed me too much. She had a lot of anger in her, too. Men had hurt her bad. And one day I was going to be a man.

When I laughed my mother said, "You shouldn't laugh at misfortune, Tommy." But she had this silly grin on her face and it caused me to crack up again. I just couldn't stop. I think now I must have been a bit hysterical from the anxiety I had been living with all those weeks while she was telling me about the telephone conversations that I wanted to hear about only part of the time.

It was dark outside, and I got up when I finished my dinner and went to the window and looked down on the street lights glowing on the wet pavement. I said, "I bet he's out there right now, hiding in the shadows, watching our window."

"Who?" Her eyes grew large. She was easily frightened. I knew this and I was being devilish and deliberately trying to scare her.

"You know, Mister Kibbs."

She looked relieved. "No he's not. He's not like that. He's a little strange but not a pervert."

"How do you know?"

By the look she gave me I knew now that I had thrown doubt into her and she wasn't handling it well. She didn't try to answer me. She finished her small, dry pork chop and the last of her bright green peas and reached over and took up my plate and sat it inside of her own.

She took the dishes to the sink, turned on the hot and cold water so that warm water gushed out of the single faucet, causing the pipe to clang, and started washing the dishes. "You have a vivid imagination," was all she said.

I grabbed the dishcloth and started drying the first plate she placed in the rack. "Even so, you don't know this man. You never even seen him. Aren't you curious about what he looks like?"

"I know what he looks like."

"How?"

"He sent me a picture of himself, and one of Temple."

I gave her a look. She had been holding out on me. I knew he was crazy now. Was he so ugly she hadn't wanted me to see the picture? I ask if I could see it.

She dried her hands on the cloth I was holding, then took her cigarettes out of her dress pocket and knocked one from the pack and stuck it between her thin pale lips. I watched her light it and fan the smoke and squint her eyes. She said, "You have to promise not to laugh."

That did it. I started laughing again and couldn't stop. Then she started laughing too, because I was bent double, standing there at the sink, with this image of some old guy who looked like the Creeper in my mind. But I knew she couldn't read my mind, so she had to be laughing at me laughing. She was still young enough to be silly with me like a kid.

Then she brought out two pictures, one of him and the other one of his sister. She put them down side by side on the table. "Make sure your hands are dry."

I took off my glasses and bent down to the one of the man first, so I could see up close as I stood there wiping my hands on the dishcloth. It was one of those studio pictures where somebody had posed him in a three-quarter view. He had his unruly hair and eyebrows pasted down and you could tell he was fresh out of the bath and his white shirt was starched hard. He was holding his scrubbed face with effort toward where the photographer told him to look, which was too much in the direction of the best light. He was frowning with discomfort beneath the forced smile. There was something else. It was something like defeat or simple tiredness in his pose and you could see it best in the heavy lids of his large blank eyes. He looked out of that face with what remained of his self-confidence and trust in the world. His shaggy presence said that it was all worthwhile and maybe even, in some ways he would not ever understand, also important. I understood all of that even then but would never have been able to put my reading of him into words like these.

Then I looked at the woman. She was an old hawk. Her skin was badly wrinkled, like the skin of ancient Indians I'd seen in photographs and the Westerns. There was something like a smile coming out of her face, but it had come out sort of sideways and made her look silly. But the main thing about her was that she looked very mean. On second thought, to give her the benefit of the doubt, I can say that it might have been just plain hardness from having had a hard life. She was wearing a black iron-stiff dress buttoned up to her dickey, which was ironically dainty and tight around her goose neck.

All I said was, "They're *so* old." I don't know what else I thought as I looked up at my mother, who was leaning over my shoulder looking at the pictures too, as though she'd never seen them before, as though she was trying to see them through my eyes.

"You're just young, Tommy. Everybody's old to you. They're not so old. He looks lonely to me."

I looked at him again and thought I saw what she meant.

•

I put the dishes away and she took the photographs back and we didn't talk any more that night about Mitch and Temple. We watched our black-and-white television screen, which showed us Red Skelton acting like a fool.

Before it was over I fell asleep on the couch and my mother woke me when she turned off the television. "You should go to bed."

I stood up and stretched. "I have a science paper to write."

"Get up early and write it," she said, putting out her cigarette.

•

"He wants me to meet him someplace," my mother said.

She had just finished talking with him and was standing by the telephone. It was close to dinnertime. I'd been home from school since three-thirty and she'd been in from work by then for a good hour. She'd just hung up from the shortest conversation she'd ever had with him.

I'd wondered why they never wanted to meet, then I stopped wondering and felt glad they hadn't. Now I was afraid, afraid for her, for myself, for the poor old man in the picture. Why did we have to go through with this crazy thing?

"I told him I needed to talk with you about it first," she said. "I told him I'd call him back."

I was standing there in front of her, looking at her. She was a scared little girl with wild eyes dancing in her head, unable to make up her own mind. I sensed her fear. I resented her for the mess she had gotten herself into. I also resented her for needing my consent. I knew she wanted me to say, Go, go to him, meet him somewhere. I could tell. She was too curious not to want to go. I suddenly thought that he might be a millionaire and that she would marry the old coot and he'd die and leave her his fortune. But there was the sister. She was in the way. And from the looks of her she would pass herself off as one of the living for at least another hundred years or so. So I gave up that fantasy.

"Well, why don't you tell him you'll meet him at the hamburger cafe on Wentworth? We can eat dinner there."

"We?"

"Sure. I'll just sit at the counter like I don't know you. But I gotta be there to protect you."

"I see."

"Then you can walk in alone. I'll already be there eating a cheeseburger and fries. He'll come in and see you waiting for him alone at a table."

"No, I'll sit at the counter, too," she said.

"Okay. You sit at the counter, too."

"What time should I tell him?"

I looked at my Timex. It was six. I knew they lived on the West Side and that meant it would take him at least an hour by bus and a half-hour by car. He probably didn't have a car. I was hungry, though, and had already set my mind on eating a cheeseburger rather than macaroni-and-cheese out of the box.

"Tell him seven-thirty."

"Okay."

I went to my room. I didn't want to hear her talking to him in her soft whispering voice. I'd stopped listening some time before. I looked at the notes for homework and felt sick in the stomach at the thought of having to write that science paper.

A few minutes later my mother came in and said, "Okay. It's all set." She sat down on the side of my bed and folded her bony pale hands in her lap. "What should I wear?"

"Wear your green dress and the brown shoes."

"You like that dress, don't you?"

"I like that one and the black one with the yellow at the top. It's classical."

"You mean classy."

"Whatever I mean." I felt really grown that night.

"Here, Tommy, take this." She handed me five dollars, which she'd been hiding in the palm of her right hand. "Don't spend it all. Buy the burger out of it and the rest is just to have. If you spend it all in that hamburger place I'm going to deduct it from your allowance next week."

•

When I got there I changed my mind about the counter. I took a table by myself.

I was eating my cheeseburger and watching the revolving door. The cafe was noisy with shouts, cackling, giggles, and verbal warfare. The waitress, Miss Azibo, was in a bad mood. She'd set my hamburger plate down like it was burning her hand.

I kept my eye on the door. Every time somebody came in I looked up, every time somebody left I looked up. I finished my cheeseburger even before my mother got there, and, ignoring her warning, I ordered another and another Coca-Cola to go with it. I figured I could eat two or three burgers and still have most of the five left.

Then my mother came in like a bright light into a dingy room. I think she must have been the most beautiful woman who ever entered that place and it was her first time there. She had always been something of a snob and did not believe in places like this; I knew she'd agreed to meet Mister Kibbs here just because she believed in my right to the cheeseburger and this place had the best in the neighborhood.

I watched her walk ladylike to the counter and ease herself up on the stool and sit there with her back arched. People in that place didn't walk and sit like that. She was acting classy and everybody turned to look at her. I looked around at the faces, and a lot of the women had these real mean sneering looks, like somebody had broken wind.

She didn't know any of these people and they didn't know her. Some of them may have known her by sight, and me, too, but that was about all the contact we'd had with this part of the neighborhood. Besides, we hardly ever ate out. When we did we usually ate Chinese or at the rib place.

I sipped my Coke and watched Miss Azibo place a cup of coffee before my mother on the counter. She was a coffee freak. Always was. All day long. Long into the night. Cigarettes and coffee in a continuous cycle. I grew up with her that way. The harsh smells are still in my memory. When she picked up the cup with a dainty finger sticking out just so, I heard a big fat woman at a table in front of mine say to the big fat woman at the table with her that my mother was a snooty bitch. The other woman said, "Yeah. She must think she's white. What's she doing in here anyway?"

•

Mitch Kibbs came in about twenty minutes after my mother, and I watched him stop and stand just inside the revolving doors. He stood to the side. He looked a lot younger than in the picture. He was stooped a bit, though, and he wasn't dressed like a millionaire, which disappointed me. But he was clean. He was wearing a necktie and a clean white shirt and a suit that looked like it was about two hundred years old but no doubt made of the best wool. Although it was fall, he looked overdressed for the season. He looked like a man who hadn't been out in daylight in a long while. He was nervous, I could tell. Everybody was looking at him. Rarely did white people come in here.

Then he went to my mother like he knew she had to be the person he'd come in to see. He sat himself up on the stool beside her and leaned forward with his elbows on the counter and looked into her face.

She looked back in that timid way of hers. But she wasn't timid. It was an act and part of her ladylike posture. She used it when she needed it.

They talked and talked. I sat there eating cheeseburgers and protecting her till I spent the whole five dollars. Even as I ran out of money I knew she would forgive me. She had always forgiven me on special occasions. This was one for sure.

She never told me what they talked about in the cafe and I never asked, but everything that happened after that meeting went toward the finishing off of the affair my mother was having with Mitch Kibbs. He called her later that night. I was in my room reading when the phone rang and I could hear her speaking to him in that ladylike way—not the way she talked to me. I was different. She didn't need to impress me. I was her son. But I couldn't hear what she was saying and didn't want to.

Mister Kibbs called the next evening, too. But eventually the calls were fewer and fewer till he no longer called.

My mother and I went on living the way we always had, she working long hours at the factory and me going to school. She was not a happy woman, but I thought she was pretty brave. Every once in a while she got invited somewhere, to some wedding or out on a date with a man. She always tried on two or three different dresses, turning herself around and around before the mirror, asking me how she looked, making me select the dress she would wear. Most often, though, she went nowhere. After dinner we sat together at the kitchen table, she drinking coffee and smoking her eternal cigarettes. She gave me my first can of beer one night when she herself felt like having one. It tasted awful and I didn't touch the stuff for years after that.

•

About a day or two after the meeting in the hamburger cafe I remember coming to a conclusion about my mother. I learned for the first time that she did not always know what she was doing. It struck me that she was as helpless as I sometimes felt when confronted with a math or science problem or a problem about sex and girls and growing up and life in general. She didn't know everything. And that made me feel closer to her despite the fear it caused. She was there to protect me, I thought. But there she was, just finding her way, step by step, like me. It was something wonderful anyway.

A Liar in Love

Quinn Eli

When a black man sits down to write about black women and relationships, the reader is well advised to take cover. Because whenever a man writes about male-female relationships in the black community and, like some cross between Cupid and Rodney King, argues that we should "all just get along," chances are that writer has an agenda up his sleeve. And that agenda, concealed in some flowery language about "preserving our unity as a people," is almost always self-serving.

I should know. I'm a male writer who spent the last couple of years in a graduate creative writing program, spinning tales about blacks folks in love. Most of my stories had some pressing conflict at their center—certainly there are enough hateful forces in the world that conspire against black love—and so I would artfully depict the way my two protagonists, a black couple in Boston or Brooklyn or Philly, beat down the conflict that threatened to tear them apart, and, hand in hand, defeated the forces of racism, poverty, and joblessness that might otherwise have destroyed them and, by implication, the entire black community.

But as I look back now from my new position as a Ph.D. candidate, a four-eyed student of literature, I can't help but think that my earlier short stories were a little too self-righteous and too assured of their own political and artistic consequence. In other words, I'm starting to think that maybe my stories were full of shit. Young writers always think we have something terribly *deep* to say and that we're the first people who ever in the history of humanity to see the world so clearly, so keenly—and so I guess it would have been a miracle if I hadn't shoveled at least a little manure onto every page I ever printed out. But what's bothering me now is the thought that maybe the shit I was dishing out—and attempting to feed to a hungry, unsuspecting public—was manipulative and self-serving.

It's an awful thought to face. If it's true that I packed my stories with self-serving messages, my only comfort is knowing I wasn't alone. Whenever a black man writes about romantic relationships, it almost always seems he's trying to preach to black women about the way they should treat us black men: A little less attitude, goes the usual refrain, a little less giving your man lip, and black love will flourish and grow and eventually defeat the menace of racism.

Some nifty trick, wouldn't you say? Putting *all* the responsibility for black liberation from oppression and injustice onto the shoulders of black women? If y'all would simply get your act together, my own stories have suggested, and quit with the mood swings and humiliating back talk, maybe we could all finally come together as a people and overthrow the devil who keeps us in chains. In the short stories I wrote, all that stood between black folks and freedom was the black woman's refusal to emotionally support her man. And since life invariably mimics art, I believe I began to carry this point of view into my own romantic relationships. Before I'd even had time to consider the absurdity of my attitude, I found myself saying to the women I dated, This is why the white man is able to keep us down—'cause we ain't unified. Every time I say one thing, you gotta say another. But you and me oughta be on the same side, baby.

In these discussions, however, "the same side" I was referring to was actually my side. And so the gist of my message couldn't have been much different from anything my father had said to my mother, back in the fifties, when she thought she might like to go to college: "You figure if you get all that schoolin'," he reportedly told her, "you won't need me around?" Like him, I guess I was afraid that if the woman in my life developed ideas and opinions that differed from my own, she would eventually come to think of me as a fool and have no choice but to leave me. But because I was a man of my times, a member of the first post–civil rights era generation—well educated, politically astute, and passionate about social causes—I was able to disguise my fear with a language that would have dazzled my father. I would simply suggest to my partner that by clinging so tightly to her own point of view she was demonstrating a "slave mentality" and thus undermining our progress as a people.

And most of the time it worked like a charm. Not because the women in my life lacked the intelligence or common sense to see through my ruse—more often than not they were much more intelligent than me in every imaginable way—but because all it takes to push a lot of black folks' buttons is for one of our own to suggest that we ain't down wit' da cause, that we done lost what it means to be black. It wasn't their identities as *women* I was challenging—on that subject they were thoroughly confident and would've stood for no instruction from a man—but rather, their identities as *black folks*. I had come from a long line of black agitators (during the sixties my brother accumulated a record with the FBI as thick as a telephone book) and so I posed convincingly as someone who could speak on such matters and who had only the best interests of the black community in mind.

Could it be, though, that all I really had in mind was my own obsessive need to be always in control? I'm a diminutive man, bookish and jittery, and I could never have gotten away with the macho posturing that some of my larger male friends had adopted (I tried once, though, with a woman I met in the Bronx, who looked at me as if to say, Nigga, you *must* be crazy, and then sat laughing at me for something like an hour, so it's possible that maybe—just maybe—I used the power of words to transform my insecurity and crazy need to control into something that sounded politically urgent, as though our very survival as a people were at stake.

It's only fair to point out, however, that overly controlling behavior, whether it's a woman's or a man's, is something that is difficult to escape in the black community. And while the behavior should never be condoned or encouraged—God knows it can have unhealthy ramifications, draining a person both emotionally and mentally—it must at least be acknowledged and understood. Like a lot of folks, I grew up in a household where money was always tight and opportunities for a better life were scarce, and because of liquor, depression, and feelings of personal worthlessness brought on by social restraints, the relationship between my parents always seemed to me like a time bomb ticking loudly through our cramped apartment, likely to explode at any minute. It made for the kind of anxiety that is still with me from childhood, and which I detect in so many other black men and women. It is any wonder, then, that when we grew into adults we sought ways to keep that anxiety at bay, to maintain a tight grip over our lives so that nothing would suddenly fly apart or spiral out of control?

When my need to control met head-to-head with a partner's need to control, the struggle that would ensue was better than anything you'd ever see in World Federation wrestling. We'd fight like we were in the middle of Madison Square Garden, two dark adversaries circling the canvas of our apartment, both of us determined to pin back the other's shoulders, to drop the opponent to his or her knees. Most of all, we each wanted to leave the struggle without surrendering too much and with our sense of personal dignity still intact. And, as all black folks know, battles like these are loud, fierce, and never really end: some part of each one comes up again in the next battle between you, or leaves emotional scars that never quite disappear. In my struggles with women, it occurs to me now, I must have been a particularly cruel opponent—because whenever I thought I was in real danger and might not survive the fight, I trotted out that old broken-record business about black unity. It was, I guess, my secret weapon—the suggestion that the disarray in the black community was due to exactly the kind of shit she was pulling right now, refusing to see things my way. And more often than not it was this accusation that brought the fight between us to its sad, bitter conclusion.

Could it be that I came to this type of behavior all on my own? Certainly my friends had their own secret weapons, their own ways of lying in love. If I had wanted, I could have borrowed a line a friend of mine uses when the women in his life assume points of view different from his and in the process threaten his sense of control. "Fine, baby," he says. "Have things your way. But it seems to me you done worked too hard and too long pulling yourself outta the ghetto to go backslidin' now."

And, man, what a panicky response he gets from these women when he reminds them of their modest beginnings—the Section 8 housing and low-income projects that they fought tooth and nail to escape—and suggests that by refusing to follow his lead they could end up back at square one. "All I'm tellin' you," I've heard him say, "is that what goes around comes around." My friend understands that for many black folks, words like these can conjure up all our worst fears about our accomplishments— Maybe it's just an illusion, we think to ourselves, another hand-out intended to keep us from complaining or to pacify some white liberal's guilt. Our professional successes often seem founded on something as sturdy as, say, a butterfly's wing, and pointing out how easily any one of us could end up back in Bed Stuy or South Central doesn't necessarily make my friend a bad person, but pointing it out to keep a woman in line puts him in league with the master who warns his house slave that one false move will land him back in the fields. What I mean is, keeping somebody back in this particular way isn't something my friend invented; rather, it's a strategy as old as the hills, the one thing that oppressors have always done whenever they've feared the oppressed. And so it doesn't take a rocket scientist to figure out from whom my friend could have learned such behavior.

The only other "secret weapon" I've ever seen used was in fact used on me. A woman I knew had a way of convincing the men in her life that her unhappiness was somehow their fault—and that this inability to make her happy was related in some way to their masculinity. The suggestion was that a woman's spiritual fulfillment—like (I guess) her sexual fulfillment—was based on her man's performance, and so any man who couldn't get the first job done right sure as hell wasn't cutting the mustard in any other regard. So in my fights with her for dominance and control, she was almost always the victor, because as soon as she felt threatened enough she'd invariably call out, "You don't know shit about being a man." And, like a balloon stabbed abruptly with the tip of a pin, I would burst and then sputter to the ground.

Despite the grimness of my encounters with this woman, I get some comfort now when I think back on her behavior: it's nice to know I'm not the only black person who ever blamed somebody else for my own failings and insecurities, and for the hurt I've experienced at the hands of an intolerant society. And lately I've seen lots of other folks doing the very same thing. Here in my West Philly neighborhood, for instance, we've got brothers standing on street corners holding their dicks, each one still swearing to anybody who'll listen that it was Whitey that kept him from going to college and getting ahead in life. Or else it was some woman—usually his mother, but it may be the old lady he's sharing his crib with now—who (figuratively) emasculated him and made it impossible for him to function as a man. Or check out some of the magazine articles and current fiction aimed at (and written by) black women: You'd be having a happy life, a rich and fulfilling life, my sister, they all seem to suggest, if these brothers of ours would simply get their acts together.

It seems there's no shortage of places to assign blame for the emptiness and dissatisfaction so many of us experience in our lives. But more often than not we point our fingers in the wrong direction—we point them at one another. Because to look inside ourselves for ways to be happy in a racist society is, admittedly, a monumental task, and to take personal responsibility for our own individual failings is just too damn scary.

So we find somebody else to blame. Or, as in my case, we find some concept outside ourselves—for me it was black unity—and, pinning all our hopes for happiness on that concept, browbeat and bully those who appear to be rocking our boat. Confused by my own need to be in control and fearful of taking any scenic excursions into my own heart, I believed the thing that would bring me happiness at last was a unified black community. But the unity I was working toward had a tyrant at its helm—namely, me—and, like some Stalin of the ghetto, I thought I could determine happiness for *all* black folks according to my own terms. Which is why I would get so impatient with those women in my life who saw the world differently than I did and who had their own ideas about how to live a fulfilling life. Some of these women had ideas as suspect as my own (I once dated a woman, beautiful and dark-skinned, who thought she'd be happy at last if she could just get herself a chemical peel), but this doesn't mean they should have let me determine the course of their lives. Looking back, I'm ashamed at the number of times that I tried to convince them otherwise.

But back in those days there was so much at stake for me. If I were to give up the concept of black unity—a concept that is, by the way, as flawed as Afrocentrism or any other concept that discusses black folks as though we were some monolithic entity—I might have to look to myself for a way to be happy. And I damn sure wasn't going to do that. It was easier and much more convenient to assume that all that stood between me and my ideal were the women, the black women, who were undermining "the cause" by insisting on their own point of view. Like the street brothers who maintain that it's Whitey keeping them down, or like the sisters who swear black men are the ones making their lives so unhappy, I was content to point fingers and pass the buck about the pain I was in, without ever once stopping to wonder if I had brought any of it on myself.

I'd love to say that I suddenly had some dramatic experience that removed the blinders from my eyes, but that kind of stuff only happens in fiction—or at least it happens an awful lot in the fiction I write. In reality, the only thing that caused me to change my way of thinking and start taking responsibility for my own life was the everyday, ordinary business of living. But I guess there were two incidents that you could say put me on a better path.

A while back I was standing on a crowded street corner—my mind wandering as usual—and without stopping to look both ways, I stepped out into a rush of traffic; of all the people who were standing near me, only one reached out a hand to pull me back to the curb. That person was a woman, the only other black person in the crowd, and if I owe my life to anyone, then certainly I owe it to her.

More recently, I was feeling pretty bleak about my life, wondering what the hell to do when I was finished with grad school, and in the meantime drinking my evenings away. But one night in a bar, a brother asked me what was wrong and patiently listened to my entire sob story. Then he gave me the name of some people he knew who were hiring at a local school and, together with his wife, made it his personal business to cheer me out of my depression.

When I think back now to the kindness of this man—and then remember the woman from the street corner incident—it's clear to me that I spent too much time in the past believing it was necessary to mobilize entire armies against the devastating effects of racism, and not enough time considering how one person can help another person to heal from those effects. A chain, after all, is only as strong as its individual links, and it seems to me now that the way to help strengthen my community as a whole is to improve the quality of my relationships—romantic and otherwise—with the individual black folks I meet every day. To do this requires tearing down all the walls I've built around myself and taking a long, hard look inside; what I've already discovered, much to my surprise, is that the view isn't really all that bad.

So, recently I finished a new short story—another romantic saga about a young black couple in love. This time, though, neither of them is more responsible than the other for whether or not their love survives—or, by extension, whether or not the black community survives. They are, quite frankly, a lot more cynical than characters I've created in the past. They know the world is an awful place and not likely to ever get much better. But they also know they've got a pretty good thing going, what Alice Walker would call "a council between equals," so they spend each day showering each other with kindness and rescuing one another from the unfriendly climate of the world outside their door. And if there's a lesson to be gathered from these two characters of mine, I'm hoping I'll be the first one to learn it.

The Sexual Diversion:
The Black Man / Black Woman
Debate in Context

Derrick Bell

Rayford Logan, the great black historian, called the period at the turn of the last century the nadir for black people. Hundreds of blacks were lynched, thousands were victims of racist violence and intimidation, and literally millions were exploited on farms and at mostly menial labor where their pay failed to cover the food and other necessities they were often required to purchase from their employers.

For Dr. Logan, the nadir meant the bottom, a status that arguably was only a small step up from slavery itself. It is a measure of the fragility of our current condition that a great many thoughtful black people now worry that we are heading toward another nadir, this one marked by far more self-destruction than anyone living a century ago could easily imagine. The statistics supporting these concerns are all too familiar.[1] Maya Angelou transforms them into words that highlight the pain of our plight:

> In these bloody days and frightful nights when an urban warrior can find no face more despicable than his own, no ammunition more deadly than self-hate and no

target more deserving of his true aim than his brother, we must wonder how we came so late and lonely to this place.[2]

If African Americans are to survive the storms we are now experiencing—and those storms now brewing on the horizon—we must reconnect ourselves, eschewing in the process divisive behaviors that distract us from the dangers lurking outside our community, dangers we know all too well and prefer to deny.

It is sad but hardly remarkable that oppressed black people vent far more of their rage on other blacks than on their oppressors. The very power that defines the status of those on the top and those on the bottom serves to deflect frustrated rage from the perpetrators of oppression to fellow sufferers. Diversion is now, and likely has always been, an important tactic in preventing the oppressed from recognizing the true sources of their oppression. Those in power recognize the value of diversion to redirect victim rage away from themselves and seldom miss the chance to promote its paranoid permutations.

Once sown, the seeds of distrust and enmity seem to flourish on their own. Those in power need do no more than appear to favor one subordinate group over another to quell even a possibility that the feuding groups will either recognize the similar character of their lowly state or identify the source of their condition. The lowly ones engage in spirited expressions of hostility against each other, exhausting time, energy, and resources that might otherwise be employed against their oppressors. In the process, their squabbling provides their real enemies with a seemingly impenetrable insulation from intergroup strife among those who, while fearing their differences, are quite similar in their subordination. Subordination, by its very nature, generates beliefs and behaviors that lead to antagonism among subordinate groups. Victims often look for the less powerful and attempt to victimize them in turn. Those harmed seek to retaliate, and soon there is a vicious cycle of hostility that creates disorder and chaos among victims of the status quo while serving to ensure the position of those in power.

The stability and even the survival of the economic system in this country depends on maintaining divisions between people based on race, gender, and class. The success of this strategy can be measured in the fact that (for example) there is little outcry about the gap in income and wealth between the rich and the rest of us, even though this gap is larger than at any time in this century. The reason is not hard to find. Those at the short end of the income and wealth gap are easily convinced that they should vent their otherwise unfocused upset on those on welfare, newly arrived immigrants, those who commit street crimes, and the society's traditional scapegoat—black people. A great many whites across the socioeconomic spectrum are vocal in their opposition to affirmative action policies that they view as aiding less qualified members of minorities at their expense; there is no similar opposition to all manner of priorities and preferences aimed at privileging those who are already well-off.

It would be a most welcome but quite unlikely miracle if black people, we who from our earliest days in this country have occupied the very bottom of society's well, were able to avoid the victim's predisposition to battle others within our group rather than those responsible for our lowly status. Alas, it is likely that because of our long history of subordinate status in this country we are more rather than less prone to this affliction. Because sexism and patriarchy are deeply rooted in this society, all too many black men have fallen into patterns of physical and emotional abuse of women, behavior that black women understandably fear and resent.

For a generation now, a host of writers—many of them black women—have been telling the world about the inadequacies of black men. This often emotional testimony ranges from mournful frustration to flat-out rage. These revelations contain both deeply felt disappointment about what often is and a yearning hope about what might be. And while there are many, many black males who do not fit the woeful patterns, we know from statistics and personal experience that these criticisms are based in reality as well as myth. Rather than either condone or condemn, I want to examine this phenomenon in the context of a society where the deflection of oppression is the norm.

Who can deny it? Life for black men in racist America is devilishly difficult. Surely, a factor in our failings is the hostility we encounter at every level. While slavery is over, a racist society continues to exert dominion over black men and their maleness in ways more subtle but hardly less castrating than during slavery, when male-female relationships between black people generally were not formalized, and even when a marriage was recognized, the black man's sexual access to his wife was controlled by the master or his sons or his overseer.

Black women also suffered the pains of slavery. Black women were exploited, abused, and demeaned, and that harm was serious. Forced to submit to the sexual desires of their masters or to slaves selected by their masters, they then suffered the agony of watching helplessly as their children were sold off. Black men were also dealt a double blow. They were forced to stand by powerless and unable to protect black women from sexual access by white men, and they were denied access to white women as a further symbol of their subordinate status. The harm done black men by this dual assault has never been fully assessed. Moreover, the assault continues in less blatant but still potent forms.

James Baldwin asserts that "the action of the White Republic, in the lives of Black men, has been, and remains, emasculation. Hence, the Republic has absolutely no image, or standard, of masculinity to which any man, Black or White, can honorably aspire."[3] The vain effort to protect black males against this ever-present danger, Baldwin explains, results in what Andy Young calls "sorriness," a disease that attacks black males. Baldwin writes:

> It is transmitted by Mama, whose instinct—and it is not hard to see why—is to protect the Black male from the devastation that threatens him the moment he declares himself a man. All of our mothers, and all of our women, live with this small, doom-laden bell in the skull, silent, waiting, or resounding, every hour of every day. Mama lays this burden on Sister, from whom she expects (or indicates she expects) far more than she expects from Brother; but one of the results of this all too comprehensible dynamic is that Brother may never grow up—in which case, the community has become an accomplice to the Republic.[4]

Women may well respond that here is one more effort, albeit a well-written one, to blame male failure on female love. There is a chicken and egg aspect to this position. This society has not much loved either black men or black women, and debate as to whether society's hostility or parental efforts to shield males from this hostility is more damaging does not move us much closer toward the relief that both need. Even so, in Baldwin's view, "this dilemma has everything to do with the situation of the Black man in the American inferno."[5]

Black women do not accept racism as the reason for sorry behavior—they have experienced it firsthand, and for them it is an excuse, not a justification. Alice Walker's character Grange Copeland speaks her mind on this subject:

I'm bound to believe that that's the way white folks can corrupt you even when you done held up before. 'Cause when they got you thinking that they're to blame for everything they have you thinking they's some kind of gods! You can't do nothing wrong without them being behind it. You gits just as weak as water, no feeling of doing nothing yourself. Then you begins to think up evil and begins to destroy everybody around you, and you blames it on the crackers. Shit! Nobody's as powerful as we make them out to be. We got our own souls, don't we?[6]

In addition to rejecting the traditional, patriarchal notion that women must be protected by men, black women cannot see why black men must try to emulate the macho sexism of their white counterparts rather than work toward a more natural and healthy equality between the sexes. As a woman student wrote in an essay, quoting Fran Sanders's "Dear Black Man,"

Talk to me like the woman that I am and not to me as that woman who is the inanimate creation of someone's overactive imagination. Look at me with no preconceived notions of how I must act or feel and I will try to do the same with you. No presumption, no assumptions, no banal rhetoric substituted for real person-to-person giving and receiving. Look at my face when you speak to me; look into my eyes and see what they have to say. Think about the answers that you give to my questions. . . . I am a woman and you are a man and I have always known it. If you love me, tell me so. Don't approach me as you would an enemy. I am on your side and have always been. We have survived, and we may just be able to teach the world a lesson.[7]

That, of course, is a wonderful homily of how life should be for sexual partners, regardless of race. It is an ideal, and as is obvious from the charges and countercharges, a far from fulfilled ideal for many black men and women.[8] It can hardly be denied that black women bear much of the brunt of black male frustration and suppressed rage.

During my twenty-five years of law school teaching, I have listened to dozens of black women—and more than a few white ones—voice their disappointments with many black men. Much of the problem is due to the paucity of black men at the professional level rather than to their behavior. The statistics regarding the number of black men who fall by the wayside long before professional school are harsh. Most law school classes contain many more black women than men. This disparity heightens black women's sense of betrayal when potentially available black men choose white women. As one of my students put it, "We black women are always being reminded of how marginal and unworthy we are. We're never smart enough or beautiful enough or supportive, sexy, understanding, and resourceful enough to deserve a good black man."[9]

Another former student, Kirsten Levingston, makes clear that she would not encourage a black woman to stay with a black man if he made her unhappy, nor would she discourage a black man from marrying a white woman who makes him happy. Even so, she believes black Americans must do all they can to unite and develop. This unity begins at home with our children, and, she contends, "the key to producing strong and proud black children is to raise them in an environment with strong and proud black parents."[10] Ms. Levingston's call for unity may be unrealistic in a society where one-half of all marriages end in divorce, but hers is a view shared by many, perhaps most, black women.

Recently, while discussing this issue in a civil rights class, two black women prepared a fictional dialogue among friends regarding interracial relationships. As reported by the black woman commentator, the black and white law students discussed the tendency of handsome and promising black men to prefer or at least look with admiration on white women, while disliking ethnic hair styles and other Afrocentric "looks" on black women. They raised the often unspoken question regarding black women's suspicion that any expression of interest in them by white men is based on the stereotype of black women as super-sensual, and discussed the refusal of some black women to date white men for that reason. The narrator shares this concern, but feels trapped by it because the "bottom line is that there just aren't enough brothers to go around." She recognizes that many black men are not very sensitive to this dilemma, resent black women who date white men, and sometimes ask, "How come a garbage collector isn't good enough for you?" The fictional group discusses several variations on this theme and then the narrator closes with this observation:

As I took a sip from my wine glass, I realized that there were no definitive answers. I could say I am black, female, and bright in a white mediocre world, but that hardly explains why I sit on the beaches of St. Croix feeling so abandoned.

In the same class, a young Indian woman, after conceding the burdening nature of male hegemony in Indian culture, posed the question,

Why is it that struggle and racial adversity create strong black women and "weak and disempowered" black men? The African-American female has fewer job opportunities and just as many stereotypes heaped upon her as does the African-American male. Why does the most oppressed class, women of color, derive strength from oppression, whereas black men may scapegoat oppression to justify unjustifiable behavior (often against women of color).

Both my student's question and the issue deserve to be more firmly grounded in the societal environment out of which they come. I shared my student's observations with a black social worker friend, Gwen Jordan, who felt that the Indian woman posed an ultimate dilemma for all people of color. When we attempt to work through the difficulties in relationships that are fundamental to the preservation of our culture and well-being in public, within the view of others who do not share our cultural issues, we unconsciously place that struggle in the context of an alien culture whose values and mores do not support—and are often hostile to—the core of our definition and being. And then it is from this perspective that we evaluate and judge the quality of these relationships and the sincerity of our mates.

In Ms. Jordan's view, African-Americans in their relationships must struggle to achieve a level of unconditional love in a systemic context—racism—which places conditions upon our being. Within that context, we trivialize ourselves when we attempt to define African-American male/female relationships in terms of the prevailing culture: we attribute to black females mystical powers and strengths that become burdensome in their superficiality, and we attribute weakness and defeat to black males. These, according to Jordan, are really just more sophisticated versions of the stereotypes that we have carried since slavery. The result is that we disempower ourselves and imperil our capacity to love unconditionally and, through that love, to grow and create together.

The threat of disempowerment is certainly real, but the effort to define differences can be both revealing and strengthening in our understanding of how we function as male and female human beings. James Baldwin, for example, provides an enlightening statement about the psychological makeup of men and their weakness, too often masked by a show of muscle and—it must be said—all too often manifested in the physical abuse of those very women who would, if given a chance, love and care for them. Baldwin writes:

> One is confronted, first of all, with the universal mystery of men—as we are, of a man, as he is; with the legend and the reality of the masculine force and the masculine role—though these last two realities are not always the same. Men would seem to dream more than women do—always have, it would seem, and very probably, always will. They must, since they assume that their role is to alter and conquer reality. If women dream less than men—for men know very little about a woman's dreams—it is certainly because they are so swiftly confronted with the reality of men. They must accommodate this indispensable creature, who is, in so many ways, more fragile than a woman. Women know much more about men than men will ever know about women—which may, at bottom, be the only reason that the race has managed to survive so long.
>
> In any case, the male cannot bear very much humiliation; and he really cannot bear it, it obliterates him. All men know this about each other, which is one of the reasons that men can treat each other with such a vile, relentless, and endlessly inventive cruelty. Also, however, it must be added, with such depthless respect and love, conveyed mainly by grunts and blows. It has often seemed to me that men need each other in order to deal with women, and women, God knows, must need each other in order to deal with men.
>
> Women manage, quite brilliantly, on the whole, and to stunning and unforeseeable effect, to survive and

surmount being defined by others. They dismiss the definition, however dangerous or wounding it may be—or even, sometimes, find a way to utilize it—perhaps because they are not dreaming. But men are neither so supple nor so subtle. A man fights for his manhood: that's the bottom line. A man does not have, simply, the weapons of a woman. Mama must feed her children—that's another bottom line; and there is a level on which it can be said that she cannot afford to care how she does it.

But when a man cannot feed his women or his children, he finds it, literally, impossible to face them. The song says, Now, when a woman gets the blues, Lord/ She hangs her head and cries/But when a man gets the blues, Lord/He grabs a train and rides.[11]

Even we black men fortunate enough to provide for our families must defend against the myriad forms of emasculation that the society has placed in our path. Success as the society measures it exacts a very real and often terrible price. None of us escapes, really, and those of us who feel we have established some limits to what we will put up with spend far more time than we should criticizing those who, by our measures, have been too willing to comfort whites in order to either get ahead or (usually) stay even.

Baldwin, I think, would urge more understanding—if not compassion—as he reminds us:

It is a very grave matter to be forced to imitate a people for whom you know—which is the price of your performance and survival—you do not exist. It is hard to imitate a people whose existence appears, mainly, to be made tolerable by their bottomless gratitude that they are not, thank heaven, you.[12]

Writer Jill Nelson speaks for many of us, men as well as women, when she describes how difficult it is to maintain one's ethical bearings in the job market. Following a series of interviews at a major, white newspaper that was considering her as a reporter, she wrote:

I've been doing the standard Negro balancing act when it comes to dealing with white folks, which involves sufficiently blurring the edges of my being so that white folks don't feel intimidated and simultaneously holding on to my integrity. There is a thin line between Uncle Tomming and Mau-Mauing. To step over that line can mean disaster. On one side lies employment and self-hatred, on the other, the equally dubious honor of unemployment with integrity. In the middle lies something like employment with honor, although I'm not sure exactly how that works.[13]

Jill Nelson got the job. Even so, it was a constant hassle, which she writes about with pain-filled humor. Increasingly, blacks—men and women—are not getting these jobs, or much of any work. The optimist might hope that frustrated employment hopes might bring humility and compassion to the Donnells of this world and their less talented brethren. Alas, for all the reasons Baldwin asserts, it usually does not. And it is unlikely that the relations between some black men and black women will improve until societal conditions improve. Even so, we must not ignore the fact that despite all the barriers, a great many—dare we say most?— black men marry and stay with their wives and families through thick and thin. Here, again, Baldwin says it well:

A stranger to this planet might find the fact that there are any Black people at all still alive in America something to write home about. I myself find it remarkable not that so many Black men were forced (and in so many ways!) to leave their families, but that so many remained and aided their issue to grow and flourish.[14]

This positive observation provides an important foundation on which to plan the coming struggle for our survival in a society in transition, one that appears more than ready to sacrifice our interests, our well-being, even our lives, in a desperate effort to avoid the dangers inherent in change. The black man/black woman debate should continue, but participants must be aware of the ever-present temptation of diversion and its potential to twist that debate in a way that comforts our enemies and betrays ourselves.

Notes

1. Typical are the figures issued by the U.S. Justice Department, reporting that young black men were almost 14 times more likely to be murdered during 1992 than the nation's general population. In that year, black males ages twelve to twenty-four were victims of homicide at a rate of 114.9 per 100,000, compared with 8.5 murder victims per 100,000 of the general population. They constituted 17.7 percent of all homicide victims, even though they were only 1.3 percent of the U.S. population. Black males age sixteen to twenty-four, were 1.5 times more likely to be victims of all types of violent crime (source: "Around the Nation," *Washington Post*, 9 December 1994, A = 10).

2. Maya Angelou, "I Dare to Hope," *New York Times*, 25 August 1991, 15.

3. James Baldwin, *The Evidence of Things Not Seen* (1985), 21.

4. Ibid., 19.

5. Ibid., 20.

6. Alice Walker, *The Third Life of Grange Copeland* (1970), 207.

7. F. Sanders, "Dear Black Man," in *The Black Woman: An Anthology*, ed. T. Cade (1970), 73, 78–79.

8. Compare Wallace, "A Black Feminist's Search for Sisterhood," in *All the Blacks Are Men, All the Women Are White, but Some of Us Are Brave*, ed. G. T. Hull et al. (1982), 5–8 ("Whenever I raised the question of a Black woman's humanity in conversation with a Black man, I got a similar reaction. Black men, at least the ones I knew, seemed totally confounded when it came to treating Black women like people"), with Staples, "The Myth of Black Macho: A Response to Angry Black Feminists," *Black Scholar*, March/April 1979, 24–32 (While black males are not free of sexism, most black men lack the institutionalized power to oppress black men, and it is their lowly societal position that most disturbs black males).

9. I used this quote in the story "The Last Black Hero," in Derrick Bell, *Faces at the Bottom of the Well: The Permanence of Racism* (1992), 75.

10. See "Racial Reflections: Dialogues in the Direction of Liberation," ed. Derrick Bell, Tracy Higgins, Sung-Hee Suh, *UCLA Law Review* 37 (1990): 1037, 1083.

11. Baldwin, *Evidence of Things Not Seen*, 20–21.

12. Ibid., 44.

13. Jill Nelson, *Volunteer Slavery* (1993), 10.

14. Baldwin, *Evidence of Things Not Seen*, 21.

Music, Darkrooms, and Cuba

Richard Perry

When the waiter had taken their orders, Adrian glanced at his companion's throat, dazed by his behavior and the realization of how long it had been since the translator had entered his dreaming. Even more time had passed since he'd seen her in the flesh, thirty-something years; she'd be well past fifty now, age he couldn't imagine her wearing.

•

The translator had come into his life in 1960, during a summer of ill-tempered heat. Residents of midtown speak fondly of that time, for on those occasions when they left air-conditioned spaces they could walk without jostling neighbors or having to confront the not yet documented homeless. Still, despite these lifestyle improvements for the well-to-do, the truth was that the summer of 1960 was insufferably hot, which is why folks in the inner city remember it as one that drained lovers of appetite for touching and drove old women to sprawl naked in the dark. What relief there was came from window fans, refrigerated drinking water, sponge baths, and dreams of ice.

All during that summer, Adrian found himself across aisles from women who fell asleep on subways, lips parted, thighs gaped beneath the pleats of pastel dresses. He'd never guessed that the world was so densely populated by women with compelling thighs, and though he thought of that summer as the year of the translator, he also remembered it as a time when thighs didn't touch, the year when he took two chances.

The first was on the "A" train, when he stared into the smoked eyes of a girl who had caught him exploring the dark cave between her knees. The second was that evening. Fired by a stranger's cunning smile and a hard rain's hammer at his window, he'd asked his wife to turn over so he could mount her from behind.

Two weeks later Adrian was part of a crowd in front of the Hotel Theresa, standing in a street whose light had been stolen from cathedrals. The day was stifling. Dense with rain's undelivered promise, a pewter sky slid down to gaunt trees lit by birds who would neither sing nor fly until dawn, then fell onto the shoulders of black boys slumped by lost desire for basketball. Adrian glanced at the man on his right. The man had an undeveloped beard. He wore a pink shirt and sucked a grapefruit wedge, a union that would have brought Adrian's camera to his eye had not the Cuban visitors chosen that moment to spill from the hotel door. The press, baffled that a head of state had deigned to stay in Harlem, surged forward, obscuring the photographer's view. Efficiently, he elbowed an improvement in his position and plunged forward into a moment defined by light shining in his eyes without the blinding. Music surged—flute, bassoon, a saxophone; he felt pain in his mouth, and his feet twitched with wanting to dance.

There at the side of Fidel Castro was a creature so arresting that Adrian had suppressed an outcry only by biting his lip. Trembling, he shot a roll in black-and-white, advancing the film so fast that his thumb would be sore in an hour. She was, simply, the loveliest woman he'd ever seen. Her nose was African, skin a deep shading of loam, hair a black sweep at her shoulders. She had full lips and hands that searched for harp strings. Only once did she frown at the stupidly shouted questions. Twice she waved away smoke from Castro's foul cigar.

When the press conference ended, the translator, on her way to the limousine, looked directly into Adrian's face and winked. Her eyes were green, and when she smiled he saw that her teeth were bad. Before he could regret this, she threw her head back, exposing a throat he'd forever insist was inviting him to weep. He didn't weep, because to do so would call attention to himself, and because in his haste to witness history he'd left home without a handkerchief. Instead, he drew deep breaths that tasted of cigar smoke and promised to protect the translator from all harm forever.

Of course he knew it was strange to be drawn to protection rather than desire, and had not the occasion been so moving, he'd have stopped to think it through. But he was pleased with the depth of his feeling, and so he only acknowledged it in the way the well-adjusted accept compliments from strangers. Then he went home beneath a clearing sky that tried to distract from its unkept promise with fabric borrowed from an old man's willing heart. On his way to the subway he walked a street where men sat listlessly on stoops. All the buildings had green plants growing stubbornly at windows, and doorways wild with shadows and a trumpet's thin spun gold. Adrian saluted the plants' persistence, forgave the men their indolence, knowing that by evening they'd look up at the translucent sky. Hard on the heels of that certainty came the bliss, so unaccustomed a feeling that it took a while to name it. He thanked God for beauty in the world, and while he did, the trumpet healed his lip and lifted his feet in dance.

Inside his Bronx darkroom, heart racing like a first-time lover, he bent to process the film. In a little while he moaned, cupped a hand to his mouth, staggered to the bathroom where he sat on the toilet and sucked his throbbing thumb. Then he lay his face against the warm, smooth sink, feeling stupid and unworthy.

None of the photographs had developed. At first he thought he'd left the lens cap on, but when he checked, the cap was in his pocket. So the film was defective. He stared at the celluloid, understanding that nothing in his life would ever match this day for disappointment. He knew this with a certainty so quiet his heart had to lean forward to hear it. He was about to say it out loud when his wife sailed into the apartment, carrying two novels and whistling a tune by Ellington.

•

Here in the restaurant, Adrian's companion was waiting with the patience of a woman who knew not to interrupt a man reliving failure in the darkroom. Twenty minutes ago, she'd stepped from shadow on the corner of 26th Street and Third Avenue, materializing like an image from solution. Shadows loomed behind her; street light nested in her hair. Her coat was blues-song red, her shoes, brown tasteful oxfords, sensible, like her hands. It wasn't until she asked if Adrian knew a decent place to eat that her head moved to reveal her throat, not until then that music flowered—an oboe, a trumpet that sang of potted plants. This time the song didn't say to dance. This time the song said that if this woman's teeth were bad, what was left of his life would change.

The street was deserted—small shops, apartment buildings—it was evening, just past seven; March was in decline. The day had been rich with a spring's soft promise, but the night bloomed raw, sliced by a wind that should have been arrested as an enemy of the people. Adrian looked again at the woman's throat and felt the impulse to protect. It wasn't that he mistook her for the translator (he was shaken by the similar appearance, but he knew she wasn't); he was overwhelmed that the ability to feel was still in him. So he chose not to think, in the way that one paralyzed by heights goes to meet his love across a bridge without looking at the water. In this way he was able to accomplish something he'd not done since the evening more than thirty years ago when he'd asked his wife to turn over. He took a risk. He invited the woman to dine with him, around the corner in a small Italian restaurant.

•

Now he listened to her voice, flat, clipped, rising at the ends of sentences. Her name was Norma Fillis, and this was her first time in New York. She'd worked for sixteen years as a practical nurse. Most of her clients were elderly, although once there'd been a young woman in a wheelchair who kept a greenhouse in which she obsessed over grapefruit that grew no larger than her fist. Norma was from Marietta, Ohio, a small city known for its prison, a maximum security facility from which, apparently, no one had ever escaped, and it was also known for its widows who tilled gardens so luxurious that in spring the entire metropolis grew sick of the smell of roses.

The words struck Adrian's forehead like frozen rain. By now, braced by a glass of chenin blanc and the smell of tomato sauce, he'd begun to recover from his folly, which was, simply, that he'd disregarded what he knew. And what he knew was this: he was old; life was armed and extremely dangerous; the only way to survive the world was to hide within it, be film that refused to develop. He'd mastered the tones of anonymity, or so he'd thought, and now he was trying to adjust to color in his life (a coat the red of blues songs), and to having invited a stranger to dinner because he was moved by her throat. He shivered at what might have happened—an accomplice hidden in a doorway, a knife, a pistol's circle frozen at his neck.

Norma paused in mid-sentence. In the interval her words collected—*Ohio, Marietta, nurse*—and Adrian swallowed and forced himself to talk. He'd been born in Paterson, New Jersey, had lived his adult life in the Bronx. He'd worked, before retiring, as a photographer.

"A photographer," Norma said, as if the profession were exotic. She leaned toward him, movement that fired the scent of avocado. "What kind of pictures did you take?"

"I worked in the garment center."

"The what?"

"It's here in New York. An industry that makes and sells clothing."

Norma lifted her wine, a red bordeaux even though she'd ordered fish. "You photographed fashions?"

"No. I photographed women modeling lingerie. For mail-order catalogues. It was all I could get then," he said, and looked past her at a silver tray that seemed glued to a waiter's fingers. He'd had some talent—a good eye, a deftness in the darkroom; he'd wanted to be another Van der Zee or Parks, but he'd had no chance to share his gift. People who bought photographs didn't see the world as he did—shades of black and white, complex and frightening. And one had to eat. Even when the white models had complained about his presence and he'd been forced to take his pictures from behind a screen, even then he'd done what he must.

When it became difficult to work without grinding his teeth, he imagined he endured this humiliation for his wife, who taught school with a devotion that inspired in her students a love for reading that caused them to turn from television and ride past subway stops. The truth was that his wife's life was nicely filled with work and books, and affection for other people's children, and when Adrian realized there was no one for whom he could do, he would think of the translator, imagine she needed money to escape from Cuba, or to fix her teeth, or was heartsick for someone to love her.

Dinner came, for him, veal in a wine sauce, for his companion, broiled flounder, linguini on the side. Norma dug in, eating with the enthusiasm of a man, then, a fork of pasta like a bee's nest at her mouth, she paused.

"How could you take pictures like that?"

"There are ways to hold the camera. I had an assistant, white, who spoke directly to the models, arranged the poses. I'd tell him what I wanted. He'd tell them."

"What did you feel?"

"It was a job."

"The women, what were *they* like?"

He shrugged. "Ordinary."

"It would have made me crazy," Norma said. She devoured the nest of pasta. "I'd have hated them. Are you married?"

"She passed away. Ten years ago."

"What was *she* like?"

"A good woman. Self-sufficient."

"Children?"

He shook his head. "Are you married?"

"Never." There was a note in her voice, strident, as if the idea had plucked a vocal chord.

"Why?"

"*Adrian.* What a question to ask a lady. I declare," and she smiled, revealing perfect teeth. Then she cocked her head to one side so that her throat was lit at an angle only just invented, and bent to attack her food. He couldn't remember the last time he'd talked to someone about his life, and though self-revelation was unsettling, it also made him feel worthwhile, concrete. Now he considered telling Norma about the translator, how once he'd have promised anything to see her, how at times the thought of her existence was all the motivation he could find for getting out of bed. But Norma might be confused, in the way the translator must be at how life had changed in Cuba. The beaches were still white, but the country was gripped by bad fortune. He'd read in the *Times* that there were shortages of food and medicine. The young people wanted to go to America; they piled into unsafe boats and drifted toward Miami, where in full view of flamingo-colored buildings they were turned away by soldiers barely old enough to vote.

Outside, a siren keened, faint, then came closer, swelled and burst in the street. Norma touched a napkin to her mouth. "Ambulance?"

"Or police."

"I've heard," she said gravely, "about your police."

"Oh?"

"That they can be brutal. That they have no respect for anyone who has no money, who isn't white."

Adrian frowned. "We have black police, you know."

"I heard that few of them are different."

"You can't," he said gently, "always believe what you hear. I'd guess they're like policemen everywhere . . . but imagine what life would be *without* them." He paused, fixed by the vengeance with which a man at a nearby table thrust his spoon into a grapefruit.

". . . Coming here, I took the train. There was a woman wearing purple sneakers, maybe fifty, a scar on her left cheek, skin the color of mahogany. When she got off she left behind a *Daily News*. I picked it up. On the fourth page, in the lower left-hand corner, was a woman's photograph. She'd been found in a vacant lot in the Bronx, in the shadow of the elevated train, her neck broken. Strangled by someone of strength. No purse. Estimated motive, robbery. It happened two blocks from my house."

"That was an old paper," Norma said.

"Old?"

"I read about it. I'd been here two days. The dead woman was a nurse. Someone saw the photograph and identified her."

"I don't usually read the *Daily News*," he said.

His companion leaned back in her chair, her eyes on the remains of her flounder. "Why would a woman carry an old newspaper? She works hard and gets behind? She found the paper, like you, and read old news to pass the time? Or was she just out of touch?

"You know, I haven't been here but what my boss-lady calls 'a New York minute,' but it's long enough to see the madness in this city. Yesterday I'm pushing the baby along the avenue, and coming toward me is this white woman, dressed to kill. She stops to put a coin down near the knee of a homeless man who's sleeping in a vestibule, on a poster for Aruba, then she walks on. Her head's dancing to some no-beat private song. She had a white glove on one hand and she was holding the other one, and with her bare hand she's running her finger along the side of a building and licking it. We were on Madison near 82nd. No one else noticed. When she passed, I heard the sound her mouth made. Like kissing."

"I've seen people like that," Adrian said. "I always imagine they're disappointed."

"At what?"

He shrugged. "Life?"

"I think they're weak. You have to be strong to live in this world."

When Adrian didn't respond, she said, "Are *you*?"

He blinked. "Strong?"

"You have a strong face."

He touched his face.

"You touch your face like a stranger."

"It's not a good face."

"I declare. What a thing to say about your own face. What's wrong with it?"

"The eyes are too close together. The chin too narrow. The mouth belongs on a taller man."

She laughed. He'd have thought her laugh would be controlled and sensible, like her shoes, but this spilled from her lips in a cackle that turned heads in the room and rekindled his discomfort.

"Well, I like your face."

"Thank you," Adrian whispered. He'd not meant to whisper.

Norma lit a cigarette. "Which way is Harlem?"

He pointed. The waiter mistook the gesture; Adrian ordered coffee.

"Why do you eat here?"

"I eat all over."

"Do you eat in Harlem?"

"Not any more. When I was young, it was the place to be. Alive. Safe. Once Fidel Castro came to visit. Did you know that?"

"Why's that so special?"

"Because now he wouldn't."

"Why?"

"It's . . . different."

When she asked how it was different, he explained that it was mostly the young, the disrespect they had for elders, boys with their hats on backwards, girls lean and hard, immodest, the booming music, sound meant to intimidate, to make it impossible to ignore them. Instead of baseballs, they carried guns, invented opportunities to use them, and their faces, nearly always furious, were those one would never photograph in color. Even their laughter disturbed him, a pitched substitute for rage.

What Adrian didn't say was how hard it was for him not to despise these children, less for their music or their hats than because they didn't understand the darkness toward which he headed. It was as if they had no old folks in their lives, as if they were strangers to death and disillusionment except as seen on screens in front of which they hunched in speechless worship. Worst of all, they killed one another with the same impunity with which they'd fire on passers-by. He was convinced that despite the slaughter, despite the blood left pooled on the pavement, which screamed their suspicion that life wasn't worth it, they didn't believe that death was real, or forever.

"Well, it isn't so," Adrian would mutter when he passed them, "death *is* forever." His voice, then, was taut with loathing, with love and the desire to be loved, with fear for the moment of their discovery and a greater fear that they'd never understand at all.

But the children didn't hear him. The truth was that they seldom saw him. It didn't matter that he was sixty-seven, and kind, or that his bitterness at having to die was all mixed up with his longing for connection. They wouldn't have cared that once he'd fallen in love with a translator from whose absence of image in his darkroom he'd not recovered.

"Well," Norma said. "They're not *all* our kids. Some of our kids are coming up right, we just don't hear about them. Lots go to college and make something of themselves. And some of what you talk about is nothing more than style. When I was coming up we had the Afro, remember? And my mama and daddy talked about my hair like I'd sold my soul to the devil. It's what the young *do*: they set their parents' teeth on edge. Then they become parents, and the same thing happens all over again. Think about it. What was the rage when you were a kid? Zoot suits? Conked hair?"

"I never," Adrian said stiffly, "straightened my hair."

"But you had a zoot suit?"

He nodded, full of shame.

"And what did your daddy say?"

"That I looked like a gigolo."

"See?"

He wanted to say, But we weren't *killing* one another.

"Anyway," Norma said. "I want to see Harlem. I'd have gone already if I had someone to go with. The woman I work for said not to go by myself. She said the Village was okay, but not Harlem. Will you take me sometime? And I want to see where you live."

"Excuse me?"

"I'm off until tomorrow. And to tell the truth, Adrian, I'd rather not spend it alone. I'm tired of alone."

He didn't understand. Then his heart stepped off a shelf, took its sweet time looking for a bottom. "I'm not prepared," he said.

"Prepared? For what?"

"For . . . guests."

"You don't have a couch?"

He nodded, and his face made her laugh again. "Adrian. Are you afraid of me?"

He shook his head. "Should I be afraid of you?"

She reached for her purse; he gathered himself. "Of course not."

"Well, then." She held an almost empty pack of cigarettes, lit one, blew smoke into his eyes. "Listen, Adrian, do you believe in things happening for a reason? Like they're fated? I think we're meant to be friends. I think something or someone brought us together. And don't worry. I'm not crazy, or *weird*, or anything like that. I'm just lonely."

He was struck by how easily she said this. He wanted to say, I am, too, and while he considered making that confession, Norma said it again, as if its persistence in her life confused her.

•

The night had sharpened. The wind came from the north, driving debris with the rhythms of an untuned engine. Norma smoked another cigarette. Her arm in his was heavy, unfamiliar—*he* was unfamiliar. The familiar was what he counted on to fill the empty in the life, to stave off danger and aloneness: patterns, schedules, the *Times* reassuringly on his doorstep in the morning. He had no thirst for change, and now his throat was dry and his heart looked for a bottom.

They moved in silence toward the corner, past a black man huddled in a doorway, who, in summer-ripe falsetto, sang a haunting lullaby. The song filled the doorway and made Adrian think of warmth and safety. At Third Avenue he looked into rushing lights and waved his arm, bracing for the inevitability of cabdrivers who would ignore him. But it was different tonight, as if the red length of Norma's coat demanded service.

As was his habit, Adrian glanced at the driver's license, committing the number to memory before he gave his destination. The driver was Palestinian. What an unfortunate country that is, Adrian thought, and told the driver to take the highway. When they reached 116th Street he said, "That's Harlem, on your left."

She twisted, sent the faint smell of avocado up his nose, said it seemed peaceful.

•

Inside the apartment, Norma stood a moment before the photograph of Adrian's dead wife's face, then moved to a living room window, looked three stories down into the street. A rumbling rolled past the building.

"What's that?"

"The elevated train."

"You live with that racket?"

He said he'd grown used to it. He took her coat. "Would you like a drink?"

"No, thank you."

She sat on the couch, slipped off her shoes. "It's very comfortable. Two bedrooms?"

"One's a darkroom."

"May I see?"

The light was harsh. Equipment lined one wall; the others were covered with black-and-white photographs of faces. Most looked away from the camera, so that in the moment Adrian's eyes adjusted to the light he had the feeling of being ignored. A thin layer of dust covered everything. He was tired, his behavior pulled at him like a sodden winter coat. A woman was in his house, in stockinged feet. She stood in the darkroom's center, watching averted faces, then with a wan smile turned, walked back into the hall. Adrian left the light on, shut the door.

"That's your bedroom?"

Reluctantly he nodded. She went into the parlor, returned with her purse, and marched into the room he slept in. The room seemed different, as if the furniture had darkened since the morning. Behind the window, a gate cut off the fire escape.

"How long has it been since you've had a woman?"

Adrian couldn't remember her name. "Eight years," he blurted. In a clear moment the odor of that woman came to him, her flesh sheened with sweat, a musk perfume that made him think of Muslims. Norma was stepping out of her dress. She had a dancer's body, one of strength. Her hands were on his shoulders, driving him to the bed.

"Please. I'm an old man."

"Adrian." She pointed to his head. "Old is here."

"It's not safe."

She was fumbling for her purse. "Oh, but it is."

He shut his eyes, allowed her to undress him. As she sheathed his member in latex, her fist like a vise at his groin, he shivered but didn't watch. Confused, but hard inside her, he let himself be taken, flat on his back, open hands above him, thinking that if there were music in the room he'd find distraction. But there was no music, only her breathing, a bed spring's rhythmic protest, the tropical smell of silence in the dark behind his eyes. In that silence men on stoops sat beneath green plants while Adrian marvelled at the wonder in his feet. It was all as he recalled from more than thirty years ago—the fragile sky, the heat—except for the smell and that there was no music.

●

In the morning her touch against his cheek awakened him. She'd pinned up her hair and wore his old brown bathrobe. "Breakfast?"

He smelled coffee, nodded.

"I'll put the eggs on now."

When she left, Adrian swung from bed, took his blue robe from behind the door. In the bathroom he washed and looked at his face and didn't think. Norma called to him; he went obediently into the kitchen. The train groaned by. He was hungry, ate without speaking. She talked of jobs she'd held: a house by the sea in Oregon, a ranch in Colorado. Adrian suffered her speech as a man endures his captor's conversation. When she excused herself and went into the living room, he began to plot his escape.

"I'm out of cigarettes. Do you have any?"

He told her where. Coming back, she moved as if she lived there. She lit the cigarette from the stove.

"My God," she coughed. "How old are these?"

"Old?"

"They're stale. Something awful." She held the cigarette beneath the open faucet. Adrian cringed when she dropped it in the sink. "I'll have to go get some."

"I'll go."

"No, finish your coffee. Where's the store?"

He told her. She hummed her way to the bedroom, came back dressed. "I just ring the buzzer to get in?"

"Yes."

"You need anything?"

For an alarming moment he considered being rude, but he only shook his head.

"Back in a minute."

And she left, taking with her all that energy, leaving a space into whose silence Adrian allowed himself to fall. Shoulders hunched, he recreated the night leading to this morning, saw her step from shadow, the light alive in her hair. She could have been a thief who smirked while the old man made a mess of emptying his pockets. He'd been lucky, and his relief ballooned so heavy that his head dropped.

Yolk from the fried eggs dried on his plate, a sickly yellow that clashed with the red in the flatware's oval center. He pushed away from the table, went to the sink and retrieved the soggy cigarette, tossed it into the trash, wiped his fingers on a towel. There was an ache in his groin and things were moving several ways inside him, a fugue of feeling more intricate than Bach—one of those complex tunes by Ellington, one that his wife used to hum, the stereo a sound-lamp on a sunlit Saturday morning. What was the name of that tune, and why had his wife died and left him? How long had it been since he'd asked *that* question? And why was he so tired and lonely and yet desperate for alone?

"Translator," he said. "Please comfort me."

In the living room, open on the low table, sat Norma's purse. When she returned, he'd ask her to leave. It was his house, his unyielding pattern; she'd disturbed it. He sat on the couch, head against the cushion, eyes closed. Her body formed behind his eyelids, strong, brown, and very hot, and his face was wet and now her thighs were tight around him, her head thrown back, laughing that strange, ungodly, high-pitched laugh, the glow of her cigarette just before he slept, too tired to say, Be careful, please, don't smoke in bed. . . .

•

He awoke into a sense of danger. Disturbed, he trudged into the kitchen, checked the clock. One-thirty. They'd eaten breakfast at eleven. He drifted back to the living room windows, opened one. The sun threw shadows across the midday roofs of cars; the air felt like October. Adrian closed the window, fumbled questions. Where was she? What had happened?

The bathroom was empty. The opening door moved dust through gloom that huddled in the darkroom's corners. He switched off the light, forced himself into the bedroom. The bed lay stained and crumpled, the way it looked after they'd come for his wife, after her gasping, her face fixed in the agony his fingers couldn't change.

He fled that room. Norma's coat still hung in the hallway closet. In the light of day it was closer to orange than red. He'd slept through the buzzer and she'd given up and gone home. There could be no other explanation. He closed his eyes and witnessed a scene that drained strength from his knees: a body in a vacant lot, skirt raised, spread-eagled thighs; birds flew from a bloodied, teeth-ruined mouth, a sky the color of water.

"No," Adrian whispered. He grabbed the purse, rummaged through it. A handkerchief, not used, a mirror with a smudge of fingerprints, a wallet. Fifty-seven dollars. Her name was Norma Fillis. A small bottle of white pills. Two condoms. A scrap of paper, a telephone number in a barely legible scrawl.

He sat waiting for the phone to ring, the hole widening in his belly. Norma knew his name. And where he lived. It was beyond his control; there was nothing he could do. For the first time that day he experienced a feeling that was tolerable. There was nothing he could do.

•

When he went again to the window the shadows were longer, the street deserted except for a woman in a yellow scarf who pawed in garbage cans. He went through Norma's purse again, read the number on the paper, took it to the phone and dialed. After three rings a voice answered.

"Hello?" It was an old man's voice.

"May I speak to Norma Fillis, please?"

"Who?"

"Norma Fillis."

"Ain't no Norma Fillis here."

Adrian explained the number in her purse. "Sorry," the voice wheezed, "ain't no Norma Fillis here."

"Excuse me," Adrian mumbled, and hung up. The buzzer growled. He answered it, moved to the front door, waited. When the steps halted at his apartment, when the bell rang, he called, "Who?"

"Me. Norma."

He opened the door. It was unlocked; he could have been set upon by thieves, by murderers. She swept past, had let her hair down. "It was nice out before," she said, "but now it's chilly."

"You were out all day?" His voice was querulous, old; it spoke of patterns interfered with.

"Well, hardly all day. A couple hours. When I came back the first time you were sleeping. Someone was coming out of the building and let me in. I'd left the apartment door unlocked. You were sleeping so good I decided to take a walk. I went past the lot where they found the woman. Is it time for lunch yet? Are you hungry?"

"No."

"Let's go to Harlem tonight. Something inexpensive. I'll treat. But for now," she said, and winked, "let's go back to bed."

He wouldn't look at her.

"Are you all right?"

He nodded.

"No, you're not. What's wrong?"

"Nothing."

"Nothing? Look at you." Her voice was patient; she touched his shoulder. "I enjoyed last night. Did you?"

"No."

She took her hand away.

"Who are you?" he rasped.

"Why, Adrian, I declare. Who *am* I?"

He could hardly speak for shaking. "That number in your purse. A man answered. An old man . . ."

"Number? What number?"

He showed her.

"Oh, Adrian, that's my sister's number. In *Ohio*. She moved and called me . . . see? That's what you get for going through a lady's purse." And she laughed that awful laugh. "Adrian, what's wrong? What are you afraid of?"

"Nothing . . . not afraid." It was difficult to breathe.

"Look at you."

"I'm not afraid."

She tried to catch his eyes with her own, but he wouldn't let her. She said, "You wear fear."

"What do you know? I'm an old man. Leave me alone."

"Old?" her mouth tightened. "What's old?"

The room gathered shadows. Her face seemed luminous, thrust shining out of darkness. "I took care of a man once, in good health, all of him dead except the fear, and that lived like small animals in a cage inside him. Don't be like that. We all have to die. But we don't have to do it in installments."

"Leave me," Adrian barked. "I don't need your pity."

"Pity?"

"Go."

"Adrian."

"Leave me alone."

She moved to her toes, her mouth set. He feared she'd leap and hit him; he remembered her strength. But once she reached the height her toes would take her she sighed and shook her head, and the light released her face.

"If you insist."

Her voice, her feet, were flat and practical again. She collected her purse, her coat from the closet. Places she touched shook in Adrian's vision, left pools of darkness in her wake. When she went past him, he caught, for the last time, the smell of avocado.

The door clicked behind her. Adrian sat on the couch. The slip of paper still lay on the table, and he picked it up, but the room was too dim to read it. There was a lamp at his shoulder, but he wouldn't turn it on. He needed to move, to drive away his heart's strange, sudden pleading. So he began to walk, not outside where there was space and cool; he walked his empty, stale-aired rooms. Bathroom to bedroom to kitchen to hallway, back again, cramped steps, but he was moving, driven by the pleading of his heart, by desire so long thwarted it was screaming, and outside the train went by.

"Translator. Oh, translator," he said, and walked, carrying his heart like dead fish wrapped in newsprint, like an infant whose fever wouldn't break. He slumped to the couch, leaped up as if he'd sat in fire, raced toward the darkroom, banged against the doorway as he entered. There he retrieved from a strong box the film he'd shot on the day the translator had come into his life. He lay the waxed envelope on the counter, fixed the reeking chemicals, slid the strips of negatives from their sleeves, blew dust away, lowered the film into the pan and waited.

While he waited evening fell. When it had come to rest against the city he went downstairs to get the *Times* that had been on his doorstep since morning.

((part four))

OUR LIVES TOGETHER

(from *Out of the Madness*)
Cool Brother

Jerrold Ladd

By the summer of 1978, I had already begun to develop strong self-reliance traits. I was coming to grips with my reality. We were children in abject poverty, separated from real America. We had parents who were trying every morning to deal with the man or woman in the mirror. The first law of nature, self-preservation, prevailed for them. They became wrapped up in big balls of grief and left us to fend for ourselves. But my mother, even in her zombielike condition, was there when I needed her the most.

She would come out of her dope trance, utter her powerful wisdom, then disappear without a trace: "Don't hang around the wrong crowd. Don't stay out too late." Times like that made me wonder how my mother would have been if she had not been put through so much, if her mother had let her go to school, if the father of her children had not abandoned her.

When she confronted me about stealing food from the shopping center (mother's intuition), she explained in two quick sentences, nothing more, nothing less, how it could devastate my life: "Jerrold, whatever I do, I'm not gonna raise you to be no thief. When people find out you're a thief, they'll never trust you again."

But I was driven by hunger and had no concern for what others thought. I had experienced enough hunger headaches to know that you can't do anything when you're cramping and swelling and every cell in your body is screaming for a bread crumb or something. It almost paralyzes you.

•

The boy who introduced me to stealing, Bad Baby, was sixteen, short, and lean. He was aggressive and would act quickly on his beliefs, which were good ones. The young girls loved his long Afro and the sharp clothes his mother, who had a speech defect, piled up for him. Of course they were a minimum-wage family, and they lived next door. Their apartment had nice cheap furniture, pictures, pots, plants, and wall-to-wall carpeting on the floor. The apartment also stayed cool and pleasant from the air conditioner in the window.

"Jerrold, are you coming over for dinner?" Bad Baby often asked.

"Naw, man, I'm not hungry," my shame would say.

"Come on over and eat, Jerrold. There's no reason to be ashamed, little brother. Ain't nothing wrong with eating at a friend's house."

Bad Baby had this kind of sympathy for my brother and me because even the poorest kids now talked about how dirty and ragged we were. They had given us nicknames. They called me Dirt Dobbler, and Junior, Dirt Mieser. But Bad Baby wasn't like them. Instead, he did nice things and never talked bad about me.

Bad Baby was also good at building bicycles from used parts. He also stole them. At times, when his mother let him, he would ride his bike out of the neighborhood. I didn't have a bike of my own, like kids from the minimum-wage group, so he would carry me along on the back of his bike. We went to visit his aunt across Hampton. We ran errands to the store. But on one trip Bad Baby took me across the Hampton bridge. It was the first time.

With Prescott, Bad Baby's older brother, we rode alongside the traffic on busy Hampton Road until we came upon a residential area. As we turned down several different streets, Bad Baby and Prescott checking in all directions, I noticed small bikes, toys, and chairs unattended on front lawns. They stopped at one corner, where Bad Baby ushered me off and pointed to a bike lying in someone's front yard.

He said, "Jerrold, this is the only way you'll ever have a bike. Go get it, man."

"I don't want to," I told him.

He and Prescott stepped away for a second, talked, and returned.

"Jerrold, you'll never have a bike unless you do it this way," he lectured.

"Bad Baby, take me home."

"If you don't get the bike, we're gonna leave you here."

Seeing that I wasn't budging, they sped off. I ran after them but they were too fast. Scared, I turned back around, hopped on the bike, and pedaled in the direction they had ridden. They stood around the corner, waiting for me. We hurried back past the traffic and back across the bridge. Along the way, Baby Baby told me that the people had plenty of money and would never miss the bike. To keep me from being whopped, he told my mom he'd built it for me. And I kept it.

•

Bad Baby had always observed what went on at our house and had always been concerned. So it was no surprise when he found out my mother was on drugs. After he gradually became closer to my brother and me, he convinced us to run away and sneak into his house late one night, even though it was only next door. He thought things would be better if my mom was reported.

Since our mother had traded the upstairs room with Junior and me, Bad Baby had to creep onto the ledge under our window and above the back door. After he was inside, he tucked clothes under our blankets to look like sleeping people, and helped us out the window. The next day, authorities from Human Resources came. This funny-looking white man, dressed in a suit, took us to our apartment. He identified himself to our mother and told her he alone would question my brother and me. She gave him a nervous "okay" and looked at us sadly, as if she knew her wrongdoing had finally caught up with her. Before the white man started, I whispered to my brother to tell the man we were okay. My brother looked disappointed.

As for me, I had gone along reluctantly with Bad Baby's plan, but this was too much. From snatches of conversations at the corners with the dope dealers, I had heard about these strange white people from the state who destroy black families. I had been warned to avoid them at all costs. But more than any verbal admonishment, my instincts compelled me not to trust them. She was my mother. This was our home.

In our room, with the door shut, the man began talking with that soft, soothing voice, the kind psychiatrists use to relax people. "Now, I don't want you to be afraid of what will happen to you boys, because no one's gonna hurt you. I just want you to tell me the truth, and I'll see if I can make things better for you, okay?"

"Okay," my brother said, already falling under the spell. But I was not to be taken. The white man began his questions.

"Now, does your mother feed you?"

"Yes, sir," I said quickly. "We eat very well."

"How often do you attend school?"

"Ooh, we rarely miss days. I love school, my momma always helps me."

"Does she take care of your sister?"

"Yes, sir."

"Does she do drugs?"

"Ooh, no, sir," I told him.

The white man started looking confused, as if he couldn't understand why neighbors would report something wrong with such happy kids and such a good mother. Before leaving, he apologized to my mother. And we never heard from the state people again.

Thereafter I was forbidden form talking with Bad Baby. Before the summer ended, he and his family moved across Hampton to the shack houses. I later learned that Prescott, Bad Baby's brother, was murdered there. His throat was cut.

•

My quiet brother, who also was experimenting with self-reliance, had learned to steal during his own adventures in the camp he'd gone to. And together, on days when our hunger would not let us rest, we stole food from the shopping center. We stole things that were easy to conceal, like cans of sardines and small packages of rice. A bowl of rice and a tall glass of water was enough for our indiscriminate stomachs.

Another hustle we used to get food was going into the shopping center late at night to steal TV guides. The newspaper companies dumped hundreds of papers on the sidewalk. So Mark, another kid named Big Mark, my brother, and I would get there about one in the morning. We would quickly sift through the piles and pick out all the TV guides. Then, when we had gathered all we could carry, we would scurry back to the lake to take the hidden trail. Back in the projects, we would go from door to door, selling our magazines for a quarter apiece.

We weren't thieves, just hungry children. Work, when we could find it, took the place of stealing. Each morning Junior and I would rise early and go looking for jobs, walking up Industrial, up Singleton, up Hampton Road. Consumed with our attempts to find work, we would stay gone all day without eating. Most places would not hire us because we were too young, just eight- and ten-year-olds. Occasionally we did stumble upon a place that needed temporary help. And my brother once landed a job for a service station that paid him about thirty dollars for a full week of work.

We worked at the shopping center, too. All day my brother and I would be at the Tom Thumb with Syrup Head and Three Finger Willie, roaming around. We would ask customers if we could carry their groceries but would not ask for a fee; instead we would just stand there, looking dirty and hungry. When we were done, some would tip us, others wouldn't. We could make a good seven bucks after a long, ten-hour day. We gave our mother sometimes all, sometimes half the money; the rest we spent on food or candy. We also dug through the trash cans behind the DAV store in the shopping center, looking for clothes, toys, change, and good pairs of shoes.

I still played Deadman, but not as often, because a body had been found in the Deadman vacant units. Between the stealing and scavenging, though, I was managing to stay away from the house, where things weren't getting any better. A bootleg family had moved in next door to us. They bought cases of beer from South Dallas, a wet part of the city, and stored it in their house. From their back door they sold each can for a dollar. Nighttime traffic was steady in and out of their house. On the corners, the heroin dealers were in full force.

•

I was on my Huffy bike all the time now. I often rode it down Fishtrap and Shaw streets, near the two candy trucks, and on Apple Grove and Morris, up and down the sidewalks and trails on the block, not stopping for the common fistfights that crowds gathered to watch or the young boys burning mattress cotton at nightfall to keep the mosquitoes away.

I would even ride my bike where rapists had once attacked me. Each time I did, a black man sitting on a porch watched me curiously. Sometimes a woman was with him. I made a mental note to keep an eye on him. If he were another rapist, I would not be his next victim.

Riding my bike on the other end of the block, I grew closer to Eric, a boy I played Deadman with. He and I were the same age and both had heroin mothers, so we had a lot in common. Eric was afraid to live in his house, a problem he discussed with me. He knew something bad was going to happen there. He told me he kept his bedroom window open, in case he needed to make the two-story jump to safety. He dreamed, he often said, of the day when his parents would stop selling dope and they all could leave the projects forever. To pass the time, we would sit out at night on the swings the authorities had built. We would swing our souls away late into the dark, starry nights. Both our young mothers had stopped coming home.

Eric also knew of the muscular, dark man who had been watching me. I pointed him out one day while he sat on Eric's porch. Eric was surprised. He said that the man had been with some of the prettiest women in the projects. He was no rapist. He was one of those settled, cool brothers, the smooth ones who know a lot about women.

One evening, instead of going up Morris, I rode past the man's house, where he was sitting on the porch with his girlfriend. He stopped me and asked what my name was, said he knew about my mother and my home situation. He said he used to be just like me when he was a boy. Looking into my eyes with his own black rubies, he told me I was good-looking.

"Women will take care of you when you're older, if you know how to move a woman's heart," he said. His girlfriend just sat there and smiled. The man wasn't threatening, and he aroused my curiosity too much for me not to go back. So I did go, all summer long.

I don't think he had children, because I never saw any. I know he didn't work. The apartment, which belonged to his woman, was sparsely furnished and had only two dining-room chairs and a couch. It was still a project unit, so it had the small rooms, which stayed hot. Everything was kept tidy and clean, even the tile floors, which required a lot of mopping. His backyard had the same wire clotheslines and red ants.

He kept food, a lot of vegetables, greens, and fish, but none of the disgusting pig feet, pig ears, and things my mother cooked from time to time. He never fried his food and said he didn't eat pork because it was worse than putting heroin in your blood. He, not his girlfriend, cooked their meals; I found that odd. Until he moved away, he gave me food, which I ate like a starved animal.

But what I recall most is his bedroom. The windows were covered by heavy blankets, forever blackening out the sun. It stayed totally dark in there. A dull, red light, like one blinking on a dark stormy night atop a tall tower, revealed the shadow of a small table next to his bed. That light and the reefer smoke made the room an enchanted setting.

While the deep rhythms of the band Parliament and Bootsy's Rubber Band softly played out of four speakers in each corner of the room, I would sit, light-headed from his reefer smoke, absorbing the almost spiritual music, and listen to this black man, who wore a net cap over his small Afro. I clearly remember two of his imperatives: "Always love your woman's mind" and "You have to take care of her, so she'll hold you up when the white man wants to crush you." Not until years later would I come to understand his advice or the rare kind of black man he was. Over time I grew to respect him because, unlike many of us, he seemed content and at peace, seemed to know some secrets about the projects, perhaps their purpose, perhaps why we were in them, that made him seem not subdued, at least in many ways.

After the sweet brother piqued my interest in women, it wasn't long before I met my first female friend, Gloria, on the day she and her family moved to West Dallas, near my unit, on the row behind Biggun's. My friendship with Eric had been dwindling away naturally, like friendships between little kids do, so Gloria came along on time.

From the first day I saw her at the candy truck on Fishtrap, Gloria was beautiful to me. Too beautiful. She was thin, her skin gleamed with natural health, and her eyes were pearls shaded by shoulder-length hair. Not even her old clothes and weathered shoes could overshadow her beauty. After I gathered enough courage I introduced myself.

"My name is Jerrold, you must don't live around here."

"How'd you know?" she asked.

"Because you're shopping at the high candy truck. If you want to, I'll show you where the cheap one is."

"That'll be nice," she said, looking as if she knew she had met her first friend. And from that day forward, that's the way Gloria and I would get along, simply, openly, and cheerfully.

I walked her back home from the candy truck and offered to help her and her family move in.

•

With the work of moving, Gloria was helping as much as her girlish strength would allow, carrying bags of clothes and boxes of pots over the barren ground, between much-needed rest periods. Her sisters, on the other hand, were bulky, strong women who could help the men carry the heavy pieces. They all worked under the admiration of the older boys, who stood around watching. Enough of them had already volunteered. And her mom, who was thin like Gloria, helped also.

Over time I learned that Gloria's two sisters had babies and her mother was on heroin. I didn't know much about her father—who mostly stayed to himself—except that he had a job somewhere and was the only support the family had. Gloria's mother shouted at him all the time. He seemed to be on heroin, too.

I admired the young girls as much as I could at that age, but Gloria was beyond them all because she was kind, gentle, and sweet, all at the same time. I can't recall ever hearing one bitter word come from her mouth or one angry expression on her face. The older boys longed for her ripeness with lusty stares. But of all of us, she liked scrawny me.

She was my first intimate contact with a woman. To share feelings and play games became the order of the day. And though we would not see each other for weeks or months, we would still say that we were going together. We would sit around together and talk on her back porch, after I climbed the tall tree back there, which was equally as important. Sometimes we held hands, being sure to stay away from the minimum-wage group, who would have teased us. We occasionally sat alone under the dark nights. We kissed only once, and I thought I experienced a little bit of that healing my cool friend had talked about, for even at that age blacks were real mature about relationships between men and women.

Sometimes Gloria would express her disappointment at her mother, who she thought could do a lot better. I would overhear Gloria questioning her mother about women things. But her mother, who didn't want to be bothered, always responded unkindly, angrily, sometimes frantically. Something else I picked up on was Gloria's serious weakness. She lacked self-reliance, something all kids had learned was vitally necessary. I hoped Gloria would also gain the skill, in time.

But for now she looked to her mother for guidance, to shape her into the fine woman she was destined to be. Gloria was enduring the projects the way my brother had when he first arrived: remaining quiet, sweet, and sensitive, even to her mother. No need to worry about Gloria, her loveliness would see her through.

Toward the end of the year 1978, however, I let a boy and his sister peer-pressure me into picking a fight with Gloria. I wanted to be accepted by the bullies, even at the cost of my love. I figured this was the better long-term investment, an example of those self-reliance skills. After they dared me, I walked up to Gloria, her knowing all along what was going on, and blackened her eye.

The two who'd put me up to it "oohed" and "aawed" and giggled. But Gloria, devastated, was crying softly. When she walked away from me that day, I saw the pain and hurt in her eyes. She wouldn't speak to me for weeks, and the bullies still chased me home. I felt terrible for months afterward. But Gloria eventually forgave me. She stopped me one day as I walked in front of her house and told me I was wrong for doing that. But when I apologized, she smiled. Regardless, we would never become close friends again. Gloria and her family would soon leave the projects. Her mother was about to have a nervous breakdown.

After apologizing to Gloria that day, I went home and found a small crowd gathered across from my window. They were watching as a black man was being wheeled from the Deadman units by paramedics. A sheet hid his face. He was Gloria's father.

Palm Wine

Reginald McKnight

This was fourteen years ago, but it still bothers me as though it happened day before yesterday. I've never talked about this with anyone, and I'm not talking about it now because I expect it to relieve me of painful memory but because, as they say in Madagascar, the bad is told that the good may appear. So. I was in Senegal on a graduate fellowship. I was there to collect and compile West African proverbs. This was to complete my Ph.D. in anthropology, which, I'm afraid, I failed to do. The things I'm going to talk about now had as much to do with that failure as did my laziness, my emotional narrowness, and my intellectual mediocrity. I was a good deal younger then, too, but that's no excuse. Not really.

Anyway, one afternoon, instead of collecting proverbs in Yoff village, which I should have done, I went to Dakar with Omar the tailor—a friend of a friend—to buy palm wine. I'd craved palm wine ever since I'd read Amos Tutuola's novel *The Palm-Wine Drunkard* in college. Tutuola never attempts to describe the taste, color, or smell of palm wine, but because the Drinkard (whose real name is Father of the Gods Who Could Do Anything in This World) can put away two hundred and twenty-five kegs of it per day, and because he sojourns through many cruel and horrifying worlds in order to try to retrieve his recently killed palm wine tapster from Deadstown, I figured palm wine had to be pretty good.

As Omar and I boarded the bus, I dreamed palm wine dreams. It must be pale green, I thought, coming from a tree and all. Or milky-blue, like coconut water. I had it in mind that it must hit the tongue like a dart, and that it must make one see the same visions Tutuola himself witnessed. A creature big as a bipedal elephant, sporting two-foot fangs thick as cow's horns; a creature with a million eyes and hundreds of breasts that continuously suckle her young, who swarm her body like maggots; a town where everything and everyone is red as plum flesh; a town where they all walk backwards; a town full of ghosts.

I really had no business going that day. I was at least a month behind in my research because of a lengthy bout with malaria. But I excused myself from work by telling myself that I had no Wolof proverbs on the subject of drinking and I'd likely encounter a couple that day. I took my pad, pencils, and tape recorder along, knowing I wasn't going to use them.

On the ride to town, I could scarcely pay mind to matters that usually fascinate me. For instance, I would often carefully observe the beggars who boarded the buses to cry for alms, their Afro-Arab plaints weaving through a bus like serpents, slipping between exquisitely coiffed women and dignified, angular men, wives of the wealthy, daughters of the poor, beardless hustlers, bundled babies, tourists, pickpockets, gendarmes, students. A beautiful plaint could draw coins like salt draws moisture.

Some beggars not only sang for indulgences but also sang their thanks. "*Jerrejeff*, my sister, paradise lies under the feet of mothers. A heart that burns for Allah gives more light than ten thousand suns." Some of them sang proverbs from the Koran. "Be constant in prayer and give alms." "Allah pity him who must beg of a beggar." Some of them merely cried something very much like "Alms! Alms!" And some of them rasped like reptiles and said little more than "I got only one arm! Gimme money!" and the proverbs they used were usually stale. They were annoying, but even so I often gave them alms, and I recorded them. I guess it was because I liked being in a culture that had a good deal more respect for the poor than my own. And I guess I tried hard to appreciate art forms that were different from the ones I readily understood.

But, honestly, as I say, that day I could think of little more than palm wine. It would be cold as winter rain. It would be sweet like berries, and I would drink till my mind went swimming in deep waters.

We alighted from the bus in the arrondissement of Fosse, the place

Omar insisted was the only place to find the wine. Preoccupied as I was with my palm wine dreams, they weren't enough to keep me from attending to Fosse. It's an urban village, a squatter's camp, a smoke-filled bowl of shanties built of rusty corrugated metal, gray splintery planks, cinderblock, cement. It smelled of everything: goatskins, pot, green tobacco, fish, overripe fruit, piss, cheap perfume, Gazelle beer, warm couscous, scorched rice, the sour sharpness of cooking coals. People talked, laughed, sang, cried, argued—the sounds so plangent I felt them in my teeth, my chest, my knees. A woman dressed in blue flowers scolded her teenage son, and the sound lay tart on my tongue. Two boys drummed the bottoms of plastic buckets while a third played a pop bottle with a stick, and I smelled *churai* incense. Two little girls danced to the boys' rhythms, their feet invisible with dust, and I felt them on my back.

A beautiful young woman in a paisley wraparound pagne smiled at us, and I rubbed Omar's incipient dreadlocks, his wig of thumbs, as I called them, and said, "Hey, man, there's a wife for you." Omar grinned at me; his amber eyes were crescents, his teeth big as dominoes. "She too old for me, mahn," he said.

"Oh, please, brother, she couldn't be older than eighteen."

"Young is better."

"Whatever. Letch."

I didn't really like Omar. He insisted on speaking English with me even though his English was relatively poor. Even when I spoke to him in French or my shaky Wolof he invariably answered me in English. This happened all the time in Senegal and the other francophone countries I traveled. People all around the globe want to speak English, and my personal proverb was, Every English speaking traveler will be a teacher as much as he'll be a student. I suppose if his English had been better I wouldn't have minded, but there were times it lead to trouble—like that day—and times when the only thing that really bothered me about it was that it was Omar speaking it.

Omar the tailor man, always stoned, always grinning, his red and amber crescents, his domino teeth, his big olive-shaped head, his wolfish face, his hiccupping laugh jangling every last nerve in my skull. He perpetually thrust his long hands at me for cigarettes, money, favors. "Hey, I and I, you letting me borrow you tapedeck?" "Hey, I and I, *jokma bene* cigarette." He was a self-styled Rastafarian, and he had the notion that since the U.S. and Jamaica are geographically close, Jamaicans and black Americans were interchangeable. I was pretty certain I was of more value to him as a faux-Jamaican than as a genuine American.

He was constantly in my face with this "I and I, mahn" stuff, always quoting Peter Tosh couplets, insisting I put them in my book (I could never get him to understand the nature of my work). Moreover, it took him six months to sew one lousy pair of pants and one lousy shirt for me, items I was dumb enough to pay for in advance. Between the day he measured me and the day I actually donned the clothes I'd lost twenty-six pounds (constant diarrhea and a fish-and-rice diet will do that to you), but I wasn't about to ask him to take them in—I only had a year's worth of fellowship money, after all.

Omar always spoke of his great volume of work, his busyness, the tremendous pressure he was under, but each and every time I made it to his shop hoping to pick up my outfit, I'd find him sitting with four or five friends, twisting his locks, putting the buzz on, yacking it up. "Hey, I and I, come in! I don't see you a long time."

In northern African they say, Bear him unlucky, don't bear him lazy. But I bore Omar anyway because he was a friend of my good friend and assistant, Idrissa, who at the time was visiting his girlfriend in Paris. I went with Omar to get the palm wine because Omar, who knew Fosse a great deal better than Idrissa did, insisted that that day was the only time in palm wine season he would be able to make the trip. He told me that Idrissa wouldn't be back till the season was well over. Originally, the three of us were to have made the trip, but Idrissa's girlfriend had sent him an erotic letter and a ticket to Paris. And money. We blinked; Idrissa was gone. And since Omar was so "pressed for time," we wasted none of it getting to the city. As I walked the ghetto with Omar I reflected on how Idrissa would often fill things in for me with his extemporaneous discussions of the history, economics, and myths of wherever in Senegal we happened to be. Idrissa was self-educated and garrulous. My kind of person. He was also very proud of his Senegalese heritage. He seemed to know everything about the country. As Omar and I walked, I told myself that if Idrissa had been there I would have been learning things. (What did I know?)

On our walk, Omar seldom spoke. He seemed unable to answer any of my questions about the place, so after about ten minutes I stopped asking. We walked what seemed to me to be the entire ghetto, and must have inquired at about eight or nine places without seeing a drop of palm wine. Each inquiry involved the usual African procedure—shake hands all around, ask about each other's friends, families, health, work; ask for the wine, learn they have none; ask them who might, shake hands, leave. It was getting close to dusk now, and our long shadows undulated before us over the tight-packed soil. I was getting a little hungry, and I kept eyeing the street vendors who braised brochettes of mutton along the curbs of the main street. The white smoke rose up and plumed into the streets, raining barbecue smells everywhere. I said, "Looks like we're not getting the wine today. Tell you what, why don't we—"

"Is not the season, *quoi*," Omar said as we rambled into a small, secluded yard. It was surrounded by several cement-and-tin houses, some with blanket doors, insides lighted mostly by kerosene or candles. Here and there, though, I could see that some places had electricity. Omar crossed his arms as we drew to a stop. "We stay this place and two more," he said, "then I and I go."

"Aye-aye," I said.

Four young men sat on a dusty porch, passing a cigarette between them. Several toddlers, each runny-nosed and ashy-kneed, frenetically crisscrossed in front of the men, pretending to grab for the cigarette. Until they saw me. Then they stopped and one of the older ones approached us, reached out a hand, and said, "*Toubobie*, mawney." Omar said, in Wolof, "This man isn't a *toubob*. This is a black man. An American brother." I answered in Wolof, too. "Give me a proverb and I'll give you money." The boy ran away grinning, and the men laughed. I drew my cigarettes from my shirt pocket, tapped out eight, and gave two to each man.

"Where's Doudou?" Omar asked the men.

They told him Doudou, whoever he was, had left a half-hour before, but was expected back very soon. One of the men, a short, muscular man in a T-shirt and a pair of those voluminous trousers called chayas, detached himself from his friends and walked into one of the houses. He returned carrying a small green liquor bottle. I felt my eyebrows arch. The stuff itself, I was thinking. I imagined myself getting pied with these boys, so drunk I'm hugging them, telling them I love them and, God-dammit, where's old Doudou? I miss that bastid. The man in the chayas unscrewed the lid with sacramental delicacy, drank and passed the bottle on. I watched the men's faces go soft when each passed the bottle on to his brother. I took the bottle rather more aggressively than was polite, and I apologized to the man who'd handed it to me. Omar winked at me. "You don't know what bottle is, *quoi*?" Omar had the irritating habit of using the tag *quoi* after most of his sentences. He did it in English, French, Wolof, and his own language, Bambara. It wasn't an uncommon habit in French West Africa, but Omar wore it down to a nub.

"Paaalm wiiine," I said in a low, throaty voice, the way you'd say an old love's name. My God, what was wrong with me? I was behaving as though, like the Drinkard himself, I had fought the beast with the lethal gaze and shovel-sized scales, or had spent the night in the bagful of creatures with ice cold, sandpapery hair, like I'd done some heroic thing and the stuff in the green bottle was my reward. As I brought the bottle to my lips, Omar said, "It's no palm wine, I and I." I drank before Omar's words even registered, and the liquid burned to my navel. It was very much like a strong tequila. No, that's an understatement. If this drink and tequila went to prison, this drink would make tequila its girlfriend. "Is much stronger than palm wine," said Omar.

My throat had closed up and it took me a few seconds before I could speak. All I could manage was to hiss, "Jeezuz!" And abruptly one of the young men, a Franco-Senegalese with golden hair and green eyes said, "Jeezuz," but then he continued in rapid Wolof and I lost him. Soon all five of them were laughing, saying, "Jeezuz, Jeeezuz," working the joke, extending it, jerking it around like taffy. My blood rose to my skin, and every muscle in my back knotted. I squinted at Omar, who looked back at me with eyes both reassuring and provocative, and he said, "He saying he like *Americain noire* talk. You know, you say—*quoi*—'Jeezuz,' and 'sheeee,' and 'mahn,' *quoi*. We like the *Americain noire* talk." His mouth hovered this close to a smirk.

I was furious, but I had no choice but to grin and play along. I lit a smoke and said, "Jeezuz," and, "Jeezuz Christ," and "Jeezuz H. Christ," cuttin' the monkey, as my dad would put it. My stomach felt like it was full of mosquitoes. My hands trembled. I wanted to kick Omar's face in. His hiccupping giggles rose above the sound of everyone else's laughter, and his body jerked about convulsively. Yeah, choke on it, I thought. But I didn't have to endure the humiliation long, for soon an extremely tall, very black, very big-boned man joined us, and Omar said, "Doudou!" and fiercely shook hands with the giant. Doudou nodded my way and said in Wolof, "What's this thing?" and I froze with astonishment. Thing? I tried to interpret Omar's lengthy explanation, but his back was to me and he was speaking very rapidly. As I say, my Wolof was never very good. Doudou placed his hands on his hips and squinted at the ground as though he'd lost something very small. The big man nodded now and then. Then he looked at me and said in French, "It's late in the season, but I know where there's lots of palm wine." He immediately wheeled about and began striding away. Omar followed, then I.

The walk was longer than I'd expected, and by the time we got to the place, the deep blue twilight had completely absorbed our shadows. After seven or eight months of living in Senegal, I had become used to following strangers into unfamiliar places in the night. But even so I felt uneasy. I watched the night as a sentry would, trying to note every movement and sound. There was nothing extraordinary about the things I saw on the way, but even today they remain as vivid as if I'd seen them the day before yesterday—a three-year-old girl in a faded pink dress, sitting on a porch; a cat-sized rat sitting atop an overflowing garbage crate; a man in a yellow shirt and blue tie talking to a bald man wearing a maroon khaftan; a half-moon made half again by a knot of scaly clouds; Omar's wig of thumbs; Doudou's broad back. I wasn't thinking much about palm wine.

It was an inconspicuous place, built from the same stuff in the same way that practically every other place in Fosse was. Perhaps half a dozen candles lit the room, but rather than clarify, they muddied the darkness. I couldn't tell whether there were six other men in the place or twelve. I couldn't make out the proprietress's face, or anything else about her, for that matter. The only unchanging features were her eyes, an unnatural olive-black and egg-white, large, perpetually doleful. But was her expression stern or soft?

As the candlelight shifted, heaved, bent, so did her shape and demeanor. At times she seemed as big as Doudou, and at other times she seemed only five-foot-two or so. One moment she looked fifty, a second later twenty-three. Her dress was sometimes blue, sometimes mauve. I couldn't stop staring at her, and I couldn't stop imagining that the light in the room was incrementally being siphoned away, and that my skull was being squeezed as if in the crook of a great headlocking arm, and that the woman swelled to two, three, four times her size, and split her dress like ripe fruit skin, and glowed naked, eggplant-black like a burnished goddess, and that she stared at me with those unchanging olive-and-egg eyes.

It's that stuff I drank, I kept saying to myself. It's that stuff they gave me. Then, with increasing clarity I heard a hiss as though air were rushing from my very own ears, and the sound grew louder, so loud the air itself seemed to be torn in half like a long curtain, until it abruptly stopped with the sound of a cork being popped from a bottle; then everything was normal again, and I looked around the room half embarrassed, as if the ridiculous things in my head had been projected onto the wall before me for all to see, and I saw that Doudou was staring at me with a look of bemused deprecation. I felt myself blush. I smiled rather stupidly at the giant, and he cocked his head just a touch to the left but made no change in his facial expression. I quickly looked back at the woman.

She told my associates that the wine was still quite fresh, and she swung her arm with a graceful backhand motion before ten plastic gallon jugs apparently full to the neck with the wine. It was very cheap, she said. Then she dipped her hands into a large plastic pan of water on the table that stood between herself and us. She did it the way a surgeon might wash her hands, scooping the water, letting it run to the elbows. In the same water she washed two bottles and laid them aside. Next, she poured a little palm wine into a tumbler, walked to the door, then poured the contents on the ground outside. I could feel excitement sparking up again in my stomach. "Is ritual," said Omar, but when I asked him what it meant he ignored me.

The woman returned to the jug, filled the bottom half-inch of her tumbler with wine, and took two perfunctory sips. After that she slipped a screened funnel into the first bottle's neck, filled the bottle, then filled the second bottle in the same way. Omar lifted one of the bottles, took a whiff, then a sip. I closely watched his face, but his expression told me little. He arched both eyebrows and nodded a bit. The woman handed the second bottle to Doudou, and he did pretty much what Omar had. I don't recall noting his expression. Then Omar handed me his bottle.

It was awful. It was *awful*. It was awful. Though Idrissa had warned me about the taste, I had had the impression that he was trying to prepare me for the fact that it doesn't taste like conventional wines. I was prepared for many things—a musky flavor, a fruity flavor, dryness, tartness, even blandness. But for me, the only really pleasant aspect of this liquid was its color, cloudy white, like a liquid pine cleaner mixed with water. It had a slightly alcoholic tang and smelled sulphuric. It had a distinctly sour bouquet that reminded me of something I very much hated as a kid. If you could make wine from egg salad and vinegar, palm wine is pretty much what you'd get.

Really, the stuff was impossible to drink, but I did my best. The ordeal might have gone more easily had Omar not been Omar—singing reggae music off key, slapping my back, philosophizing in a language he didn't understand, toasting a unified Africa, then toasting the mighty Rastafari, toasting me, then Doudou. But the thing that made the ordeal in the bar most unpleasant was that Doudou glared at me for what felt like ten unbroken minutes. He stared at my profile as though my face were his property. I couldn't bring myself to confront him. He was just so fucking huge. He was not merely tall—perhaps six-foot-eight or so—but his bones were pillars, his face a broad iron shield. He gave off heat, he bowed the very atmosphere of the room. Wasn't it enough I had to drink that swill? Did I need the additional burden of drinking from under the millstone of this man's glare? Just as I was about to slam my bottle to the table and stalk out, Doudou said in French, "An American."

"Americano," I said.

"Amerikanski," he said.

"That's right. We've got that pretty much nailed down."

"Hey," Omar said, "you like the palm wine?"

Before I could answer, Doudou said, "He doesn't like the wine, Omar."

"Who says I don't?"

Doudou cocked an eyebrow and looked at the low-burning candle on our table. He rolled the bottle between his fingers as if it were pencil-thin. "I tell you he doesn't like it, Omar." Then he looked at me and said, "*I* say you don't." I felt cold everywhere. A small painful knot hardened between my shoulder blades, as so often happens when I'm angry.

"You know," I said, stretching my back, rolling my shoulders, "I'm not going to argue about something so trivial." Then I turned to Omar and said in English, "Omar, the wine is very good. Excellent."

Omar shrugged, and said, "Is okay, I think. Little old."

We were silent after that, and Doudou stopped staring, but it got no more comfortable. Two men started to argue politics, something about the increasing prices of rice and millet, something about Islamic law, and when it got to the table-banging stage, Omar suggested we leave. I had suffered through two glasses of this liquid acquired taste, and Omar, much to my regret, bought me two liters of the wine to take home. I did want to go home, and said so, but Doudou said, "You must stay for tea." Omar said yes before I could say no, and I knew it would be impolite to leave without Omar. We walked back to Doudou's place and I saw that the young men were still quietly, getting happy on the Senegalese tequila. Doudou sat in a chair on the porch and sent the young man in chayas into the house; he returned with a boom box and a handful of tapes. He threw in a Crusaders tape, and immediately two of the men began to complain. They wanted Senegalese music, but Doudou calmly raised his hand and pointed to me. The men fell silent, and I said, "I don't have to have American music."

"Sure you do," said the big man. He leaned so far back in his chair that its front legs were ten inches off the porch and the back of the chair rested against the windowsill. His feet stayed flat on the ground.

"Your French is good," I said.

"Better than yours," he said. He was smiling, and I couldn't see a shred of contempt in his expression, but that remark burned up the last of my calm. It was full dark, but I could see his broad, smooth face clearly, for the house's light illuminated it. It hung before the window like a paper lantern, like a planet. Looking back on it, I can see that I must have offended him. He must have thought I was evincing surprise that, he, a denizen of Fosse, could speak as well as he did. Actually, I was just trying to make conversation. When the bottle came my way I tipped it and drank a full inch. "Thanks for the hospitality," I said. Doudou folded his arms and tipped his head forward, removing it from the light. "Amerikanski," he said. One of the men chuckled.

Omar sat "Indian-style" a foot to my right. He rolled a very large spliff from about a half-ounce of pot and an eight-by-ten-inch square of newspaper. He handed it to the man sitting across from him, the Franco-Senegalese with the golden hair. The comedian. "Where's the tea?" the man asked in Wolof. "Eh?" said Doudou, and then he pointed to the boom box. The man in the chayas turned it down. The golden-haired man repeated his question. Doudou's only reply was, "Ismaila, get the tea," and the young man in the chayas rose once again and came back quickly with the primus stove, the glasses, the sugar, and the tea.

"Omar tells me that you're an anthropologist," said Doudou.

"That's right," I said.

"The study of primitive cultures." Doudou said this as though he'd read the words off the back of a bottle. A dangerous sort of neutrality, as I saw it. It grew so still for a moment there that I jumped when Ismaila lit the stove; the gas had burst into blue flame with a sudden *woof* and I found myself glaring at Ismaila as though he'd betrayed me.

I cleared my throat and said, "That's only one aspect of anthropology . . ." I struggled for words. When I'm nervous I can barely speak my own language, let alone another's, but I managed to say, "But I study the living cultures." There, I thought, that was nice. I went on to explain that the discipline of anthropology was changing all the time, that it had less to do with so-called primitive cultures and more to do with the study of the phenomenon of culture and the many ways it can be expressed.

The light from the stove's flame cast ghostlight over the four of us who sat around it. A short man with batlike ears sat behind me and Omar. He was in silhouette, as was Doudou, up there on the porch. The man with the strange ears tapped my shoulder and handed me the spliff. I took a perfunctory hit, and handed it to Omar. "Ganjaaaa," said Omar.

"I knew an anthropologist once," said Doudou, "who told me I should be proud to be part of such a noble, ancient, and primitive people." He paused long enough for me to hear the water begin to boil. Then he said, "What aspect of anthropology do you think he studied?"

"Couldn't tell you," I said.

"Too bad."

"Maybe," I said, "he was trying to tell you that primitive . . . . I mean, that in this case 'primitive' means the same thing as 'pure.'"

"Really. 'In this case,' you say."

"I can only—"

"Was I supposed to have been offended by his language? Are you saying we Africans should be offended by words like 'primitive'?" He placed his great hands on his knees, sat up straight. It occurred to me that he was trying to look regal. It worked. I could feel myself tremulously unscrewing the top of one of my palm wine bottles, and I took a nip from it. My sinuses filled with its sour bouquet. "Well . . . you sounded offended," I said.

"Who studies *your* people?"

"What?"

"Do you have anthropologists milling about your neighborhood? Do they write down everything you say?"

"Look, I know how you must—"

Doudou turned away from me. "Ismaila, how's the tea coming?" he said.

"No problems," said Ismaila.

"Look here," I said, but before I could continue the man with the pointed ears said, "I get offended. I get very offended. You write us down. You don't respect us. You come here and steal from us. It's a very bad thing, and you, you should know better."

"What, because I'm black?"

"Black," said Doudou.

"Is fine, I and I. Is very nice."

"What the fuck's that supposed to mean, Omar?" I said. "Look, I'm trying to help all black people by recovering our forgot things."

"Your 'lost' things," Ismaila said quietly as he dumped two or three handfuls of tea into the boiling water.

"'Lost' things," I said. "My French is pretty evil."

"Your French is poor."

He removed the pot from the flame and let it steep for a few minutes. One of the men, a bald, chubby man with a single thick eyebrow, rose from the ground and began fiddling with the boom box. He put in a tape by some Senegalese group and turned it up a bit. The guitar sounded like crystal bells, the bass like a springy heartbeat; the singer's nasal voice wound like a tendril around the rhythm. As Ismaila sang with the tape, he split the contents of the pot between two large glasses, filling each about halfway, and dumped three heaps of sugar into each glass.

While he worked, I kept nipping at the palm wine like a man who can't stop nipping at the pinky nail of his right hand even though he's down to the bloody quick. The more I drank, the odder its flavors seemed to me. It was liquid egg, ammonia, spoiled fish, wet leather, piss. The taste wouldn't hold still, and soon enough it wholly faded. The roof of my mouth, my sinuses, my temples began to throb with a mild achiness, and if I'd had food in my belly that evening I might have chucked it up. Ismaila began tossing the contents of the glasses from one glass to the other. I could see that Omar was following his movements with great intent.

"What's all this about, Omar?" I said in English. "Why are these guys fucking with me?" I hoped he'd understood me, and I hoped that no one among his friends would suddenly reveal himself as a fluent speaker of English. I also ended up wishing Idrissa was there when Omar said, "No worry, I and I, the tea is good."

"Things lost?" said Doudou. "That must mean you're not pure, *quoi*. That you think you can come here and bathe in our primitive dye."

Omar and I exchanged looks, our heads turning simultaneously. I was encouraged by that speck of consanguinity. It emboldened me. "Want some palm wine?" I said to Doudou. "It really tastes like crap."

The giant shifted slightly in his chair. He said nothing for maybe fifteen seconds. "How does it feel," he said, "to be a black *toubob*?" I felt my face suddenly grow hot. My guts felt as if they were in a slow meltdown. I took a large draft of the wine and disgust made me wince. "By *toubob*," I asked, "do you mean 'stranger' or 'white'? I understand it can be used both ways."

Doudou leaned forward in the chair and it snapped and popped as if it were on fire. It appeared for a moment that he was going to rise from his chair, and everything in me tightened, screwed down, clamped, but he merely leaned and said, "In Wolof, 'toubob' is 'toubob' is 'toubob.'"

The blood beat so hard beneath my skin I couldn't hear the music for a few seconds. I tried to breathe deeply, but I couldn't. All I could do was drink that foul wine and quiver with anger. I stared for a long time at some pinprick point in the air between me and Doudou. It was as though the world or I had collapsed into that tiny point of blackness, which, after

I don't know how long, opened like a sleepy eye, and I realized that I'd been watching Ismaila hand around small glasses of tea. First to Omar, then to Doudou, then to the golden-haired man, then to the man with the bat ears, then to the chubby bald man with the uni-brow. Ismaila didn't even look my way. I sat there with blood beating my temples. Their tea-sipping sounded like sheets tearing.

Then Ismaila brewed a second round of tea, but I received no tea in that round, either. When everyone finished Ismaila simply turned off the stove and began gathering the cups and things. It was the most extraordinary breach of Senegalese etiquette I'd seen in the year I lived there. No one, not even Omar, said a word. Omar, for his part, looked altogether grim. He leaned toward me and whispered, "You got no tea, huh?" I could hear the nervous tremor in his voice.

"It's no big deal, Omar."

"I and I, you tell him for give you the tea, *quoi*."

"Skip it."

"*Quoi?*"

"Forget about the tea. I got this." I raised the bottle and finished it.

"He *must* give you the tea."

"Omar, that big motherfucker don't have to 'must' shit."

Omar relit the spliff and said, "Is bad, mahn, is very bad." He offered me the spliff, but I waved it off and opened up my second bottle. Omar often displayed what one could call displacement behavior when he didn't understand me. He'd swiftly change the subject or say something non-committal. You might think that this was one more thing that bothered me about him, but actually I found it rather endearing, for some reason. "Is bad, I and I. He do bad."

"Fuck it."

The other men had moved closer to the big man. Two sat on the ground, two squatted on the porch. They spoke quietly, but every so often they burst forth with laughter. I drank and stared at the bottle. "Listen in you ears, I and I," said Omar. "You must strong Doudou. You must put him and strong him."

"Speak French, Omar."

"No, no. You must. He do this now and every day—*quoi*—every day. Only if you strong him he can't do it."

I took this to mean that unless I "stronged" Doudou he would treat me badly every time he saw me, but I wasn't figuring on seeing him again and I whispered as much to Omar—in French, so there'd be no mistake.

"And besides," I said, "as your countrymen say, The man who wants to blow out his own brains need not fear their being blown out by others." I raised the bottle but couldn't bring myself to drink from it this once.

"No, mahn, strong him. He do this and then 'nother man, then 'nother, then 'nother man. All the time. All day."

"Sheeit, how on earth could—"

"Believe in me, I and I—"

"—anything to do with how other people treat me, man. Let's get out of here. I can't just—"

Omar clutched my knee so firmly I understood—or thought I did—the depth of his conviction. "You make strong on him now, and it will be fine for you." Then he removed his hand from my knee and touched it to his chest and said, "For me, too."

It was then that I realized that the incident with the tea was meant for Omar as much as for me. Omar had brought me as an honored guest, or as a conversation piece, or as his chance to show his friends just how good his English was. But why was it up to me, either as symbol or as a genuine friend, to recover his luster? I was the guest—right? I told myself to just sit there and drink, then leave. But suddenly the men around Doudou burst into laughter again, and I distinctly heard the golden-haired comedian say, "Jeeezuuuz!" and I felt my body rising stiff from the ground in jerky motions. I walked straight up to Doudou, dropped my half-empty bottle at his feet and slugged him so hard I'm sure I broke his nose. I know for certain I broke my finger.

Doudou went tumbling from his chair and landed face down on the porch. He struggled to get up, but fell forward, his head rolling side to side. His blood looked like black coins there on the porch. All the men rushed up to him, except the chubby man, who shoved me off the porch. I went down on my ass, but sprang up almost immediately. I was still pugnacious, but in a very small, very stupid way. Omar removed his shirt and pressed it to Doudou's nose.

I said, "Is he okay?"

No one replied.

I said, "We can get him a cab, get him to a doctor. I'll pay for the cab. I'll pay the doctor." And someone told me in Wolof that I could go out and fuck a relative. I stepped closer to the lot of them, out of shame and concern rather than anger, but Omar handed his shirt to Ismaila, stepped toward me with his palm leveled at my chest. "You go now," he said.

"But I thought you said—"

"You are not a good man." He turned back toward Doudou, whom they'd moved to the chair. The man with the strange ears left with a plastic bucket to retrieve fresh water. They all had their backs to me. I stood there a good long while, sick to my stomach from palm wine or shame, or both. After some minutes, Omar turned toward me for the briefest moment and said, "Don't come again, Bertrand." He said this in French.

I left the little courtyard and immediately lost my way. I wandered Fosse for what must have been ten years. On my way, I encountered an army of headless men who chased me with machetes. Blood gushed from their necks like geysers. Later I was eaten and regurgitated by a creature with three thousand sharp fangs in its big red mouth; it had the head of a lion, and its long snaky body bristled with forty-four powerful baboon arms. Months later in this strange new world, I discovered a town where everyone ate glass, rocks, wood, dirt, bugs, etc., but grew sick at the sight and smell of vegetables, rice, couscous, fish. They captured me and tried to make me eat sand, but I brandished a yam I'd had in my pocket, and when they all fell ill at the sight of it I ran away. In another town I met a man who was handsome and elegant in every way, and I followed him to his home simply to jealously gaze at him. But while on the way to his own home, I saw him stop at other people's homes, and at every place he stopped he'd remove a part of his body and return it to the person from whom he'd borrowed it. At each place he'd leave a leg, or an arm, or a hand, and so forth, so by the time he got home I discovered he was but a skull, who rolled across the ground like a common stone. It made me sad to see his beauty vanish so, and I walked all the way back to my home in Denver with my shoulders rounded and my head bent low. And when my people asked me what I found on my long, long journey, I told them, "Palm wine. But it wasn't in season, so I have nothing to give you."

The Black Family

Amiri Baraka

Take this as a note from a black man
reflecting on the fundamental social unit in which most of us (bm) exist. Therefore
this is meant as a clarifying basis for any serious discussion of "the black man,"
impossible without identifying the socioeconomic and cultural matrix, the basic
human context, in which he exists, and drawing from that the politics which defines
that context.

The black family, in its nuclear or
extended form, is the most ancient family unit in the world. And as such
it has reflected the entire history of human social change on earth!

The most ancient family structure was the communal family, the
horde, in which all males and females could mate. The children, obviously, were part of the collective, but could trace their parentage only
to the mother.

Ancient communalism, so-called primitive communism, was the earliest form of social organization. And women held a predominant and naturally powerful status in that kind of society and in that kind of family.
They were the only known parents, and lineage naturally flowed through
them.

As social relationships changed, based on economic and political changes in society, the structure of the family reflected these and changed as well. Many other variations precede the nuclear monogamous family.

The pairing family, the Punuluan family, were changing models, as the single hordes got larger and larger, eventually dividing, excluding the parents from collective sex, then, later, brothers and sisters.

Women in all these early family units were powerful, as groups of women controlled the home and the newly developed sciences of agriculture and the domestication of animals (developed by women). When the societies developed *surpluses* and these surpluses (larger herds of cattle and the bounty of the new, metal-tipped spears) and wealth became privately held, usually by men, this was the beginning of the end of the matrilineal development of society. It was also the beginning of classes in society.

It is the private ownership of wealth (by men, in the main) that is the catalyst for the social revolution that ends communalism and brings in the mode of production called *slavery*.

With slavery (ancient slavery, worldwide), the family structure undergoes a radical change, reflecting the radical change of society itself! The overthrow of communal society brought an overthrow of *motherright*. The matrilineal structure of the mainstream of human development was overthrown, and women were, literally, enslaved. They still are.

The overthrow of women and motherright, and the emergence of slavery as the dominant mode of production also accompanied the overthrow of Africa and the "southern cradle" (i.e., the origin of humanity and human civilization), and the rise and ultimate world rule of peoples from north of the Mediterranean.

With each change of the mode of production (how society produces food, clothing, and shelter), the structure of the family changes as well.

Monogamy, as Engels said in *The Origin of the Family*, *Private Property*, *and the State*, has existed only for women; prostitution rises with monogamy. The purpose of monogamy is to fix the line of inheritance, of wealth and power, through the male. (The Greek word for "housewife" is neuter, it has no sex. Homosexuality becomes an observable social feature of ancient slave-holding, post-matrilineal societies.)

As world society has gone through its development past slavery to feudalism and past feudalism to capitalism, the family has changed as well. By the end of feudalist society, Africa was the source of a new world-enslaved population. The rise of capitalism corresponds to the decline and enslavement of the African peoples in Africa and worldwide.

The enslaving of Africans and the colonization of Africa (and indeed of the whole Third World) has made historic, profound, and tragic changes in the black family. The slave trade has existed since the fifteenth century; the triangular trade (Africa–New World–England) was the basis for world trade, the Industrial Revolution, and the primitive accumulation of wealth responsible for U.S. and European world domination!

As modern slaves, black people were *chattel* slaves, owned as *property* by their masters. The estimated number of Africans who died in the Middle Passage and slavery is 50,000,000 (Du Bois), 300,000 (Toure).

The African family, even in its feudal state of development and its placement of women as less powerful and subservient to men, still maintained many essentials of its matrilineal character. And the black queens—the Shebas, Nzingas, Aminas, Cleopatras—attest to the prominent place of African women throughout history.

Under Western slavery, the black family was *legally* destroyed. Marriage between slaves was illegal (and, to the slavemasters, even the occasion for slapstick "coon" comedy).

As property, black people had no humanity, they were part of the means of production—tools, machines. The U.S. Constitution ruled us three-fifths of a human being. The Dred Scott decision (1859) said we had no rights the United States had to recognize!

Children produced by slaves were the property of the slavemasters, to be dealt with by them as they desired. Families were routinely separated, parents sold in one direction, children in the other. Genocide and social degradation always accompany slavery. Self-consciousness is dangerous and history the dim analogy of religious parables. Education for blacks is outlawed, along with the *drum* (witness the inherent politics of our art!). Marriage itself becomes a subversive activity, only practiced "underground," like the railroad that led to freedom. "Jumping the broom," we called it. A ceremony held in the forests surrounding the plantation, through which, even as slaves, black people defied slave society by declaring the continuing sanctity and sacredness and will to self-determination of the black family.

Chattel slavery and the slave trade are together the single most destructive assault on the black family in the history of the world! Any working-class family is weakened and dispersed by the negative pressures of capitalism. Even in the nineteenth century, Marx and Engels showed how child labor and long work hours for parents away from the children contributed to the weakness of English working-class families. Consider that for black people this class assault was added to by slavery and the national oppression that followed it and still continues to this day. (In the

United States we have been slaves for 244 years and "free" for only 127 years!)

It was the struggles of the African American slaves and the antislavery movement that ended slavery, and this should have marked a great positive step for the black family toward stability and self-determination. But Reconstruction was always partial and insincerely attempted. (There are "loopholes" and still unpracticed aspects of the Thirteenth, Fourteenth, and Fifteenth Amendments—and Ralston-Purina and *them* got our forty acres and a mule!)

By 1876, Reconstruction had been destroyed (by the Hayes-Tilden compromise, the repeal of civil rights bills, the installation of the racial-fascist "Black Codes," the withdrawal of the Union armies, and the rise of the KKK).

By the end of the century, segregation—U.S. apartheid—was the law of the land (1896, *Plessy v. Ferguson*), ratified by Booker T.

Throughout our history in the United States, the Afro-American people have struggled for freedom, equality, self-determination, democracy! As a result of our struggle, there are three distinct eras of Afro-American history. Periods in which our continuous struggle reached high peaks: the nineteenth-century antislavery movement, the early twentieth-century Harlem Renaissance, and the Civil Rights and Black Liberation movements of the 1950s and 1960s. American apartheid did not legally end until 1954 (*Brown v. Bd. of Ed.*), and you know the reality of that!

The rising and falling motion of black struggle I characterize as the *Sisyphus syndrome*, after the Greek myth of the man punished by the gods by having to continuously throughout history roll a huge boulder up a mountain, only to have it rolled back down on him at the end. As soon as we have managed to mobilize a sharp, revolutionary upsurge in our struggle, as in the three periods mentioned, the forces of reaction and white supremacy forcibly roll the rock back down on us, though hopefully not as far down as before. Langston Hughes called this phenomenon "white backlash."

The nature or status of the black family reflects almost directly the rise and fall of our national "fortunes" here in the United States. When the Afro-American people are in periods of vigorous and progressive advance, through the focused intensification of our struggle, our lives are improved, even amidst the shouts and chants, marches and gunshots, and the confrontations of the period. (For instance, the 1960s black income was higher than it has been since—jobs, housing, education, etc. See *The*

Social and Economic Status of the Black Population, 1790–1978, U.S. Department of Commerce.) Political confrontation forces concessions. No struggle, no progress, to paraphrase Fred.

When the upsurge comes to an end and the negative aspect of the Sisyphus syndrome dominates, then the fortunes—the structure, the political and economic conditions, the social stability—of the black family are also under assault and clearly weakened!

Compare the black family, in its most recent period of self-consciousness, unity, and political focus (the 1960s) with the condition of the black family today. The condition of the black family today is directly attributable to the same state assault, corporate cooptation, and class betrayal that sent the Black Liberation Movement into decline.

No one should have to be told that, of the black family, black youth are most directly under attack—pushed out of schools, unemployed, stereotyped as public enemies and with blacks in general as a criminal class, often locked up, assaulted even by each other and by the police, and even killed (by police and racist civilians alike)!

The black woman is *triply oppressed*, by race, class, and gender—the slave of a slave.

The weakness of the black family is a direct reflection of economic exploitation and the national racial and social repression of the Afro-American people.

To strengthen and stabilize the black family it is necessary to strengthen and stabilize the whole of the black nation!

The first focus must be political! The gaining, maintaining, and use of power. Political organization is key. The term Black Power was put forward in the 1960s, but it came to be coopted by black petty bourgeois politicians, including the Black Congressional Caucus, to mean electoral politics under the wing of the Dems or the Reps, two wings of the same vampire.

The larger black family of the Afro-American people must be brought together, including all of the various class and ideological forces in the black nation. This united front, joining together all segments and sectors of the people in collective struggle around concrete issues—in this case, our own self-determination—is the strong political "kinship" necessary to reunite and strengthen our big national family, to strengthen and create a developmental paradigm for our smaller families and a powerful instrument of change.

We know also that the even larger black family of the Pan-African peoples must be brought together in the same manner, to create both an OAU and an OAAU that see one African American nation as well as one Africa and one Pan-African family.

The largest family of all includes the peoples of the whole world. And all but those uninformed by history should know that (as quiet as it's kept) this too is a *black* family—every human being on the planet is of African descent!—even though quite a few of the chi'ren backward and some even dangerous. Eventually, this is the largest challenge of family reorganization and reunification there is!

Fade to Black: Once Upon a Time in Multiracial America

Joe Wood

New Orleans. It was late and the show was finished. We were hungry and drunk. Adolph said Mulé's was probably closed by now but he knew a place to eat on the other side of town. "Maybe you'll see some of *them* over there, too," he said. Adolph is a scholar of African-American history and politics, and he was raised in New Orleans and knew how *they* looked and where *they* ate. They liked Mulé's, a seventh-ward diner that serves the best oyster rolls in the city. The other place, Adolph said, was also good for observations, but far below seventh-ward culinary standards. It turned out to be an all-night fast-food joint, lighted too brightly, with a listless crowd of party people waiting in broken lines for some uninspired fried fare.

For a moment I forgot entirely about *them* and *they*. I wanted to try an oyster roll but there were none left, so I ordered a chicken sandwich "dressed" with lettuce and tomato and mayonnaise. The woman at the cash register seemed bored by my enthusiasm, and sighed, and in response I noted her skin color. She was dark. I turned my head and checked out two sleepy-eyed girls in the next line. They looked tired in their frilly prom dresses; their skin was waxen, the sad pale finish of moonlight. I knew—oh, I hesitated a moment, because I could see how a hasty eye might have thought them white, but *I* knew. Turning to

Adolph I whispered "creole" and made a giant drunken nod in their direction. Adolph looked and confirmed it: they were, in fact, *them*.

And they were us, black like us. I bet that virtually no one in the crowd had any trouble spotting the girls' African blood, and not only because we happened to be standing in an establishment that catered to black people, and not only because the girls did not look scared or determined not to look scared, as white girls in such situations usually want to. We all knew because we all were in some elusive sense family, and family can—or imagines it can—recognize itself, detect itself, see its own self no matter the guise.

So there stood the girls, their tired moonish looks telling us everything. Now I really eyed them and discerned the secret layer of brown just underneath the surface of their faces and arms. With practiced accuracy my eyes took in the other hints: a certain weightiness of hair, a broadness of lip, a fullness of hip and nose. (When I was a child it was something of a sport to fish for evidence of our presence, to seek ourselves in the faces of "whites" such as Alexander Hamilton or Babe Ruth.) Each detail made plain the girls' "blackness" as surely as a look in the mirror, and gave me the old sense of triumph, until a moment passed and I remembered why we could never really be the same: we were in New Orleans and these girls were creole and I am not.

•

Adolph, you hold the key to this story. The reason—you and I are family, but you are on the other side of the creole difference, a strange distinction made of nothing but stories and lies, lies and stories, the forces that conjure family. While you and I would both like to think of the creole tale as one more plotline in the black story, because that's all it is, really, we both know that true believers say creole is a separate thing altogether; you and I know how they say, Look at us. How they say, Watch us go. How they enjoy being them, and not us.

Them and us. How strange. I realize now that we have never talked about the differences in our looks, your light and my dark. Neither of us, I suspect, has consciously *avoided* this discussion. It simply hasn't been an issue: there are so many things to talk about—why waste time on such foolishness? But there it was, during the trip down home to New Orleans, there was the difference stuck in our faces. It broke our silence, compels me to speak on the absurd—let me first describe our looks with as cold an eye as I would any character.

I have chocolate-brown skin, generous lips, the kind of ordinary kinky hair many black women still get mad at. I wear a goatee and sometimes glasses. I am thirty years old and I'm not in great shape because I don't like working out. You've got a couple of decades on me but you're probably in better condition. I don't recall seeing too many gray hairs on your head last time I saw you, though your hairline is ebbing. Your hair is straight and heavy like a South Asian's; your skin is amber brown, your features are round but strong: You've even been mistaken for a countryman by several natives of India. But you are black, definitely, and creole.

We've been friends for several years now, and though there is no explaining friendship, there are a few reasons I want you to know I see. We both love to watch people do their hustles. We laugh at the same absurdities, and mostly get hurt by the same absurdities. We have similar politics, and we aren't sellouts. (Which is not normal, which is why the sellouts call us cynics.) There is a lot more, of course. The stories of people's affections are oceanic in number and complexity. In this way we are very ordinary.

But the subject at hand is the black and the brown. Surely this is one of the stories that makes us up, as it makes up every other African American, and with any examination, every white or Asian or Latino or anybody else on these shores. Though we haven't talked about our own colors, you and I have talked about how much social meaning is attached to shade difference, even today. You've lived it and tried to forget it because the debate is absurd. I don't like tracking that stuff inside, either. I've cracked jokes about those confessional pieces describing the pain of being dark, or the pain of being light, or the pain of being mixed and in-between—seldom is anything real said. We've laughed about how white people eat up that stuff, but for the moment I will stop laughing because I've decided to put in mind that conflict.

•

My sister is light with broad features. Adolph, you and she have met, but you don't know how much she favors my mother. They are both light—my mother says her father had a lot of Native American in him. In the photograph she keeps in the basement he looks creole. Mom told me that several of his brothers and sisters were so light they lost the mossy accent and turned Jewish or Italian or WASP, and vanished into the white world. Mom's mom was as dark as navy blue, and she couldn't hide her slave history. We don't name the rest of the races that made her, but you can bet she had some other tribes inside.

Remember that Tito Puente concert that night in the municipal ballroom by the waterfront? Remember checking out all those Latinos, those creoles, those light-skinned black people? Remember the way I eyed Jeannine, her light color? I remember thinking of a brotha I know whose skin is very dark, and then I could *see* him at the table. I could hear him, too, accusing me—I felt for a second like a Negro banker hunting for a suitable wife.

Of course this was an easy comparison. Everyone knows that the powerboys who choose "suitable wives" are sick about this sort of thing, and everyone knows that the young Negroes in the theater on 125th Street who laughed when Alva Rogers was on the screen in Spike Lee's *School Daze* are sick, too. You and I know that the equation between femininity and light skin is ubiquitous in the culture, as is the equation between light skin and intelligence, and light skin and beauty. Negroland's self-described iconoclasts, especially the boys, are no less sick this way. You've seen brotha writer and brotha artist and brotha filmmaker walk more proudly holding the hand of the Mulatto Ideal. And why not? In the movies or on television brotha man's semen always produces a mulatto child, no matter the skin color of the mother. At bottom, light skin and white features and *multiracial* make males in Hollywood happy, and most employers in America happy, and many social planners and other futurists, too; I had to wonder whether the same story fashioned my desire.

I took refuge in the way the story failed to determine my sense of my own body. Each day this "I" of mine faces the mirror; I blindly see *me*, and fail to wonder enough what the brownness means to others. Usually I even forget that old refrain "the darker the berry the sweeter the juice," its equation between dark skin and blackness, the way it insists that one's fidelity to the race rises directly with an increase of melanin. I suppose my being dark makes it relatively easy to see through that old affirmation; I know it is not as easy for lighter sisters and brothers, who are often made to feel as if they should pay us in blood for their skins. But I think a more fundamental reason is that I, like most everyone else, don't really like to live racially. No one I know takes much pleasure in trying to measure how racism shapes his or her life; no matter how much folks celebrate or hate being black, they ordinarily forget about it. Who has the time when thanking God that the newborn is not deaf, when worrying about why the tax man is phoning you at work, when marveling at the way the sun lights up the metal on the scaly top of the Chrysler Building? Of course, there *are* those moments when you and I are forced to shoo away un-imaginative opinions about who we are: the veteran cop, the prospective landlord, the Afrocentric professor often make judgments that follow tired and expected patterns. But most of the time I, like you, dispose of such takes the moment they enter the skull, because I live here.

There is, of course, much more and much less to say about all this. Here is another story about Adolph and me. A beginning and an end and another beginning.

•

One of the last nights I was in New Orleans, Adolph took a bunch of friends to a bar in the seventh called Pampy's. It was the kind of speakeasy you find in black neighborhoods all over the country. There was a jukebox against the wall playing old r & b songs; the walls were seasoned with posters for local concerts and handwritten signs about "house rules"; the drinks were poor. A gang of dressed-up people in their forties sat on stools at the bar, hungry, bathed in an encouraging red light. Even so, I could guess everyone's complex-ion, including the guy sitting at the other end of our table.

Gary was just a little bit darker than the light-skinned girls at the be-ginning of my journey, and I was already pretty certain he would call himself creole—no, by now I *knew* he'd say he was. Still, I asked. Gary and the woman sitting next to him both said yes. It turned out that they were lovers. She was darker than he, the syrupy brown of coffee with ex-tra sugar mixed in, brown like me, so her claim surprised me a little. But I didn't say anything out loud. Maybe, I reasoned, she's a genetic specter; even the best cultivation fails sometimes.

I could tell that Gary was a nice guy, though his looks made it hard to take him seriously. His face was almost perfectly flat; its most active fea-ture was his mouth, a messy thing. He wore his dental bridge a little too high on the upper gum, which would have been all right if his incisors didn't hang down the way they did. Each time he opened his trap he looked like a clownish Dracula, and even though he spoke with consid-erable honesty and earnestness, it was hard not to laugh.

Gary had grown up nearby, in a project where poor creoles lived along with noncreoles. That equation of higher class and lighter skin—not nec-essarily. Class status didn't, however, seem to cause Gary much anxiety. Now in his late twenties, he was a waiter at a downtown hotel, and, from the looks of it, doing fine. His girlfriend didn't really talk much, except to say again that she was creole. I asked one more time about the differences between creoles and other blacks. "Sometimes they like to blame us for looking good. We look good," he said, in a sincere drawl. I noticed that Gary's eyes were a little too high on his face and his hair was a little too low; I considered how the difference between looking inbred and not is a question of millimeters.

"Like my hair. I got good hair," he continued, smiling in the generous red light. He pulled a comb smoothly across his scalp. "Not like yours." I recalled something Adolph once told me about *them*: the first questions people ask when a baby is born is what kind of hair, then what color is it, then does it have two heads or whatever. Gary was a nice guy, and he didn't especially mean anything by "good hair" or "like yours," he was just repeating the things he'd heard; he was saying, Look at me—can't you see?

I could only laugh. A few minutes later Gary and his girlfriend left. I recounted the scene to Adolph, and he just doubled over laughing about how the nigga was so low-class he didn't even know enough not to say that absurd shit. So that's why you're laughing? I thought as I laughed, too— it was very, very funny. I stopped when I remembered that Gary had been very kind to utter his family's open secret, its story of itself, and I realized the smugness of my own laughter. Then I sensed with horror the oldest future, its familiar story: *Our family is better than yours.*

Where We Live: A Conversation with Essex Hemphill and Isaac Julien

Don Belton

At the twentieth century's close, independent filmmakers Marlon Riggs, Isaac Julien, and poet Essex Hemphill are likely the artists/activists whose work most richly articulates and extends the represented range of black gay men's identity. Their daring interventions advance the project of healing the whole of black masculinity by celebrating acts of dialogue, compassion, and love between black men across the spectrum of sexual orientation, as well as between black men and black women.

Riggs's landmark documentary *Tongues Untied*, along with Julien's *Looking for Langston*, a cinematic meditation on the life and legacy of the closeted Harlem Renaissance writer Langston Hughes, served stunning notice that black gay male silence and invisibility had ended. For two decades, Hemphill has crafted elegant poems that illuminate the life-giving geography of black men's love and grief.

Riggs died on April 5, 1994, of complications due to AIDS. In December of 1994, I brought Julien and Hemphill together for a conversation around the completion of Riggs's film *Black Is . . . Black Ain't*, which explores the nexus of black identity and masculinity. Hemphill appears in the film, along with cultural activists bell hooks, Michelle Wallace, Cornel West, and Angela Davis. I met with Julien and Hemphill at

Hemphill's apartment in West Philadelphia. Hemphill showed an advance cassette copy of the film. The following is excerpted from conversation between Julien and Hemphill that afternoon.

HEMPHILL: I find myself resisting popular notions of black masculinity while at the same time being attracted to them. Early on, I learned ways to protect my masculinity or, I guess I should say, my homo-masculinity. I wasn't inclined to be athletic. In the black neighborhood I came from, there was an emphasis on being able to play basketball or football. I, instead, was attracted to gymnastics because of the way the body looked. But I knew instinctively that if I had said, "I want to be a gymnast," among the fellas I ran with I would have been labeled a sissy. As an adult, I've had to resist the idea that I'm not a man because I don't have children or a woman.

JULIEN: I think this is a good place to start. Initially, masculinity was about living up to the fiction of normative hetereosexual masculinity. Growing up, I remember men in the community who were a part of my parents' circle commenting in Creole about how I was such a *petit macqot*, which is a small boy, *un petit garçon*. It was also a way of calling a young boy a sissy. A means of saying he's already displaying feminine traits. Maybe I wasn't interested in trying to conceal that part of my identity. So, in a way, it began a war early in my life, but not a bloody war. It was a war of positions in the sense I did not want to totally participate in being a straight black male in the conventional framework. My feelings for boys my age happened very early on—I must have been eight years old. In the playground, I saw the shorts fall off the goalkeeper's waist during a sports match. I remember feeling very erotically charged by the image. There was already in circulation the idea of black men having this hypermasculinity that was tough and resilient. It was tough growing up in London in the 1970s. You had to be tough to physically contest the everyday racist treatment by the police, by various authority figures and institutions. Therefore, you understood that this toughness was a mask and a defense. Questions around being black and male came to the forefront for me when I began to pursue my education and most of the other young men around me were being arrested.

HEMPHILL: We're faced with redefining what masculinity is. We're faced with constructing a masculinity for all of us, one that will be useful as opposed to disempowering. I think that, given issues like economic oppression, we feel safe holding onto the model constructed out of athletics, around street toughness and other conventional models of masculinity. You know, "My gun's bigger . . ." The gun is supposed to be an extension of you or your anger, and it's the bullet that strikes, not the fist. I can't think when I last saw two black men physically fighting. And not that I'm endorsing fighting, but I think the gun has become an apt metaphor for our isolation from our own rage and frustration. Our increasing isolation from one another's humanity. Then there's the masculinity that we're getting via television, film, and magazines. We need a masculinity that brings us more into contact with one another. A masculinity that is intimate and humane. A masculinity that allows if I feel like being soft my softness won't mean I'm a sissy or a punk.

JULIEN: In *Black Is . . . Black Ain't*, bell hooks and Michelle Wallace talk about the language of sexism and the presumptions around gender. That's really where everything begins to shut down. We both grew up experiencing scenes in which black men could not cry or express fear. Growing up, I very much identified with trying not to reproduce the dominant ideas of being a man. There's an overvaluation of strict gender codes in the black community. "Only sissies cry." When that was told to me, I said, "Fuck this. I'm not going to live like this." Those stories or fictions of "real" masculinity are learned early in life and then become ways of toughening young boys. That sort of information isn't useful to our community. I think there should be more of an investment in unlearning those codes, because they end breeding a certain inhumanity. Our redemption as a people is *not* a "dick thing," as bell hooks points out in the film.

HEMPHILL: I believe that many of the destructive lessons taught in our childhood homes is the result of the desperation of our parents. They were children at one point and were made to learn those same lessons. I don't know how we begin to unlearn that behavior.

JULIEN: Well, it's true that the codes we're meant to adhere to—masculine and feminine—are prescribed in childhood. As black boys and girls growing up in families attacked by racism from the outside, we are made to feel a kind of double restriction on the expression of ourselves in any way that might go against the grain of dominant ideas. We, as black men especially, are supposed to instill and police these codes within ourselves. But where are these codes coming from? I think that in America, but not only in America, there is this obsessive concentration on the family—the notion that everything can be resolved within the family. But this middle-class notion of "family" seems to me the space where we first learned how to fear one another and to fear the free expression of ourselves. As a result, the debate around black masculinity in the U.S. has become so topical with films like *Jungle Fever* and *Boyz in the Hood*. One of the problems with the *New York Times* article/symposium on black men [*Who Will Help the Black Man? New York Times*, 4 December 1994, v. 1, 74:1] is that it is exclusively a discussion by and about black middle-class, presumably heterosexual men. The question at the center of that discussion is really, How can we get black people, black men in particular, to get over in the American Dream? It should be obvious by now that's just a poor question. I also think the street tough machismo identity is bankrupt. It's just producing a competitive, nihilistic environment for black men to destroy themselves and each other. It's difficult to have a position on this without talking about the disappearance of real economic opportunity for the black working poor and the infiltration of drugs in our communities in both the U.S. and London. Marlon's film carries an important critique of black manhood along these lines.

HEMPHILL: Yes, and the critique bell hooks provides [in the film] of the black macho pose of the 60s and 70s is so powerful because if the sum of black political struggle is about empowering the black phallus at the expense of all other cultural issues, we cannot succeed. Or else that success will have no meaning. Our masculinity must encompass diversity and nuance. There should never be a question about whether Sally can drive a rig or whether Tommy can raise the children. There are also important class issues. The *Times* piece represented the black male middle class. I'd like to see that [discussion] take place with representatives from a broader range of possible black male identity. I'd have loved to have heard someone who flips hamburgers for minimum wage talk about how he views himself as a man. A construction worker. An emergency room doctor. I had problems with one of the participants in that article referring to working-class blacks as "black trash." Its a simple-minded analogy he was trying to draw—that you have white trash and you have black trash. Well, come on, baby [laughs], . . . who says any group of society is to be regarded as trash? So for me the *Times* piece was not a broad enough conversation. It was a safe conversation for the *New York Times*. Safe for the particular men who were included. And self-serving.

JULIEN: It became a spectacle, a symbolic discussion of black masculinity in a white newspaper, a discussion where very little was actually said. The patronizing and vindictive tone toward black working-class people, even by the one speaker who actually does work with young black men from impoverished backgrounds. . . .

HEMPHILL: The absence of debate on gender issues. . . . The absence of any gay voice. . . .

JULIEN: It's a question of power. Black men have been rendered powerless by the dominant society, and it's that drive to have power at any cost, no matter what is silenced or dismissed. It isn't very different from ways in which blacks are excluded from the representation of "true" American masculinity.

HEMPHILL: Yes. It's important to realize it isn't black women who are gunning down one another. Black women are not gunning *us* down and beating us to death. *We* are doing this.

JULIEN: We won't be able to abate this hatred and annihilation of self by flattening out and silencing differences within our community. These differences are vital to our mutual survival.

HEMPHILL: In a recent issue of the Nation of Islam's newspaper, *The Final Call*, Louis Farrakhan called for a "million-man march" on Washington, D.C. A march of one million black men on the nation's capital. The call itself is historic, though I've heard nothing about it in the mainstream press. But who's going to be on the stage when those one million black men assemble in Washington? You? Me? Would Marlon have been invited to speak? Hardly. It will be men who are considered safe. Safe for me equals ineffective—men who will not take risks in their intellect and who will not take risks in their compassion. I think of the ending of *Black Is . . . Black Ain't*, where bell hooks speaks about replacing the notion of black unity with the notion of communion. The root meaning of communion suggests that our union is based on a willingness to communicate with one another. It's a beautiful idea to pursue. [In the film] Michelle Wallace says, "I always get the feeling that when black people talk about unity and community that it's a turf war thing, you know—we're gonna get together and this is gonna be our block, and if you come on our block, you know, we're gonna kick your ass." Michelle says, "I always think I'm gonna be the one whose ass is gonna get kicked." I've always felt like that as well. I'm as black as anyone, but not by the criteria the nationalists construct.

JULIEN: It's about wanting attention and power in the system. Farrakhan demands this march on Washington. It's about another spectacle of middle-class black straight men claiming ownership of blackness. It's just another bankrupt political discourse.

HEMPHILL: But if this march happens, it will have historic ramifications. A new kind of power will be unleashed—a power that shows us the possibility of unity among black men. I think black gay men need to at least bring the issue of our participation to the table. We should press to have gay voices at the podium.

JULIEN: I think that within a Farrakhan march of black men on Washington, anyone attempting to read its meaning in any way that could be considered homoerotic would be dealt with. I don't see where the intervention can be made there.

HEMPHILL: Given some of the dangerous places gay men are often willing to go in the name of love or desire, why would intervening at the Farrakhan march be any less dangerous?

JULIEN: I say just the opposite. I would say we should be going back to the communities we are a part of and working on a grassroots level to get the black community to challenge hetero-normative assumptions. I think that would be the way from a grassroots level to change destructive assumptions about blackness, gender, and sexual identity. Otherwise, we just become a part of Farrakhan's spectacle.

HEMPHILL: I still think we need to bear witness in the representation of black male identity. Those black men who will march will largely be lower- and working-class men—your grassroots level. The march may not be framed around their identities, but they have always been the essential part of the Nation of Islam's political base. Of any black political base. For that reason, I believe we ought to try to participate. So at least, for the record, there is the fact that we were there to claim our membership in our communities.

JULIEN: Why should we try to claim membership in black masculinity through the Nation of Islam?

HEMPHILL: Big spectacle-oriented groups like the Nation of Islam are winning minds and support among everyday black people. Either we are a part of black communities or we aren't. Our presence has always been crucial to our communities, yet within those communities and the larger society we're still rendered as nonexistent. We're still considered to be not interested in something like this. There is a danger in that. As black gay men we need a politic that touches the vast majority of our brothers where they're at. Otherwise as gay men we only represent a breakdown. . . .

JULIEN: I think failure is something that should be celebrated. I don't want to be in a formation of black male identity where one has to hold oneself in a rigid way—as in a march—even against how we might feel about ourselves in terms of our pain, our skepticism, lack and self-doubt. All these things are as much a part of black male identity as the things we might want to parade, like toughness and unity. We have to be willing to engage in a process of thinking through our failure as black men in this society. Black masculinity has always been a "failed masculinity" in relationship to white male colonialism. Black macho discourses of empowerment will never truly reach us where we live. There is something interesting we can learn from our so-called failure, because our failure also contains our resistance. Failure to live "up" to oppressive masculinity is a part of what it means to be queer. That's what my work has been about. What your work is about. Being black itself is seen as a failure in the white world. We want to remember that, and there is a way we can use that failure to critique white supremacy. If you want to be a black version of white supremacy, of course you end up with a Farrakhan.

HEMPHILL: So where do we intervene?

JULIEN: Use the media. If you're going to make the intervention it would be, "This is a problem, and you know . . ." If, when they march, you have an interview on CNN, and CNN runs it only five times that day, then you'd have a larger audience than their march on Washington.

HEMPHILL: Definitely, yes. But I still come back to the power of the possibility of black men coming together. I'm not being romantic here. When Marlon was working on *Black Is . . . Black Ain't*, I went with him to a theater in South Central Los Angeles to film a meeting between the Bloods and the Crips gang members. It was historic. Some of that is in the film. I will never forget stepping out of the van when we arrived at the theater and looking up, and along the rooftops of the theater and the houses on the block were these SWAT teams of uniformed policemen holding guns. There were at least one hundred men, most of them white, which underscores this nation's real terror of black men cutting back on the violence against one another and creating a space to come together.

JULIEN: But what are these black men coming together to do?

HEMPHILL: Don't quash it yet, Isaac, [Isaac laughs] without taking into account that an agenda would have to be defined. Maybe it's desperation that draws me to the march despite my aversion to Farrakhan. We can't just attack his ideology. What good is that? I can't look at television without seeing negative representations of a black male. He's either in handcuffs or he's been shot by one of his brothers over whatever foolishness is out there.

JULIEN: I don't think it's a matter of desperation. The desperation is that people are looking for black straight men to provide political leadership against white patriarchy. The problem is with these very selective representations. We're dealing here with white society's own anxiety and fear about black men and about the black underclass, the working-class populace.

HEMPHILL: How can we control it?

JULIEN: That question is part and parcel of the postslavery experience. I don't know how one negotiates oneself out of it.

HEMPHILL: I don't think you addressed my concern [about] whether or not there's a necessity for black men to assemble anywhere in this country.

JULIEN: I just question the whole premise. I can see a homoeroticism in it, perhaps, but I have to see it for what it is—a fantasy.

HEMPHILL: You're not in any way interested in a million black men assembling?

JULIEN: No.

HEMPHILL: Okay. I guess that's our first point of contention. [Both laugh.] So what is the perfect site for our resistance?

JULIEN: An intervention like *Black Is . . . Black Ain't*.

HEMPHILL: What about the troublesome issues of Marlon's dying of AIDS and his sexuality? There are public television stations and schools that won't run it because of Marlon's candor.

JULIEN: You have this distribution out of, say, Sony Classics. That film can be seen in twenty cinemas in New York alone. That sort of intervention would be profound, and it could be marketed toward black people.

HEMPHILL: This isn't about art cinema. I'm talking about addressing raw black life.

JULIEN: Yes, and that's what I'm addressing as well. I'm talking about the apparatus of mass culture. Which is Sony. Miramax. We don't own the means of production. Even certain aspects of our blackness are being experienced through what comes through the marketplace.

HEMPHILL: I see your point, and I respect that. But, I guess, with your hypothetical way for intervening . . . what comes to mind is that I come to the table with an idea and you come with an idea, but now we have to take our ideas to something that doesn't come from us, the media, corporate distribution. . . . For me, the way I live, my blackness is the priority. Period. Be it my identity as a gay person or as a person with AIDS or my identity as a writer . . . I'm still dealt with as black, first and foremost.

JULIEN: I think it's a product of segregationist thinking about sexuality and gender that we have to prioritize our identities.

HEMPHILL: I don't want you to misunderstand me. In 1991 or '92, when I was on tour in England, I had trouble with customs, and the trouble I had had everything to do with me being a black man in bomber jacket, in jeans and construction boots. All these other people are flowing by me in customs with no problem, but they stopped me every time, because I fit a certain profile. That's why my blackness has to be there first for me. It's a battle around that place where I am desperate and wanting to see some of the dying stop.

JULIEN: But a march won't stop that. Anyway, I think the image of one million black men marching on Washington is phallocentric and misogynist. I don't know. Maybe I'm just cynical.

HEMPHILL: I don't think it's cynicism. We share a similar concern and pessimism. I think we articulate it differently. I agree with you about the phallocentrism and misogyny. . . . I stopped three or four young brothers on my street last spring, and they were bigger than me. It was after school, after business hours. These young fellas had taken magic markers and written all over the storefront windows. And something in me just snapped. I'm sick of there being no intervention. I told them, "Don't do that. That's a black business. You're destroying property." I was scared to death, but I wasn't going to my apartment and locking my door. The truth is I might not be sitting here now because of that act. Even a simple intervention could cost our lives.

JULIEN: Generally, there's a breakdown of the civil society in America.

HEMPHILL: Various horrifying themes occur in all our communities. Why is there such tremendous disrespect among black men towards women, regardless of our sexual orientation? Even a statement like, "Miss Thing is gonna take me to a new level of sensuality." I was wondering why it's never "*Mr*. Thing." Why is it "*Thing*"?

JULIEN: I thought "Miss Thing" was about a parody of a sexist comment.

HEMPHILL: Think about the things you've heard among gay brothers about women. How much different are some of those statements from the ones by some heterosexual brothers? There hasn't been much discourse among black gay men about that. But I know sisters are anxious for that. Not just conversation, but deliberate work. I don't think current notions of masculinity work for any male. I don't think they work for anyone.

((speak my name))
218

JULIEN: I think the social complexities around contemporary male identity are just deepened by issues of blackness and gayness.

HEMPHILL: This is why, for various reasons, including expediency, I've elected not to take a white lover when that option has been there. I feel like this is the worst country to try to love outside the race. I can't imagine what you deal with in your relationship [Mark Nash, Julien's life-partner of seven years, is white].

JULIEN: My experience being in America with Mark has not been one where I've been rejected. If blacks or whites want to reject me, they're not my friends and I don't feel I've lost anything.

HEMPHILL: It seems so incredibly important, the way that Marlon's use of the slogan "Black men loving black men is *the* revolutionary act" in *Tongues Untied* has been so fucked by so many people [because Marlon's partner, Jack Vincent, is white].

JULIEN: I just don't agree with a slogan like that. Who's to say what *the* revolutionary act is, anyway? Who can prescribe that? If I'd grown up in America, I don't know what I would be like. The positioning of a slogan like that—the way it is positioned in the film—is fine, I suppose, but when it's used as some kind of moral code to police interracial desire, then I think it's really about our shame about the range of our own desires.

HEMPHILL: The act of black men loving black men isn't only about our sexual expression. It means everything, including intervening downstairs when those young black men were defacing their neighborhood. That was about my love for them. If I didn't love us, I wouldn't care. You know—"Just go ahead. Get your magic markers and do the block. Do the block!"

JULIEN: I think it's very complicated, the discourse of love in relationship to yourself. Unlearning self-hatred and fear is hard work. I've had to be in America to really begin to understand that, being so marginalized here.

HEMPHILL: In some ways, I think we *have* failed.

JULIEN: We have to be willing not to reject that failure out of hand. That's essential to experiencing humanity.

((part five))

HEROES

Voodoo for Charles

Don Belton

On Christmas morning in 1991 I telephoned my nephew. I have two nephews: Charles, who had only just turned nineteen the week before, and Wayne, Jr., who is somewhere in his middle twenties by now. These are the children of my brother's first marriage. My nephews grew up in Newark, New Jersey, where much of my early childhood was spent, but that was before the conflagration of the 1967 riot and the razing of what remained of the city by the local, state, and federal governments in the name of an urban renewal which is yet to come. While Newark was not an easy city to live in, it was still, in any case, from the late 50s to the mid-60s (when I lived there with my great-grandmother in the black district called the Hill) a city. Today Newark is the ghost of a city. Its statistics for AIDS, black-on-black crime, infant mortality, and unemployment bear witness to dissolution.

Charles was living in Newark in 1991. I had not spoken to him in over four years. I hadn't seen him in a longer time. The last time we'd spoken was by telephone. (For several years now, I seem to talk to the members of my family only on the phone.) By 1991 I still felt unresolved about our last conversation. I had been visiting my parents' house in Philadelphia, while they were away on a trip. "Uncle Don," Charles had said to me on the phone back then, "Where's Grandad and Gramma? I want to tell them I got shot."

His father had divorced his mother when Charles was six. My brother had married again after renouncing the street life he'd embraced almost his entire youth. His second marriage was to a middle-class black woman nine years younger than he (and one year younger than I). She was a preacher's daughter. My brother soon became an evangelical preacher himself. Since my brother has renounced what he often calls, from the pulpit, the sin and shame of his former life, he has also, tragically, renounced his sons. He is uncomfortable with them. It is as if they are his doubles. They *are* him, but with a frightening difference. They are projections of all the parts of himself that he has disowned in order to achieve his new life. They still know little more than the brutal reality of the streets he fled. They also remember him as the junkie who beat their mother, and they still bear the mental and spiritual wounds of that. He does not talk to them, any more than our father spoke to him, because to talk to them might mean confronting the past from which he is always running; allowing that past into his present. Instead, he quotes the self-hating apostle Paul when I criticize his abandonment of his sons, proclaiming himself a new creature in Christ. "All old things," he assures me, parroting Saint Paul, "are passed away." My brother now has three young daughters with his new wife. When his new wife was pregnant with the last girl, she called me on the phone and said, "Your brother wants a boy, but I pray it's another girl. It's easier for black girls than it is for black boys."

In the four years since I'd spoken to Charles, his mother had been murdered in the housing project where both she and her children were raised. Had it been easier for her? After having been shot (almost fatally, for refusing to run drugs for a neighborhood syndicate), Charles recovered and began his career as a drug lord in Newark. Recently he had been sentenced to three to seven years in prison for attempted murder, a sentence from which he was on the lam on Christmas, 1991. He was *nineteen*.

The phone rang several times before there was an answer at the number that another relative had provided. The voice that answered was a man's, husky, low. I wondered if this was the new voice, the man's voice, for the mercurial black baby boy whom I'd helped to raise. I asked if Charles was there.

"Who is this?" the voice asked, gruff.

"I'm sorry," I said. I'd been told he was in hiding. "This is his uncle, Don."

"Uncle Don?" I listened to the voice come alive, filling with pleasure, softening, turning into a boy's. "Uncle Don?"

Suddenly I was afraid, awed by the power of the telephone to create the illusion that pushing a sequence of buttons was all that was required for me to reach Charles. He was, after all, now speaking into my ear— this was his voice, we had each other on the line. I also felt regret that it had taken me so long to complete such a simple action.

He wanted to know where I was calling from. He said he'd heard I lived in Maine. I told him I live in Saint Paul, Minnesota.

"Minneapolis?" he asked. "Where Prince lives?"

"Yes."

He told me he'd seen the book I'd written, at his great-aunt's house in Newark. He said he wanted to read it. I promised to send him a copy. I told him I was writing another, a section of which I had dedicated to the memory of his mother when it was published in a literary journal. I don't really know much that is certain about his mother, though I knew her, except that she was mellow-voiced and pretty when she was young. Her skin was the color of yellowed ivory, she had freckles, and her name was the same as my own mother's.

"You're a teacher, aren't you? At a college?"

"Yes," I said. "I teach literature."

I wonder what Charles thinks of my life. I know he's been told I am a success, though I doubt he understands why. I doubt he knows mine is a success I sometimes can barely feel, though I live in a multicultural (predominately white, middle-class) neighborhood, where my white heterosexual neighbors tolerate my homosexuality, my blackness, my intellectual bent. A number of the neighbors have adopted children of color from the American South, Peru, Korea. Others are busy making babies. The parents accept me ostensibly, but they make certain I never babysit. I wanted to tell Charles I'm gay. I came out to most of the adults in my family years ago. I wanted him to learn from me that his uncle loves men.

I also wanted to tell him what it has been like for me teaching at a college whose faculty I joined in 1990, a college that has failed to tenure a single black professor in twenty years, about the stress of sometimes confronting a racism so covert and insidious our ancestors could not have imagined it. I wanted to tell him that although I was preparing a lecture I would give in a few weeks in Paris at the Sorbonne, my life felt permeated by a soul-sick sadness I inherited from my father and my father's father (both of whom were named Charles) and share with my nephew's father. Obviously Charles is a part of this, and I believed that if I could discuss this sadness with Charles (surely he was now old enough for this conversation), could share my names for it with him and hear the names he gave to it, then we might touch that hurt together and help each other heal. But something prevented me. I wasn't afraid that he would cease to look up to me if he knew my life isn't the magazine of success our relatives want to pretend it is; I was afraid of the incoherence that stretched out before me when I thought of naming the pain we were both a part of. Any words I might speak would have to be words used in faith, since I did not know their exact power to hurt or heal. To speak them I would have to trust myself and trust Charles, trust love. And I was unable to speak those words of faith that morning.

I did the best I could. I opened the door as wide as I could to my nephew, hoping he might, because of his youth or recklessness, push it further. "So how are things with you?" I asked him. "I haven't seen you in so long. Talk to me."

I listened as my nephew brought me up to date on his life with the same adolescent mixture of nonchalance, anxiety, and wonder with which I had once reported to my parents about a backpack trip to Quebec City in 1975, life in my college dorm, or meeting James Baldwin at his brother David's apartment on Manhattan's West Side when I was a sophomore.

Trying to listen beneath my nephew's words for his feelings—for his life and my own—my mind wandered over all I already knew of Charles's life. He had been out of my life for so long, and more importantly, since he had once been in part my responsibility, I had been out of his. I wondered would I even recognize my nephew were I to pass him by chance on the street in my city, or see his face in a video clip accompanying the all-too-familiar TV news narration about another anonymous (even when named) young black male criminal murdered, imprisoned, standing trial, beaten.

I thought about the times when my nephews were little. Even though I was only thirteen when Wayne, Jr., was born and sixteen when Charles was born, I took my role as their uncle quite seriously. My brother had become a junkie shortly after Wayne, Jr., was born, and though my brother was clean when Charles was conceived, he'd begun using again before Charles was delivered. Between the births of my nephews, my star had begun to ascend. I received an academic scholarship to an exclusive Quaker boys' school in Philadelphia. Education, it seemed, was the sword I could use to vanquish racism. If I hewed the assimilationist line, studied and got good grades, dressed and spoke properly, went to church, I would become something better than a criminal or a corpse. I soon tried to pass these values on to my nephews—even though I had begun to feel a certain amount of ambivalence, distance, and irony in relation to these values even then. I knew instinctively from the moment I first saw my nephews that they were born into a world full of trouble.

I used to take them everywhere with me whenever I could be with them. I dragged them to the library, bookstores, plays. I remember, later, the train trips down from my exclusive New England college, arriving at Newark station—a monstrosity always under construction and restoration, a sad remnant of the populuxe shrine to mobility I'd traveled through when I was a child, the times I shuttled back and forth between Philadelphia and Newark, between belligerently bourgeois parents and my Southern immigrant great-grandmother, a hickory-skinned crone with long, puff-of-smoke hair.

When I took the train down for my nephews, it was invariably a trial to find a cabdriver—black or white—willing to transport me to the notorious housing project where my nephews lived. I remember walking up stinking stairways and through dark hallways to find their apartment, sometimes finding their mother high on drugs with her boyfriend and her sister, or finding no one at home at all.

"Oh, Uncle Don," Charles was saying on Christmas morning in 1991, "did I tell you Aunt Geraldine died of AIDS?"

I remember searching the grounds of the project when no one was home, and finding Wayne and Charles in some glass-strewn play yard amid the wild bedlam of unsupervised children—unsupervised except for the foxlike vigil of men and women whose preying on children takes various forms, all deadly. I would take my nephews to a friend's place in the country or to the city, to a planetarium, a museum, a movie, a historical site, *any*place that said to them there *is* someplace—some *way*—other than this.

By the time I moved from college to graduate school, I was spending more time with Charles because he was still young enough to be at home, while Wayne, Jr., grew harder to locate during my visits. Wayne, Jr., was running with a bad crowd, picking up the legacy his father had escaped and left for him in Newark's streets. When I did see my oldest nephew, I realized that in my absence he was rapidly becoming a man I didn't understand. (This was before the violent, misanthropic music he now favored and the disaffected style of dress he'd adopted was appropriated and commodified by the white media.)

I was worried about Wayne, Jr., increasingly unsure with him now that he was becoming a man. I went back and forth, reaching out to him and hoping he would reach out to me. I worried that it might not be good for him to spend too much time with me anymore, that I knew too little about that street world in which he was striving. I knew that though I'd come from Newark, the destruction waiting in its streets had not remained the same. It had metastasized. In that world he would have been my mentor. I might encourage his tenderness, and that might be his undoing in that world. I couldn't give him what he needed to survive there. He knew that. I hoped to share with him some of what he might need to get out. If he wanted it. And I'd hoped to give him that from the first time I carried him across a room.

But Charles was still a child. He clearly needed me. I struggled to give him everything I'd given his brother too late, the experience of being prized. It had been an experience I'd somehow created or been given, perhaps by my great-grandmother, in my own early childhood. My storytelling, "part-Indian" great-grandmother with the smokecloud hair was off-and-on my primary care-giver from my birth until I was nine years old. She chose me, chose me to invest with her stories and accumulated legacy, which is to say she loved me. With Charles I was in a hurry, because I knew that the world I left him in every time I returned him to his mother's apartment was a world in which children became old abruptly, without warning.

I told him the same stories I'd taught his brother. I told him about his great-great-grandfather on my mother's side, who moved his wife and children all over South Carolina before he came to Philadelphia around the turn of the century, always a step ahead of the Klan, because he refused to accept the large and small indignities white men meted out to colored men. In Saluta, South Carolina, he'd been the first black man to attend the auction of cotton he raised on his homestead, not because he was granted a special permission but because he demanded a basic right. In Philadelphia he had a "contract" with movie princess Grace Kelly's father, John B. Kelly, the brick magnate, to supply the work crews for building operations, though I cannot imagine what a contract between a black man and an Irishman looked like in the early nineteen teens. He moved his family into a big house in the once-progressive neighborhood near Girard College in North Philadelphia.

I once took Charles to the ruin of this house, near Girard Avenue. We stood at the entrance and called our ancestor's name. We could see from the entrance to the backyard. A tree was growing through the kitchen into the second floor. For a time Great-Grandfather had rented the house next door to help an ongoing chain of relatives from the South relocate and find work. He lost his mind after the unionization of his trade empowered newly arrived white ethnics and ousted black men from the professions of carpentry and masonry. My mother grew up with him living on the third floor of her family home, a withdrawn, bitter, old man who occasionally came to life when he took his fiddle down from the mantle and ordered his grandchildren to dance until they went crying to their mother, "Please, make Grand Pop behave!"

Charles learned old songs from my collection of reissued recordings by Louis Armstrong, Bessie Smith, Cab Calloway, Ethel Waters. There was one Waters song that always broke him up; it had the spoken line *Take it easy, greasy, . . . you got a long way to slide*. Charles loved singing and language. He was a miraculous dark bird when he was little, always echoing and articulating. Before he turned two he had a good command of adjectives and adverbs. He was always narrating his experience. I am told small children usually exhibit exceptional verbal skills or advanced physical skills early. Charles exhibited both. He loved to run and climb and dance. He was fondest of his push toys. When he was four or five, I bought him toy boxing gloves and we practiced his jabs and footwork. I'd make the sound of the opening bell and he would start bobbing, weaving, and hooking. He had the classic combination down pat: the left jab followed by the right cross. I called him Kid Chocolate, after the legendary 1920s black boxer. I used to tell him his boxing technique was pure voodoo.

Charles was my heart. I was his uncle, almost his father, even if only for the day, the weekend, the week or summer we were together.

Once Charles fell riding his tricycle and split his tongue. I rushed him to the hospital emergency room and had to curse out the receptionist before he was admitted. "We can't admit him without the consent of his parent—that means a mother or father," the receptionist had told me from a barred cage. I was standing there with Charles's blood drenching my polo shirt. "*I'm* his goddamned parent!" I railed. "What's it to you? What kind of shit is this?"

I believe I am being objective when I say Charles was the most beautiful baby I have ever seen, more beautiful than his brother, who was perfect, and, if pictures are any indication, more beautiful than his father or I had been. His skin was darker than ours at the same time it was more brilliant. He shone. His was a preternatural blackness dedicated to the light. His round face was like a thundercloud with the lightning of his eyes and teeth flashing constantly inside it. Charles was the resurrected promise of all our childhoods going back generations for our manhood. I loved that boy better than my life. He was my life. Only better. Even before he was born, I was always talking to him, reading to him. When his mother was pregnant with Charles, I used to sit by her and touch her stomach and read to him inside her womb. I read him James Baldwin's letter to his nephew from *The Fire Next Time: "You can only be destroyed by believing that you really are what the white world calls a* nigger. *I tell you this because I love you, and please don't you ever forget it."*

But as I've said, by the time Charles was born, his father was back on heroin. My brother tried many times to save himself, to heal, to redeem himself, and no one knows better than I do that he was born into a world of trouble. And maybe the reason I loved his sons so much was because I loved my brother and I hoped I could redeem him if I could help redeem them.

•

The following is one of my earliest memories. It emanates from both my memory and my imagination. It is literally true, however, in terms of the organic infrastructure informing my life, it has the quality of supertruth. Once, when I was four and staying in Philadelphia for the summer, my brother and I were walking home from Sunday school. The afternoon was sultry-hot. We were in no hurry to get home. I held his hand, as I always did when we walked down the street together, and he swung our arms in a jovial way. Soon we heard thunder and saw the zig-zag lightning. The swinging of my arm slowed. As we walked, we were caught in the downpour.

The rain pounded so hard it hurt my small body. I had never been outside in weather like that, away from home, in the street, without my mother or my father. All I had was my brother to protect me. He was lanky, athletic, almost as tall as my father. We began to run. The rain poured like a mirror of heaven. My brother held my hand tight. Lightning flashed, thunder rumbled, and I began to scream and cry.

I stopped running, and my brother stopped. I couldn't move. I was too terrified. I believed I would die. God was angry. He was tearing up the world and washing it away. I fully realize now what I only realized then in part, that my brave fourteen-year-old brother was terrified too. But he said, "It's all right. I'm with you. I'll get you home." This vow was punctuated by a burst of thunder so loud it threatened to crack open the street before us. My brother took me and ran first in one direction and then another. We rushed along the flowing curb. Then we were standing near a tree. We had reached the elementary school building two blocks from our house.

"We're almost there," my brother shouted over the ringing wind. "Do you want me to carry you?"

"No," I said, "I'm scared."

"All right," he told me. "We'll rest for a little while."

We ran from the tree to the awning leading into the school building. As soon as we came up against the closed glass entrance, there was a big burst of lightning. For an instant the world went white. The skin of my neck and arms tingled. We held each other. I felt his heart leaping just above my head, but he held me, and I didn't cry. We stood there holding each other until the rain slowed. Then we walked home in silence.

My father was sitting in the living room, reading the newspaper. My mother came out from the kitchen. I was excited. I wanted to tell them how my brother had saved me from the storm and brought me home safe like he promised. "You better take off those wet things," my mother said immediately. "Go on upstairs." As we turned on the stairs, my father said my brother should leave his clothes off when he removed the wet things and remain upstairs in the bathroom. He said that he'd received a call from church, that Wayne had stolen money from the Sunday school collection. My father had also found money missing from the coin collection he kept hidden in our basement. He was going to whip my brother.

The terror I'd felt in the storm returned. My father was a strong but soft-spoken man. I waited in the bathroom with my brother until our father came in with the piece of ironing cord. Wayne and I had been sitting on the rim of the bathtub. He was naked except for his blue jockey shorts. I had dressed myself in my Daniel Boone outfit. I held my brother's hands, telling him not to worry. His saffron body was still marked from the last beating he'd received from our father that summer.

Our father put me out, but I turned and stood at the door. I could see him through the slightly opened door, lashing my brother's legs and back with the cord. At first Wayne fought back and my father lost his balance for a moment near the sink. He righted himself and bore down on my brother, muttering and striking him, lashing him into the floor with the ironing cord. I ran downstairs to my mother in the kitchen. I told her to call the police. I said Daddy was killing Wayne. She did not move. Had she ceased to be our mother? It was a long time that we stood in the kitchen, listening to the lashing and crying upstairs before she said flatly, "He's got to learn. Your father is beating him because he loves him. He's beating him so the police won't have to."

•

The last time I saw my nephew Charles he was fourteen or fifteen years old. I had taken him to lunch at a restaurant inside the John Wanamaker department store, an historic, illustrated text of upward mobility in downtown Philadelphia. I had been told by his mother that he was having trouble in school. This was nothing new. From the time Charles began school, though he entered able to read, write, count, multiply, and divide, he was labeled a problem child by teachers who were either unwilling or unable to address the accelerated needs of a child like Charles in an overcrowded Newark classroom.

At Wanamaker's, I talked to him about school, which he thoroughly hated by then, and about his young life, which he was coming to hate as well. As I listened to him I could hear that he had already arrived at his youth's end. His voice grumbled with loss.

"Listen here, Kid Chocolate," I said, about to launch into my value-of-education talk.

"Don't call me that," he pleaded. "I hate my color. I hate it. I wish I was light-skinned like you, Uncle Don."

"Baby. Man," I said, "first of all, your uncle is *not* light-skinned," and I laughed (*how could I?*), "and even if I were, you're beautiful, man. You've always been beautiful."

But he wouldn't laugh. Not even for me. I think he even hated me a little that afternoon for trying to turn the light on his dark brilliance, since to be conspicuous by one's brilliance in the world to which he was always returned was only, to him, another liability.

I should have shaken him right in that restaurant in the bright, white department store. I should have shaken him. Held him. Rocked him. I should have told him what my great-grandmother told me in one way or another every day we were together, "*You're* the one the ancestors prayed for. *You're* all our hope." I should have told Charles, "You're the one. It belongs to you. You can't give up. You better win. Remember the Kid. Kid Chocolate. Knock that mean shit out. Where's your footwork, baby? Weave. Let me see your combination. Where's that spooky jab-hook-jab? Where's your voodoo?"

But I could see the enemies of my nephews and me knew how to manufacture the antidote to our voodoo and were now able to kill a black man-child's spirit early—and the work had already been accomplished in Charles. It was harder and harder for a black boy in Newark to slip through the system as I had done—which is not at all to suggest that my passage had been an easy one or that this nation sets no other snares for young black men besides ghettos.

Four years later, on Christmas morning in 1991, Charles was living with a thirty-year-old woman, waiting for his first child to be born. "As soon as the baby is born," he was telling me, "I'm going to turn myself in. I can do three years stiff. I'm not saying it's going to be all that easy, Uncle Don, but I can do it. Most of my friends from around the way are already in prison anyway."

"Guess what," he said, after I told him I loved him, that I believed he could still turn his life around, though I had no idea what I was talking about. I think I was in a mildly shocked state. I'd been hearing my own voice speaking to Charles as if from a distance.

"Guess what," Charles said again with a cheerfulness that finally undid me. "Now in Newark they even have surveillance cameras in the street lights."

We both realized it at the same moment: He was already in prison. He's been in prison most of his life. And because he, my heart, is in prison, so am I.

When I hung up I turned off the telephone. I sat at the house until it was dark, listening to records. Jelly Roll Morton. Marvin Gaye. Wayne Shorter. Sam Cooke. The Soul Stirrers. Albert Ayler. Jackie Wilson. Dexter Gordon. It was as though, through the voices of these black male artists I was calling a phalanx of ancestors to rise and protect my nephew. In the evening I made a light meal. I had planned to attend a dinner party. I plugged in the telephone long enough to excuse myself. "I'm fine," I assured my hosts. I said "Merry Christmas" and my hosts and I made plans to get together "soon."

Next, I cleaned my house. I swept dust from corners. I moved furniture, sweeping. I got on my knees and scrubbed the floors in the kitchen and the bathroom. I put clothes I no longer wore away in boxes, ready for the next week's trash collection. I did the wash and changed my bed. When I was done I felt better. I got into bed and fell into a hard sleep.

I awoke when it was still dark, the sheet and blanket twisted around my torso. In my sleep I had been dreaming and conjuring. I had awakened myself shouting, *"I'll get you home."*

The Black Man: Hero

Walter Mosley

1.

I recently watched a TV nature show in which a very small mouse was confronted by a large snake in the dead end of her own hole. The mouse, instead of giving in to fear, leapt on the snake's head, confusing him momentarily, and then ran up the length of his body to escape.

This tiny mammal proved herself as a hero. That is, she faced up to and survived against an overwhelming foe. It was real heroism: life under threat of death as it occurs every day for every species—including our own.

The mouse not only overcame the snake but she soon returned to her nest. You see, that was the only home she had and she was pregnant. That death trap was also a home for her future babies.

Later on I saw the same mouse (or one that looked a lot like her) kill another mouse and eat his brain in order to enrich her milk with the high nutritional content of that organ. That was a bloody scene, and it did not make me like her more, but neither did it alter her as a hero in my mind. Survival is a dirty business and heroes are not saints.

The end of the show was this dainty mother teaching her young to defeat and devour tarantulas, darkling beetles, and scorpions. Not all of the babies would survive this schooling.

It's a tough life.

•

It seems appropriate to begin an essay on black male heroism with a female example. Appropriate because heroes come in all forms and all of those forms are related.

The truth is that heroism isn't defined by male or female, good or bad, black or white. Heroism isn't even limited to humanity. Heroism, to my understanding, is simply survival. And, to make my very human definition even more so, it is really only the attempt to survive.

Heroism is in our blood, life itself—at least in part.

It is not my purpose here to say that black men are more heroic than others. It's not my goal to make saints out of men who are anything but saints. Neither do I want to exclude our mothers or even our enemies from this discussion.

I hope that this gesture of inclusion might invite others to open their minds to include some of the great tragic heroes of American history—African-American men.

2.

Heroism, as a rule, is not a studied thing—one does not risk his own life if he has other options. It's when we are cornered, like that mouse, that we stand up and try to do the impossible. And survival is the most impossible thing because death is waiting for all of us—evilly, without sense, without memory, without even a name.

Without a name.

Black American men and women were robbed of their true identities centuries ago, so long that one might wonder why we haven't gotten over it yet. One might wonder, that is, if they didn't know history, if they hadn't followed the history of the slavery, violence, and humiliation that have been visited upon black bodies and black minds from the seventeenth century up to, and past, Rodney King.

We lost—and have been systematically kept from—our names and our cultural memories for generations. All we have left, then, are our sensations. The senses have been our strongest link to life.

But even in this realm, our experience has often been nearly unbearable. Lives filled with pain, poverty, hunger, extreme violence, and love so harsh that it might just as well have been hatred.

Sometimes the pain would subside—temporarily: *a kind* master inherited the plantation; a moment of elation after the false emancipation.

In those moments we created the blues, we built the South, we wrought prayers that became a foundation for faith. And when we finished, the pain returned and what we had made was taken from us.

Robbed and then robbed again; the scene was set for heroes to emerge. But you must remember—one man's hero is another man's villain. When that mouse murdered another rodent for his brain she didn't do it to be remembered fondly by his clan.

3.

Black women and men have been driven down different paths to heroism toward a shared survival.

Women have been the nucleus, the producers of children and the beasts of burden. Raped and reviled, they became the roots of what culture we could approximate. They held the home and church together and made politics work. They stood strong because there was no place to run with children to be raised. They surpassed themselves with intellect, emotional strength, and, when necessary, with physical strength too.

Men were shorn early from their mothers. We became solitary laborers, silent martyrs of pain. Black men became the economic and cultural warriors of the new world. Juke-joint poets, cowboys, sharecropping fools. Black men danced to the sounds of grunts and wails—all the while whispering our tales on street corners, in elaborate codes that became the secret rhythms of the whole world.

Together black men and women not only survived, we also made names for ourselves. We did the impossible and we wept with joy and pain.

•

These acts of heroism are not chronicled properly in the literature of America. They aren't because we weren't supposed to do all that we've done. Our women were supposed to be the nursemaids of their rapists (an interesting irony), while the men were destined for loose-lipped whining and shuffling, afflicted with large genitals and no intelligence to speak of.

For generations these stereotypes were forced on us. We were humiliated and oppressed. Only in our secret hours and our secret hearts could we make our names. And even in those moments we chafed against each other and fought.

We had great cultural heroes such as Marcus Garvey and Langston Hughes. We had great sports heroes like Jack Johnson and Joe Louis. George Washington Carver rejuvenated the whole South, black and white, with his chemistry.

(There were women, too. There are always black women. Sojourner Truth, Mary McLeod Bethune, Zora Neale Hurston. But I'm talking about men right now.)

These men were all heroes, great not only in their actions but also in their ability to succeed against hatred and the threats of American white racism.

These were great men whose battles to maintain their names are heroic epics worthy of Homer.

These heroes were denied access to the mainstream of culture. Their words went out of print almost as soon as they were published, their deeds were never recorded in "serious" works of history. They were called primitive because they did not have the benefits of Western progress. And so these heroes moved forward like ancient men carrying fire in the night and burning their bodies to protect their burden from the rain. So many stories and dreams were extinguished. But still we survived. We passed on our stories wrapped in the hatred for our oppression.

Hatred because they tried to kill our dreams. Dreaming itself became a threat to life. Dreaming could bring death; success became synonymous with demise.

Hank Aaron received death threats for approaching Babe Ruth's record. Fats Waller and Bessie Smith died because no white doctor would admit them to the hospital.

You wake up one morning and find a snake the size of a fire truck in your home. What do you do?

4.

His name was Raymond but we called him Mouse because he was small and had sharp features. We could have called him Rat because Ray really wasn't very nice, but we liked him and so the name Mouse stuck on him. . . .

These lines were the first words in a series of stories that I've been writing about a fictional L.A. hero named Ezekiel "Easy" Rawlins. Easy is a friendly, introspective kind of guy who believes that he has a right to make it in this country in spite of his color (which is black). He is courageous, articulate, and, most of all, empathetic. He understands pain and wants to make a better world.

When Easy says that Raymond wasn't very nice, he means that Mouse is a remorseless killer who could gut a man and then sit down to a plate of spaghetti. Raymond is a thief, a great lover, fast with a smile and a story. Raymond is cold inside and unable to care about the pain of others.

Mouse and Easy are friends because the world Easy inhabits is hard and unfair. In the Deep South and deep in the ghetto black men often find that they need someone to cover their backs, and Raymond is better coverage than any insurance policy you could buy from the Rock.

I've written quite a bit about Easy and his world. Often Mouse enters into the tale. And when Mouse comes around everyone knows that there's bound to be blood—innocent blood, ignorant blood, usually the blood of black men born from black mothers.

•

When I talk to my readers they often ask me, Why does Easy maintain a relationship with Mouse? My pat answer is that Easy needs Mouse because when somebody's out after him, 911 just won't work. That answer is true enough, but there's another answer that has come to me over the years—Easy chronicles the world of black America in the second half of the twentieth century; he tells of the names we have given ourselves and the oppression we have had to fight in order to keep those names; he tells of heroism in all its hues and is even a hero himself.

But the hero of the world that Easy inhabits is Mouse.

Easy tells you how black men have suffered in America. How we've been beaten, turned away at the door, segregated, and humiliated. In the world that Easy came from, black men have had to learn to do without or to beg. That was his reality. That was everyone's reality. Everyone except Mouse.

You didn't fuck with Mouse. Mouse would kill you. He didn't care if you were white, black, or polka-dotted. He didn't care if you had the muzzle of your gun jammed up against his eyeball. If you went up against Mouse you would wind up dead.

For a group of oppressed people a man like Mouse is the greatest kind of hero. He's a man who will stand up against bone-cracking odds with absolute confidence. He's a man who won't accept even the smallest insult. And for a people for whom insult is as common as air, that's a man who will bring joy.

I know freedom is possible as long as there's a man like Mouse on the streets. That's what someone might say about Mouse. And if you asked that person, *But isn't all that violence wrong?* he would answer, *Sure it's wrong! It's been wrong all these years when they been doin' it to us but that didn't stop it.* And then you say, *But he kills black people as well as whites.* But you probably know the answer before it comes—*I know it, and I hate it. But this is a kind of war. We're fightin' in ourselves and against our great enemy. Mouse got the cops scared. They don't come around him all arrogant and sure of themselves. They don't come around for no reason an' they check their guns twice if they do. They respect Mouse because of the violence he's willing to do. And I tell you, man, respect is worth it at any price.*

•

It isn't only Mouse who is a hero of this kind. When Adam Clayton Powell was giving the white man hell down in Washington, his Harlem constituency backed him all the way. Malcolm X exhorted his followers to use violence when violence was used against them.

Often black men have to cross the white man's rules because we know that those rules never applied to us anyway. The laws and the lawmen were there to protect the property of dominant whites—there was no door for us to make our petitions.

5.

I suppose that it's not much of a coincidence that the first words in Easy's long tale and the first words in this article are both concerned with mice. The irony probably isn't lost either: just because we're small or outnumbered doesn't mean that we can't be great.

This is not a polemic or a call to violence. I'm not saying here what actions I think people should, or shouldn't, take. What I'm trying to do is to let the concept of Black Male Heroes breathe a little bit. Men who suffer violence also study it. If you think there's a man waiting out in the street for you with a club, you have three choices: you can go out there and take your beating, you can run out the back door, or you can try to stand up under the hail of blows—you can try to wrest the club from the hand of your foe, you can turn the tide of force, or you can die trying.

Which is the action of a hero?

That answer is for you, and those who depend on you, to come to.

Pain and Glory:
Some Thoughts on My Father

Quincy Troupe

I grew up in a community of exiles and outcasts, a family of people who were systematically denied the full rights of citizenry in this country with the exception that we had to pay the same amount of taxes as our white American counterparts. This is nothing new. Everybody and his mama knows it by now—the evidence is everywhere, is irrefutable and undeniable.

My father, Quincy Trouppe, Sr., was forced to play baseball in the all-Negro leagues almost all of his career. He made the major leagues for only six months, when he was thirty-nine years of age, because he came along "20 Years Too Soon." My father came along before integration allowed players like Jackie Robinson, Willie Mays, Don Newcombe, Roy Campanella, Monte Irvin, Larry Doby, and Henry Aaron—all products of the old Negro leagues—to show their great gifts to a sometimes appreciative and other times unappreciative nation, by playing in the then almost all-white major leagues. The glory and the pain of his life and how that impacted my life and the lives of others around me is a great story, one filled with anguish, pathos, sadness, and pain. At the same time, it is filled with unbelievable achievements, incredible joy and happiness. It is a complex story of an extremely complex man who, had he been born later, would probably have lived to see his name become instantly recognizable throughout American households, like the names of Willie Mays, Jackie Robinson, Henry Aaron, and Roy Campenella. This is mere speculation on my part, because people are shaped by their times, and who can say with certainty what might have happened had my father been born later, during the generation of those great African-American baseball players—giants!—that I have mentioned above? Maybe he would have been more interested in medicine, or the law, or perhaps even basketball or football, or boxing, another sport at which he excelled. What we *do* know is that my father *was* born twenty years too soon, that he *did* come along before a lot of opportunities were there for African-American men and women. These are the facts, and while he *did* achieve great, even extraordinary things—many say he was the second or third greatest catcher of all time in the old Negro League, after the immortal Josh Gibson—in his lifetime his lack of opportunity to display his vast skills in the major leagues caused him extreme pain that lasted until the day he died.

But my father was more than a baseball player, more than merely a great athlete. He was also a manager of baseball teams and a historian as well, not only of the Negro leagues but of the Puerto Rican, Cuban, Venezuelan, and Mexican baseball leagues; my father played baseball ten or eleven months every year during his career, dividing his time equally between the Negro leagues and Latin America and the Caribbean. My father played on and managed the Kansas City Monarchs and the Cleveland Buckeyes to championships. He was a player and manager in Mexico and in Puerto Rico. He lead Ponce, Puerto Rico to five straight championships as a player and manager. He wrote his thoughts down about many things outside of baseball—about the politics of the day, about the great musicians and entertainers he liked and knew, like Lionel Hampton, Charlie Parker, and others. He loved music and fashion, and he spoke Spanish fluently and a passable French. He was also the first African-American baseball scout for the St. Louis Cardinals, after he finished his playing and managing career. He recommended that the Cardinals sign Roberto Clemente, Juan Marichial, Vic Powers, Willie McCovey, Orlando Cepeda, and other great players of color, but the Cardinals refused to sign these gifted players because of their own rampant organizational racism.

My father was a tall man, six-foot-three, strong and handsome. He was brown-skinned, a very dapper dresser, and wore the latest and best of fashions—wide-lapel suits and sports coats, oversized, with two buttons; loosely draped pants and "bad to the bone," two-toned Foot Joy shoes; wide-brimmed Panama hats and gold Rolex watches. He always drove a new Cadillac or Chrysler. Only the best was good enough for my father. And his smile was so radiant that it stripped the clothes right off the bodies of many a fine lady who loved him dearly and whom he loved too—which probably had something to do with why my father and mother divorced in 1948. That and the arguments they had over whether my mother's mother should live with them or not. My father didn't want her to and my mother did, so my grandmother—"Mama," we called her—stayed. But my father left or was thrown out (according to whose side of the story you believe) when I was nine, an event that traumatized my brother and me for years to come.

My father was a catcher whom some (as I already said) called the second or third greatest catcher of all time in the old Negro Baseball League. The greatest, without a doubt, was Josh Gibson, whom many believed was the greatest catcher that ever lived, regardless of race. My father agreed that Josh was a more powerful hitter than he was, but not a better hitter in terms of average. And he downright disagreed about Josh being a better catcher than he was defensively, or in the way that they both handled pitchers behind the plate. On this, my father—and, I might add, others like Satchel Paige and Monte Irvin—felt he had a decisive upper hand and was better. But baseball legends aren't made by the way a catcher might have handled a bunch of pitchers, or thrown out a score of runners trying to steal second or third, or the style and grace in which they might have caught a bushel load of towering pop flies behind the plate or along the first and third base foul lines. Baseball legends are made in the way that someone swings a bat, and in this area Josh Gibson was head and shoulders above the rest, numero uno, bar none, just as Satchel Paige was as a pitcher and Cool Papa Bell as a base runner. According to eyewitness accounts, Gibson was a colossus, hitting baseballs further than anyone else ever hit them in the history of the game. The only films of those days are the ones my father made, and he never caught Josh on any of them swinging his bat.

Even so, it is as a historian, a recorder of events with his camera (both 8-millimeter home motion pictures and still photographs) and his words—through his memoir, 20 Years Too Soon—that I feel my father will leave his lasting mark on baseball history. The motion pictures taken of the old Negro leagues are the films of my father, the only true historian of his kind during those long-gone days. My father's pictures are the definitive records that we have of those incredible African-American players and their days in the sun! For this alone I am absolutely proud of him.

Once, in the middle to late 1980s, my wife, Margaret, and I were returning from a vacation in Guadeloupe, in the French West Indies. Our American Airlines flight brought us through customs in San Juan, Puerto Rico. Now, I wear my hair in the Jamaican dreadlock style and in many places in the West Indies this is perceived as a sign of a potential drug dealer, or at least of someone who might use drugs. So when the Puerto Rican customs officer saw me coming I sensed him watching me closely.

"Passports and open up all your bags," he demanded of Margaret and me.

I handed over my passport, lifted our bags into his work area and opened all of them. Meantime, the customs officer, an older man perhaps in his late fifties or early sixties, looked at my passport. Suddenly he lifted his eyes, fixing me with an intense gaze.

"Quincy Troupe. Is that your name?"

"Yes," I said, preparing myself for the worst.

"Are you any relations to the baseball catcher named Quincy Trouppe?" he asked. My father added a *p* to his last name because of the way they pronounced it in Latin America: *Troup-pe*!

"Yes," I said. "He is my father."

"Really!" the man said joyously, his eyes widening in great surprise. "He was a great, great player and a very fine man. A gentleman," he said, "I saw him play many, many times. He played on the team in Ponce, Puerto Rico, my hometown, and led them to five straight Puerto Rican championships." The he gave me back my passport, and without even looking through them, told me to close our bags (we didn't have any contraband anyway). Then he called out to all other customs officers: "Hey, this is the son of Quincy Trouppe!" and many of them turned around and saluted me with big smiles.

"Is he still alive?" the man asked.

"Yes," I told him, clear in that moment I was speaking what was most deeply true. "He's still alive."

"Well, when you see your father, you tell him for me that the people of Ponce, Puerto Rico, still remember him and love him for what he did for us while he was here. And you tell him also that if he wants to he can come back to Ponce to live, because there will always be a place for him there. Tell him to come and visit. Will you tell him that for me?"

"Yes, I will tell him," I said, proud as all get-out.

Then he shook my hand and smiled a beautiful smile at me and Margaret as we left his area.

((speak my name))

"Don't forget to tell him that we remember him, Okay?" the man said again as we began moving past customs.

"I won't," I yelled back as we cleared security with the eyes of most of the American passengers who'd heard the conversation on my back. They were probably wondering who in the hell I was, without even a clue of who my father was. This is what I mean when I say most African Americans are outcasts and exiles. If these same passengers had heard the names of Mickey Mantle or Babe Ruth, most of them would have known who was being spoken of.

My father was the only athlete in Missouri's history to make All State in baseball, basketball, and football and win the Open Division Golden Glove Heavyweight Boxing Championship. Had he been a White American with the same talents, accomplishments, and charisma, his sports history and athletic achievements would not be obscure. Even until his death, the state of Missouri never acknowledged his great contributions. But my father is not the only African American with great achievements to suffer this fate in this country. There are countless others whose accomplishments during this nation's history must be, in time, brought out into the light of day for all to see—and they must be celebrated—if we are to ever know our *true* selves as a people and the *real* history of this complex land.

Race, Rage, and Intellectual Development: A Personal Journey

Haki R. Madhubuti

This is not fiction, nor is it complete autobiography. I share this slice of my life only to make a connection to readers that may indeed be impossible to make in any other way. I do not believe in victimology, even though I am a victim. As an intelligent, productive black man, husband, father, poet, teacher, publisher, editor, community cultural worker, political entrepreneur, and "brother," my story, with all its horror and unforgettable heartbreaking insights, is not unusual in the context of growing up in urban America. However, in the final (and hopefully most revealing) analysis, self-examination, self-realization, and self-definition in the context of a known and understood history are the first steps toward enlightened empowerment.

If I extend my hand as a willing victim of American racism (white supremacy) and leave it at that, I do you—the reader—no good and ultimately fail myself. It is easy, yet debilitating and weakening, to be a victim. Being a victim, living as the object of victimization, is the denial of the possibility to become more than others (others who don't like you or your family) think you can become. A victim is not a contributor; rather, he or she is but a childlike participant, looking for the easy and less difficult or responsible way to survive. Victimhood is modern enslavement, with invisible reinforced steel chains firmly placed around one's legs, arms, and mind. Anytime you capture a person's mind, nine times out of ten you have his or her body as well. Victimhood is the prerequisite to self-hatred and dependency, political and economic neutralization, and joyless living. I ask myself two questions every day: (1) What good can I do for myself, my family, my extended family, black people, and others today? (2) How can I continue to rise above the limiting expectations of others, especially my enemies?

I now share these factual slices from my life only to place myself in a cultural and historical context.

I grew up on the Lower East Side of Detroit and the West Side of Chicago, in a family that lived too often from week to week. My mother, sister, and I represented the nucleus of our family. In 1943, my mother migrated from Little Rock, Arkansas, moving, as John O. Killens would say, 'up-South' to Michigan. She came with my father, who stayed long enough to father my sister, who is a year and a half younger than I. I was born in 1942.

Those years, the 1940s and 1950s, were not kind to us, and my father wandered in and out of our lives from the day we hit Detroit. My mother, alone with two children and no skills, ended up working as a janitor in an apartment building owned by a Negro preacher / undertaker. My earliest memory is of her cleaning that three-story, sixteen-unit building each day, carrying garbage cans on her back to the alley once a week. Seldom did I see her without a broom, mop, or washcloth in her hands. By this time I was eight years old, and my sister was seven. We helped as much as possible because we knew that staying in our basement apartment depended upon our keeping the building clean. I did not know then that our housing also depended upon my mother's sexual involvement with the Negro building owner. These encounters took place when we were at school or while we were asleep. My mother began to trade her body quite early in order for us to live. In the 1950s there were few "safety nets" for single women with children. Consequently, my mother became a victim in a white supremacist, monied system which allowed some black men to become surrogate oppressors.

With no family in Detroit, and left to her own limited resources, my mother sought to survive with her children in a way that would have the least possible negative impact on us. However, due to the violent nature of her relationship with the landlord, we stayed in our Lower East Side apartment only until she was able to find work less threatening and taxing on her, physically and psychologically. At least that is what my sister and

I thought. What I've failed to tell you about my mother is that she was probably one of the most beautiful women in the world. I've seen her beauty not only stop traffic but compel men to literally get out of their cars to introduce themselves to her. Her beauty, which was both physical and internal, was something that only the few women she associated with could handle. Women would stare at her with dropped mouths. Her beauty would ultimately place her in an environment that would destroy her.

My mother's next job was that of a barmaid. She started serving drinks at one of the newest and classiest locations in Detroit, Sonny Wilson's. Along with this job came the slow but destructive habit of alcohol consumption. Also, she began to run in very fast company. She was named Miss Barmaid of 1951, carrying with that title all of the superficiality and glitter of the Negro entertainment world of that time. To cut to the bone of all of this is to note rather emphatically that my family's condition of poverty drove my mother into a culture that dictated both her destruction and great misery for my sister and me. By the time I was thirteen, my mother was a confirmed alcoholic and was fast losing her health. When I turned fifteen, she had moved to hard drugs and was not functional most of the time.

My sister, who had just turned fourteen, announced to us that she was pregnant. This was in the late 1950s, and pregnancy out of wedlock was not a common or acceptable occurrence. I went looking for the man who had impregnated her. He was a local gang leader, twenty-one years old, who had as much potential as a husband or father as I did at fifteen. After briefly talking to him about my sister's condition and getting virtually nowhere, I did what most "men" did in similar situations at that time—I hit him. And he, in a rather surgical fashion, responded by literally "kicking my ass." After I reported this to my mother, she, in a drunken stupor, gave me another whipping for getting whipped.

Shortly after that incident, my mother's need for alcohol and drugs increased. She prostituted herself to feed her habit. Many nights I searched Detroit's transient hotels looking for her. Needless to say, I had grown up rather quickly and felt that there was no hope for me or my sister. Just before I turned sixteen, my mother overdosed on drugs and died. She had been physically and sexually abused by someone so badly that we were not able to view her body at her funeral. My sister was pregnant again. By the time she was twenty she had three children; before she was thirty she had six children and had never been married. She has endured a life of pain and difficulty that has often been the exact duplicate of our mother's. To this day she lives in great pain.

I could not cry at my mother's funeral. My heart was cold and my mind was psychologically tired. I felt a quiet feeling of relief and release at her death, but also an underlying tone of guilt. At sixteen, I felt that I had not done enough to save my mother. It was clear to me that her final days had been filled with long hours of tragic suffering over which she had no control. All I could do was watch in confused pain, hostility, anger, resentment, and rage.

At first I could not understand my anger. Why did she have to die so young and so viciously? Why were my sister, her baby, and I alone without help or hope? Why were we so poor? It seemed that my life was one big fight. There was no escape from problems and very little peace. And I guess my mother's death brought a moment of peace. The fight to survive remained uppermost in my mind. Yet it seemed I was being torn apart from the inside. A part of my own fear was connected to how my sister and I were going to survive. I had seen and been a part of too much destruction and death in my young life. I knew that the only person who really cared about our future was me, and that was not enough.

I had few friends, partially because of my economic condition; I had little time to play because I had to work. Also, my social skills were not the best and the path of the loner best suited me at that time. I did not realize then that my solitary existence was to eventually save my life.

Color in America

A part of the problem that my mother, sister, and I faced in America was that our skin color was neither black nor white, but yellow! The unusual beauty that centered in my mother was not only due to the distinctive bone structure of her face and her small, well-connected body. It also had to do with the fact that all of her physical beauty was wrapped in yellow. Yes, we were Arkansas blacks, but my mother could easily have passed for Puerto Rican or dark Italian if she did not have to open her mouth. Her language was Southern Black English, and it carried in it the rural slowness that urban America does not have pity on.

However, it was her beauty, illuminated by very light skin color that attracted the darkest of black men and, of those I remember, the most abusive of black men. They seemed to be steaming in anger, hatred, and internal rage. It seems as though by being with her they were as close to white women as was allowed at that time. And their often intense love/ hate relationship with her was only a mirror of the fight they were having daily with themselves and the white world. They could not touch or physically retaliate against white people, but my mother was there for many of them to play out their deepest hurt in their "loving" and abusive treatment of her. I was not to understand, until much later, the deep color-rage that plagued them and that lay at the surface of my own reality.

Being a "yellow nigger" in urban America was like walking on roasted toothpicks hanging from the mouths of brothers who did not like the taste of wood or understand themselves. Many of the black men who populated my early life used self-defacing language twenty-four hours a day. The two operative words used constantly were "nigger" and "mothafucka." We had not only been seasoned to dislike or hate the "us" in us, but also had adopted the language of self-abuse and self-hatred. I learned early to walk the fine line between black and white. I began to understand the anger, hatred, and rage in me by studying black literature and black music.

What Saved Me?

At thirteen, my mother asked me to go to the Detroit Public Library to check out a book for her. The title of the book was *Black Boy*, by Richard Wright. I refused to go because I didn't want to go anywhere asking for anything "black." The self-hatred that occupied my mind, body, and soul simply prohibited me from going to a white library in 1955 to request from a white librarian a book by a black author, especially one with "Black" in the title.

I and millions of other young blacks were products of a white educational system that at best taught us to read and respect the literary, creative, scientific, technological, and commercial development of others. No one actually told me, "You should hate yourself," however, the images, symbols, products, creations, promotions, and authorities of white America all very subtly and often quite openly taught me white supremacy, taught me to hate myself.

This white supremacist philosophy of life was unconsciously reinforced in black homes, churches, clubs, schools, and communities throughout the nation. Therefore, my refusal to go check out *Black Boy* was only in keeping with a culture that twenty-four hours a day not only denied me and my people fundamental rights and privileges as citizens, but refused to admit that we were whole human beings. Few articulated it in popular culture at that time, but we lived in Apartheid, U.S.A.

However, *Black Boy* had somehow attached itself to my mother's mind and would not let go. I went to the library, found the book on the shelf myself, put it to my chest, found an unpeopled spot, and began to read the book that would profoundly alter my life.

For the first time in my life I was reading words developed into ideas that were not insulting to my own personhood. Richard Wright's experiences were mine, even though we were separated by geography. I read close to half of the book before the library closed. I checked *Black Boy* out, hurried home, went into the room I shared with my sister, and read for the rest of the night. Upon completing *Black Boy* the next morning, I was somehow a different type of questioner in school and at home. I had not totally changed, but the foundation had been planted. Deeply. I became more concerned about the shape of things around me. I also read Wright's *Native Son, Uncle Tom's Children*, and *12 Million Black Voices*. Richard Wright painted pictures with words that connected to the real me. I could relate to Bigger Thomas because his fears, doubts, and internal rage were the same that I experienced. Layers of ignorance were being removed by just opening my mind to a world that included me as a whole person. Wright entered my life at the right time.

After my mother's death, I took the Greyhound to Chicago, where I stayed with an aunt for a while, then I rented a room at the Southside YMCA. I completed high school in Chicago and ended up in St. Louis, Missouri, where I joined the United States Army.

The military was the poor boy's employment. On the way to basic training at Fort Leonard Wood, Missouri, I was reading Paul Robeson's *Here I Stand*. When we arrived at boot camp, the white, middle-thirtyish drill sergeant ordered us off the bus. We were about two hundred men. Three black men, including myself, and one hundred ninety-seven white men. The black men had all joined voluntarily, but most of the white men had been drafted. This was 1960, and the Army was practicing "integration."

As I stepped off the bus, the white drill sergeant sighted Paul Robeson's face on my book and snatched it from my hand. He pulled me out of line and barked into my face, "What's your Negro mind doing reading this black communist?" Of course, many thoughts ran through my head as potential responses to his question. This was the first time I had heard a double negative used so creatively. The drill sergeant ordered all of us up against the bus and commenced to tear the pages from the book, giving a page to each recruit, and telling the recruits to use the pages for toilet paper. By this time I was questioning my own sanity about joining the military, and examining my options.

Luckily, I was also reading John O. Killens's *And Then We Heard the Thunder*, a powerful and telling book about black men in Europe's War on the World Number Two (commonly referred to as World War II). What I learned from Killens was the importance of using one's time wisely and never to speak from the top of one's head in anger when outnumbered. As I stood, lips closed, cold and shaking with fear, anger, and loneliness—while the sergeant destroyed my copy of Robeson's work—I decided four things that would stay with me for the rest of my life:

1. I would never, never again apologize for being black. I am who I am, I realized then, and if black literature has taught me anything, it clarified for me that I was a man of African descent in America serving time in the United States Army rather than the United States prison system.

2. I would never again put myself in a cultural or intellectual setting where people outside of my culture or race would know more about me than I knew about myself. This meant that I had to go on the offense and put myself on a reeducation program that prepared me internally as an African in America, as a black man.

3. I was in the United States Army because I was black, poor, and ignorant of the forces that controlled my life and the lives of other men— black and white—with whom I was to train. These forces were racial, economic, and political, and I needed accurate information on all of them. While many of the other brothers in my platoon searched for fun, I visited the libraries. Few could understand why I chose to be alone with books. The reason was that I found new friends, uncritical friends, in the literature. I was a sponge. Reading became as important as water and food.

4. If *ideas* were that powerful and could cause such a reaction, then I was going to get into the *idea* business. For that drill sergeant to act so violently against a book that contained ideas that he probably did not even understand was frightening. He was reacting to the image and idea of Paul Robeson that had been created by monied, political, and mass-media white power brokers.

From that day on I have been on a mission to understand the world and to be among the progressive men who want to change it for the benefit of the majority who occupy it.

My two years and ten months in the military were essentially my undergraduate education. I read close to a book a day, concentrating in history, political science, black literature, and (of course) black poetry—the written / oral music of our people. I read and reread, studied the history and culture of black people, and extended my study into the areas of political economy. One of the most influential writers to impact my thinking was W. E. B. Du Bois.

Du Bois had already articulated that the problem of the twentieth century would be color. As I studied his work, I began to see possibilities for myself for two reasons: (1) Du Bois was a high-yellow black man who had devoted his life to the uncompromising development and liberation of black people, and (2) his writing represented liberating medicine for my mind. All of Du Bois's work, whether in sociology, politics, fiction, or poetry, led to the reconstruction of the black mind. The passage that both freed me intellectually and gave meaning to the rage that continued to tear me apart came from *The Souls of Black Folk*:

> After the Egyptian and the Indian, the Greek and Roman, the Teuton and Mongolian, the Negro is a sort of seventh son, born with a veil and gifted with second sight in this American world—a world which yields him no true self-consciousness, but only lets him see himself through the revelation of the other world. It is a peculiar sensation, this double consciousness, this sense of always looking at one's self through the eyes of others, of measuring one's soul by the tape of a world that looks on in amused contempt and pity.
>
> One ever feels his twoness—an American, a Negro; two souls, two thoughts, two unreconciled strivings; two warring ideals in one dark body, whose dogged strength alone keeps it from being torn asunder. The history of the American Negro is the history of this strife—this longing to attain self-conscious manhood to merge his double self into a better and truer self.

Yes, I knew that I was different and black. However, it was Du Bois's analysis that brought me to where I could appreciate and begin to reconcile the different "selves" in me. Color and psychology, color and history, color and enslavement, color and politics, color and economics, color and rage, took on new meanings for me. I came to understand that the white images and symbols that assigned me to certain roles in life had nothing to do with the quality and content of my history or my mind.

My search for authenticity was being led by the literature of W. E. B. Du Bois and others.

However, Du Bois's *Black Reconstruction* and *The World and Africa* were the two books that ultimately unlocked my brain and liberated my own thought. Dr. Du Bois was a black intellectual who remained true to his calling in that he not only wrote and documented history, he, by his actions, via the NAACP (National Association for the Advancement of Colored People) and other progressive organizations, tried to change the world for the best. He went to his grave in Ghana in 1963 at the age of ninety-five, never giving in to the "long and comfortable compromises." Du Bois was a political activist for life.

I left the military in August 1963. In September of that same year, four little girls were murdered in Birmingham, Alabama. They were bombed in their church while praying to a God who did not even look like them. This violent act against our children confirmed for me the course of my life. For two years and ten months, I had been trained to be a killer in the U.S. Army. Later I realized that all the targets I shot at were either black or colored, however, I knew even then the color of the people who were blowing up our children. To this day, they, and the millions of brain-mismanaged Negroes that they control, continue to tapdance on the dreams of our children.

I am against dancing to and entertaining the enemies of the world. As a young man, I reeducated myself. The poet-writer that I've become is directly connected to my education and political involvement over the last thirty-four years. Each day I also realize that I too am an activist for life, and that serious struggle and organizing will only bear fruit if it is ongoing, institutionalized, rethought, updated, involves the young, remains honest, and is open-minded and combative. Struggle must be renewing and productive if it is to grow. Additionally, one must struggle with like-minded people.

The rage that I and most sane people feel toward the death and human damage inflicted upon the weak by this society and others must be channeled and released in a healthy manner. Otherwise we internalize it or let it loose on those persons closest to us.

Often our lives may seem like pieces of slave fiction; however, by seriously studying history and political economy, we can come to understand that one way we can have an impact on the nightmare that covers the lives of most people is through organized struggle at every level of human involvement. If such cultural work is to be fruitful, we must con-

((speak my name))

centrate on that which we are *for* as opposed to only fighting and articulating that which we are *against*.

This is not rhetoric or playground boasting. If the condition of our
people and that of the majority of the world's people is not recognized as
proof enough of the destructive path we are on, we are truly lost. Our
greatest tasks remain (1) discovering a way to neutralize racism and
oppression without becoming racists and oppressors ourselves, (2) destroying an abusive economic system while trying to create something
better, (3) reversing destructive habits with the knowledge of that which
is best and better. We cannot build on the "anti" only. I am African, I am
black (a political, cultural, and color designation in the U.S.), even though
my skin complexion is what is loosely described as high yellow. Yet, to
look at me any time of the day or night few would conclude that I am any
person other than one of African descent. I am clear about this fact just
as I am certain that all black people descended from the continent of Africa. That this is still debatable in some quarters speaks highly of the
global effects of white world supremacy propaganda (see Frances Cress
Welsing's *The Isis Papers: The Keys to the Colors*, John Henrik Clarke's *Notes
for an African World Revolution*, Marimba Ani's *Yurugu: An African-
centered Critique of European Cultural Thought and Behavior* and Chancel-
lor Williams's *The Destruction of Black Civilization*).

I have traveled to Africa at least eight times. I am not sure of the number because I stopped counting after I realized that my journeys were
about me centering myself, rather than going to give papers, participate
in international gatherings, or to read my poetry. Africa had become the
source, a connecting spirit that revitalized me, a place where I could
gather new knowledge and the best cure for Africa romanticism.

Again, it was the literature that pointed me to Africa—Du Bois, yes,
but also Carter G. Woodson, Alaine Locke, Langston Hughes, Marcus
Garvey, and Richard Wright (especially his 1954 book on Ghana and
Kwame Nkrumah, *Black Power*). My life changed as the knowledge I absorbed lifted me into the African world community of builders, creators,
inventors, and producers. Reading and studying, reflecting and inter-
nalizing the words and works of black (African) authors represented a
type of cultural food that would shape me into the culturally conscious
man that I am today. Ideas about the African (black) reality became liberating food. I consumed black (African) ideas and literature like a desert
taking to raindrops. I learned to stop making excuses for black people as
well as for whites. It should be a given fact that everything black is not

right. There are many good white people in the world—the problem is that they are in the minority and do not hold power.

There is no separation between my cultural self and my political, professional, business, familial, and writer selves. I am one, and I am clear—always open for new knowledge, ideas, and revelations, but firmly anchored and connected to the millions of African (black) women and men that led the way for my enlightenment and normalcy. Those of us that understand this heritage must be at the forefront of creating, producing, and building that which we are for and of sharing such development with our families, extended families, community, and world. It is easy to be against any number of ideas and institutions. The larger task is to fight that which we consider evil by building that which we consider good, just, and correct.

The role of the black intellectual is not only to understand the text but to write his/her version of the story, not only to teach the young the positive objectives of life but to be involved at a community level—where theory is often untested—in making real and substantive, long-term changes in the lives of those who are truly suffering.

This is transforming work. It is moral and ethical work. The monetary rewards are few, if any. However, the love generated by the hope in the eyes of our children as a result of such work is for me the best payment. We must give our children a fighting chance in a world that long ago counted them out, diminished their chances of success to below zero. To see the yes in their eyes is also to hear the yes in our own heartbeats. This is why the drum is our magical instrument: you cannot kill the beat of hungry hearts.

Rickydoc: The Black Man as Hero

Arthur Flowers

I am Flowers of the delta clan Flowers and the line of O Killens. I wanna be a hero. I wanna be a hero bad.

In fact, I think everyman is potentially a hero. I think that deep down inside, where he really lives and rarely shows, any man worth his keep considers himself a hero, a champion of the tribe, in shield and spear, with his finger plugged into the dike that was assigned to him.

•

How I got to this questionable and possibly foolish state of mind is traceable. First off it's personal. It's in me to be a hero. Too many marvel comics, delta myths, legends and tall tales when I was a kid.

Furthermore, I come from a heroic line, the delta clan Flowers. My mama and my daddy were heroes, and so too are a great many of my relatives. My mama was the flashy type, she never accepted the status quo of the old south. A race woman, Im proud to say, who never left a battle undone. My daddy was a quieter model, a classic crusty old general practitioner who felt a distinct responsibility for the health of all the colored folks of south Memphis. It's said in old Memphis that half the kids on the southside still belong to Doc Flowers cause they were never paid for. (I love that line.) And my mama and daddy passed that sense of social responsibility on to me.

An equally significant part of my state of mind is that Im a child of the 6os. Flower Power. Civil Rights. Black Power. The whole bit. I remember the day the King was killed, my senior year at Hamilton High School in Memphis. I remember pitched battles with the police the next day. We would charge them with sticks and stones and they would drive us back with batons and tear gas but they couldnt come on the school grounds. We'd retreat, regroup, and charge again. I had just been elected Mr. Brain of the senior class and Ms. Martha P. Flowers, a notoriously demanding english teacher and another one of the delta clan Flowers heroes, told us that anybody who walked out of her class to join the street battle outside wouldnt graduate. The whole class looked at me as if to say, She's your aunt, what you gon' do, Mr. Brain? What could I do? I upped and walked (what kind of graduation would it be without Mr. Brain?) and the rest of the honors class followed me. Standing at the crossroads. One of my first steps in the Struggle. The Almighty Movement. A luta continua.

And, understand, the 6os were more than street battles or sex, drugs, and rock 'n' roll, the 6os were about "commitment." We cared. We tried. It was important (and doable) for us to "make a better world." It was important to "save the race." And it still is.

For all our excesses, we felt a responsibility to be forces for good and drummajors for righteousness. And still do.

And then there was Nam. In the middle of my black power thing, along came Nam. I brought back from Nam a sense of racial solidarity that can never be broken. Never. My commitment is absolute. I was already a black militant when I got there, all afro and attitude. And Nam was, shall we say, a hostile environment. Not just the war, but blackfolks was still being dumped upon. Being dumped upon in Nam was potentially lethal. Blackmen in Nam responded with a sense of racial solidarity that was phenomenal. Any blackman of my generation who experienced what we called blackinization will testify. I tried to in my first novel and didnt touch it. We survived—brotherme, brotherblood, brotherblack. I been a warrior ever since. I have been at times a chief and at times a spear-carrier. I've often stumbled and tacticswise I've zigged and zagged, but by Ogun's beard I'ma live and die a warrior.

The next jewel in my shield was John O Killens and the Guild literary movement. One day I will have to sit down and tell the tale of John O Killens, cause he dont get nowhere near the respect he deserves. I tell you the half aint never been told. John O Killens and the Guild school taught me not only how to be a writer but how to be a historical force. An ideological orchestrator. A master player. Even more, John O filled me with the "divine responsibility" of a master of the word.

John O's luminous love for blackfolk and all humanity gathered unto him a cadre of young writers whose destinical influence has not yet begun to be felt. John O taught us how to be "longdistance runners." John O gave us vision.

•

So by the time I come to the hoodoo way, Im ready to play. Learned my early hoodoo licks from Ishmael. Mumbo Jumbo & Conjure. Literary hoodoo I call it. Efforts of mystically inclined black writers such as Zora Neale, Ishmael, and myself to manifest hoodoo, the indigenous African-American spiritual tradition, through our works. To operate as contemporary shamans & medicine-workers. Cultural custodians. Archetypic guides and guardians of the tribe. Its destiny and its generations. Conjurors & Rootdoctors.

Using longgame vision to peer as far into the future as possible. Determine what challenges the tribe will have to face. Prepare the tribal soul to meet them.

The hoodoo way. The most westernized of the family of African religious retentions in the Newworld. Voodoo, Santería, Macumba, Ocha, Obeah, et al. The hoodoo way had degenerated into a primarily magical system. Until Ishmael made it a functional 20th-century Afrocentric ideology.

An African Way of God. Neither hoodoo nor African religion in general are respected in the world spiritual tradition. There are those, even righteous blackfolk, who would passionately declare there is no such thing as an African Way of God. We disagree. Antiquated perhaps, outdated perhaps. Contemporary hoodoo consequently striving to update the hoodoo way. Update the entire multitudinous African religious tradition. Synergize and refine it. Illuminate it. Make it a contemporary instrument of spiritual and political redemption. Compatible with the 21st-century mind. And soul.

Ase.

•

We of the Hoodoo Way understand. The way of the spirit is a more profound instrument of redemption than that of politics. Jesus has turned more heads than Marx ever thought of.

The test of a good healthy spiritual tradition: its adherents lead good healthy lives. Brimming with strength and meaning, beauty and grace. They build good healthy communities.

Look at the condition of blackfolks worldwide. Everywhere blackfolks on the bottom of their respective societies. Cant blame Everywhere on nobody else. Aint nobody's fault but ours. A race that must look deep inside. Find and finesse the weaknesses that have crippled us in global competition. Transform them into strengths.

Each person, each generation, has its own tasks. Its own mission to be found.

Increasingly clear, is it not? Ongoing struggles against competitive and/ or hostile groups must always be subordinate to the struggle within. A strong, illuminated people cope with and adapt to any assault. Human or natural. KKK or AIDS. A strong people cope, a weak people fold. We generally fold. Genocidally weak. Mere survival no longer sufficient. If it ever was.

For this is. A time of testing. Gods instrument. Forged. Tempered upon the anvil of adversity.
For life is Trial. & Tribulation. And it is only through adversity. That we are truly challenged.

Do what you do. With style and grace. Maintain serenity of purpose. Savor life's fleeting joys.

For we must. Ennoble ourselves. Find again the high ground. Heal thyself. Be the great and mighty people we were meant to be—the Children of the Sun.

·

Look at the tribal soul. Manifested as a given culture's spiritual tradition. The primary instrument through which perceived survival knowledge passed from generation to generation. All other efforts incremental. Swallowed by the sheer immensity. And comprehensiveness. Of our problems. Of life. A strong spiritual tradition will permeate every aspect of our lives. All our efforts. Enhanced. Work dem roots, chi'dren. Rootdoctors all.

Not a couple of months, years, or even a lifetime. Orchestrating the tribal soul, you thinking in generations. Longgame.

What we know in our heads, our children will know in their hearts, our generations in their souls.

Rootwork. The thought becomes the act—the act becomes the reality.

·

Shalabongo: Gods-Will be done.

Longgame. Geas by rickydoc: not only responsibility for shaping our own destiny but also responsibility for all the peoples of the planet. Enhancement of the human condition. And even further. The orchestration of cosmic harmony. Spiritual responsibility equals spiritual power. Y'all listen up now. Stay with me. Dis here de old rootdoctor. And he talking big truth: to lead you must serve.

Firstborn. Living ancestors of humanity. Some of the most spiritual people on the planet. But the essence has been warped. Witness dysfunctional cultures and lifestyles.

We must reclaim our legacy as Gods Instrument. Strive to become the most illuminated peoples on the planet. In the cosmos. Humanity's spiritual guides.

The chosen people syndrome.

A greater destiny for all.

Strive, then, o ye firstborn. To be the most righteous peoples on the planet. Gods true chosen. Be ye of the righteous and God shall watch over you with a special care. For God doth love a righteous people.

Oluddumare Mojuba: Gods Blessings on us all.

•

                              Im from the oldschool. If a race is conquered and oppressed their men were weak. Say what? Thats right. Weak men. Including me.
So just what does it mean to be a strong black man?

Rickydoc's Generic ShortList: *commitment and responsibility. love. compassion. power. quiet composed game. hard, strategic work. right thought, right words, right deeds. magnanimity in abundance. honor. discipline. service. humility. dignity. righteousness. tolerance, tolerance.* I could go on, etc., & on. Basically the old boy scout oath. Basically saying, Carry yourself well, brother.

But in the final analysis I keep getting back to a personal thing. Each man has to decide for himself. In his own context. Just what it means. To be a strong black man.

Heroship in front of the multitudes is easy pickings. The real work of heroship is often done in the quiet spaces. Drudgery. Often alone, unsung, unappreciated, and without pay. Simply because it is the right and righteous thing to do.

History sees everything, God sees all.

Flashy myself, I admire the quiet ones. The dependable brothers who. Quietly take care of business. Fathers who stay, love, honor & obey, raise families, man block associations, vote, build institutions. Stable secure types who *do*. The real work.

Me as hero? Well. More joke than not. Artist and mystic. Delta Griot. Bluesman. Hoodooman. Sorcerer & Wouldbe Prophet. Being strong for me just aint the same as for other folk. It aint. I got unique struggles. So I got to assume there is no one way. To be a strong blackman.

Just do it.

•

Irie. All tings.

Most folk dont understand good longgame. Cant let that concern you. Got to play for real and not to the gallery. As de High Hoodoo once wrote, "Just cause you cant see the stones dont mean I aint building."

Kinda embarrassing. To be out here. Selling these wolf tickets like this. But thats I job. Both conjuration and ideological orchestration. I got to prepare the ground for my seed, I got to make my trip real in the world, I got to publicly validate the hoodoo way in the world spiritual tradition.

I am. Not only a writer and a spokesperson of my culture and my age. I am. The Voice of Oluddumare.

•

Dont care if you understand it. Dont care if you believe it. Magic and prophecy work both best in the shadows of mystery. Im just a ole regulation delta hoodooman doing my job best I know how. An ideological orchestrator strategically placing my destinic vision into the historical record and leaving a message for future generations:

I am Rickydoc
when you need me
call me
I will come.

Contributors

HOUSTON A. BAKER, JR., is a professor of English and the Albert M. Greenfield Professor of Human Relations at the University of Pennsylvania, where he also directs the Center for the Study of Black Literature and Culture. Among his many publications are *The Journey Back: Blues, Ideology, and Afro-American Literature*; *Modernism and the Harlem Renaissance*; *Black Studies, Rap and the Academy*; and *Workings of the Spirit*.

AMIRI BARAKA has written twelve volumes of poetry and eight works of nonfiction. His novels are *The System of Dante's Hell* and *Tales*. His many plays have been produced internationally for more than twenty-five years. He has edited a number of anthologies, most notably *Black Fire* and *Confirmation*. He lives in Newark, New Jersey.

DERRICK BELL, author of *Confronting Authority*, *And We Are Not Saved*, and *Faces at the Bottom of the Well*, is currently a visiting professor at New York University Law School.

DON BELTON, author of *Almost Midnight*, teaches at Macalester College. A former reporter for *Newsweek*, he has been a fellow at MacDowell, Yaddo, and the Rockefeller Center in Bellagio, Italy.

CECIL BROWN was born in North Carolina and educated at Columbia University and the University of Chicago. He is the author of three books, including his critically acclaimed novel *The Life and Loves of Mr. Jiveass Nigger*. He recently received his Ph.D. in English and is currently teaching at the University of California at Berkeley.

LOUIS EDWARDS is the author of the novel *Ten Seconds*. He has won both a Guggenheim Fellowship and the Whiting Writer's Award. NAL/Dutton will publish his novel *N* in 1996. He lives in New Orleans, Louisiana.

QUINN ELI, a native of the Bronx, New York, has written about books for *Emerge*, *Black Warrior Review*, and other publications. He is a regular contributor to the *Philadelphia Inquirer* and has recently completed a collection of short stories. He lives in Philadelphia.

TREY ELLIS, the author of *Home Repairs* and *Platitudes*, lives in Santa Monica, California.

ARTHUR FLOWERS is the author of *DeMojo Blues* and *Another Loving Blues*. He teaches writing at Medgar Evers College in Brooklyn, New York.

HENRY LOUIS GATES, JR., is the author of *Colored People* and *The Signifying Monkey*, for which he received an American Book Award. He has edited several works, including *Our Nig* by Harriet Wilson, the thirty-volume *Schomburg Library of Nineteenth Century Black Women's Writings*, and *The Works of Zora Neale Hurston*. He is the W. E. B. DuBois Professor of the Humanities and Chair of the Department of Afro-American Studies at Harvard University.

ESSEX HEMPHILL is the editor of *Brother to Brother: New Writings by Black Gay Men*. He is the author of *Ceremonies: Prose and Poetry*, winner of a 1992 ALA literature award.

ISAAC JULIEN is a critic and filmmaker whose work addresses issues of race and gay sexuality. Among his most recent productions are *Looking for Langston*, *Young Soul Rebels*, *Black and White in Color*, *The Attendant*, and *Darker Side of Black*.

ROBIN D. G. KELLEY is a professor of history and Africana at New York University and the author of *Hammer and Hoe: Alabama Communists During the Great Depression* (1990) and *Race Rebels: Culture, Politics, and the Black Working Class* (1994).

RANDALL KENAN's first novel, *A Visitation of Spirits*, was published in 1989. His collection of stories, *Let the Dead Bury Their Dead*, was nominated for the 1993 National Book Critics Award and won the Whiting Award.

JERROLD LADD is a single parent living in Dallas, Texas. He has written for the *Dallas Morning News*, the *Philadelphia Inquirer*, *Texas Monthly*, and North Carolina's *Sun Magazine*. A commentator for National Public Radio and a recipient of the Robert F. Kennedy Journalism Award, Ladd is the author of *Out of the Madness: From the Projects to a Life of Hope*.

DANY LAFERRIERE was born in Port-au-Prince, Haiti, where he practiced journalism under Duvalier. He went into exile in Canada in 1978. In 1985 he published his first novel, *How to Make Love to a Negro (Without Getting Tired)*, which was a bestseller both in the original French and in English (1987) and was made into a feature film. His other books are *Eroshima* (1991); *An Aroma of Coffee* (1993); and *Dining with the Dictator* (1994). Laferriere now divides his time between Montreal and Miami.

WILLIAM HENRY LEWIS is the author of *In the Arms of Our Elders*, a short story collection. He teaches writing at Mary Washington College in Fredericksburg, Virginia.

REGINALD MCKNIGHT won the O. Henry and the Kenyon Review Award for Literary Excellence for the story "The Kind of Light that Shines on Texas." The author of the novel *I Get on the Bus*, he is also the recipient of a National Endowment for the Arts Grant for Literature. His first collection of short stories, *Moustapha's Eclipse*, was awarded the 1988 Drue Heinz Literary Prize.

HAKI R. MADHUBUTI, writer, poet, and lecturer, is the author of *Black Men: Obsolete, Single, and Dangerous* and the founder of the Third World Press. He is professor of English and director of the Gwendolyn Brooks Center at Chicago State University. Madhubuti lives in Chicago with his wife and children.

CLARENCE MAJOR is the author of five novels, most recently *My Amputations* and *Such Was the Season*, and several volumes of poetry. He is the editor of *Calling the Wind: Twentieth-Century African-American Short Stories*.

BRUCE MORROW is an associate director of the Teachers &Writers Collaborative in New York and an advisory editor of *Callaloo*. Currently, he is coediting an anthology of black gay men's short fiction, to be published by Avon Books in 1996.

WALTER MOSLEY, a native of Los Angeles, now lives in New York City. His first Easy Rawlins mystery, *Devil in a Blue Dress*, was an immediate international success, nominated for an Edgar Award, selected by two book clubs, and published in seven languages. The equally acclaimed *A Red Death*, *White Butterfly*, and *Black Betty* followed. Heralded by President Bill Clinton as his favorite mystery author, Mr. Mosley's next novel is *RL's Dream*. *Devil in a Blue Dress* will soon be a major motion picture starring Denzel Washington.

ALBERT MURRAY is the author of several collections of essays, including *The Omni-Americans* and *Stomping the Blues*, as well as an autobiographical work, *South to a Very Old Place*. He lives in New York City.

DAVID NICHOLSON is an assistant editor of the *Washington Post Book World* and the founding editor of the magazine *Black Film Review*.

RICHARD PERRY is the author of the novels *No Other Tale to Tell* and *Montgomery's Children*. He lives in Englewood, New Jersey.

QUINCY TROUPE is a poet, journalist, and professor of creative writing at the University of California, San Diego, in La Jolla. His essays and articles have appeared in the *Village Voice*, *Spin*, *Musician*, and many other publications. He is the editor of *James Baldwin: The Legacy* and coauthor of the bestselling and award-winning *Miles: The Autobiography*. Troupe is currently at work on a Hollywood film adaptation of the Miles Davis biography.

JOHN EDGAR WIDEMAN is the author of ten highly acclaimed works of fiction, including *Fever*, *Damballah*, *Hiding Place*, *Sent for You Yesterday*, and *Philadelphia Fire*, the last two of which won the prestigious PEN/

Faulkner Award. He is also the author of two works of nonfiction, *Brothers and Keepers* and *Fatheralong* (both National Book Critics Award finalists). He lives in Amherst, Massachusetts.

DENNIS A. WILLIAMS is the author of *Crossover*, a novel, and coauthor with John A. Williams of *If I Stop I'll Die: The Comedy and Tragedy of Richard Pryor*. He teaches writing at Cornell University in Ithaca, New York.

AUGUST WILSON is at work on a series of plays about the black experience in America. He is the recipient of many awards, including Pulitzer Prizes for *Fences* and *The Piano Lesson*. He lives in Seattle, Washington.

JOE WOOD is a writer living in Brooklyn, New York. He writes a column for the *Village Voice* and is the editor of *Malcolm X: In Our Own Image*.

BAKER "On the Distinction of 'Jr.'" by Houston A. Baker, used by permission of the author.

BARAKA "The Black Family" by Amiri Baraka, used by permission of the author.

BELL "The Sexual Diversion: The Black Man/Black Woman Debate in Context" by Derrick Bell, used by permission of the author.

BROWN "Go Home to Your Wife" by Cecil Brown, used by permission of the author.

EDWARDS "Albert Murray on Stage: An Interview" by Louis Edwards, used by permission of the author.

ELI "A Liar In Love" by Quinn Eli, from *Testimony*, edited by Natasha Tarpley. Copyright © 1994 by Natasha Tarpley. Reprinted by permission of Beacon Press.

ELLIS "How Does It Feel to Be a Problem?" by Trey Ellis, reprinted by permission of the author.

FLOWERS "Rickydoc: The Black Man as Hero" by Arthur Flowers, used by permission of the author.

GATES Excerpt from *Colored People* by Henry Louis Gates, Jr. Copyright © 1994 by Henry Louis Gates, Jr. Reprinted by permission of Alfred A. Knopf, Inc.

HEMPHILL & JULIEN Interview with Essex Hemphill by Isaac Julien with Don Belton, used by permission of Essex Hemphill and Isaac Julien.

KELLEY "Confessions of a Nice Negro, or Why I Shaved My Head" by Robin D. G. Kelley, used by permission of the author.

KENAN "Mr. Brown and the Sweet Science" by Randall Kenan, used by permission of the author.

LADD "Cool Brother," excerpt from *Out of the Madness: From the Projects to a Life of Hope*, reprinted by permission of Warner Books/New York. Copyright © 1994 by Jerrold Ladd.

For all St. Joe students
and in appreciation for
their Catholic education.

Patricia Mc Neal

Harder than War

Harder than War

Catholic Peacemaking in Twentieth-Century America

PATRICIA MCNEAL

Rutgers University Press

New Brunswick, New Jersey

Library of Congress Cataloging-in-Publication Data

McNeal, Patricia F.
    Harder than war : Catholic peacemaking in twentieth-century
America / Patricia McNeal.
        p.   cm.
    Includes bibliographical references and index.
    ISBN 0-8135-1739-7 (cloth) — ISBN 0-8135-1740-0 (pbk.)
        1. Peace—Religious aspects—Catholic Church—History—20th
century.   2. Catholic Church—Doctrines—History—20th century.
I. Title.
BX1795.P43M36   1992
261.8'73'09730904—dc20   91-16814
                                                                CIP

British Cataloging-in-Publication information available

For my sons,
Patrick and Mark,
and their generation,
that they may be peacemakers

Contents

Preface

THIS BOOK BEGAN TWENTY years ago when I wrote my doctoral dissertation, "The American Catholic Peace Movement, 1928–1972." During the intervening years three significant changes took place that led me to update my research and write a more comprehensive study of American Catholic peacemaking in the twentieth century.

The first change took place in 1983 when the American Catholic hierarchy began to assume an important role in American public life by issuing pastoral letters that addressed society's main social problems. By explicitly stating the church's moral position and values, the hierarchy hoped not only to educate its members but also to occupy a central place in the public discourse about public policy in the United States, and thus to make a distinctive contribution to the life of a pluralistic society. The pastoral that received the greatest press coverage and discussion was *The Challenge of Peace: God's Promise and Our Response*. In this document, the Catholic hierarchy fully embraced the legitimacy of Catholic peacemakers who rejected the just war doctrine and looked to the Gospels as the source of their pacifist and nonviolent positions.

The second change was the historical study of the Vietnam War. A plethora of books on Vietnam filled the marketplace and a new field of study was created. Two recent political studies of the antiwar movement of the Vietnam era—Charles DeBenedetti and Charles Chatfield, *An American Ordeal: The Antiwar Movement of the Vietnam Era*, and Melvin Small, *Johnson, Nixon, and the Doves*—made me acutely aware of how significant and distinctive a force religion was in the American Catholic peace movement when compared with the broader antiwar movement. Though Catholic pacifists were always

ix

attempting to stop a war or the threat of a war, they were also trying to respond to Christ's call to be peacemakers and to bring forth a peacemaking response from the institutional church.

The final change was the rise of neoconservatism following the election of Ronald Reagan to the U.S. presidency and the election of Pope John Paul II to the papacy. The continual military buildup and displays of force and intervention in our government's foreign policy and the continual retrenchment from Second Vatican Council reforms on the part of important Vatican leaders have created a climate wherein the "neoconservatives" whose right-wing politics are more important than their Christian beliefs are now heralded as "the best and the brightest" in the American Catholic church. This book attempts to set the historical record straight about American Catholic peacemakers.

The purpose of this study is to document the growth of pacifism, nonviolence, and nuclear pacifism within the American Catholic community and assess their impact on the church and the nation. Support for pacifism among American Catholics is a relatively new phenomenon. Catholic pacifism that opposed all war did not emerge in the United States until the 1930s when Dorothy Day, cofounder of the Catholic Worker movement, proclaimed it. Prior to Day's proclamation, those Catholics who opposed war based their opposition on the just war doctrine. Among Roman Catholics the pacifism of the primitive Christian church, like other features of the radical Gospel, largely disappeared with the Age of Constantine. The just war doctrine with subsequent modifications remained the dominant Catholic position on war from its formulation by Augustine until the Second Vatican Council. In 1983, the National Conference of Catholic Bishops in the document *The Challenge of Peace* established pacifism, nonviolence, and nuclear pacifism as well as the just war doctrine as valid positions for Catholics in the United States to hold. The document stated: "We believe the two perspectives support and complement one another, each preserving the other from distortion."[1]

Dorothy Day was the one person most responsible for the shift in American Catholic thought away from the just war doctrine toward pacifism. By the end of World War II, she had added to the Catholic theological agenda the concepts of pacifism, conscientious objection, and nuclear pacifism. Although she did not articulate a theological rationale for these positions—this would evolve in the writings of

Thomas Merton—she did not hesitate to proclaim her pacifism as a moral response generated by the teaching of the Gospel. Her witness challenged the church's theology.

The military tactics of obliteration and atomic bombing during World War II also challenged the relevance of the just war doctrine to modern warfare. These military tactics violated the just war principle of proportionality and the principle of "double effect," which applied to the killing of noncombatants. The tensions between pacifists who contend that the just war doctrine is no longer relevant to modern warfare, and the just war theorists, who contend it is the only moral criteria available to address government decision makers on public policy issues of war and peace, is a dominant theme in the history of American Catholic peacemaking.

The first official Catholic peace organization in the United States (1927) was the Catholic Association for International Peace (CAIP), an elitist lay organization under clerical leadership and financially supported by the American hierarchy. Working independently of the broader American peace movement, CAIP operated out of an internationalist vision that opposed interwar isolationism and sought to awaken in Catholics a sense of collective responsibility as well as support for a world organization. This view depended on a concert of power in the political realm, the degree of collective cooperation among nations determining the type of security that could be devised to prevent war. The CAIP looked to the nation state as the arbiter and authority on issues of war and peace. Its approach to war issues emphasized the political and moral responsibilities of the decision maker to use power, but with normative restraints as delineated in the just war doctrine.

Unlike CAIP, Day and the members of the Catholic Worker movement emphasized the individual and not the state. Day believed that "at a time of war, the coercive power of the state reached its zenith."[2] She saw a nation's decision to declare war as the most extreme opposition to active love and the Gospel message of peace. Day believed that peace depended on the actions of individuals and not nations or world organizations; her internationalism resided in human solidarity and the doctrine of the Mystical Body of Christ whereby the action of each individual affected every other individual. To be consistent with the Worker ideal, Day believed a pacifist response was necessary. Thus, she opposed the draft and the Catholic Worker was the only Catholic group that assisted Catholic conscientious objectors.

Though the differences between CAIP and Day's Catholic Worker movement were great, both witnessed to the inseparable link between justice and peace in the Catholic tradition. Both were self-consciously Catholic and aimed to reconstruct America on the principles of social and economic justice. These domestic concerns for creating a just order led into international issues, particularly those of war and peace.

In the 1950s, Catholic pacifism moved to a new level with the incorporation of the theory of Gandhian nonviolence. Robert Ludlow wrote of the compatibility of Catholic pacifism and nonviolence and Ammon Hennacy showed Catholic Workers how to practice nonviolence. Pacifism opposed all war, but nonviolence provided a way to posit actions for peace and a way to address public policy issues never before available in pacifism. During the Vietnam War, Catholic Workers such as David Miller and Tom Cornell burned their draft cards and moved nonviolence to resistance by this practice of civil disobedience. Daniel and Philip Berrigan escalated that resistance when they destroyed draft files. Later these brothers used the same model of resistance when they symbolically poured blood over and hammered nuclear weapons to awaken the national conscience to the life-ending effects of nuclear warfare.

Dorothy Day, through the Catholic Worker movement, became the midwife in the formation of Catholic pacifist peace organizations such as PAX and the Catholic Peace Fellowship during the Vietnam War. The focus of PAX was to lobby the church to officially recognize both conscientious objection and selective conscientious objection as valid positions for Catholics to hold. The Catholic Peace Fellowship focused on draft counseling and worked with the broader antiwar movement. Its members became leaders in the Catholic Resistance. In 1972, Dorothy Day and the Catholic Worker were present when PAX gave birth to Pax Christi-USA. This organization would not be a solely pacifist organization, but would attract mainline Catholics, members of the American hierarchy, and just war theorists under its umbrella. Members of these groups cooperated with the broader peace movement in the United States and their main focus became opposition to nuclear warfare and nuclear weapons. These were the Catholic peacemakers who were able to proclaim the Gospel message of peace even when their nation proclaimed war.

The major conclusion of this study is that Catholic peacemakers had the greatest impact not on the government but on the institutional church. In 1971, the American hierarchy judged that the Vietnam war was not a "just war." For the first time in the United States, and possibly in history, a national hierarchy announced as unjust a war being waged by its own nation. In the 1983 peace pastoral *The Challenge of Peace*, the leaders of the institutional church condemned the use of nuclear (and conventional) weapons of indiscriminate effect even in retaliation. Though the church still clung to the just war doctrine and believed it alone offered a mediating language with which to address the nation on public policy, on the individual level, the church for the first time officially recognized and embraced its members who in conscience were pacifists, nuclear pacifists, practitioners of Gospel nonviolence and nonviolent resistance, conscientious objectors, and selective conscientious objectors.

The historical record reveals clearly the effectiveness of the moral witness of the American Catholic peace movement on its hierarchy and mainline Catholics. The record also reveals the ineffectiveness of their witness on the policies of the U.S. government on war and peace issues. This ineffectiveness is also characteristic of church policy makers who operated out of the just war ethic. But members of the American Catholic peace movement would be justified in asking "Who has been politically effective?" Americans continue to reap personal benefits from the war machine while at the same time apologizing for its existence. Perhaps the greatest contribution of the American Catholic peace movement is its message that peacemaking requires great personal sacrifice and a religious commitment that can sustain an individual in face of political ineffectiveness—peacemaking is harder than war.

One cannot complete a study of this magnitude without expressing the sincerest gratitude to the many people who made it possible. In the first place I wish to thank all those workers in the American Catholic peace movement who gave their time and support during interviews, especially Daniel and Philip Berrigan and Bishop Thomas Gumbleton. James Forest shared his memories, library, and correspondence with me. Thomas Cornell did the same, and together we loaded my car with boxes of Catholic Peace Fellowship material to take to the archives at the University of Notre Dame to begin its collection. James Douglass gave me his private collection of statements and correspondence relating to his work at the Second Vatican Council. Carol and Jerome Berrigan were most gracious in their concern and hospitality and allowed me access to their basement archives on Daniel and Philip Berrigan. Gordon C. Zahn, professor of sociology at the University of Massachusetts, aided portions of this study with a critical reading and valuable insights. I also want to thank Carole Roos for helping me to write a better book and Delores Fain, secretary at the Cushwa Center at the University of Notre Dame, for her technical assistance.

There were others who also assisted me, particularly the archivists at the Catholic University of America, Marquette University, the University of Notre Dame, and the Peace Collection at Swarthmore College. Financial assistance for travel was provided by grants from Indiana University at South Bend. And I am most grateful to faculty and staff at the Institute for International Peace Studies at the University of Notre Dame, which granted me a Visiting Faculty Fellowship to complete the book.

I also want to thank Professor Allen F. Davis of Temple University who directed my doctoral dissertation almost twenty years ago. Above all I want to thank my husband, Jay P. Dolan, who has constantly encouraged, supported, and helped me to complete this work.

Harder than War

1

Origins of the Catholic Peace Movement

ON 5 APRIL 1917, the day before the U.S. Congress declared war, James Cardinal Gibbons, speaking on behalf of the Catholic hierarchy and the American Catholic church, proclaimed that, "In the present emergency it behooves every American citizen to do his duty and uphold the hands of the President . . . in the solemn obligations that confront us. The primary duty of a citizen is loyalty to country. This loyalty is exhibited by an absolute and unreserved obedience to his country."[1] In pledging the loyalty of American Catholics to the nation Gibbons was reaffirming a tradition of Catholic "patriotism in wartime." This tradition, wrote one historian, "has been a hallmark of the American Catholic community," evident since the earliest days of the nation.[2] It was reinforced by a reaction to the anti-Catholicism prevalent in Protestant America and supported on a theological level by the just war doctrine.

As members of an immigrant church, Catholics in the United States continually sought to dispel the label of foreigners put on them by American nativists.[3] Their enthusiastic support of the nation's wars "has remained one of the most frequently used, if not logical retorts to answer any aspersions on Catholic loyalty to American principles."[4] The general antipathy of the American people for Catholicism was rooted in the virulent anti-Catholicism of the Protestant Reformation and strengthened periodically by waves of immigration, during which between 1790 and 1920 approximately 9,395,000 Catholic immigrants arrived in the United States. In response to the needs of this immigrant population, the church hierarchy was largely concerned with domestic rather than international issues. Church leaders had to turn their attention to building up the institution—churches, schools, and other organizations for

1

the spiritual welfare of the people. This domestic concern was influenced by Catholic social doctrine that emerged at the end of the nineteenth century when Pope Leo XIII, in response to problems posed by the industrial revolution, wrote the encyclical, *Rerum Novarum*, "On the Condition of the Working Man" (1891). The principal issues addressed in the document were "the role of government in society and the economy, the right of laborers to organize, the principle of a just wage, and a Christian critique of both capitalism and socialism."[5] *Rerum Novarum* was not a blueprint for the reform of the world, but "a broad theological and philosophical framework of social analysis" which exhibited not only concern for the individual but for the general welfare of society.[6] Though American Catholics were mainly attracted to Leo XIII's message relating to the reconstruction of the domestic order, the pope had also expressed a new attitude toward peace in *Rerum Novarum*. His central concern was for a new international order in which peace was based on justice and love rather than on military defense, and he called for a reevaluation of the justice of defensive wars in a technological world. He also asked Christians to follow Peter's call to obey God above humans, beginning a new era in which the church would declare independence from any particular social order for the first time since Constantine.[7] Though Catholics in the United States paid little attention to his international message before and during World War I, in the aftermath of the war, American Catholic reformers attempting to reconstruct the domestic order became involved in international issues. In addition, subsequent popes with their emphasis on rights, justice, and order strengthened the connection between justice and peace issues in Catholic social doctrine during the twentieth century. By the Second Vatican Council, the development of Catholic social doctrine had led the international hierarchy to call for a new theology of peace after questioning the adequacy of the just war tradition in the church's teaching.

The previous acceptance by the church of the just war doctrine as normative made legitimate the Catholic acceptance of the state's decisions pertaining to issues of war and peace. The just war doctrine has a long history in the church, originating with Ambrose and Augustine in the fourth century. At that time the pacifism of the early church was complicated by the conversion of Constantine and his transformation of the Roman Empire into a Christian state. According to Augustine, the father of the just war doctrine, every society seeks peace but may have to wage war to preserve that peace. Since Christians live in society, they are bound to share society's responsibilities, possibly including participation in war. However, Christians' motives for their participation would be different from those of pagans in that they wage war to establish peace and their defense of their earthly city is secondary to their fulfillment of the divine will.

During the Middle Ages, Thomas Aquinas refined the doctrine with such great precision that his formulation has remained the traditional interpretation. The just war doctrine presupposes that war is a rational and moral activity when it is governed by rules justifying the resort to violence and the nature of the violent force. Though the doctrine admits a variety of interpretations developed by both Catholic and Protestant theologians, the core of its teaching lists several conditions for going to war. First, war must be declared by a competent authority. Then, there must be a just cause for engaging in war; that is, a grave wrong to be corrected or right to be defended. Third, the likely beneficial results of a war must outweigh the evil results, the so-called principle of proportionality. The fourth condition states that war must be waged only as a last resort, after all peaceful means have been exhausted. Fifth, war must be waged with the right intention; that is, a war can be fought legitimately only if its purpose is to achieve a just end, not the uncharitable activities which usually accompany war.

The conditions for waging war are, first, that the means used are proportional to the likelihood of achieving just ends. And second, that no matter how militarily effective, no means can be employed that is immoral in itself. This last prohibition would apply to the killing of noncombatants. However, according to the principle of the double effect, an attack in which civilians were killed could be morally permissible if the intended object of the attack had been a legitimate military target that could not be dealt with in any other way, and the deaths of the civilians were incidental to the intention of the attacker.[8]

In the just war doctrine the presumption of justice is granted to the state as is all responsibility for war. The state thereby becomes the decision maker for all individual consciences. Where the individual disagrees with the state, the burden of proof rests with the individual.

With this understanding, American Catholics expressed their patriotism through military service and the hierarchy did not hesitate in supporting the government's position in World War I. The outbreak of this war provided the Catholic hierarchy with an opportunity to demonstrate its patriotic Americanism. In support of President Woodrow Wilson's crusade "to make the world safe for democracy," they formed the National Catholic War Council. Founded in August 1917, it functioned throughout the war "as a highly effective medium in almost every phase of Catholic participation in the war effort, from providing material assistance to chaplains serving with the troops to acting as an official agency designated by President Wilson to promote the war-loan drives."[9]

A few months after World War I ended in Europe, the American bishops issued their first pastoral statement since 1884. This document, entitled *Lessons of War* and issued in September 1919, urged the United States to accept its unique role to "restore peace and order" according to "principles of reasonable liberty and of Christian civilization." In effect, the hierarchy condoned the war as a crusade and like many Americans they were now looking toward the reconstruction of American society.[10]

The success of the war council as a national coordinating agency for the church persuaded its supporters, principally, Bishop Peter J. Muldoon of the Diocese of Rockford, Illinois, to continue its operation after the war as a way for the church to maintain a national focus. The name was changed to the National Catholic Welfare Council (NCWC) and its headquarters was in the nation's capital. It became the primary agency to coordinate and promote Catholic interests and activities at a national level. Though there was initial opposition from some bishops who feared the council would limit their autonomy and authority, NCWC did succeed in providing the church with the type of national organization it needed and gave the bishops a national consciousness that taught them to think about issues that transcended local diocesan concerns.

The council originally had five departments: education, lay activities, press, missions, and social. But the one department "that has probably impinged more than any other on the national consciousness is the Social Action Department."[11] In 1920, the American Catholic hierarchy selected John A. Ryan to direct the new department, which was primarily concerned with social reform at home. However, under Ryan's leadership, social justice was linked for the first time to the broader international interests of war and peace.

John A. Ryan was the oldest of eleven children. Born in 1869 to Irish immigrant parents, he lived his youth in the small farming community of Vermillion, Minnesota. Ryan later acknowledged that his upbringing provided him with "an interest and love of economic justice, as well as political justice."[12] After ordination to the priesthood in 1898, Ryan went to the Catholic University of America to study moral theology. For completion of his degree, he wrote a doctoral dissertation entitled A Living Wage: Its Ethical and Economic Aspects. When it was published in 1906 Ryan began to receive public attention. At the time he was professor of moral theology at St. Paul's Seminary in St. Paul, Minnesota, and was writing articles on social reform for Catholic publications and giving many lectures. He was also mingling freely with reform groups not associated with the Catholic church. In 1915, Ryan returned to Catholic University as a professor and continued to teach there until his forced retirement in 1939. In 1916, he wrote another major book, Distributive Justice: The Right and Wrong of Our Present Distribution of Wealth, which provided a synthesis of his ethics and economics. In his position as director of NCWC's Social Action Department, he gradually emerged as the principal architect of Catholic social concern. At his death in 1945 he was still the dominant American Catholic social theorist.[13]

The genius of Ryan was his ability to merge Catholic social thought with the American current of reform. The basis for this merger was natural law tradition.[14] Pope Leo XIII had positioned the natural law at the foundation of Catholic social ethics in his encyclical, Rerum Novarum. Ryan took this aspect of papal social thought and applied it to the American economic and industrial environment. From this basic principle flowed Ryan's emphasis on a living wage, the importance of labor unions, and the need of the state to intervene and effect change in the social order. This positive role for the state in Catholic social theory did not mean an absolute trust in a particular government or administration that necessarily led to endorsing policy. Rather the natural law provided a language that allowed discussion of the morality of public policy in a pluralistic society.

After World War I the Catholic bishops wanted to present their own program for reconstruction of American society and set up their own committee to draft a document. The priest John O'Grady, secretary of the Committee on Reconstruction, had the responsibility to produce such a plan. He turned to John A. Ryan, who at the time was writing his own program of reconstruction. O'Grady begged him for it and in February 1919 it appeared as the "Bishops' Program of Social Reconstruction." Without a doubt it was "the most forward-looking social document ever to have come from an official Catholic agency in the United States."[15]

Avid criticism of the 1919 statement did occur. Some segments of the Catholic community labeled it as "partisan, pro-labor union, or socialistic propaganda."[16] Nevertheless, it pointed the direction toward which many Catholics were moving in the years after World War I. One visible omission in this quest for social reform was the international issue of war and peace.

As was evidenced in World War I, Catholics were eager to prove their loyalty to the United States, and in seeking social reform they never challenged the place of the nation in the international community. Raised in an immigrant community, Catholic reformers were also not inclined to challenge the country's basic social system. They wanted reform, but only within the boundaries of the accepted American tradition. They looked to the government for help, not to criticize it. Thus, it was inevitable that one of the last issues Catholic reformers would confront was the responsibility of the United States in war and for peace. Moreover, the just war tradition worked against any consideration of this issue.

Ryan typified this acceptance in World War I when he wrote in his autobiography that "I acquiesced in the declaration of war because I assumed that the President and Congress were in a better position than I to make the right decision."[17] Like Ryan's system of social ethics, the just war had its basis in the natural law tradition. For Ryan the state was necessary, and its authority was both real and binding. This did not, however, mean that the state is above the law or that the state is the final arbiter of right and wrong. According to Ryan the state stands under the law and must be judged according to the principles of natural law.[18]

During World War I, however, Ryan was greatly influenced by the proposals of Pope Benedict XV (1914–1922) for ending World War I and reestablishing international order and peace. During his pontificate, Benedict XV was faced with the full impact of world war and its aftermath of hatred and destruction. A former papal diplomat, Benedict XV opposed war in any form and rejected the theory of the just war as historically outmoded and theologically inadequate. He earned the title Pontiff of Peace.

Pope Benedict XV was more in line with the humanist peace tradition within the church, which he expressed in his direct moral appeal to individual conscience, than to the internationalist tradition that emerged after the Council of Trent and was promulgated with qualification by Leo XIII. The internationalists placed their hopes for peace on the diplomatic efforts and military balances of Europe's governments. Benedict XV issued the encyclical *Ad Beatissimum* at the outbreak of World War I. The encyclical outlined the causes of war and the methods for attaining peace. For Benedict XV the causes of war were lack of mutual love, disregard for authority, class war, and gross materialism; the path to peace embraced the Beatitudes and Christ's command that "you love one another as I have loved you." He called for a peace without victory and an end to hostilities, prophetically reminding the belligerents that true Christians must make the first offer of peace. "He was as close to a pacifist as any pope since Benedict XII during the Hundred Years War."[19]

Although the messages of Leo XIII and Benedict XV did not persuade the majority of Catholics nor Ryan to question the decisions of their government, Ryan was greatly influenced by the rejection of Benedict XV's proposal for ending World War I and reestablishing peace, which was sent to the belligerents on 14 August 1917. In responding to the international crisis Ryan established himself as the foremost advocate of the League of Nations. Ryan gave one of the first talks in support of the league at a meeting of the Knights of Columbus in Louisville in December 1918, five months before the covenant of the league was written into the Treaty of Versailles. In May 1919, he stated that the league was "the only means in sight to save the people of Europe from experiences perhaps worse than those of war."[20]

Ryan addressed his most urgent appeals for the league to Catholic bishops, whom he hoped would provide leadership on the issue; he also appealed to editors of the Catholic press because he believed that "the Catholic press was never more than 'spasmodic and half-hearted' in applying principles of Catholic political ethics to international questions."[21]

After 1920, other individuals also identified with the Social Action Department of NCWC took up the cause. Their aim was not to criticize the actions of the government, but rather to encourage it to move toward establishing an international organization that would assure peace. Although the leadership in the Social Action Department was primarily concerned with social reform at home, they attempted for the first time to link their quest for a domestic order of social justice to an international order based on social justice. The Catholic tradition, after all, had always stressed the inseparable link between justice and peace.

Catholic spokespersons for the league often met bitter popular opposition. Charles Fenwick, a Bryn Mawr professor and a nationally known Catholic, spoke out in favor of the league before Catholic audiences in the East and Midwest. Reinforcing his talks with quotations from Augustine, Thomas Aquinas, and the popes, he found that

> not only were Irish Catholics upset because of the failure of President Wilson to do anything about the independence of Ireland, but that German Catholics felt that Germany was being choked to death by the loss of needed territory like the busy Rhine, the iron and coal of the Saar and Alsace-Lorraine, the valuable mines of Silesia and reparations that would last until 1987. Italian Catholics were incensed at the loss of Fiume.

Fenwick also reluctantly admitted that he "never won a single debate, or converted a single audience."[22] Similar experiences were related by Francis McMahon, a professor at the University of Notre Dame, who was met with the charge that the league "was invented by Wilson and taken to Geneva, the ancient city of Calvin, to make it anti-Rome." Others told him that "its instigators were the international Masons." Another charge against the league, McMahon reported, was "its failure to include the Vatican in its organization."[23]

A closely related crusade that attracted Ryan in the 1920s was international peace through disarmament. Not historically literate, Ryan was, nevertheless, well informed on matters within his own memory and he understood European problems, especially economic ones. He gave particular attention to the excessive burden the war debt placed on the German people; he believed this would be a source of continuing threat to world peace.[24] In 1928, Ryan appeared before the House Naval Affairs Committee as a representative of the Church Peace Union, an interdenominational group, to oppose the construction of new capital warships. The *Buffalo Catholic Union and Times* did not approve and demanded to know "How long, O! Lord! would Catholics have to put up with the intrusions of Father Burke and Dr. Ryan into political questions in the discussion of which they have no authority to speak except for their own ill-formed and ill-considered convictions?"[25] Ryan also applauded the Treaty of Locarno, the Kellogg Pact, and the World Court.

In 1922, while visiting England, Ryan met a British peace advocate, Joseph Keating, S.J., from whom he learned about England's Catholic Council for International Peace. After returning to the United States, Ryan discussed with some of his friends the idea of founding a similar Catholic peace organization. He received support from Robert Mc-Gowan and from Carlton J. H. Hayes of Columbia. Worth M. Tippy, Charles S. Macfarland, and especially Sidney L. Gulick, all of the Federal Council of Churches for Prevention of War, urged him to organize a peace movement among Catholics.[26] Frederick J. Libby, executive secretary of the National Council for the Prevention of War (NCPW) was also urging Ryan forward. Ryan at this time was serving on the board of the NCPW. These men propelled Ryan into a territory that Catholics had not entered. The popes had spoken vigorously for peace; the bishops had echoed them. But there it ended. Ryan did not exaggerate in 1925 when he said, "he could tell the whole story of American Catholic peace sentiment in a fraction of the sixteen hundred words that the *NCWC Bulletin* wanted him to write."[27]

The diversity of positions later evidenced in the 1930s by these individuals who had counseled Ryan in the formation of a Catholic peace movement reveal how loosely related peace societies were in the 1920s. In 1922, Ryan did not want to start an American Catholic peace movement, but he did want to form a group of Catholics who could serve as a pressure group to lobby for significant legislation on issues of war and peace in Congress.[28] Ryan's primary focus was the issue of social action, yet he did agree with the judgment of Bishop Peter J. Muldoon, episcopal chair of the Social Action Department, that "the department was not doing enough to educate Catholics on world affairs. It concentrated on domestic social justice alone."[29] Another priest, Joseph Burke, C.S.P., finally pushed Ryan in the direction of organizing a peace group among Catholics. He suggested that Ryan and his assistant, Raymond McGowan, also a priest, "get leading Catholics together at the 28th Annual Eucharistic Congress to be held in Chicago in 1925," and together they could begin to discuss the issue of international peace.[30]

The proposed meeting of fifty Catholic leaders took place following the close of the congress. The assembled group did not draw up any specific plans, but expressed a desire to meet again and established an organizing committee headed by Colonel P. H. Callahan of Louisville, Kentucky. The next conference took place in Cleveland on 6 October 1926; here a committee system was adopted to study, report upon, and help promote Catholic understanding and action on problems of world peace. An organizational meeting was then scheduled for April 1927, at the Catholic University of America in Washington, D.C.[31]

For this meeting Ryan was to chair the subcommittee on international ethics and prepare a working paper for discussion. His final product drew substantially from *The Church and War* by Franziskus Stratmann, O.P.; Stratmann believed no modern war could be just. Ryan's pamphlet became the principal manifesto of the new association when it was published in 1927 with the title *International Ethics*. This report rejected Stratmann's pacifist position, but attempted to limit the characterization of a just war and warned of the need for caution in invoking force. Ryan stated that "righteousness would surely not be protected if wicked men were permitted to have a monopoly on physical coercion."

With the problem of creating a Catholic group in mind, the subcommittee noted: "Justice requires a state to promote peace for the sake of its own members, while charity obliges it to pursue the same ends for the welfare of both itself and other nations. These duties rest not only upon governments, but upon peoples, particularly upon those persons and organizations which can exert influence upon public opinion and upon political rulers."[32] This 1927 meeting realized the goal of a Catholic peace organization: It adopted a constitution, elected officers, and chose a name, the Catholic Association for International Peace (CAIP). Its motto was that of Pope Pius XI's reign, "The Peace of Christ in the Kingdom of Christ." It was the first Catholic peace organization in American history.

> The Association did not look for mass support, but planned to seek to educate Catholics and non-Catholics on the Catholic point of view on international affairs, as drawn from what the Holy Fathers, the Bishops of the United States, and Catholic scholars had said on the principles of attaining world peace through justice and charity.[33]

Studies were to be made by experts and reports published on the principles of peace and their application to current issues. In addition, the association would promote annual conferences, lectures, and study circles to present Catholic opinion on subjects relating to international morality. CAIP was allotted office space in the NCWC headquarters in Washington as an independent branch of the Social Action Department and was given the use of NCWC facilities, including the news service.

In attempting to analyze the ideology, structure, and tactics of CAIP, it is impossible to separate the association from NCWC's Social Action Department because of the central roles of Ryan and McGowan in both organizations. During this period, Ryan's reputation as "American Catholicism's foremost social reformer" enabled him to link American Catholics and liberal, progressive groups.[34] McGowan, however, assumed primary responsibility for CAIP's organization and vision.[35] Both men believed that "highly trained laymen and laywomen would join priests in furnishing the material for the program of education for and the actual re-creation of the social order. Catholics should remake social institutions by gaining positions of power in business organizations and civil life."[36] Thus, the structure of CAIP was elitist from the beginning though it intended to reach the general population of the laity.

People invited to participate in the formation of CAIP and later to serve on its committees were leaders from church, business, military, and university life. Bishop Thomas J. Shahan, rector of the Catholic University of America, was elected honorary president of CAIP. The first secretary was Francis Riggs who served but a short time before he left to become chief of police in Puerto Rico. Other prominent people in the early activities of the organization were Parker T. Moon and

Carlton J. H. Hayes of Columbia Univesrity; John LaFarge, S.J., editor of *America*; Francis Haas of Grand Rapids, later bishop of that diocese; Marie Carroll, librarian of the World Peace Foundation; Vincent Ferrer, O.P., of Rosary College; Archbishop Robert E. Lucey of San Antonio, then a priest of the Archdiocese of Los Angeles; and George Shuster, editor of *Commonweal* and later president of Hunter College.[37] These prominent and influential people belonged to an institutional world of decision making that spoke in political terms of compromise and mediation.[38]

The CAIP's focus was on peace education. Because it was part of the official church bureauracy, NCWC, the association "was to eschew anything like direct action."[39] Its relationship with the NCWC favored the organizational approach of issuing statements from the top of the hierarchical structure rather than working directly with people at a grass-roots level. As a result, CAIP conducted its best work through its pamphlets, which it distributed to its members and existing Catholic organizations. Its campaign of peace education was most effective, not in preventing war but in instructing people in the value of internationalism.

The key organizational component of CAIP was the committee. These were formed to present "a united front against isolationist mentality,"[40] and expressed the internationalist viewpoint of CAIP. The association developed a concept of internationalism that was based on the desire for cooperation among individual nations through a world organization that would mobilize the moral and physical resources of the great majority of nations against aggression. This view depended on a concert of power in the political realm. The degree of collective cooperation among nations would determine the type of security that could be devised to prevent war. CAIP, therefore, was a proponent of collective security and supported America's entrance into the League of Nations and the World Court. After 1937, they would support President Franklin D. Roosevelt's advocacy of collective security.

As early as 1930, the Ethics Committee issued a pamphlet on *The Causes of War* which argued that the primary cause of illegal warfare was the action of "unmoral" states. An unmoral state was defined as one dominated by excessive nationalism and aggressive materialism. In CAIP the major critic of excessive nationalism was Carlton J. H. Hayes, whose pamphlet *Patriotism, Nationalism and the Brotherhood of Man* stated that Catholics were all too quick to subordinate their loyalty to Catholic principles to those of nationalism, chauvinism, and antiforeignism. He went on to argue that there was no basic difference between the selfishness of America's political and economic policy and that of other nations. He did point out, however, that fascism and Nazism were the twentieth century's most extreme forms of virulent nationalism and that such political philosophies were unacceptable to the Catholic church since they exalted the state as the supreme and exclusive object of the individual's loyalty.

The association also attacked aggressive materialism. In its economic reports aggressive materialism was cited as a major source of discord and distrust among nations. In a 1938 report, *World Trade Patterns*, it demonstrated that the economic life of the world was moving, not toward a just distribution of the goods of nature, but toward divisive ideological political blocs of economic control. This was true of all forms of government, democratic, fascist or communist with the most blatant example being Germany's domination of eastern Europe. Like other conservative peace groups, CAIP in 1937 urged that a World Economic Conference be held to remedy the economic ills that seriously contributed to Europe's major troubles. The proposed guiding principle for the conference was the "reaffirmation of the moral unity of mankind and that an injustice done to one nation is an injustice done to all."[41]

Prominent in CAIP's international position was the legitimacy of just war. In 1932, Cyprian Emmanuel, chair of the Ethics Committee, wrote a pamphlet, *The Ethics of War*, presenting the conditions of a just war for the moral nations of the twentieth century. The criteria for such a justifiable war included the basic conditions of the just war doctrine.[42] Since it adopted the just war doctrine, CAIP was able to endorse the Stimson doctrine and the Geneva Disarmament Conference. It also supported the denunciation of Nazism, the revision of neutrality legislation, and ultimately the acceptance of World War II as a just war.

The person most responsible for coordinating the work of CAIP was Elizabeth Sweeney, secretary of the association. Sweeney had previously been a secretary in NCWC's Social Action Department. Extremely competent as a secretary, she was an active member of many Catholic organizations and knowledgeable on the workings of Washington, D.C. One of her principal accomplishments was directing publication of twenty-eight pamphlets between 1928 and 1938. The funds needed to publish these pamphlets were donated by member institutions such as Mount St. Joseph's College, Rosary College, and Rosemont College.[43] CAIP also received contributions from organizations that sympathized with the association's principles and work, such as the National Catholic Welfare Conference (NCWC), National Council of Catholic Men (NCCM), National Council of Catholic Women (NCCW), National Federation of Catholic College Students (NFCCS), and Newman Club Federations.

CAIP's first effort in disseminating peace education material consisted of distributing pamphlets to already existing discussion groups in the hope that groups would focus on the issue of international peace and ultimately to become members of CAIP. Elizabeth Sweeney applied this tactic when she was invited to address the annual convention of NCCW in 1933 on the topic of international peace. After her address, NCCW adopted the topic as the discussion theme for the year and CAIP pamphlets were then used as source material in dioceses throughout the United States.[44]

CAIP also worked with existing nondenominational organizations in order to recruit new members. In Los Angeles, Robert Lucey, a Catholic priest, established an active branch of CAIP out of the existing League of Nations Association. After Lucey left the diocese in 1932, Mary Workman, an active member in the parish, attempted to coordinate activities, but without strong clerical leadership, the group became increasingly less active.[45]

On the college level, CAIP devoted most of its energies to Catholic institutions. As early as 1928, Elizabeth Sweeney proposed to facilitate the distribution of CAIP material to peace study groups in Catholic colleges. Two years later the executive committee suggested that all Catholic colleges should encourage student participation in peace programs on Armistice Day. The first program CAIP organized was at the College of Notre Dame of Maryland; it was led by Elizabeth Morrissey, a member of CAIP on the college faculty.[46] In the early 1930s, more than 150 Catholic colleges adopted Peace Week Programs. There were attempts to initiate CAIP chapters on every campus, but there was also an alternative policy of affiliating with existing clubs, such as the Student Mission Crusade, the Catholic Action Movement, or the International Relations Club.[47] Affiliate members were then organized into geographic units known as Student Peace Federations. In 1936, the association sponsored two Student Peace Federation Conferences modeled on CAIP's annual conference.[48] The Middle Atlantic colleges met at St. Elizabeth College in New Jersey and the Middle Western colleges met at Rosary College in River Forest, Illinois.

During the 1930s, CAIP faced the question of whether or not the Reserve Officers Training Corps (ROTC) programs, which began to emerge on Catholic campuses, were compatible with its mission. In 1931, only three Catholic universities had an ROTC program: Boston College, Fordham University, and Georgetown University. All three colleges offered it as an elective and the total number of students involved was 1,169.[49] However, by 1937 many more Catholic universities had adopted the program. CAIP saw no basic conflict with the ROTC mainly because of its just war presupposition and its commitment to collective security.

CAIP also tried to bring the message of peace to the secondary and elementary levels of education.[50] That such a need existed was obvious from the results of a study made by Monsignor Maurice Sheehy, *National Attitudes in Children*, published by CAIP. The study, which surveyed elementary and high school students in the large metropolitan centers of thirty states and Puerto Rico, revealed the consciousness of racial or national differences among children and youth. This study was supplemented two years later by a pamphlet, *Peace Education in the Curriculum of the Schools*, written by Monsignor J. M. Wolfe of Dubuque, Iowa, chair of the Peace Education Committee, which called for a new curriculum that would present a broad, comprehensive program for cultivating "peace mindedness" among young people.

CAIP attempted to gain support for its principles in Congress through lobbying tactics. In 1933, when Congress voted on the Arms Embargo Bill, ten Catholic Democrats and all seven Catholic Republicans voted against the bill. Members of the association were distraught because five of these legislators were on the sponsoring committee of the annual conference of CAIP which had just met and endorsed the Arms Embargo Bill.[51] Such voting patterns of Catholic legislators suggest that the CAIP had little influence in persuading members of Congress to follow its recommendations. Differences between CAIP and Catholic legislators continued throughout the 1930s.

The CAIP urged its members to work within the framework of all existing organizations devoted to the cause of peace in the world, but it did little more than send pamphlet material upon request or provide a speaker for a peace rally. Some individual members did serve on national committees of various peace organizations. Ryan had served several years on NCPW's executive board. When the board in 1933, over Ryan's repeated protests, decided to intervene between the government in Mexico and the Catholic church, he resigned. President Roosevelt had instituted a "good neighbor" policy toward Latin America during the height of Mexico's anticlericalism, which resulted in antagonism between his administration and the Catholic church. Some American Catholics made Josephus Daniels, the newly appointed U.S. ambassador to Mexico, the scapegoat in their attempt to pressure the Roosevelt administration into meddling in the internal affairs of Mexico in support of the church. Between 1932 and 1936, "it was the most severe strain imposed on the generally harmonious relationship between Roosevelt and American Catholics."[52]

Thus it was the "Mexican question" and not pacifism that led to Ryan's resignation from NCPW. In his autobiography, Ryan admits that he was aware that many of the members of NCPW were pacifist, but it did not cause him any "unpleasant complications" in the years he was with them. Ryan goes on to say that it would have caused his resignation in 1939 when the council took a strong stand against President Roosevelt's recommendation to Congress to lift the embargo on the sale of arms in favor of Great Britain and France and again when they fought against the program for national defense adopted by Congress in 1940. Ryan's main criticism of NCPW was that they had become "hopelessly isolationist."[53] In his autobiography he writes, "Because I still have faith and hope in world peace through international action, and because I still believe that the precepts of the moral law bind nations as well as individuals, I reject and detest isolationism under any and every guise."[54]

CAIP's relations with peace organizations outside the United States were similar with those at home. To establish contact with Europe, Elizabeth Sweeney, as early as June 1929, wrote on behalf of CAIP to Franziskus Stratmann, head of the German Catholic Union for Peace, who in turn urged the need to prepare the way for an international peace conference. Stratmann held that no modern war could be a just war and also urged that war service and military service be declared an absolute contradiction of the teachings of Christ and of the Catholic church.[55] From this position he urged Sweeney to contact Joseph Clayton in England who had written on peace for the English Dominican periodical *Blackfriars*, the Polish Jesuit Graf Rostoworowski, Professor Ude of Graz University, Professor Keller of Freiburg University, and the War Resisters' International. CAIP, however, gave little cooperation beyond publishing a pamphlet called *Catholic Peace Organizations in Europe*. It also worked with the Carnegie Endowment for International Peace in publishing for American readers a five-hundred page work on internationalism and Catholicism. The work, *The Catholic Tradition of the Law of Nations*, was written by John Eppstein under the auspices of the Catholic Council for International Relations of Great Britain.

By 1937 CAIP's internationalism had resulted in opposition to neutrality legislation. CAIP contended that the Neutrality Act made no distinction between the aggressor nation and its victim.[56] In 1938, it reiterated its position by objecting to the "narrow conception of national interest upon which [the] Neutrality Act was based—[an] attitude of washing our hands of responsibility in present crime—[and it was] concerned primarily not with the prevention of war but with [the] avoidance of its consequences."[57] This paved the way for the CAIP to embrace wholeheartedly Roosevelt's move away from neutrality toward collective security.

The only stumbling block in this process for the CAIP was the Spanish Civil War and the ensuing debate between 1937 and 1939 over the Embargo Act. During this time President Roosevelt did not advocate a change in the Neutrality Act of 1937 and a lifting of the Embargo Act. Yet, in his "Quarantine Speech" at Chicago on 5 October 1937 he discarded the doctrine of neutrality for the United States and espoused the idea of collective security—the cardinal principle of internationalism. Despite this, he never lifted the embargo. Like Roosevelt CAIP was also ambiguous. It seemed logical by 1937 that CAIP was ready to reject strict neutrality but the American bishops and the "official" church statements from the NCWC came out in support of Franco in Spain and were against the repeal of the embargo, which would favor the Loyalists. Because of CAIP's close relationship with the NCWC, it chose to remain silent rather than confront the position of the "official" church.

Ryan, however, spoke out on the issue when he joined a group of
174 Catholic laymen and clergymen to defend the American church's
support of the insurgents in the Spanish Civil War. The group issued a
statement that insisted on the right of revolution against a government
that made persecution of the church an integral part of its program.
Ryan made no apologies about signing the statement. He had no
affection for fascism and he believed the coming struggle in Europe
would be between communism and democracy rather than between
democracy and fascism. Even though this view set him off from most
liberal opinion in America, he reminded himself that where religion
was involved, liberals were likely to be "muddleheaded."[58]

After Franco's victory in Spain in 1939, such a conflict of loyalties
would never again confront CAIP. Because the "official" church opposed Nazism, CAIP was able to speak out against strict neutrality
when it touched on the German situation.

The shift of CAIP from support of neutrality legislation to endorsing
collective security reflected the transformation taking place among
other non-pacifist peace groups such as the Carnegie Endowment for
International Peace, the Church Peace Union, the World Alliance for
International Friendship through the Churches, and the League of
Nations Association. All these organizations rallied around the concept
of collective security and formed the Non-Partisan Committee for
Peace Through the Revision of the Neutrality Law. Through this organization and others, the non-pacifist peace groups prepared the nation for war by emphasizing collective security rather than a position of
neutrality. As a spokesperson for the committee in late 1939 Ryan
expressed the consensus of the group when he stated in a radio broadcast that all Americans were "morally obliged to do all they reasonably
can to defeat Hitler and Hitlerism."[59]

By 1940, Ryan was firmly convinced of his position on war and
Hitler. In an article that appeared in *Commonweal* and was reprinted
as a pamphlet *The Right and Wrong of War*, he wrote:

> The extreme pacifist position, that war as such is always wrong because
> it involves violence, does not deserve formal discussion. With the
> position of some recent Catholic authorities, that in our day war is
> practically never justified because of its awful consequences, I have
> considerable sympathy; but if Hitler and his government intend to

substitute paganism for Christianity not only in Germany but in foreign territories which they have annexed in the last two years and if they are aiming at world domination, then I have no hesitation in saying that a successful war against this immoral Nazi program would be the lesser evil. In other words, such a war would be justified, despite the enormous ensuing destruction of life and property.[60]

When the United States declared its formal participation in World War II, CAIP unhesitatingly continued the Catholic tradition of patriotism in wartime.

When bombs came down on Pearl Harbor, Catholic debate of foreign policy ceased. The isolationism CAIP had tried to combat disappeared among American Catholics. The historian, George Q. Flynn, in his book *Roosevelt and Romanism*, contends that there was a moral clarity reflected in the American Catholic conscience on World War II, which had little to do with politics and everything to do with theology. A study of the statements of Catholic leaders concerning World War II, according to Flynn, reveals that Catholics believed Hitler was a demonic force in history and the United States held a special place in God's plan of creation that placed God on their side during the war. These two religious assumptions, states Flynn, combined with the dominant teaching of the just war doctrine, turned the war effort into a moral crusade to promote a world of liberty and goodness. Catholics might have put some qualifications on their commitment, realizing that to identify God with any nation was a heresy in doctrine. Yet, Flynn contends that there were no such reservations voiced by Catholic spokespersons. Catholic leaders and their flocks had been trained to think in religious terms, thus it is understandable that they could "be lifted out of history and into a morality play."[61] By approaching the war as a moral crusade, Flynn concludes that Catholic leaders were left with an atrophy of their ethical feelings concerning the objects, tactics, and strategy of the conflict. They had become one with the Roosevelt administration in the attempt to win the just war.

Prior to World War II, CAIP never claimed a membership of more than five hundred.[62] However, because of the prestige of its members, especially John A. Ryan, the ideals of the association reached a wide audience. CAIP's identification with NCWC opened the doors to all other recognized Catholic organizations. Most of the work was coordinated by Elizabeth Sweeney who labored to help CAIP attain the goals of its constitution: "To further accord, with the teachings of the Church, the 'Peace of Christ in the Kingdom of Christ' through the preparation and dissemination of studies applying Christian teaching to international life."

While CAIP claimed to be the "official" peace organization within the Catholic church, other movements representing alternative perspectives on war and peace issues began to emerge in the 1930s. These movements also traced their roots back to the social question, the principal concern of Catholics between the two great wars. The financial crash of 1929 and the ensuing depression focused the concern of Americans on social issues and more than one citizen devised a plan for rebuilding the nation. Among those was Charles E. Coughlin, a Catholic pastor in Royal Oak, Michigan, who gained national prominence through his weekly radio program.[63]

Coughlin's strength was his personality, which he conveyed in his powerful oratory over the radio. He attracted thousands of listeners, the majority of whom lived in Eastern and Midwestern cities. Many became members of his organization, the Christian Front. In his addresses, this "shepherd of discontent" was able to put into words the fears and frustrations of his listeners.

Coughlin was not a peacemaker. He was both a demagogue and an ardent nationalist who believed that the United States was synonymous with Christendom; anything that sapped the strength of this "Christian Commonwealth" had to be eradicated. To this end, capitalism and communism, in Coughlin's opinion the two main evils of the 1930s depression, had to be eradicated from American society. By 1938, his belief in the threat of "international jewry" reinforced his views on capitalism and communism. In his opinion, jewry advanced the evils of capitalism and communism and all three forces threatened the "Christian Commonwealth" both from within and without. An equally passionate isolationism reinforced Coughlin's view of America's place in the world community.

Surfacing during the years of the Great Depression as a social reformer, Coughlin eventually emerged for some Catholics as a spokesperson against World War II. Anything that diverted the energies of the nation away from its reconstruction was to be opposed, and World War

II did just that. Coughlin's main concern was not peace but war as a threat to the Christian nation, America. He remained firm in his isolationism and his opposition to the war became a moral crusade.

One might legitimately ask why Coughlin is being mentioned in a study of the Catholic peace movement. The reason is that Coughlin opposed the participation of the United States in World War II. He did not identify himself with any of the existing peace groups, though at times he found himself standing with them on a particular issue. More significantly, Coughlin's stance against America's entry into World War II represented a new departure in American Catholicism. By challenging America's participation in the war, Coughlin broke with the Catholic tradition of wartime patriotism. However, his motives were not rooted in a concern for peace. Coughlin was an isolationist who challenged the role of the state in this particular war because he believed that American participation would support the wrong side—a side that in his opinion was dominated by British capitalists and Russian communists, and therefore was inconsistent with his view of America as the new Christendom. Thus, despite his extreme nationalism, Coughlin challenged the role of the U. S. government, and some of his followers, members of the Christian Front, even became conscientious objectors.

The third group of Catholics who addressed themselves to the issues of war and peace was centered in the Catholic Worker movement. Founded in 1933 in New York City, it was unique in the history of American Catholicism, being fundamentally a movement of Catholic lay people. Moreover, the Catholic Worker held a position of pacifism and thus became the first Catholic group in the United States to follow this ideal. Like Coughlin and the social actionists of the CAIP, the Catholic Worker first emerged as a group of people concerned about the social reconstruction of America.

The co-founders of the Catholic Worker movement were Peter Maurin and Dorothy Day. Maurin was a French peasant who had abandoned the Christian Brothers to join Le Sillon, a lay movement whose goal was to Christianize modern democracy. Becoming disillusioned with the Sillon movement and seeking to escape the draft in France, he immigrated to Canada in 1909. These experiences had helped to form Maurin's philosophy of Christian personalism. He believed that at the core of Christianity was personal responsibility that the chaotic conditions of modern society destroyed. Each person could affirm his or her personal responsibility by integrating the spiritual and material aspects of life through active participation in the political, economic, and social concerns of the world. If each individual Christian pursued this course, a restoration of unity in the Christian world would result.[64] Wanting to share his vision, Peter Maurin became a peripatetic teacher, who eventually made his way to the United States.

Dorothy Day was by occupation a journalist. After dropping out of college for financial reasons, she was involved with radical movements such as the Industrial Workers of the World and with communism; she was also a feminist.[65] As soon as Day heard Maurin speak, she quit her job as a journalist with the sole desire to join Maurin in building the Catholic Worker movement. As Dorothy Day herself was to say many times of Peter Maurin, "He was my master and I was his disciple."[66]

Dorothy Day managed to find concrete ways of embodying Maurin's ideas. First, she began a newspaper, the Catholic Worker, that sold for a penny a copy. She also opened a House of Hospitality on Mott Street in New York City where workers and intellectuals could meet and hold "round-table discussions." Later, she began a farm commune in Easton, Pennsylvania. As the Catholic Worker movement spread beyond New York, the concept of a newspaper, a house of hospitality, and a fascination with the simplicity of the rural life continued to define the movement.

The Catholic Worker movement was not an organization but rather a gathering of diverse people. Those who joined (actually more a matter of self-identification and working with others in the movement) were cosmopolitan scholars and reformers who, unlike members of CAIP, identified themselves with the disinherited.[67] They embraced a life-style of voluntary poverty and focused their attention on economic and social changes that were consistent with the goals of Christian personalism. While these people did not wait for clerical leadership, the Catholic Worker was recognized by the church hierarchy, and the Archdiocese of New York requested its members to accept a chaplain. The founders did so, but the chaplain stayed very much in the background. Dorothy Day, then as always, followed the directives of her church superiors, but the Catholic Worker movement was never dependent upon the institutional church or any other organization for financial support. Voluntary contributions provided what monetary assistance was necessary.

Because of the depression, Catholic Workers focused all their energies on ways to relieve human suffering and to remedy the injustices of American society. They based their program of social reconstruction on Christian personalism and upon Pope Leo XIII's injunction in *Rerum Novarum* to "go to the workingman, especially to the poorest of them." Catholic Workers favored a new economic system to replace what they viewed as a decadent capitalism. Though steeped in the thought of American and European social and liturgical thinkers, they centered the core of their beliefs on the Gospel, showing their love for God by carrying out the corporal and spiritual works of mercy.[68] Thus, in their call for a new social order members favored direct action aimed at countering the evils of industrial society and demanded an unbloody revolution. An explicit concern for peace was not apparent in the early days of the Catholic Worker, but as Dorothy Day was to say before the outbreak of World War II: "For eight years we have been opposing the use of force—in the labor movement, in the class struggle, as well as in the struggles between countries. . . . By working for a better social order in our own country, by working for the 'tranquillity in order' which is the definition of peace, we are working for peace."[69] The Catholic Worker saw the incidents of aggression during the 1930s and the world's response to them as power politics. In its view the League of Nations and the concept of collective security to prevent war seemed to fail each successive test. Thus, the movement developed and acted upon a pacifist rationale.

This pacifist position became explicit at the time of the Spanish Civil War. The Catholic establishment was decidedly pro-Franco, but the Catholic Worker did not support his cause and condemned every aspect of Franco's revolt. In doing this the *Catholic Worker* stated that it was adopting a position of strict neutrality, yet by remaining neutral, it was already in opposition to the mainstream of Catholics in the United States. The paper printed the message of love and Christian pacifism: "Love your enemies; do good to them that hate you, and pray for them that persecute and calumniate you."[70]

The *Catholic Worker* was not the only Catholic publication to profess neutrality during the Spanish Civil War. *Commonweal*, a monthly magazine published by Catholic lay people, and the diocesan paper, the *Echo*, in Buffalo, New York, were neutral during the Spanish Civil War. The *Echo*, also professed pacifism. These are the only known Catholic publications to adopt positions similar to the *Catholic Worker* during this war.

By 1935, the distribution of the movement's newspaper had increased to 110,000 copies and it was also appearing in England and Australia.[71] The paper consistently opposed efforts to involve the United States in war and provided clear statements of its peace position interspersed with articles on the popes' messages on peace, on the morality of war, and on conscription. It denounced Roosevelt's foreign policy and opposed preparedness measures. It urged Catholic Workers not to manufacture munitions and, later, not to purchase defense bonds. Individual Catholic Workers also joined demonstrations and boycotts, appeared before Congressional hearings and attempted to organize Catholic pacifists in resistance to conscription.

Strict neutrality became for the Workers the only viable way to prevent America's entrance into World War II. This stance clearly revealed the ideological differences between the Catholic Worker and CAIP. Ironically, the Catholic Worker found itself aligned with Coughlin in advocating strict neutrality, although Catholic Workers were internationalists (not in CAIP terms of world government, but in religious terms of human solidarity and the Mystical Body of Christ) and the Coughlinites were isolationists. The differences and similarities that emerged among Catholics over the issue of neutrality legislation were identical to those found among all pacifist groups, all advocates of collective security, and all isolationists during the 1930s. Once America entered the war, the pacifist rationale of the Catholic Worker logically required its members to reject participation in the war as a means of resolving the conflict. This was also true of all pacifist peace groups.

The Catholic Worker had little direct cooperation with other groups during the 1930s,[72] although the articles in its newspaper provided some cooperation. In December 1934, the *Catholic Worker* ran an ad for CAIP and it utilized the NCWC news service on items relating to peace. As late as 1939 in its October editorial, the newspaper asked:

How many Catholics know that in Washington we have a Catholic Association for International Peace . . . , an association which is headed by Most Reverend Edwin V. O'Hara, Bishop of Kansas City? Among the vice presidents there are many friends of the Catholic Worker. . . . It is absolutely necessary that our groups and cells and as many of our readers as possible should write and obtain literature that is available and form study groups to prepare themselves for the work of peace.

The *Catholic Worker's* pages also praised the work of the Women's International League for Peace and Freedom (WILPF) and the National Council for the Prevention of War.[73] The paper often used resource material from the National Council for the Prevention of War.

In its attempt to offset the influences of anti-Semitism and anti-communism among American Catholics, the *Catholic Worker* also touched on issues crucial to peace. Peter Maurin argued in his newspaper articles that "America is big enough to find a refuge for persecuted Jews." Dorothy Day stated that the Catholic Worker "defended Jews during times of stress."[74] And in 1939 the newspaper reported Archbishop Stritch of Chicago as decrying "the slanders and untruths being printed about the Jews" and his condemnation of the anti-Semitism of Coughlin and the Christian Front.[75]

The Catholic Worker's founders deplored red-baiting as much as anti-Semitism. Day was convinced by her early association with communists "that often the Communist more truly loves his brother, the poor and oppressed, than many so-called Christians."[76] In July 1937, the *Catholic Worker* replied to Coughlin's charge that its members were communists by contending that the movement was not communistic and affirming that the only true "international" was the Catholic church.[77]

The founders were also aware of the great fear of communism and saw it often as the real motive behind Catholic statements on war and peace issues. In October 1936, the Catholic Worker agreed to cooperate with John Noll, bishop of Fort Wayne, in his anticommunist drive, but explained its participation by stating that "it joined mainly because it believed that man was not subject to the state but to Christ and that this message should be delivered to the leaders of all nations not just the communist leaders." The *Catholic Worker* opposed peace groups controlled by communists such as the American League Against War and Fascism, on the grounds that these groups still advocated class war.[78] People interested in these groups were advised to contact the Catholic Worker for more information and urged Catholics to start their own peace groups so that communists would not be the only ones claiming to work for peace.

The pages of the *Catholic Worker* in 1936 pleaded with bankers not to lend money to nations at war.[79] It opposed the cash-and-carry clause of the Neutrality Act of 1937 because it "only served to line up Fascist against Democratic powers."[80] It also admitted, with the defeat of the Ludlow Resolution in the House by only twenty-one votes, that there was no way left for the American people to prevent a presidential declaration of war. This position remained constant and in 1939 the *Catholic Worker* opposed the lifting of the Arms Embargo and declared that the United States "should not export arms to any country in peace or at war."[81]

As the situation in Europe worsened, the *Catholic Worker*'s position remained clear and consistent, and like other pacifist peace groups in America it supported the Keep America Out of War campaign after 1939. Increasingly it turned to the needs of its own constituents, particularly to the needs of Catholic conscientious objectors. Pearl Harbor was anticlimatic. President Roosevelt had already won approval to extend American military and economic goods to the Allies, had accepted an anti-German naval commitment in the Atlantic, and had removed most of the fetters from neutrality legislation.[82] Unable to alter national legislation and defeated in their demands for strict neutrality, the *Catholic Worker* remained faithful to its pacifism and refused to support the war when it was finally declared.

The Catholic Worker movement like CAIP and Coughlin was led into the arena of war and peace through its concern for social justice. By moving to the left on the political spectrum in America, the Catholic Worker stepped out of the whole intellectual and social ethos of Americanism. Strengthened by deep religious faith, the movement gradually worked out a stance of pacifism, but any degree of intellectual sophistication concerning this position would not be reached until after World War II. The significance of the Catholic Worker for American Catholic history in the 1930s is that it provided a pacifist alternative to war.

The internationalism of CAIP, on the other hand, left the association with no alternative to war once it was declared. Ryan and his associates wished to achieve world peace through social justice, and the greatest strength of their approach to international problems was their economic interpretation and their clear recognition of the necessity of worldwide planning and control. In the absence of a strong international organization and with no ethic but the just war doctrine, CAIP ended up acknowledging the state as its final decision maker in matters of war. For all the association's opposition to extreme nationalism and to the Coughlin hysteria, CAIP accepted the decisions of its nation for international ends. In the face of Hitlerism its way to peace was through war.

Despite Coughlin's moral crusade against political evils, he was unable to stop the United States from entering World War II. Coughlin was not against participation in war; he believed that America was fighting on the wrong side in this particular war and therefore men should not fight. The irony of this stance is that Coughlin was mainly condemned for his extreme nationalism, yet, at the time of World War II, he stood in opposition to his nation.

The structure and tactics of all three Catholic groups influenced and attracted as members portions of the American Catholic public. CAIP, the "official" Catholic peace organization, attracted middle- and upper-class Catholics, and once war was declared reflected the majority opinion, not only of Catholics, but of all Americans. Coughlin's demagogic approach appealed to the lower class and the more disaffected members of society in his offer to raise their standard of living by rooting out evil. The Catholic Worker attracted those Catholics seeking an intensified life-style of commitment to the Gospel message of "love of neighbor." In all three groups only the Catholic Worker offered a life-style and a supportive community that enabled its members to provide a Christian witness to peace, an alternative to the American way of life.

Neither Coughlin nor the Catholic Worker was able to influence national legislation to the extent of maintaining strict neutrality, even though minor victories were achieved, such as the 1939 delay of the lifting of the arms embargo during the Spanish Civil War. The defeat of strict neutrality and the United States entrance into World War II cancelled out the minor victories. Coughlinites and the Catholic Worker, together with all isolationist and pacifist groups during the 1930s, could not determine national legislation. CAIP's move to collective security in national legislation placed it in the victorious camp of the Roosevelt administration and ultimately in the midst of World War

II. The belief that Hitler had to be stopped, even by war, was a greater cause than the maintenance of peace. In this case, CAIP was no different than the other peace groups that advocated collective security.

The diversity in American Catholicism's quest for peace represented by these three groups contradicts the generally accepted view of a united Catholic front on the issues of war and peace. The three positions of pacifism, internationalism, and isolationism provided the basis for ideological diversity among Catholics as well as among all Americans during the 1930s. The major difference between Catholics and other Americans was that Catholics reinforced these positions with a Catholic theological rationale.

Until the 1930s, the just war doctrine had been the normative ethical position in American Catholicism. With the appearance of the Catholic Worker movement this tradition was challenged for the first time in American history by the earlier Christian tradition of pacifism. After the war, the ethical stance of pacifism became more widespread among Catholics and as a result the just war doctrine considerably less acceptable.[83] The demagogic rhetoric of the crusader Charles Coughlin has disappeared and one reason for its demise was its emphasis on hatreds and negativism rather than on positive ethical values. Though CAIP continued to publish pamphlets and issue statements on war and peace, it had little impact on the Catholic peace movement after the opening of World War II.

The group that would provide the American Catholic peace witness during World War II and for the next forty years would be the Catholic Worker. In order to understand the place of pacifism within the Catholic Worker movement and its impact on the American Catholic church it is necessary to know more fully the thought and action of Dorothy Day. Through the Catholic Worker, she offered a new direction in the American Catholic peace movement and launched what she described as a "permanent revolution" in American Catholicism.[84]

2

Dorothy Day
Mother of American Catholic Pacifism

PRIOR TO THE TWENTIETH CENTURY, pacifist in the United States was a term with a broad connotation and was applicable to anyone advocating international cooperation for peace. The definition narrowed with World War I and came to be "malevolently" applied to anyone who would not support even a "war to end war."[1] The government further narrowed the definition in its selective service legislation to include only those opposed to "war in any form." It was this definition that provided the legal recognition of conscientious objection in the United States during World War II.

Among Roman Catholics the pacifism of the primitive Christian church, like other features of the radical Gospel, largely disappeared with the Age of Constantine. Only in the twentieth century did American Catholics rediscover this heritage in their attempt to address contemporary issues of war and peace. The first American Catholic to challenge the accepted just war teaching was Dorothy Day. Perhaps, because she was a convert to Catholicism, she did not initially confront the just war tradition or offer an intellectual critique; she merely proclaimed her pacifism.[2]

Dorothy Day was born in Brooklyn Heights 8 November 1897 the daughter of John I. Day, a sportswriter. Essentially a conservative, John Day attempted to combine respectability with journalism. The Days were an austere Scotch-Irish Presbyterian family and Dorothy found the coldness of their family life unsatisfying. "There was never any kissing in our family, and never a close embrace," she wrote years later. "There was only a firm and austere kiss from my mother every night. . . . We were like most Anglo-Saxons."[3]

Unable to embrace her parents, Day embraced the poor and the

29

oppressed. As a young girl in Chicago, where her father was a sports editor of *Inter Ocean*, she began reading radical literature, the Russian Kropotkin especially. Initially unaffected by World War I, she entered the University of Illinois at Urbana on a scholarship which she supplemented by caring for children and doing house work. During her two years at college, formal academic disciplines did not capture her interest, she missed classes and disdained the customary patterns of college social mixing. She read everything by Dostoevsky, who impressed her profoundly, along with the works of Gorky and Tolstoy and she became preoccupied with poverty, misery, and the class war, eventually joining the campus Socialist club. As she put it, "I was in love with the masses."

Leaving college in 1916 because of academic dissatisfaction and financial need, Dorothy Day moved with her family to New York, where her father had taken a job on the *Telegraph*. Soon after they arrived she went to work as a reporter and columnist on the Socialist *Call*. Her father's disapproval led her to rent a room on Cherry Street, in the slums of the lower East Side, and never again did she live with her family. Day believed "her father's greatest unhappiness came from her ideas which he thought were subversive and dangerous to the peace of the country."4

On her own at nineteen, Day spent the next two years in the tumult of Greenwich Village life. While on the job at the *Call*, she reported on and often participated in strikes, picket lines, peace meetings, and antiwar demonstrations. She also joined the Industrial Workers of the World, because she shared its anarchistic verve and distrust of Marx. In April 1917, Day left the *Call* and went to work for the Anti-Conscription League before joining the staff of the radical *Masses*, which folded by the end of the year due to enforcement of wartime postal censorship. She worked at various jobs during the winter of 1917–1918, one of which was with the *Liberator*. She left Greenwich Village early in 1918 to begin nurses training at King's County Hospital in Brooklyn, after deciding that the step was not contrary to her pacifist principles. In her autobiography, *The Long Loneliness*, Day reflected on her pacifism during World War I and cryptically wrote "I was pacifist in what I considered an imperialist war though not pacifist as a revolutionist."5

During these years Day did have brief moments when she experienced religion. In 1917, she joined sixty other women to protest the treatment of imprisoned suffragists. Though as a radical Day never intended to vote, she and others were arrested for their demonstration of support and when they refused bail they were sentenced to thirty days in the Occoquain Prison. While in jail, an attendant brought her a Bible, and she read it. The Psalms comforted her, yet she decided that the comfort received from religion was a sign of weakness.[6] In 1918, at the Golden Swan saloon, she first heard Catholic poet Francis Thompson's "The Hound of Heaven" recited from memory by friend Eugene O'Neill. Many mornings, after staying up all night with Village friends, she attended early morning Mass at Saint Joseph's Church on Sixth Avenue. At King's County Hospital she attended Sunday Mass on a regular basis. Despite these religious experiences, at this point in her life, Day can best be seen as "an old-time native American radical who reflected the strong but nondoctrinaire dissent against the corporate capitalist state that existed in the United States."[7]

While at the hospital Day fell in love with Lionel Moise, a former *Kansas City Star* reporter and moved in with him shortly after the November 1918 Armistice. The war had ceased but Day's personal struggle had just begun. She proceeded to spend the next seven years of her life pursuing unsuccessful and often tragic personal relationships that ended in suicide attempts, an abortion, a marriage, and a divorce. Day tried to keep these seven years of her life hidden and never spoke of them.

During these years, Day spent her time between New York and Chicago, working as a reporter, a proofreader, a librarian, and even as a clerk at Montgomery Ward's. She still managed to write, and in 1923 A. & C. Boni published her first novel. It was about life in the Village and very autobiographical. Though it was not very successful, the publisher sold it to Hollywood on the strength of the name, *The Eleventh Virgin*. Day, however, did receive a payment of $2,500 for her novel which she used to buy a cottage on the shore of Raritan Bay, at Huguenot, Staten Island.[8] A few months later she began to live with Forster Battingham, a young biology instructor. She continued to view herself as a writer. Within a year her second novel, *What Price Love?* was bought by the Bell Syndicate for newspaper serialization.

On 3 March 1927 she gave birth to her daughter Tamar. She was happy though Tamar's father was not. Battingham wondered what point there was to bringing another person into a world of hopelessness and injustice. In her autobiography, Day tells how the birth of her child compelled her to become a Catholic.

> Forster had made the physical world come alive for me and had awakened in my heart a flood of gratitude. The final object of this love and gratitude was God. No human creature could receive or contain so vast a flood of love and joy as I felt after the birth of my child. With this came the need to worship and adore. I had heard many say they wanted to worship God in their own way and did not need a Church in which to praise Him. . . . But my very experience as a radical, my whole make-up, led me to want to associate myself with others, with the masses, in praising and adoring God. Without even looking into the claims of the Catholic Church, I was willing to admit that for me she was the one true Church.[9]

This choice on Day's part meant that she would have to leave her mate, who was deeply irreligious and found all that he needed in nature. Her choice of Catholicism also meant parting with her lifelong radical friends. In some aspects, Day's choice is not entirely incomprehensible. She ultimately seemed to be searching for something that her past experiences had not satisfied. She had never been attracted to the intellectual life; she had found the class-conflict interpretation of Marx inadequate to explain the plight of the masses; and one-issue causes such as women's rights did not long hold her attention. Journalism and writing were still her profession, but she did not view herself as very successful in these areas. Her conversion signified a belief in a deeper reality. This belief was so strong that she was willing to leave all for it.

Day first had her daughter Tamar baptized. Then on 28 December 1927, Dorothy Day was baptized a Catholic in the Church of Our Lady, Holy Christians, in Totenville, Staten Island. The action was almost wholly mechanical. There was no consolation. For the next five years, Day explored her faith, raised her daughter, wrote, worked for a short time for the Fellowship of Reconciliation, and at times did manual labor jobs. She also traveled to Hollywood, to Mexico City, and to Florida to visit her mother—but always returned to New York. Then, while on a writing assignment for *America* and *Commonweal* to cover the Washington hunger march, she noted the total absence of the church's presence on behalf of the poor and knew that somewhere the faith that she had embraced had been turned aside from its true historic mission. She was aware of a frequent dichotomy between the doctrinal ideals of Catholicism and their implementation by church members, and in her autobiography she wrote that she "loved the Church for Christ made visible. Not for itself, because it was so often a scandal to me."[10]

After the hunger march was over Day went to the National Shrine at the Catholic University and prayed that she would discover how the mission of the church could become vital. As she knelt there she also realized that "after three years of Catholicism my only contact with active Catholics had been through articles I had written for one of the Catholic magazines. Those contacts had been brief, casual. I still did not personally know one Catholic layman."[11] Now, this was all to change. Day wrote, "When I returned to New York, I found Peter Maurin—Peter, the French peasant, whose spirit and ideas will dominate . . . the rest of my life."[12]

Maurin's message, whether oral or written, was essentially that of Catholic radicalism. He believed that "the most traditional Catholicism was of supreme social relevance to modern humanity, and that it was only necessary to 'blow the dynamite' of that ancient church to set the whole world afire."[13] His vision was antithetical to liberalism, which is dependent on the changing currents of history and the doctrine of progress. His vision was also unlike liberalism because he did not accept the state as the primary source of community that holds together the change and flow of the material world. And finally, Maurin rejected technology as the means of assuring progress in the world. In place of the liberal myths of nation state, technology, and progress, Maurin drew extensively on the central teaching of orthodox Catholicism and posited the Garden of Eden, the Fall, the light of the Beatitudes, the darkness of oblivion, sacred community, and sinful alienation as central to his social vision. Thus, the radical ideal of Peter Maurin was rooted not in the material world but in the realm of the spirit. His goals would be achieved at the end of time—with the second coming of Christ. Thus, the vision was eschatological and therefore beyond history. It demanded that history submit to it and not the reverse.[14]

Besides this eschatological view of history, the other distinctive feature Maurin presented to Dorothy Day was personalism. "The personalist idea holds that the primacy of Christian love should be brought from its position of limbo where human affairs are concerned and infused into the process of history. The central fact of existence should not be process, with men holding on in whatever spot they found most tolerable, love should redeem process itself. Faith in love is the ultimate reality."[15] This concept of personalism—coupled with a view of freedom that meant the capacity of an individual to turn from tyranny of sense toward the spirit—involved suffering and even tragedy. It basically meant that individuals would reenact in their own lives the mystery of the crucifixion of Christ.

Peter Maurin saw the expression of personalism in individuals who embraced voluntary poverty and at the cost of personal sacrifice performed the works of mercy proclaimed in the Beatitudes. Maurin believed the individual should daily practice the corporal works of feeding the hungry, clothing the naked, and sheltering the shelterless.

Personalism rather than political analysis appealed greatly to Dorothy Day. She had been attracted in vain to political groups such as Socialists and the Industrial Workers of the World in hopes of finding solutions to the plight of the poor. In Christian personalism the solution resided with the individual and was not dependent on historical circumstances. Victory also was assured because of a power beyond history—Christ. Day's commitment to pacifism would be founded in "a matrix of personalism, which called for a heightened sense of personal responsibility for one's neighbors and involvement in struggles for justice on their behalf."[16] It would be Dorothy Day's activism combined with Christian personalism that would keep the Catholic Worker movement embroiled in the messy affairs of society rather than only writing or talking about them.

Maurin was careful to point out what he believed to be the greatest enemies to attaining the Worker ideal in contemporary America: nationalism and capitalism. According to him, the nation had become the symbol of community and had put too much of its use to the ends of competitive power. He opposed capitalism because of its glorification of struggle. He believed capitalists were always in pursuit of their own aggrandizement and used the nation for their own imperialist ends. Maurin did not believe that there was anything new in his analysis of the twin enemies, but he did believe that his solution was new. The Worker ideal presented a viable alternative to the American way of life.

It was the twin enemies of nationalism and capitalism that led Day to apply to herself the term "Catholic anarchist."[17] She did this during the 1930s when the authority of the federal government had become almost sacred to millions of people who perceived the New Deal to be the one and only hope to solve society's ills. Day's anarchism, on the other hand, meant increased reponsibility of one person for another, of the individual to the community along with a much lessened sense of obligation to or dependence on the "distant and centralized state."[18]

Maurin had no blueprint for the decentralization and simplification of American society. The Worker ideal was all very vague and, at best, all he could offer were a few general principles.[19] Yet, these general principles were all that Dorothy Day needed to begin her work. According to William Miller, Day's biographer, "What Peter Maurin did for Dorothy was to reorient her vision from the object to the subject, from collectivisim to Christian personalism. He also provided her with something she had not had—an understanding of the meaning of the Church and her position in it."[20]

Dorothy Day believed that the Worker ideal was a positive Christian alternative and that it should be made available to every individual who desired it. For this to occur, it was first necessary to present the ideal to others. Day's first effort was related to what she knew how to do best—start a newspaper. She entitled it the *Catholic Worker* to announce a Catholic presence and concern for the poor and oppressed in opposition to communists and other radicals who were identified with the poor and oppressed. The publication of the first issue caused Maurin to disappear for a month. He had wanted the paper to devote itself exclusively to the printing of his own essays which appeared under the title of Easy Essays. Day had different ideas and wanted a broader focus on current issues by many contributors. Peter eventually returned.[21]

Day also managed to find other ways of carrying out Maurin's vision. She opened a House of Hospitality on Mott Street in New York City where roundtable discussions between workers and intellectuals occurred. She raised enough money to buy land to start a farming commune in hope of achieving a simplified way of life in contrast to the dehumanizing aspects of the capitalist economy. These three endeavors—the paper, the House of Hospitality, and the farm—provided visibility, place, and work for individuals who also desired to embrace the Worker ideal. The main work of Catholic Workers was administering food, clothing, and shelter to the poor. Since Maurin spent most of his time on the road trying to spread his vision to others, Day was left to direct, order, and maintain the Catholic Worker. Under her leadership Workers not only performed the corporal works of mercy but also began to spend much time protesting the dehumanizing aspects of nationalism and capitalism through their newspaper, by participation in strikes, and by demonstrations against social injustice.

Within a few years of the founding of the Catholic Worker movement, it became evident that it was not the depression, but war that was the major crisis confronting Americans. The *Catholic Worker* stated that "during a time of war the nation state was invested with all the marks of power in the form of military might. At a time of war, the coercive power of the state reached its zenith."[22] A nation's decision to declare war was thus the ultimate question to be faced by the individual. For Day, war was the most extreme opposition to active love, the antithesis of the radical Christian vision she had embraced. Having been opposed to war before her conversion to Catholicism, she now clearly saw that the Gospel message was peace. For Day the only alternative to violence was nonviolence or what she called Catholic pacifism. Her emphasis was on the individual and not the state. She would not cooperate with the state in any way concerning the issue of war. In opposition to war Day brought together the personalism and anarchism of the Worker ideal of love. In this sense her Catholicism enhanced her pacifism of old and placed it within a revolutionary context. As historian Mel Piehl stated, "After 1945, it was the issue of pacifism that most effectively represented the Catholic Worker's gospel idealism."[23]

Peter Maurin never reached the point of making his pacifism a pronouncement. As a young man in France, in November 1898 he had been called to military duty, and he served as a soldier in the 142nd Infantry Regiment of Mende at Lodeve until the following September. According to Marc Ellis, Maurin's most recent biographer, "This was a disturbing, perhaps even transformative experience for him, for his superiors and his brother Celestin confirmed that he strongly objected to military service. The organization of people toward a dubious end undoubtedly disturbed him. His background as a peasant, with its lack of emphasis on nationhood, and as a Brother, with its emphasis on the poor, clashed with the assertion of national aspirations and protection of wealth bound up with the military."[24] Maurin received an honorable discharge and was placed in the reserve. The reserve called him back for two short periods in 1904 and 1907. Maurin's continuing involvement with the military was undoubtedly a major factor in his decision in 1909 to immigrate to Canada where there was no conscription.

There is no clear explanation of why Maurin would not proclaim pacifism. In his Easy Essays he often pointed to the evil and futility of war. John C. Cort, a young Catholic Worker of the 1930s wrote that "Dorothy says that Peter was a pacifist, but I don't recall seeing anything he ever wrote or hearing anything he ever said that supports that. The subject didn't seem to interest him, or else he didn't feel confident enough to challenge the traditional Catholic view that there are just wars and there are unjust wars."[25] Eileen Egan, who knew both founders of the Catholic Worker movement, wrote that "On the subject of the Spanish Civil War, Maurin did not speak out, though he made it clear that his way was the Franciscan way, a way that excluded violence. For a man intent on finding 'concordance,' the confrontation of the Worker movement with modern war, and the bitter criticism it evoked, was hard to bear. 'Perhaps silence would be better for a time than to continue our opposition to war,' he said to Dorothy Day as World War II began. 'Men are not ready to listen.' "[26]

Maurin's reluctance, however, did not prevent Day as editor of the *Catholic Worker* from announcing that pacifism was the paper's position. She viewed pacifism as a part of the total vision that was presented to her by Peter Maurin. The Catholic Worker was a total way of life and to be consistent with the Worker ideal during a time of war, Day believed a pacifist response was necessary, flowing naturally and perhaps supernaturally from the total Worker ideal. As early as October 1933, the newspaper stated that its "delegates" would "be among those present at the United States Congress Against War" and they would be representing 'Catholic Pacifism.' " Since this was the first such collective statement in American history of a group of Catholics, they well knew that they scarcely represented more than themselves.

In 1933 the only American Catholic peace activity came from semiofficial CAIP. The leaders of CAIP disdained mass organization and antiwar action, preferring instead the more genteel peace activities of lobbying, lecturing, and publication prevalent in America before World War I. In Europe, on the other hand, World War I had produced the German Catholic *Friendensbund* and the French *Ligue pour la Paix.* Associated with these mass organizations was a small but influential group of intellectuals and theologians who urged the church to declare herself unequivocally against war. The best known were Father Johannes Ude of Graz University and the German Dominican Franziskus Stratmann. Within the first year of the *Catholic Worker* publication, Stratmann's works, particularly *The Church and War*, were favorably reviewed and quoted in the paper.[27] What was meant by American Catholic pacifism in terms of an intellectual rationale was still undefined.

Catholic Worker pacifism derived from Dorothy Day's personal commitment. In the late 1930s, some of Day's followers were able to elaborate her basic conviction about Catholic pacifism in an attempt to develop a Catholic case against war. The first of these were Paul Hanly Furfey, William Callahan, and Arthur Sheehan. Furfey, a pacifist priest and educator from the Catholic University of America as well as a friend of the movement, foreshadowed the theological rationale that would eventually form the basis of Catholic Worker pacifism in an article he wrote for its newspaper in 1935. He based the antiwar case on the Gospel counsel of perfection. The article centered on an imaginary debate between Christ and a patriot. Furfey based the theological principle for pacifism in the debate, not on the just war theory but on the Christian's calling to a kingdom of love and peace that takes precedence over one's calling to obedience to the state. He urged abandonment of the "Constantinian Compromise" with the war-making state and a return to the eschatological pacifist vision of the early saints and Church Fathers. This was the first statement that reflected a pacifism based on the Gospel message of peace, and with it the American Catholic peace movement mothered by Dorothy Day was born.

Because of the dominance of the just war theory in the Catholic tradition, it was logical for Catholics to attempt to apply it to pacifism. The first theoretician of the just war rationale for Catholic Worker pacifism was young Bill Callahan, managing editor of the paper during much of the decade. In December 1935 he gave a talk to the Catholic

Social Club of Brooklyn entitled "Catholics Should be Conscientious Objectors in Time of War."[28] Then, in October 1936 he announced through the *Catholic Worker* "the formation of a Catholic organization of conscientious objectors." Four months later the group was named PAX and Bill Callahan became its director. The logic of the group was based on the presupposition that the war in question was not just.

Catholic pacifism, however, did not become a central issue of the Catholic Worker movement until the Spanish Civil War, 1936–1939. When the war erupted in July 1936, Dorothy Day proclaimed pacifism and neutrality in the pages of the *Catholic Worker.*

> Poor blood-drenched Spain is the most talked about subject today. . . . Who is right and who is wrong? We are inclined to believe that the issue is not so clear cut as to enable either side to condemn the other justifiably. . . .
>
> Our main concern is that the "members of Christ tear one another." . . .
>
> Spain doesn't need favorable publicity for the rebels. She doesn't need condemnation of the loyalists. What she needs is the prayers of the rest of the Mystical Body. Please to God that Members stop hating each other. . . .
>
> The *Catholic Worker* makes this appeal to its readers: Forget your anger. Let your indignation die. Remember only that the Body is rent asunder, and the only solution is Love.[29]

Ironically, the issue of pacifism was overshadowed by anti-Communism. American Catholics had found a rallying point for their anti-Communism in the war. Thus, it was not the *Catholic Worker's* voicing of Dorothy Day's position of pacifism and refusal to take sides in the war that raised the ire of American Catholics, but her refusal to support Franco against the Communists. In the *Catholic Worker's* attempt to offer a Catholic counteropinion to the "propaganda in favor of Franco and rebel Spain," it provoked the strongest reaction against the *Catholic Worker* since its inception.

The experience of the Spanish Civil War inspired Arthur Sheehan to attempt to clarify the meaning of Catholic pacifism by examining the application of the just war criteria to modern warfare. Sheehan used evidence from the Spanish Civil War to show that in modern war each side typically asserted the complete justice of their cause. He argued that modern warfare could not be waged according to the traditional criteria, particularly those concerning pure intentions and the protection of noncombatants. The vast destructive capability of technological weaponry guaranteed that no side could pursue self-defense without perpetuating a great moral evil, a violation of the just war principle of proportionality. Because of modern technological warfare no war could be just, and pacifism was the only option.[30] As a just war pacifist, Sheehan provided the rationale that other Catholic Workers reiterated when defending their position as just war pacifists. Dorothy Day and other Catholic Workers, however, did not look to the just war doctrine, but to the Gospel message of peace for the basis of their pacifism. Thus, debate among Catholic Workers continued on the topic. A clearer analysis of Catholic pacifism based on the Gospel message of peace would not emerge until the outbreak of World War II. Even then the issue of Catholic pacifism would be initially blurred by historical interpretaions of the causes of war and justifications for conscientious objection.

The Catholic Worker's preoccupation with the twin enemies of nationalism and capitalism influenced their interpretation of the cause of World War II. The *Catholic Worker* contended that wars were the work of the big capitalists. In its interpretation that World War II resulted from a conspiracy of high finance, the *Catholic Worker* was joined by the followers of Charles Coughlin and by a notable member of the American hierarchy, Archbisop John T. McNicholas of Cincinnati. But McNicholas and the Coughlinites added the proposition that it was also of Communist inspiration. When the war did break out, the *Catholic Worker* continued to insist that it was a repetition of 1914. It gave its position in a front page statement: "We Are to Blame for New War in Europe."

Peter Maurin believed that the combination of external competition for markets and internal protection of industry had led to the increasing power of the state and the hostility of England and Germany in World War I. This war had ushered in the era of finance capitalism and had resulted not in the establishment of democracy but its antithesis: Marxism in Russia, fascism in Italy, and Nazism in Germany. The world depression in 1929, according to Maurin, had ushered in the last watershed, state capitalism. This decline symbolized the triumph of a secular world guided by self-interest over a religious world once guided by tradition. The end of cultural and religious tradition involved in the decline devalued the individual because the economic, political, and military systems left fewer avenues for the individual to recognize and follow the soul's longing for eternity. Maurin saw World War II as a continuation of the historical forces of capitalism and nationalism.[31]

Maurin's historical interpretation of World War II had a profound effect on Dorothy Day's pacifist rationale. Through 1939, Day and the *Catholic Worker* had used history-based arguments to justify Worker pacifism. This was understandable because the just war tradition had taught Catholics to distinguish between a just war and an unjust war in history. By late 1940, however, it became evident that World War II was not a repetition of World War I and that Catholic pacifism could not be based on the just war tradition whose criteria were themselves based on the actions of a nation in the objective material world. Day realized she had to turn to the spiritual realm beyond history and look to the Gospel message of peace and the individual's conscience as the basis of decision making concerning issues of war and peace.

By 1940, Dorothy Day believed that the Worker's pacifist position had to be put to the test of close theological analysis. She also knew that she was not equipped to provide such reasons herself, and increasingly relied on John Hugo, a young Pittsburgh priest, for spiritual direction. In a note to Day, Hugo wrote: "No doubt [pacifism] is all clear to you; but then you have not tried to work it out doctrinally. If you knew no theology, it would probably be simpler to make a solution. Yet the decision must be based on doctrine. Pacifism must proceed from truth, or it cannot exist at all. And of course this attack on conscription is the most extreme form of pacifism."[32]

John Hugo attempted to answer Day's challenge with a series of articles in the *Catholic Worker* which were reprinted in pamphlet form under the title *Weapons of the Spirit*. In the introduction Hugo began by rejecting the just war tradition and positing the Gospel law, which he believed modern war negated. "While I believe that war may be just, at any rate in theory," he said, "I am also convinced that it is not Christ's way." He then stated that Christ's way is based on faith and love and this sets it above man's way, which is based on reason. The individual is called to live out Christ's love particularly during a time of war. Hugo, like Maurin, contended that modern war is capitalistic and imperialistic. Hugo invited the individual to embrace spiritual means—prayer, fasting, and penance—to overcome the evil of war. Though he never used the word pacifism in his writing, he did invite the individual to live "the more perfect" life in Christ and reject all war. He also stressed the devotions of the Rosary and the Sacred Heart as spiritual aids for those who sought to live the more perfect life.

Dorothy Day's view of nationalism and capitalism as twin enemies had led her to an incorrect interpretation of the cause of World War II, but the Gospel message and Christian personalism would not let her err in her spiritual conviction of pacifism —of that she was convinced. But the cost of such witness to Dorothy Day and the Catholic Worker movement was great. Her pronouncement of pacifism caused dissension among members of the movement across the country. The Chicago House of Hospitality in particular was not pacifist. This house, with John Cogley as editor, had been publishing its own newspaper, the *Chicago Catholic Worker*, which did not reflect the pacifist position of the New York paper. At the St. Francis House of Hospitality in Seattle, the Workers stopped distributing the *Catholic Worker* because it was filled almost entirely with pacifism and instead distributed the *Chicago Catholic Worker*. In June 1940, Dorothy Day sent a letter to all Workers concerning the issue of pacifism.

> We know that there are those who are members of 'Catholic Worker' groups throughout the country who do not stand with us in this issue. We have not been able to change their views through what we have written in the paper, or by letters, or by personal conversation. They wish still to be associated with us, to perform the corporal works of mercy.

" 'And that,' she said, 'was all right.' But there had been other cases when some associated with the movement had taken it on themselves to suppress the paper. In such instances she felt it would be necessary for those persons to disassociate themselves from the movement."[33] By the end of 1942 sixteen of the houses or one half of them had been closed.[34] Dorothy Day even admitted in the May 1942 issue of the *Catholic Worker*, that she had been accused of splitting the movement from top to bottom by her pacifism.

As the war progressed the issue that involved Catholic Workers more than anything else was the draft. Dorothy's pacifism made her an advocate of total resistance to the draft. She believed the individual should not cooperate in any way with the U. S. government concerning the draft. Moreover, her respect for the individual, the heart of Christian personalism, enabled her to reach out and assist all men, regardless of their degree of resistance, who became conscientious objectors (COs) in World War II.[35] Thus, it was the Catholic Worker movement alone, among all American Catholic groups, that offered assistance to individuals who conscientiously objected to World War II.

Prior to Pearl Harbor, the Catholic press opposed conscription or the draft. Archbishop McNicholas even urged men to become conscientious objectors. In March 1938, he issued a pastoral letter that recommended the formation of "A Mighty League of CO's." The *Catholic Worker* published the full text of the letter. McNicholas also denounced the 'war makers' who were advancing the present capitalistic system and who "did not deserve the name of patriots."[36]

This statement coming from a member of the Catholic hierarchy, encouraged the members of PAX to redouble their efforts.[37] Through a regular monthly column in the *Catholic Worker*, PAX attempted to secure signatures to support a Catholic's right to conscientious objection. Moreover, they dared to print a box in the *Catholic Worker* urging men not to register for the draft. The government chose to ignore this legal offense; the Catholic ecclesiastical authorities did not. They thought Dorothy Day and the *Catholic Worker* "had gone too far" and Day was called to the New York Chancery and told, "Dorothy you must stand corrected." She remarked that:

> I was not quite sure what that meant, but I did assent, because I realized that one should not tell another what to do in such circumstances. We had to follow our own consciences, which later took us to jail; but our work in getting out the paper was an attempt to arouse the consciences of others, not to advise action for which they were not prepared.[38]

PAX was active until 1940 when military conscription became imminent. By that time, Bill Callahan had left the Catholic Worker and Arthur Sheehan was given the job of directing and reorganizing the group. Sheehan changed the name of the group from PAX to the Association of Catholic Conscientious Objectors (ACCO) in order to be self-explanatory. By not forbidding the name, the church tacitly recognized the association and with it the right of practicing Catholics to be conscientious objectors.[39] The group received many requests for information about conscientious objection and attempted to keep informed about Catholics who were conscientious objectors and those who had gone to jail for noncooperation with the draft.

The issue of military conscription, like the Spanish Civil War, made apparent to Catholic Workers that there were at least two types of Catholic pacifism operative in the movement—just war pacifism and pacifism based on the Gospel message of peace. In both cases the end result was the same. More importantly, both emphasized the right of the individual in conscience to refuse participation in war. This right had long been part of Catholic teaching and modern popes and traditional defenders of the just war theory professed to uphold individual conscience when the issue of conscription and war were matters of public concern. This right of individual conscience would provide the basis of unanimity among Catholics concerning conscription.

In an exhaustive series of articles in the *Catholic Worker* in 1940, Monsignor Barry O'Toole of Catholic University, developed with scholastic thoroughness the objections of Catholic moral theology to a permanent system of conscription. O'Toole argued that selective service could never be endorsed by Catholics because "the citizen cannot be forced to be free by his government, whether in the form of a totalitarian party or the liberalistic majority." Quoting Aquinas, Vittoria, and Franziskus Stratmann, O'Toole put selective service to the test of the just war and concluded that no war in which men were forced to fight against their will could pass the traditional criteria. O'Toole never mentioned pacifism, but under modern conditions, opposing war fought by conscripts would in effect mean opposing all war.[40] In arguments concerning selective service it was just war pacifism that dominated Catholic thought and writing. Even John Hugo's booklet *The Immorality of Conscription*, originally published in the *Catholic Worker* in 1944, used the just war arguments to oppose the idea of compulsory military service, while adding complaints about family disruption and the possibility of women in combat.[41]

The proposed Burke-Wadsworth Bill in Congress in 1940 confronted the American public in a new way concerning the issue of conscription. The bill favored the use of conscription in a time of peace and to many

Americans this was a complete break with their democratic tradition and an indication of the government's desire to enter the European conflict. In July, the Catholic Worker joined a number of peace groups in carrying the anticonscription message to Congress. Barry O'Toole, Dorothy Day, and Joseph Zarrella, a young draft-age Catholic Worker, testified before the House Military Affairs Committee that conscription was contrary to the church.[42] The church always maintained both the right of an individual to choose a vocation and the duty of every individual to serve one's country. It taught further that when the conscience of a citizen prevented the individual from serving in a military vocation, the individual's conscience would be respected. Monsignor Michael J. Ready, the official spokesperson for the Catholic hierarchy also testified before the committee. Though Ready also maintained the right of freedom of conscience in his testimony, his main concern was stated as follows: "The bishops are opposed to provisions in this bill which include for compulsory military service students for the priesthood and those under vows to serve the works of religion."[43] Dorothy Day's testimony on the other hand pointed out that she was speaking for Catholic lay people. When asked by Senator Burke if the clause in the proposed selective service bill that granted exemption from combat for any member of a "religious sect whose creed or principles forbid its members to participate in war in any form" would protect lay Catholics, Day replied: "It does not protect Catholics, no, it may protect the Quakers, the Mennonites, the Dunkards, but not Catholics. . . . There is nothing in the Catholic Creed which would entitle us to that exemption. It does not deal with Catholics."[44]

A Cleric from the National Catholic Welfare Conference who happened to be at the hearings questioned Dorothy's right to speak for Catholics on the issue. She answered in a few words: 'We are speaking for lay people, and they are the ones who fight the wars.' "[45] On 16 September 1940 after eighty-six days of emotional congressional debate, the Burke-Wadsworth Bill was passed by a narrow margin. When it expired, the House of Representatives passed the Selective Service Extension Act on 18 August 1941 by a single vote—293 to 292.[46]

After the Japanese attack on Pearl Harbor on 7 December 1941, attitudes changed dramatically. Congress quickly responded to the attack by passing within six days an amendment to the Selective Service Act that removed the restriction that limited the service of draftees to the Western Hemisphere and stipulated that their period of military service would continue from the time of induction until six months after the end of the war.[47]

Concern for the rights of individual conscience receded into the background and the obligation of the individual to obey the state and support its just cause now became apparent. Neither the Catholic hierarchy nor Catholic intellectuals denied the right of an individual to be a conscientious objector after World War II was declared, but they did nothing to support such individuals. The next major project the Catholic Worker assumed was direct support for Catholic conscientious objectors. Arthur Sheehan, the founder of ACCO, was the self-appointed Catholic representative who approached the selective service for permission to operate a Civilian Public Service Camp (CPS) for Catholic COs. The federal government approved such camps as the legal alternative service system for individuals who had been granted CO status by local draft boards.

To Catholic Workers, especially Dorothy Day, it became evident that an individual conscience shaped in the just war tradition would not lead to pacifist conclusions for most Catholics. Day acknowledged this, and confessed that "it is a matter of grief to me that most of those who are Catholic Workers are not pacifist, but I can see too how good it is that we always have this attitude represented among us. We are not living in an ivory tower."[48] Most Catholic Workers entered military service. John Cogley, one of this group, later remarked, "Most of us still feel that the war on Nazism was a morally justified enterprise, . . . It was better to have fought that evil, even at the price of slaughter, than to have acquiesced in it."[49] Tom Sullivan, an editor of the *Catholic Worker*, served in the Pacific. Jack English, formerly from the Cleveland House of Hospitality, was a gunner on a bomber that was shot down and he spent a year in a Rumanian prison camp. Day's comment on English was, he "has theologian friends whose opinions keep him away from the extreme pacifist position."[50] Other young men helped at the Catholic Worker as long as the draft board permitted and, as Day put it, "talked the issue over constantly." She maintained that their discussions raised the following questions:

> Can there be a just war? Can the conditions laid down by St. Thomas ever be fulfilled? What does God want me to do? And what am I

capable of doing? Can I stand out against state and Church? Is it pride, presumption, to think I have the spiritual capacity to use spiritual weapons in the face of the most gigantic tyranny the world has ever seen? Am I capable of enduring suffering, facing martyrdom? And alone? Again the long loneliness to be faced.[51]

Neither Dorothy Day nor the *Catholic Worker* was able to supply adequate arguments in response to the evils of Hitler and Japanese aggression; in fact, the pages of the newspaper reflect a conspicuous absence of attempting to deal with these historical realities. Instead what is found in its pages is an undaunted pacifism and advocacy of conscientious objection. "We are still pacifist," the editorial read, "and our manifesto is the Sermon on the Mount, which means that we will try to be peacemakers."[52] Because of its pacifist position, the circulation of the *Catholic Worker* decreased from 130,000 copies a month in 1939 to 50,500 copies a month by November 1944. A wider circulation would not resume until April 1948, when 73,000 copies of the *Catholic Worker* were printed.

In 1943, Dorothy Day decided to absent herself from the Catholic Worker for a year. She had become involved in the Lacouture retreat movement, and under the spiritual direction of John Hugo her faith deepened as she tried to live a more perfect Christian life. In an attempt to evaluate her life, she removed herself from responsibility for the movement and turned over editorship of the paper to Arthur Sheehan; she also took her name off the masthead. World War II was bringing death and destruction to large areas of the globe and desolation to Dorothy Day. Her Catholic pacifist stance had exacted a great toll on the movement, reducing the number of houses of hospitality by 50 percent, and it did the same to the circulation of the paper. The flow of invitations to speak at parishes, schools, and seminaries around the country had ceased. Even Peter Maurin had said that "perhaps silence would be better for a time than to continue our opposition to war." The demands of peacemaking on Dorothy Day were as great as the demands of war. Whatever doubt may have arisen concerning her life at the Worker before her sabbatical, she was back with the Catholic Worker in six months, never to leave again until her death.[53]

Though the *Catholic Worker* would not shift from its position of pacifism during World War II, there was a shift in its theological rationale for pacifism. After the war the Catholic Worker abandoned the just war doctrine. Though Sheehan had argued that the application of the doctrine led to pacifist conclusions in modern warfare, it obviously had not for most American Catholics. Dorothy Day had never embraced the doctrine and had never used it in her writings. When it came to war, Day never gave any consideration to the traditional obligations to render obedience to legitimate authority. She always placed the emphasis on the Gospel message of peace, the core of the Worker ideal, as the reason for its pacifism. Even during World War II, there was no theological development of her Catholic pacifism, which had been foreshadowed by Paul Hanly Furfey. Nonetheless, a significant development had taken place among American Catholics. Pacifism had finally become an option practiced by members of the American Catholic community. Though it would take another twenty years for the church to "officially" recognize pacifism as a legitimate option, Dorothy Day continued to be its most powerful advocate. Her repudiation of war, rather than the search for justifications, has become the dominant thrust of contemporary theology. The Catholic Worker would continue to be the heart of the Catholic peace movement in America to the present day.

3

World War II and the Just War Tradition

WITH THE 1941 ATTACK by the Japanese on Pearl Harbor, the United States became the victim of an aggressor and thus the duty to defend America became paramount. The attack outraged Americans and the American Catholic response was identical to the nation's. Francis J. Spellman, archbishop of New York, reflected this sentiment with great emotion when he said,

> With fire and brimstone came December 7, America's throat was clutched, her back was stabbed, her brain was stunned; but her great heart still throbbed. America clenched the palms of those hands oft-stretched in mercy to the peoples of the nations that struck her. America's brain began to clear. America began the fight to save her life.[1]

This statement summarized the attitude of the Catholic hierarchy and of most Catholics who saw the attack as justifying participation in the war. However, some Catholics challenged the traditional just war doctrine by becoming conscientious objectors. For a few others the just war doctrine provided the rationale to speak out against the obliteration bombing of Dresden and Berlin as well as the atomic bombing of Hiroshima and Nagasaki. But these Catholics were voices in the wilderness. The vast majority of American Catholics supported the nation throughout the course of the war. An important reason for this was that the statements of both the popes and the American hierarchy supported the state.

The reign of Pope Pius XI (1922–1939) coincided with the rise of fascism, Nazism, and communism and the destruction of democracy in Europe. Pius XI at first attempted to work with the new totalitarian governments. In 1933, he accepted the Nazi government's offer of a concordat, but he gradually realized the party's hostility to Christianity. In 1937, he condemned Nazism in his encyclical *Mit brennender Sorge*, and five days later he issued *Divini Redemptoris*, a condemnation of "atheistic communism." "When Pius' response came it was almost too late," wrote historian Ronald G. Musto.[2] At Pius XI's death in February 1939, the college of cardinals, who would elect a new pope, realized that a skillful and experienced diplomat would be needed to direct the church through the coming war.

Eugenio Pacelli, who was dedicated to the internationalist approach of his predecessors, was elected to succeed Pius XI and chose the name Pius XII. With the outbreak of war in Europe in September 1939, he could do little but acknowledge his helplessness. His first encyclical, *Summi Pontificatus* (20 October 1939), summarized his approach to war and peace. He condemned Nazi and Soviet aggression plainly and denounced the evils of the totalitarian state; but once again the state was "the framework for all Pius's thinking."[3] In his 1941 Christmas message, *Nell' Alba*, he continued the papal emphasis on rights, justice, and order and stressed the "rights of minorities, economic equality and justice, and freedom of religion, but he did so 'within the limit of a new order' based on the primacy of the nation-state and the recognition of treaty rights, international agreement, and ruling elites."[4] Never did Pius XII mention conscientious objection in any of his addresses nor did he refer to Scripture or pacifism in the early church. Pope Pius XII relied solely on the just war tradition throughout World War II and granted the state the paramount position in conducting what he viewed as a just war in face of the evils of Nazism and fascism.

Pius XII, however, did use the just war doctrine as the basis for his criticism of the state in three instances during the course of World War II. In 1943, he was highly critical of the bombing of Rome, but his reluctance to protest the obliteration bombings of Dresden or Berlin suggests that his condemnation of Rome's bombing was rooted more in self-interest than in just war principles. In his Christmas broadcast of 1944 the pope acknowledged the will of the people and their role in bringing about peace, "the first time since the Middle Ages that a pope had mentioned the role of the Catholic laity" rather than the state in bringing about peace.[5] When atomic bombs were dropped on Hiroshima and Nagasaki, the pope criticized the actions of the U.S. government.[6] After the war Pius XII began to speak in earnest of the emptiness of new defensive systems and the hollowness of even the most just war fought in the modern world. The horrors of modern warfare were finally beginning to change the pope's attitude toward war itself.

During World War II the American Catholic hierarchy issued five statements on the issues of war and peace that reflected the papal position, but with a distinctively American twist. The framework for their thinking was the just war tradition, but nowhere in their public statements did they condemn the savagery of means used in obliteration and atomic bombing. Despite intense pressure from the Vatican, the American hierarchy refused to condemn publicly the bombing of Rome, although they did attempt to change the government's policy through private correspondence and talks with key officials. It appeared that "the American bishops had to balance their allegiances";[7] they wanted to support the pope's concern over the bombing of Rome, but they would not publicly criticize the government's policies as the Holy See wanted.

The neoconservative George Weigel contends that the American hierarchy's five "remarkable" statements during and immediately after the war have been completely ignored in the contemporary American Catholic debate on war and peace. They have been largely ignored by peacemakers because they reflect the bishops' preoccupation with communism and its impact on them in establishing a new international order after World War II. Their significance is not, as Weigel contends, that they "both challenged the Roosevelt and Truman administrations to make the promises implicit in the origins of U.S. involvement in the war (particularly the program laid out in the Atlantic Charter), and contributed to the further development of the Catholic theory of peace as dynamic political community," but because they explain the basis for the relationship between the American hierachy and the U.S. government in foreign affairs during the Cold War.[8]

In the most important of the five statements, *International Order*, issued in November 1944, the American Catholic hierarchy proclaimed the end of isolationism among its ranks and announced a quickly developed concern for the world beyond the United States. The opening line of the statement: "We have met the challenge of war. Shall we meet the challenge of peace?" clearly reflected the hierarchy's desire to help define the new world order. The hierarchy attempted to enunciate the Thomistic principles for a just peace and remind America of its own ideals of what is right in determining the fate of weaker nations. The enunciation of such principles placed the hierarchy in the forefront of the attempt to prevent the domination of Eastern Europe by the Soviet Union, thus entering "into a whole-hearted alliance with the United States government for the preservation of the world order against international communism."[9] The statement demonstrated that the world government heralded by John A. Ryan and CAIP after World War I and during the isolationist ascendancy of the 1930s was suddenly acceptable to many by 1944. CAIP's plea for an international organization to guarantee the rights of all peoples and to see that nations would abide by international law became the type of peace the bishops wanted.

This vision of an international organization, however, was not totally compatible with the United Nations. In their fifth and final statement, *Man and Peace*, issued in November 1946, the American bishops claimed that the basic issue now was human rights and that the new international order under the United Nations, because of the position of power of the USSR in the UN, was in violation of these basic rights. The hierarchy believed that their battle cry throughout the war was the defense of native freedoms against Nazi and fascist totalitarianism; the aftermath of the war revealed a victorious Soviet totalitarianism just as antithetical to these freedoms.

In the years following the war the American Catholic hierarchy tried to unite the just war tradition with the theory of democratic pluralism in hopes of establishing a new order of peace. They did this through the CAIP, which held observer status in the United Nations. CAIP's anti-communist position fused the objectives of the American Catholic hierarchy with those of the U. S. government. But, unlike Pope Pius XII, the American bishops were uncritical of any U. S. government policy that was performed to stop Soviet aggression. In issues of peace as well as war, the state, not the principles of the just war, were victorious. Thus, more was "rendered unto Caesar" than was consistent with justice and peace.

Despite a concern for the rights of people in communist-occupied countries, the bishops made no mention of the right of an individual Catholic to be a conscientious objector in any of their five statements. The first opportunity for the American hierarchy to address this issue had been occasioned by the Military Draft Bill of July 1940. George Flynn has claimed that the Catholic church took what amounted to an official stand opposing the bill since it initially deferred clergy and did not exempt them as in World War I. This status aroused resistance from the American bishops and as a result of this opposition the final version of the bill granted exemption to Catholic clergy. Flynn states: "The entire episode reveals the degree of unity achievable by American Catholics on a nontheological problem, and deep distrust of most clerics for militarism and foreign adventure, and the effectiveness of Catholic pressure on Congress."[10] Recent research reveals that a deep division within the hierachy prevented it from taking a solid stand for or against conscription before the attack on Pearl Harbor and that they were only concerned about exemptions for priests, brothers, and seminarians; there was no concern for lay Catholics who might be conscientious objectors to the war.[11]

In their annual meeting of 1939, the bishops discussed the possibility of draft legislation coming to the Congress, and voted merely to maintain its opposition to the drafting of priests, religious, and seminarians. Archbishop John Glennon of St. Louis recalled that in 1917 several archbishops had testified before a Senate committee and obtained the needed exemptions. Now, it was decided to leave the defense of their position to Michael Ready who was "recognized by the Government as expressing the mind of the Bishops."[12] At the meeting there was no expressed concern for the Catholic laity. Ready asked for the clerical exemptions when he testified before a House committee and also warned against rushing such important legislation, asking that a one-year, voluntary enlistment program be tried before conscription. Fearing he had gone beyond the mandate of the bishops, he wrote a letter of explanation to the committee. Samuel Stritch, archbishop of Chicago, defended Ready's position and blamed the reason for Ready's excess on "the animosity of much of the Catholic press to conscription and noted that some 'important' ecclesiastics [thought] that the Board should have taken this attitude."[13] The bishops gained their desired exemptions in the final bill, which was signed into law on 16 September 1940. Over the next three years they faced several changes in the law. They were especially concerned when the draft age was lowered to eighteen because this affected minor seminarians. This issue was resolved on local levels between individual bishops and draft boards. The hierarchy's response to conscription reflected a position of total self-interest. They did not hesitate to seek exemptions for their own clergy who were necessary to staff church institutions during a time of war, but they would not exert their influence to defend a lay person's right to be a conscientious objector even though the U. S. government granted such an exemption in the draft law during World War II.

Among Catholics in general, support for conscientious objection before World War II was not impressive. *America*, the Jesuit weekly, in November 1939 published the results of a survey of 54,000 Catholic students of both sexes in 141 Catholic colleges and universities. They were asked to respond to a statement of Francis J. Beckman, archbishop of Dubuque, who had declared, "Catholics should give serious thought to the question of whether or not they should be conscientious objectors if this country should enter the war."[14] The results of the survey showed that 20 percent of young Catholics would volunteer for military service, 44 percent would accept conscription, while 36 percent would conscientiously object.[15] Such statistics illustrated the continued strength of traditional patterns of patriotism among two-thirds of these American Catholic students. Once war was declared the one-third who claimed that they would be conscientious objectors dissipated.

For the men who did choose to be conscientious objectors during World War II, the choice necessitated a direct confrontation with the U. S. government. Everyone eligible for military service was required to fill out a selective service questionnaire. The religious objector was recognized by the Selective Service and Training Act of 1940 since the government exempted from combatant service those who, "because of religious training and belief," were opposed to all war in "any form."[16] In completing the questionnaire the individual was allowed to request a special form for conscientious objectors if he so desired, and this form (DDS-Form 47) became the basis for selective service classification.[17]

Under the operation of the overall conscription program, there were three distinct types of conscientious objection. First, men were classified I-A-O who, on the basis of religious opposition to war, refused all combatant military service or training, but were willing to perform noncombatant military service under military direction within the armed forces. Second, men whose opposition to World War II involved the actual violation of the Selective Training and Service Act by either refusing to register or failing to report for induction or assuming some other posture of noncooperation were imprisoned and considered draft "delinquents." The third group was opposed to war and to all military service, combatant or noncombatant. Nonetheless, they were willing to cooperate with the government and fill out DDS-Form 47. Classified IV-E, these men were assigned to the Civilian Public Service camps, which were under civilian direction.

It is important to note that this complex means of classification applied to but a small percentage of the U. S. population. The highest estimate of the total number of COs during World War II was 2.4 percent of the population. The highest estimate of the number of Catholic COs was 135 out of a church whose membership then numbered 19,913,937, or .0001 percent of that membership. This was a tremendous increase over World War I when, at most four Catholics had been COs.[18] In World War I, 345 different churches were listed by the COs as the source of their religious grounds for objection. All conscientious objectors during World War I were sentenced to twenty-five years imprisonment since the complex classification system for COs did not exist at that time.

Although the selective service system did not keep accurate or complete records on COs during World War II, it estimated that during the life of the Selective Training and Service Act, it ordered the induction of 25,000 men classified I-A-O and 11,887 classified IV-E, and it imprisoned 6,086 COs. Thus, 42,973 of the 10,022,367 males ordered to report for induction into the armed forces were COs. Most striking was the increase in the number of imprisoned COs, which jumped from 450 in World War I to 6,068 in World War II, an increase of 400 percent. Every sixth man in the federal prisons during World War II was a CO.[19]

Because of a lack of accurate records, there is no way to determine the number of Catholics who were classified I-A-O. Statistics are available on the number of Catholics imprisoned and the number of Catholics in the Civilian Public Service camps. The National Service Board for Religious Objectors (NSBRO) compiled a list of sixty-one Catholics imprisoned in sixteen of the twenty-eight federal prisons. The Danbury Federal Prison had the largest number of Catholic COs—eighteen men. These sixty-one men were sentenced for anywhere from eighteen months to five years; the largest number, thirty, were sentenced to three years' imprisonment. Furthermore, on the entire list only one man was cited as being released from a five-year prison sentence to serve in the Army.[20] When the sixty-one Catholic COs in prison are deducted from the total of 135 known Catholic COs the remaining seventy-four COs were classified IV-E and assigned to the Civilian Public Service (CPS) camps.

The idea for founding the CPS camps originated with the historic peace churches. Leaders of the Quakers, Mennonites, and Church of the Brethren, with the support of peace groups concerned about the protection of the rights of COs, met with President Roosevelt on 10 January 1940 to propose a program for COs. They suggested the establishment of an alternative service program under their direction in which COs could perform work of a humanitarian nature.[21]

The actual establishment of the alternative service system, however, forced the pacifist leaders to compromise in a number of ways. First, American law would recognize conscientious objection solely on religious grounds. Second, no exemption would be granted to men who in good conscience could not accept compulsory government service even if it were in the form of labor in the CPS camps. While final plans were being made for the establishment of the CPS camps, certain unwanted conditions were imposed concerning the administration of the camps. President Roosevelt suddenly expressed opposition to the proposed system of camp autonomy and "advocated putting all the men to work under army direction."[22] The leaders of the historical peace churches became fearful and agreed to assume all costs of the alternative service program in order to eliminate military control. This meant that COs in the CPS camps would work without pay. In the end the government granted that old Civilian Conservation Corps camps could be converted into CPS camps with the historical peace churches providing the operational expenses. The government, nevertheless, maintained final supervision over the camps. When Brigadier General Lewis B. Hershey was asked to explain the way funds were provided for the CPS camps, he stated before the Congressional Subcommittee on Conscientious Objection in 1941, "You see, we have three major historical creeds. They underwrite those costs. If the boy has $35 a month, he pays it; and if he has not, his church pays it; if neither has it, the three religious groups pay it."[23] In total the administrative cost to the historical peace churches for the CPS camps amounted to $7,000,000. There were 12,000 pacifists in 151 CPS camps from 1940 to 1946 with a sum of 8,000,000 man-days of free work for the United States.[24]

The leaders of the historical peace churches formed NSBRO to administer the CPS camps. Arthur Sheehan, head of ACCO, which had been formed to help Catholic COs at the Catholic Worker house in New York City, felt a responsibility toward these Catholics and became the self-appointed Catholic representative on NSBRO. The Catholic Worker alone of all the existing Catholic organizations and groups came to the aid of lay Catholics who opposed conscription. Dorothy Day was personally opposed to any form of cooperation with the draft, but she believed individuals had to follow their own conscience in the matter of cooperation. She believed that they needed support from other Catholics for their position and wholeheartedly supported all Catholic Worker endeavors to support Catholic COs regardless of their degree of resistance to the draft.

Arthur Sheehan approached the selective service for permission to operate a camp in the interest of Catholic COs. The government granted a forestry camp at Stoddard, New Hampshire, that would accommodate fifty men, and the Catholic Worker, through small donations, attempted to meet the yearly expenditure estimated to be $12,000. The camp was opened on 15 August 1941, with sixteen men; Dwight Larrowe was camp director, and Joseph Zarella assisted him. Both of these men were from the New York Catholic Worker community and active in ACCO.

The Catholic church, unlike the historical peace churches did not support the CPS camps.[25] This absence of moral and financial assistance inflicted grave hardships on the COs. Since ACCO was a creation of the Catholic Worker movement and financially dependent on it for support, ACCO's source of revenue became as precarious as the Catholic Worker's, which depended on the personal contributions of readers of its paper and people familiar with its houses of hospitality. The CPS camps were never far removed from absolute poverty at Stoddard or later in the other Catholic camp at Warner, New Hampshire.

The opening of the CPS camp at Stoddard was "in a very real sense, the first corporate witness against war and military service in the history of American Catholicism. Indeed, the claim might even be made that it was the first such witness in the entire history of the Church."[26] The irony of this witness, according to Gordon C. Zahn, is that it could not have occurred without the elaborate CO classification system designed by the federal government during World War II. However, he does not give sufficient credit to the Catholic Worker in establishing this Catholic corporate witness.

Zahn's book, *Another Part of the War: The Camp Simon Story*, gives a complete account of the Warner experience based on his own participation as a CO. In the book, he treats the Catholic camps at Stoddard and Warner as two separate phases of one camp experience and calls it Camp Simon. Zahn notes that the Catholic COs were older and more highly educated than their Protestant counterparts in the CPS. Also, 72 percent gave no affiliation with an existing peace organization. Eleven men did mention affiliation with the Catholic Worker, ACCO, or PAX. Zahn believes that a greater amount of maturity was necessary for Catholics to be COs because they were "taking a deviant stand on religious principle *without* the support of the religious community."[27]

The men at Stoddard faced many hardships. Their daily schedule was highly structured and the camp's location—a virtual Siberia—made obtaining supplies and attending Mass difficult.[28] Government trucks were available for work, but not religious purposes, even to travel to Mass on Sundays. The lack of finances for the camp caused additional problems, including the lack of adequate food, especially meat.[29] Dorothy Day told the following story of the camps:

> At first the boys themselves did the cooking. Then began the era of apple dumplings, apple strudel, apple sauce, apple pie. The camps were in the middle of an apple orchard and nothing went to waste. The fellows even sat around at night and sliced apples for drying so that they could be assured of their diet of apple pies for the duration.[30]

The men suffered psychological and emotional strains from doing work for which they were not trained professionally, which they did not believe to be of "national importance," and for which they were not paid. Zahn asserts that the daily schedule at Stoddard was applied to Warner, but it was not kept. He states that very little work was done because CPS was in violation of the two basic principles upon which alternative service was based: "The work was to be of national importance and performed under civilian direction." As a result, the two principles "were distorted and circumvented until they became little more than a grotesque farce."[31]

Conflicts among the men also arose, particularly in the antagonisms caused by the anti-Semitic Christian Front group and by the chapel group (deeply religious men who believed the others were not "Catholic" enough and whose sole aim was to erect a chapel at the camp).[32] Because of the hardships, a few men believed that they could no longer cooperate in *any* way with military conscription and left the camps to assume the extreme position of non-cooperation with the selective service system.[33]

Zahn contends that among the COs at Camp Simon "nothing approaching consensus in principle or application with respect to their opposition to war" existed.[34] Not all the men there were Catholic and the Catholics who were there felt out of place in CPS, "trapped into a situation not of their making, obliged to accept deprivations imposed by a set of concessions and compromises arranged without their approval or participation between the military officers who ran the show and the Protestant peace church leaders."[35]

The absence of consensus on the relationship of Catholicism to the COs' stand against war, is confirmed by Paul Fitzgerald, a Catholic CO who left Camp Simon for the army almost as soon as he arrived. Fitzgerald wrote:

> You must remember that the thinking of most of us, indeed our statuses as COs, was a product of non- war thinking. Few of us were pacifists, except for Dorothy [Day] and a few others. Most of us were products of a time when Thomism was all, . . . when a position on a moral matter was strictly a matter of applying our philosophies to a particular event. And yet, until World War II came about, there was no particular event. So you can see that the actual outbreak of the war threw some of us into an agonizing necessity for making decisions. The circumstances of the war (remember, this was at the time and we had no chance for the 20/20 vision of hindsight) made it most difficult for a moral decision. If we had been pacifists, it would have been a different story. But, again, remember we had no clear-cut theology for pacifism; the years between World War II and the Vietnam war provided that. We had to contend with the murderous attack on Pearl Harbor, Hitler's treatment of the Jews, etc.[36]

In an earlier book, *War, Conscience and Dissent*, Zahn attempted to classify the religious beliefs of these Catholic COs. A major handicap in doing so, he believed, was that there was no definite way of judging the relationship and impact of an individual's Catholic faith on his decision to become a conscientious objector.

> It is hard to generalize about men holding essentially individually determined positions. The source of strength for the conscientious objector in World War II came from personal conviction that he was conforming to the true norms of social living as defined by the great humanitarian thinkers and teachers of the past. True he would still remain a deviant; but his deviation would have something of a supra-social encouragement behind it in the identification with certain ideals which for him, at least, transcended temporal and national considerations.[37]

Despite this difficulty, Zahn constructed five categories to explain the theological positions of Catholic COs. The first was "individual" positions, which consisted of Christian Fronters who were scornful of the pacifism of others and believed the United States was fighting on the wrong side, and one or two COs who traced their objection to personal revelations of a presumably supernatural origin. The second category included those who made no religious references, since their position was based on a philosophical or humanitarian ideal. The third position was "evangelical," men who avoided formal theological arguments and stated their objections in terms of an antithesis between the "spirit of war" and the "spirit of Christ." Arguments offered by this group were based upon the unifying element they found in Redemption and the doctrine of the Mystical Body of Christ. Somewhat more theological was the "perfectionist" position, which was based upon a literal interpretation of the counsels of perfection as outlined in the Sermon on the Mount. Holders of this view refused to limit themselves to a just war analysis though they would agree to it. They believed the Christian was called to follow a supernatural ethic which went beyond justice to charity. This position was held mainly by the men associated with the Catholic Worker movement. Finally, there was the "traditionalist" position based on the "just war—unjust war" distinction developed by the writings of St. Augustine, St. Thomas Aquinas, Vittoria and Suarez, Gerald Vann, G. Barry O'Toole, and Franziskus Stratmann. Only nineteen of the sixty-one men at Camp Simon held this position.

In a later book on Camp Simon, Zahn classified the COs in the following manner: the Chapel Group, the Catholic Workers, the Coughlinites, College Boys and Intellectuals, the Artists, the Disrupters, the Workers, the Loners, and the Oddballs. In this study Zahn abandoned his previous attempt at religious classification and concluded that for more than half (thirty-six of the sixty-one) of the men at Camp Simon their Roman Catholic affiliation had no direct relationship or bearing in their decisions to become COs. The importance of both sets of Zahn's categories is that they illustrate both the diversity of positions among Catholic COs in relation to the role religion played in their decision and how difficult it is to determine or define an individual's religious belief.

The Stoddard CPS camp was in existence for one year when its forty-seven members were moved to larger facilites at Warner in October 1942. Two weeks before the Warner CPS camp closed on 17 March 1943, twelve men from the Catholic CPS camp went to the Alexian Brothers' Hospital in Chicago. This was the first instance in which COs were able to leave the camps and work elsewhere as a form of alternative service; the practice became more frequent after 1942. A unique aspect of this program was that living expenses for the COs were not paid by the historical peace churches but by the agency where the men worked.[38] Many reasons explain the closing of the camp at Warner and the cessation of ACCO to attempt to maintain a separate Catholic CPS camp: the men were generally dissatisfied; more meaningful work was opening up in the hospitals; New Hampshire residents wanted the camp removed; and finally, ACCO was not financially capable of meeting the government regulations necessary to keep the camp operating.[39]

After the camp closed, over sixty of the Catholic COs went to Swallow Falls near Oakland, Maryland, CPS camp No. 89. In June 1944, Rosewood Training School in Maryland opened and took many Catholic COs. There the men spent twelve hours a day caring for the mental patients and received an allowance of $15 a month. Other Catholic COs went to Cheltenham, Maryland, and worked in a training school for boys. The chapel group went to a CPS camp for Native Americans sponsored by the American Friends Service Committee in North Dakota and finally realized their dream of building a chapel; Bolton Morris, a member of the chapel group and in later years a well-known Philadelphia architect, designed the building. When the Catholic COs moved from Warner, NSBRO willingly accepted the financing of the men. In NSBRO records, the expense absorbed for the Catholic COs by the Mennonites was $5,975.34 and by the Quakers, $32,707.31.[40]

Besides working in the camps, over five hundred COs, including several Catholics, volunteered as "guinea pigs" for medical research. Two thousand COs served in forty-one mental hospitals and seventeen schools for the mentally deficient.[41] Over fifty Catholic COs served in the hospitals after 1943. The historical peace churches had originally been training some COs for overseas work, but wartime hatred of COs induced Congress to attach a rider to an appropriation bill making this illegal. An offer was made to a group of Catholic COs to go to England to establish a Catholic Worker hospitality house, but passports were refused these volunteers.[42] One intellectual venture of the CPS was a research study program at Columbia University on war relief and reconstruction. Fifteen men, including George Mathues, a Catholic CO, took part in this program even though they had to pay for it out of their own pockets.

In an attempt to keep the now scattered Catholic COs united and informed about one another and thus provide moral support, Arthur Sheehan along with two Catholic COs, Raymond Pierchalski and William Strube, began a quarterly newspaper, the *Catholic CO*, in January 1944. It came out of the Catholic Worker office in New York and sold not as the *Catholic Worker* for a penny a copy, but for twenty-five cents until it went up to fifty cents a copy in 1945. The funds from subscriptions were used to support the publication of the newspaper and to finance the Catholic COs in the CPS camps. After the first edition, the paper was taken over by the responsible men at the Rosewood Training School. The editors who served during the four years of the paper's existence were all Catholic COs: William Strube, Richard Lion, Gordon Zahn, Ray Pierchalski, and Robert Ludlow. Sheehan assisted them in the work. These men felt there was a need for a Catholic newspaper that focused solely on war and peace issues.

The *Catholic CO* took over the peace writings and peace news usually covered by the *Catholic Worker*. The two constant columns in the *Catholic CO* were "In Passing," which contained news about the men in the camps, and a book review. The main feature of each issue discussed conscientious objection, pacifism, or possible alternatives for peace. All the articles attempted to come to grips with the growing militarism in the United States. By 1945, the atomic bomb and the withdrawal issue were discussed in length. In 1946, much space was given to ACCO's withdrawal from NSBRO and Federal Judge James E. Fee's declaration that the CPS camps were illegal. The *Catholic CO* also took time to protest the ultra-nationalism of NCWC and CAIP when they stated that Pope Pius XII was "not in sympathy with a negotiated or compromising peace."[43]

In June 1948, the editors discontinued the *Catholic CO*. They stated their reasons in an article that appeared in the *Catholic Worker's* PAX column. They recognized that members of ACCO had very little in common except their opposition to the war; once that ended there was little else to bind them together. They also felt that the nation no longer needed a separate newspaper to cover war and peace issues; the coverage in the *Catholic Worker* would suffice.[44]

Meanwhile, after the closing of the Catholic camps and the 1944 founding of the paper, ACCO withdrew from NSBRO on 30 October 1945. Arthur Sheehan explained that ACCO had continued its membership in the NSBRO in hopes of working out the difficulties of the CPS and ultimately bringing a fair interpretation of the CO's status, but ACCO now felt at last it was being honest with itself in admitting that CPS was a form of slavery; scarcely any good resulted from the camps and in the end the program proved a failure. Sheehan also urged honesty on the part of NSBRO and hoped as well for its repudiation of CPS. NSBRO soon followed ACCO's act of repudiation.[45]

Robert Ludlow described CPS as "a program of involuntary servitude without compensation, nothing more than a program of slave labor offered by the State as an alternative to outright imprisonment."[46] Though the statement is strong, Zahn contends that it honestly reflected the position of the Catholic men serving in the program. If anything positive can be said about CPS it would be that the hardships, injustices, and wasted talent of the men in the system did not match those endured by the World War I objectors. Nevertheless, with the court system declaring CPS illegal in 1946 there can be no doubt that it was a form of slave labor and imprisonment.

Of the sixty-one Catholic COs who had taken a stand of noncooperation and were sent to prison, Arthur Sheehan managed to arrange parole
talks for eighteen who were incarcerated at the Danbury Federal Prison.
All but two of the seventeen men at the meeting called by Warden
Alexander had one-third of their sentences commuted and were assigned to hospitals in New Haven, Boston, and Baltimore.[47] When
paroled, a CO was assigned to a hospital and required only to appear for
work each day. Thus, these men fared better than the COs in the CPS
camps.[48]

The prison witness was not totally unproductive. Recent peace movement histories point out that these imprisoned COs were responsible for
effective prison reform conducted through hunger strikes, sit-ins, and
other forms of organized nonviolent action. Compared to the COs in
alternative service, these men were more likely to come out of the experience convinced of nonviolence as an effective strategy for peace in the
future, and many made contributions to the postwar peace movement.

Generally speaking, however, Catholic opposition to war was very
feeble, consisting only of the Catholic Worker and 135 known Catholic COs. Most mainstream Catholics viewed the Catholic Worker as
radical and of doubtful orthodoxy; COs in prison went unrecognized.
Nevertheless, the demands of peacemaking on these individuals were
as great as the demands of war.

In assessing the value of the Catholic COs' witness in the CPS
camps, Zahn contends that only those men in CPS offered a corporate
witness in the sense that their witness was for the church and in the
name of the church. He also states that the friendships formed by the
men at Camp Simon were of lasting value and these men have no
regrets about their witness. Zahn cites the following changes since the
end of World War II as proof of the value of their witness: First, the
Catholic Worker and the historical peace churches agreed never again
to cooperate with the government in administering CPS camps as an
alternative service program. Second, the Catholic church has significantly changed its teachings on modern war and conscientious objection, a change in part that can be attributed to the prophetic stance
taken by the Catholic men in the CPS camps:

> If . . . taken to imply that those who refused to serve were directly
> responsible for the crucial changes in theological stance and interpreta-

tion that have developed since, it would be claiming too much. On the other hand, if it refers to nothing more than the recognition that their stand anticipated, and and may even to some extent have prepared the way for, a more unambiguous commitment to peace and nonviolence among important segments of the Catholic community, the Warner witness was a prophetic witness. It met the test of the two characteristic notes of the prophetic tradition; it affirmed, and exercised, the competence of the individual conscience to pass adverse judgment on the acts of principalities and powers; and it insisted that, by doing so, it was fulfilling moral obligations that should have been recognized by all.[49]

Whatever changes occurred in the Catholic church after the war, the fact remains that it was a silent bystander on the issue of conscription throughout World War II. Catholic COs found reasons for their positions in a tradition not encompassed in the normative or popular teaching of Catholicism in the first half of the twentieth century. Although there was little connection between Catholic teaching and the individual's decision to become a CO, the Catholic church in the United States never denied the right of an individual to become a conscientious objector. At the same time the church never articulated its support for this right. The reason for this is not hard to discover— the church had always remained loyal to the nation in time of war. The apparent legitimacy of World War II in face of the evil of Nazism, coupled with the official just war doctrine of the church served to justify such uncritical patriotism.

The means used in the waging of World War II, such as the obliteration bombing of European cities, introduced another challenge to the just war doctrine. Although Pope Pius XII only criticized the bombing of Rome and the American Catholic hierarchy only privately questioned the use of such actions, some segments of the Catholic community, especially pacifists, did criticize the war tactic.

The person most responsible for developing a theological rationale for this moral protest was John C. Ford, S.J., teacher at Weston College. In a scholarly article, "The Morality of Obliteration Bombing," published in 1944, he became the only American Catholic moral theologian during World War II who challenged the bombing of cities as not admissible under traditional just war criteria. In the article Ford defined obliteration bombing in the following terms:

Obliteration bombing is the strategic bombing, by means of incendiaries and explosives, of industrial centers of population in which the target to be wiped out is not a definite factory, bridge, or similar object, but a large area of a whole city, comprising one-third to two-thirds of its whole built up area, and including by design the residential districts of workingmen and their families. [50]

Ford contended that such bombing was immoral, basing his position in international law, the laws of humanity, and natural law. He pointed out that the question of obliteration bombing leads to the more general one of the possibility of a just modern war: "For obliteration bombing includes the bombing of civilians, and is a necessary practice which can be called typical of total war, and if all modern war must be total, then a condemnation of obliteration bombing would logically lead to a condemnation of all modern war." [51] Ford, however, admitted that he did not intend to go that far and believed that it was possible for modern war to be waged within the limits set by the laws of morality. [52]

While Ford did not accept pacifism and believed that certain wars could be just, he maintained that there were some things, such as the use of poisonous gas and obliteration bombing, which were inadmissible in warfare. He based his argument against obliteration bombing on the distinction between combatants and noncombatants and referred to the writings of many theologians who were firmly convinced of the distinction. One of these writers was the American Catholic theologian, John K. Ryan, author of *Modern War and Basic Ethics*, which was published by CAIP before United States entry into World War II. Ford considered soldiers under arms as combatants, but was not clear about the status of civilian munitions workers, leaving it to international law to decide. However, the rest of the people were clearly seen as innocent noncombatants, and their rights were being violated by obliteration bombing. Ford concluded his argument with a section on "The Mind of the Holy See." Here, Ford cited the condemnation of aerial bombardment of civilians by Benedict XV in World War I, the condemnation of the bombing of cities in Spain during the Spanish Civil War by Pius XI, and the lament of the bombing of Rome during World War II by Pius XII. From such statements, Ford concluded that if the words of the popes "do not contain an implicit condemnation of obliteration bombing as I have described it, then it is hard to see what they do condemn."[53]

Ford was careful to point out that his article was insufficient to impose obligations on the conscience of the individual. "A clear violation of natural law can be known to the ordinary individual soldier in a case of this kind through the definite pronouncements of the Church, or of the hierarchy, or even through a consensus of moral theologians over a period of time. On the question of obliteration bombing we have no such norms."[54]

A few Catholics, as Ford pointed out, had condemned obliteration bombing. James M. Gillis in the "Editorial Comment" in *Catholic World* took such a stand. The editors of *Commonweal* flatly condemned obliteration bombing as murder. The *Catholic Worker* speaking from its pacifist position condemned obliteration bombing and published the statement of Gerald Shaugnessy, D.D., S.M., of Seattle, the only American bishop who spoke out during World War II on the immorality of this tactic.[55] The *Catholic Worker* also printed the words of Monsignor Paul Hanley Furfey's condemnation of obliteration bombing.[56] Thus, there were a few Catholics who protested the United States policy of obliteratiion bombing during World War II. Most Catholics, even the CAIP, never addressed this issue. One Catholic periodical, *America*, urged precautions concerning obliteration bombing.

If the protestations of American Catholics and others had been stronger against the government's policy of obliteration bombing, President Truman would have found it more difficult to drop the atomic bomb on Hiroshima and Nagasaki. As it was, he made the decision to drop the bombs, and one observer noted that "the general American reaction, is one of stunned disquiet. It is not jubilant, yet it contains no real feeling of guilt."[57]

Despite the "stunned disquiet" of most Americans, some did protest the bombing of Hiroshima and Nagasaki. Editors of Catholic publications were spurred on by the pope's criticism of the bombings. Catholics, however, who subjected the American decision to sharp attack were the same ones who had previously challenged the policy of obliteration bombing. The reasons for their protest stemmed from the same reason for their opposition to obliteration bombing; knowledge pertaining to the unique destructive power of nuclear weapons was still unknown. Gillis in the *Catholic World* responded by proclaiming, "I here and now declare that I think the use of the atomic bomb, in these circumstances, was atrocious and abominable; and that civilized peoples would reprobate and anathematize the horrible deed."[58] Dorothy Day in the *Catholic Worker* began her pacifist condemnation of the atomic bomb attack with extreme sarcasm as she talked of the president. "He went from table to table on the cruiser which was bringing him home from the Big Three conference," she noted, "telling the great news, 'jubilant,' the newspapers said. JUBILATE DEO. We have killed 318,000 Japanese." She placed the responsibility for the atomic bomb on "scientists and captains of industry." In her Gospel manner she asserted that Christ had already given his judgment of the act: "What you do unto the least of these my brethren, you do unto me."[59] John J. Hugo's article "Peace Without Victory" also appeared in the same issue of the *Catholic Worker*. Hugo termed the dropping of the atomic bombs "the culminating crime" and attributed it to the United States' capacity to "out-Nazi the Nazis" by using means that do not justify the end, by accepting tribal morality, and by acquiescing in obliteration bombing.

While indignation and dismay at America's use of atomic weapons held the initiative in these Catholic circles many Catholic leaders were not united behind the discontent. This was true among clerical leadership of every denomination in the United States.[60] Catholic groups who abstained from judgment on obliteration bombing, such as *America*, the American Catholic hierarchy, and the CAIP, did the same when the atomic bombs were dropped on Hiroshima and Nagasaki. The principles of the just war doctrine which provided the moral imperative for Catholics to support World War II were insufficient for these same Catholics to criticize the means used by the government to win the war.

After the war in 1947, the CAIP finally spoke out on the issue of the atomic bomb. During the war CAIP, like other peace groups that were advocates of collective security, supported the policies of the government during the war and focused its attention on planning for a postwar community of nations. When the United States helped to build the United Nations, CAIP made many recommendations for a strong UN. It was in this context that the CAIP proposed the UN have "legislative powers . . . to make effective atomic control and inspection and general disarmament."[61] CAIP stated that the use of atomic bombs was illegitimate or unjust when (1) atomic bombing was used to break peoples' will to resist; (2) atomic total war was pursued as an end in itself; and (3) a war was started with a shower of atomic bombs. The use of atomic bombs was just, however, in the following situations: (1) for counteruse by a nation in a defensive war when other means were insufficient and (2) that the United Nations may use atomic bombs against an aggressor nation if the nation's preparations and objective were clearly to enslave the world or a large part of it. CAIP concluded by declaring that "the United States was obliged to stop production of the A bomb and publicly announce this due to suspicion aroused in Russia and the armaments race."[62]

This statement of CAIP probably went beyond dominant Catholic opinion. Though there are no statistics available on exclusively Catholic public opinion, on 8 August 1945, a poll found that only 10 percent of the American population opposed the use of atomic bombs on Japanese cities, while 85 percent approved.[63]

On the question of the use of the atomic bomb, American Catholics evidenced a variety of positions: The majority approved or were silent; the American Catholic hierarchy was silent; CAIP applied the just war doctrine to the new weapon and tried to bring it under the control of the United Nations and develop a rationale that would limit the use of nuclear weapons. For CAIP, the just war theory still provided an ethical rationale that permitted them to support their government in war, even "limited" atomic war if it were necessary for the defense of their nation. *Commonweal,* the *Catholic Worker,* and the *Catholic World* opposed the use of the atomic bomb under any condition. They came to call themselves nuclear pacifists.

The just war doctrine had enabled some few Catholics to become conscientious objectors, to protest obliteration bombing, and to condemn atomic warfare during World War II. Ironically, those who had looked to the just war doctrine for a Catholic justification of their opposition had become increasingly disillusioned with the doctrine in the face of modern warfare. After the war they proclaimed that no modern war, especially nuclear war, could be just. They also became more like the pacifists in the Catholic Worker tradition by looking to the Gospel message in hopes of creating a new peace ethic within Catholicism. The just war doctrine was not dead in the American

Catholic church, but it had been dealt serious blows. Nevertheless, the majority of American Catholics and the hierarchy would continue to view the just war doctrine as the normative teaching of the church on issues of war and peace for the next forty years. During this time Catholic pacifists would continue to gain strength as their Gospel message combined with the theory of nonviolence and nuclear pacifism. The increasing escalation of the nuclear arms race, the growing knowledge of the effects of nuclear warfare, and the unjust war in Vietnam eventually propelled pacifists to a position of parity with just war traditionalists within American Catholicism.

4

The Birth of Nonviolence
From World War II to Vatican II

FROM WORLD WAR II to Vatican II the main focus of the Catholic Worker, as well as the American peace movement, was the development of the concept of nonviolence as a means of social protest. Among American Catholics concerned about war and peace issues, the Catholic Worker alone moved beyond pacifism into nonviolence under the leadership of Robert Ludlow and Ammon Hennacy. The CAIP had no interest in nonviolence but aligned itself instead with the "realist" school of theologians led by John Courtney Murray, S.J., who attempted to apply just war principles to American nuclear policy. Both CAIP and the Catholic Worker, as well as the entire American peace movement, were greatly influenced during this time period by the Cold War.

After World War II, the Cold War between the Soviet Union and the United States permeated every aspect of American life. The peace movement retreated in face of the issues raised by the Cold War, such as the fear of communism, the arms race, and defensive security. The loyalty-security mania of the early 1950s led to McCarthyism, the domestic counterpart of the nation's foreign policy.[1] Ironically, the Cold War accelerated the very forces the peace movement sought to restrain. Peacemakers continued their struggle by formulating alternatives to American military policies (CAIP) and by serving as prophets of nonviolence (Catholic Worker).

The American peace movement had a long-term interest in Gandhian nonviolence. Nonviolence is "the force which is born of Truth and Love" (satyagraha) and exercises "power or influence to effect change without injury to the opponent."[2] Nonviolent resistance is a technique of action that employs noncooperation and civil disobedience. "Non-cooperation is simply the refusal to cooperate with a requirement which is taken to violate fundamental 'truths' or refusal to cooperate with those responsible for such violations. Civil disobedience is the direct contravention of specific laws."[3] Young pacifists during World War II found these tactics most useful in dealing with the injustices in American race relations, the CPS camps, and the prisons. The use of these tactics to correct injustice achieved the greatest success when performed by the pacifist noncooperators in the prisons.[4]

After the war many of the COs who had been in the CPS camps and prisons held new ideas about the functions of a peacemaker gained from their experiments with nonviolent resistance. For a time there was a split between traditional pacifists and this young generation, who were termed radical pacifists, as revealed in the two oldest pacifist groups in the United States, the Fellowship of Reconciliation (FOR) and the War Resisters League (WRL). In 1946, however, the radical pacifists who had joined FOR's Congress of Racial Equality sponsored the first Freedom Ride, which was a definite victory for the radical pacifists because it was a tactic of nonviolent resistance. In June 1947, the executive committee of WRL adopted a resolution declaring that it would "adopt its literature and activities to the promotion of political, economic, social revolution by nonviolent means."

Though the radical pacifists had greatly influenced traditional pacifist groups, they still attempted to form their own peace organizations; the first of any size and permanence being the Peacemakers. The focus of the new group was war resistance. The most unique of their programs called for the nonpayment of taxes to protest war. Recalling the actions of Henry David Thoreau over a century earlier, this tax resistance was unique as action performed by a group of people in opposition to war.[5]

Radical and traditional pacifists alike joined in an attempt to secure amnesty for COs imprisoned during World War II. They also cooperated in the struggle against the proposal of President Truman to continue compulsory military training into the postwar era. In their opposition they again applied the tactics of nonviolent resistance. In February 1947, five pacifists burned draft cards in San Francisco's Union Square. In the same month sixty-three draft cards were burned at a meeting in New York.[6]

By 1950, three government policies brought an end to the American peace movement. The first was the heightening of the Cold War; the second, was President Truman's continuation of tests on the hydrogen bomb; and finally, the outbreak of fighting in Korea. The Korean War came as the final blow because world government organizations almost universally accepted the American role in the conflict.

The American Catholic segment of the peace movement also experienced the effects of these government policies. After World War II, the Catholic peace movement was represented by the relatively few Catholic conscientious objectors who had performed alternative service and their even fewer supporters. "Basically, it dissolved completely until nothing remained to show for it but the Catholic Worker, its principal benefactor throughout the war period."[7] For the most part, Catholic Worker pacifists returned to their roots of social justice concerns and administered the corporal works of mercy to the poor. The pacifist witness remained during the 1950s, however, in the writings on nonviolence by Robert Ludlow in the Catholic Worker and in symbolic actions of nonviolent resistance as Ammon Hennacy led Dorothy Day and other Workers in the extension of their pacifism.

The other group of Catholic peacemakers, CAIP, focused attention on the United Nations, where it held observer status.[8] CAIP was directly linked with the NCWC through Rita Schaefer, former secretary of CAIP, who served as the representative of both groups in a consultant position at the United Nations.[9] Her main effort during this period was devoted to the drafting of the International Covenant on Human Rights. Her efforts were also supported by the National Catholic Conference of Women and the National Federation of Catholic College Students, both of which were affiliated with NCWC in America. The Sword of the Spirit, a periodical of Catholic peace groups in London and the British Society for International Understanding collaborated with her on this project.[10]

Though CAIP always aimed at combating nationalism and building cooperation among nations for peace, it was particularly unsuccessful at both after World War II. Because of pronouncements by government leaders in America against communism and the pope's condemnation of atheistic communism, CAIP was very conscious of the need to combat it. This fear of communism was most evident in the association's policy toward China. On the one hand, it worked toward bringing to a vote the admission of Communist China into the United Nations, but at the same time it went on record as opposed to Communist China's entrance into the world organization.[11] CAIP also viewed the Korean War as an example of Communist aggression.[12]

During the post–World War II period, the CAIP was also represented at the State Department's "off-the-record" meetings concerning issues before the U.N. At these meetings discussions focused on American foreign policy in relation to the Korean situation and technical assistance to underdeveloped nations of the world.[13]

Through the association's statements, reports, conferences, and pamphlets an attempt was made to reiterate papal teaching on social and international themes such as disarmament, peacetime conscription, and foreign aid. However, this did not result in any significant modification of the Catholic obsession, encouraged by the hierarchy, that the anti-communist crusade was the only real international issue.[14] Even a mild attempt to broaden the discussion during the early Cold War period met with a note of caution from America's most distinguished liberal theologian, John Courtney Murray, as evidenced in his comment on a CAIP paper, "Co-Existing with Communism": "It seems to me that the relations between the Christian concept of man and the Communist concept are better characterized by the word 'war' than by the term 'co-existence.' I mean of course a war that is carried on purely by intellectual and spiritual means."[15] Although American Catholics were sorely anti-communist, many Catholics were at great variance with the views of Catholic Senator Joseph McCarthy and his followers. The anti-communism of most Catholics was rooted in spiritual rather than political concerns. The pope had set the tone with his condemnation of atheistic communism and the American hierarchy had been disillusioned in the peace settlement when Russia took control of Eastern Europe. Catholic prayer books from the postwar era stated that it was a Catholic's duty to resist communism. In their "Prayers After Low Mass," Catholics prayed for the conversion of Russia, a practice which continued until the Second Vatican Council. Because of their religiously ingrained anti-communism, Catholics often transferred the evil of atheistic communism to political issues. Even liberal and radical Catholics preferred to work alone rather than seek a social or political alliance with the Left in America during the early Cold War period.[16] For American Catholics this combination of religious and political anti-communism created a climate of fear and a support of the arms race and defensive security that left the Catholic Worker standing not only isolated, but also subdued in its efforts for peace.

The Catholic Worker movement, though subdued, was not intimidated by the Cold War. In the immediate postwar period, Catholic Workers like all American pacifists concentrated their energies on opposing conscription. In 1946 and 1947, the Catholic Worker joined for the first time with other pacifist groups—the Protestant Fellowship of Reconciliation, the War Resisters League, Peacemakers, and the Committee for Nonviolent Revolution—in a campaign against President Truman's proposed peacetime draft and Universal Military Training (UMT). When the peacetime draft was passed in 1948 without UMT, the *Catholic Worker* continued in its tradition of advocating noncooperation with the draft and offering support to men prosecuted for draft resistance. The case receiving the most attention was that of Larry Gara, a history professor who was imprisoned in 1949 for urging a student to refuse to register if it violated his conscience. The Catholic Worker, however, never performed any actions with the newly formed groups such as the Federation of Atomic Scientists, the United World Federalists, or the World Citizen Movement which had risen to prominence in America and were the forefront of the popular antiwar movement from 1946 to 1949. Though concerned about the issues of atomic arms control and world government, the Catholic Worker was too pacifist, too personalist, and too anarchistic to cooperate with them.

The Catholic Worker was most concerned with continuing its pacifist witness. Experiences in the CPS camps and the dropping of the bomb on Hiroshima and Nagasaki had convinced Workers of the irrelevancy of the just war doctrine, which never appeared again as a basis for their discussion and writing on war and peace issues. From 1948 to 1955 the writings of Robert Ludlow dominated the movement's thought on pacifism and led Catholic Workers to embrace Gandhian nonviolence. Robert Ludlow, a Catholic convert, had just joined the Catholic Worker when he had to confront the prospect of fighting in World War II. He chose not to do so and as a conscientious objector he took his place along with other Catholic COs at the Rosewood Training School in Maryland. During the war he wrote for the *Catholic Worker* and the *Catholic CO* and gained a reputation as the most articulate radical among the Catholic pacifists.

After the war, Ludlow joined the Workers at the House of Hospitality in New York. "Joining" simply meant going to the house and, after a while finding a job that became one's own. Ludlow was an associate editor of the *Catholic Worker* for the next decade and wrote on a variety of topics, but he tended to concentrate on pacifism, anarchism, Gandhian nonviolence, and mental illness. Historian William Miller claims that "Ludlow's contributions to the *Catholic Worker* in this era helped much to make it a distinguished paper."[17] John Cogley described Ludlow as "the predominant intellectual figure of the movement" during this period and credits him along with John A. Hugo and Ammon Hennacy as the main figures who partially reshaped the movement. The reason for the word "partially," Cogley explains, is that "the abiding imprint of the movement has always been that of Miss Day herself, whose genius it has been to cut through all kinds of distractions, abstractions and intellectual complexities to get at the heart of Christianity itself."[18] The first historian, however, to analyze Ludlow's thought and give him his rightful place within the Catholic Worker movement was Mel Piehl.

Piehl contends that Ludlow was "the first Catholic pacifist to understand and to appropriate the Gandhian theory of nonviolence as a comprehensive method of religious peacemaking." He was also "the first to see Catholic pacifism not simply as the witness of a small minority to the counsels of perfection, but as the forerunner of a possibly historic shift in the whole Catholic Church's attitude toward war."[19] Ludlow basically followed the lines of Paul Hanly Furfey's views in the 1930s, but went further in assessing the Catholic Worker's relation to prior Catholic social thought. According to Ludlow, in condemning anarchism, Catholic theologians and philosphers had failed to distinguish between society and the state to the extent that was necessary. Service to the people by the state and coercion and violence against the people by the state were not adequately defined by church doctrine. He believed that an anarchism which preserved social cohesion and authority and at the same time discarded coercive state violence was permissible. Thus, his work consisted of many tirades against the violent actions of the state. In developing a response for the individual in face of the coercive violence of the state Ludlow took Catholic Worker personalism and pacifism and added Gandhian nonviolence. Because Gandhian nonviolence rested on a spiritual vision of life,

Ludlow in the pages of the *Catholic Worker* in 1949 and 1950 hailed satyagraha as "a new Christian way of social change" that would be both politically effective and morally uncompromised. The individual could resist the coercive violent state through the spiritual practices of disciplined social struggle and suffering. In the end nonviolence would remove from pacifism its constant criticism of being individualistic, passive, and sentimental.

Ludlow also provided Catholic pacifists with a more satisfactory interpretation of their own insistent departure from the church's position on just war. While some pacifists saw their position only as a witness of personal conscience, Ludlow argued that war would turn out to be an instance of Cardinal Newman's theory concerning the development of Catholic dogma: the church arrives at many tentative judgments on the way to truth and may even tolerate for a time such unchristian practices as human slavery, which was long permitted but eventually condemned. In such an evolutionary course, Newman had observed, some within the church must risk going beyond the official positions of the time. Ludlow argued that this was true of war and that Catholic pacifists should not fear to differ with leaders of the church on a matter not defined in terms of formal doctrine. "We act in accordance with the belief that war will eventually be condemned" he wrote, "and must try by our actions to add our very small contributions to the time when pacifism may be the norm of society." The moral progressivism of this approach appealed to American Catholic pacifists, who wanted to be not only prophetic but effective. The idea that their pacifist witness was not only a counsel of perfection intended for a few saints, but somehow represented the true "mind of the Church" better than its current voices, gradually shaped the pacifists' self-understanding and relations with other Catholics.[20] Thus, Ludlow's integration of nonviolence into pacifism gave Catholics the means to confront the warmakers and by their example to show how the end of war among nations might be accomplished.

Ludlow's writing on pacifism was featured in the PAX column of the *Catholic Worker* and he often looked back to his CO experiences during the war. One of his main themes was that the Christian pacifist would be considered abnormal or psychotic because of the growing irrationality of modern society which was becoming fragmented by a rapidly expanding technology. This theme increased in significance when President Truman announced that he was sanctioning the testing of the hydrogen bomb. Ludlow's reponse to the announcement was that " 'The whole thing has become unreal and fantastic.' If nothing else nuclear weapons testing would bring man to 'the conclusion that absolute pacifism is the only answer. . . . We live in a world of hate and we can only oppose it by going to the opposite extreme.' "[21]

In the PAX column Ludlow also wrote an occasional report on Catholic conscientious objectors. Once, he thought it necessary to make clear that Catholic Worker COs had nothing to do with Coughlinite COs. In his opinion all Coughlinite COs were anti-Semitic; thus, they were not true pacifists. This return to the past as a source of keeping the issue of pacifism alive during the post-World War II period was also apparent in April 1948, when the paper reprinted the full text of John Hugo's "The Immorality of Conscription." Seventy-five thousand additional copies were printed for handout distribution. This was one of the Catholic Worker's ways of combating the increasing talk in America of establishing universal military training.

Ludlow's contribution to peace after World War II was in promulgating the intellectual and theoretical rationale for a Catholic pacifism that included nonviolence; he combined this with an optimistic view of the moral and political value of such witness. Day herself called him "doctrinaire and dogmatic, and yet the mildest of mortals, meek and disciplined in his personal life."[22]

During the Korean War, the more moderate pacifist groups disbanded or changed their emphasis, the radical groups met much public hostility, and the *Catholic Worker* was more subdued in its antiwar writings than during World War II. In the first issue of the *Catholic Worker* following the invasion of South Korea by the North Koreans, Dorothy Day reiterated her position against all war. "It is heartbreaking once again to see casualty lists in the *New York Times*," she wrote. "We believe that not only atomic weapons must be outlawed, but all war, and that the social order must be restored in Christ."[23] Day focused on the centrality of love in resolving the conflict and not on the actions of the U. S. government. She also talked about the poor whom she identified not only as American soldiers fighting in subzero weather in Korea, but also the Koreans who were the victims of bullets and bombs. During the war the paper constantly featured articles condemning the immorality of conscription, but there was also a warning to objectors not to oppose war "with pride, with condemnation of others, with bitterness."[24] And during the entire Korean War, only one occurrence of direct, protesting action was reported. The one event was when Ammon Hennacy picketed the Phoenix Tax Office to oppose President Truman's declaration of a state of emergency.[25] The Catholic Worker had clearly reached an all-time low in peace activity.

Though the writing in the *Catholic Worker* was more moderate during the Korean War, the pacifist spirit of the Worker remained strong. When Michael Harrington joined the Catholic Worker movement in 1951, he contended that it affected him so that it almost led him to prison as a conscientious objector. His refusal to attend rifle practice as a volunteer for the Army Medical Reserves resulted in several crises with military authorities. Harrington wrote: "What maintained and stiffened my will was that almost primitive Christian sense of mission that pervaded the Worker."[26] There were Catholic COs during the Korean War but their numbers are unknown because the classification forms used did not provide for a religious affiliation category. There were also no CPS camps during the Korean War. From the pages of the *Catholic Worker*, it is known that Catholic conscientious objection to the war was advocated, but how many Catholic COs were assisted by the Worker is unknown.

The impact of the early Cold War period upon the Catholic peace movement was great, but nevertheless, Day and Ludlow kept writing. Day wrote frequently to counteract the increase of anti-communist sentiment. Along with Robert Ludlow and Irene Naughton at the *Catholic Worker*, Day published a statement on anti-Communism:

> Although we disagree with our Marxist brothers on the question of the means to use to achieve social justice, rejecting atheism and materialism in Marxist thought, we respect their freedom as a minority group in this country. . . . We protest the imprisonment of our Communist brothers and extend our sympathy and admiration for having followed their conscience even in persecution.[27]

During this period the *Catholic Worker* opposed the anti-communist Smith and McCarran acts and reacted with horror to the trial of Julius and Ethel Rosenberg and co-defendant Morton Sobell. The writings reflected an attempt to stop the mounting anti-communism among

Catholics. In June 1953, as the Rosenbergs were awaiting their execution, a despondent Ludlow revealed these concerns:

> It is not a just age we live in. It is an age where guilt by association is
> fast becoming the accepted method of judging. . . . And our patriotic
> Catholics and our wretched publications do not see this as the leaders
> of the Church in France did not see it before the Revolution and as the
> leaders in Spain did not see it. And when they do see it (of course they
> never really do) then they will envision themselves as the innocent
> victims of devils. . . . May all Catholics, in union with the Supreme
> Pontiff who has already asked that clemency be granted the Rosen-
> bergs, send one last plea that these lives be spared.[28]

Many supporters of the anti-communist crusade in America had taken
issue with the *Catholic Worker's* willingness to defend Communists as
"our brothers," and to join with them in opposition to certain aspects of
capitalism. Senator McCarthy himself took notice of the *Catholic
Worker* and his proclamations put some pressure on the movement.
"McCarthyites hinted darkly of the paper's communist ties and nick-
named Dorothy Day 'Moscow Mary,' as some reactionaries still call
her."[29] FBI agents were sent to interrogate Day and Monsignor Edward
R. Gaffney at the chancery in New York City, questioned her about the
paper's use of the word "Catholic" in its title.[30] Because of their daily
performance of corporal works of mercy to the poor in the name of
Catholicism, the Catholic Worker movement was left relatively un-
troubled by the witch hunt.

By the mid-1950s even liberal Catholics began voicing concern
about the mounting anti-communism. John Courtney Murray, wondered whether "we prove our Americanism and our Catholicism simply by being vociferously anti-Communist." He seriously questioned
whether Americans were "spiritually and intellectually equipped to
meet the communist threat at its deepest level." He called the engage-
ment with Communism on the domestic scene a "basic fiasco."[31]
Murray avoided the public debate on communism. His primary concern as a theologian was "to establish the compatibility of American
pluralism and Catholicism in the eyes of both the Roman Catholic
church and of the American people. Murray's chief legacy to American Catholics was his demonstration that it is possible to be both an

American and a Catholic without being disloyal to either."[32] This Catholic Americanism, more than anti-communism best characterizes the desires and aspirations of the "realist" school of theologians during the Cold War period.

Beginning in the late 1950s, a renaissance of the American peace movement occurred when attention was focused upon thermonuclear weapons. The immediate cause of this was the atmospheric testing of the hydrogen bomb. Despite the sudden commotion at the bombing of Hiroshima and Nagasaki, the American people had never truly appreciated the possibility of wholesale slaughter until the Soviet Union detonated a series of hydrogen bombs during the middle and late 1950s. Although the Soviet breakthrough in thermonuclear weaponry spurred an acceleration of the American "defense effort," it also cut the other way. Prominent political and military leaders now began to talk about the impossibility of victory in a war that rendered survival unlikely.[33]

Catholic concern for peace in face of thermonuclear warfare arose once again from CAIP and the Catholic Worker. CAIP showed its concern mainly through the tactic of lobbying in the United Nations to establish a criteria for the use of nuclear weapons. CAIP, however, refused to embrace nuclear pacifism. Again, Murray's influence on CAIP cannot be underestimated. He provided the justification for CAIP's position on nuclear issues through the just war doctrine by asserting that "the use of nuclear force must be limited, the principle of limitation being the exigencies of legitimate defense against injustice. Thus the terms of public debate are set in two words, 'limited war.' All other terms of argument are fanciful or fallacious."[34] He believed that to say "limited war" could not be created by intelligence, energy, and under the direction of moral imperative was to succumb to some sort of determinism in human affairs.

Murray also countered Catholic opinion that the just war was irrelevant in relation to modern warfare. In his most noted article, "Morality and Modern War," first published in 1958, Murray provided what would become the standard explanation of the relevance of the just war doctrine. He contended that objections are raised not against the doctrine itself but about the usefulness of the doctrine, "its relevance to the concrete actualities of our historical moment."[35] He contended that these questions arise because the doctrine had for so long not been used even by Catholics. And that the indictment should not be placed on the doctrine but on everyone who failed to make the tradition relevant. He argued that the just war tradition is the solvent for the dangerous type of thinking which dichotomizes two extreme positions, "a soft sentimental pacifism and a cynical hard realism." The second false dilemma that the doctrine resolves is the desperate alternative of either universal atomic death or complete surrender to communism, a dilemma which denies moral reason and submits to technological or historical determinism. Murray believed that the strength of the traditional doctrine "is a will to peace, which, in the extremity, bears within itself a will to enforce the precept of peace by arms. But this will to arms is a moral will; for it is identically a will to justice."[36] Thus he rejected the notion that the big problem is to "abolish war" or "ban the bomb." For Murray, the just war tradition's value is that it serves as a standard of casuistry on various kinds of war and has the capacity to set the right terms for rational debate on public policies bearing on the problem of war and peace in today's world of international conflict and advanced technology. Murray believed that the church's just war doctrine still fulfilled its triple function: "to condemn war as evil, to limit the evils it entails, and to humanize its conduct as far as possible."[37] His writing encouraged other Catholics who viewed themselves as "realists" to continue to write about nuclear issues from the basis of the just war doctrine.

In 1955, Monsignor George Higgins was appointed head of the Department of Social Action in the NCWC and automatically became executive secretary of CAIP. Higgins, like Ryan and McGowan, was mainly concerned with the problems of labor[38] and had very little grasp of international affairs.[39] The program of CAIP immediately after World War II changed little under his direction: It continued to play an indirect role in public policy formation by functioning as a Catholic lobbyist group and as an invited observer at the United Nations and the State Department. The committee system still served as the core unit of the association and publication of policy statements, pamphlet reports, and a monthly newsletter, *CAIP News*, served as the chief means of carrying out the program. Under the directorship of Higgins, CAIP became almost undistinguishable from NCWC. The aim of CAIP, as always, was to make known to its Catholic constituency the "official" position of the Catholic church on the issues of war and peace.[40] The normative position was always the just war doctrine.

The most significant group in the CAIP from 1958 through the Second Vatican Council was the arms control subcommittee of the International Law and Juridical Institutions Committee. Key members were Edward A. Conway, S.J., member of the advisory committee to the United States Arms Control and Disarmament Agency; Alain C. Enthoven, deputy assistant secretary of defense for systems analysis; Charles M. Herzfeld, deputy director, Advanced Research Projects Agency, U.S. Department of Defense; William J. Nagle, director of external research, Department of State; John E. Moriarity, Department of State, colonel, U.S. Air Force and formerly with Weapons Systems Evaluation Group, Department of Defense; James E. Dougherty, St. Joseph's College, assistant director of the Foreign Policy Research Institute, University of Pennsylvania, and professor at the National War College in Washington (1964–65); and William V. O'Brien, professor of international law and chair of the Institute of World Policy, Georgetown University, as well as author of a number of books and articles on the legal and moral aspects of modern war, and an active reserve officer in the United States Army.[41] This committee of one priest and many active laymen in leadership positions in the government wrote CAIP statements on modern warfare and delivered lectures, sponsored symposiums, and compiled literature on the topic.

In 1960, William Nagle edited a book for the CAIP called *Morality and Modern Warfare* on the question of nuclear weapons. Nagle admits in the introduction that since the book "has the character of a pioneer effort fifteen years after Hiroshima indicates something of the failure of the Christian community to come to terms with that event." He attempted to account for the absence of nuclear pacifism and the persistence of the just war criteria in the writings of American Catholics by stating, "[The contributors to the book] are citizens of the nation that has the major responsibility for the defense of the free world. The question here is not one of patriotism but responsibility."[42]

Nagle was careful to point out the noticeable difference between his *Morality and Modern Warfare* and a book published a year earlier in Britain on the same topic. In the British book, *Morals and Missiles: Catholic Essays on the Problem of War Today*, the tone is strongly pacifist.[43] Nevertheless, Nagle concluded his introductory essay with a defense of the just war tradition by quoting the address of Bishop John J. Wright of the Diocese of Pittsburgh at the 1958 CAIP meeting.

Wright said, "It is unfortunately not yet possible for honest theologians to deny that justice may require of us duties from which charity would prefer to shrink."

Several contributors to Nagle's book were members of the arms control subcommittee of CAIP, James E. Dougherty, John E. Moriarity, and William V. O'Brien. All the contributors except for the pacifist, Gordon Zahn, a member of the Sociology Department of Loyola University of Chicago, were just war theorists who were employed by the U. S. government either in the Defense or State departments.

In 1962, CAIP and the Adult Education Centers of the Archdiocese of Chicago co-sponsored a two-day convention in Chicago on "Christian Conscience and Modern Warfare."[44] Most of the speakers were members of CAIP and contributors to Nagle's book: Nagle, Moriarity, Dougherty, and Conway. Zahn was also present to represent the pacifist viewpoint. The most significant address of the conference was delivered by Thomas C. Donahue, S.J., project director of the Center for Peace Research at Creighton University, Omaha. Donahue noted what Catholic moralists in the United States had been saying about nuclear warfare, basing much of his analysis on the scholarship of the men represented in *Morality and Modern Warfare*. He divided American Catholic views on nuclear warfare into the following seven major categories:

> The first theme is that of the theologians who have an *apocalyptic* preoccupation, seeing the most important element of our age as a race to extinction. They believe we are unable to prevent the doom that is sure to encompass us.
> The second approach is that of *prevention*. These moralists say we simply have to prevent a major war because it just doesn't make sense to destroy ourselves. No one can win a nuclear war, they believe.
> The third theme centers around the idea of *justification*. This school of thought among the moralists holds that we are unable today to justify a war under present circumstances and that the principle of justifying a defensive war is inapplicable here.
> Theme number four is that of *innocence*. It notes that too many innocents (noncombatants, civilians) would be killed in any kind of nuclear warfare. Indeed, one writer feels the old theory of a just war is intrinsically altered.[45]

The fifth theme stresses the idea of *public responsibility* and raises many questions about what the government can do morally in a situation when force is required if that force is nuclear.

Theme number six is concerned with problems of *policy*. It discusses the morality of certain aspects of foreign policy and matters such as the use of war as an instrument of policy.

And, finally, among the moralists who have been writing and speaking on the Christian conscience in a nuclear world, one group lays stress on the use of *deterrents*. Many of them seem to feel that the emphasis on counterforce seems praiseworthy, but they realize there are grave difficulties involved in the use of effective deterrents for if the deterrents fail to deter, mass destruction on both sides will result.[46]

Thus, in the United States, "the Catholic view" had not established a position of consensus in 1962. Unlike Nagle, Donahue did not defend just war theorists, rather, he pointed out that "American Catholics are not even agreed on two or three major positions of what moral theologians have been saying."[47] By noting the absence of any agreement on moral criteria for nuclear warfare at the conference, he unintentionally launched a frontal assault upon the whole Catholic tradition of just war in relation to modern warfare.

Despite the results of the conference, the CAIP continued to hold firm to the normative position of the just war criteria. The next year, in 1963, CAIP and Chicago's Adult Education Centers again cosponsored a conference on "Peace and World Order" with emphases on *Pacem in Terris*, the peace encyclical written by Pope John XXIII, the role of the United Nations, and the moral and political implications of the Cold War. Within such a context, the just war criteria remained the underlying presupposition.

By the time of the Second Vatican Council there was no doubt that CAIP held as strongly as ever to the just war doctrine. Neither World War II nor the possibility of nuclear warfare had raised any serious doubts as to the validity of this normative position within the Catholic concern for peace. The small liberal membership of the association, with their key positions in the church, in universities, the State Department, the Defense Department, and the military, believed that they had done much to apply Catholic moral teaching to public-policy issues and the just war had served them well. CAIP members believed that they could look back on the period after World War II and point to the many accomplishments of which they had been a part: the United Nations as the first international organization chartered to promote world peace and understanding, the nonadmittance of the People's Republic of China into the United Nations, and the Korean War, which had prevented the extension of communism. Above all CAIP believed it had established a just criteria that limited the possibilities of a nuclear war. CAIP's efforts for peace, however, continued its tradition of nonidentification with the American peace movement.

A revival of the peace movement occurred in the late 1950s. The immediate initiator was the atmospheric testing of the hydrogen bomb with the health hazards attached to nuclear "fallout." Around this issue the National Committee for a Sane Nuclear Policy developed. In 1957, they ran their first ad in the November 15 issue of the *New York Times*. The group was open to pacifists and non-pacifists alike. By 1958, the group had 120 chapters representing approximately 25,000 Americans.[48]

The onset of the nuclear-testing issue also caused a renaissance among the radical pacifists. In June 1957, a small group of pacifists committed to nonviolent resistance organized an ad hoc committee, Non-Violent Action against Nuclear Weapons, which reorganized in 1958 as the Committee for Non-Violent Action (CNVA). Perhaps the most successful project of CNVA was the 1958 voyage of the protest vessel *Golden Rule* into a bomb-test area.[49] CNVA also sponsored other actions and became most noted for its peace walks throughout the world.

The revival of the Catholic Worker movement's peace witness during the 1950s can be attributed to Ammon Hennacy, an American radical from the Midwest. He began his "one-man revolution" in 1950 just when most peace action was receding into oblivion. His motivation came from his own vision, the object of his crusade was the state, and his aim was to live apart from any aspect of an institutional life that contributed to the power of the state to do harm to people. He had refused to serve in World War I because as a socialist he would have nothing to do with a capitalist war. In World War II he was a Christian anarchist and would not serve the government.[50]

Hennacy also wrote his autobiography, *The Book of Ammon*,[51] and subtitled it, *The Autobiography of an Unique American Rebel*. Dorothy

Day is quoted on the back of the book jacket as stating that "The story of his prison days will rank with the great writings of the world about prisons." The rationale for his "one-man revolution" is also proclaimed in the book.

The reason that Hennacy's "one-man revolution" merged with the Catholic Worker movement was not because of any deep reflection, but because he admired Dorothy Day and got what he called a "crush" on her.[52] "Ammon had thoughts that perhaps he and Dorothy would marry which annoyed Dorothy. She resented Ammon's suggestions to third parties that something might develop between them, and she let him know it."[53] It was because of her that Hennacy gave seven years of his life to the Catholic Worker and was baptized a Catholic, but it must be pointed out that much of his thought was consistent with the movement and his personal journey paralleled that of Day's. Since the 1950s were the low point of peace activities in America, Hennacy may also have been searching for a community that would provide support and access to the American public.

Like Day, Hennacy had grown up in the Midwest, made radical friends at college, and dropped out before graduating. He was born into a Baptist family in Negley, Ohio, on 24 July 1893. Politics were a central part of his home environment because his father held local elective office as a Democrat in a Republican area. At sixteen, Hennacy joined both the Socialist party and the Industrial Workers of the World. He went off to college in 1913 and attended three different schools over the next three years. At each campus he organized activities on behalf of the Socialist party. He was not yet a pacifist and even took military drill on campus. He left college to provide financial assistance at home for his seven brothers and sisters.[54]

Like Day, Hennacy viewed World War I as an imperialist war. As chair of the local Socialist party chapter, he spearheaded an antiwar and anticonscription campaign. He also refused to register for the draft. He was arrested and stood trial for his leadership role in an antiwar rally and was sentenced to two years in the Atlanta Federal Penitentiary. Still he refused to register for the draft, and an additional nine months in the county jail was added to his term. Midway through his prison term he had his first conversion experience. He wrote of this experience in his prison account:

I had passed through the idea of killing myself. This was an escape, not any solution to life. The remainder of my two years in solitary must result in a clear-cut plan whereby I could go forth and be a force in the world. I could not take any halfway measures. . . . I read Jesus who was confronted with a whole world empire of tyranny and chose not to overturn the tyrant and make Himself king, but to change the hatred in the hearts of people to love and understanding —to overcome evil with good will. . . . Gradually I came to gain a glimpse of what Jesus meant when He said, "The Kingdom of God is Within You."[55]

Upon his release from prison, Hennacy described himself as a "nonchurch Christian." He was met at the gate and immediately arrested for refusing to register for the second draft while in prison. He spent another seven weeks in prison awaiting trial. This time he had a copy of Tolstoy's *The Kingdom of God is Within You*, which led him to believe that bullets and ballots were useless, exchanging one system of power and coercion for another. Hennacy had fully embraced anarchism but brought to it a Christian dimension rooted in himself and his individual relationship with God. Day's religious vision on the other hand saw the church as mediator between time and eternity and the place where the redemption of community occurred. Though Hennacy's life was modeled on Jesus and the Sermon on the Mount, he was individualistic and political in the expression of his belief and rejected all institutions, including an institutional church.

According to his most recent biographer, Patrick Coy, "Hennacy crusaded for one great human value, freedom. At the end of freedom's rainbow was the classical anarchist paradise, where oppression, injustice, and institutional violence were done away with, where no state or church chould divide people and plant seeds of discontent and oppression."[56] Yet, like Day's personalism, the bases for Hennacy's belief were personal responsibility and a heart full of compassion that did not participate in government nor depend on it to correct social injustice. He also embraced poverty and led a life of hard physical labor mainly to avert cooperation with evil institutions so as to remain true to his vision. This quest for personal purity led Hennacy by 1942 to separation from his wife Selma and their two daughters.

World War II led Hennacy to again refuse to register for the draft; at this time he was forty-six years of age and this probably was the reason he was not prosecuted. He notified the government of his refusal and also published in the May 1942 issue of the *Catholic Worker* his statement of refusal to register for the draft. In 1943, he refused to pay income taxes and contended that the position of Dorothy Day and the Catholic Worker had led him to the belief that to pay taxes was un-Christian.

Coy contends that "Hennacy's anarchism and pacifism were two sides of the same coin."[57] His pacifism had always been active and when he studied Gandhian nonviolence it resonated with his personal experience. This led Hennacy to set himself up as the perfect radical and explains his use of the phrase, "one-man revolution." It also accounts for his harsh and critical attitude toward other peace activists and their organizations. Karl Meyer, a Chicago Catholic Worker said, "Ammon was impatient with meetings and seldom went to them. . . . He was unlike Gandhi and A. J. Muste who both made political compromises to build coalitions. . . . He didn't want to be limited. . . . He was not able to work in cooperation or coalition with other people."[58]

Hennacy believed warfare and militarism were the greatest threat to humanity and that pacifists should refuse absolutely in matters of the draft, taxes, and loyalty oaths to the government. The fact that Day's beliefs on these issues were the same as Hennacy's was another reason that he joined the Catholic Worker. In 1952, he moved to the New York Worker House and was baptized a Catholic. His official membership in Catholicism would last fifteen years (1952–1967).

Hennacy was unable to forgive the church for what he perceived as its marriage to corruption and tyranny. His anarchism led him to develop the notion "that it was up to him to show the world—both secular and religious—that one could be a Christian AND an anarchist, indeed, that that was the only way to keep alive the ideals of the Sermon on the Mount."[59] In fact, he began to use the term, "Catholic anarchism" in the *Catholic Worker*, and wrote an unpublished 150,000-word manuscript on the subject. The implication of the term "Catholic anarchism" led Robert Ludlow to disavow its use in the *Catholic Worker*. Because of a personality conflict with Hennacy, Ludlow eventually left the Catholic Worker movement. "The story around the Worker at the time was that Tom Sullivan wanted Bob Ludlow to move out, and that he invited Ammon to come to Chrystie Street knowing that Bob and Ammon would clash, compete for the attentions of the same coterie, argue over personalism and anarchism and that Bob would give up the battle. So it was."[60]

Hennacy argued that "Catholic anarchism" was a valid term even given the hierarchical/clerical nature of Catholicism because the church was not the clergy or the hierarchical structure:

> The REAL Church consists of the Mystical Body of Christ in those who grasp the meaning of the Sermon on the Mount and who do not seek to change the world by ballots or bullets, but by changing themselves daily in that daily communion which the Catholic Church furnishes them. . . . The Catholic Church does offer in daily mass a method of spiritual growth and a world view of brotherhood entirely compatible in method and in ideal to the anarchist dream which envisions a world made different not by wholesale pushing around of crowds but by the individual revolution within the heart of each individual.[61]

With such writing, Hennacy seems very close to Day in her belief in the church, but even Day could not root out Hennacy's anticlericalism and anti-institutionalism. In the end, Hennacy saw his conversion to Catholicism as something of a mistake.

It must be pointed out that within the Catholic Worker movement Hennacy found individuals who shared many of his same concerns. Though the vision of Peter Maurin dominated the movement, it had always been open to the visions of others. Gandhian nonviolence had long been a matter of concern with the Catholic Worker and the movement had always advocated and practiced fasting, picketing, and leafleting as means to correct the evils of social injustice. It had resisted payment of taxes from its inception and had also advocated resistance to conscription. What Hennacy brought to the Worker was the breezy self-confidence of a fighter who possessed a self-discipline and bravery that made him appear invincible. With these personal characteristics he led the Catholic Worker movement into a new level of pacifist activism that was labeled nonviolent resistance. His emphasis was on civil disobedience. The tactic called for the conscientious violation of an unjust law in response to obedience to a higher law that would challenge the public policy of the government and at the same time provide a moral witness to truth. Thus, he integrated both the theory and practice of nonviolence into the existing pacifist witness of the Catholic Worker and led it to a new level of peacemaking.

Hennacy had begun practicing civil disobedience in 1950 in Phoenix, Arizona, where he fasted and picketed the Tax Office for five days to protest tax money being spent on bombs and troops in Korea and in penance for the dropping of the bomb on Hiroshima.[62] He continued to perform this action annually, adding an additional day for each year since the tragedy had occurred. In 1954, he experimented with a variation of this action, which led the Catholic Worker movement into the most widely publicized act of civil disobedience to have occurred in the United States. The focus of the resistance was New York City's air raid drill, participation in which was required by the Civil Defense Act.

In 1954, Ammon Hennacy, Dorothy Day, and a few other Catholic Workers refused to take shelter during the drill. On 15 June 1955, Hennacy, Day, and five Catholic Workers were joined by twenty-three others, mainly members of the WRL and FOR. The following year they repeated their performance and were sentenced to five days in jail. Every year thereafter, a dozen or more practitioners of nonviolent resistance appeared, committed civil disobedience, and served prison sentences for it. A. J. Muste, America's most acclaimed peace activist, expressed their attitude when he told the director of Civil Defense in New York that, "Civil defense, after all, is an integral part of the total preparation for nuclear war. We, on the other hand, are convinced that the only way to a secure defense is for people to refuse to participate in any way in the preparations for war."[63] In response to an article in the *Village Voice* and a letter in the *New York Post*, several newcomers arrived to take part in the 1959 demonstration. When they suggested broadening the 1960 demonstration, the regulars, mostly CNVA members, agreed and organized the Civil Defense Protest Committee to spread the word.

On 3 May 1960, approximately two thousand students and adults throughout New York City resisted the yearly drill.[64] Ten minutes before the sirens were scheduled to blow, about five hundred persons assembled in Central Park, with many more arriving all the time. Among those present were writers Nat Hentoff, Dwight Macdonald, Norman Mailer, and Kay Boyle. It was the largest direct action demonstration against nuclear warfare, and was covered by radio and television as well as the *Village Voice, Nation, Commonweal, New York World,* and the *New York Post.* This demonstration marked the new strategy the American peace movement would use in the 1960s. The tactic of calling together massive numbers of individuals to commit civil disobedience to change the public policy of the U. S. government was a form of nonviolent resistance already being successfully used by the civil rights movement.

The air raid drill demonstration also marked a new spirit of cooperation among Catholics with other peace groups in the United States. The Catholic Worker, Peacemakers, WRL, FOR, and CNVA all practiced the more radical response of nonviolent resistance. These groups also joined with the National Committee for a Sane Nuclear Policy (SANE) in advocating unilateral disarmament.[65] Karl Meyer, a tax resister and member of the Catholic Worker in Chicago, joined the San Francisco to Moscow Walk for Peace sponsored by the CNVA. Dorothy Day helped to lay the plans for the CNVA Polaris action, a Gandhian assault on submarines bearing nuclear-tipped missiles stationed in the town of New London, Connecticut. Ammon Hennacy, Karl Meyer, and Tom Cornell were the only Catholic participants in the project. Cornell contended that "Ammon's involvement made it easier to line up the CW with that kind of experimental nonviolent action early in the game."[66] Catholic Workers also participated in the first General Strike for Peace begun in January 1962, and in many sit-ins and vigils held at the Atomic Energy Commission's office in New York. Fallout shelters were also picketed.[67] Nuclear warfare was the focus of all of these actions: It was not until after the election of President Johnson in 1964 and the escalation of the war in Vietnam that the focus of the peace movement's efforts shifted away from nuclear warfare to the draft.

During these years with the Catholic Worker, Ammon Hennacy had not limited his activity to New York City. He often took his anniversary Hiroshima demonstration to various parts of the United States. In 1957, he went to Las Vegas because the Atomic Energy Commission was conducting a series of nuclear tests near there; in 1958, he was in the nation's capital; and in 1959, he took his "one-man revolution" to Florida to protest another government installation. One of the last episodes in the confrontation that Hennacy had with the federal government in his role as a member of the Catholic Worker was going "over the fence," as he called it, at an Omaha missile base.

This act of going "over the fence" had cost other pacifists six months in jail; one of them had been a Catholic Worker from Chicago, Karl Meyer. He had participated in this act because the construction of missile sites and the continued testing of atom bombs had struck him as a hideous madness that required the most desperate resistance. Hennacy, very attracted to the action, wanted to perform it himself and was also given six months for his act of civil disobedience, which he served in Sandstone, Minnesota's federal penitentiary. He left Sandstone in January 1960.

On 2 January 1961, Hennacy left the Catholic Worker to make his home in Salt Lake City, where he remained until his death on 14 January 1979. However, he did not desert his work. He continued as usual to write his column for the *Catholic Worker*, calling it "Joe Hill House," the name of his own House of Hospitality. The name honored the IWW songwriter who was executed in the state of Utah in 1915.[68]

Though Ammon Hennacy did not leave a lasting impression on the Roman Catholic church in the United States, he did leave his mark on the Catholic Worker movement. By his undaunted actions, he had introduced to the movement the way of nonviolent resistance. Ludlow had said that Gandhian nonviolence and Catholic Worker pacifism were compatible, but Hennacy had demonstrated how to join the two together and how to apply these nonviolent tactics to the issue of peace in America. Thus, practitioners of nonviolence were not left waiting for the state to apply moral principles to nuclear issues, but were able to be the initiators of change in public policy. They were no longer just pacifists saying no to war; they were positing actions for peace. They considered themselves peacemakers.

The radical pacifists in the American peace movement had already begun to perform such actions immediately after World War II. Catholic Workers would begin to collaborate with them as never before after the peace movement's revival in 1957. However, Day envisioned the Catholic Worker movement as much broader than the peace movement. Concern for the poor and oppressed remained a priority as well as did the issues of civil rights and labor. The issues of justice and peace were inseparable. Nonviolent tactics could be used not only to bring the Gospel message to war-and-peace issues but to all areas of social injustice. Day would remain faithful to Maurin's broad vision, but also would incorporate Hennacy's vision into the Catholic Worker. She best described the difference between Ammon Hennacy and Peter Maurin when she wrote, "Ammon is deep and narrow, but Peter was so broad that he took in all the life of man, body, soul and mind."[69]

By the early 1960s, it became clear to many Catholic Workers that the peace issue was of such significance that a Catholic group solely dedicated to peace should be formed. One idea was to reactivate PAX; the other possiblity was to form a Catholic Peace Fellowship (CPF) under the auspices of FOR. The CPF idea was rejected because of the old Catholic suspicion of Protestants. As one *Catholic Worker* editor put it at the time, "All they want to do is use you."[70] Though a high level of cooperation had been achieved among peace groups during the late 1950s, Catholic Workers wanted to maintain their own identity. Self-consciously Catholic, yet critical of the existing militaristic and capitalistic American system, they were ever mindful of the encroachments of other groups, even of other Catholic groups. Stressing autonomy, the idea of reactivating PAX was adopted.

Eileen Egan, a life-long Catholic Worker and close friend of Dorothy Day, was mainly responsible for the organization. She held an executive position in Catholic Relief Services and had also written the book *The Works of Peace*. PAX was affiliated in England with PAX, whose most prominent member was Archbishop Thomas D. Roberts. The archbishop stressed the need for autonomy and told the group to be sure to keep PAX totally free of hierarchical control, especially financially. He pointed to CAIP as an example of what happens if autonomy is not maintained.[71] Sponsors of America PAX included: Thomas Merton, Edward Rice, Marion Casey, Gordon Zahn, Robert Hovda, Dorothy Day, Robert McDole, Anne Taillefer, Robert Fox, Helen Iswolsky, Rosemary Sheed, Dorothy Dohen, and Arthur Sheehan.

Because of financial difficulties, PAX grew slowly, but it succeeded in issuing a valuable quarterly magazine, *Peace*, begun in 1963 under the editorship of Eileen Egan. PAX also observed an annual peace Mass in commemoration of Hiroshima and sponsored an annual conference at the Catholic Worker farm in Tivoli, New York, as well as conducted monthly meetings in a room above the Paraclete Bookstore in Manhattan.

Founders of PAX proclaimed no official position though they themselves were pacifists. Emphasis on the individual as the one who applies the tradition and teaching of the church on issues of war and peace pervaded all of their statements. Ironically, PAX devoted most of its energies not to individuals directly, but to lobbying for peace within the institutional church.

The main reason for PAX's emphasis on the institutional church was that in the same year of its founding, 1962, more than 2,400 bishops from every continent in the world had assembled in Rome for the solemn opening of the Second Vatican Council. Three years previously, 25 January 1959, Pope John XXIII had announced that he would convene the Council. The proposed agenda for the meeting touched on many issues confronting the church in the latter half of the twentieth century, including the issue of peace. This topic came up for debate in 1964 when the council fathers were composing what was ultimately to be one of the council's more significant documents, *The Pastoral Constitution on the Church in the Modern World.* The drafts, proposals, amendments, and debates on the issue of peace centered on Schema 13 of the document during the third and fourth sessions of the council held in 1964 and 1965.

Prior to convening the Second Vatican Council, Pope John XXIII had issued his world renowned encyclical on peace, *Pacem in Terris,* on 11 April 1963. This encyclical was to set the tone for discussion at the council. In it Pope John, like Benedict XV, moved in a pacifist direction and repudiated nuclear war in the modern world, stating that "in an age such as ours which prides itself on its atomic energy it is contrary to reason to hold that war is now a suitable way to restore rights which have been violated."[72] In this statement, John XXIII condemned not just nuclear war but all war in the nuclear age. By repudiating the suitability of war as a means of restoring violated rights he implicitly rejected the theory of the just war. *Pacem in Terris* heralded a new approach to warfare and a revolution in the meaning of Catholic peacemaking.

The reason for this shift in thought can be attributed to Pope John's humanist approach. He built his arguments in the encyclical on the principles of the freedom of the individual and the validity of natural law. John XXIII believed that truth, solidarity, and justice undergirded a universe held together in the harmony and order of peace, and this order was not imposed from above but one that sprung forth from each individual.[73] Each individual was called forth to "observe, judge, act" because it was the individual acting for the common good that would bring forth peace. In *Pacem in Terris* he provided a clear statement of which rights were necessary to preserve the human dignity of each person in society, and he chose to stand with the rights of individual conscience, even over and against the rights of political authority. The pope made clear the priority of the individual conscience and the duty to obey God above human beings.

Consequently, when discussing the authority of the state, Pope John said that "civil authority must appeal primarily to the conscience of individual citizens, that is to each one's duty to collaborate readily for the common good of all."[74] Thus, in *Pacem in Terris* the primacy of the individual right and duty to work for peace is what ultimately informs and judges the actions of governments and organizations.

John XXIII explicitly expressed a hatred of nationalism, repudiated force because it violated the dignity of the person, condemned the arms race and the balance of terror on which the arms race rested, and rejected fear in favor of mutual trust. An emphasis on nonviolence in his writing transcended the old moral categories of the just war and pacifism. Moreover, *Pacem in Terris* called for structural reform of the international political and legal system to deal with the world's problems.

It is important to note that there is no explicit endorsement in this encyclical of the right of self-defense for peoples and for states. Later official documents of the Roman Catholic church, however, continued to assert the right of legitimate defense for states and often made no attempt to reinterpret *Pacem in Terris*. Thus, the door was wide open on the issue of peace when the council convened.

At the Second Vatican Council the positions of the just war and pacifism collided. By 1964 the Cold War, the possibility of a nuclear holocaust, and the pope's encyclical on peace had suggested to a number of bishops throughout the world that a just war was no longer possible.

Thomas Merton, a Trappist monk in Gethsemani, Kentucky, sent an Open Letter to the hierarchy at the Second Vatican Council in 1964.[75] The letter focused on two aspects that he considered to be crucial to the issue of peace in the nuclear age. According to Merton, the moral problems involved in the use of nuclear weapons and the right of a Catholic to be a conscientious objector to war had to be faced by the bishops gathered in Rome. He believed that the writings of Popes Pius XII and John XXIII had already implicitly condemned nuclear weapons and affirmed individual conscience.[76] In his opinion, it was up to the council to make these points explicit. Significantly, Merton's letter pinpointed the two main areas of debate that would emerge at the council.

The first draft of Schema 13 presented at the third session of the council condemned total war, and the condemnation was accepted without debate. The draft, however, also contained a similar condemnation of the use of nuclear weapons, on which point debate flourished.[77] In order to understand what part the American peace groups had in determining the final statements of Vatican II on the issues of war and peace, it is necessary to clarify their different approaches.

In 1963, Harry W. Flannery, president of CAIP, worked closely with CAIP's subcommittee on arms control. Flannery, a firm believer in the just war, urged the members of the subcommittee to prepare a statement to be sent to the bishops at Vatican II. In a letter to a CAIP member concerning nuclear warfare, Flannery said,

> No subject is of more importance today, as you well know, and I am pleased to hear that you are planning to try to get something out to the Council. The European pacifist influence in Rome may need to be offset. Here, too, we need to speak out because of the formation of PAX. Like all extremists, they may have most persistent, devoted and possibly persuasive adherents.[78]

Six active Catholic laymen, Alain C. Enthoven, Charles M. Herzfeld, William J. Nagle, John E. Moriarity, James E. Dougherty, and William V. O'Brien, all members of the subcommittee on arms control of the International Law and Juridical Order Committee of CAIP, prepared a critique of the nuclear war passages in the schema.

The critique was not a formal CAIP statement since the committee believed that there was not time nor need for it to go through the necessary procedures. On 5 August 1964, a copy was sent to Bishop John J. Wright of the Diocese of Pittsburgh. Catholic pacifist lobbyists at the council referred to it as the "secret memorandum." Essentially, the statement declared "the right to have recourse to war in extreme cases is justified by the present defective state of international society, law, and organization."[79] The just war ethic pervaded the entire statement.

Because of CAIP's close relationship with and, by the 1960s, its total financial dependency on NCWC, it is clear that the CAIP statement on nuclear war did not basically conflict with the beliefs of the American hierarchy. Members of CAIP saw no need to go to Rome to lobby for acceptance of their critique of Schema 13. William V. O'Brien in a memorandum, "Morality, Nuclear War, and the Schema on the Church in the Modern World," written in October 1964, perceptively gave the reasons why the Council could not condemn nuclear warfare and would therefore accept the recommendations submitted by CAIP.[80] His main reason was not the threat of Communism but the age-old form of nationalism peculiar to American Catholics known as "Americanism"—if Catholics did not obey their lawfully elected leaders they would be considered disloyal Americans.[81] O'Brien writes, "if the Council were to adopt such a schema [the condemnation of nuclear weapons], it would place close to fifty million American Catholics in an awesome dilemma as to whether to listen to the solemn findings of a Vatican Council or to the hitherto accepted assurances of their government that America's nuclear deterrent is the foundation for international stability and the sine qua non of the defense of the United States."[82] Thus, the only action taken by CAIP in reference to the Second Vatican Council was to prepare and send to Rome a critique of the nuclear war passages in Schema 13.

The pacifist branch of the American Catholic peace movement, however, took a more direct approach. In 1964, some members of the Catholic Worker and PAX went to Rome in hopes of encouraging the council fathers to condemn nuclear weapons and affirm the right of conscientious objection. There were two types of peace witness offered by these American Catholics at the council. The first type consisted of a group of women headed by Dorothy Day who fasted and prayed and discussed the issues with the members of the hierarchy.[83] This type of witness was intensely personal and spiritual. The other type of witness consisted of three members of PAX who self-consciously performed the tasks of a political lobby. Eileen Egan, Gordon Zahn, and James Douglass,[84] a young lay theologian and close friend of Thomas Merton, were tireless in their efforts to produce a positive statement in condemnation of nuclear warfare. They worked simultaneously on two issues in Schema 13, the condemnation of nuclear weapons and the affirmation of conscientious objection.

James Douglass's work on these two issues accounts for the major American contribution to the final statements at Vatican II. Douglass was both a theologian and a lobbyist who worked hard at locating members of the hierarchy throughout the world that were already sympathetic to these two positions. He had done his homework as a theologian and had well-drafted arguments for the positions. On the issue of nuclear warfare he attempted to show the hierarchy exactly how to condemn it within their own traditional framework of the just war ethic. Douglass, greatly influenced by Merton, believed that the just war categories were inadequate in face of the present world crisis, yet he attempted to use the theory with which the council fathers were most familiar. At the same time, Douglass also tried to move them toward a new ethic of peace based on the Gospel, the rights of personhood, and nonviolence.

It is important to note that the inclusion of the subject of nonviolence in the *Pastoral Constitution on the Church in the Modern World* was the result of the tireless lobbying at the council of Jean and Hildegard Goss-Mayr of the International Fellowship of Reconciliation.[85] The document mentions the use of nonviolence as an alternative to war: "We cannot fail to praise those who renounce the use of violence in the vindication of their rights and who resort to methods of defense which are otherwise available to weaker parties too, provided this can be done without injury to the rights and duties of others or of the community itself."[86] The American Catholic peace lobbyists Douglass and Zahn, and Merton who prepared statements for them, would all write books on nonviolence after the Second Vatican Council. Day, of course, had not assumed the role of lobbyist.

At the end of the third session, Bishop John Taylor, the American bishop of Stockholm, Sweden[87] submitted an intervention on Schema 13 that Douglass had prepared.[88] Taylor's statement began with a reference to Merton:

> Thomas Merton, one of the most profound mystical theologians of our times, has written that total nuclear war would be a sin of mankind equal only to the crucifixion of Christ. Modern means of war threaten the very existence of man. Moreover, the Council has a sacred duty to

respond with all its moral power to this threat of mankind's self-destruction.[89]

The intervention changed the technical term "uncontrollability" to the moral term "indiscriminant" based on the rights of non-combatants, supported conscientious objection, and pleaded for nonviolence. Copies of Bishop Taylor's statement were also distributed by the peace lobby to twenty-five council fathers, some of whom used sections of it for their own interventions.

During the third session, the text of Schema 13 was revised and again presented to the council for discussion in its fourth session in 1965. In article 98, "Modern warfare, and in particular so-called 'total' war," the term "indiscriminant" was used rather than "controllability." This was a definite achievement for the peace lobby. Philip Hannan, the auxiliary bishop of Washington, D.C., however, challenged Schema 13's revised text, with the support of nine bishops, three of whom were also Americans—Francis Cardinal Spellman of New York, Bishop Patrick O'Boyle of Washington, D.C., and Lawrence Cardinal Shehan of Baltimore.[90] The challenge claimed that total war had never been condemned in such a manner by "recent popes," as the final draft of the Schema stated. Bishop Hannan also wanted to keep the term "controllability." The Council voted against the challenge and accepted the revision. Article 98 in its final form reads as follows:

> All these considerations compel us to undertake an evaluation of war with an entirely new attitude. The men of our time must realize that they will have to give a somber reckoning of their deeds of war for the course of the future will depend greatly on the decisions they make today.
>
> With these truths in mind, this most Holy Synod makes its own the condemnations of total war already pronounced by recent popes, and issues the following declaration:
>
> Any act of war aimed indiscriminately at the destruction of entire cities or extensive areas along with their population is a crime against God and man himself. It merits unequivocal and unhesitating condemnation.[91]

The exact role of the American hierarchy in the revision of Schema 13 is not clear. After the third session, Gordon Zahn in the March

1965 issue of *Ramparts* charged that some American bishops were circulating a "secret" memorandum and trying to block the condemnation of the use of atomic weapons by the Second Vatican Council. Certainly Bishop Hannan's statements in both sessions and the circulated CAIP critique (secret or not) give some weight to Zahn's charges.

Monsignor George Higgins of CAIP, NCWC, and a council consultant, issued a NCWC news release on 22 February 1965, refuting Zahn's charges. Higgins's release first berated Zahn as a pacifist for having an "infuriating holier-than-thou attitude" and for writing an "outrageously superficial article." Higgins claimed in his article "that the American bishops, with few exceptions, have never even seen the so-called 'secret' memorandum referred to . . . and are certainly not carrying on a concentrated effort, either singularly or collectively to block condemnation."

Higgins's position is supported by several events that occurred during the fourth session. First was the absence of a CAIP lobby in Rome. Second, before Bishop Hannan spoke during the fourth session, there were efforts on the part of other members of the American hierarchy to modify his speech. At the annual NCWC meeting in Rome, Hannan had introduced the topic of nuclear warfare, but Joseph Cardinal Ritter, who was presiding, ruled him out of order and encouraged those interested to stay for discussion after the meeting. Several bishops did remain and tried to persuade Bishop Hannan to modify his position but they were unsuccessful.[92]

The last significant event that supports Higgins's argument was the intervention submitted by Joseph Cardinal Ritter at the council. During the fourth session three British prelates, Abbot Christopher Butler and Bishops Gordon Wheeler and Charles Grant, had spoken against a clause in Schema 13 that upheld nuclear weapons as a deterrent. Ritter then submitted a written intervention asking that the very possession of total-war arms be clearly condemned. Peace lobbyists conjectured that Cardinal Ritter delivered the intervention in writing rather than raising the issue on the floor because he feared provoking a scandalous opposition from some of the more nationalistic American bishops.[93]

Cardinal Ritter represented clearly a very different position from Bishop Hannan at the council. The degree of diversity among the American council fathers is unknown. The fact that there was a compromise position on the part of the bishops on the issue of deterrence illustrated that there was diversity among all council fathers. The final Constitution did not make an "absolute condemnation of the possession of arms which involve the intention or grave peril of total war," as Cardinal Ritter suggested.[94] Nor did the final Constitution affirm the possession of such arms as the more nationalistic bishops would prefer. Instead, the Constitution remained silent on the morality of deterrence since it would not pass judgment on the intention of nations in possession of nuclear weapons.

The council fathers did not transcend the just war criteria. *The Pastoral Constitution on the Church in the Modern World* proclaimed that "As long as the danger of war remains and there is no competent and sufficiently powerful authority at the international level, governments cannot be denied the right to legitimate defense once every means of peaceful settlement has been exhausted."[95] Thus, war could only be condemned if in its execution indiscriminate acts of bombing were committed either by nuclear weapons or traditional methods of warfare.[96] By not explicitly condemning both the intention and execution of modern methods of warfare, the council failed to draw explicit conclusions on deterrence and military defense. Bishop Hannan feared, as had CAIP technical experts' critique, that if the council had acted otherwise, Schema 13 would have meant a wholesale withdrawal of Catholic support from every nuclear arsenal in the world. The council did provide norms on modern warfare, but logical objection and national loyalties could still subject them to the priorities of nations.

The peace lobby was more successful in the council's explicit affirmation of the right to conscientious objection. The thrust for such a provision had come from Archbishop Roberts who spoke at both sessions.[97] After the third session Thomas Merton wrote to Archbishop George Flahiff of Winnipeg suggesting ways of strengthening the provision on conscientious objection. Merton urged that the right to be a conscientious objector had to apply to all wars, not just Vietnam, and that it should not be expressed negatively. Merton suggested that the provision in the draft be changed from "encouraging the consciences of the faithful to submit to the decision of authority in cases of doubt," to a "positive statement using the words of *Pacem in Terris*, 'Those who are morally convinced of the necessity of nonviolent conflict resolution, and who reject war as a solution which will hardly be reasonable in our time.' " He concluded his letter with a plea to get away from the idea of pacifist to the real truth of Christian resistance to evil on a nonviolent basis.[98]

The only American objection on the floor of the council to a provision on conscientious objection came from Francis Cardinal Spellman, the head of the military ordinate for the U. S. armed forces and in effect the bishop of Catholics in the services. Cardinal Spellman asked for a provision in Schema 13 which would make military service obligatory. In a speech before the assembled council fathers he said, "the responsibility for judging the necessity of drafting men for service belongs to civil authorities and individuals cannot refuse their obedience to the state."[99] It is noteworthy that Cardinal Spellman praised the rest of the revised draft on Schema 13.

The final text on conscientious objection adopted by the council clearly upheld the rights and duties of individual conscience and recommended legal provisions for those who resist military commands. The final text also dropped the negative statement that presumed the duty of a person to obey lawful authority until its injustice was clearly manifest.[100]

The peace lobbyists at the Second Vatican Council wanted to shut the door on the scholastic just war doctrine as a viable ethic for modern warfare. They hoped to do it with a condemnation of nuclear weapons and the affirmation of the right of conscientious objection. They were most successful in achieving the latter and the Council's final statements on modern warfare were the result of a series of compromises.

Nonetheless, the door was partially shut on the just war. The development of nuclear warfare and the Cold War had sufficiently influenced the council fathers to attempt to reevaluate the traditional just war doctrine in which they had been trained, but the attempt did not result in the development of a new ethic. This incapacity on the part of the entire assembly had already been experienced by the peace activists themselves, by individual members of the hierarchy, and by theologians throughout the world who had previously made the same attempt. At best, the council fathers opened the way for a new ethic of peace based on their affirmation of the dignity of personhood, the Gospels, and nonviolence. Thus, the very small parts played by all of these participants at the council who desired to see the condemnation of nuclear weapons were only partially successful. The new ethic was yet to be born.

The role of the American hierarchy in working towards the condemnation of nuclear weapons was almost nonexistent except for the intervention of Cardinal Ritter. The statements of other members of the hierarchy throughout the world, particularly of the bishops from England and the solemn and clear condemnation of all nuclear warfare by Patriarch Maximos of Antioch did more for the partial successes achieved on the issue than did the actions of any American. Viewed in these terms, the work of PAX, particularly its representative James Douglass, pales in significance. Yet, he was able to do a great deal, especially in providing the final wording of statements, and was listened to by many members of the hierarchy. This was a great accomplishment since he possessed no power other than the moral power of his message of peace.

After the Second Vatican Council, the just war tradition remained normative in addressing the war-and-peace policies of governments. Pacifism and nonviolence were also recognized as viable positions, but were viewed solely as options for individual Catholics not for nation-states. Vatican II affirmed the right of a Catholic to be a conscientious objector and encouraged all Catholics to work toward the development of a new ethic of peace. The American Catholic who had spent much of his life writing on peace and whose drafts and letters had great influence at the Second Vatican Council was Thomas Merton. Though not a trained theologian, his efforts to develop a new ethic of peace in the face of nuclear warfare and the war in Vietnam would provide spiritual leadership for the American Catholic peace movement during the 1960s and 1970s.

5

Thomas Merton at the Crossroads of Peace

THE PERIOD BETWEEN WORLD War II and Vatican II was a crucible for the later development of the American Catholic peace movement. This was the time when the theological rationales for the just war doctrine and pacifism were being severely challenged and the new ethic of nonviolence was born. The war in Vietnam would complete the process in the 1960s when nonviolent resistance became the movement's main means to stop the war. Thomas Merton stood at this crossroads and attempted to evaluate the Catholic tradition on war and peace in three areas: just war, pacifism, and nonviolence. His writings changed once and for all how American Catholics would henceforth think about peacemaking.

Thomas Merton was born in Praedes, France, on 31 January 1915. Six years later his Quaker mother died. He spent most of his young adult life studying in France or England. When he was not in school, he frequently travelled throughout Europe with his father, who was an artist and was always in quest of ideas for his paintings.

In 1934, after attending Cambridge for one year, Merton came to the United States and completed his formal education at Columbia University, where he obtained an M.A. degree in English. Like Dorothy Day, he had flirted with socialism and communism, but found them disillusioning because they were too focused on society with insufficient emphasis placed on personal responsibility. While completing his master's thesis on the religious and mystical elements of the writings of William Blake, he took the advice of a Hindu monk and began to read St. Augustine and the early Church Fathers. By the end of his first year of graduate study, Merton had led himself to a firm commitment to the Catholic faith.

In November 1938, Thomas Merton was baptized a Roman Catholic at Corpus Christi Church in New York City. In *The Seven Storey Mountain,*[1] an autobiographical account of his spiritual pilgrimage, he wrote that he had been converted from "rank savage paganism, from the spiritual level of a cannibal or of an ancient Roman, to the living faith."

Within two years of his baptism, Merton decided that he wanted to become a priest. This desire to do so was initially frustrated when his application to the Franciscan Order was rejected. Accepting this decision, he went to teach in a small Franciscan men's college, St. Bonaventure, located in Olean, New York. While teaching there, the conviction grew in him that he would dedicate himself to the contemplative life and in 1942 he applied to and was eventually accepted into the Trappist Abbey of Gethsemani in Kentucky.

While making this decision, Merton was faced with the draft. In conscience he knew that he could not kill anyone and would not carry a gun. By personal conviction he was a pacifist. As a new Catholic and older pacifist, Merton decided "the war would have to be defensive, and since the average person could not know whether it was or not, he would simply have to trust the leadership in Washington."[2] In November 1940, he registered for the draft as a noncombatant objector, agreeing to serve in the medical corps. Ironically, after agonizing over this moral dilemma, he failed his physical examination and was not drafted. After the attack on Pearl Harbor, the standards for induction were lowered and he was recalled for the draft. But the military was too late; Merton had already entered the monastery.

On 10 December 1941 Thomas Merton was welcomed into the abbey and given the name Brother Louis. At the monastery he was ordained a priest in 1949 and he became a U.S. citizen on 22 June 1951. During his twenty-seven years as a Trappist monk, Merton wrote, edited, and translated fifty books and three hundred articles, reviews, and poems for periodicals. Because of his writing, he became the most distinguished and well-known Catholic monk in American history. Thus, his writings on peace gave the Catholic peace movement a respectability and wider audience than previously experienced.

Merton himself divided his writings into three periods. The writings of the first period, from his conversion in 1938 to his ordination in 1949, were ascetic, intransigent, and somewhat apocalyptic in outlook.

Written in his "first fervor" days, they represented a rigid, arbitrary separation between God and the world. The second period extended from 1949 to 1959 and was mainly one of transition in which Merton sought to discover ways to integrate God and the world. Readings in depth psychology, Zen Buddhism, and existentialism greatly influenced him and led him to develop a positive view of the individual, which he combined with the theological doctrine of the Incarnation. The integration, however, did not appear until the third period beginning in 1959, when he increasingly focused on contemporary social issues.[3]

It was during the third period that Merton wrote on peace. He was not a systematic theologian like John C. Murray, who followed the logical and linear just war tradition of Augustine and Aquinas. Merton was more literary. He employed a language that was creative, dialogical, and inclusive. In his way of thinking he attempted to raise new questions and present new solutions to peace that challenged the just war tradition. He was the only Catholic writer whose extensive study of the question of peace considered the full variety of approaches: just war, pacifism, and nonviolence. Though by personal conviction a pacifist, Merton attempted to develop a theology of peace that all Catholics could embrace to become peacemakers. In his writings he provided an appreciation of the problems and contradictions of the various approaches to the issues. The focal point of his writings on peace was his belief in the eschatological dimension of the Judeo-Christian vision of a "new heaven and a new earth." According to Merton, the ultimate triumph of the vision would be achieved in the Eschaton. Daniel Berrigan termed Thomas Merton's vision of peace "the long view" and mourned his death because there was no one of Merton's stature who could provide the historical tradition and the eschatological vision of peace to the world.[4]

The international issue of the Cold War and the much discussed issues of the Christian-Marxist dialogue provided the background that eventually led Merton to address the dangers of nuclear war. Most of his writing on nuclear war was completed before the Test Ban Treaty of 1963. Because both the United States and the Soviet Union possessed nuclear weapons, Merton saw the Cold War as the most serious threat to international security.[5] He opposed the extreme nationalism of both the United States and the Soviet Union for fear that technological knowledge might trigger a nuclear war in a time of ideological conflict. His most explicit response to this struggle was written in "Letter to Pablo Antonio Cundra Concerning Giants":

> The two great powers are like sorcerer's apprentices, spending billions of dollars on space exploration and nuclear weapons while failing to feed, clothe, and shelter two-thirds of the human race. They are like the twins Gog and Magog in the book of Ezechiel, each with great power and little sanity, each telling lies with great conviction. . . . If a citizen is not properly classified, Gog shoots him while Magog deprives him of a home, a job, a seat on the bus. In both, life and death depend on everything except who you are.[6]

Merton opposed the Cold War primarily because he feared that an escalation into a nuclear confrontation would destroy the world. He believed that there was no effective control over the use of nuclear weapons and that the Cold War was releasing forces that would eventually lead the great powers into national suicide.

Merton was one of the first theologians to see that the Cold War threat of nuclear war had warped traditional Christian ethics. He held that the normative Catholic teaching of the just war doctrine was inadequate in the nuclear age and required reevaluation. He believed that if there was to be a new theology of peace, Christians had to free themselves of the overpowering influence of Augustinian assumptions concerning war. He was the first American Catholic to proclaim that the only posture that was both reasonable and Christian in the modern world was that of "relative" or "nuclear" pacifism. Such a position, Merton wrote in 1962, "admits the traditional doctrine of a just war by conventional weapons, but . . . insists that nuclear disarmament, or at the very least a completely effective arms control is an absolute moral obligation."[7] A careful reading of all of his writing on nuclear warfare reveals that the term, nuclear pacifism, meant that a Catholic would condemn the use of nuclear weapons by any nation under any circumstances and would refuse to participate in any aspect of a nuclear war from the making of nuclear weapons to the firing of them.

In developing his position, Merton first looked at the just war tradition. He established the historical roots of this tradition in early Christianity with Augustine. He wrote that Augustine imposed many limits on the Christian soldier and that these were not entirely unrealistic in a less destructive age, but he had an excessive naivete with regard to the good that could be attained by violent means.[8] Merton concluded his writing on Augustine with the following analysis: "The twofold weakness of the Augustinian theory is its stress on a subjective purity of intention which can be doctored and manipulated with apparent 'sincerity' and the tendency to pessimism about human nature and the world, now used as a JUSTIFICATION for recourse to violence."[9]

The arguments for the just war were expounded by St. Thomas Aquinas, but Merton, who had been trained in Thomistic philosophy, did not attempt to build a systematic argument against each point of the doctrine. Rather he wrote in a spiritual and literary manner about the qualitative difference between nuclear warfare and traditional forms of warfare. He believed that nuclear weapons had altered the nature of war by bringing instant death to millions of noncombatants and had consequently altered the traditional Catholic doctrine of the just war.

Merton believed that when the Japanese bombed Pearl Harbor "there was no question about the morality of America's entering the war to defend its rights. There was a very clear example of a 'just cause' for war."[10] But the obliteration bombing of cities on both sides, culminating in the massive destruction of Hiroshima and Nagasaki, had completely changed the nature of war. According to Merton, "traditional standards no longer applied because there was no longer any distinction between civilian and combatant. Even the moral principle of double effect was not valid when it 'permitted' the slaughter of fifty-thousand civilians in order to stop production in four or five factories. There was no proportion between the 'permitted evil' and the 'intended good.' "[11] Merton asked how the traditional doctrine of the just war was "so profoundly modified that it is almost ready to permit any outrage, any excess, any horror, on the grounds that it is a 'lesser evil' and 'necessary' to save our nation?"[12]

For Merton the just war theory completed a cyclical process during World War II:

A country begins a defensive "just war." It starts by declaring its firm adherence to the ethical principles held by its Church, and by the majority of its civilian population. The nation accepts unjust suffering heroically. But then the military begins to grow impatient, seeing that its own methods of retaliation are not effective. It is the military that changes the policy. The new, more ruthless policy pays off. The civilian protest is silenced before it begins. Those who might otherwise have objected come to believe what they are told: "This will save lives. It is necessary to end the war sooner, and to punish the unjust aggressor."[13]

In the end, Merton wrote, "the methods of the Allies eventually became as ruthless and as inhumane as those of the enemy."

After World War II, American Presidents Harry S. Truman and Dwight D. Eisenhower relied increasingly on a massive retaliation strategy based on nuclear arms to deter Soviet aggression against the United States and its allies. Under President John F. Kennedy, Secretary of Defense Robert S. McNamara announced a plan to develop the means to strike at Soviet military installations as well as the cities of the Soviet Union. He was attempting to "limit" nuclear warfare. In America prominent Christian "realist" theologians such as John Courtney Murray welcomed McNamara's effort to limit the effects of a nuclear war. Like Merton, Murray stated that an all-out nuclear war would be immoral. But he also argued that to halt the expansion of Soviet Communism, which he considered the primary threat to Western civilization, a limited nuclear war might be necessary and would also be morally permissable under the criteria of the just war doctrine.

In the early 1960s, Merton was one of the first and one of the few Catholics to speak out on the "illogical logic of deterrence." Merton attacked the proliferation of nuclear weapons and the immorality of massive retaliation. In theory Merton admitted that a limited nuclear war could satisfy the just war criteria for a moral war, but in practice it would be impossible to restrict a nuclear war. He wrote:

> It may be quite true that . . . Popes have . . . affirmed a nation's right to defend itself by just means, in a just war. It may also be true that a theological argument for the use of "tactical nuclear weapons" may be constructed on the basis of some of the Pope's statements. But when we remember that the twenty kiloton A-bomb that was dropped on Hiroshima is now regarded as "small" and as a "tactical device" and when we keep in mind that there is every probability that when a force that is being beaten with small nuclear weapons will resort to big ones,

we can easily see how little practical value can be found in these theorizings.[14]

For this reason, he began to attack Murray and the "realists" who were creating a strong and articulate body of theological opinion in the church in America which favored nuclear deterrence as necessary to an "adequate posture of defense." Merton sarcastically censured Murray's position in the following manner: "He takes his stand on the natural law and on the traditional Just War theory. He believes that defensive wars may be necessary and they ought to be fought with conventional weapons or with small nuclear bombs . . . it is adequate on paper, but the 20 kiloton bomb dropped on Hiroshima would be small according to Father Murray."[15] Merton also cited one of Murray's footnotes which seemed to indicate that a preemptive strike could be regarded as "defensive." "One wonders," Merton conjectured, "if this does not after all tend to validate morally everything that goes on at Cape Canaveral or Los Alamos."[16]

Merton concluded his criticism of the "realists" by stating that "the theoretician who splits hairs about 'just war,' and makes nice distinctions in journals for experts is actually supporting the military mind and military policies, which imply no such fine distinctions at all. . . . Men with nuclear weapons will use them when they think the situation is sufficiently critical. And they will not use them with regard for restraints demanded by moral theologians. To cooperate with them now is to share in the responsibility then."[17] Merton believed nuclear warfare was always total and offensive. "In our age," he wrote, "there is essentially a new kind of war and one in which the necessary conditions for a 'Just War' are extremely difficult to maintain. A war of total annihilation simply cannot be considered a 'Just War' no matter how good the causes for which it is undertaken."[18]

Merton also looked for direction in his analysis of the just war in the writings of the popes. He was disturbed that none had formally condemned the use of nuclear weapons, and in various articles he tried to justify this neglect, not only to his readers but also to himself. His writings reflected his own ambiguous feelings on the matter. As Merton viewed it, the popes had not formally condemned the use of hydrogen bombs because to condemn a specific weapon would leave some critics free to make the pope appear to be approving other kinds of weapons.[19]

Another time he contended that the popes had not condemned nuclear weapons because the weapons condemned themselves. Merton also utilized the statements of the popes that condemned certain aspects of war before the discovery of nuclear power to build his case, for example, Pope Pius XII's statement that a weapon is immoral when it becomes so destructive that it cannot be controlled. In the end, Merton contended that Popes Pius XII, John XXIII, and Paul VI had said in so many words that the new means of warfare inherently transgress the permissible limits established by the traditional just war norms of morality and make any resort to nuclear war illegitmate or immoral. Thus, according to Merton, this new kind of war made the concept of a just war impossible to achieve.

Merton also believed that the traditional just war doctrine was irrelevant because the testimony of history is clear in that an attempt to subject the irrationality of war to the rule of reason alone fails miserably. He was convinced that the power of Pope John XXIII's encyclical, *Pacem in Terris*, was that it made clear the key to the meaning of peace lay not in

> a casuistical treatment of the problem of nuclear war but in the profound and optimistic Christian spirit with which the Pope lays bare the deepest roots of peace, roots which man himself has the mission to cultivate. (This necessitates a free commitment to the ethic of Christianity which goes beyond logic to the spiritual and mystical rooted in deep and simple love for God which is also love for His creation and for God's child: man.)[20]

Though he proclaimed the just war doctrine to be irrelevant in the nuclear age, by using it himself, Merton did not break with the doctrine. He had turned to the historical tradition of the just war within the Catholic church to provide legitimacy for a nuclear pacifist position and in the process had ironically reaffirmed the relevancy of the just war doctrine for many Catholics.

According to his biographer, Michael Mott, Merton believed the just war doctrine was irrelevant for three reasons. First, Merton had come to see that to have a "just war" was an ideal as elusive as Aristotle's "perfect ruler" or Plato's "philosopher-prince" in the political theories. Second, the theory of the just war by definition referred to a war of defense and according to Merton almost all war began in defense of something and that this ruled out nuclear weapons because nuclear weapons could only be used to threaten and never as a weapon of defense. And finally, that the just war theory was developed by Augustine to preserve Christianity and the Roman Empire. Yet, the Roman Empire disappeared and Christianity would conquer the conquerors of the empire. Merton's main point here, which he made over and over in the mid-1960s was that "those who tied their faith in Christianity to faith in a single culture and a single political structure served only the structure and had no faith."[21]

It must be pointed out that Merton's writings on nuclear warfare occurred in the first few years of his attempt to address social issues, in the beginning of which stage he looked to the historical tradition within the Roman Catholic church to provide him with a degree of legitimacy. In October 1961, he wrote in his journal:

> I am perhaps at the turning point in my spiritual life: perhaps slowly coming to a point of maturation and the resolution of doubts—and the forgetting of fears. Walking into a known and definite battle. May God protect me in it. The Catholic Worker sent out a press release about my article [on peace], which may have many reactions—or may have none. At any rate it appears that I am one of the few Catholic priests in the country who has come out unequivocally for a completely intransigent fight for the abolition of war and the use of non-violent means to settle international conflicts. Hence by implication not only against the bomb, against nuclear testing, against polaris submarines, but against all violence. Non-violent ACTION, not mere passivity. How am I going to explain myself and defend a definite position in a timely manner when it takes at least two months to get even a short article through the censors of the Order, is a question I cannot attempt to answer.[22]

In 1961, Merton's *Original Child Bomb* was published. It used various accounts of the first atomic bombs dropped on Hiroshima and Nagasaki. In September 1962, *Breakthrough to Peace: Twelve Views on the Threat of Thermonuclear Extermination* was published. Merton admits that he edited the book to counter the written and spoken statements of nuclear "realists." Unable to find American Catholics with a nuclear pacifist position besides Gordon Zahn, Merton drew on other American writers, "faithful to the Judeo-Christian tradition on which our civilization was built." He was inspired to take such action by the influence of Walter Stein in Britain who edited in 1961, *Nuclear Weapons and Christian Conscience*. After publication of *Breakthrough to Peace*, Merton was silenced on writing about war by his religious superiors. He resorted to a mimeograph machine to print his "Cold War Letters," which he circulated to friends until a new abbot general lifted the ban on his war and peace writings in the summer of 1964.

The lifting of the ban carried with it a directive to Merton that he could "write about peace, not war—he was not to show pessimism."[23] Merton believed that this meant he could "radiate sweetness and light but not condemn the bomb." When a letter from the order came, however, saying that Merton's article, "Peace in the Post-Christian Era," could be published in his next book, *Seeds of Destruction*, Merton was jubilant. The book appeared on 16 November 1964 and also contained a selection from the "Cold War Letters." Merton would continue to condemn the bomb and proclaim nuclear pacifism.

The second major theme in Merton's writings on war and peace was pacifism. Merton proclaimed himself a nuclear pacifist and contended that it should be the normative position for all American Catholics to assume in any discussion of nuclear issues. After 1964, Merton left the just war doctrine behind him in his writings on war and peace as he did not believe that it was adequate to address the issues raised by the Vietnam War. He began instead to write of nonviolence. Merton's position on pacifism is the starting point for his writings on nonviolence. Although contradictions may often be found in Merton's writings on pacifism, David W. Givey points out in *The Social Thought of Thomas Merton*, that they were not seen as negative elements by Merton, but as reflective of his life, which he saw as "almost totally paradoxical." Givey contends that Merton's thought was a dialectical process that continued over and over with each step leading him nearer to reality and truth.[24]

Like Day, as a convert Merton had brought his pacifism to Catholicism. On numerous occasions in his writing, he declared that he was not a pacifist, at least in the traditional sense, for fear that readers would reject his writing if he proclaimed pacifism. Personally he had embraced pacifism but his primary concern was creating a new ethic of peace that would replace the existing traditions as the normative position for all Catholics so that they could be peacemakers.

Merton gave four reasons why he did not call himself a pacifist. First, pacifism depended solely upon the conscience of the individual Christian and had no inherent social orientation. The individual witness of the pacifist was not concerned with trying to change public policy. He believed pacifism was inherently passive and a Christian was called to action, to be a "peacemaker." Second, he believed that "the religious ambiguities in the term 'pacifism' gave it implications that were somewhat less than Catholic." A pacifist who believes in peace as an article of his faith, warned Merton, will end up "contending that Christians who are not pacifists are apostates from Christianity."[25] Third, Merton did not like the facile caricature of the pacifist and wanted to disassociate himself from it publicly. Bloom in *Ulysses* best represented this caricature for him.[26] The best explanation of why he did not want to label himself a pacifist was that even though he would not carry a gun nor kill another human being, he believed a Christian could never be forbidden to fight and he refused to admit that a war could never be just.[27]

Concern for the oppressed people of the world was the fourth reason Merton gave for his rejection of unqualified pacifism. Merton affirmed the right of an individual to resort to violence to restore rights wrongfully denied or to reestablish an order necessary for decent human existence. Because of his identification with the oppressed, Merton lamented the hidden violence that masqueraded as just authority in oppressive and highly organized societies. "Those who in some way or other concur in the oppression—and perhaps profit by it—are exercising violence," Merton contended, "even though they may be preaching pacifism. And their supposedly peaceful laws, which maintain this spurious kind of order are in fact instruments of violence and oppression."[28] He summarized his position on this point in the following manner: "If the oppressed try to resist by force—which is their right—theology has no business preaching non-violence to them. Mere blind destruction is, of course, futile and immoral: but who are we to condemn a desperation we have helped to cause!"[29]

By qualifying his pacifism, Merton came into open disagreement with Dorothy Day. Merton had been a contributor to the *Catholic Worker* since the publication of his autobiography, *The Seven Storey*

Mountain in 1948. By 1959, the year of their first extant letters, a steadfast friendship had developed. In November 1961, the relationship was tested when Merton wrote for the *Catholic Worker* an article entitled, "The Shelter Ethic." It was in response to an *America* article by L. C. McHugh, S.J., which argued that in a case where a possessor of a backyard shelter was confronted by a less provident neighbor during a nuclear attack, it would be licit for the owner of the shelter to defend against the intruder at gun point.[30] Merton's response was not concerned with the rightness or error of the ethical response of the owner of the shelter. He was willing to grant that an individual did have the right to kill someone if there was no other way to protect self or family. What Merton objected to was seeing the issue completely in these terms. He held that the owner's response was not Christian since it gave the impression that every individual was for self—such an attitude was wrong even on a purely natural level and disastrous to the political interests of the United States. Because of her pacifism, Day took issue with Merton. She could not justify killing another human being under any circumstance. She held that a Christian should not take the life of another even in self-defense.[31] Beyond this single incident there is no evidence of any other disagreement between Merton and Day. Day was grateful for Merton's writings because she believed his was the first voice for peace among the theologians since John Hugo in World War II.[32]

The war in Vietnam caused Merton to shift the emphasis in his writings on peace away from nuclear warfare to limited warfare. All of the distinctions made by him pertaining to nuclear pacifism, the just war, and pacifism seemed ultimately to disappear when he considered the issue of limited warfare in reference to the war in Vietnam.[33] Though Merton had contended that a limited nuclear war could never be just, he had also contended that a limited war without nuclear weapons could be just. This distinction became tenuous in Merton's writings, when he stated that even limited wars (however just) presented an almost certain danger of all-out nuclear war. Thus, it became highly questionable for Merton if any war could be just. He, however, did cite the uprising in Hungary in 1956 as an actual situation where the waging of war was a defensive war and a just war. Merton did not provide any other examples.

The essential evil of the United States in Vietnam for Merton was as Gordon Zahn put it, "the total commitment to violence in utter

disregard for the rights of individuals that the war had come to represent."[34] Reflective of his writings on World War II, Merton once
again bitterly attacked the ready willingness of the American people to
rationalize and excuse acts of large-scale terrorism and a war-making
policy that he believed verged on genocide. The American people
had entered a psychological state of obsession with the need to "completely wipe out" the enemy. For Merton, Vietnam was also a symbol
of the eschatological moment when a nuclear holocaust could result.
He wrote in his preface to the Vietnam edition of No Man Is an
Island, "The War in Vietnam is a bell tolling for the whole world,
warning the whole world that war may spread everywhere and violent
death may spread over the entire earth."[35]

But the Vietnam War had further implications for Merton. It led
him to search for a new theology of peace that would enable the
individual to speak against the United States' unleashing of a campaign
of destruction upon the Vietnam people. He found it in nonviolence
and for the rest of his short life he worked at formulating a Catholic
theology of nonviolence.

Merton looked to the doctrine of nonviolence as a means that would
provide Catholics with a new social ethic to meet the moral problems
of the nuclear age and replace the inadaequate doctrine of the just war.
He also hoped that nonviolence would aid pacifists in advancing beyond a position of conscience, which he saw too closely tied to "passive-
ness," to one that would speak more effectively to public policy and the
problems of the world. Merton looked to nonviolence as the basis for a
new theology of peace.

Merton's solution to the violence in Vietnam was nonviolence. He
had arrived at the position by linking the issues of justice and peace. In
Merton's writing about racial injustice in America, he had consistently
blamed the problem of racial violence at home on the white man and
had singled out the work of Martin Luther King, Jr. "as the most
Christian and effective plan for achieving racial and national unity at
home."[36] The influence of King on Merton can not be overestimated.
Mahatma Gandhi was King's inspiration in his nonviolent civil rights
campaign in America. Merton's admiration for King led to a study of
Gandhian nonviolence that resulted not only in understanding nonviolent techniques and requirements, but in believing that only nonviolence could break the endless cycle of violence. Thus, "in the field of
international affairs he most admired the work of King's guiding spirit,

Mahatma Gandhi."[37] Merton explained Gandhi's significance for Christians:

> One of the very few men of our time who applied Gospel principles to the problems of a political and social existence in such a way that his approach to these problems was inseparably religious and political at the same time. . . . [For Gandhi] political action had to be by its very nature "religious" in the sense that it had to be informed by principles of religious and political wisdom. To separate religion and politics was in Gandhi's eyes "madness" because his politics rested on a thoroughly religious interpretation of reality, of life, and of man's place in the world.[38]

Showing how Gandhian nonviolence was consistent with the Gospel and the Catholic tradition of peace, Merton turned first to Scripture and the writings of the early Church Fathers. He affirmed that, neither blessed nor forbidden by Jesus, war belonged to the world outside the Kingdom which He came to establish. It was the Apocalypse, according to Merton, that presented the eschatological view of peace in its symbolic description of the critical struggle of the nascent church with the powers of the world. War in the Apocalypse was the "Rider of the Red Horse" who, Merton stated, was to prepare the destruction of the civil power structure. Merton asserted that the Holy Roman Empire was clearly understood by the early Christians to possess a demonic power, and this was evident in the Apocalypse where "the battle was non-violent and spiritual, and its success depended on the clear understanding of the totally new and unexpected dimensions in which it was to be fought."[39] There is no indication whatever in the Apocalypse, concluded Merton, that "the Christ would be willing to fight and die to maintain the 'power of the beast,' in other words to engage in a power-struggle for the benefit of the Emperor and of his power."[40]

Merton next explored what Origen and other early Church Fathers such as Clement of Alexandria, Justin Martyr, and Cyprian had written about the Christian's right (or duty) to bear arms. He discovered that the Church Fathers during the first four centuries A.D. taught that Christians should not take up arms in any war. Merton believed he had discovered in Origen, the author of *Contra Celsus*, a theory very different from Augustine's. Origen, said Merton, denied that the early Christians were violent revolutionaries, or that they intended to bring about the overthrow of the empire by force. Origen, himself, did not believe in the need of war because the time would come for all people to be united in the Logos, though this fulfillment most probably awaits the Second Coming of Christ. Origen believed that human society had been radically transformed by the Incarnation, and that, among other things, Christians, who desired the good of all people, should be united against war in obedience to Christ. Because Christians are a "royal priesthood," they did more by their prayers to preserve peace than they could by force of arms. Origen also argued, Merton added, that nonperformance of military service did not free early Christians from their fair share of the responsiblities for maintaining the commonwealth, but their role was primarily spiritual and transcendent. "In a word," Merton explained, "if peace is the objective, spiritual weapons will preserve it more effectively than those which kill the enemy in battle. For the weapon of prayer is not directed against other men, but against the evil forces which divide men into warring camps. If these evil forces are overcome by prayer, then both sides are benefitted, war is avoided and all are united in peace. In other words, the Christian does not help the war effort of one particular nation, but he fights against war itself with spiritual weapons."[41] Merton believed Origen's position was very close to nonviolence and would use the early Church Fathers to show the compatibility between nonviolence and Catholicism. Based on these sources Merton called for a new theology of peace in place of the just war criteria.

At this point, what we have in Merton is the presentation of the Christian myth that provides a vision of the future without any attention to specific means for its achievement. It is focused on the individual and does not address the state as the just war doctrine does, rather it presupposes the existence of a Christian state, which Merton claimed has never existed. All extant ages, according to Merton, have been pre-Christian or post-Christian. He also contended that the New Testament says nothing about politics. Rather than building a new theology of peace whereby the church provides a moral criteria to be followed by the state as in the just war theory, Merton was searching for an ethic not contingent on the actions of the state but based on the actions of individual Christians who could address the political issues of the state. Merton's theology of peace, therefore, began with the conversion of the heart that rejected violence and then subsequently transformed passive ideas of peace into actions that would bring about peace through nonviolence. He realized that he was shifting the responsibility of war and peace away from the state to the individual peacemaker and he found support for his position in the the words of Karl Rahner, who stated:

> Thus the political action of the Christian does not become confused with projects centered around an official and clericalist "party line," nor is it inevitably associated with the propagation of a dogmatic message which the rest of the world is not disposed to hear without challenging it. But on the other hand, this Christian action is concretely ordered to advancing the work of Redemption and deepening the penetration of grace into the realm of society and nature. . . . It is the "action of Christians but not action of the Church."[42]

Accepting Christ's Sermon on the Mount as the basis for ethics, Merton linked the Beatitudes with natural law in his attempt to justify the peacemaker's political action. He stated that "the Beatitudes indeed convey a profound existential understanding of the dynamic of the Kingdom of God, . . . a dynamism of patient and secret growth. . . . This is not merely a matter of blind and arbitrary faith. The early history of the Church, the record of apostles and martyrs remains to testify to this inherent and mysterious dynamism of the ecclesial 'event' in the world of history and time."[43]

Merton, rooted in a Catholic tradition that looked not only to the New Testament but also to its doctrine of natural law for its principles, realized that the church adopted the natural law from pagan philosophy and made it a basis for much of its doctrine and practices. Thus, the natural law became the basis for Christian doctrine concerning the social order. But Merton pointed out that "once the Law of Christ has been promulgated, it is no longer possible to isolate the natural law in a sphere of its own. The natural law itself acquires a Christian perspective from the Sermon on the Mount. It has an aim higher than the mere avoidance of brutality, savagery, and sin. It becomes obligatory for the Christian to orientate all his conduct according to the law of love and to make use of non-violent means of persuasion whenever it is humanly possible. He must do this out of generous love both for his neighbor and for the truth."[44] What Merton was trying to do was move the Christian from passive resistance (a conscientious negative response to participate in a political action by the state that the individual deemed wrong) to a more active resistance (positing direct actions against political decisions by the state which the individual conscience has judged is wrong). It was at this point that Merton proclaimed nonviolence as the Christian's way to peace.

According to Merton, Gandhi provided a means that would involve human beings in the decision-making process and in the discipline of meaningful participation. This means would enable participants in actions of nonviolence to correct the evils of the existing social order without demanding the participants engage in and become part of the evil social structure they were attempting to correct. Thus, Gandhian nonviolent resistance provided a dynamic for social change that was contingent on individuals positing actions to help create the new order. Gandhian nonviolence was consistent with the Catholic faith, according to Merton, because it rested on the Gospel principle of willingness to endure suffering rather than to inflict it upon another and also because its primary goal was truth. Thus, Catholic nonviolence like Gandhi's satyagraha did not seek power but truth. Merton tried to summarize this meaning of Catholic nonviolence in his statement, "It does not say 'We shall overcome' so much as 'This is the day of the Lord and whatever may happen to us, He shall overcome.' "[45]

Merton took Gandhian nonviolent resistance and added the eschatological dimension that provided for the ultimate triumph of truth and love only with the Second Coming of Christ. It was Merton's hope that if enough individuals made a free commitment to the love ethic of Christian nonviolence, a new earth would exist and the problem of force-dominated politics of the state would cease. His eschatological vision, which was dependent on personal conversion and nonviolent action, was consistent with Day's and Maurin's concepts of Christian personalism and revolution.

The ethic of nonviolence reconciled with the concepts of eschatology and individual responsiblity constituted the basis of Merton's writings on peace. Merton was plagued by the contradiction between politics and the New Testament and by 1968 in a letter to a friend, said that he was interested in any insights on the problem, but would leave the area alone. He felt himself moving into a kind of "post-political eschatology" which he could not articulate. He hinted that appeals to politics lacked firmness and to accept politics as a religious area of reality would only contribute in the end to the slide into "technical totalism." What Merton called for was a radical rethinking of politics.[46]

Merton himself pointed out his own limitations in attempting an integration of religion and politics. He could add nothing to Gandhian nonviolence in this area. Aware of his lack of political astuteness and removed from participation in direct action in his monastery, he contended that he was not primarily concerned with the tactical strategy of building a peace movement. Rather Merton had come to see the monastery as the model of the nonviolent Christian life of community, conscience, and witness. He summarized the role of Christian monasticism in these terms: "The monastery is not an 'escape from the world.' On the contrary, by being in the monastery I take my true part in all the struggles and sufferings of the world. To adopt a life that is essentially non-assertive, non-violent."[47]

The monastery, however, had not prevented Merton from being a long-standing member of the Catholic Worker. He had joined the Fellowship of Reconciliation, and had lent his name as sponsor in 1962 to the American PAX Association and in 1964 to the Catholic Peace Fellowship. Merton had even desired to become personally involved in the "Peace Hostage Exchange" project and praised and supported the demonstrations of civil disobedience protesting the New York air raid test and the Golden Rule, Phoenix, and Everyman projects. He had also counseled young men seeking conscientious objection status during the Vietnam War. Merton had reservations about the tactic of draft card burning and draft file destruction and was most upset by the self-immolation of Roger LaPorte, a young member of the Catholic Worker. Merton advocated most strongly the need for pastoral and educational work in the area of peace.[48] Practical strategies concerning the means of nonviolence were beyond Thomas Merton. It was nonviolence as a Christian way of life, not as a political strategy, that consumed his thought and writing.

Merton acknowledged that he could not develop what he termed a "systematic theology of love," which, in crisis situations might support actions of resistance. He admitted that, at best, he was only examining "principles and cases which help an individual to see the unacceptable ambiguities of a theology of 'might makes right' masquerading as a Christian theology of love."[49] He was certain, however, that the new ethic required a person to be aware of the dangers posed by the state.

In order for the individual to be a peacemaker in the United States during the nuclear era, Merton believed that the individual must first recognize the predominant myths operative in the country. Merton portrayed America as a "sick nation" where "people are fed on myths" and "are stuffed up to their eyes with illusions" so that "they can't think straight." The two great American myths blinding the individual, Merton asserted, were that "force is the only alternative" and that "power is the only basis for human relationships."[50] Predominant during the Cold War these myths were supported and reinforced by the mass media, according to Merton, and they cultivated a "state of mind" that prevents the individual from grasping the plight of the present situation. This "state of mind," he warned, has taken over the role of morality and conscience and will, and rationalized its prejudices with convenient religious and ethical formulas to condone what has occurred in the United States since World War II.[51] This "state of mind" increases the enslavement of people and the possibilities of personal destruction, because as Merton pointed out, the massive power structures are the only benefactors. As a result, the power structures within that nation exploit the individual and ultimately conscript him into warfare.

After asserting that the individual was in great danger of being swallowed up by the Leviathan state, Merton urged individual Christians to look upon the acts and demands of their nation's leaders with intense suspicion and recognition that there was a high probability of jeopardy to their personal spiritual responsibilities and well-being if they obeyed such leadership. For Merton authority in America was suspect. The reason he gave is that it seeks to compel obedience by increasingly resorting to external force or to the law of fear. Though Merton documents this position by a reference to Pope John XXIII, he gives no concrete examples. "When authority ignores natural law, human dignity, human rights, and the moral order established by God," he concludes, "it undermines its own foundation and loses its claim to be obeyed."[52]

Merton saw this sickness that infected the state reflected in the

Catholic church in America, especially in its stands on the issues of war and peace. In his view this sickness accounted for the ambiguity of so many Catholics on the war question, or worse the frank belligerency of the majority of them. He lamented the failure of his church to inspire its members to be peacemakers and oppose America's militaristic ethos and the arms race, even though it was clear that he did not see the church as an effective agent for social change. His hope for change rested on the actions of individual peacemakers and he viewed spirituality as the basic dynamic in human behavior for durable social change.

Moreover, the "state of mind" which existed in "sick" America, according to Merton, threatened not only the spiritual basis of society but also the democratic process itself. If such a "state of mind" continued among the majority of American people, he feared that America would become the equivalent of Nazi Germany or totalitarian Russia. He compared the spiritually sterile man in America to Adolf Eichmann. In *Raids on the Unspeakable*, Merton noted that Eichmann was considered to be a "sane" man even though he felt no guilt at the extermination of the Jews.[53] The refusal of Eichmann and men like him to accept the imperatives of personal responsibility and oppose Hitler made a Nazi Germany possible.

In contrast to Eichmann, Merton in *Faith and Violence* celebrated such responsible individuals as Alfred Delp, Max Josef Metzger, Franz Jagerstatter, Dietrich Bonhoffer, and Simone Weil, whom he considered authentic Christians. These people defied the totalitarian power of the rulers of Nazi Germany by their acts of resistance and for Merton their nonviolent resistance was a measure of their faith.

Hence, the problem for Merton was not how to change the state, but how to change individuals into peacemakers in America. The question became for Merton how to transform the present "state of mind" into a new consciousness that would result in human liberation and a capacity to act responsibly in face of totalitarian power. Merton gave some impetus and direction to such a process. He insisted that individuals be properly informed, not only about the situation in which they found themselves, but also about nonviolent resistance; moreover, individuals must exercise their rights to protest or resistance. Both of these demanded the recognition of individual conscience. Merton stressed the need for the individual conscience to be based on spiritual principles for the processs to succeed. The means of nonviolence would enable the individual Christian to act in such a way as to have direct relevance to the state and society.

Merton's insistence on a spiritual base as a prerequisite for nonviolent resistance seemingly contradicted some of the statements in his writings on peace where the only prerequisite for the end of war and the unity of humankind was the human response. In the essay "Nhat Hanh Is My Brother" he pointed to the overarching nature of the concept of human solidarity. Nhat, a Vietnamese, deplored war, as did Merton, and for the same reasons: human reasons—reasons of sanity, justice, and love. As Merton put it,

> I have far more in common with Nhat than I have with many Americans, and I do not hesitate to say it. It is vitally important that such bonds be admitted. They are the bonds of a new solidarity and a new brotherhood which is beginning to be evident on all the five continents and which cuts across all political, religious and cultural lines to unite young men and women in every country in something that is more concrete than an ideal and more alive than a program. This unity of the young is the only hope of the world. [54]

In his essay "Taking Sides on Vietnam" Merton says, "The side I take is, then, the side of the people who are sick of war and want peace in order to rebuild their country." [55]

Finally, in what was Merton's most famous statement on the entire issue of peace, first written in a letter to James Forest, and later reprinted and widely circulated by A. J. Muste, the same human dimension is paramount.

> It seems to me of course that the most basic problem is not political, it is a-political and human. One of the most important things to do is to keep cutting deliberately through political lines and barriers and emphasizing the fact that these are largely fabrications and that there is another dimension, a genuine reality, totally opposed to the fictions of politics, the human dimension which politics pretends to abrogate entirely to themselves. Is this possible? I am accused of being too ready to doubt the possibility, though I am as ready as anyone to put some hope in it. At least we must try to hope in that, otherwise all is over. But politics as they now stand are hopeless. Hence the desirability of a manifestly non-political witness, non-aligned, non-labeled, fighting

for the reality of man and his rights and needs in the nuclear world in some measure against all the alignments.[56]

Merton's insistence on the human dimension, however, did not preclude the spiritual. His definition of the "spiritual" or "religious" dimension always presupposed the human which it sought to elevate or perfect. The distinction between human and spiritual is most apparent in Merton's writings when he addressed himself to the eschatological dimension. For him, the inner change in the individual and the consequent change in the social order, which the reign of justice and love demanded, was inextricably bound up with the Second Coming of Christ or the Eschaton. Only at the Eschaton would a revolution that established the primacy of Christian love over force be successful. Only at that time would each individual have undergone the inner change that Merton considered a prerequisite for what he called the "revolution" of society and the reign of justice and peace. Merton's insistence on the inseparable association of personal and social change, and the role of nonviolence in both, was articulated in the following passage: "Never was it more necessary to understand the importance of genuine non-violence as a power for real change because it is aimed not so much at revolution as conversion."[57]

The insistence on the prerequisite of personal conversion together with his long view, which places all of his writings on war and peace within the Catholic tradition and the Second Coming of Christ, defined Merton's concept of revolution. The revolution he called for could not be realized until the Second Coming when all creation would be fulfilled. Therefore, the revolution Merton envisaged is impossible to achieve in human history. Yet, because of his optimistic view of person, where the individual is capable of transcendence and of acting responsibly, the revolution of love that he called for could be realized in human history to the extent that individuals are willing to let Jesus Christ and His Spirit work through them as peacemakers.

In his writings on peace, Merton turned toward Gandhian nonviolence as a way for individual believers to translate their own Christian beliefs concerning peace into a life-style and behavior that would realize, at least partially, his view of revolution. He recognized nonviolence as a viable way for individuals to use their reason, religious faith, and courageous spirit of self-sacrifice to resist the evils of injustice and war and give meaning once again to the ideals of Christianity and democracy.[58]

Merton's optimistic view of the person enabled him to make great demands on the individual as a peacemaker. As he saw it, the crucial link between Christianity and nonviolence as espoused by Gandhi was faith in the meaning of the Cross and the redemptive death of Jesus who instead of using force against his accusers, took all the evil upon himself and overcame the evil by suffering. Merton saw this stance as a basic Christian pattern. It was a realistic theology that

> will give a new practical emphasis to it. Instead of preaching the Cross *for others* and advising them to suffer patiently the violence which we sweetly impose on them, with the aid of armies and police, we might conceivably recognize the right of the less fortunate to use force, and study more seriously the practice of non-violence and human methods on our own part when perhaps, as it happens, we possess the most stupendous arsenal of power the world has ever known.[59]

Merton's major contribution to a Catholic theology of peace was to integrate Gandhian nonviolence into Christianity. In the pamphlet *Blessed are the Meek: The Christian Roots of Non-Violence* Merton sets forth for the peacemaker a list of criteria as touchstones for a relative honesty in the practice of Christian nonviolence. These coincide with many of the points made by him in all of his writings on war-peace issues. They call for a transformation of the present state of the world by a peacemaker who is free from all association with unjust use of power, who stands in solidarity with the poor and underpriviledged, who is free of self-righteous blindness, who avoids the fetish of immediate visible results, who is concerned with manifesting, not obscuring the truth, and who grounds action in Christian hope. For Merton power can never be the hallmark of Christian peacemakers. Rather the "key to non-violence is the willingness of the non-violent resister to suffer a certain amount of accidental evil in order to bring about a change of mind in the oppressor and awaken him to personal openness and to dialogue."

It is evident from his writings on peace that Merton repeatedly stressed that the burden and responsiblity was with the individual. He assured the reader of his own conviction that "the witness of genuine non-violence has been incontestable."[60] He also pointed out that "the non-violent ideal does not contain in itself all the answers to all our questions. These will have to be met and worked out amid the risks and anguish of day to day politics. But they can never be worked out if non-violence is never taken seriously."[61] Finally, Merton offered the peacemaker a bleak promise: "It is the 'men of good will' the men who have made their poor efforts to do something about peace, who will in the end be the most mercilessly reviled, crushed, and destroyed as victims of universal self-hate of man which they have unfortunately only increased by the failure of their good intentions."[62] Indeed, for Merton the demands of peacemaking on the individuals were harder than demands of war.

Thus, Merton's notion of nonviolence affects both the individual and society, for it demands that the ends and means of a peacemaker's action be compatible. Though his work on war-peace issues begins with conscience seen in the light of the history of moral law as both social and individual, both rational and "beyond reason," he argued that when conscience assumed the compatible means offered by nonviolence, peacemakers were able to preserve their own integrity and at the same time act with relevance and effectiveness in bringing about social change. Christian peacemakers who have embraced the means of nonviolent resistance, according to Merton, will provide an alternative to, rather than a cooption into, the means of interest-group democracy or power politics. He also believed that Christian nonviolence could open the road to a new policy, more in keeping with the self-interest of the individual and the good of society as a whole.

Merton's primary concern with the role of the Christian against the massive power of the state and his own solitary life as a monk did not enable him to address himself to the question of individuals joining together in building a peace movement. He believed that "Christianity is against all mass movements, for they are intrinsically detrimental to man's well-being. . . . Leaders of movements place their trust in money or technology rather than God."[63] His opposition to such movements extended from Nazism to communism and even in a modified way to the peace movement in later years. For Merton, mass movements mentally portrayed the individual not as a real person but as a part of a group; it labeled people who were part of the group as friends and others outside the group as enemies. Jesus, according to Merton, was mistaken for the enemy and was killed because he did not conform to the pattern of behavior dictated by the dominant group of his day.[64] In no way did Merton promise an effective and successful revolution of love in terms of human history. He offered only the hope that individuals would bring about "a new heaven and a new earth" and he assured peacemakers of Christ's promise of suffering and death and ultimate resurrection. Merton's writing on peace became a source of support to the action of prophetic individuals who embraced Christian nonviolence in America.

In November 1964, Merton conducted a retreat on the "Spiritual Roots of Protest." Six of the men in attendance were later to be in prison for "crimes" of nonviolent resistance. They were Daniel and Philip Berrigan, Robert Cunnane, James Forest, Thomas Cornell, and John Peter Grady. Two other participants were Protestant peace leaders, A. J. Muste and John Howard Yoder. Merton also maintained correspondence over this entire period with American Catholic peace leaders such as Dorothy Day, Daniel Berrigan, and James Forest. He also maintained an extensive correspondence with individuals around the world.

Merton did make a difference by proclaiming the inadequacy of the just war doctrine and pacifism within the Catholic tradition. He was successful at the Second Vatican Council in writing on behalf of the individual's right to become a conscientious objector, but he was unsuccessful in procuring a condemnation of nuclear war and weapons. Yet, Merton would write often that "truth" not "effectiveness" was the criteria of Christian nonviolent action. He spent his years after Vatican II emphasizing the compatibility of nonviolence with Catholicism and urging individuals to practice it in their efforts at peacemaking. He asked his readers not to consider the peace movement as simply another of several new ideologies in a never-ending cycle for power. Like Dorothy Day, he urged each individual to see peacemaking and nonviolence as a completely new way of life, a life that would liberate each individual from the logic of power and power relationships. He also called upon individual Christians to serve the community of humankind, a service that was radical insofar as its aim was to replace a dominating society of force with a society dominated by love. His long view, based on faith, assured a revolution of love.

Thomas Merton provided the spiritual impetus to many American

Catholic peacemakers in their struggle against the American war in Vietnam. He was undoubtedly one of the greatest influences upon the Catholic peace movement in the United States. He gave the movement respectability and he struggled constantly to awaken his readers to their vocation as peacemakers. Numerous Merton Centers for the Study of Peace have appeared across the country. Many colleges and universities have courses on Merton and incorporate his thought into courses dealing with justice and peace. The far-reaching aspects of his influence certainly extended to the bishops, for many of the challenges and statements that he issued were adopted not only at the Second Vatican Council, but also by the National Conference of Catholic Bishops.[65] Individual American Catholics would attempt to embrace nonviolence, if not as a way of life, at least as a strategy for stopping the war. The number of American Catholics involved in working for peace would reach proportions never before experienced in our nation's history. By Merton's death in 1968, the Catholic church in the United States was undergoing an internal revolution that would transform it from a predominantly conservative and patriotic body, whose hierarchy always exhorted its members to obey the nation's lawfully constituted government in matters of war and peace, to a new outlook on peacemaking for the rest of the century.

6

The Catholic Peace Movement and Vietnam

IN LESS THAN A year after the adoption of *The Pastoral Constitution on the Church in the Modern World* at the Second Vatican Council, Pope Paul VI undertook a series of pilgrimages for peace. For the first time in American history a pope visited the United States. The highlight of his visit occurred on 5 October 1965, when the pope addressed the General Assembly of the United Nations on its twentieth anniversary. In his address, Paul VI confirmed the teachings of the peace encyclical, *Pacem in Terris*, and the new approach to the issues of war and peace stated in the pastoral directives of the Second Vatican Council.

The pope's message reached its climax when he proclaimed: "No more war, war never again! Peace, it is peace that must guide the destinies of peoples and of all mankind."[1] The pope elaborated on this point by stating:

> If you wish to be brothers, let the arms fall from your hands. One can not love while holding offensive arms. Those armaments, especially those terrible arms, which modern science has given you, long before they produce victims and ruins, nourish bad feelings, create nightmares, distrust and somber resolutions. They demand enormous expenditures, they obstruct projects of union and useful collaboration. They falsify the psychology of peoples.[2]

The pope's message, like that of John XXIII and the council, called for a new approach to the issues of war and peace. In 1967, in his encyclical *Populorum Progressio* he approved conscientious objection and alternative service and connected justice and peace by spelling out the relation between the arms race and the poverty of the Third World.[3] In

131

December 1966, he called for a negotiated settlement of the Vietnam War and in May 1968 he offered the Vatican as a site for peace talks.[4]

During the Vietnam era (1963–1975), Catholicism would pass through the most turbulent period of its short history in the United States. Catholics not only had to cope with changes in American society, they had to contend with changes in their church initiated by the Second Vatican Council. The combination of these events would give birth to the largest Catholic peace movement in American history.

John XXIII opened the Second Vatican Council with a call for *aggiornamento*, that is, to bring the church up to date. At the very first session, some bishops protested the proposed agenda and the people selected for major committee positions. Immediately the papers carried the headlines "Bishops Revolt." "This marked the beginning of an open Council and an open church, in which debate and dissent became accepted. . . . As a result of the Council, . . . Catholics acquired the authority to dissent."[5] The process of implementing the changes unleashed by Vatican II affected the entire hierarchical structure of the church. Vatican II encouraged the role of the laity in the church and the concept of collegiality, or shared authority. The new emphasis on the individual and conscience in the council's "Declaration on Religious Freedom" and the concept that the church was the "people of God" led American Catholics to challenge the authoritative decisions of their church and also the policies of their government.

At Vatican II the bishops also went on to make social justice a top priority and continued the Catholic tradition of linking justice with peace. This tradition would have a profound impact on American Catholics in the 1960s as social changes swept across the land. The civil rights movement, the birth of a women's movement, and a mounting concern with poverty and urban blight involved many Catholics who were committed to establishing a just order in American society. Involvement in these domestic nonviolent struggles for social justice in American society provided a stepping stone for many American Catholics into the peace movement as the United States escalated its role in Southeast Asia.

During the Vietnam War, many Catholics were involved in social justice issues domestically. On the labor front where church leaders had traditionally evidenced support, Cesar Chavez organized the National Farm Workers Association. In 1970, when the association signed the first of several labor contracts with California growers, George Higgins, a priest associated with the United States Catholic Conference was a central figure in the negotiations. The involvement of bishops in these negotiations and in the farm workers' movement was part of a new trend.[6]

Nothing shocked the nation like the civil rights crusade and the racial violence that erupted during the 1960s. The race crisis drew the church into public life to deal with a problem that affected a group who were for the most part not Catholic. Nevertheless, Catholic religious orders like the Josephites had traditionally committed themselves to work solely for blacks. Philip Berrigan, a Josephite, and his brother, Daniel Berrigan, a Jesuit, along with Richard Wagner, another Josephite priest, attempted to join the Freedom Ride in Mississippi led by James Farmer in the summer of 1961 but their religious superiors denied them permission. When one of the most significant marches took place in Selma, Alabama, in March 1965, clergy of all religions took part, including over four hundred Catholic priests, numerous nuns, brothers, and lay people. The American church hierarchy began to encourage priests and sisters to work with the black community and this gave a new prominence to social ministry. In 1967, the Milwaukee priest James Groppi made national news when he led open-housing marches throughout Milwaukee. In 1970, the National Office of Black Catholics was opened and for the first time in over a century, black priests were appointed to the hierarchy.[7]

Race was not the only issue in which many Catholics became involved. Poverty, inadequate housing, and job discrimination in the cities where Catholics lived led many Catholic clergy to become involved in urban affairs. The bishops supported the war on poverty launched by Congress and President Johnson in 1965. John Egan, a Chicago priest, together with social action priests trained in Saul Alinksy's community organizing techniques, founded the Catholic Committee on Urban Ministry (CCUM) in 1967. Within a decade over five thousand men and women had joined the organization. Geno Baroni, a priest in Washington, D.C., who was noted for his work with ethnic groups in the cities, joined Egan to establish the Campaign for Human Development, a national program funded by the bishops in an effort to eliminate poverty.

The parish also took on a new look in the 1960s and 1970s. Many became community institutions committed to serving the needs of all people regardless of race or religion and the church hall became a community meeting place. In New York City, the showcase of this new-style parish was St. Gregory the Great, on the city's West Side. Pastor Henry J. Browne, an important community leader in the 1960s, was aware of the transformation that had occurred and was sensitive to some old-time parishioners who were not pleased with the change. Browne was not surprised when one of them wrote to him: "I would also like to point out at this time that I feel St. Gregory is now a Political Organization and a meeting place for the liberals, hippies, anti-establishment, etc. characters, and since the many incidents of the past year . . . it is with regret that now after more than thirty years, I am no longer a parishioner."[8]

Among this array of social justice activities, the Catholic connection between justice and peace was made and support both directly and indirectly was given to the American Catholic peace movement during the Vietnam era.[9] Many Catholics remained committed to a single issue such as race or community organizing and only indirectly supported the peace movement; other Catholics moved from their social justice work into the peace movement; some integrated the two works. Some Catholics like Mario Savio, leader of Berkeley's Free Speech movement, Tom Hayden, the author of the "Port Huron Statement" which launched the Students for a Democratic Society (SDS), and Timothy Leary, who urged the use of LSD as a sacrament in the counterculture of the 1960s made no connection between their religion and society's problems and left the church. On the other hand, Jack Kerouac, the "beat" novelist and guru of the counterculture, could not abandon his Catholicity.[10] Beyond a doubt, the impact of social changes in American society and the changes within Catholicism after the Second Vatican Council were causing an identity crisis among American Catholics. They were rethinking the meaning of Catholicism in American society and were becoming very visible and vocal in their criticism of the injustices they found.

The connection between justice and peace for American Catholic social justice activists was complicated by the policies of President Johnson. They as well as many other Americans supported the president in his domestic policies of civil rights and the War on Poverty, but many opposed his foreign policy in Vietnam. Others did not want to jeopardize their domestic social gains by opposing the war. Martin Luther King, Jr., more than any other leader, provided the link that enabled the social-justice activists to embrace the peace movement. On 25 February 1967 at an institute sponsored by *Nation* magazine, King delivered his first speech devoted entirely to Vietnam, "one of history's most cruel and senseless wars." In the speech he indicated that the war was limiting the effects of the war on poverty. "The promises of the Great Society have been shot down on the battlefields of Vietnam," he declared. He called for union as a goal for a better America: "We must combine the fervor of the civil rights movment with the peace movement. We must demonstrate, teach and preach, until the very foundations of our nation are shaken."[11]

American Catholics, more than any other group, had a tradition of a conservative and patriotic hierarchy that exhorted its members to obey the nation's lawfully constituted authority, especially during a time of war. As the historian David J. O'Brien has pointed out, "the history of American Catholic responses to international events is more complex than that." He then points to the American hierarchy's opposition to American arms shipments to the Loyalist government during the Spanish Civil War and to the bishops' private conversations during World War II to the president concerning their reservations about war-time policies toward the Soviet Union. O'Brien, however, does not go far enough in his analysis. In both cases the hierarchy was motivated by their anti-communism. This was not sufficient motivation, however, to oppose U.S. entrance into World War II nor obliteration or atomic bombing, but it was the only sufficient rationale for criticism by the hierarchy during that period. O'Brien does make the observation that "For many understandable reasons Catholics were early and active cold warriors, but their anti-Communist militance could and did lead them to become very critical of the government and its policies."[12]

Church leaders favored containment policies in Europe and were concerned about communist expansion in Asia. The victory of communism in China had given rise to a powerful anti-communist lobby in the United States. When the French withdrew from Vietnam in 1954 and left behind in South Vietnam a non-communist government dominated by Catholics led by Ngo Diem, Cardinal Spellman and such Catholics as Senators John F. Kennedy and Mike Mansfield of Montana supported the pro-Diem lobby in Congress. The medical missionary Tom Dooley reinforced this anti-communist position by popularizing a view of Indochina as a battleground between communism and democracy. Thus, the Catholic hierarchy as well as its members along with other Americans were initially sympathetic with American efforts to counter communism in South Vietnam.[13]

The election of the first Catholic president, John F. Kennedy, assured a continuation of these American efforts in South Vietnam. Kennedy's administration established for Vietnam "a political guideline that would be respected by decision-makers for the next thirteen years: in its effort to ensure an anticommunist regime in Saigon."[14] Presidential policymakers disagreed with those on the Right who wanted to use nearly any means in order to maintain an anti-communist regime in Saigon and they also disagreed with the Left who argued that U.S. objectives for Vietnam were unattainable and immoral. Kennedy's choice of a middle course of action gained the support of the majority of Americans who considered themselves neither hawks nor doves, but in the political center.

During Kennedy's administration the American peace movement had been reconstituted on the issue of atmospheric testing. There were basically two wings in the movement. The first was the liberal wing, which used the politics of persuasion and advocacy but experienced frustration in not being able to popularize an agenda of disarmament and a negotiated end to the Cold War. On the other hand, the radical wing emphasized individual acts of moral protest. The only Catholic group identified with the American peace movement was the Catholic Worker, which often joined the radical wing in moral actions of protest against nuclear testing.[15]

The successful passage of the test-ban treaty of 1963 cut through the newly constituted peace movement like a two-edged sword. Since the peace movement proposed a comprehensive test-ban treaty, disarmament and disengagement from the Cold War, the liberal wing was left without its primary issue of atmospheric testing, and liberal groups, like SANE, rapidly declined in membership. The radical wing of the peace movement, however, began to align itself with the student New Left that was emerging out of the civil rights movement and focused on the Indochina policy. Members of the radical wing and the student New Left were often joined by activists in the social and cultural movements. Historians Charles DeBenedetti and Charles Chatfield contend that this realignment signaled the transition from peace advocacy to war opposition in the American peace movement.[16]

The shift of the American peace movement from nuclear issues to opposition to the Indochina policy was also reflected among Catholics involved in the peace movement. The writings of Thomas Merton clearly reflected this change. The year 1963 marked a transition in his writing from a focus on nuclear pacifism to nonviolence as the basis for developing a new ethic for peace as he called for an end to the Vietnam War. This shift within the peace movement became complete after the election of 1964 when President Johnson defined the Vietnam War as "limited" and stated that its escalation excluded the use of nuclear weapons in favor of an air war of obliteration bombing conducted with new electronic and bio-chemical methods.[17] Merton's comment on Johnson's position at the time revealed the hold that the just war doctrine had on him.

> Still Johnson is as much a fire breather as there is when it comes to Vietnam, and that is what is most tragic. There is not a shred of justification for war there. It is a pure power policy, without necessity, a brute piece of stupidity and frustration on the part of people who have no imagination or insight and no moral sense. Because a few people in America want power and wealth, a lot of Vietnamese, Chinese, and Americans have been and will be sacrificed. It is a complete travesty of justice and right and liberty. I do not think it can meet any of the requirements of the traditional "just war."[18]

Official leadership among American Catholics, on the other hand, characteristically continued to support the war for the next five years.

The issue of the draft, however, provided Catholics with a means to address not only the public policy of their government in Vietnam, but also the official stance of the church on conscientious objection and the morality of the war. Some Catholics would protest the Vietnamese policy of the United States by resistance to the draft. Others who were not willing to challenge the war itself, still used the issue of the draft as the focal point for creating change in the teaching of the church in America.

The right of an individual Catholic to become a conscientious objector (CO) had been proclaimed at the Second Vatican Council.

Conscientious objection did not necessitate a judgment against the public policy of government on the part of the individual, it merely required that the individual be opposed to all war. In the case of a selective conscientious objector (SCO) the individual judges the government to be involved in an unjust war and thereby refuses to fight in that particular war. Thus, the same individual could not be both a CO and a SCO. The American Catholic hierarchy would not endorse the right of a Catholic to become a conscientious objector until after the Second Vatican Council. But when it did, the American Catholic hierarchy also recognized selective conscientious objection.

Prior to Vatican II the statements of the Roman Catholic church had been ambiguous on this issue. This ambiguity was reflected as recently as 1954 when Pope Pius XII in his Christmas message had said that "a Catholic citizen cannot invoke his own conscience in order to refuse to serve and fulfill those duties [of combat that] the law imposes." Yet, later in the same address he conceded that, "there are times in which only recourse to higher pinciples can bring peace to consciences. It is therefore consoling," the pope concluded, "that in some countries, amid today's debates, men are talking about conscience and its demands."[19]

The right of a Catholic to be a conscientious objector was invoked by individual Catholics in the United States even before the Second Vatican Council had ended. A few years after Vatican II, the Catholic church came into conflict with the U.S. policy of conscription by supporting the right of an individual Catholic to be a selective conscientious objector, a status that was not recognized by U.S. law. By supporting the right of a Catholic to be a CO or a SCO, church leadership was able to respond in a pastoral manner and on an individual level to its membership in parishes and on college campuses. In this support, church leadership did not have to declare the immorality of the government's policy in Vietnam but it did enable the church to support its members who in conscience had reached such a position. The church hierarchy never advocated or supported noncooperation or resistance to the draft for those acts directly protested the legitimacy of the government's actions by denying its right to draft an individual. The majority of Catholic individuals who refused to be drafted chose to be COs and register their dissent within the law.

Although there are no accurate counts of the number of Catholics who resisted the draft or applied for SCO, records do exist for those who received CO classification: From September 1967 to November 1968, 2.8 percent of men classified for alternative service as COs were Catholic; between November 1968 and September 1969 the percentage of Catholic COs rose to 7.8 percent.[20] This was a larger percentage than of any other single denomination. In addition many others were denied recognition of their SCO position, and some left the country or went to prison for refusing to register for the draft or for burning their draft cards.

Since individuals were powerless to alter directly the means of warfare employed by the U.S. military in Vietnam, the focus for organizing protest against the war became the draft. This opposition enabled individuals to assume personal responsibility and visibly take a stand to reflect their moral commitment. In turn, pressure was applied on the hierarchy as individuals turned to the church for support of their position. Thus, for Catholics the draft became the main organizing tool for peace activists and this constituted their main contribution to the entire antiwar movement during the Vietnam era.

Since for more than thirty years, the Catholic Worker was the only Catholic organization that had provided support to conscientious objectors and advocated noncooperation, it was natural for it to be in the forefront on the draft issue. By the early 1960s, the Catholic Worker in cooperation with other pacifist peace groups had advanced the support of nonviolent resistance with an emphasis on the activist imperative. Symbolic acts of nonviolent resistance against the draft in the 1960s enabled the intense personalism and moral commitment of Catholic Workers to witness against the war in Vietnam. This emphasis on peace pervaded the energies of the Catholic Worker movement after 1964 while other issues such as poverty, labor, and civil rights receded into the background. Houses of hospitality, farming communes, and the paper still continued to flourish. Despite the emphasis on peace in the movement and the formation in 1962 of PAX, a group solely dedicated to bringing a new vision of peace to the institutional church, a significant new Catholic pacifist group directly linked to the broader antiwar movement was formed: the Catholic Peace Fellowship (CPF).

One reason for the formation of the new group was that though it was a pacifist group like the Catholic Worker, its sole focus would be peace and an effort to effect change in the government's public policy in Indochina. CPF would advocate nonviolent direct action and resistance, making it very different from PAX, which continued to focus on institutional changes for peace within the church and basically rejected nonviolent resistance tactics. To reach the hierarchy, PAX embraced not only pacifists but also adherents of the just war theory into its membership. Eileen Egan, friend and traveling companion of Dorothy Day, was mainly responsible for the organization. She directed the energies of the small group increasingly toward achieving institutional changes in the Roman Catholic Church in America on the issue of conscientious objection.

The formation of CPF was the result of the efforts of John Heidbrink, a Presbyterian minister and interfaith director of the Fellowship of Reconciliation (FOR), which had been established in England just after the outbreak of World War I by Henry T. Hodgkin, an Anglican priest. In 1915, he traveled to the United States and established the American FOR. It was a membership organization and individuals could apply for admission on the basis of their agreement with a statement of principles that included the refusal of personal participation in any war. In 1960, Alfred Hassler became the executive secretary of FOR in America and assigned John Heidbrink the task of finding a way to organize the Catholics into a FOR affiliate. Heidbrink went to the Catholic Worker to recruit. There he found James H. (Jim) Forest, "a high school dropout who sought refuge in the Navy, but found the Church and pacifism instead. He was released from the Navy as a conscientious objector and high tailed it to the Catholic Worker. Jim was then nineteen years old and helped in every aspect of the house work and the paper in 1960–1961."[21] Heidbrink persuaded Forest to call together a few people to lay the groundwork for a Catholic Peace Fellowship; but the end result was the formation of PAX. Heidbrink tried again, "incessantly" as Forest says, from 1962 to 1964, when the Christian Peace Conference in Prague provided the occasion for accomplishing his hope. Heidbrink secured a gift from an anonymous donor and organized an American group to participate in the conference. They included Jim Forest, Daniel Berrigan, Hermene Evans, and James Douglass, together with Heidbrink. This group determined to form a CPF within FOR upon their return from Europe.[22]

In 1964, Daniel and Philip Berrigan asked three Catholic Workers, Jim Forest, Thomas (Tom) Cornell, and Martin Corbin to work with them in forming a new peace group.[23] A letterhead listing sponsors was put together, a mailing list compiled from personal Christmas card lists of the organizers and two hundred names from FOR were collated, and an invitational mailing enlisting membership and support for a Catholic Peace Fellowship was sent in August 1964. The organizational membership of CPF was similar to FOR but its daily operation to the Catholic Worker. Those who came to help at the CPF did so on a volunteer basis and directors received only a nominal salary.

The successful formation of CPF under the auspices of FOR was due to the increased cooperation between Catholics and other peace groups in America by the 1960s. Catholic suspicion and distrust of other religions had greatly dissipated since the birth of the ecumenical movement that produced in 1948 the World Council of Churches and later the National Council of Churches in the United States. The Second Vatican Council had also encouraged ecumenism and had devoted one of its sixteen major documents to supporting union rather than separation. The ecumenical spirit affected the American peace movement and CPF became the first Catholic peace group to exist under the auspices of an interdenominational organization—FOR provided financial and organizational support.[24]

The stated purpose of CPF was to affirm life and denounce war: "War has been the way of life of the majority of mankind throughout history, and we only deceive ourselves if we think it is not just as much the life of our times, the impulse of much of our economy, and the preoccupation of our politics. But war is not life, nor even a necessary part of life."[25] The founders viewed their job as that of educating Catholics and others on the issue of peace.

As an educational agency, CPF hoped to address itself to many areas of concern, including building interest in and opposition to the war in Vietnam, raising medical relief for victims on all sides, and providing draft information and counseling services.

Self-consciously Catholic, the founders of CPF also wanted to develop a "theology of peace" with an emphasis on the principles and techniques of nonviolent resistance, and in accordance with the Second Vatican Council, a "vision of a Church that is peacemaking to its very core." Forest was the catalyst, and engaged in lengthy correspondence with Thomas Merton and Daniel Berrigan. He kept in touch with various leaders in the antiwar movement. He wrote and talked and organized Catholics on a day-to-day basis using the talents of each for CPF and also using CPF to assist them in their labors for peace.

The most significant accomplishments during the initial period of CPF were the planting of articles in Catholic journals and the publishing of a booklet by Jim Forest, *Catholics and Conscientious Objection*, with Cardinal Spellman's imprimatur. Free ads offering a criticism of the Vietnam War and written primarily by Gordon Zahn and Jim Douglass were placed in several Catholic journals. Some modest educational activities were undertaken as well as a few demonstrations. Both Forest and Cornell helped to pull together the anti–Vietnam War coalition known as the Mobilization to End the War in Vietnam. But CPF's day-to-day work centered on counseling Catholic conscientious objectors. Implicit in their concern was the desire to build a future constituency for war resistance.

In the fall of 1966, Jim Forest decided to accept an offer to join the FOR staff at Nyack, as special projects coordinator, working two-thirds of the time for FOR and one-third for CPF. Cornell remained in the Manhattan office until 1969. Both operated CPF in the Catholic Worker tradition and utilized the organizational structure and contacts of the FOR for CPF's benefit. Cornell contends that the work of CPF "stimulated the debate on [the Vietnam War's] morality that culminated in the erosion of liberal Catholic support for the war and indeed, in its renunciation by the American Catholic Bishops in 1969."[26]

CPF faced many difficulties due to jail sentences, finances, and personal responsibilities of its leadership. When Tom Cornell was released from prison for burning his draft card in 1969, he decided to accept a paid position for FOR in Nyack, working as the representative at the United Nations on the Non-Governmental Organizations Disarmament Committee where he served on its executive committee. Jim Forest, realizing that he would soon be in jail for his involvement in the Milwaukee 14 destruction of draft files, expressed his concern to Cornell about what his move to Nyack would do to the CPF. Forest wrote to Cornell saying that "Yet, it would be a great blow to the New York scene not to have you here and in it, and to the New York CPF situation. It could conceivably have the effect of moving the CPF into its last days."[27] Cornell had no intention of abandoning the CPF, but as a married man with three children, a paid position offered a little security and the move assured a home in Newburgh for his family. When Cornell moved to FOR in Nyack, the CPF moved to 339 Lafayette Street in New York City. There the office would remain. Since the CPF office was staffed by volunteers its leadership often changed because of the constant turnover in volunteers in the New York City office. Tom Cornell and Jim Forest always maintained control of the organization.

Soon after CPF had been reorganized and Forest was in jail, Tom Cornell received a letter from Alfred Hassler, executive director of FOR, saying that the CPF had a $10,000 deficit with FOR in the last fifteen months.[28] Cornell immediately decided that the best course of action was a fund appeal letter to members of CPF. The financial crisis precipitated a five-page letter from Cornell to Forest after Forest suggested severing any institutional connection with FOR. Cornell's reply provides an assessment of CPF from one of its leaders in relation to FOR and its Catholic Worker tradition.

Cornell first replied to Forest's criticism of the FOR. "The FOR is not what it should be, that emphasis on publications, speaking and 'superficial' contact with individuals coordinated by a top heavy bureaucracy is not what we want. It's not what we have, either. The CPF is quite other as you know and in no way has it been hindered in being quite other by its integration into FOR." Cornell also admitted that he felt at times the religious component in Nyack "is superficial and even fake." Yet, he also admitted that the most positive feature of FOR was its ability to accomodate to different styles and to be a center of communication for the religious groups: Protestant, Catholic, and Jewish. He also believed that the FOR was attempting to meet the needs of the peace movement in general by releasing Ron Young to work on the New Mobilization. Cornell finally did not want to sever his and CPF's financial relationship with FOR. He explained his position to Forest in the following words. "Because I need the security of knowing that the check is coming. Because they do our mailings and take care of bookkeeping that I can not do and you are not here to do. Because it gives CPF more weight in the circles of the movement. Yes, it does. Because it keys us in to other people and is an example of ecumenism. . . . I find that the reason you give for dissolving the ties to FOR are ephemeral, lack substance, even meaning."[29]

Cornell then spent the next few pages attempting to clarify Forest's

144 ◆ Harder Than War

expectations of the CPF working within the Catholic Worker tradition.[30] He tried to distinguish between the myth and reality of the Catholic Worker. First, he dealt with "community" and stated, "We [CPF] have helped some people to be more aware of each other and more supportive to each other's common longings for some way to work for peace. But if you mean 'community' in the way that we are used to thinking of it, community is a living together, a sharing of resources. This we have not done." Second, he tried to come to grips with the term, "voluntary poverty." Cornell pointed out that after "five years of marriage and two children, now three children, my wife has at last a washing machine! . . . We live with precarity all the time. That is the essence of poverty. Simplicity is the rest. You do not know of another organization or group that works with such precarity or simplicity as the CPF." Third, Cornell dealt with the concept "works of mercy" and said that CPF takes care of that as individuals. And finally he wrote cryptically, "Decentralization. We've got it. Resistance. We started it."[31] In the end Cornell accused Forest of purism and stated that none of these values were antithetical to FOR's values. Unlike Forest and the Berrigans, Cornell was more deeply rooted in the Catholic Worker tradition. Personally, he never went beyond traditional nonviolence and like Dorothy Day, he would never directly confront the church. After Forest was released from prison in 1971, he too continued to work for CPF and assumed a paid position with FOR as editor of *Fellowship*.

CPF remained within the Catholic Worker tradition. The center for CPF remained in New York City, where with a staff of volunteers and a minimal allowance members operated a speakers' bureau, a tape and film library, a publication program, and a production of the bi-monthly *CPF Bulletin*.[32] CPF also collaborated with other peace groups for demonstrations, marches, beg-ins, prayer vigils, and fasting in New York City and in Washington, D.C. The main work of the group on a day-to-day basis was always the providing of free draft counseling for conscientious objectors, sometimes as many as fifty to one hundred a week.[33]

Other CPF groups were founded in major cities throughout the United States. Though each group was autonomous, it could draw on the resources of the New York group. Activities of each CPF group varied greatly and there was no serious attempt made to coordinate

these groups. Some groups devoted their energies solely to draft counseling, others to organizing demonstrations against either the government or the church. The Washington chapter made an effort to
influence the American bishops before their fall national conference
in 1966. The group received most attention when they placed an ad
in the recently founded, *National Catholic Reporter,* a newspaper
independently owned and operated by lay people that was seeking to
keep liberal-minded Catholics up to date on developments in the
church. The CPF ad read:

When is A
BISHOPS'
meeting a
HAPP
EN
ING?
maybe when
Pentecost first occurred
maybe when John
called a Council maybe when our Bishops
show they are bothered by the same things we are. The rightness of
continuing massive civilian casualties in north and south Vietnam—the
draft—conscientious objectors to unjust wars going to prison—plans for
universal training—laws against showing love of enemy. As Christians and
Americans these things bother us. We ask for some concern, some sharing of
our difficulties. In the problem of war, we ask that Bishops go as far as Paul
VI and call for an immediate end of the fighting "even at the expense of
some inconvenience or loss."[34]

Despite the efforts of CPF's public call for the bishops to condemn
the war in November 1966 the bishops issued their pastoral, *Peace and
Vietnam,* which stated, "In light of the facts as they are known to us, it
is reasonable to argue that our presence in Vietnam is justified."[35] In
1966, members of the Catholic hierarchy were recognized for speaking
out in support of the war rather than for speaking critically of it. Most
notable among the hierarchy were Cardinal Spellman and Archbishop
Robert E. Lucey, who as a young priest had worked zealously to build
the CAIP. The cardinal's position on the Vietnam War was no different
than his position on World War II. As the head of the U.S. Military
Vicariate, his annual Christmas messages to the American troops

received wide publicity[36] when he consciously discarded the normative just war tradition by proclaiming his support of "my country right or wrong."[37] In "Peace and Vietnam" the bishops made no mention of other war and peace issues such as conscientious objection, conscription, or efforts to provide medical relief to areas of the world labeled "enemy" by the government.

The New York City CPF issued a statement on the issue of medical aid in 1967 after the *National Catholic Reporter* and the *New York Times* revealed that the Catholic Relief Services provided material assistance to members of the South Vietnamese Popular Forces, yet refused assistance to war victims in North Vietnam.[38] The *National Catholic Reporter*, at a great financial investment it could ill afford, had sent Michael Novak as a correspondent to Vietnam for a few weeks in the summer of 1967, and while on assignment there Novak discovered the Catholic Relief Services' involvement. CPF asked Catholics in their statement to withhold contributions to Catholic Relief Services and to send their money to Caritas Internationalis, the Vatican's relief-coordinating body that provided material assistance to the North Vietnamese Red Cross as well as participating in relief efforts in the South. Since Eileen Egan of PAX worked for Catholic Relief Services, she resented the embarrassment caused by her Catholic pacifist friends in the CPF.[39] Tragically, Catholic Relief Services resolved the conflict by dropping all relief to Vietnam. These efforts gained publicity and gave visibility to those Catholics who opposed the war in Vietnam.

From Vatican II until the end of the war, the Catholic Worker, CPF, and PAX were united in their desires for peace and their opposition to the war. The majority of Catholics and the American hierarchy could not identify with them. Catholics viewed members of these groups as pacifists, radicals, and perfectionists. Most of the bishops dismissed them as a "fringe" group within Catholicism. But as more time passed their prophetic messages concerning the war were recognized as the major contributions of American Catholics to peace and the antiwar movement.

Catholic Worker action in support of traditional nonviolent resistance reached a high point ten days after Pope Paul VI had spoken at the United Nations. On 15 October 1965, a young Catholic Worker named David Miller stepped to the front of a platform and said, "I believe the napalming of villages is an immoral act. I hope this will be a significant political act, so here goes." And then he burned his draft card.[40]

Destroying draft cards was nothing new to the American peace movement, nor was it the first such act performed by a Catholic Worker. At a series of nationwide demonstrations on 2 February 1947, some four or five hundred Americans either publicly destroyed their draft cards or mailed them to President Truman.[41] At a rally in Washington Square at the end of the second worldwide General Strike for Peace in November 1963, Tom Cornell, who was then an associate editor of the *Catholic Worker*, destroyed his draft card along with twenty-five others. He and Chris Kearns, also a Catholic Worker, led a draft card burning at an anticonscription rally in Union Square on Armed Forces Day, 16 May 1964. This rally was sponsored by the War Resisters League, the Student Peace Union, the Committee for Non-Violent Action, and the Catholic Worker.[42]

Also in 1965, a nationwide coordinated National Assembly of Unrepresented Peoples was held in August. *Life* magazine ran a long article on the demonstrations; it contained a picture of Chris Kearns dropping his draft card into a flaming cooking pot. In direct reaction to the picture, Representative Mendel Rivers of the House Armed Services Subcommittee rammed a bill through Congress that made draft card burning a crime punishable by $10,000 fine and/or five years imprisonment. President Johnson signed the bill into law on August 31.[43] Thus, David Miller's action on October 15 became a test case for the act.

Miller had joined the Catholic Worker the previous June following his graduation with a degree in sociology from LeMoyne College. Miller's action acquired unusual visibility since it took place at the largest nationwide antiwar rally to date in New York City. He appeared on the program not as a representative of the Catholic Worker but of draft noncooperators, later to become known as draft resisters. James Peck of the War Resisters League introduced him. Three days later Miller was arrested.

At a rally on 6 November 1965, in front of the Federal Court House in New York City where 150,000 people had gathered to protest the Vietnam War, five more men burned their draft cards. Dorothy Day and A. J. Muste introduced the men. Three of the five were members of the Catholic Worker movement, James Wilson, Roy Fisher, and Tom Cornell.

Cornell, the spokesperson for the group, prefaced his statement by citing the futility of previous protests and the continuing escalation of the war. He claimed that the Rivers Bill outlawing the burning of draft cards was merely an attempt to stifle protest. He summed up the reason for his course of action by quoting a letter from Karl Meyer of the Chicago Catholic Worker to his draft board; it was printed in the October 1965 issue of *Catholic Worker*. Meyer, who was known for his witness of draft and tax resistance, had written: "I am sending to you with this letter, pieces of a Selective Service Registration Certificate and Notice of Classification which I have destroyed by tearing them in half, to signify my resistance to the new law. . . . The mutilation of human beings in Vietnam has become a civic virtue; now, the mutilation of a scrap of paper becomes a grave crime against the state." Cornell added to Meyer's words: "The grave crime, we are told, is not the destruction of life but the destruction of a piece of paper."[44] The five protesters were arrested.

David Miller went to trial on 9 February 1966, claiming that the act of burning a draft card was "symbolic speech" and thus guaranteed by the First Amendment. He was found guilty and a unanimous Court of Appeals later upheld the conviction.[45] Of the five draft card burners who participated in the November 6 rally, one, Jim Peck pleaded guilty and received a two year sentence.[46] The other four pleaded not guilty and based their case on freedom of speech as had Miller. They too were found guilty and were each sentenced to six months in prison.[47]

After these acts of civil disobedience and nonviolent resistance in October and November 1965, many others followed the path of the Catholic Workers. Thus, the draft-resistance movement, later known as "The Resistance" was born. Since over 3,500 draft cards had been publicly destroyed in various ways, the Rivers law was unenforceable and the movement proved to be a success. CPF as well as the Catholic Worker worked closely with the Resistance.

Even more remarkable was the extent to which Catholics who, for reason of sex or age, were not subject to the draft, nevertheless were willing to take risks and make sacrifices in their attempt to stand in solidarity with the young men facing the draft. The most dramatic example of this took place on 17 May 1968, when Daniel and Philip Berrigan together with seven other Catholics removed four hundred draft files from the Catonsville, Maryland, Draft Board office to a nearby parking lot, and burned them with homemade napalm. In a statement released after their arrest, this group called themselves the Catonsville Nine and justified their action on the grounds that "some property has no right to exist." This action began what was to become known as "The Ultra-Resistance."

The Catonsville Nine action began a series of draft board raids from the Milwaukee Fourteen to the Beaver Fifty-five to the East Coast Conspiracy to Save Lives to the Camden Twenty-eight. The exact number of draft board raids is unknown and estimates of their number range from 53 to 250 from the years 1967 to 1971.[48] Often arrests and trials followed. Support groups sprang up around the country. The movement ended when Attorney General John Mitchell announced that a federal grand jury had indicted Philip Berrigan and five others on charges of conspiring both to blow up the heating system of federal buildings in Washington and to kidnap Henry Kissinger. The Harrisburg trial followed.

Rosemary Reuther, a well-known Catholic theologian, and the priest-sociologist Andrew Greeley criticized the Berrigans for their political perfectionism and extremism because it alienated more people than it attracted. The old pacifist groups in the antiwar movement such as the Catholic Worker, the War Resisters League, the Fellowship of Reconciliation, and various Quaker groups, though supportive and sympathetic of the motives of the Catonsville Nine, could not support the destruction of property as a valid nonviolent tactic even in the symbolic violence of draft file destruction.[49] Despite the controversy among Catholics and others involved in the Catholic resistance that resulted, the Berrigan brothers were still acclaimed for their willingness to "pay the price" to stop the war in Vietnam and recognized as the leaders of the American Catholic peace movement.

The issue of the draft was also the catalyst on Catholic college campuses in building support for the antiwar movement. Draft-counseling services were provided as an initial response since there were always a few Catholic priests or lay faculty who believed it was part of their pastoral duty to aid young men facing the draft. As the war escalated, however, a diversity of responses appeared on the college campuses. What happened at the University of Notre Dame provides a good example of how Catholic college students responded to the war in Vietnam.

All college campuses were affected by the free speech movement and the founding of the Students for a Democratic Society (SDS). The most significant events on Catholic college campuses, however, were the 1965 "teach-ins," which were organized by University of Michigan faculty members and spread to the country's leading campuses. These teach-ins legitimized dissent at the outset of the war and their effect was eventually felt on all Catholic campuses.[50] The University of Notre Dame's day-long teach-in took place on 16 October 1965. Faculty, students, and two non-University speakers debated American involvement in Southeast Asia for over twelve hours. The political spectrum of the students represented the nation in microcosm: SDS, Young Americans for Freedom, political realists, conservatives, cold-war liberals, pacifists, and radicals. Two students, Joel R. Connelly and Howard J. Dooley, who wrote about their undergraduate years at Notre Dame in the 1960s, contended that the 1965 Vietnam symposium set the temper of the Notre Dame student protest movement for a decade. They wrote that a pattern emerged on that day which signaled the tone for protest on the campus for the remainder of the antiwar period. "Notre Dame students remained by and large non-ideological in their anti-Vietnam stance, thus avoiding much of the factionalism and irrational one-upmanship which made a shambles of the ideologically committed New Left. Notre Dame students also, for the most part, remained tactical moderates, preferring peaceful demonstrations to bear witness to their concern rather than violent activism."[51] The fact that during the day of the teach-in a Mass for Peace was celebrated on the campus may have been the greatest factor explaining why students preferred peaceful demonstrations, though the student observers made no mention of it. The tradition of celebrating a Mass for Peace also provided a religious dimension to the days of protest on campus and this practice continued during the entire period of campus unrest at Notre Dame. During the homily of every Mass for Peace the ethical and moral issues rather than the political issues concerning the war were constantly being raised. This focused the terms of intellectual debates on moral issues and may account for the absence of political ideology on campus.

After the teach-in, student unrest manifested itself sporadically. In 1967, two hundred students, faculty, and religious demonstrated against the job interviewing that was being conducted at the University

Placement Bureau by Dow Chemical Company, because Dow was producing the napalm used by the U.S. military in the Vietnam War. Then in 1968 the student unrest escalated, but it took various directions. Several different student newspapers appeared on campus protesting the university's administrative policies concerning the lack of a totally open speakers policy, disciplinary regulations and parietal restrictions, the ROTC (Notre Dame had the largest program of any Catholic university), the small number of minorities at the school, campus job interviewing by the Central Intelligence Agency, and the escalation of the Vietnam War. As each issue came to the fore, demonstrations and counterdemonstrations were held. Thoughout 1968 student unrest was creating havoc and when the students returned to campus in 1969 after Christmas break their enthusiasm for such activities persisted.

To avoid future embarrasment and disruption of the university's normal activities, its president, Theodore Hesburgh issued an eight-page letter to the university comunity. This letter set forth what became known in the national media as Notre Dame's "Tough Fifteen Minute Rule." The letter permitted dissent but would not permit disruption of the Notre Dame academic community. Students, faculty, or staff who violated this principle would be given fifteen minutes to reflect on their actions; if they continued their disruption, their identity cards would be seized. In his autobiography, Hesburgh states that "after the letter was distributed, the crisis on campus quieted down, at least temporarily. Resistance to violence, incivility, and boorishness began to stiffen. The letter was at least partially responsible for that. But it had another effect that I never anticipated. It made me a kind of folk hero among the hawks, who saw the solution to the student revolution in terms of truncheons and police action. Maybe that explains why I spent so much time after 1969 trying to get people to understand why the students were legitimately upset and what was good about their concerns. A hawk I was not."[52] Debates on the legal and moral limits of the right to dissent persisted at faculty councils and among the student press. Confrontations also continued to occur. At a national conference on institutional racism sponsored by the National Student Association at Notre Dame, Hesburgh was heckled by students who demanded greater minority enrollment while others called for the withdrawal of academic credit from ROTC programs and an end to the U.S. military involvement in the Vietnam War.[53]

In October 1969, Hesburgh and other U.S. college and university presidents signed an open letter calling on the government to accelerate its withdrawal of military forces from Vietnam, and Hesburgh joined with the students in observing the Vietnam Moratorium Day, which had been announced by the New Mobilization Committee. A peace rally took place on campus and it included a Mass for Peace attended by over 2,500 students, faculty, and staff. Archbishop Thomas Roberts of England spoke of the Christian's obligation to resist immoral behavior by the state and affirmed the action of four students and two assistant professors who destroyed their draft cards during the Offertory of the Eucharistic service when he said, "You may be the only university in the world where the Mass has been connected with the offering of draft cards but when you and I go to daily Mass, more often than not we celebrate the feast of a martyr who was put to death for some form of civil disobedience. We have learned from [the martyrs] that we ought to obey God, not man."[54]

Student protests against the Vietnam War continued when Dow Chemical Company and the CIA tried to recruit on campus again in 1969. Students attempted to take over the administration building and Hesburgh invoked the Fifteen Minute Rule. Five students were expelled and five students were suspended. With the invasion of Cambodia and the killing of students at Kent State University and Jackson State University in the spring of 1970, outrage swept the campus. Mass meetings, memorial liturgies, protest rallies, and Masses for Peace were held. A student strike was also proclaimed. Around-the-clock discussions were held about the university community's proper response to the events. President Hesburgh made provisions for students who felt in conscience that they needed to strike, but he kept the university open for those who did not want to strike. Hesburgh also issued an unequivocal public statement declaring his personal opposition to the war and decrying the paucity of moral leadership in America. Students collected over 23,000 signatures from South Bend residents who agreed with Hesburgh's opposition to the Vietnam War and sent it to Congress.[55] The excellent leadership of Hesburgh during these years of student unrest and the constant incorporation of religion and the message of peace no doubt reduced the level of violence and disruption at the academic institution. In one sense the Catholic college campus looked very much like other college campuses in America during the student unrest period of the 1960s. On the other hand the added religious dimension provided by Masses for Peace that were an integral part of protest demonstrations and the constant structuring of the terms of debate and discussion in moral and ethical language distinguished the Catholic campus from its secular counterparts. The Catholic college campus seemed to be the one institution in American Catholicism that enabled all Catholics, regardless of their beliefs on the Vietnam War, to find a place where they could witness to their convictions.

The college campus was also the place where many young men confronted the issue of the draft. And the proper response to the draft was often a topic of debate. Some students accepted the draft when their number was selected or they were part of the ROTC program on campus. Others received deferments or exemptions from the draft, or left their country for Canada or Sweden to escape the draft, and still others chose the path of resistance. Most students who opposed the war, however, preferred to register their dissent within the laws of American society by applying for CO status. In order for a young man to qualify for CO status a knowledge of the law together with an ability to express beliefs and convictions in a written statement and verbally before a draft board required a certain level of education as well as some counseling. A college student definitely held the advantage in such cases over a high school graduate who went directly into the work force. The position of some of these Catholic men was further complicated by the lack of a legal provision for a selective CO status. Three Catholic groups, CPF, PAX, and CAIP, tried to help the young Catholic men seeking CO status. PAX and CAIP attempted to help them, not directly as CPF did by draft counseling, but by lobbying the church and the government.

The PAX group of the Vietnam era was very different from the first PAX group of the World War II era. The earlier group attempted to offer support to Catholic conscientious objectors. The aim of the new PAX group was to change the positions of both the Roman Catholic church and Congress on conscientious objection.

In *U.S. v. Seeger* in 1965 the Supreme Court extended the privilege of CO status to include as "religious" certain beliefs not identified with conventional religions and thus identified conscientious beliefs with religion. [56] Congress's response was to omit the Supreme Being clause from the 1967 Draft Act. The Seeger decision aided many young men who were not identified with an official church in applying for CO status. It also aroused hopes that the courts or Congress would extend the privilege of COs to selective conscientious objectors. The rationale for SCO was advanced by three theologians who were noted for their work on the just war theory: John Courtney Murray, a Catholic theologian at Woodstock; Ralph Potter, a Protestant theologian at Harvard; and Paul Ramsey, a Protestant theologian at Yale.

Murray developed the Catholic case for SCO. In the mid-1960s, President Johnson had appointed a commission, chaired by Assistant Attorney General Burke Marshall, to consider the question of selective conscientious objection.[57] While serving on the commission, Murray advocated that "the revised [selective service] statute should extend the provisions of the present statute to include not only the absolute pacifist but also the relative pacifist; that the grounds for the status of conscientious objector should be not only religious or non-religiously motivated opposition (Seeger decision) to participation in war in all forms, but also similarly motivated opposition to participation in particular wars."[58] After considerable debate, Murray's position was rejected by the majority of the commission, which was unwilling to extend the right of conscientious objection to include those who dissent selectively. In effect, the commission disavowed the relevancy of the just war tradition for conscientious citizens engaged in public discourse about war. No presidential recommendation was made to Congress on the issue. There was no indication on the part of Congress or the courts that either would extend CO to SCO.[59]

At the time of his death, Murray believed that the issue was not satisfactorily settled and that it should be kept before the country. One of his last acts was to lend his support to the "official" Catholic peace group, CAIP, in planning their 1967 conference on the topic of "Selective Conscientious Objection." The prestige of Murray as a theologian and the fact that he believed the Vietnam War to be justifiable meant that his position on SCO would carry great influence among the just war believers in the Catholic community. This was especially true among the hierarchy.[60] Since Murray used the just war doctrine to develop his position of SCO, for the first time in the twentieth century the just war doctrine was being used not only to measure the actions of the state but also was found to be applicable to the individual. The individual was now being called upon to apply the criteria of the just war theory to an existing war and in conscience make a decision about the morality of that war. Thus, on moral grounds, an individual who had supported World War II could oppose the Vietnam War. Selective conscientious objection has yet to be legally recognized in the United States.

After the Second Vatican Council, PAX's desire to effect change in church and state institutions on the draft resulted in the development of a strategy that would include both pacifists and just war traditionalists. The tactic was the pioneering of a Rights of Conscience Campaign. The campaign had a twofold purpose: "1) to have the Bishops of the United States issue a clarifying statement that a Catholic had the right to be a conscientious objector and further to be one on the grounds of the traditional Catholic teaching of the just war which makes 'selective conscientious objection' a valid Catholic position and 2) to change the draft law so that those who follow the just war tradition should not be discriminated against when they claim the right of conscientious objection."[61]

To help achieve these goals, PAX published *The War That Is Forbidden: Peace Beyond Vatican II*, which was sent free to every bishop in the United States. The organization also sent two memoranda to the bishops before the Selective Service law was extended in 1967. PAX even inserted in *Commonweal* magazine a paid announcement on the rights of conscience campaign and gathered signatures from a wide range of supporters, including theologians, educators, writers, and seven Catholic bishops. The book, the memorandum, and the *Commonweal* statement were also sent to every member of Congress, and Representative Donald Edwards of California read the PAX statement into the *Congressional Record* and urged that Congress take into account the validity of its arguments.[62] Despite the efforts of PAX, Congress remained unfavorable to SCO.

Though the CAIP supported the war in Vietnam and would not work directly with the "too pacifist" PAX, it did work to bring about the same desired change on the issue of conscientious objection in the institutional church. PAX realized this would happen and knew that CAIP was a dying organization after the Second Vatican Council and that as it had not expanded its membership since World War II, it had even fewer resources. Since CAIP was the only "official" peace organization in the church, PAX rightly assessed the need for its support to effect any change in the institutional church.

By the 1960s, CAIP had been totally absorbed into NCWC. Monsignor George Higgins, executive secretary of the CAIP by virtue of his position as director of the Social Action Department, managed to keep CAIP alive by issuing a monthly newsletter, *CAIP News*, and maintaining its annual conferences. Nevertheless, NCWC had refused to allot sufficient funds for a full-time CAIP staff.[63] In 1967, the reorganization of the NCWC into the United States Catholic Conference (USCC) brought along with its new name a new Commission for World Justice and Peace. USCC announced that the duties of the new commission duplicated the work of CAIP. Because of CAIP's total dependence on NCWC and the fact that it had become a very small and inbred group which was out of step with the times, it had no choice but to go out of existence. CAIP's leader and dominant spokesperson, William V. O'Brien of Georgetown University, was the only one capable of keeping it alive, but he did not have the required time, energy, or resources.

The other reason for CAIP's demise was its inability to depart from its conservative political position (what its members called political realism: "more realistic 'power political' approaches to war which emphasized the political and moral responsibilities of the decision maker to use power, but with due appreciation of normative restraints"[64]). CAIP's advocacy of the natural law and the just war doctrine could have attracted the general Catholic population who were looking for a Catholic peace group that would speak to them in those terms as they moved in opposition to the war during the 1960s, but CAIP's inability to depart from political realism precluded that possibility. Thus, CAIP, the first American Catholic peace organization, ceased to exist in 1968.[65] George Higgins stated that his main regret was that it was a lay organization and it died just when lay leadership was being encouraged by the church. Meanwhile, the vision of the new USCC's Commission on Justice and Peace was headed in the opposite direction. It wanted to establish a branch of the commission under clerical leadership in every diocesan office in America.[66] By 1970, these offices began to appear.

Following the Second Vatican Council, the American bishops voted to reorganize themselves and establish the National Conference of

The Catholic Peace Movement and Vietnam ◆ 157

Catholic Bishops (NCCB) as well as the USCC. The NCCB and USCC are separate organizations with the latter serving as the secretariate of NCCB. Generally speaking, the USCC develops policy and programs for approval by the administrative board and the body of bishops. Within the USCC is the Office of International Justice and Peace, which deals with military and political issues affecting other nations, human rights, the arms race, and global economy. It was this office that was responsible for addressing the issues related to the war in Vietnam. Monsignor Marvin Bordelon was appointed the director of the Office of International Justice and Peace at the USCC. The commission itself consisted of Patrick McDermott, S.J., Patricia Ringel, and James R. Jennings.

In the April 1967 bishops' meeting, there was no mention of the Vietnam War. In the November meeting, however, the national conference praised the Johnson administration for "repeated efforts to negotiate peace" and refused to repeat their 1966 endorsement of the war as just. The bishops' next pastoral, the *Resolution of Peace*, criticized the extremism of both left and right but acknowledged that the antiwar protestors represented "responsible segments of our society." Finally, in November 1968 the National Conference issued the important pastoral letter, *Human Life in Our Day*, the American reply to Paul VI's *Humanae Vitae*. The letter tackled two divisive issues in American Catholicism in 1968, the church's position on birth control and Vietnam.[67]

In *Human Life in Our Day*, the bishops recalled Vatican II and explicitly condemned aggressive wars and total war.[68] In relation to America's nuclear capability, the bishops again repeated the message of Vatican II condemning the "indiscriminate destruction of whole cities or vast areas with their inhabitants [as] a crime against God and man."[69] They endorsed the partial test-ban treaty and the nonproliferation treaty, condemned the antiballistic missile (ABM), and the doctrine of nuclear superiority, and escalation of the arms race.[70] This section on nuclear war in the document had not received very thorough discussion because of the attention focused on the first part of the document which dealt primarily with sexual ethics.[71] Turning to Vietnam, the bishops declared their opposition to the peacetime draft and posed several questions about the war in Vietnam. They did not proclaim the Vietnam War to be an unjust war, but stated that valid moral questions could be raised concerning the war effort.[72] The most significant part of the pastoral, however, was its proclamation of the right of a Catholic to be a conscientious objector or a selective conscientious objector to war. In Chapter 2, "The Family of Nations," the bishops not only endorsed the principle of conscientious objection but further recommended that the conscription law be changed to admit selective conscientious objection. [73]

> We recommend a modification of the Selective Service Act, making it possible . . . for so-called selective conscientious objectors to refuse— without fear of imprisonment or loss of citizenship—to serve in wars which they consider unjust.
>
> Whether or not such modifications in our laws are in fact made, we continue to hope that, in the all-important issue of war and peace, all men will follow their consciences. [74]

It is significant that this statement was only a small section in the larger pastoral that engaged Rome's encyclical reaffirming its teaching on birth control. What the American bishops were doing was attempting to place the issue of birth control within a broader context in which they could affirm the right of conscience in decision making and, by affirming the right of conscience in the broader context rather than in the context of the birth control issue, deflect their criticism of Rome's statement on birth control. [75] This was also the beginning of the bishops linking of abortion and war within a broader context of pro-life issues. Basically, it was all too subtle for anyone (Roman or American) to grasp. Regardless, through the labor of one person, Patrick McDermott, the bishops recognized the right of a Catholic to become a CO or an SCO.

Patrick McDermott had worked diligently to secure a statement from the American bishops on conscientious objection. After attending a retreat under the direction of Daniel Berrigan, McDermott decided to work at the Office of International Justice and Peace. [76] He was a friend of both pacifists and just war theorists and wrote the drafts for and did the organizing among the American hierarchy on the issue of conscientious objection.

McDermott continued his work on CO and SCO and wrote a pamphlet entitled, *Statement on the Catholic Conscientious Objector*, 15

October 1969, which was issued by USCC a year after the endorsement of the positions in *Human Life in Our Day*. The concluding
paragraph in the pamphlet states:

> We should look upon conscientious objection not as a scandal, but
> rather as a healthy sign. War will still not be replaced by more humane
> institutions for regulating conflict until citizens insist on principles of
> non-violence. John F. Kennedy once said, "War will exist until the
> distant day when the conscientious objector enjoys the same reputa-
> tion and prestige as the warrior does today."

In 1969, Richard Fernandez, the director of Clergy and Laity Concerned About Vietnam, after experiencing frustration at trying to rally
support for war resisters, "voiced his displeasure that a number of
religious bodies, including the National Conference of Catholic Bishops, the Lutheran Church in America, and the Union of American
Hebrew Congregations, had endorsed the concept of selective conscientious objection, but had failed to follow through with supporting actions."[77] In October 1971 the USCC issued a *Declaration on Conscientious Objection and Selective Conscientious Objection* that called on
Catholic organizations to show their support for both COs and SCOs
by hiring them.

> It is clear that a Catholic can be a conscientious objector to war in
> general or to a particular war "because of religious training and be-
> lief." . . . Catholic organizations which could qualify as alternative
> service agencies should be encouraged to support and provide meaning-
> ful employment for conscientious objectors.[78]

This endorsement of support for COs and SCOs from the Catholic
hierarchy during the Vietnam War was radically different from World
War II when, as Dorothy Day said, "I didn't particularly want to help run
a CO camp, but the Quakers, the Mennonites and the Brethren, they
nobly offered the government to go the second mile. . . . The Quakers,
the Mennonites and the Brethren would send the bills [for providing for
Catholic COs] to the Catholic Bishops, none of whom paid. Can you
imagine this? Well, fortunately, some of the Catholic institutions got in

on the deal at the hospital in Chicago and they offered their COs not only to take them in and help with the work but to give them training as male nurses, anesthetists, and laboratory technicans."[79]

James Jennings, reflecting on the USCC Division of World Justice and Peace's work for CO and SCO, believed the greatest influence on them at the time was not the Catholic peace groups but the tremendous amount of mail inquiries and telephone calls from the grassroots: young men, parents, pastors, and draft boards wanting to know what the position of the church was on conscientious objection.[80] It is very doubtful, however, that these individuals would have approached the USCC with such questions if they had not seen or heard the priests, nuns, and laity whose acts of resistance were frequently reported by the press. It is difficult to ascertain how many nuns, priests, brothers, and lay people were involved in the Catholic peace movement. Michael True in *Justice Seekers Peace Makers*, provides portraits of John Leary, a young Harvard graduate, and Kathy Knight, a wife and mother, who were at the center of Catholic peacemaking in Boston.[81] They are representative of Catholics throughout the United States involved in peacemaking.

Whatever the ultimate reason for the American Catholic hierarchy's support of CO and SCO, it reflected PAX's effective strategy of combining the pacifist CO position with the just war SCO position. PAX's choice of the human rights campaign pinpointed the possibilities and limits of the institutional church on the issue of the draft. It failed, however, to change the position of the government on SCO. In 1971, the U.S. Supreme Court announced that it could find in the Constitution no right to exemption from military service for one who claimed to be an SCO.

The general Catholic population, however, which was moving in opposition to the war seemingly in proportion to the war's escalation under the Johnson administration, had no Catholic peace group with which to identify. CPF was a pacifist group whose members were performing nonviolent resistance that seemed very foreign to the teachings of the just war tradition and traditional patriotism. PAX was not so much speaking to the laity but to the hierarchy trying to effect change in the church's teaching on CO and SCO. These Catholics were sought after by the peace movement when the ecumenical thrust among Catholic, Protestant, and Jewish clergymen formed an organization called Clergy (later Clergy and Laity) Concerned About Vietnam (CALCAV). Its initial leadership, Richard Neuhaus, Abraham Heschel, and Daniel Berrigan, held a news conference in the United Nations Church Center on 25 October 1965 to announce the formation of the group. This group wanted to move the churches and public opinion into opposition to the war and maintain a witness to the American tradition of dissent. It embraced both pacifists and just war traditionalists and assumed a middle ground since it did not call for an immediate withdrawal from Vietnam. As the war continued to escalate year after year, however, CALCAV increasingly denounced the war as immoral and moved beyond protest to acts of civil disobedience in its attempt to reverse the U.S. government's policy in Vietnam.

As early as 1963, clerical and lay church leaders had begun moving outside of established organizations to speak against the war in Vietnam. Reinhold Niebuhr, Harry Emerson Fosdick, John C. Bennett, president of Union Theological Seminary, Robert McAfee Brown of Stanford University, and Harvey Cox of Harvard Divinity School were among the first. Also in the summer of 1965, Martin Luther King, Jr., gave indications that he would join other religious leaders in opposition to the Vietnam War.[82] Daniel Berrigan was the one Catholic priest known to these Protestant leaders who was willing publicly to join the new venture. He did not stay with CALCAV very long because his Jesuit superiors sent him to South America early in 1966 to silence him for his public opposition to the war. Upon his return to the United States, Berrigan did occasionally join the group, but his move to Cornell University took him out of the Manhattan area and he lost touch with CALCAV.

Catholics who were not pacifists but were opposed to the war in Vietnam were attracted to CALCAV because of its religious witness. Two Catholics who rose to national prominence as spokespersons for CALCAV were John B. Sheerin, C.P.S., editor of *Catholic World*, and Michael Novak. Sheerin had chastised Catholics for their silence on the war and in the opinion of one historian he "provided a more consistently moral appraisal of the war earlier than most other clergymen. He found the conflict unsupportable when judged by the traditional Catholic doctrine of the 'just war.' "[83] Michael Novak, a writer, became part of CALCAV when in 1967 he collaborated with Robert McAfee Brown and Abraham Heschel on the book, *Vietnam: Crisis of*

Conscience. Novak as well as Sheerin later wrote for CALCAV's paper, *American Report,* which began in 1970.

CALCAV wanted a member of the American Catholic hierarchy to join them in their first national mobilization attempt. In December, CALCAV called "American clergymen of all faiths" to meet in Washington, D.C., for two days beginning 31 January 1967 to discuss "Vietnam: The Clergymen's Dilemma." CALCAV spent several weeks attempting to attract at least one Roman Catholic bishop or cardinal. They hoped that Bishop John J. Wright of Pittsburgh would attend, but after his refusal the executive committee sent night letters to all 250 bishops in the United States urging their approval and participation. Only about a dozen responded, a few of them in very hawkish terms. Two thousand five hundred Christian and Jewish clergy attended; not one Catholic bishop was there.[84]

After the mobilization, Archbishop Paul J. Hallinan of Atlanta refrained from endorsing an open letter against the war signed by 800 Catholic priests and laity, Auxiliary Bishop James Shannon of St. Paul-Minneapolis, and ten Roman Catholic college presidents. In February, however, he traveled to New York to speak out at a CALCAV-sponsored ecumenical study conference on "Vietnam and the Religious Conscience." At the symposium Hallinan sided more strongly than ever before with the opponents of American policy in Vietnam. The alternatives that Hallinan suggested in his talk seemed inadequate, for he urged an end to the stockpiling of weapons and support for the peacekeeping efforts of the United Nations. He also linked the civil rights movement in the United States with the war in Vietnam when he called for a "Selma for Peace," that would lead to the end of the Vietnam War.[85] Hallinan's speech was the closest that he had yet come to an outright condemnation of the war; but in the months following the talk he stepped back from his position because the antiwar activists tried to associate him with a project called Vietnam Summer.[86]

It was not Hallinan but James Shannon who eventually became one of the leading Roman Catholic voices within CALCAV. In 1968, Bishop Shannon joined CALCAV for the first time in a silent prayer vigil at the Arlington National Cemetery. Nearly 2,500 people gathered at the foot of the Tomb of the Unknowns and participated in a ceremony led by Martin Luther King, Jr. Shannon concluded the service with "Let us go in peace."[87] Other well-known Catholic clergy, Robert

Drinan, S.J., and Richard McSorley, S.J., supported CALCAV on its various projects. Many Catholic priests like William Hogan of the Archdiocese of Chicago were also involved with CALCAV at the local level.

Catholic involvement in CALCAV was very meager in the beginning years. There had only been five Catholics in the founding group. By 1971, the group's director was still Richard Fernandez, an ordained minister of the United Church of Christ, and its executive committee was still approximately two-thirds Protestant, but in addition to the inclusion of women, over time the most significant change was the proportional decline of Jews and an increase in Catholic participation.[88] In August 1971, when CALCAV sponsored its first national conference in Ann Arbor over four hundred people from thirty-six states attended. "Eighty-four percent claimed some religious affiliation with the same percentage active in at least one peace organization. The largest represented religious groups were Catholic, 21 percent; Methodist, 14 percent, Episcopal, 9 percent; United Church of Christ, 9 percent; Presbyterian, 8 percent; and Quaker, 7 percent. Only 2 percent were Jewish."[89] The increase in Catholic participation is significant for it meant that CALCAV provided a religious organization where Catholics who could not identify with the radical and pacifist organizations like the Catholic Worker and CPF could feel at home in their attempts to stop the war. It had also provided a place for individual members of the American hierarchy to test the waters as they spoke out as individuals against the war in Vietnam. Unfortunately, these same individuals did not speak out against the war before their fellow bishops at the NCCB meetings.[90]

At various times during the 1960s some members of the American Catholic hierarchy while addressing their Catholic constituency did challenge the morality of the Vietnam War. The earliest collective statement of protest concerning the war in Vietnam signed by members of the American Catholic hierarchy appeared in the scholarly journal, *Continuum*, in the summer 1965 issue. The protest came in response to the bombing of Hanoi and was called "A Declaration on the Threat of Bombardment of Civilian Centers." It was written by Justus George Lawler and stated: "Unlike other church issues concerning the war in Vietnam on which there is necessary and justifiable debate, the possibility that either side may bomb any purely civilian center would entail a clear and direct violation of Christian ethics and must be denounced as an immoral action."[91] The following bishops signed the declaration: Henry J. Grimmelsman of Evansville, Marion F. Forst of Dodge City, Hugh A. Donohoe of Stockton, Maurice Schexnayder of Lafayette, Robert J. Dwyer of Reno, Walter W. Curtis of Bridgeport, Mark K. Carroll of Wichita, John J. Russell of Richmond, and Charles A. Buswell of Pueblo.

As opposition grew with the escalation of the war, so did the pressure on the American bishops to take a stand. Not only peace groups like CPF, PAX, and CALCAV were applying such pressure, but as early as 1966 the New York Times observed that, unlike most American religious leaders, the Catholic bishops had been largely silent on the question of Vietnam.[92] The National Catholic Reporter immediately picked up on the statement and sent a questionnaire about the war to 225 bishops but received replies from only three, Leo Pursley of Fort Wayne-South Bend, Alphonse J. Schladweiler of New Ulm, and George J. Rehring of Toledo, all of whom supported the war in varying degrees.[93]

The earliest written statement by an individual member of the American Catholic hierarchy that raised any doubts concerning the war came in June 1966 when Lawrence Cardinal Shehan issued a pastoral letter, Vietnam, Patriotism and Individual Conscience, which was to be read aloud at all Masses celebrated in the Archdiocese of Baltimore. Since this was the first official pronouncement by a prominent Catholic ecclesiastic to give any indication of moral misgivings or reservations regarding the war in Vietnam, it received widespread attention in the American press when it first appeared. The pastoral letter presented a restrained and carefully balanced set of reminders of the traditional limits to be observed in warfare and a cautious endorsement of conscientious objection.

Less than two months later, the cardinal, believing the peace people had gone too far in their claims, explicitly repudiated what he described as attempts "to interpret my pastoral as a condemnation of American presence in Vietnam."[94] In a letter to the national commander of the Catholic War Veterans, he made his position clear. "Our presence in Vietnam and the reasons which have prompted us to involve ourselves there are honorable. The alternative of the withdrawal could well have catastrophic results under the present circumstances."[95] So determined was the cardinal to correct the "distortions" he ordered that the printed copies of the original text distributed by the Baltimore chancery also include the full text of his subsequent clarification.[96]

A few months later Hallinan and his auxiliary bishop of Atlanta, Joseph L. Bernardin, jointly issued a similar pastoral letter. They made it clear in their letter that their continued support for the war depended on the kind of war that the United States was waging in Vietnam. They quoted Cardinal Shehan's warning: "If our means become immoral, our cause will have been betrayed," and then added their own statement: "We must protest, therefore, whenever there is a danger that our conduct of war will exceed moral limits. A Christian simply cannot approve indiscriminate bombing, methodical extermination of people, nuclear arms designed for "overkill" or disregard for non-combatants."[97] Just as with Shehan's pastoral, both hawks and doves claimed it for support. But peace people this time contented themselves with saying that the bishops had not gone far enough. Neither pastoral was effective because a moral yardstick by which to measure the war was not presented. Both pastorals receded into oblivion.

When the number of American troops in Vietnam rose to 475,000 and the casualty figures reached 80,000 during 1967, antiwar demonstrations became larger. The failure of continued American bombing of North Vietnam to hasten military victory in South Vietnam increased the frustrations of many Americans. During this period a few more individual members of the hierarchy critical of the war began to speak out. Fulton J. Sheen, bishop of Rochester, New York, called for the withdrawal of U.S. troops from Vietnam in 1967.[98] Four Catholic bishops, Victor Reed, John Dougherty, James Shannon, and Paul Hallinan, endorsed the group Negotiations Now. In a joint statement, the four bishops said that in conformity with the plea for peace made by Pope Paul VI at the United Nations, they called upon the U.S. government to set a time and place for negotiations.[99] Richard Cardinal Cushing of the Archdiocese of Boston in his 1967 Christmas message pleaded: "For God's sake we must bring this war to an end." Yet, Cushing could not be persuaded in the following year to lend support to efforts to put the National Conference on record in support of selective conscientious objection. He did, however, endorse the Vietnam Moratorium Committee in the fall of 1969.[100]

There was only one American prelate prior to 1969 who consistently spoke out publicly in opposition to the war in Vietnam, James Shannon, an auxiliary bishop in the Archdiocese of St. Paul, Minnesota. It was mainly due to Shannon's persistence that the bishops took a stand in support of conscientious objection in 1968. It was also the frustration which this bishop experienced on the Vietnam issue that partially accounted for his resignation from the priesthood in 1969.[101] Auxiliary Bishop Bernard A. Kelly of Providence, Rhode Island, followed Shannon's opposition to the war and participated in an antiwar demonstration at the naval base in Newport, Rhode Island. He also urged the bishops to take a stand regarding the war at their meeting in the spring of 1971. He was upset that no collective presentation was prepared by the bishops on matters of economic justice or world peace and he too resigned from the priesthood in June 1971.[102] Bishop Thomas Gumbleton of Detroit had made a similar plea at the same meeting. Gumbleton assumed a leadership role among the hierarchy in opposing the war in Vietnam and in working for peace with justice.

By 1968, the bishops were saying that valid moral questions could be raised concerning the war effort and that Catholics could conscientiously object to the war in Vietnam not only because they were pacifists but because they believed the war in Vietnam to be unjust. It was mainly the effort and writing of Bishop Thomas Gumbleton who, with the USCC staff, managed to incorporate the series of questions concerning the morality of the Vietnam War into *Human Life in Our Day*.[103] According to church journalist, Jim Castelli, "It was Gumbleton who ultimately got the U.S. bishops to oppose the Vietnam War."[104] The bishops' pronouncements were not forming but following the lead of Catholic opinion during the Vietnam years. As early as 1965, *Continuum*, a Catholic scholarly periodical, condemned as immoral American plans for the bombing of Hanoi. Two days before Christmas 1966, the Catholic laity's periodical *Commonweal* pronounced the Vietnam War "a crime and a sin."[105] In October 1967, *Commonweal* became the first Catholic publication, excepting of course, the *Catholic Worker*, to take a stand in favor of civil disobedience as a legitimate form of antiwar protest when it editorialized:

> The resistance envisioned is a passive disobedience in the tradition of Thoreau. This might take the form of withholding of taxes, counseling, aiding or abetting young men on avoidance of the draft . . . , or

disruption tactics of various sorts. Such conduct might sound extreme to some, but as Robert McAfee Brown writes in a recent issue of *Look*, the war is so wrong and ways of registering concern about it have become so limited, that civil disobedience is the only course left.[106]

The *National Catholic Reporter* followed *Commonweal* when it called for the immediate withdrawal of U.S. troops from Vietnam and supported draft resistance, conscientious objections, and tax resistance.[107] These periodicals represented the intellectual position of Catholic liberals. There was a significant change not only among the liberal press, but among the Catholic press in general during the Vietnam era as John Deedy, editor of *Commonweal*, points out: "The Catholic press in general shifted from avid support for the struggle to a call for negotiations as a way of ending it [Vietnam War]."[108] The views of the Catholic press in general, like their bishops, grew directly from the traditional doctrine of the just war. As historian David O'Brien points out, it was only the liberal press that regarded pacifism and nonviolent resistance sympathetically. Yet, even these Catholic liberals for the most part remained loyal to the approach and categories of the just war.[109] Catholic liberals and intellectuals clung to the just war doctrine and contributed to maintaining it as the dominant position in the church. The position stated by James O'Gara, one of *Commonweal*'s editors in September 1967, remained typical:

> The war in Vietnam is a tragic and bloody mistake. . . . We have become reckless in our use of power and undercut the goals we seek, so much so that the war cannot be justified morally or politically. If the traditional Christian norms of just means and right proportion mean anything, we should vigorously seek negotiation and get out of Vietnam as quickly as possible.[110]

Thus, despite the image of Catholics as authoritarian, conservative, ultrapatriotic, and militaristic during the days of the Cold War, American Catholics were more critical of the Vietnam War than has often been supposed. According to Gallup Poll data, when the war began, "they were more hawkish than other Americans, when it ended, they were more dovish. And they have remained that way for a generation."[111] In July 1967, a plurality of Catholics for the first time disapproved of President Johnson's handling of the war. "Fifty-five percent of Catholics said it was not a mistake to get into Vietnam to begin with, but, by a 52–36 percent, Catholics opposed Johnson's plans to send another 100,000 men to Vietnam—a larger portion than that among Protestants (47–42 percent) and the general population (49–40 percent). In November 1966, the U.S. bishops issued a statement saying that the Vietnam War met the church's criteria for a 'Just War'; at that point, they were moving in a direction opposite to that of their own people."[112] In November 1969, Catholics described themselves as doves by 60–27 percent. The invasion of Cambodia revealed that Catholics were split, opposing the invasion by 47–44 percent while Protestants supported the move by 54–29 percent. In January 1971, Catholics supported a plan to bring all American troops home by the end of the year by 80–16 percent, Protestants by 68–23 percent. It took the American Catholic hierarchy until November 1971 when they concluded that "Vietnam no longer met the 'Just War' criteria—[that] they had caught up with their people."[113] In fact, the American Catholic hierarchy had almost missed the opportunity to condemn the immorality of the war in Vietnam.

In 1971 the United States Catholic Bishops issued the collective statement entitled *Resolution on Southeast Asia* which concluded that,

> At this point in history, it seems clear to us that whatever good we hope to achieve through continued involvement in this war is now outweighed by the destruction of human life and moral values it inflicts. It is our firm conviction, therefore, that the speedy ending of this war is a moral imperative of the highest priority.[114]

This was the first time in the modern world, not only in America, that during a war a nation's Catholic hierarchy had publicly judged their government's actions unjust.

The question of the significance of the resolution for American Catholics generated much discussion. The conservative press such as the Catholic newspaper, the *Wanderer*, and the journal, *National Review*, considered the resolution a disaster. The liberal press basically said, "Too little, too late." And *Commonweal* observed that the National Council of Churches had condemned the war six years earlier. And as Bordelon pointed out, when the NCCB resolution reached the floor at the November meeting it generated heated debate, and an earlier version had to be softened in order to gain the necessary two-thirds vote. This division among the hierarchy on the issue was evident to the public in a press conference after passage of the resolution when Bishop Gumbleton said anyone who agrees with the bishops "may not participate in the war." And Archbishop Hannan of New Orleans immediately disagreed with that conclusion.[115] For American Catholics the discussion did not end in 1971 nor did the Vietnam War. The condemnation of the war by the American Catholic hierarchy had no more impact on the U.S. government in stopping the Vietnam War than did the nonviolent acts of resistance of Catholic pacifists or the actions and judgments of Catholic just war theorists. Despite President Nixon's effort to discredit the antiwar movement and to continue the war through the air while bringing the troops home, there was peace at last with the fall of Saigon on 1 May 1975. Finally, after thirteen years, the longest war in American history stopped.

Pacifism was the heart of the American Catholic peace movement during the Vietnam era. Introduced into American Catholicism by Dorothy Day and the Catholic Worker movement in the 1930s, by the 1960s it had become a recognized option for Catholics. Tom Cornell attempted to define this Catholic pacifism when he wrote:

> We are opposed to the war in Vietnam not only because it is unjust, but because it is a war. If the United States government were fighting on the other side we would be in opposition also, but we would have different and fewer allies. Catholic pacifists are opposed to war because it is the planned, mass taking of human lives for political purposes and violates God's exclusive dominion over human life. We are opposed to abortion, euthanasia, capital punishment, and economically enforced starvation also, on the same basis.[116]

Nonviolence and nonviolent resistance developed from the concept of pacifism. The draft became the catalyst for the development of nonviolent resistance during the Vietnam era because the draft placed the individual in a position whereby a decisive action had to be taken. The Catholic Worker advocated noncooperation with the draft and when one of its members, David Miller, burned his draft card at a rally in New York City the resistance was born. Catholics beyond draft age identified with these young men who were going to jail because of their convictions and some of them decided to pour napalm over selective service files. These actions gave birth to the Ultraresistance led by the Berrigan brothers. Their commitment and willingness to pay the price of jail placed them in the vanguard of the American peace movement. It also raised the question of "effectiveness" in terms of stopping the war. This led to the question, what will the Gospel message of peace allow in terms of actions necessary to stop the war?

It must be remembered, however, that during the 1960s a far greater number of young Catholics chose to register their dissent against the war within the law as conscientious objection rather than choose the path of noncooperation or resistance. This indicated that the pacifist element was increasing and continued to predominate even though the element of resistance was far more visible because of the publicity generated by the media. Thus, the role of PAX in lobbying on behalf of conscientious objection both at the Second Vatican Council and before the National Conference of Catholic Bishops in America cannot be underestimated.

Finally, although pacifism was the core of Catholic peace activism, the just war doctrine was still the dominant position among Catholics during the Vietnam War. It was the CAIP and the hierarchy that maintained the just war tradition in their peacemaking efforts. John Courtney Murray expanded the just war doctrine so that it not only applied to the state but to each individual in judging the actions of the state during a time of war. Catholics for the first time were using the just war doctrine to condemn their nation's war effort and demanding that their "lawfully constituted authority" end the war.

The leaders in the American Catholic peace movement during the Vietnam era could have been counted on less than ten fingers. Because they all identified with the Catholic Worker tradition there was no claim of leadership by any single individual and there was no one community, or action, or position. Rather, a network of friendship and support developed that sustained all of them. The Berrigan brothers were obviously very close. Tom Cornell and Jim Forest were friends and they kept the CPF together. Forest was also good friends with Daniel and Philip Berrigan and Thomas Merton. Tom Cornell was close to Dorothy Day. Eileen Egan and Dorothy Day were friends and

Eileen Egan and Gordon Zahn kept PAX alive. Zahn also kept close to Tom Cornell at the CPF. Each one of these persons was very independent, and their Catholic faith motivated and sustained them. As a result all were self-consciously Catholic. Every action they posited for peace was religiously motivated and was done for the purpose of bringing peace to American society and persuading the leaders of the Roman Catholic church to adopt a new ethic of peace.

Because its leadership was religiously based, the American Catholic peace movement *was* a peace movement and not an antiwar movement. The Catholic peace movement was alive to the same elements in American culture that affected the antiwar movement. In their study of the Vietnam antiwar movement Benedetti and Chatfield have listed five major components that comprised the movement: changes in liberal thought, the rise of student-led protest, the emergence of the new radical left, the challenge of a nonviolent civil rights campaign, and the growth of the counter-culture.[117] According to their interpretation, politics held these components together. Also, because the American Catholic peace movement came out of the Catholic Worker tradition, there was a basic identification of its leadership with the various analyses of the injustices of American society by both the old and new Left, but the leadership always placed them within a religious context and the solution to the injustices was never in solely political terms. The relationship between politics and religion often left the leadership in a quandary. Members of the Catholic peace movement never used political terms such as liberal or Marxist to identify themselves. Both Dorothy Day and Daniel Berrigan called themselves "personalists" and "fundamentalists," and they also used the term radical, but in a religious sense in terms of living "the radical Gospel message." The leadership in the American Catholic peace movement also saw itself as part of a counterculture, but again in the Catholic Worker tradition where community, poverty, and the Gospel Beatitudes were its trademark. Thus, members of the Catholic peace movement were never particularly attracted to liberal thought, the New Left, or the counterculture. Instead, they tended to work most closely with other pacifist groups such as FOR, WRL, and CNVA or nonpacifist religious peace groups such as CALCAV. They also spent a great amount of energy educating Catholics about peace within existing Catholic institutions by speaking at parishes and schools and working with existing Catholic organizations and groups. Though they were not exclusively, they were self-consciously Catholic.

The most important impact of the American Catholic peace movement was that it helped to persuade large numbers of Catholics to oppose the Vietnam War. Within a few brief years the hawks had turned into doves and this desire for peace has remained a characteristic of American Catholics throughout the 1980s. These Catholics also brought their church hierarchy to a position of declaring the immorality of the Vietnam War. The American Catholic peace movement's most significant contribution to the antiwar movement was in its leadership roles in the Resistance and the Ultraresistance as it attempted to end the war by extending pacifism with new tactics of nonviolent resistance. The American Catholic peace movement also attempted to change the public policy of the U.S. government on the issue of conscientious objection by trying to include SCO in the CO classification. Though this attempt failed with the government, it was successful with the American Catholic hierarchy in its pronouncements of the right of a Catholic to be a CO or an SCO. The American Catholic peace movement also made pacifism and nonviolence a valid option for Catholics. It would take another decade before the American Catholic church would put this in writing, but it would come.

The most important leaders of the American Catholic peace movement during the Vietnam Era were the Berrigan brothers. A look at their personal lives and their quest for justice and peace provides many insights into what it meant to be Catholic and American during this most turbulent time. It also reveals that for the individual the demands of peacemaking are as great as the demands of war.

7

The Berrigan Brothers and the
Catholic Resistance

ON 17 MAY 1968, nine men and women entered Selective Service Local Board No. 33 at Catonsville, Maryland. The group seized records and burned them outside the building with napalm, which they had manufactured themselves following a recipe in the Special Forces Handbook published by the U.S. government. Within a few minutes the local police arrived and heard Daniel Berrigan, S.J., lead his companions in praying the Our Father as a thanksgiving for the completed action. The police waited until the end of the prayer, then handcuffed the "criminals for peace" and loaded them into a paddy wagon. The Catonsville action symbolized the high point of American Catholic resistance to the Vietnam War in the 1960s. For Catholic peace activists, Catonsville signaled a dramatic move to the Left in their resistance to war. After this action, two of the nine participants, Daniel Berrigan and his brother Philip, emerged as the architects of a new political and theological movement.

The American press labeled this movement the Catholic Left or the New Catholic Left[1] and used these terms consistently and without distinction when describing events related to the Berrigan brothers from Catonsville in 1968 to the Harrisburg Seven Trial in 1972. The press estimated in 1972 that the Catholic Left had grown in size from the Catonsville Nine to several hundred participants and several thousand sympathizers in a church of 47,000,000 American Catholics.[2]

The term Catholic Left or New Catholic Left, however, was a misnomer. Within the antiwar movement there was a coalition of the Left formed by the old Left (Communists and Socialists), the new Left (mainly students led by the SDS who were against those who opposed communists and socialists), and militant pacifists (the radical wings of the traditional peace churches and groups like WRL and CNVA). All of these groups viewed the war in Vietnam as a direct expression of America's military-industrial complex which they felt stood against the social forces of revolution in Southeast Asia. As a result, this coalition viewed American foreign policy as imperialistic and neocolonial. This view was tied to a vision of an American political system that was also considered to be unresponsive to the social-justice demands of its own society. Therefore, instead of relying on electoral politics, this coalition called for resistance to a state that they believed had become illegitimate.

Since the Catholic Resistance also supported many of these same political positions, it is understandable that the press would label them the Catholic Left. It is important, however, to recognize that the Catholic Resistance did not come out of this coalition of the Left. Rather it was a religious group whose aim was not only to stop the war in Vietnam, but to work for justice and peace in both the church and society. Their religious motivation was rooted in a basic revulsion against the secular values of American society that they believed were manifested in a materialistic, racist, and militaristic culture. Communism had little to do with their analysis for, like Merton, capitalism and communism were two sides of the same evil coin. Their journey into resistance first began with their involvement in social-justice issues such as poverty and civil rights. The injustice of the Vietnam War then led them to work for peace. Their resistance escalated as the war continued year after year and the American political system failed to respond to their efforts to bring forth justice and peace. As a result they kept increasing their actions of nonviolent resistance against that system. The term Catholic Resistance rather than Catholic Left makes more sense and is a more accurate term.

The draft board raid at Catonsville marked a new departure in the escalation of resistance on the part of peace activists because the action was planned in secret and destroyed government property.[3] The Catonsville Nine claimed that the raid was a nonviolent direct act of civil disobedience that had both secular and religious implications. By attacking law and property, the bulwarks of a value system the participants believed lay at the roots of exploitation, racism, violence and war, they hoped to expose the evils in the social-value system of America. At the same time they hoped to call the church to heed its message of justice and peace. The participants dramatized the act of civil disobe-

dience by placing it within a theological context of prayer at Catonsville, thus proclaiming that they had attacked the false values of America, especially the Vietnam War, while affirming human life in a
Christian context.[4]

The idea for the destruction of draft files and the organization that
led to Catonsville was the work not of Daniel Berrigan, but of his
brother, Philip Berrigan, S.S.J. In April 1964 Philip was sent by his
religious community to St. Peter Claver parish in Baltimore, where he
worked in support of housing for blacks and for peace. In a desire to do
more to stop the Vietnam War, Philip Berrigan along with Robert
Alpern, Thomas Lewis, Harry Trabold, and James Harney formed the
nucleus of a small peace group. They first organized and practiced civil
disobedience on several occasions at Fort Myers, Virginia, where most
of the Joint Chiefs of Staff resided, but according to Berrigan there
were no arrests because too many clergy were present. In the summer
of 1967, Philip Berrigan returned to New York City to finish his book *A
Punishment for Peace*, and in September he went back to Baltimore to
seek a more effective tactic to stop the war. The idea of bombing draft
boards was first contemplated by the small Baltimore peace group but it
was regarded as too violent. As members of the white middle-class
society they maintained that they had no right to resort to violence;
other options were still open to them. Finally, Philip Hirchkopf, a
Virginia lawyer and head attorney for the Pentagon March in October,
came up with the post-Christian era symbolism of pouring blood on
the draft files.[5] Daniel Berrigan, of course, was told of the proposed
action at the Custom's House in Baltimore, but he did not feel free to
join.[6]

Twenty years later, Daniel Berrigan would write in his autobiography *To Dwell in Peace* that when Philip told him of the action "It was
all quite simple. It was also unprecedented, calculated to set the head
spinning." Daniel wrote to him after the revelation that he "continued
to see my [Daniel's] work as standing by the students in their travail;
nothing more." Daniel goes on to say that his brother responded with
"considerable impatience." He then explains his brother's action:

> Philip's instinct, on the other hand, was to seek out an occasion, at his
> own time and place, to take the offensive and force the government to
> respond.

He had come on a way to do this: a moral assault on purportedly sacrosanct territory. An act, he insisted, very much in the spirit of King and Gandhi; but as a tactic, something utterly new. Something, as he must have known, bound to raise towering waves, to erupt in controversy, denunciation, passionate pros and cons, even spite and scorn.

The proposed act was entirely in line with his temperament. His life had been a steady rhythm of improvisation and discipline. He was a surprising spirit; he dug deep and came up with directions, modes, arguments, lights in dark places. And equally of import, he had a capacity to beckon others along; he made virtue attractive. In his presence, as I saw time and again, less hardy spirits such as myself breathed deep, stopped out.[7]

On Friday, 27 October 1967 Philip Berrigan and three others, David Eberhardt, Thomas Lewis, and James Mengel, poured blood on selective service files at the Customs House in Baltimore, Maryland.[8]

It was the combination of the brothers Berrigan that would provide the leadership of the Catholic Resistance. Daniel emerged as spokesperson after Catonsville. Thomas Merton had already articulated the theological rationale for traditional nonviolent resistance, but the monk had never left his monastery to participate. Even Catholic Workers who had limited their actions to traditional forms of nonviolent resistance were not participants at Catonsville, though some of them would follow the example of the Berrigans in subsequent draft board raids. As a writer, a poet, a theologian, and an activist, Daniel Berrigan was able to combine the tradition of the Catholic Worker, the activism of his brother Philip, and the contemplation and writing ability of his friend Merton.[9] Because of his writing and speaking ability, he was able to articulate for the American public a rationale for nonviolent resistance. By conveying sincerity and commitment through his participation, he also brought visibility and a following to the Catonsville action. Thus Daniel, who reconciled the paradoxes of the Catholic peacemaker within his own being, became a symbol of the possibilities and limits of the American Catholic peace movement as it confronted both church and state in resistance to the Vietnam War.

It is difficult to ascertain exactly what led the brothers to take such a daring risk at Catonsville. Some authors attribute it to the authoritarian character of their father or to the authoritarian structure of the Roman

Catholic church and its religious communities; others attribute it to the "supposed sibling rivalry" between the Berrigan brothers. Though these all may have contributed, the best explanation lies in their faith in the Gospel message and the combination of people and events that influenced their thought and action. These experiences led them to new thoughts and actions concerning what it meant to be both Catholic and American.[10]

The Berrigan brothers were not converts to American Catholicism but products of the "immigrant church," sons of a German-born mother and a second generation Irish-American father.[11] Philip was the youngest and Daniel the second youngest of six sons. Their father, Thomas Berrigan, was a strong-authoritarian Irish Catholic who enforced a rigid and often abusive discipline in his home and had no rapport with his sons. He was a great lover of poetry, which he bellowed through the house or silently attempted to write. "His literary rejection over the years soured his heart, and intensified his sense of being a neglected genius."[12] He made his mark in his community in Syracuse with his physical strength, his support of unionism at the light company in Syracuse, and his involvement in social-justice concerns with the poor and civil rights. His home was always open to those who sought relief, and extras were shared with everyone coming to their door during the Great Depression years. Politically he was a Democrat, but he also supported Charles Coughlin during the depression and subscribed to the *Catholic Worker*.

When Daniel tried to evaluate what his father had given him, he attempted to give the answer in terms of faith. "One could console himself in any easy homiletic way—he gave us faith. That would put things simply—and uselessly. That statement would be true, and just as clearly untrue; for what he gave with one hand, he took back with the other."[13] But he went on to say that "he offered something other than faith or a viable or attractive religious sense. Something of persistence, stubbornness, skepticism, a queer kind of gnarled integrity, a sixth sense for the right order of things, thrashing out in all directions. If only this could have been disciplined and directed, what a strength!"[14]

The mother, Frida, was the real spirit in the family. A gentle, fragile, and humble woman of great faith in God and people, she was able to instill confidence and hope in her sons as they confronted each new situation. Daniel's position in the family was different from the other boys; he was pale and delicate, he helped with the work inside the house while the stronger boys, like Philip, did the outside work on their small farm. Daniel and his mother suffered greatly from the physical and psychological strains of the family. As a result a special bond existed between them.[15] Daniel writes of his mother,

> And our faith, as we came to know, had another source than him; it came from our mother. Strangely; for with regard to things religious, she was reticence personified. But in the midst of all, and stuck as she (and we) seemed in a cul-de-sac, her example could not but be noted, even by the blind. It counted for nearly everything, the patience, plain goodness, long-sufferance; and now and then, the right word filling the space, and the religious piety that was never once overbearing or showy, but that carried its burdens, carried others along, and finally carried the day. Oh (as the Irish never conceded), she had a way with her!"[16]

When Philip writes of his parents' influence, he is much less revelatory, but he too stresses the faith they passed on to him. Philip stated, "We were all perfectly aware and deeply pained by the imperfections of Frida and Tom—their marriage was sometimes stormy, contentious, unhappy. But toward others, especially the poor and outcast, they were people of towering compassion and justice."[17] He reiterates repeatedly their background of deprivation and struggle and contends that "Frida and Tom took the Gospel to heart—to a depth unprovided by a lifetime of conventional Catholicism. Their faith was due undoubtedly to experience with desperate need, deprivation, misery, discrimination, oppresssion. Their analysis of social injustice might prove lacking but they understood profoundly the command to care for 'the least of these.' "[18]

All the Berrigan brothers attended St. John the Baptist Academy in Syracuse. Except for Daniel, the boys were average students and participated mainly in athletic activites. During high school Daniel wrote poetry, acted in plays, and learned to dance. His enthusiasm for life even led him to become a cheerleader, for which his brothers relentlessly chided him. Toward the end of his high school years, Daniel applied to the Society of Jesus for acceptance. At first the society would not accept him and told him to go home and improve his Latin. After a year of study, the rejection was rescinded and he entered the Society of Jesus on 14 August 1939.

Daniel underwent the thirteen years of Jesuit training with its emphasis on the intellectual and spiritual life. In these years the training made no provisions for the social apostolate except for three years reserved for teaching. Daniel later wrote of the effect the training had on him:

> We were being asked to accept the truth that the past had something to offer living men. We could accept the truth, abstractly, but we could in fact offer men very little; for our theology, was not a living science. It was a dead one. . . . It was almost entirely an exercise in memory; it ignored living questions on principle; its vernacular was almost as far from man's thoughts as its Latin; it had no urgent need to confront Protestant or Jewish traditions, except as opponents. And in moral questions, it gave a view of the world only as large or liberating as could be gained from the upper storeys of a Roman ivory tower.[19]

He went on to say, however, that it did do one thing, "It made me teachable." It also seems to have provided him with a strong foundation of basic values and a sense of direction that served as a sounding board to evaluate the onslaught of everything new.

After ordination on 21 June 1952, Daniel went abroad for his tertianship. He studied at the Gregorian University in Rome and at the Maison la Colombiere, Paray le Monial, in France. It was during his stay in France that he associated himself with the Worker Priest Movement. The impact of these priests would shape the rest of Daniel's life.

The Worker-Priest Movement was founded after World War II under the guiding spirit of Emmanuel J. Suhard, the cardinal archbishop of Paris. The horrifying experiences of Hitler's atrocities and the incredible inhumanity of World War II in "Christian" Europe, coupled with the moral paralysis of the churches in face of such a disaster, had summoned a few to a rethinking of the social dimensions of Christianity. The worker-priests rejected the Enlightenment notion that religion was a personal private matter and emphasized an involvement in temporal and social spheres. Their political philosophy was largely socialistic and anticolonial. For Daniel the worker-priests combined the personal commitments most emphasized by his parents: a strong support for the workers and a deep faith in God that could translate Christian belief into personal charity. It also showed him an attempt to revitalize Christianity against the encroachments of secularism. Association with these men brought Daniel into contact with the writings of such progressive European theologians as Dietrich Bonhoeffer, Henri de Lubac, Yves Congar, and later Teilhard de Chardin. These contacts were to be among the most important influences on Daniel Berrigan's later writings and actions. The French underground experiences of some of the worker-priests as German prisoners affected Berrigan's theories of civil disobedience; the progressive theologians' concepts of Christianity demanding social involvement confirmed his call to public action, and Teilhard de Chardin's optimistic view of history would contribute to the eschatological dimension that he would attribute to such actions as that at Catonsville. [20]

After returning from Europe in 1954, Daniel Berrigan was not with the workers in America, but with the students. He was assigned to teach high school at Brooklyn Preparatory. His extracurricular interest in these years centered on combating poverty. He first began working with Puerto Ricans in lower Manhattan and later became chaplain for the Young Christian Workers, a Catholic group of high school students involved in social justice concerns. In 1957, he was assigned to teach theology at LeMoyne University in Syracuse. The young liberal college students, especially the activists of the 1960s, shared much in common with Berrigan: Catholicism, gender, higher education, middle-class values, and concern for the oppressed at home and abroad. Besides teaching theology and English, he continued his social-justice involvement by moderating a professional sodality, a group of middle- and upper-class adults whose social action he directed toward housing for the poor and interracial work in the community. He also established an International House on campus after President John F. Kennedy announced his Peace Corps and Alliance for Progress. Such projects brought Daniel Berrigan into a close working relationship with his brother, Philip. This personal relationship would grow during the years and be the most significant and sustaining influence on both men. It would ultimately produce the action at Catonsville and the Catholic Resistance. [21]

Philip Berrigan had taken a different route. Upon graduation from high school, Philip worked for a year scouring soot-caked locomotives at the New York Central Yards to earn college money. He spent a semester at St. Michael's College in Toronto before he was drafted in 1943. The army served as a unique training ground. Philip underwent Field Artillery training in the Deep South, Georgia, Florida, and North Carolina, where he saw black poverty and second-class citizenship. His own account of his army career was written in a brief paragraph to the religious community he later entered. "Went overseas with a field artillery unit as a sergeant. While in Germany volunteered for officer's training in the infantry in the futile and foolish hope of seeing some action. By the time I was commissioned, the war had ended."[22] Philip rarely speaks of his experience in the army and when asked directly, he replies briefly or mentions some account of racial discrimination he witnessed.

After his discharge in 1946, he enrolled at the College of the Holy Cross in Worcester, Massachusetts, where he completed work for his B.A. degree under the G.I. Bill of Rights. Upon graduation in 1950, he entered the Josephite Fathers, whose apostolate is service to African Americans. Philip entered the Society of Saint Joseph because of their apostolate to the African Americans and his own identification with these people and because their period of preparation for ordination was briefer than that of the Jesuits. The final factor in his decision was that his brother Jerome was also a member of the society. Philip had always been closest to this brother. Jerome left the Society of Saint Joseph just before ordination, married and adopted four children, but he continued to help blacks by joining the Catholic Interracial Council and working with his brother Daniel in the professional sodality. Philip continued his studies and was ordained a priest in 1955. From 1956 until 1963, he taught in an all-black high school, St. Augustine, in New Orleans. During these years Philip and Daniel grew closer together as they shared ideas and activities concerning their students, and increased their involvement in the civil rights movement in America and the liturgical movement in the church.

Philip Berrigan spent these years in New Orleans not only in the classroom, but also in outdoor work, maintaining the physical plant of the high school and repairing homes in the black community, where he spent hours of his free time organizing drives for clothes, food, and housing. Obtaining first-class citizenship for African Americans was his top priority. He often read and clipped articles on current events in order to keep abreast of changes in the church and in American society. These years cannot be underestimated in their impact on him as he moved from administering corporal works of mercy to searching for ways to empower the African American community to achieve its own goals.[23] "Phil," as his friend James Forest has said, "looks like an ad for a wheaties boxtop—a Mr. All-American." During these years he was known as a man's man, courageous, strong, direct, fearless, and a man who constantly confronted injustice. In sum, Philip Berrigan spent all his time during these years teaching and working in the social-justice movement for black equality in the South. Daniel Berrigan often sent his LeMoyne students to his brother's high school to work in summer projects for poor African Americans and aided Philip in securing college scholarships for the most able black students.

The impact of the general climate of evolving social protest, especially the civil rights movement, had a profound impact on the Berrigan brothers, as on many thinking Americans. The various church-related, social-action groups had the greatest impact, especially the Southern Christian Leadership Conference under the direction of Dr. Martin Luther King, Jr. This group gave nonviolent direct action and civil disobedience a new dignity by the courage of a conscientious few in the midst of growing awareness of the urgent need for massive social change.

Spurred on by such actions for social justice, the Berrigan brothers confronted the question of civil disobedience for the first time in the summer of 1961. Along with Richard Wagner, another Josephite priest, he decided to participate in the Freedom Ride in Mississippi led by James Farmer. For the first and last time the two asked their religious superiors for permission to follow their consciences in an act of civil disobedience. Daniel Berrigan could not obtain permission, but Philip Berrigan and Richard Wagner received affirmation from their religious superior general, George O'Dea. The two priests got as far as Atlanta, Georgia, where a phone call prevented them from reaching Mississippi. The Congress of Racial Equality (CORE) had released their names to the press two hours before their scheduled arrival. This exploitation of the priests' presence resulted in the bishop of Jackson, Richard Gerow, demanding the removal of the two priests from his diocese.[24] Obeying their religious superiors, the priests did not participate, but the experience left them no less convinced of the value and need for priests to give such witness. Since civil disobedience was a matter of individual conscience, the priests never again asked their religious superiors for permission to follow their own consciences.

It was also during the period of the late fifties and early sixties that the Berrigan brothers experienced the changes occurring in the church. Prior to the Second Vatican Council, the new emphasis on the emerging laity and the liturgical movement occurred. The liturgical movement viewed the ritual of the earthly church as the visible expression of Christ's worship, and the mission of the church (including the social apostolate) as the visible expression of Christ's love for the world. It encouraged full participation on the part of the laity and thus introduced the vernacular language and a simple and clear liturgy designed to educate the faithful. Though Daniel Berrigan rose to national prominence in the liturgical movement, it was Philip Berrigan and not Daniel who had first published a significant article on the topic in *Worship* magazine.[25] Philip lost interest in the liturgical movement, however, because he was more interested in work for social justice and did not have the time or temperament (much like Dorothy Day) to spend explaining it theologically. He continued to devote his attention to finding ways to aid the African American community.

Liturgy, on the other hand, greatly influenced Daniel and helped him to develop a stronger theological basis for his social involvement. At LeMoyne this enthusiasm for liturgy was reflected in the chapel he and his family built in the new International House on campus. The austere lines of the table altar and the stone floor were designed to emphasize the celebrant, which in Berrigan's case sometimes led to an excessive use of gestures in his attempt to express the symbolic. The significance of the liturgical movement resided in its new emphasis on the Paschal Mystery as an on-going reality at work in the lives of men and women in their efforts to develop a new world. The sacraments, expecially the Eucharist, were not merely a remembrance of God's past activity in Christ, but of God at work in Christ's new body, the community of discipleship, transforming the believing community and through them the world. Along with all of this was the liturgical movement's emphasis on salvation-history theology—that in Jesus Christ the Kingdom was begun, and now history, through the actions of men and women, moved toward the fullness of the Kingdom and the reign of love, justice, and peace. It was this new emphasis that Daniel Berrigan used to explain the motivation behind acts of nonviolent resistance. He extended the theology outward and not inward on a worshipping community.

Thus, Daniel used these theological emphases of the liturgical movement to move him toward more radical social and political action. The transition from liberal to radical was evidenced in both his theology and politics. By acting with other persons in community against the evils of social injustice and eventually against the evil of the war in Vietnam and his government which perpetrated them and his church which was used to sanction such evils, he believed that he was moving history through such action toward the fullness of the Kingdom—the day of love, justice, and peace.[26]

The ecumenical movement beginning during this period also influenced Daniel greatly. First, it helped to build an increased solidarity among clerics who held similar convictions about theology and action being combined to fulfill the Kingdom. During the early 1960s at Mount Saviour Monastery, Daniel Berrigan and John Heidbrink, the director of church relations for FOR, led Roman Catholic and Protestant retreats for clerics. This ecumenical probing and inquiry established their friendship. John Heidbrink believed he helped "to liberate" Berrigan in the area of ecumenical relations.[27] Heidbrink would often accuse Daniel of legalism in the liturgy and of holding the Apostle Paul in such reverence that he became the fourth member of the Trinity. He also introduced him to the Fellowship of Reconciliation (FOR), which Berrigan joined in late 1962 and which later provided him assistance in the founding of a new Catholic peace organization, the Catholic Peace Fellowship (CPF). Heidbrink commented on the kind of changes Daniel Berrigan was undergoing in the early 1960s.

Dan was, in the early sixties, a thorough-going artist with a sensitivity for the sensuous which shocked me at times. He was moving into a Hebrew [biblical] grasp of reality in a unified matter-spirit unity. This was before the Teilhard manuscripts were released. But Dan sensed the organic relationship of matter and spirit and would begin soon his efforts to unite these substances so long divided. . . . Dan's ecclesiology underwent a massive change and it was then that his often bold and angry iconoclasm began and took such radical forms.[28]

While at LeMoyne, Daniel Berrigan wrote a great deal and his writings reflected the changes in his thought concerning theology and social involvement. Berrigan became most widely known during this period for his poetry and he published two books of poems, *Time Without Number* and *Encounters*. His first prose work, *The Bride: Essays in the Church*, reflected his competence as a biblical scholar and liturgist. In these writings he was concerned with exploring nature, the church, suffering, grace, sin, and the sacraments. His Thomism, legalism, and views about the dichotomy between the spiritual and the natural were quite evident, especially in his defense of the statement "There is no salvation outside of the Church" in *The Bride*. His writing very much paralleled Merton's during this time period. In later years, Dan referred to this prose work as a "sin of his past."[29]

By 1961, however, in his prose work, *The Bow in the Clouds*, and especially in his book of poetry, *The World for a Wedding Ring*, all dichotomy disappeared and the wedding of the sacred and profane was finally achieved. Significantly, this last book of poetry was dedicated to three Catholic social activists: Tony Walsh, Dorothy Day, and Karl Meyer. Suffering was no longer a spiritual agony for Daniel, but a moment of intense anxiety and ultimate rebirth. He found Christ in all nature and in the universe. He began to see the church as a part of a larger movement to serve the world. He saw behind the symbols the realities that the church had betrayed for the sake of acceptance and status. He also altered his view of authority and began to stress service. In his next book, *They Call Us Dead Men*, Daniel attempted to place the individual in a concrete context of social involvement. From this book the person emerges as a sacrament when service is rendered to a brother or sister in need. All issues for Daniel Berrigan were now viewed as religious issues.

At this time he was also publishing in journals such as *Worship*, *Critic*, *Perspectives*, and *Today*. His topics ranged from sacred art, to the Christian in modern times, to the role of the church, to freedom, and to nonviolence. The emphasis in all the writing is on the individual's reaching the fullness of personhood by consciously confronting things as they really are and trying to change them to fulfill the King-dom of God.

Many of the changes reflected in Daniel's writing were the result of the knowledge he had gained while trying to serve human needs in the social apostolate. But even more important, he was observing, listening, and questioning every person and event that passed before him. He had a series of way stations that provided him these contacts. He maintained his relationship with Tony Walsh at the Benedict Labre House for the poor in Canada,[30] he would stop by the Catholic Worker, he would either make or give retreats at Mount Saviour Monastery in Pine City, New York, and visit or address the Association for International Development (AID) in Paterson, New Jersey.

The years at LeMoyne, however, also supplied negative influences. Daniel experienced increasing opposition from influential people in the Syracuse community because of his activities in civil rights. He was disappointed and angry when the Jesuit censors refused to sanction publication of a book he and his brother Philip had collaborated on. The reason given was that Philip Berrigan's writing was too secular, too hard hitting, and too radical on issues such as civil rights.[31] Despite the anger, Daniel Berrigan accepted the Jesuit censorship of Philip's writing. As a result, Daniel wrote his own book, *They Call Us Dead Men*, and Philip published his own work as *No More Strangers*. Also, and perhaps most difficult to bear, was the inhuman action and constant opposition Daniel received from his rector the last two years at LeMoyne. In 1964, Daniel explained this situation to his provincial while he was on visitation at LeMoyne and asked for a sabbatical. The request was immediately granted.

By 1964, both Berrigan brothers had begun to increase their involvement in the issue of peace, especially opposition to the war in Vietnam. Philip had been concerned about the nuclear issue, but moved to focus his energies on the Vietnam War. One reason for this increase of concern about peace was Pope John XXIII's encyclical, *Pacem in Terris* and the Second Vatican Council's reiteration of Pope John's social orientation. At the time of the council, the church was emphasizing that it is a pilgrim people whose primary task is the transformation of the social order in light of the Gospel message. The Berrigans took this teaching seriously and sought ways or actions that symbolized the ability of Christians to break out of their privatized spirituality and involve themselves with the great social and political questions facing humankind.

By 1963, Philip had become increasingly aware of the issue of peace. He began to see the war in Vietnam as diverting the energies of the American people and government from the struggle for civil rights. He was impatient and dissatisfied with his effectiveness in the civil rights movement while working out of a high school in New Orleans. He was also becoming aware of his own paternalism while trying to assist African Americans. The increased emphasis on black separatism and militancy also persuaded him to realize that he might do more not only for civil rights but for his country as a whole if he devoted his energies to trying to stop the war in Vietnam. Unsure of his feelings and not desiring to leave the struggle for civil rights, he first accepted an assignment as a fund raiser for his religious community in New York City. During this time he arranged for a consulting firm to study the Josephite community and submit recommendations on how the order could better fulfill its mission of service to the African American community. The consultants proposed that $2 million be raised to enable the Josephites to play a more prominent role in the fast developing civil rights revolution. The order's ruling council rejected the proposal, a setback that finally convinced Philip that he could best accomplish his goals on the edge of his community rather than try to change the organization of the religious community itself. [32]

While fund raising, Philip was also serving as a consultant to priests in Harlem who had not yet freed themselves from the attitude of being protectors of the blacks. He often worked with John P. Grady, whose house became the center of many Berrigan meetings in the city. [33] In March 1964, Philip was assigned to teach at Ephiphany Apostolic College in Newburgh. He left the college in April 1965, because the politically conservative community had harrassed the seminary for maintaining him on its staff. They had objected to Philip's positions and activities in civil rights and peace. Philip Berrigan was then assigned to an African American parish in Baltimore, St. Peter Claver. Greatly upset by the fact that his religious superiors had acquiesced to the pressures of the people in Newburgh, Philip asked his brother Daniel to drive to Baltimore with him so they could talk. At that time they made a solemn agreement that regardless of the actions of the church against them, they would not leave the priesthood of their own volition.[34]

Prior to Philip's transfer to Baltimore, Daniel had been revisiting Europe. While in France during 1964, he was again affected by the Worker Priest Movement. This time the question of relevance began to loom large in his thinking. The worker priests taught him that relevance needed to be rooted in being brother to the world—to serving those in need. This was also the time when the memory of France's involvement in Vietnam and Algeria was still viewed as a tragic mistake. The church's role had been mixed, but Berrigan soon learned that all respected European Catholics were pacifists and heavy supporters of the Fellowship of Reconciliation. After his stay in France he concluded that the church in America was not really Christian for it often put him in a position of choosing either for the church or for humankind. "From time to time, it is asked of man to choose between obedience on the one hand, and fidelity to the poor, or the Negro, or the workers, or the Algerians, or the Jews, or a hundred other actual men and situations," he wrote. "But I know, too, that Christ is in His Church; even though silenced, or put to shame, or drowned out by cynicism or politics or cowardice."[35]

More aware than ever of the issues of war and peace, Daniel was asked by FOR to join with twenty other Protestants and Catholics in a new experiment in peripatetic ecumenism through the socialist countries. These men were together for most of the summer of 1964 on a tour that included visits to Prague, Hungary, and the U.S.S.R.. While in Prague, they attended the All Christian Peace Conference. Before leaving the socialist countries, the FOR group decided on a series of resolves. The first and most significant was the "necessity of doing our own part in the peace movement in our churches at home." Another stressed the need for "imaginative and prophetic work at home."[36]

The time abroad had also included a visit to Iona Island off the coast of Scotland and a trip to South Africa. These experiences helped develop Daniel Berrigan's ideas on the church and the individual and provided him with a new vision of America and its role in the world. He also felt that the times had changed enough to permit his ideas a possible area of implementation. In his view the Second Vatican Council had stressed the need to remove the church from the power system and, according to Vatican II's document the *Pastoral Constitution on the Church in the Modern World,* encouraged the Christian to see the church's issues as synonymous with the individual's and to start serving the world by applying the Beatitudes literally. Also, the pressure of world conscience was upon the church, allowing her to remove herself from methods of repression and coercion as evidenced in the Vatican II's *Declaration on Religious Freedom.* This new vision of America and its role in the world would be applied to the war in Vietnam as it continued to be escalated. [37]

In September 1964, Daniel returned to the United States to serve as assistant editor of *Jesuit Missions* magazine, headquartered in New York. He again frequented Mount Saviour, AID, and the Catholic Worker but as a new man fortified by his European experience. The question now paramount in his mind was what should he do in face of the war. Daniel and Philip, at the urging of John Heidbrink, gathered together individuals from the Catholic Worker to begin CPF. Daniel Berrigan and John Heidbrink worked out the structures of CPF and raised enough money for the salary of the first director, James Forest. Convinced by Philip Berrigan to assume the directorship of CPF, Forest and Philip along with Martin Corbin became the national co-chairs. [38] Daniel Berrigan together with Dorothy Day, Archbishop Thomas Roberts, Thomas Merton, and a few others served as national sponsors.

Involvement in the peace issue did not mean the end of other participation. In March 1965, both Berrigan brothers joined the civil rights group in Selma. They also continued their priestly functions of celebrating liturgy and counseling those with personal problems, but most of their energies were spent in working for peace and developing CPF. Both brothers spent as much time as possible writing and speaking on peace. While Daniel Berrigan was the best known nationally, Philip spent more time in the actual running of CPF during its formative period. Both men contributed most of what they earned on the road to the CPF, and it in turn provided a community of conscience for them as for all the others involved. Who was influencing whom at this time is difficult to measure. [39] Jim Forest and Tom Cornell both felt that they had contributed significantly toward Daniel Berrigan's becoming a full-blown activist. Certainly Philip Berrigan always was an activist. [40] In any event, Daniel was beyond the activism of these men as they all attest, for his action was always rooted in the theological, and his vision of the dimensions of each action went beyond history and gave the Catholic peace movement a prophetic, eschatological quality.

In October 1964, a number of clergymen felt compelled to protest the charges which had been lodged against dissenters, particularly against the young people opposed to the draft. About twenty clergymen of the New York area called a press conference. It was Rabbi Abraham Heschel who gave the most definitive assurances to the press when they were asked about continuing activities. So in a sense it might be said that he conceived the idea of forming an organization that later became known as Clergy and Laity Concerned About Vietnam (CALCAV). The group caucused on the question that afternoon and Rabbi Abraham Heschel, Daniel Berrigan, and Richard John Neuhaus were chosen co-chairs. Berrigan was actively engaged in the planning and organization of this ecumenical group of clerics until he was sent on his Latin American journey.[41]

In March 1965, after President Johnson took a crucial escalatory step and ordered retaliatory bombing attacks against North Vietnam, Philip and Daniel Berrigan were the only American Catholic priests to promise total "noncooperation" with the nation's Vietnam policies by signing a "Declaration of Conscience." The statement advocated draft resistance. Among other signers were Martin Luther King, Jr., and Bayard Rustin from the civil rights movement and Benjamin Spock from the peace movement. The repercussions of the act came in October 1965, when David Miller, a former student of Daniel's at LeMoyne and a member of CPF, burned his draft card after passage of the law that made such an act a felony. On 6 November 1965, Thomas Cornell, co-chair of CPF along with four other members of the American peace movement also burned their draft cards. The actions of these men, especially the Catholic Workers and CPF members weighed heavily on the consciences of the Berrigan brothers. Miller and Cornell were risking so much and even going to jail for peace—what were they as priests doing for peace?

In November 1965, Daniel faced a crisis within the Society of Jesus just as Philip had previously met at Newburgh—the only difference was that the disciplinary action taken against Daniel was more severe. It not only meant a transfer, but literally an exile to South America to silence him on the peace issue in the United States. Because of the contradictions in accounts in the *New York Times*, the *National Catholic Reporter*, and *America*, it was evident that there was duplicity on the part of the church authorities concerned. In his autobiography, Daniel was to write about this Jesuit attempt at a cover-up. "Exile? Of course not," he said. "I was sent on a 'routine assignment' to Latin America, as editor of a Jesuit magazine, to file reports on the work of Latin Jesuits. It was contemptible and saddening. For the first time, I had cause to be ashamed of my order, its honorable name, the history of holiness and probity I treasured."⁴² At the time when Daniel was exiled, two other Jesuit priests, Francis Keating and Daniel Kilfoyle of St. Peters College in New Jersey, were also silenced because of their activities in the peace movement.⁴³

Daniel Berrigan's exile generated a quick reaction. Heschel and Neuhaus issued a joint statement of protest when Berrigan, a co-chair of CALCAV, was exiled. Fifty Fordham students picketed Cardinal Spellman's residence and other people demonstrated at Marquette, St. John's, and Fordham universities demanding Berrigan's return. The Protestant *Christian Century* stated, "These actions appear to be a high-handed exercise of ecclesiastical authority to silence Priests who champion unpopular views."⁴⁴ On 5 December 1965, in the *New York Times* an ad appeared entitled an "Open Letter to the Authorities of the Archdiocese of New York and the Jesuit Community in New York." The ad was financed by an ad hoc organization, the Institute for Freedom in the Church, composed of lay Catholics who protest, Daniel said, "if someone gets kicked around." And several hundred young Jesuits threatened to leave the order if he was not recalled. Without this public protest and display of united effort for an individual's freedom of conscience within the church, Daniel would probably never have been permitted to return to New York and to continue his peace activities. The authorities of the church could not silence the conscience of Daniel Berrigan and never again would they attempt to silence or discipline the Berrigan brothers in their quest for peace. This would not be true, however, of the government of the United States.

The exile in Latin America lasted three months. While there Berrigan wrote *Consequences, Truth and . . .* in which he presented the church at the edge of new opportunities. To be successful, he contended, the church must be a revolutionary force in society by rejecting power and prestige and choosing to serve all of humankind by making institutions more humane. The exile served only to radicalize him and intensify his commitment to peace. After Berrigan's return he participated in many peace actions all over the country, but especially in New York City. On 30 March 1966, he participated in the Interfaith Peace March, which included a prayer service at St. Patrick's Cathedral in New York City. On 4 July 1966, he spoke of the need to stop the bombing and to begin negotiations. By June 1966, however, he was working mainly out of the CPF—partly because of his individual style and also because other organizations such as CALCAV were too bureaucratic and concerned about their middle-class constituency.

During this period, Daniel Berrigan continued to write. His poetry received increasing attention and criticism because it was said to have lost its universal quality by alliance with a particular ideology. Even *No One Walks Waters* was criticized in this manner by the *New York Times*. His most unique book, *Love, Love at the End*, a collection of poems, fables, and prayers, received the severest criticism because of its obscurity. Daniel was also finding difficulty locating a place for himself within the Jesuit community. In September 1967, he accepted the offer to become the associate director for service on the Cornell United Religious Work staff. By this time Berrigan felt that the contribution he could make to the specifically Catholic structure was pretty well ended. In an article, "Berrigan at Cornell" he explained his decision and went on to state that the times called for Catholics to integrate and reform themselves and make their values amenable to those who were passionately interested in entering communion with the Catholic tradition, and that humankind was in desperate need of such resources. Yet, he also contended that the church and society were almost at the dead end of their resources and that the moral individual would only take on an understanding of self through the poet, the sacrificial student, the African American, and the inner-city community. This alone, according to Berrigan, would provide the humaneness to which the Gospel offers its widest options.[45]

In his life at Cornell University he was associated with all and closed to no one. His student contact was as wide and diverse as the people at the university. He worked in the resistance movement and still functioned within CPF. Once again he assumed the role of teacher with courses in modern drama and the New Testament.[46]

In October 1967, Daniel Berrigan attended the March on the Pentagon with the Cornell University contingent. At midnight, October 22, he was arrested at the Pentagon for a misdemeanor for "refusing to move on when told" and was placed in jail for the first time. In his "Letter from Three Jails" he wrote that two reflections occurred to him: "1. Why was I so long retarded from so crucially formative a happening? 2. What's the big joke, You there?" On Friday, October 27, just after his release, he heard a radio report of the arrest of Philip and three others for pouring blood on selective service files in Baltimore.

In February 1968, Tom Hayden invited Daniel Berrigan and Howard Zinn to be representatives of the resistance in America and go to Hanoi to obtain the release of three war prisoners: Captain John D. Block, Major Norris M. Overly, and Ensign David P. Matheny. It was again time for Berrigan to witness the horrendous sights of poverty and death. But this time more trauma would result because he would be under the fire of his own country's bombs and witness the war atrocities caused by his countrymen. He was to label Vietnam as the "land of burning children," a recurring theme to be used by the Catholic Resistance. As Berrigan reflected on why he had had this experience he wrote: "I do not as yet know what its import is but I shortly will. . . . To have seen the truth has its price attached."[47]

When Daniel returned home he attended Philip's trial and wrote "My Brother, the Witness."[48] The trial resulted in a conviction of Philip Berrigan and the three others who had joined him. The trial was not widely publicized and Philip's testimony at the trial was direct, simple, and hard-hitting. There was no drama. Philip Berrigan just laid things out as he saw them. By Easter of 1968, he and Tom Lewis were planning a second action drawing on their experience from the October event. Philip Berrigan was doing most of the contact work, approaching people at Cornell, in Mobile, in Boston, and in New York. David Darst was the contact in St. Louis and George Mische was instrumental in getting the Melvilles involved. The idea of napalm came from Tom Lewis and Philip Berrigan, who saw firsthand that the people did not perceive the symbolism of pouring blood, but were convinced that they could not miss the one of napalm. The courage of Philip Berrigan and Tom Lewis and the constant reaffirmation of their presence in the action and of the price they would have to pay strengthened the wills of the others. Daniel decided to be a part of the action only five days before the event occurred.[49] Even the night before, if he did not call his brother Jerome by ten in the morning, it meant that he had decided to act. The final decision was an extremely difficult one for Daniel Berrigan to make.

Many factors entered into the final decision. For years Daniel had lived with the peace movement. He had tried every legitimate means to bring about peace. His friends and followers had even been jailed with no cleric going with them. He had written books and lectured widely on peace and as he told his friend, Paul Mayer, "They slap me on the back and tell me how great I am and nothing happens."[50] All of these things were true of his brother Philip as well, he realized, as he attempted to make the final decision. Daniel Berrigan had also traveled around the world and had seen the poverty and suffering of the majority of people and could not help but compare it to the affluence of America and America's erroneous foreign policy. Though his brother Philip had been limited mainly to sights of poverty in America, especially African American poverty, Daniel knew that he had come to the same conclusions. Next, Daniel Berrigan carried the Society of Jesus with him in his every action. This was an extremely significant factor, for relations with the Jesuits had become increasingly tenuous as his actions for peace escalated. Yet, his brother had similar experiences with the Josephites though they were a less prestigious religious community. Finally, on the eve of the Catonsville action, Philip and Daniel spent the night discussing the pros and cons of the action. With Philip's emphasis on the practical and political and Daniel's emphasis on the ideal and spiritual, it was a soul-searching time for both brothers. The end result was that Daniel joined Philip and the seven others the next morning at Catonsville. After the arrests, the nine were released, each on $2,500 bail. While awaiting the trial on 7 October 1968, the nine began an extensive speaking tour to explain the reasons for their action at Catonsville.

Ironically, the Jesuits did not evict Daniel Berrigan from the community as a result of Catonsville. Rather, a movement began among the rank and file to support him. The Jesuits used the theme: "Our Brother Is In Need," and stressed the right of freedom of conscience. During the week the trial began the Jesuit church and hall of St. Ignatius Parish in Baltimore was used as the gathering place for the nine. Religious services and rallies were held. Peace activists from all over the United States came to participate in a parade to protest the trial of the Catonsville Nine. The trial proceeded for three days during which time the defendants admitted that they had napalmed the files. Just before the verdict was returned, Federal Judge Roszel C. Thomsen engaged in a rather informal discourse with the Catonsville Nine. It seemed to be painful for the judge to arraign people whose intensity of moral passion and accumulated years of service to others rendered them anything but "convicted felons." After all was said, Daniel Berrigan ended the trial the way he had ended the action at Catonsville by praying the Our Father.

The action and the trial of the Catonsville Nine left no doubt to many observers that their moral commitment to peace was so great that it had called them forth to this ultra form of resistance. This commitment revealed to the public that they believed civil disobedience was the required action for those who wanted to follow Christ. It was necessary because the evils in America had become so great. The seriousness of poverty, racial conflict, urban riots, and returning missionaries in reaching negative judgments about U.S. foreign policy combined with the illegality and immorality of the war in Vietnam to create in the Catonsville Nine an alienation from U.S. society. The nine attempted to express this link between injustice and war in their trial. They tried to explain that the evils of injustice and war had extended into every aspect of American life and necessitated an action such as theirs from a moral people. Through civil disobedience these people sought to overhaul the inefficient, cumbersome, and corrupt governmental machinery and its archaic policies of war, racism, and exploitation. Despite their moral plea, a verdict of guilty was returned against each defendant on each of three counts: destruction of U.S. property, destruction of selective service records, and interference with the Selective Service Act of 1967. The convicted proceeded to appeal the decision.[51]

The action itself had been an open and peaceful violation of the law done in obedience to their conscience. It was a so-called "stand-by" action where people openly remained awaiting arrest. These protestors emulated Gandhi, Thoreau, and Martin Luther King, Jr., and other apostles of civil disobedience who were prepared to go to jail for violating the law, even though they thought the law was unjust. Some members of the traditional peace groups believed that they had gone too far by destroying property and breaking and entering. Even though

Dorothy Day was critical of their destruction of property, she continued to support them.

Soon after Catonsville, similar draft board actions occurred in Milwaukee and Chicago, cities with traditionally strong centers of the Catholic Worker from which participants could easily be recruited. These individuals prided themselves on individual acts of conscience and while they admired the Berrigans, they considered neither them nor anyone else to be their leaders per se.

At the time Catonsville occurred, publicity reached a high point and focused on the Berrigan brothers. "Support groups" surrounding the nine began to flourish and a defense committee to raise funds for the trial was also formed. Basically, the nine, the support groups, and the defense committee began to promote themselves as a Christian community. It was a fragile group of volunteers who based their community on love and trust and advocated civil disobedience as the form of protest against the war in Vietnam. Initiation into the inner core of the community was an act of civil disobedience at a draft board. The action was meant to symbolize their unwillingness to allow or permit the uncritical adaptation of Christianity to the society in which they lived. Consequently, the emphasis was on Christianity's conflict with the present war-making policy of their country.

In 1969, the Catholic Resistance underwent significant changes. First, a group calling themselves the D.C.-Nine raided the Dow Chemical office in the nation's capital. This attack on a corporation broadened the targets of the movement to include corporations that produced war materials such as napalm. Second, the members of the New York Eight draft board group did not stand by and await arrest after their action. This group destroyed the draft files at night and later "surfaced." The choice of a night tactic was first used by the New York group to avoid any possible harm to individuals in the selective service office at the time of the raid. The New York Eight's tactic of "surfacing" consisted of calling a press conference and at it Neil McLaughlin, a Baltimore priest, read a statement signed by the eight which claimed moral responsiblity for the draft board action.[52] Surprisingly to the participants, no arrests followed. The reason was lack of evidence. Up to this point most people who had performed draft board actions had come from the Catholic fold: priests, nuns, and lay people who were highly educated and middle class.

The tactic of "night actions" and "surfacing" was adopted by subsequent groups, such as, the Boston Eight, the Beaver Fifty-five, the East Coast Conspiracy to Save Lives, the Flower City Conspiracy, and the Camden Twenty-eight. The exact number of draft board actions to occur between Philip Berrigan's first draft board raid at the Custom's House in Baltimore on 27 October 1967, to the Camden Twenty-eight action on 22 August 1971 is unknown. Theodore Glick, a draft resister and participant in the East Coast Conspiracy to Save Lives and the Flower City Conspiracy, and indicted conspirator in the Harrisburg trial, has estimated that over 250 draft board actions occurred during the time period.[53] Philip Berrigan estimates the number at two hundred actions. And Charles Meconis, a Catholic writer and resister, claimed that altogether some fifty-three draft board actions took place.[54] As the number of actions increased and the members of the resistance became more diverse, the term Catholic Resistance began to lose some of its denominational significance. Many non-Catholics joined the movement and did so from humanitarian and political motivation. Change from the more traditional stand-by action of civil disobedience to night actions and surfacing signalled another departure in the Catholic Resistance. Both represented a decline in emphasis on Christian witness and symbolic action and a greater desire for political effectiveness.

In addition to these actions, one other raid of significance occurred during the time period—a raid on the files of the FBI office in Media, Pennsylvania. This was a night action, but no one ever surfaced to assume moral responsibility, nor was anyone ever prosecuted for the action.[55] The documents taken from the raid were published in the periodical WIN. The newspapers carried front page stories on the documents and some excerpts. The documents did detail FBI success at infiltrating college campuses with informers who gathered information on professors as well as students and there was also an internal memorandum that proposed actions to intensify paranoia within the peace movement over infiltration by the FBI.[56]

The man who attempted to build this community of resistance and organize draft board actions was Philip Berrigan. After Catonsville, Daniel Berrigan returned to Cornell University to resume his teaching duties and to write and speak on behalf of the peace movement. Philip, on the other hand, was relieved of any specific duties by his religious superior, and resided at the Josephite Provincialate in Baltimore. From this point of official residence he spent most of his time traveling in hopes of locating people who sympathized with the draft board action and would be possible recruits for future actions. Philip Berrigan believed the draft board community was too elitist and wanted to widen it, but the lack of developing any tactic beyond draft board and corporation raids limited the possibility. Catholicism and the church were central to Philip Berrigan's personal motivation for action, but he did not make this motivation a prerequisite for participation. The only requirement that he had was that participants shared his political analysis and wanted to stop the war in Vietnam through nonviolent direct acts of civil disobedience. With night actions and surfacing even the degree of risk and assumption of personal responsibility was lessened as a prerequisite—there was now a possibility that one would not have to go to jail. The technique used by Berrigan for building such a community of resistance was called a retreat, one or more weekends to discover whether or not an individual would engage in such an action. Philip served as a benevolent facilitator and counselor, being sure that people of like mind were brought together, that people's needs were taken care of, and that precautions and planning had been carried out in full. Philip's long-time friend, John P. Grady, often assisted the participants in the planning of the action. The decision to act and the actual plans of the action were worked out by the members themselves in the group they had formed. Thus, technically, Philip Berrigan was not the leader and not a participant in each action that occurred.[57]

The switch to night actions and surfacing also reflected a change in attitude concerning arrest and jail. Some members were no longer willing to await arrest and go to jail for an action they believed to be morally correct while the draft and complicity of corporations continued unhampered in its perpetuation of an immoral war. This change in the Catholic Resistance also had its effect on the Berrigan brothers themselves.

By 9 April 1970, the appeals of both Berrigan brothers after the Catonsville trial had expired and they were to report to jail on that day. Between October 1967 and April 1970, Philip Berrigan had not spent a full year in jail and Daniel had spent only a few days in jail. Both brothers agreed not to report, but rather to appear publicly first and afterward be hauled away by federal marshals. Daniel Berrigan was to appear at the Cornell Peace Rally on 19 April 1970 and Philip was to appear at the Church of St. Gregory the Great in Manhattan's Upper West Side two evenings later.

On April 19, Daniel Berrigan appeared before ten thousand people at the Cornell peace rally weekend, which was held in his honor and called "America is Hard to Find." At the evening "freedom Seder" Berrigan appeared and gave an impassioned plea for resistance. After the Bread and Puppet Theater had finished its mime of the Last Supper, the lights went out. At that point Daniel was concealed under an immense papier-mache head of an apostle and made his escape. In the darkness of the auditorium he hopped into the figure and walked outside into a truck. In minutes he was transferred to a car and successfully began his four-month underground escapade as a fugitive from justice. The engineer of Daniel Berrigan's underground existence was at the time the relatively unknown Pakistani, Eqbal Ahmad, a fellow at Chicago's Adlai Stevenson Institute for International Affairs.[58]

The FBI agents, embarrassed by his escape, began a series of frantic searches for Daniel. Afraid that Philip would attempt the same type of escape, they sought to capture him before his appearance at the peace rally at 8:00 P.M. at St. Gregory the Great Church. Philip along with David Eberhardt, a fellow fugitive from the Baltimore Four draft board conviction had slipped into the rectory before dawn on April 21. At mid-afternoon the FBI agents entered the rectory and located Philip and David Eberhardt in a closet in the bedroom of the pastor, Henry Browne. The closet was in reality an "inner closet" which had been overlooked by all but one agent.[59] The fugitives were taken to the Federal House of Detention in New York City.

Despite the arrest, over five hundred people assembled at the evening rally. Howard Zinn, a political science professor at Boston University who had accompanied Daniel Berrigan on the trip to Hanoi, Eqbal Ahmad, and Felipe Luciano, a Young Lord, were the featured speakers. Over one hundred FBI agents were also present hoping to capture Daniel Berrigan. The pastor, Henry Browne, presided over the rally and blended together the menagerie of hippies, peace movement people, Black Panthers, Young Lords, professors, middle-class sympathizers, nuns and priests, FBI agents, and even a group of parishioners who staged a counterdemonstration in protest of the church being used as a sanctuary for Philip Berrigan.[60]

The next day Philip Berrigan and David Eberhardt were taken to

Lewisburg Federal Prison and placed in maximum security for the four months that Daniel Berrigan was underground. The two men believed that prison officials unduly punished them in order to put pressure on Daniel Berrigan in the hope that he might give himself up.

Philip Berrigan had never considered the underground as a viable political option for himself, and for the week before they surfaced, Daniel and Philip engaged in heated debates as to its viability. Daniel Berrigan strongly favored it and Philip opposed it.[61] Philip Berrigan's arrest was no shock, but the constant hassle of prison authorities and being placed in maximum security at Lewisburg was. In fact the imprisonment began to affect the psychological stability of both Philip Berrigan and David Eberhardt. On 20 July 1970, Robert Coles, a Harvard research psychiatrist examined both men and found it to be so.[62] Senator Charles Goodell of New York and others were recruited to confront the director of the Bureau of Prisons, Norman A. Carlson, about the harrassment. In July 1970, a demonstration at the prison was held to protest the maximum security confinement. There was no let up on the treatment by prison officials until Daniel Berrigan's capture. On 25 August 1970 Philip Berrigan was transferred to the federal prison in Danbury, Connecticut.

Because of Daniel Berrigan's talents as a writer, he viewed the underground as a means of amplifying—not muting—his propagandizing ability through the media. He believed the media would be more likely to publish the words of a fugitive priest than of a cleric not on the run. He also saw his fugitive status as a way to involve more and more middle-class people in a much deeper commitment to the peace movement by harboring him than they otherwise would make.[63] Thus, Berrigan mainly viewed the underground as an experiment—once there he did not know what would happen. While he was underground, both of these beliefs were realized. On 26 April 1970 the *New York Times* published an interview with him held in a Manhattan walk-up apartment. The following month the *Saturday Review* featured Berrigan writing on the twenty-fifth anniversary of the death of Dietrich Bonhoeffer, a German Lutheran clergyman executed on Hitler's orders for his role in the resistance inside wartime Germany. In August, the premier of his play, *The Trial of the Catonsville Nine*, occurred in Los Angeles. And on Sunday, August 2, John C. Raines, an assistant professor of religion at Temple University, invited Daniel Berrigan to preach at the First United Methodist Church in Germantown, Pennsylvania, where Raines's brother was pastor. Berrigan's sermon lasted twenty minutes, received wide press coverage, and caused great embarrassment to the FBI. During his four months underground, Daniel stayed with thirty-seven families and over two hundred people assisted in making arrangements for his resistance.

But in August, Daniel Berrigan did not follow the advice of his underground organizer Eqbal Ahmad, who had warned him to stay away from life-time friends. Berrigan went to the home of William Stringfellow and Anthony Towne on Block Island, twelve miles off the coast of Rhode Island. While staying there, he spent much of his time working on the manuscript for his *The Dark Night of Resistance*, which he dedicated to his two friends: "To Bill and Tony, for I was homeless and you gave me shelter." On August 11, FBI agents, posing as birdwatchers, arrested him.

The reason for the capture was that Elizabeth McAlister, R.S.C.J., in her letters to Philip Berrigan at Lewisburg prison had mentioned that Daniel Berrigan was going to stay with William Stringfellow. At the time neither Elizabeth McAlister nor Philip Berrigan knew that their smuggled letters were being read by prison officials and FBI agents.[64]

Daniel Berrigan had considered the underground an experiment and from the very beginning he did not know how long it could be sustained. His success at living this form of resistance had serious implications for the future of the Catholic Resistance. First, it considerably escalated and intensified the widening gap between conscience and cooperation with the government. The reason Berrigan gave for his underground experiment was:

Can Christians unthinkingly submit before such powers (war makers)? We judge not. The "powers and dominations" remain subject to Christ; our consciences are in his keeping and no other. To act as though we were criminals before God or humanity, to cease resisting a war which has immeasurably widened since we first acted, to retire meekly to silence and isolation—this seems to Phil and me a betrayal of our ministry.[65]

The resistance and refusal to accept jail on the part of Daniel Berrigan offended not only government authorities but also traditional adherents of civil disobedience who willingly accepted jail for violations of the law.

Second, Berrigan's underground existence encouraged the overreaction of government officials who in 1970 were filled with fear of bombings, political kidnappings, and security leaks in Washington, D.C. The Watergate hearings in 1973 revealed that the threat which the Berrigan brothers posed and the fear that this engendered on the part of government officials was greater than anyone imagined three years earlier.

Third, Daniel Berrigan's writings during his underground experience repeatedly contended that the social institutions in America were corrupt and that idolatry undergirded the value system of America. The writings called no longer for reform, but for revolution. The underground symbolized his radical break with existing American institutions.

By August 25, both Philip and Daniel Berrigan were behind bars in Danbury Federal Penitentiary. Ironically, jail was not to mean silence and isolation for the Berrigan brothers, but rather a new and intensified position of national prominence. This change can be credited to the efforts of J. Edgar Hoover, director of the Federal Bureau of Investigation.

On November 27, before a Senate Appropriations Committee hearing and to the press, Hoover hinted at an East Coast Conspiracy to Save Lives, whose members he alleged were planning to kidnap and bomb to achieve their ends. These people were a great threat to the internal security of the United States. Seven weeks later on 12 January 1971 major newspapers were called to send correspondents to a Justice Department public information meeting. John W. Huske of the department appeared carrying stacks of a four-page press release and an eleven-page indictment. Both handouts made no mention of Hoover's previous statement and his Senate testimony outlining a plot and alleging it to be the work of the East Coast Conspiracy to Save Lives.[66] Six persons were indicted on charges of plotting to blow up heating systems of federal buildings in the nation's capital and also to kidnap presidential advisor Henry Kissinger. The six people who were indicted were: Philip Berrigan, Elizabeth McAlister, Eqbal Ahmad, Anthony Scoblick, and two diocesan priests from Baltimore, Neil McLaughlin and Joseph Wenderoth. The punishment indicated in the indictment if they were convicted of the kidnap conspiracy count was a maximum of life imprisonment and/or a general conspiracy conviction with a five-year maximum in prison. Philip Berrigan and Elizabeth McAlister were also charged with three counts each of attempting to smuggle communications in and out of Lewisburg Penitentiary with a conviction of a single count punishable of up to ten years imprisonment.

The indictment also contained a list of twenty-two overt acts beginning 1 April 1970 and named seven co-conspirators: Daniel Berrigan, Jogues Egan, R.S.C.J., Beverly Bell, S.N.D., Majorie Shuman, Paul Mayer, William Davidon, and Thomas Davidson. Guy L. Goodwin was named the government's attorney. On January 13, Goodwin began a grand jury investigation in which Jane Hoover and Betsy Sandel, Patricia Rom, Zoia Horn, Robert Joynt, his sister Patricia Chanel, and Jogues Egan were subpoenaed to testify. After being granted immunity, all testified before the grand jury except Sister Jogues Egan who was cited with contempt.

The efforts of Egan's attorney, Jack Levine, a young Philadelphia lawyer, resulted in her case being heard by the Pennsylvania Supreme Court.[67] In 1972, the court rejected the stance taken by the Justice Department in the Jogues Egan contempt case. It established the precedent that grand jury witnesses threatened with contempt for refusing to testify could require the government to disclose whether they had been subpoenaed because of information gained from wiretaps. If the government refused to reveal such information, contempt charges would be dropped. It was a choice prosecutors did not make in this case.

The Jogues Egan case became significant not only in legal history and subsequent Senate investigations of Watergate but also to a reconvening of the Harrisburg grand jury. Two weeks after the indictment had been issued, William S. Lynch, the most able prosecutor in the Criminal Division of the Justice Department, was assigned to replace Goodwin as chief prosecuting attorney in the Harrisburg case. The reason for this change was the desperate desire of J. Edgar Hoover, John Mitchell, and Robert C. Mardian, assistant attorney general for the Internal Security Division, to win the case.

Lynch agreed to take the case on the condition that he could issue a "superseding indictment." The new indictment was structured in such a way that the government would not have to prove either the kidnapping or the bombing allegation in order to obtain a conviction on the overall conspiracy charge. Draft board raids would be sufficient for conviction. The new indictment added two defendants, Mary Cain Scoblick and John Theodore Glick, who was already serving time for the Flower City Conspiracy draft board raid. The indictment dropped as coconspirators Daniel Berrigan, Paul Mayer, and Thomas Davidson. Thus, one Berrigan, Daniel, was subtracted from the case, but Glick joined Joseph Wenderoth as the second member of the eleven-member East Coast Conspiracy to Save Lives to be indicted. Before the trial began Susan Davis, S.N.D., another member of the East Coast Conspiracy, and John Swinglish, head of the Catholic Peace Fellowship in Washington, D.C., were added to the list of named coconspirators.

The new indictment also included a maximum of five years imprisonment upon conviction. The irony of the "superseding indictment" was that it was issued without any new evidence being obtained.[68] On April 20, ten days before it was issued, twenty-five persons were subpoenaed to testify before the grand jury in Harrisburg. The people subpoenaed were all linked to the Catholic Resistance through draft board raids or the Harrisburg Defense Committee work. The exception was the in-laws of Eqbal Ahmad, Mr. and Mrs. Abraham Diamond. Of the twenty-five people subpoenaed only the Diamonds testified. Everyone else refused to testify and seven of the twenty-five received contempt sentences. No one was placed in jail pending the Jogues Egan case. As a result, no one cited with contempt, except for Jogues Egan, ever went to jail. Because of the silence of the subpoenaed (unlike Lynch's experience in criminal cases in which individuals talked in exchange for immunity), no new information pertaining to the case was gained by the grand jury. Despite these events, the superseding indictment was still issued on April 30.

Those indicted in the Harrisburg Eight case began meeting weekly at the Danbury Federal Prison to prepare their defense. Three nationally known lawyers were selected by the defendants, Ramsey Clark, Leonard Boudin, and Paul O'Dwyer.[69] Before the trial began Theodore Glick was dropped from the case because he wanted to defend himself. Finally on 25 January 1972 the three-month trial of the Harrisburg Seven opened in the Middle District of Pennsylvania. Judge R.

Dixon Herman, a Nixon appointee and former juvenile court judge, presided. Six of the seven indicted at the time were Roman Catholic clergy—priests and nuns—members of the Catholic Resistance.

Central to the case of the Catholic team of prosecutors, William Lynch, John Connally, and John Cattone, were letters between Philip Berrigan and Elizabeth McAlister written during Berrigan's imprisonment. Boyd Douglas, a convict turned informer had been the carrier of the letters. He had copied the letters and turned the copies over to the FBI.[70] In retrospect, since the public announcement of the marriage of Elizabeth McAlister and Philip Berrigan on Memorial Day 1973, the letters can now be viewed in their proper perspective and understood in terms of love, fidelity, duty, and fantasy between a couple dedicated to a cause. These considerations far outweigh the apparent political naivete of the letters. If there had been no love relationship there would not have been any letters. The final judgment of Boyd Douglas's direct relationship with the FBI as an informer, provocateur, and/or entrapper remained unclear even at the end of the trial. The dramatic readings of the letters and the lengthy testimony of Boyd Douglas provided the bulk of the testimony presented by the prosecution.

Ramsey Clark held the privilege of initiating the case for the defense. He surprisingly stood up and declared: "Your honor, the defendants will always seek peace, the defendants continue to proclaim their innocence—and the defense rests." This decision of silence on the part of the defense had been made by a four to three vote on the part of the defendants. Ahmad, Berrigan, and McAlister had voted against it—desiring to confront the government. Ironically, the person who assumed the leadership in this final decision was not the publicly acclaimed Philip nor the intellectual Eqbal, but the small community of four lesser figures, the Scoblicks and McLaughlin and Wenderoth. The four believed that they made the decision by default of leadership. Ahmad had looked to Berrigan as leader and because of Philip Berrigan's ambiguity between his commitment to resistance and his desire to protect Elizabeth McAlister, he was unable to lead.[71]

The concluding arguments by the lawyers were made and the judge charged the sequestered jury, which had been carefully screened for any religious or political bias during their selection. The verdict was a hung jury with a count of ten to two in favor of acquittal. A mother of four sons who were conscientious objectors to the war in Vietnam and a grocery store owner were the only ones who voted for conviction. Berrigan and McAlister were convicted of smuggling communications in and out of a federal prison. The outcome of the trial resulted in a legal and political victory for the defendants, and a setback for J. Edgar Hoover and President Nixon's Justice Department. Ironically, it was also the deathblow to what had come to be known as the Catholic Resistance.

The Harrisburg prosecution showed clearly in its presentation of evidence, actually its lack of evidence, that the case would never have been brought to trial had not J. Edgar Hoover made his accusations against the Berrigan brothers. Four weeks after the trial had ended, Hoover died of natural causes—a seventy-year-old heart giving out. The decision to prosecute illustrated how susceptible the career staff of the Justice Department could be to non-judicial influences of those running the department. The tactic of a political trial to discredit and destroy the antiwar movement under Nixon's administration was not new. It had been used in the conspiracy trials of Benjamin Spock, the Chicago Seven, the Black Panthers, and after the Harrisburg Seven it would be used again in the Angela Davis trial and the Ellsberg trial. Ironically, the government would lose every case in the courtroom. Yet, it would successfully accomplish the goal of eradicating dissident groups in American society. The government seemed to be losing every battle yet winning the war.

By means of pretrial motions, the defense lawyers were able to win victories through the courts to challenge the illegal practices of the FBI and the Justice Department, such as the use of wiretapping, the use of an informer, illegal search procedures, the use of the grand jury as a fishing expedition, and the use of conspiracy laws for political purposes. All such procedures indicated that the Justice Department under President Nixon's administration had become highly politicized in its efforts to eradicate dissent in the name of internal security and the law. [72]

Even the Bureau of Federal Prisons emerged as subject to the Justice Department's pressure. For no given reason, Philip Berrigan and David Eberhardt had been kept in maximum security rather than the usual procedure of putting draft resisters in minimum security. And the special study release program for prisoners, a rare privilege granted by the U.S.

Bureau of Prisons in Washington, D.C., had been granted to an informer, Boyd Douglas, who was paid by the FBI for his information.[73]

All of these factors take on a new significance in American history since the Senate investigations of Watergate. The politicization of American institutions revealed by Watergate was already evident at the Harrisburg Seven trial where the government served as prosecutor and not as defendant.[74]

During the trial the Roman Catholic church offered no official support for the defendants. Since Catonsville, however, there was personal support from some church leaders. Lawrence Cardinal Shehan, archbishop of Baltimore, had visited the men in jail and had designated the archdiocesan lawyer, Francis X. Gallagher, as one of the defense lawyers. There was also bail money provided and character defense testimony given for the defendants by several priests of the Archdiocese of Baltimore. Individual Catholics and some Catholic groups as well as many individual Americans and groups supported the Harrisburg Seven either through financial donations or participation in functions planned by the publicly accountable Harrisburg Seven Defense Committee. Over one half million dollars was raised by the committee and all except $20,000 was spent on trial expenses.[75]

Tragically, the government's use of a political trial to destroy a dissident group in America once again proved effective. But the demise of the Catholic Resistance and the Berrigan brothers efforts had already occurred even before the trial began. The Vietnam antiwar movement in general had declined early in the Nixon presidency, but regrouped to mount massive demonstrations in the fall of 1969. A brief resurgence occurred with the invasion of Cambodia begun on 30 April 1970. At Kent State on May 4 Ohio national guardsmen fired into a milling crowd of students killing four, wounding thirteen, and raising the American crisis to a new level of anguish. Within days, about half a million students left classes and shut down about a fifth of the nation's campuses for periods ranging from one day to the rest of the academic year. On May 14, Mississippi state police and national guardsmen attacked a dormitory at Jackson State University killing two students. On May 9, over 100,000 people on short notice gathered in Washington to protest Cambodia and Kent State, but it dissipated quickly without leadership. A politics of confrontation seemed to have played itself out among a public afflicted with war weariness.[76] Though the Catholic Resistance and the Berrigan brothers had been a separate peace group within the antiwar movement, they relied heavily on the general antiwar atmosphere. Once troop withdrawal began and the promise of peace appeared imminent, the cause of the Catholic Resistance was no longer of immediate concern to the public. The Harrisburg Seven trial kept it before the public, but the end of the trial abruptly signalled the end of a Catholic resistance to the war in Vietnam.

The group itself also contained its own elements of self-destruction. One factor was that it was a voluntary association of highly mobile and widespread people with no day-to-day leader or community to hold it together. Both Philip and Daniel had very independent styles of operation. Another element that weakened the group was that in the face of troop withdrawal the members themselves became increasingly convinced that the tactic of draft board and corporation raids was no longer an effective means of stopping the war. And finally, the high price of long prison sentences was too great for many of its members to withstand. Thus, a retreat from resistance followed.

Philip Berrigan returned to jail after the trial. Daniel Berrigan who was paroled during the trial, refused in any way to assume the role of leader for the Catholic Resistance and sought a new college teaching position. He did, however, continue to make public-speaking engagements and even appeared on the Dick Cavett Show. On national television, he seemed to alienate his audience. The other defendants in the Harrisburg Seven trial also appeared to seek retreat. The Scoblicks bought a small house in Baltimore and so did McLaughlin and Wenderoth. All four of these defendants sought to live normal lives in a changing neighborhood. Eqbal Ahmad returned to his work at the Adlai Stevenson Institute and Elizabeth McAlister returned to her religious community and assumed a part-time teaching position in a small secular college in New Jersey. McAlister did continue to speak publicly about the future direction of the peace movement, stressing the need to keep building small communities of resistance. This would have to have to wait, however, until Philip Berrigan was released from prison. None of the defendants participated in acts of civil disobedience against the war in Vietnam after the trial and all except McAlister wanted to convey to the American public that they viewed the trial as an intrusion on their personal lives.[77]

Ironically, the prosecution of the Harrisburg Seven achieved a national prominence for these defendants in a way that they could never have achieved by themselves. And in the process, the FBI director was revealed as so powerful a man that the president of the United States chose to ignore Hoover's blatant violation of the Bill of Rights. Such actions seemed only to leave a pall of despair rather than hope across the nation. The trial itself confirmed the Catholic Resistance's critical stand against American institutions. This critical position had its roots in the participants' identification with the oppressed in American society and by 1965 extended to the oppression experienced abroad as the result of the Vietnam War. The religious belief of the Berrigan brothers and the Catholic Resistance motivated their actions on behalf of peace and strengthened them as they attempted to confront their own government and bring it to a position of justice and peace. This religious faith made them unique in the Vietnam antiwar movement. Their religious motivation separated them from the political and secular orientation of the New Left. The political ideology of communism held no attraction for the Catholic Resistance though it reached similar conclusions as the New Left in relation to capitalism and imperialism in America.

Despite the Catholic Resistance's efforts to offer an effective peace witness that would awaken the consciences of the public against the war in Vietnam, the power of the U.S. government prevailed. The more it prevailed, the more the resistance escalated. As the resistance escalated the level of personal commitment required for such a peace witness also increased and not many people were willing to pay that price. For this reason the Catholic Resistance was not able to build a broadly based community of resistance. The significance of the Catholic Resistance was that the people involved did offer a peace witness in face of such power and at great personal sacrifice. As Daniel Berrigan wrote: "Peacemaking is hard hard almost as war."[78]

The Berrigan brothers and their witness for peace emerged from the American Catholic pacifist tradition. As they often acknowledged, they together with the Catholic Resistance came out of the Catholic Worker tradition of pacifism and nonviolence. Dorothy Day put it more bluntly when she said, "The Berrigans came and stole our young men away into the peace movement."[79] Like Day, Philip Berrigan addressed the public order by positing actions for peace and in doing so he escalated the level of nonviolent resistance. Daniel Berrigan because of his theological training and writing ability continued more in the tradition of Thomas Merton rather than Dorothy Day. Just as Merton had attempted to provide a theological rationale for nonviolence within Catholicism, Daniel tried to express a new theology of peace from his experiences within the Catholic Resistance. Like Day and Merton, faith was the center of existence for each brother as they embraced poverty and rooted their faith in the Gospel message and an eschatological vision. The combination of Philip's and Daniel's unique strengths and talents enabled them to bring forth the message of peace to their church and country in a way never before experienced in the history of American Catholicism. The impact of their prophetic message and witness for peace is still being experienced as American Catholics struggle more than ever to determine what it means to be both Catholic and American in a nuclear age.

8

Catholic Peacemaking

IN MAY 1983, THE National Conference of Catholic Bishops (NCCB) issued a pastoral letter on war and peace, *The Challenge of Peace: God's Promise and Our Response*. It was a watershed in the teaching of the Roman Catholic church in America on the issues of war and peace. For the first time since the early Christian period, pacifism and nonviolence were officially recognized as part of the Judeo-Christian tradition. The document also emphasized the different levels of church teaching on war and peace and in an unprecedented manner emphasized the role of individual conscience and the right to dissent. Thus, the document permitted individual Catholics to legitimately disagree on various aspects of war and peace and still remain Catholics in good standing.[1] *The Challenge of Peace* was an attempt to create a new vision of peacemaking for American Catholics. The letter concluded with the following injunction: "Peacemaking is not an optional commitment. It is a requirement of our faith. We are called to be peacemakers, not by some movement of the moment, but by our Lord Jesus. The content and context of our peacemaking is set, not by some political agenda or ideological program, but by the teaching of His Church."[2] The efforts of the American Catholic peace movement to build a pacifist constituency solidly within the institutional church contributed greatly to NCCB's pastoral letter. These efforts to influence the institutional church became most effective in the post–Vietnam War period.

The Catholic peace movement maintained its vigor while the broader American peace movement collapsed after the withdrawal of American soldiers from Vietnam and the end of military induction. The most important reasons why the Catholic peace movement grew in strength was the emergence of a resistance community, Jonah

211

House, the founding of a new organization, Pax Christi–USA, and the publication of the bishops' pastoral. Thus, the Catholic peace movement not only continued its witness after Vietnam but even broadened its constituency among mainline Catholics as it shifted its focus from Vietnam to nuclear issues and concern for Central America.

Although the Catholic Resistance stopped its raids on draft boards after the Harrisburg trial, it gained a new life when Philip Berrigan and Elizabeth McAlister founded Jonah House, which began to function in June 1973 when Berrigan and McAlister, together with a few others, rented a house in the inner city of Baltimore and began what they called a resistance community. Here they pledged to share their incomes and hold property in common and to live a life of voluntary poverty. They also set forth a few principles which would guide their new community:

—Nonviolence, resistance, and community are interchangeable— their effects are identical.
—Contemplation (in whatever form—prayer, meditation, reflection, analysis) gives sustenance to spirit and resistance.
—Holding property in common is essential to justice.
—The Scriptures hold the vision of a society faithful to God whose members are loving toward each other, reverent toward all of life. [3]

In September 1973, Philip Berrigan and Elizabeth McAlister also made public their marriage and were subsequently excommunicated from the Roman Catholic church because neither had been dispensed from their religious vows. Jonah House would be their home during the 1970s and 1980s and there their children, Frida, Jerome, and Katy, were born and raised while the two attempted to build and live a resistance community. Jonah House was in the Catholic Worker tradition but it emphasized resistance rather than the corporal works of mercy.

Members of Jonah House continued their resistance while the broader antiwar movement in America was winding down in 1973. They continued their acts of nonviolent resistance against the war— they would not give up. Again, voluntary acts of civil disobedience were performed to make their point against the war effort and jail sentences were served. Moreover, they always tried to link a religious spirit to their acts of resistance. A brief look at some of their actions in 1973 and 1974 provides some understanding of how they attempted to integrate religion and resistance.

In the summer of 1973, a number of Sisters of Notre Dame de Namur, one of whom lived at Jonah House, began the White House Pray-Ins. Each day two to six people were arrested for kneeling and praying during the White House tour. The pray-ins called for a halt to the intense bombing then under way in Cambodia. At Thanksgiving, Jonah House joined with the Community for Creative Nonviolence (CCNV) in Washington, D.C., at the home of Secretary of State Henry Kissinger where they presented him with a world globe into which was plunged a carving knife and fork. At Christmas, Jonah House again joined with CCNV at the White House, where they celebrated the Feast of Holy Innocents in solidarity against the slaughter of innocent lives resulting from the Christmas bombing of North Vietnam. They also performed the morality play, *Herod and the Kings*, which was followed by a liturgy at the Treasury Building.

In 1974, on the January 27 anniversary of the signing of the Paris Peace Accords, a form of theater was staged in front of the White House to protest the Thieu regime. Each Friday during Lent demonstrations were staged at what Jonah House believed were various seats of oppression in Baltimore: the Baltimore City Jail and Maryland State Penitentiary, the Maryland National Bank, the National Security Agency, the Catholic Center and Cathedral, and the Westinghouse plant. In the summer Jonah House participated in the Tiger Cage demonstrations outside the Capitol Rotunda. And in the fall, three members of Jonah House demonstrated at the National Catholic Shrine in Washington, D.C., during the annual conference of the American Catholic bishops. In March 1975, sixty-two people, including Daniel Berrigan and five others from Jonah House, were arrested at the White House for sitting in as a protest to President Ford's amnesty program. These were the type of activities that Jonah House promoted and over 116 such acts of resistance were performed between 1973 and 1988.[4]

The end of the American presence in Indochina in April 1975 coincided with the beginning of Jonah House's antinuclear work. The primary focus of their resistance was a continuing presence at the Pentagon. Disarmament was the aim. Other demonstrations were held at the White House, the State Department, the Congress, the Department of Energy, and the Air and Space Museum. When Philip Berrigan was in jail again in 1977, he began to focus on the "bomb." The issue consumed him more and more. He believed that it threatened not only human life but the planet itself, that he had to do something to prevent a nuclear holocaust. Berrigan searched for ways to respond to the situation and returned to the draft board actions of the Vietnam era. He decided to use the Judeo-Christian symbol of blood, which he would pour over nuclear warheads. Standby actions whereby he would await arrest rather than night actions would be the preferred course of action because it was more in accord with traditional nonviolence.

On 9 September 1980 Philip Berrigan and his brother Daniel along with six others entered a General Electric plant in King of Prussia, Pennsylvania, where the nose cones for the Mark 12A nuclear warheads were manufactured. There they enacted the biblical prophecies of Isaiah 2:4 and Micah 4:3 to "beat swords into plowshares" by hammering on two of the nose cones and pouring blood on documents. Daniel Berrigan has written regarding the action: "We have been at this for years—dramatic events orchestrated, arbitrary but intensely traditional, liturgical, illegal, in every case wrenching the actors out of routine and community life to face the music, face the public, face the jury."[5] In February 1981, the eight underwent a jury trail in Norristown, Pennsylvania. Because the court suppressed individual testimony about the reasons for their symbolic destruction of the warheads in protest of U.S. nuclear war—denied the right to bring forth testimony during the trial—the eight were able to appeal their guilty verdict. The Pennsylvania Superior Court reversed their conviction in February 1984, but the State of Pennsylvania then appealed that decision and the case went to a Superior Court of Appeals panel. The case was finally resolved ten years later. On 11 April 1990, Judge James E. Buckingham of Montgomery County Court of Common Pleas told the eight defendants that they would have to serve twenty-three months in county jail if they were convicted of any more antiwar activity in the next twenty-three months, "a condition that the defendants told the judge they might not be able to fulfill."[6]

Convinced of the significance of the Plowshares actions, three years after the incident at King of Prussia, Elizabeth McAlister and other resisters entered Griffiss Air Force Base near Rome, New York, and damaged some nuclear bomb-carrying equipment in a hangar before being detected by security police. McAlister served two years in prison. Philip Berrigan served as both father and mother to his children during McAlister's imprisonment. From 1980 to 1986 a total of seventeen Plowshares and related disarmament actions were performed. Twenty people who had participated in these disarmament actions were serving prison sentences ranging from one year to eighteen years, while a few others were on probation.[7] By 1990, an estimated total of thirty-five similar demonstrations by other Plowshares groups at nuclear weapons factories and military bases in the United States and Europe had occurred.[8]

In each of the jury trials following the Plowshares actions the participants were denied use of the defense that their actions were legally justified due to the threat posed by nuclear weapons and they were not allowed to present expert testimony. This had not been the case with the draft board actions of the Vietnam era. Moreover, lengthy prison terms applied by the judges in some of the cases were extreme compared to those given to the participants in the draft board actions. The price attached to performing such actions in the 1980s was much greater. Furthermore the absence of testimony in the court rooms denied the drama necessary to attract media coverage.

Daniel Berrigan raised the question of why an individual should perform such actions and answered in the following manner:

> Worth it for ourselves . . . —yes. Such an act must be taken. . . . The value of the act is thus measured by the sacrifice required to do it; an old and honored Christian idea. . . . We held our liturgy the night before, broke the bread, passed the cup. Light of head, heavy of heart, we nonetheless celebrated by anticipation the chancey event of the following day; and the trial to come; and the penalty. Our Logic? the body was "broken for you," the cup "poured out for all."

He goes on to try to answer the larger meaning of the Plowshares action and its value for the church and the public:

> Value is created, so to speak, in the breach, in a decision to gather, unite voices in an outcry, to precipitate a crisis that, will strip away the mask of evil.

But I know of no sure way of predicting where things will go from there, whether others will hear and respond, or how quickly or slowly. Or whether the act will fail to vitalize others, will come to a grinding halt then and there, its actors stigmatized or dismissed as fools. One swallows dry and takes a chance.[9]

The only two people continually living at Jonah House from 1973 to 1990 were Philip Berrigan and Elizabeth McAlister. Daniel Berrigan has always lived with other Jesuits in New York City. This raises the question of how Philip Berrigan and Elizabeth McAlister sustained themselves for so many years in trying to build a resistance community. For them the foremost reason was their marriage. As they put it: "Our marriage was a grace. . . . We were able to keep each other's courage up, to gain new perspectives, new energies."[10] They also had Jerome and Carol Berrigan whose home in Syracuse was a home away from home, as well as Daniel's encouragement, support, and frequent participation in actions. In the attempt to build community at Jonah House many people came and left. Some moved in other directions and some moved out to begin their own resistance communities. Philip Berrigan and Elizabeth McAlister explained the tribulations of trying to form a resistance community when they wrote the story of their lives at Jonah House, *The Time's Discipline: The Beatitudes and Nuclear Resistance*.

During those early years there was never a question of simple progress in one direction. There were layers upon layers of solitude and loneliness, profound yearning for community, moments when we were blessed with a sense of community, only to undergo a bitter cycle again.[11]

In many ways it was similar to the experiences of Dorothy Day at the Catholic Worker when she attempted to build community. Yet, it was very different—Philip and Elizabeth were married and had children. They were both committing acts of resistance that were often followed by long prison sentences. After both were unexpectedly in prison at the same time in 1977 they agreed that they would not be in jail again at the same time so that one of them would be with the children. Also, since they performed acts of resistance and not corporal works of mercy on a daily basis they could not depend on voluntary contributions for their support. Philip made a living doing carpentry work and painting houses. They did not publish a paper but Philip did write books: *Widen the Prison Gates* and *Of Beasts and Other Beastly Images: Essays Under the Bomb*. Finally, unlike Dorothy Day and the Catholic Worker, they confronted not only the injustices and evil they found in American society but also in the church when they viewed it in complicity with evil and injustice. Their life together is unique in the Catholic Resistance. Formerly, the Resistance had been the preserve of men and even during the Vietnam era only women without the responsibility of children had been involved.

When Daniel Berrigan had been released from prison in 1970 because of a spinal condition he returned to his Jesuit community in New York City. He had decided in prison that he would never again take a permanent position on any college campus. He explained this decision in his autobiography *To Dwell in Peace*: "I liked less and less what I saw there. I would come and go, for a semester at the most, teaching in a way that freed me and the students from the paper chase; and then would depart, no strings, no tenure track, nothing lost."[12]

For the next twenty years, Daniel Berrigan would go where the cause of peace led him. He became a traveling evangelist for peace confronting injustice wherever he saw it and witnessing to peace by his actions. A great preacher, teacher, and writer, he was often in demand. His celibate life-style and membership in the Jesuit community provided him great freedom of movement. His prophetic witness conveyed a consistency that affirmed peace and life over war and death and as a result he often provoked great controversy.

On 19 October 1973 he was invited to speak before the Association of Arab University Graduates in Washington, D.C. A week after the event, an antiwar periodical in New York published the speech, and as Daniel wrote, "the skies fell in."[13] His speech was viewed as vitriolic anti-Semitism. B'nai B'rith, castigated him as did the National Council of Churches. This was true also of the pages of *Commentary*, *Worldview*, *Commonweal*, *Village Voice*, and the *New York Times*. The debate raged for over a year. What Daniel Berrigan had done to merit such a response was to criticize the militarism of the State of Israel and defend the human rights of the Palestinians within Israel. He also urged the Palestinians and their supporters to put aside their reliance on violence and terrorism and adapt instead the practice and spirit of nonviolence.

Jim Forest attempted to come to Daniel Berrigan's defense through his work at Fellowship of Reconciliation (FOR) and the Catholic Peace Fellowship (CPF). He personally wrote a letter to the *National Catholic Reporter* and an article in *Fellowship* over the continuing debate. He also managed to have published a book, *The Great Berrigan Debate*. Forest believed the extreme reaction to "Daniel's speech was rooted in the fact that the Left in general still judges nonviolence and pacifism to be thoroughly counterrevolutionary and indeed reactionary."[14] Forest believed that "pacifist criticism of Israel is certainly no more marked than criticism of Arab and Palestinian groups. But the Press, for whatever reason, had generally ignored pacifist criticism of the Arabs while concentrating heavily on criticism of Israel—and rebuttals to such criticisms."[15] After a month-long, fact-finding trip in Israel, Forest along with Paul Mayer held a press conference on 19 May 1974 on the Palestinian question and supported the need for Israel to recognize the human rights of the Palestinian people in Israel.

Over a decade after the controversy, Daniel Berrigan wrote that he was grateful for having spoken the truth as he saw it. He also linked the situation in Israel with the Nicaraguan situation in the 1980s and contended: "The Nicaraguans are not alone in constructing, by force of brutal necessity, a fortress state. What a cruel necessity, a forensic nightmare, self-fulfilling! Israel is caught in the same cruel web. Inevitably, one might think: because insecurity, danger, and the imminence of terror are hardly conducive to political generosity, an open society."[16] Today, Berrigan is angry with Israelis, Nicaraguans, and Americans for repeating what he terms the oldest sophism of history: "To make peace, prepare for war."[17]

As the Vietnam War was winding down, Daniel Berrigan was again involved in another controversial issue. The issue focused on the human rights of political prisoners held by the government of North Vietnam. This time a split among the pacifists in the antiwar movement resulted. Daniel first expressed his concern on the issue of violence in relation to revolutionary movements and political prisoners when he wrote to Jim Forest in late 1972:

We must make clear to the North Vietnamese and to the Vietcong, that we reject any overt or unlimited violence, any truly military gains won at the price of civilian deaths, or any executions, political or otherwise carried out against the conquered or captured enemy. . . . There is a great unwillingness naturally on the part of all of us to enter into the Vietnamese life and death struggle with some sort of critical treatment of their conduct. On the other hand, I know that history is going to judge not only the crimes of the American military and political leaders; we also are going to be judged if we have "taken sides" on death, without making clear, even to our friends across the other line, that we object to death for no matter what pretext of what kind of gain.[18]

Forest sent a copy of Berrigan's letter to Alfred Hassler at FOR with a letter of his own expressing his agreement and concern for future direction on the matter.

On the other hand I do think the antiwar movement has become dangerously superficial, as Dan says in his own way in the letter, and that the widening enthusiasm for violence, so long as it is supposedly revolutionary, does have to be challenged. The question is how to do it in a way that contributes to the purpose of nonviolence, that being— in the most radical sense—reconciliation.[19]

In April 1973, Daniel and Philip Berrigan wrote a letter to Pham Van Dong of the delegation of the Peoples' Democratic Republic of North Vietnam asking him to respond to the allegations of the torture of American prisoners of North Vietnam.[20] Their concern for political prisoners was a result not only of their own experience in prison, but also of reports of such torture from the pacifist Unified Buddhist Church in Vietnam which worked during the war for the organization of a coalition government with the National Liberation Front and the North Vietnamese Communists. Alfred Hassler had always placed great hope in the Buddhist presence in Vietnam and in 1966 he had been instrumental in arranging a lecture tour in America for Thich Nhat Hanh, a leading Buddhist monk and poet who became a member of FOR. It was at that time that Daniel Berrigan and Thomas Merton became friends with Nhat Hanh. Berrigan supported Nhat Hanh and kept in close contact with him through the Unified Buddhist Church in Paris. In May, a letter from Tren Trong Quat on behalf of Pham Van Dong in Hanoi refuted the charges of the treatment of prisoners by simply stating it was nothing but a "campaign of slander" on the part of the United States government against the government of North Vietnam.[21] Unsatisfied with the response, the Berrigan brothers, who were also dissatisfied with the way other peace activists had responded to the allegations made by returned prisoners and the Buddhists, criticized the peace movement's admiration for an admirable enemy that had gradually turned into idolatry of that enemy. "A kind of human manifesto: that we would not countenance, or ourselves inflict, physical torture or moral degradation, on any other human. Whatever the provocation whatever the crime."[22] Daniel Berrigan then wrote to Jim Forest on the day of Rabbi Heschel's death asking Forest to call on world religious communities to ask the pope to visit North and South Vietnam and speak there in the name of all religious traditions about the bombing and suffering and make a plea for human rights, especially for those of political prisoners. Daniel said that Eqbal Ahmad would be in charge of the project and Jim Douglass would help organize it.[23] The idea, however, never worked.

From his position as editor of *Fellowship*, Jim Forest attempted to address the issue. In the summer of 1973, he published an appeal on behalf of imprisoned Soviet dissidents. Some critics called the article a revival of the cold war. In the article Forest quoted in length a letter by Aleksandr Solzhenitsyn in which the Nobel laureate pleaded for a more forthright condemnation of violence committed by the communist countries. In the article Forest also referred to the thousands of Vietnamese allegedly tortured and incarcerated by the Saigon government. He wrote, "But there is a mandate to respond to prisoners of conscience elsewhere as well, including those in the USSR. Our first allegiance is, after all, to the planet, not to any state or political group."[24] Besides continuing to write on the issue of political prisoners in *Fellowship*, Forest along with Tom Cornell organized "An Appeal to North Vietnam to Observe Human Rights."[25]

This appeal coincided with the final withdrawal of U. S. troops from Vietnam and was a result of Forest's fears that the new Vietnam might merely substitute a new, even more ruthless tyranny for the old system of arbitrary power. Forest believed the pacifist Buddhists would be among the first victims. After the fall of Saigon, the Unified Buddhist

Church had gone out of its way to demonstrate its good will toward the new regime. Uninvited, nine hundred monks and nuns had participated in the victory celebration held in Saigon 15 May 1975. A few days later, on May 19, twenty thousand Buddhists had gathered in front of the An Quang Pagoda for a tribute to President Ho Chi Minh in celebration of his birthday. Yet little justice was to be forthcoming, and the communists soon demonstrated that they had no use for these would-be allies. Pagodas were seized or destroyed, religious statues smashed, orphanages confiscated, and social service centers closed. Thich Tri Quang, the monk who had led the Buddhist movement of protest against Ngo Dinh Diem and who as recently as 31 May 1974 had participated in a demonstration calling for the resignation of President Thieu, was arrested on August 12 after giving a sermon that queried the new government in Vietnam about its promise of concord and reconciliation. Concerned about the information they were receiving from the Buddhists about the disregard for human rights in North Vietnam, Jim Forest and Tom Cornell initiated the appeal.

In the fall of 1976, Richard Neuhaus, a former antiwar activist associated with CALCAV, joined Jim Forest, a representative of both FOR and CPF, in drafting and circulating an "Appeal to the Democratic Republic of Vietnam to Observe Human Rights." In the appeal they mentioned reports of widespread violations of human rights, including the detention of large numbers of people in so-called reeducation camps. They also wrote to the Vietnamese observer at the United Nations, asking for a response to these charges. Forest followed the announcement of the appeal with an article, "Vietnam: Unification without Reconciliation," in the October 1976 issue of *Fellowship*. Because of the names of Neuhaus and Forest, CALCAV and CPF and FOR became indirectly involved in the appeal.

The timing of the Forest-Neuhaus appeal split the pacifist wing of the peace movement apart. In June 1976, the American Friends Service Committee (AFSC) board had approved a campaign to collect one million signatures on a petition calling for normalizing of relations and reconstruction aid for the Democratic Republic of Vietnam. The petition also made reference to amnesty for American draft-law offenders and rehabilitation support for veterans. Supporters of this appeal believed the Forest-Neuhaus appeal would contribute to the hostile atmosphere in the United States towards Vietnam. Dave McReynolds of the

War Resisters League (WRL) would also have nothing to do with the appeal and spoke adamantly against it. The FOR staff was also split over the appeal. Regardless of the intentions of its sponsors, many pacifists believed it played into the hands of the U. S. government and others who opposed UN membership for Vietnam and normalization of relations between the United States and Vietnam. Forest was accused of being too pure in his quest for human rights and in turn was hurting the broader aims of the movement.

Forest, however, would not relent in his pursuit of protecting the rights of political prisoners. In December 1976 he resigned as editor of *Fellowship* and assumed the post of coordinator for the International Fellowship of Reconciliation (IFOR) headquartered in Holland. Forest continued his efforts on behalf of human rights from that position though he knew it was causing a factional split within the peace movement. From Holland, Forest remained focused on the issue of political prisoners whether it was those in detention camps, or the persecution of Buddhists in Vietnam, or the boat people arriving in the United States. These three groups documented for Forest the violence of the North Vietnamese and justified his continued attempts to stop it.

Forest would often forward letters written by Daniel Berrigan to Pham Van Dong asking "for release of religious peoples, and an international team to go in," always advocating that Amnesty International organize such a team.[26] In 1975, Daniel Berrigan collaborated with Thich Nhat Hahn on *The Raft if Not the Shore*. In Holland in 1978 Forest published a pamphlet on *The Unified Buddhist Church of Vietnam: Fifteen Years of Reconciliation*. Then in 1978, Daniel Berrigan threatened to resign from FOR because it refused to support a vigil at the Vietnamese embassy on behalf of Buddhist monks who were being held as political prisoners. The issue was never resolved to Forest's or Berrigan's satisfaction, but the Catholic peace movement had made a significant contribution to the human rights effort that would continue around the world. When Forest left for Holland, Daniel Berrigan was to lose his main organizer for peace in the United States. Through Forest's new international position, however, he was often able to include Daniel Berrigan in various international peace projects.

During these years, Daniel Berrigan also lent his name and voice to many other causes. In the 1970s and 1980s he was attempting to integrate every issue into his position of nonviolent resistance and to develop a consistent message of peace and life, not war and death. In conjunction with the Center for Constitutional Rights in New York, Daniel and Philip worked for the improved welfare of federal prisoners. On 24 September 1973, Daniel Berrigan and fifty other religious among several hundred U. S. and Canadian citizens signed a public advertisement in the *New York Times* condemning the military takeover in Chile; it asked the U. S. government not to recognize the new regime in Santiago and urged the United Nations to guarantee the human rights of all persons in Chile.

As the keynote speaker at the 27th Annual New England Congress of Religious Education at the University of New Hampshire, Daniel Berrigan turned his attention from foreign policy to the homefront and talked about the family as an "Instrument of Violent Society." He strongly attacked the family when he said that "the family has allowed itself to be reduced to a tool of the materialistic economy, so that it is little more than a 'consuming unit, a tax paying unit, a biological unit, for the next war—producing sons for the cannons.' " And on 3 May 1974 he was a featured speaker with Paulo Freire, Richard Barnett, and Harvey Cox at Marygrove College for a week-end seminar "Is Peace Possible" sponsored by the Archdiocese of Detroit's Commission for World Justice and Peace. In private correspondence with Jim Forest in April 1975 Daniel Berrigan raised the issue of abortion when he wrote "Is the dignity of the women's movement served by an (essentially western, war ridden, itchy, competing, mechanistic) position like control of our bodies? . . . Maybe the most crucial and hopeful statement of the seventies is a nonviolent statement 'Everyone should live.' "[27] It would not be until the late 1980s that Daniel would join a pro-life group and commit civil disobedience in opposition to the abortion laws in the United States. He received many awards at colleges and from peace groups. Promoting Enduring Peace, Inc., gave him the 1974 Gandhi Peace Award and in the same year the WRL presented him their annual peace award.

Daniel Berrigan also continued to accept visiting professorships in the 1970s and 1980s in Europe, Canada, Detroit, Berkeley, and the Bronx. But again, his prophetic witness for peace provoked controversy. When he was at the Jesuit seminary in Berkeley, Daniel could not abide the fact that degrees were granted by the University of California that he believed "provided cover for the malignant Livermore

Laboratories, a vast nuclear weapons research center some thirty miles distant from Berkeley."[28] While teaching in Berkeley, Berrigan led hundreds of people on Ash Wednesday to the administration building where a request was made to meet with the president of the university concerning Livermore Laboratories. Around midnight the campus police cleared everyone out. The Ash Wednesday action as well as other demonstrations against Livermore Laboratories continued through the 1980s. But as Daniel Berrigan says of the action, "With the exception of a small number of students, no one was troubled at Berkeley."[29] And perhaps Daniel's greatest disappointment while teaching at Berkeley was when his fellow Jesuits did not welcome him as a peer.[30]

In the early 1980s, Daniel Berrigan taught three successive summers at Loyola University in New Orleans. While there he was confronted with another moral dilemma. Once again living with his fellow Jesuits at a Jesuit institution of higher learning, he believed he had to resign his teaching position because the university supported an ROTC program. This time the experience for Daniel was to prove positive, for in 1987 the ROTC program was removed from Loyola and Daniel returned to teach there in the summer of 1988.

Teaching at universities, however, was not Daniel Berrigan's main work. He often joined Jonah House in their demonstrations at the Pentagon and, of course, joined his brother Philip in the King of Prussia Plowshares action. He also spent a great deal of time writing and by 1987 had published thirty-seven books. Attempting to comprehend as fully as possible the meaning of life and death, Daniel Berrigan decided to do volunteer work first with dying cancer patients and later with dying AIDS patients in New York City. Rather than volunteering at a soup kitchen or a homeless shelter, he found that his hospital work became his way of administering the corporal works of mercy. Many of his books written in the 1980s reflect his experiences with the dying.

His efforts on behalf of with AIDS victims inspired a renewal of his work with homosexuals, which had begun at Cornell University. A brief look at some of this work reveals again the consistency of Daniel's message of peace and life. First, the issue brought him into direct conflict with the Jesuits and his church. Whenever conflict with his religious order occurred, Daniel Berrigan always experienced great pain and suffering. Drawing on his past experience of being silenced and exiled for his work for peace, Daniel offered to help his fellow

Jesuit John McNeill, who had published his book *The Homosexual and the Church* in 1977 and had been silenced by church authorities from writing and public speaking on the topic of homosexuality. Daniel Berrigan with the assistance of McNeill published an article on the whole matter, but it did not help and John McNeill was dismissed from the Jesuits. Daniel wrote of the experience:

> John appears as yet another courageous victim of the attempt underway to ravel the seamless robe of the Second Vatican Council. Precious gains must be set back, the personal and social freedom of Catholics reduced to tatters. . . . McNeill's predicament was my own, it was simple as that. My own freedom was assailed when McNeill's was.[31]

Second, his work with homosexuals like all work for Daniel was viewed in terms of peace and life. This was obvious when he was asked to address the gay fellowship of the Unitarian-Universalist church in San Francisco. Daniel told his audience that if the gay rights movement were to be taken seriously, it had to have a vision that included the larger suffering of the world. Berrigan offered them his own vision and pointed out to them the nuclear arms race, epitomized a few miles from Berkeley in the Livermore Laboratories. Daniel then pleaded with them to connect their own lives with the lives of the poor, the powerless, and the homeless. In other words, to link the many injustices they experienced as gays with the injustices experienced by other Americans under the larger umbrella of peacemaking.[32] As this incident suggests, Daniel Berrigan's words and actions were always rooted in peace and life. Again, the issue did not change Berrigan's message. Homosexuality, abortion, the Middle East, Nicaragua, political prisoners, and every other issue that Daniel Berrigan confronted he linked to peacemaking and an affirmation of life.

In practice both Daniel and Philip Berrigans' approach to peacemaking remained essentially the same from the 1968 Catonsville draft board raid. Following the ancient Judeo-Christian prophetic tradition, they hoped to offer themselves as moral witnesses to their brothers and sisters in the church and the world with the hope that the consciences and concerns of enough people might alter the destructiveness that injustice and war wrought. Unable to devise a new action that would answer their critics' protestations against the destruction of property, they were able to reject the controversial night actions in attempting to keep within the guidelines of traditional nonviolence. Their antinuclear Plowshares protest in King of Prussia continued in the same tradition and their protest was "one of the best-known antiwar incidents in this country since the Vietnam War."[33] But more important was the daily witness of peacemaking these two men have offered over the past twenty-five years. Again, Philip was more focused and limited in his resistance. He wanted to stop the production of nuclear weapons as he had wanted to stop the war in Vietnam. Philip served as the convener of Plowshare actions and organizer of demonstrations at the Pentagon from Jonah House. Daniel, the traveling peace evangelist, tried to link all that he experienced into a consistent peacemaking ethic. Both have tried to break through encrusted public apathy and penetrate the country's larger sense of fatalism with a new spirit that has sparked many Americans in popular outcries over the years. Their message of peace and life over war and death has affirmed the dignity of the individual and the right of conscience and human rights. They have courageously stood up to the U.S. government when evil was being perpetrated and also to their church when it seemed to be in complicity with the government. They have not been able to resolve the tensions between religion and politics to the satisfaction of their critics, but this has not prevented them from attempting to be prophets of peacemaking within the American Catholic peace movement.

By looking at their lives what is found is an increasing alienation from American society and a radicalization of their political views, especially of the U.S. government, which they came to believe had lost all legitimacy because of its policies of militarism, racism, and exploitation. This position has been complicated by their position as priests in the Roman Catholic church. Dorothy Day had experienced alienation and radicalization before her conversion to Catholicism and brought her pacifism with her. Because the Berrigan brothers were born and raised within traditional American Catholicism, they wanted to correct the evils they found not only in their country but also in their church. Thus, their journey to reach the same conclusions as Dorothy Day took much longer.

The CPF, founded by Daniel Berrigan in 1964, was the main vehicle for organization and support of his actions until his friend, Jim

Forest, left CPF and FOR to assume a position with the IFOR in Holland in 1976. During the last years of the Vietnam War, CPF spent a great deal of time and energy working with the Berrigans. In 1972 CPF wrote in behalf of Daniel and Philip Berrigan for the Nobel Peace Prize. In 1973, CPF assisted the Harrisburg Defense Committee and began work on the series of appeals for political prisoners.

CPF has always been a membership organization. At its peak in 1974, it had a membership of 3,000 people. Control of CPF had always been in the hands of its co-chairs, Jim Forest and Tom Cornell, who ran CPF from their FOR offices in Nyack. The main office for CPF was in New York City and was staffed by volunteers who received direction from Nyack. Forest and Cornell never attempted to democratize CPF. The main focus of CPF was always draft counseling and the publication of the *CPF Bulletin*. The volunteers in the central office kept these two aspects functioning and then organized or participated with other groups in campaigns and demonstrations against the Vietnam War.

CPF always had local chapters throughout the United States, but most often with no help from the central office in New York City. The work of each chapter varied greatly. For example, the Northern California CPF under the direction of Vincent O'Connor, and with the cooperation and the thanks of administrators and counselors, entered every Catholic high school in several counties of the state to bring teams of draft resisters and COs to the students. The rate of conscientious objection to the Vietnam War increased significantly wherever this was done. The New England CPF established an annual conference that attracted hundreds every spring, most of whom were not members of CPF. Chapters ebbed and flowed around the country.

After Forest left for Holland, Tom Cornell remained committed to CPF and continued to chair the organization. Forest's influence on CPF continued, however, through correspondence. Jim Forest would write to Cornell about significant international peace issues and request that Cornell organize support for these efforts in America. In addition, when Forest went to Northern Ireland in support of the Peace People in Belfast and organized a small conference on nonviolence, he wrote an article on the Peace People for the *CPF Bulletin*. The same was true when he went to Latin America to promote nonviolence and to South Africa for a conference on apartheid. At Forest's request,

Cornell successfully coordinated the Catholic Worker, CPF, WRL, CALC (Clergy and Laity Concerned—they dropped "About Vietnam" after the war), and FOR in a support for Aldolfo Perez Esquivel and his nomination for the 1977 Nobel Peace Prize. Forest also placed the Mobilization for Survival in contact with Cornell. Cornell in turn kept Forest informed of events in America, for example, the work of Cesar Chavez and news of the Catholic Worker in New York and the activities of the peace movement. Basically, the friendship of the two men within CPF under the larger umbrella of FOR enabled them to bring forth CPF support for international issues. Forest provided the information and network while Cornell did the organizing in New York.

By June 1977, however, Forest was expressing dissatisfaction with the CPF Bulletin when he wrote to Cornell: "Finally, wasn't much impressed with the last Bulletin—can't remember why, except I thought it could have been published by the World Humanist Association. No Catholic scent to it, or did I miss something?"[34] By August 1977, Forest was suggesting to Cornell to close down CPF at the 339 Lafayette address. Cornell, however, was determined to keep the CPF in existence.

In September 1979, Tom Cornell was fired from his position with FOR. This was a result of restructuring within FOR, budget cuts, and the arrival of new leadership within the organization. For the next two years Cornell attempted to keep CPF alive at 339 Lafayette and directed its activities from his home in Newburgh, New York, while he sought employment and a new direction for his life. A few people did send support money to Cornell after he lost his job at FOR.[35]

The issue of Central America consumed most of his energy during the fall of 1979. In the name of CPF, he lobbied Congress against the intervention in Nicaragua. Along with John Quigley of USCC he tried to organize local assistance for the U.S. Support Committee for Central America. In January 1980, at the request of Forest and the Goss-Mayrs at IFOR, Cornell organized in America the International Days for Justice and Peace in Central America. About thirty groups across the United States participated in the observance. Cornell sent the money collected at the New York service to San Salvador Archbishop Oscar Arnulfo Romero.[36] In June, he sent letters in the name of CPF opposing aid to Central America to the President of the United States and ten congressmen.

In December 1979, the Red Army invaded Afghanistan to shore up a faltering communist government under siege by Moslem rebels. President Carter shelved SALT-II, suspended shipments of grain to Russia, initiated an international boycott of the 1980 Summer Olympics in Moscow, and proposed a reinstitution of the draft in America. It was the reemergence of the draft issue that gave Cornell the idea of offering draft-counseling seminars through church diocesan offices. Since Cornell had always maintained that draft counseling was the top priority of CPF and he had over twenty years experience in the work, he believed it would be a way to keep his family and CPF alive. After consulting with Gordon Zahn, he wrote to Bryan Hehir, the director of the Office of International Justice and Peace at USCC, enclosing a letter of recommendation from Zahn and asking Hehir to write a letter of support for his draft-counseling program to all the diocesan offices. Cornell also had the support of Patrick McDermott at the USCC, who promoted his program. Hehir wrote the letter. By July 1980, Cornell had given draft counseling training seminars in the dioceses of Davenport, Richmond, Bridgeport, and Peoria. Within one year he had educated seven hundred people on the draft and had made a total of $3,500.[37] In November 1980, Cornell went to press with Jim Forest's revision of his pamphlet, *Catholic Conscientious Objection*, and acquired the imprimatur for the pamphlet from the Archdiocese of New York.

Cornell could not continue without a more adequate means of support for his wife and children and so in 1981 he left New York for Waterbury, Connecticut, where he took a job with the World Council of Churches running a soup kitchen serving three hundred people a day. He remained in this work through the 1980s. CPF continues in the old office at 339 Lafayette Street with Bill Ofenloch as coordinator and Tom Cornell's name remains on its letterhead as national secretary. This existence continues at a minimal level of operation waiting for the next crisis with the draft to occur. Befittingly, Tom Cornell's last organizing effort before his departure from New York was the memorial service for Dorothy Day held at St. Patrick's Cathedral in January 1981.

The main reason for the decline of CPF was the unexpected growth of a new Catholic peace organization, Pax Christi–USA. Just as PAX and CPF had its origins in the Catholic Worker, so too did Pax Christi–USA. In 1971, a critical moment for PAX occurred when the British PAX Society merged with Pax Christi International and left the American PAX without an international link. Eileen Egan and Gordon Zahn, the founders and cochairs of PAX, explored the feasibility of bringing Pax Christi to the United States. In Europe, Pax Christi worked closely with the Roman Catholic hierarchy and a bishop was president of each national section. Bernard Cardinal Alfrink was the international president and Carel ter Maat was the international secretary. But Egan and Zahn did not want the new organization under the control of the American hierarchy either financially as CAIP had been or in terms of decision making as it was in Europe. Thus, they agreed on an episcopal moderator rather than a president for the new group and approached Thomas Gumbleton, auxiliary bishop of Detroit, because of his leadership on the peace issue in NCCB.[38] In November 1971 he accepted the role of moderator. At Pax Christi's International Council meeting in April 1972, Eileen Egan proposed that PAX be the basis for the U.S. branch of Pax Christi. At the meeting, Pax Christi International formally recognized the existence of Pax Christi–USA.

In June 1972 at Oakridge, New Jersey, an organizational meeting was held. At the meeting Tom Cornell represented the CPF, Dorothy Day and Patrick Jordan were there from the Catholic Worker, Jim Forest and Harriet Godman came from Emmaus House, and Edward Guinan, a Paulist priest, and Rachelle Linner were there from the Community for Creative Nonviolence (CCNV). Egan explained that the new organization would appeal not just to pacifists but to a broad range of American Catholics concerned about peace. The aim of the new group would be to "lay stress on peace education through a nationwide 'Peace Week' on a given theme, and through the publication of a bulletin giving news of European Pax Christi programs and peace developments throughout the world. The activism of demonstrations would be the work of other peace organizations."[39] Cornell supported Egan's idea because it would further clarify CPF as a pacifist organization. Thus, Pax Christi–USA was born that weekend. Edward Guinan was named general secretary, Clare Danielsson was the treasurer, Eileen Egan and Gordon Zahn were named co-chairs of an eight-member directing committee, and Bishop Gumbleton was the moderator. Later that year, Egan invited Carroll T. Dozier, bishop of Memphis, to join Bishop Gumbleton as episcopal comoderator of Pax Christi–USA. Dozier, a newly appointed bishop in January 1971, had issued a pastoral letter, *Peace: Gift and Task*, that December. In the letter he advocated the strongest position on peace ever taken by an American bishop when he said that "we must stop the war in Vietnam," which he called "sinful" and "not justified."[40]

Edward Guinan returned to CCNV where he established the secretariat of Pax Christi–USA. CCNV was a community that ran a soup kitchen, a hospitality house, a shelter for the homeless, and a legal aid program for the needy in Washington, D.C. CCNV viewed itself as a community called to give a prophetic witness to the world and this ultimately meant activism and demonstrations. Thus, from the very beginning the aim of Pax Christi–USA—peace education for mainline Catholics—was in opposition to the vision of CCNV, but this fundamental conflict was not anticipated in the beginning. Another planning meeting was held at the Catholic Worker in New York on 23 June 1973, where it was decided that a fall national assembly would be held at George Washington University and a regular publication containing Pax Christi–USA news and articles of peace interest would be published. The publication would be called *Pax Christi Thirdly*. Ed Guinan was responsible for both projects.

In the summer, Guinan and CCNV became involved in the protest actions at the White House with the prayer-ins supported by Jonah House. Eileen Egan who did not want Pax Christi–USA's first public event, the October national assembly, to be characterized by such activism in which the CCNV was involved wrote to Guinan, "In confidence, I feel we have to open many doors, to bring to the peace movement many Catholics hitherto alienated from it. That means to me no Berrigans since their drama . . . would drown the Pax Christi message and twist the whole message out of context."[41] Guinan ignored the letter. He and CCNV worked hard on the national assembly and it was a success. A few days after the assembly, however, CCNV continued to attract national attention by its demonstrations. At a peace conference in Washington, D.C., commemorating the tenth anniversary of *Pacem in Terris*, Guinan and several CCNV members equipped with laughing boxes disrupted Henry Kissinger's talk and were removed from the gathering. Bishop Dozier who was present at the gathering let it be known to Pax Christi–USA's board that he was upset. [42]

Guinan's next demonstration occurred when the new archbishop of Washington, William Baum, purchased a $500,000 home. Guinan began a "fast to death" in opposition to what he believed was the scandalous posture of the archbishop toward justice and the poor in the city. Guinan had identified himself to the press as Pax Christi–USA's general secretary. Again, Bishop Dozier was upset. [43]

Despite time spent demonstrating, Guinan successfully conducted the daily operations of Pax Christi. He responded to all phone calls and mail inquiries and helped to set up Pax Christi–USA groups in different cities. [44] Guinan also made available for $5. to Pax Christi–USA members a "peace packet," which contained *The Nonviolent Cross* by James Douglass, *Kill for Peace?* by Richard McSorley, S.J., *Catholics, Conscience and the Draft*, edited by Eileen Egan, six Thomas Merton essays, and an annotated bibliography on peace. He also published three issues of *Pax Christi Thirdly*. The first issue focused on "Conscience," the second on "Liberation in Latin America," and the third on "Women in the Church." Guinan was also planning the next general assembly to be held in 1974 and had secured Cesar Chavez, William Stringfellow, and James Douglass as keynote speakers for the event. To prepare for the assembly Guinan had arranged for John McKenzie, S.J., the scripture scholar, to come to Washington to speak with the Pax Christi–USA officers to prepare them for the assembly. After McKenzie's presentation there was a business meeting at which time Egan told Guinan to "dis-invite" Douglass.

After lobbying for peace at the Second Vatican Council, James Douglass became well known in the American Catholic peace movement following the publication of his books *The Non-Violent Cross* (the first statement on Christian nonviolence to issue from an American Catholic) and *Resistance and Contemplation*. He assumed a teaching position at St. Mary's College, Notre Dame, and later became a director of the Program in Nonviolence at the University of Notre Dame. After a divorce and remarriage, Douglass left Notre Dame for a professorship at the University of Hawaii. Imitating the draft board actions of the Berrigans, he destroyed files at Hickham Air Force Base in resistance to the Vietnam War. Douglass was arrested and convicted for his act of resistance; then he travelled to Canada in violation of his parole. Since he would be on a speaking tour in the eastern part of the United States at the time of the Pax Christi–USA assembly, he accepted the invitation. Since Guinan did not want to "dis-invite" Douglass, he sent a letter to the episcopal moderators and cochairs of Pax Christi–USA which stated that "The problem if we can speak in such terms, is not with Jim Douglass, but with reactionary attitudes within Pax Christi. Have we not matured enough to embrace those who have jeopardized themselves within the Gospel context, and who provide the most articulate, real commitment to Pacifism and Nonviolence in the North American Church? I believe that it is imperative that we reinstate the invitation with full force of Moderators and Officers. . . . My continuation as the General Secretary of Pax Christi and the Secretariat's continuation here in Washington, D.C. would depend upon this decision."[45]

Almost immediately, "An Open Letter to Pax Christi," was drafted and circulated to the press. *Commonweal* printed it in full. The letter was in support of Guinan's position at Pax Christi–USA and was signed by Daniel Berrigan, Jim Forest, Ned Murphy, S.J., Judy Peluso, S.N.D., Phil Berrigan, Elizabeth McAlister, Robert Hoyt, Rick Gaumer, and Bill Ofenloch. Both Jonah House and CPF were responsible for the letter. This public display of infighting among American Catholic peace movement groups only served to alienate the officers and moderators of Pax Christi–USA even further from Guinan. Eileen Egan, who was employed by Catholic Relief Services, which was the target of a similar open letter organized by CPF during the Vietnam War, was particularly furious. On 22 August 1974 Edward Guinan resigned. The October assembly was canceled and Pax Christi–USA was back to the organizational drawing board.[46]

There was no way that Eileen Egan and Gordon Zahn would relinquish control of Pax Christi–USA. From the beginning they had stated that they wanted to educate mainline Catholics about peace and that demonstrations would be left to other groups. They wanted a "respectable" American Catholic peace group in Pax Christi–USA and they wanted to keep it on course. Guinan's style was too extreme for them. Nevertheless, over the next ten years, Pax Christi–USA's umbrella would extend far enough to embrace even a Guinan as well as many other Catholic antiwar activists of the Vietnam era. But these activists never assumed a leadership position at the national level.

Bishop Dozier and Eileen Egan were most responsible for rebuilding Pax Christi–USA. Dozier wanted a sound organizational structure and a clear statement of purpose. The restructuring began with the naming of a fourteen-member executive committee.[47] Joseph Fahey, a professor at Manhattan College in New York and director of its Peace Studies Program, agreed to do the administrative work and serve as the organization's general secretary. The new executive committee resolved that Pax Christi–USA would be committed to its role in the institutional church, respectful of the church's traditions, and sensitive to the majority of Catholics. Its mission was to convert individual Catholics to peace and through them to make the Roman Catholic church in the United States an instrument of peacemaking. Both pacifists and just war traditionalists would be welcomed in the organization, but the focus would be "to move into the mainstream of Catholic life with a realistic approach to nonviolence."[48] There was no confusion as to the purpose of Pax Christi–USA when its new general secretary, Joe Fahey, said that he saw its aim as reaching in two directions—"up" to the hierarchy, and "down" to the people in the parishes.[49] The executive committee also agreed that Pax Christi–USA would focus on four areas of concern: disarmament, amnesty, selective conscientious objection, and the United Nations.

In less than ten years, Pax Christi–USA achieved its goals. Under the secretariat of Joseph Fahey the foundations of the organization were firmly put into place. To secure its ties with Pax Christi International, representatives of Pax Christi–USA attended the yearly meetings of the executive committee of Pax Christi International and Joe Fahey and later Bishop Gumbleton became very involved in the international committee work. At home, a national assembly was held annually. A *Pax Christi Newsletter* was started by Gerald Vanderhaar in Memphis. Annual elections were held for the executive committee in order to keep the organization democratic. When the level of individual membership reached 365 in 1976 a regional structure was put in place. Memphis, New York, Boston, and Chicago were the centers of the four regions and each one had its own coordinator and annual assembly. Pax Christi–USA also sent representatives to such national church gatherings as the Eucharistic Congress and the Call to Action. At these meetings it was successful in witnessing to the church's role in peacemaking. Conscious of its aim to reach "up," it also sponsored three annual Bishops' Masses for Peace after which Bishops Dozier and Gumbleton invited their fellow bishops to join Pax Christi–USA. It also attempted to reach "down" when Mary Evelyn Jegen, S.N.D., prepared a Lenten educational program on peace and justice for the National Federation of Priest Councils to be used in local parishes. Bishop Gumbleton also received a small grant to pay for the publication of a slim blue booklet *The Church and the Arms Race* written by Mary Lou Kownacki, O.S.B., which was made available to the membership and for use by local discussion groups and was one of its most successful publications.

During Fahey's secretariat the basic elements of Pax Christi–USA's organizational structure and focus were in place, and by March 1976, fifteen bishops had become members.[50] In the same year it restated its purpose in its newsletter and proclaimed that "Pax Christi seeks with the help of its episcopal members to establish peacemaking as a priority for the American Catholic Church. To accomplish this, Pax Christi–USA will work with various Catholic communities and agencies, and will collaborate with other groups committed to nonviolent peacemaking." In 1977 the name of the Bishop of Richmond, Virginia, Walter Sullivan, was added to the group's letterhead as episcopal moderator along with that of Dozier and Gumbleton. By the end of 1977, the organization had 970 members from forty states and it had grown from four regions to eight regions. The budget for that year was $6,954.49, the bulk of which came from voluntary contributions.[51] There was so much administrative work that Joe Fahey had to hire a part-time staff associate, Kathleen Kramer, C.S.J., to assist him. By March 1978, the task had become so great that the executive committee decided to make the secretariat a paid full-time position. At the same meeting the main priorities for Pax Christi–USA were reshaped into the following categories: disarmament, primacy of conscience, a just world order, education for peace, and alternatives to violence.

On 1 January 1979 Mary Evelyn Jegen, assumed the full-time position of national coordinator of Pax Christi–USA. She served in that capacity for three years and maintained a delicate balance between all segments of the Catholic peace movement. Under her leadership the organization experienced phenomenal growth. By 1982, it had 5,500 members, forty-six of whom were bishops, and a $90,000 yearly operating budget with six paid staff members.[52] Under Jegen's leadership it maintained the internationalist perspective and the tactic of lobbying Congress and the church that had characterized the no longer existing CAIP and PAX. Pax Christi–USA also expanded its pacifist core membership. Like the CPF and the Catholic Worker, Pax Christi–USA reached out to the broader peace movement and formed coalitions with groups committed to nonviolence. It also publicly supported and worked with the Catholic Resistance spearheaded by the Berrigans and Jonah House and, while maintaining this delicate balance, attracted mainline Catholics and individual bishops to its organization.

Jegen hired staff people to work in regional development and to encourage Pax Christi–USA groups in parishes throughout the country. Policy decisions were confined to the national executive council, which included Jegen, as national coordinator, the episcopal moderators, and the elected representatives from the membership. The primary means of communication with its membership continued to be the *Pax Christi Newsletter*. Under Jegen it was given a professional look, assuming a magazine format, and was called *Pax Christi–USA*. The magazine covered major peace issues and activities nationally; there were feature articles and, like the newsletter, it had a section on regional news and the activities of Pax Christi International.

Jegen also established a Pax Christi–USA press service that distributed two articles a month on peace to sixty diocesan newspapers and Catholic newsletters. She made available peace supplements for parishes to insert in their Sunday bulletins. She increased the organization's publications by issuing a disarmament package and a *Book of Prayers for Peacemakers*. Jegen encouraged the formation of reflection/action groups concerned about the links between the Bible, international systems, and poverty to come together for the stewardship program and those interested in the link between armaments and poverty to join the Swords into Plowshares project. She enabled others to offer workshops on spirituality and nonviolence and seminars in nonviolent training. She promoted and handled Zahn's film, *The Refusal*, on the life of Franz Jaegerstaetter. She also annually promoted the planning of liturgies and vigils and demonstrations in conjunction with Hiroshima Day and the Pope's World Peace Day. Jegen organized the annual national assembly and through all of these means kept the organization's aim of education for peace its paramount goal.

By maintaining close contact not only with other Catholic groups, but with the broader peace movement, especially pacifist groups with a religious identification, Jegen was able to establish Pax Christi–USA as an integral part of the peace movement in the United States. Her work on FOR's national council assisted her greatly in forming coalitions with other peace groups. While maintaining the delicate balance of attracting all Catholics concerned about peace under the Pax Christi–USA umbrella, Jegen gradually moved the organization away from the just war tradition and toward pacifism and nonviolence as the most viable Catholic attitude toward peacemaking.[53]

The major reason for Pax Christi–USA's popularity during Jegen's administration was the awakening that many Catholics experienced in their attitudes toward the state. The reason for this was the government's policy on issues of war and peace. In 1980, the agenda set forth by the new Reagan administration differed greatly from that of the hierarchy, especially on social issues. At the November 1980 meeting in Washington, D. C., the American Catholic bishops voted to go forward with proposals for two pastoral letters. The first, on nuclear war, was entrusted to Archbishop Joseph L. Bernardin of Cincinnati and the second of these, on the economy, was given to Archbishop Rembert Weakland of Milwaukee to oversee. At the meeting, the bishops had just completed a *Pastoral Letter on Marxism* and the combination of these three letters would set the hierarchy on a collision course with the Reagan administration.[54] It would be the pastoral on nuclear war that directly challenged the U.S. government's policies on the issues of war and peace. Pax Christi–USA's criticisms of these policies were more vociferous and extreme than that of mainline Catholics and the hierarchy. Its criticism focused on three main areas of concern: the draft, Central America, and nuclear warfare and disarmament.

After the Soviet invasion of Afghanistan and a political campaign that sought to use the draft as a test of loyalty and anti-communism, Pax Christi–USA opposed registration for the draft and established a bank that would store the written statements of COs and SCOs. The statements were crucial as evidence of an individual's claim to conscientious-objector status since the new computerized draft registration forms, unlike those of old, did not provide a place for individuals to declare themselves COs. Pax Christi–USA also issued new materials on conscientious objection for Catholics: a pamphlet by Eileen Egan, *Catholic Conscience and the Draft: The Right to Refuse to Kill*, and a reprint of a *National Catholic Reporter* article by M. Evelyn Jegen, "Conscience Doth (Not) Make Cowards." The organization also supported and promoted Tom Cornell's draft-counseling program being offered in various dioceses. A $50,000 grant for the development of a "national draft program" was received from an anonymous donor. Cornell wrote that "I voted to accept [the grant], although I would much have preferred that the anonymous donor had given CPF the dough. We can do a better job, finally, this Draft Counseling Training Program is my family's principal means of keeping a leaky roof over our heads."[55] Gordon Zahn administered the grant and established the Center on Conscience and War in Boston. Pax Christi–USA also supported the bishops' *Statement on Registration and Conscription for Military Service* issued 14 February 1980, which again affirmed the Catholic right of CO and SCO. The bishops approved the general idea of draft registration, but they declared that the state must show convincing reasons for its particular action. And despite the approval, the bishops affirmed their opposition to the draft at the time, condemned a draft of women, and recommended that draft counseling be available in Catholic schools and agencies.[56]

Pax Christi–USA's national council took the most extreme position on the draft when it passed a resolution on 8 October 1982 which stated: "Although we neither advise nor encourage such action, Pax Christi–USA recognizes non-registration for the draft based on conscientious objection to conscription and opposition to growing militarization of this nation as a valid Christian witness deserving the respect and support of the entire Christian community."[57] With this resolution the organization placed itself in the pacifist and nonviolent resistance tradition of the Catholic Worker and CPF on the issue of the draft, but on other justice and peace issues remained open to other perspectives. In June 1983, Pax Christi–USA joined other religious groups in calling for an end to draft registration.[58]

Another area of concern was Central America. Political and social turmoil in this region had intensified during Jegen's tenure as national coordinator. Central America was the one issue on which Pax Christi–USA followed the bishops rather than trying to lead them. As early as

1977, it had become involved in Latin America at the request of Miguel D'Escoto, M.M., director of communications at Maryknoll. Bishop Gumbleton along with six other Pax Christi–USA bishops wrote to Bishop Obando y Bravo of Managua expressing support for the Nicaraguan church in the difficult struggle the country was experiencing in the overthrow of Anastasio Somoza. The dictatorial Somoza family had ruled Nicaragua since 1936 and were long-time allies of the United States. The revolutionaries called themselves Sandinistas after the Nicaraguan who had fought American marines in the early 1930s. Joe Fahey wrote to President Carter and three congressional leaders in the name of Pax Christi–USA urging an end to aid for Somoza.[59] One of Pax Christi–USA's first actions of support of the hierarchy on Central America was to respond to the call of the secretariat of the Bishops Conference of Central America and Panama to "unite with us in a campaign for a deeper understanding of the Gospel and the vindication of human rights."[60] In 1980, Pax Christi–USA joined CPF and John Quigley at the USCC in support of the International Days for Justice and Freedom in Central America. It also recommended that its members write to the president, Congress, and State Department "urging withdraw of aid, especially arms transfers to dictatorial and repressive regimes in Central America."[61]

In November 1981, the USCC issued its *Statement on Central America*.[62] Gone was the just war approval of the early stages of the war in Vietnam. Instead, the bishops affirmed the Second Vatican Council, and the statements from the general conferences of Latin American bishops held at Medellin in 1968 and Puebla in 1979 that confirmed the tradition of liberation and peace. They mourned the martyrdoms of Archbishop Oscar Romero and the four American churchwomen in El Salvador and confirmed their solidarity with the members of the church in Central America. The bishops called for an end to U.S. military intervention in Central America and stated that the problem was not communism, but the internal condition of poverty and the denial of basic human rights. Pax Christi–USA urged Catholics to support the bishops who called on the U.S. government to "stop military aid to El Salvador."[63] It asked members to write to the Coalition for a New Foreign and Military Policy, the Interreligious Task Force on El Salvador, and/or the Religious Task Force on El Salvador. In the fall of 1982, Pax Christi–USA established an ad hoc committee to help respond to the current situation in Central America and stated that "Nicaragua is struggling to overcome its own interior divisions at the same time it is faced with massive military pressure and economic destablization from the U.S. Educated action is urgently needed to stop the escalating U.S. involvement."[64]

The major problem that confronted Pax Christi–USA in the Central American crisis was not the institutional church's response to public-policy issues in Central America but the question of theology. Liberation theology, which had developed from the Latin American experience, permits violent actions on behalf of the oppressed. Pax Christi–USA promoted a theology and spirituality of nonviolence. Such opposing views forced many of its members to ask if the organization allowed room for violent actions or did it restrict its political options to nonviolent ones? Jegen did not accept this simplistic interpretation of liberation theology and answered such questions by stating that as a U.S. organization it was permitted only nonviolent actions, but in relation to the revolutionary situation in Central America and liberation theology it would continue to support the efforts of the oppressed peoples of the world. Thus, despite the theological tension, Jegen and Pax Christi–USA stood with the poor and oppressed of Central America while they attempted in a nonviolent manner to stop U.S. military aid to Central America.[65] Its attempts to stop U.S. involvement in Central America would become the main focus of Pax Christi–USA's work for peace after the demise of the antinuclear movement in the mid-1980s.

The third area of concern was nuclear warfare and the antinuclear weapons protest movement. This consumed the greatest part of the energies of the organization during the Jegen years. The reason for this was the flourishing of the nuclear weapons freeze campaign. In the early 1980s, Ronald Reagan, the new president, kept his campaign promise to direct a massive buildup of American military forces. Despite Reagan's popularity, support for the freeze increased dramatically: by 1982 it was active in all fifty states. By 1983, 140 Catholic bishops had endorsed the freeze. This was a dramatic change not only for the bishops, but for all Catholics in the United States when these actions are compared with the antinuclear-weapons movement of the 1940s and the Ban-the-Bomb movement of the 1950s and 1960s, which only Catholic Workers and a few individual Catholics like Thomas Merton supported. The success of the freeze campaign was short-lived, however, and by 1984 it was in decline and faded into the background when it merged with SANE in 1987.[66]

Pax Christi–USA first became involved in the antinuclear weapons issue on 16 May 1978 when the UN hosted its first Special Session on Disarmament to which religious leaders from all over the world were invited. Pax Christi International presented to the preparatory UN Special Session on Disarmament, a statement which called for the banning of nuclear weapons, the condemnation of indiscriminate warfare, and the abstention from war and claimed that the funds spent on the arms race killed the poor.[67] After the close of the disarmament session, Pax Christi–USA had its own Mass at Holy Family Church near the UN. Bishop Thomas Kelly, O.P., general secretary of the USCC, came from Washington to take part in the Mass. Such a sign of support for Pax Christi–USA from the USCC made Fahey comment, "I really felt we had made it, that one of our key goals was met."[68]

On 18 October 1978 Bishop Gumbleton, Joe Fahey, and Gerald Vanderhaar were invited to attend the Conference on SALT II for Religious Leaders at the State Department in Washington, D.C. After listening to three testimonies on why the treaty would not weaken the defense of the United States, all three Pax Christi–USA representatives believed the treaty should not be supported.[69] This decision proved to place the group in the difficult position of calling for nuclear arms reduction yet rejecting a nuclear arms reduction treaty because it was too minimal. Pax Christi–USA wanted more and for this reason it supported the Hatfield amendment for a nuclear moratorium.

The debate on the ratification of SALT II wrecked havoc not only in the broader peace movement, but also among the bishops. Bishop Gumbleton spoke strongly against ratification in NCCB. USCC believed that Gumbleton's position threatened to unravel all that they had done to persuade the bishops to address the public policy issue on control of nuclear weapons. Debate on the issue flourished and Bishop Gumbleton and Pax Christi–USA modified their position by supporting SALT II with an amendment. In 1979, the bishops supported SALT II, but their collective statement of support for the treaty was made only after a highly unusual session of the bishops' administrative committee, an elected body that acts in the name of the entire conference between general meetings. "SALT II A Statement of Support" was delivered by John Cardinal Krol, archbishop of Philadelphia, before the U.S. Senate Foreign Relations Committee on 20 September 1979.[70] Krol's support of SALT II did not rest solely on the minimal accomplishments of the treaty, but also reflected concern about the morality of deterrence:

> As long as there is hope [of meaningful and continuing reductions], Catholic moral teaching is willing, while negotiations proceed, to tolerate the possession of nuclear weapons for deterrence as the lesser of two evils. If that hope were to disappear, the moral attitude of the Catholic Church would almost certainly have to shift to one of uncompromising condemnation of both use *and* possession of such weapons.[71]

Pax Christi–USA's moral position condemned both the use and possession of nuclear weapons which went beyond the point reached by the bishops. This position had been spelled out by Pax Christi International at the first UN Special Disarmament Session in 1978. At that time, Pax Christi International unequivocally accepted the nuclear-pacifist position and said no to nuclear war and to nuclear weapons of any kind. The 2 August 1979 issue of *Commonweal* announced that Pax Christi–USA was launching a "Campaign to Help Stop Nuclear Weapons," calling for "an end to all research, development, testing, manufacturing and development of any new nuclear weapon that is not yet fully developed."[72] That same year a local Pax Christi–USA group led by Bill Hogan, a Chicago priest, "sat-in" at the Commonwealth Edison nuclear plant in Zion, Illinois, and the local in Washington, D.C., led by Richard McSorley, S.J., joined the Nuclear Moratorium.[73]

In early 1980, Pax Christi–USA's executive council wrote a "Call to Conversion" and invited individuals and groups to sign its pledge, which stated "I am prepared to live without the protection of nuclear armaments. As a Christian, I wish to take a stand in our country for the political development of peace without nuclear arms."[74] At the same time, it announced that Daniel Berrigan would be its keynote speaker at its national assembly in the fall, And in March 1981, it was among the 275 participants invited to attend the national strategy session on the freeze in Washington, D.C.

Pax Christi–USA continued to increase its disarmament efforts in the early 1980s by applying pressure on corporations, the government, and the church. It called for a boycotting of nuclear weapons manufacturers and listed the responsible companies in its magazine. It also pledged itself to work with other groups on disarmament. It joined with sixty groups in sponsoring, "Ground Zero," a week of educating Americans on the nuclear issue, which had been modeled on Earth Day activities. Pax Christi–USA was also one of the founding groups along with FOR of a New Call to Peacemaking, Sojourners, and World Peacemakers in launching the New Abolitionist Covenant, which attempted to coordinate efforts among the churches to get a "freeze" on any new nuclear weapons. The New Abolitionist Covenant explained its purpose in the following manner:

> The purpose of the covenant is to place before the churches the abolition of nuclear weapons as an urgent matter of faith. The nuclear threat is a theological issue, a confessional matter, a spiritual question, and is so important it must be brought into the heart of the church's life. [75]

Pax Christi–USA viewed the formation of the group as a continuation of its position during the SALT II debate, when it pressed for the Hatfield amendment for a nuclear moratorium.

The freeze drew strong support from the religious community, particularly Catholic bishops. At the suggestion of Bishops Gumbleton and Sullivan a statement on the freeze was sent to all the bishops in the United States along with a card on which to indicate support. At this time Pax Christi–USA had fifty-seven bishops in its ranks. The mailing drew an amazing response. [76] At the Nuclear Weapons Freeze national press conference held in Washington, D.C., on 26 April 1982, Bishop Joseph Francis of East Orange, New Jersey, announced that over 138 bishops of the Roman Catholic hierarchy had endorsed the Nuclear Weapons Freeze. [77]

Pax Christi–USA also participated in the second UN Special Session on Disarmament from June to July 1982. Joe Fahey had assumed primary responsiblity for drafting Pax Christi International's statement for the session. He had consulted theologians and met with the military vicariate about the document. [78] The core of the statement reflected a nuclear pacifist position, which differed, however, from the Vatican's position at the session. On June 11, the Vatican secretary of state,

Agostino Cardinal Casaroli, delivered an address to the session in the pope's name. His talk echoed Vatican attacks on the arms race and contained the following statement on deterrence that was to be quoted endlessly during the ensuing debate: "Under present conditions, deterrence based on balance—certainly not as an end in itself, but as a stage on the way to progressive disarmament—can still be judged to be morally acceptable."[79] Pax Christi International's nuclear pacifist position went beyond Pope John Paul II's position by calling for a bilateral freeze. In order to try to accelerate the process toward a position of nuclear pacifism at the UN some Pax Christi–USA members joined the antinuclear activism, which ranged from liturgies to civil disobedience surrounding the disarmament session.

Within Pax Christi–USA the effort to educate mainline Catholics on the disarmament issue had resulted in a popular nuclear disarmament movement among Catholics that was well connected with the broader peace movement in America and was symbolized by the efforts of Helen Caldicott of Physicans for Social Responsiblity and Carl Sagan of the Union of Concerned Scientists. Pax Christi–USA had successfully popularized for Catholics an issue that was previously confined to government circles. The organization's emphasis on local and regional development provided a network that combined spirituality, intellectual debate, and a call to nonviolent action in support of nuclear pacifism.

A new ingredient was added to the antinuclear movement when Catholic pacifists tried to develop a pro-life argument linking abortion with the nuclear arms race. At the outset, a group of women at the PAX Center in Erie, Pennsylvania, started an organization called Prolifers for Survival.[80] Jonah House picked up on the linking of abortion with the nuclear arms race and sponsored a "Prolife Week at the Pentagon." Both Prolifers for Survival and Pax Christi–USA supported the event. The purpose of the event was to make obvious to mainline Catholics and the hierarchy that consistency in the church's teaching was necessary. Since the church condemned abortion because it killed human life, it should also condemn nuclear war and the arms race which could kill not only all human life, but the entire planet.[81] In 1981, Pax Christi–USA issued its statement "The Unborn Child and the Protection of Life."

The linking of antinuclearism and antiabortion gained considerable momentum in the mid-1980s when Joseph Cardinal Bernardin, the archbishop of Chicago, presented his consistent ethic of life speech in the William Wade Lecture at St. Louis University on 11 March 1985. Since Bernardin was the chief architect of the peace pastoral and in 1986 would chair the Pro-Life committee of NCCB, he attempted to link the issues of abortion and nuclear warfare into part of a total pro-life position by the Roman Catholic church. Bernardin would insist that the

> systemic vision of a consistent ethic of life will not erode our crucial public opposition to the direction of the arms race; neither will it smother our persistent and necessary public opposition to abortion. . . . A consistent ethic of life does not equate the problem of taking life (e.g., through abortion and in war) with the problem of promoting human dignity (through humane programs of nutrition, health care, and housing). But a consistent ethic of life identifies both the protection of life and its promotion as moral questions. It aims for a continuum of life which must be sustained in the face of diverse and distinct threats. . . . It is not necessary or possible for every person to engage in each issue, but it is both possible and necessary for the Church as a whole to cultivate a conscious explicit connection among its several issues. [82]

The key figure in helping Bernardin to develop his consistent ethic of life was J. Bryan Hehir.

A Boston priest with a doctorate in theology from Harvard University, Hehir became the director of the Office of International Justice and Peace at USCC in 1973, and he remained in that position until 1984, when he was promoted to secretary of the more comprehensive USCC Department of Social Development and World Peace. [83] Hehir officially left USCC in 1987, but he continues to act as a consultant. During his years at the USCC Hehir created a framework for foreign-policy analysis that many bishops followed.

While with USCC, Hehir spent a great amount of time giving talks to Catholics across the nation informing them that justice and peace were "constitutive" parts of their faith and calling them to live out the church's teaching on these issues in their daily lives. Bryan Hehir also cooperated with Pax Christi–USA from the time of its reorganization under Bishop Dozier. Though Hehir was never a member, he remained in dialogue with this organization since he believed it represented the post-Vietnam Catholic activists and intellectuals concerned about peace.

Hehir worked with the hierarachy, with mainline Catholics, and with Pax Christi–USA because he viewed himself as a mediating force in the American Catholic debate on war and peace. Like John Courtney Murray he believed in and worked out of the just war tradition, but on nuclear issues he departed from Murray's call for the evolution of nuclear weapons that would meet the just war standards. As regards nuclear issues, Hehir believed there was an absolute moral imperative of non-use for weapons of indiscriminate effect, speaking more in the tradition of Merton than Murray.

He was a nuclear pacifist.[84] But unlike Merton, he worked systematically within the just war tradition, never abandoning it for nonviolence. He viewed nuclear pacifism as an alternative for Catholics that would serve as a point of convergence between traditional pacifists and just war theorists. As a result, many individuals from all segments of the church viewed Hehir as a friend and ally in their opposition to nuclear war and the arms race. In the early 1980s, however, while working on *The Challenge of Peace*, Hehir came to believe that the position of nuclear pacifism was not tenable because the split between use and deterrence was too absolute. He therefore rejected nuclear pacifism as a viable moral position for the official church in America to promulgate. Thus his position and the one of the pastoral letter on peace are the same. As Hehir states, "Close to nuclear pacifism but not quite."[85] Because of his influential position in the church, he has had a very significant impact on the development of American Catholic thought on the nuclear issue.

Before Hehir arrived at the USCC in 1973 the bishops had already issued a statement that discussed the nuclear issue.[86] The 1968 pastoral letter *Human Life in Our Day* had included a lengthy discussion of arms-control issues and noted that nothing suggested the anti-life direction of technological warfare more than the neutron bomb. The bishops did not again address nuclear issues until 11 November 1976 when to commemorate America's bicentennial anniversary, the bishops issued a lengthy pastoral on moral life called *To Live in Christ Jesus: A Pastoral Reflection on the Moral Life*. Though only one section of the pastoral dealt with war and peace issues, it did contain a significant paragraph on nuclear weapons:

> With respect to nuclear weapons, at least those with massive destructive capability, the first imperative is to prevent their use. As possessors of a vast nuclear arsenal, we must also be aware that not only is it wrong to attack civilian populations, but it is also wrong to threaten to attack them as part of a strategy of deterrence. We urge the continued development and implementation of policies which seek to bring these weapons more securely under control, progressively reduce their presence in the world and ultimately remove them entirely.[87]

The declaration that it is wrong to threaten to use nuclear weapons against civilians was the most dramatic change in the NCCB/USCC teaching on nuclear war since the Second Vatican Council; ironically it was adopted without any substantive discussion. The concept originally came from the pen of Russell Shaw, the USCC secretary for public affairs. "I felt honestly at the time it was a new step for the bishops," Shaw said. "It was logically consistent with things individual bishops and the conference itself had said. It was another step forward in a logical progression."[88] Hehir incorporated Shaw's paragraph in the final draft of the pastoral which spoke of "the need to control rigorously nuclear weapons" and closed with a few words on human rights in foreign policy.[89]

Hehir again addressed the nuclear issue in the first collective statement of the bishops since the Vietnam War devoted solely to the issue of war and peace, *The Gospel of Peace and the Danger of War*, issued 15 February 1978. The statement focused on disarmament and the SALT II negotiations and the upcoming UN Special Session on Disarmament and said "the primary moral objective is that the arms race must be stopped and the reduction of armaments must be achieved."[90]

While Hehir was working within USCC alerting bishops to the moral significance of the nuclear issue, Pax Christi–USA was encouraging bishops to join their organization. The buildup of the Nuclear Freeze Movement and increased press coverage of the issue across the nation also influenced the bishops. As a result, an increased activism on the nuclear-disarmament issue by individual members of the hierarchy occurred. Between 1980 and November 1981 over forty bishops had spoken out on the issue.[91] The two bishops who attracted the most attention during this period followed their statements with a public action that fostered a new consciousness among other members of the hierarchy and mainline Catholics about what their faith demanded in response to nuclear disarmament.

The most notable member of the hierarchy to address the issue was Raymond Hunthausen, archbishop of Seattle.[92] In a series of statements in 1981 and 1982 he publicized his nuclear pacifist position and dealt directly with the issue of Trident nuclear submarines that were located in Puget Sound, an area under his episcopal jurisdiction. Hunthausen was challenged to speak because the construction of the Trident was in conflict with the church's "first-strike nuclear doctrine."[93] In a pastoral letter to his archdiocese dated 28 January 1982, he went beyond letter writing when he announced that "after much prayer, thought, and personal struggle, I have decided to withold fifty percent of my income taxes as a means of protesting our nation's continuing involvement in the race for nuclear supremacy."[94] He did not urge such action for the members of his diocese, that was a matter of individual conscience, but meant his action to be a means to awaken them to a better path of peace than through nuclear deterrence.

Pax Christi–USA kept its members well informed of Archbishop Hunthausen's words and deeds and in 1983 the national executive council approved the proposal that it "recognizes tax resistance as an important and valid Christian witness at this time"[95] Though it had always supported the World Peace Tax Fund Bill in Congress, this was the first time Pax Christi–USA had supported tax resistance. Among Catholic peace groups, the Catholic Worker Movement alone advocated and practiced collective and individual tax resistance as a form of nonviolent resistance to the state. Until Archbishop Hunthausen, no member of the hierarchy had ever advocated, much less practiced it.[96]

Like Archbishop Hunthausen, Leroy T. Matthiessen, bishop of Amarillo, addressed the nuclear disarmament issue in relation to the effect it was having in his own diocese. Matthiessen was particularly angry at the Reagan administration's decision to deploy the neutron bomb. The Pantex plant, located fifteen miles from Amarillo, was the final assembly point for U.S. nuclear weapons, including the neutron bomb. On 21 August 1981, Matthiessen issued his statement, "Nuclear Arms Buildup." His condemnation of neutron warheads was a logical progression from statements in the 1968 pastoral *Human Life in Our Day* and a statement by Archbishop John Quinn of San Francisco issued in 1978 in support of President Carter's decision to defer production of neutron warheads.[97] The conclusion of Matthiessen's statement set forth a new precedent when he said: "We urge individuals involved in the production and stockpiling of nuclear bombs to consider what they are doing, to resign from such activities and to seek employment in peaceful pursuits."[98] Bishop Matthiessen followed up on this when he created a Solidarity Peace Fund to financially assist employees who in conscience resigned from their arms-production jobs at the Pantex Plant. Pax Christi–USA immediately solicited contributions for the fund and encouraged its members not to work for arms-production industries.[99]

Ironically, it was not only the Catholic Resistance but also the actions of individual members of the hierarchy who moved Pax Christi–USA further away from a just war position toward a pacifist position. The nuclear-disarmament issue illustrated its best efforts during the Jegen years. It always supported members of the American hierarchy and united them in Pax Christi–USA with the old core pacifists of PAX and CPF; it managed to support and work with the Catholic Resistance and still attract mainline Catholics. From this position in the center of the Catholic peace movement in the 1970s and 1980s Pax Christi–USA was able to link Catholics with the broader peace movement in the United States.

The most publicized Catholic action for peace and against nuclear warfare and nuclear weapons was the aforementioned pastoral letter, *The Challenge of Peace*, issued collectively by the 350 bishops who comprised the American Catholic hierarchy. The institutional church's pastoral, however, would not have been possible without the threat of nuclear annihilation and the peace witness of Catholic laymen and women that began with the founding of the Catholic Worker fifty years earlier.

The immediate impetus for *The Challenge of Peace* was a proposal for new business submitted to Bishop Thomas C. Kelly, general secretary of the NCCB/USCC, in the summer of 1980 by P. Francis Murphy, an auxiliary bishop of Baltimore. Murphy proposed that the bishops consider a statement on the Catholic teaching on the morality of war and peace and urged educational efforts to make that teaching more widely known. At the November 1980 NCCB meeting discussion on the proposal focused on the subject of nuclear weapons and the bishops formally agreed to address the issue. Two months later Archbishop John Roach of St. Paul-Minneapolis, president of the NCCB, appointed an ad hoc committee on war and peace to draft the bishops' statement. The chair of the committee was the highly respected Archbishop Joseph L. Bernardin of Cincinnati, who was known for his ability to build consensus. The four other committee members were Auxiliary Bishop Thomas Gumbleton of Detroit, Auxiliary Bishop John J. O'Connor (of the military ordinariate), Bishop Daniel Reilly of Norwich, Connecticut, and Auxiliary Bishop George Fulcher of Columbus, Ohio. Neither Reilly nor Fulcher had been previously identified with the nuclear issue.[100]

The USCC staff who worked with the committee were Bryan Hehir and Edward Doherty. The principal outside consultant and the individual who actually drafted the final text of the 1983 pastoral was Bruce Russett of Yale University, editor of the *Journal of Conflict Resolution*. The committee staff was completed with the appointments of Richard Warner, Indiana provincial of the Congregation of the Holy Cross, as representative of the Conference of Major Superiors of Men, and Juliana Casey, of the religious community of the Immaculate Heart of Mary, as representative of the Leadership Conference of Women Religious.[101]

The committee heard testimony from thirty-six formal witnesses on all aspects of the issue. They ranged from Tom Cornell and Gordon Zahn of the Catholic peace movement to Defense Secretary Caspar Weinberger and Arms Control and Disarmament Agency head Eugene Rostow. Biblical scholars, military officers, a physician, a conflict-resolution specialist, and two former defense secretaries also gave testimony. The most important testimony, due to its influence on Reilly and Fulcher, came from former Defense Secretaries James Schlesinger and Harold Brown. Reilly recalled that the two were "so forceful in resistance to nuclear war, in saying that nuclear war has to be avoided at all costs as unthinkable madness. They were very affirming of the committee's work."[102]

The four key figures throughout the writing of the letter were Bernardin, Hehir, Gumbleton, and O'Connor. Bernardin had announced at the first committee meeting that the group's one ground rule would be that "it would not, under any circumstances, support unilateral nuclear disarmament"[103] and he continually urged the committee to move "back toward the center."[104] Hehir's role was different. According to Gumbleton, Hehir determined the agenda and what issues had to be resolved. Bernardin also constantly looked to Hehir for clarification.[105] The two extremes on the committee were Gumbleton and O'Connor. Gumbleton, who had experienced a conversion to pacifism, represented the prophetic and personal peace elements in the church. He wrote the sections of the pastoral on pacifism and nonviolence. O'Connor represented the just war tradition and support for the military in America. According to Gumbleton, no single individual was responsible for writing the pastoral; as he put it, "he could personally point to each paragraph and name the member responsible for it."[106] Because Hehir determined the agenda and was intellectually committed to the just war doctrine as were O'Connor, Bernardin, and the other members of the committee, the just war doctrine would provide the moral principles and framework for the document.

The pastoral went through three drafts, which were made public, and extensive debate and compromise took place before the final letter was passed by the bishops. On 2 July 1982 a major portion of the first draft appeared in the *National Catholic Reporter*. Jegen reflected the disappointment of many members of the peace movement when in response to a letter to Gordon Zahn she wrote:

> I see no way of avoiding a split over the pastoral. The important thing is to handle it with charity and a desire for continuing dialogue and eventual consensus. I simply cannot praise the overall thrust of the piece, as you sincerely can. . . . I certainly agree that Tom Gumbleton should not bear the brunt of our criticisms. He is, after all, only one member of the committee.[107]

Like Jegen many other Catholics wanted a more prophetic statement and criticized the hierarchy's accommodation to power and the just war tradition. They also wanted a condemnation not only of the use but also the possession of nuclear weapons.

Other Catholics condemned the pastoral for going too far in the direction of pacifism. Philip Lawler, director of studies at the Heritage Foundation, formed a group of lay Catholics to "call public attention" to the church's traditional teachings on war and peace. Michael

Novak, author and lay theologian, organized a group of fifty prominent Catholic laymen to be called the American Catholic Committee to counter the move of the bishops toward pacifism and return them to the teachings of St. Augustine, St. Thomas Aquinas, and the Catholic just war tradition. Ed Marciniak, a Catholic lay leader in Chicago, who had formed a National Center for the Laity for Catholics, thought the bishops have gone too far on the nuclear issue.[108]

Between the second and third drafts, a consultation was held at the Vatican on 18–19 January 1983. American participants in the consultation were Bernardin, Roach, Hehir, and Monsignor Daniel Hoye, general secretary of the NCCB/USCC. The meeting involved other bishops and specialists from France, West Germany, Great Britain, Belgium, Italy, and the Netherlands. Vatican participants included Joseph Cardinal Ratzinger and Agostino Cardinal Casaroli and other representatives of pontifical commissions. The proceedings were confidential, but insights into the meeting can be gleaned from a synthesis prepared by the priest Jan Schotte, secretary of the Pontifical Justice and Peace Commission, and published as "a point of reference and a guide to the U.S. bishops in preparing the next draft of their pastoral letter." The text of the Schotte synthesis was released to the NC News documentary service, Origins.[109] The synthesis characterized the consultation as "centered on five main themes: the precise teaching role of a bishops' conference; the application of moral principles to the nuclear weapons debate; the use of scripture; the relationship between just war theory and pacifism in Catholic tradition; the morality of deterrence."[110] On each of these points alterations were made in the third draft.[111] It must be remembered, however, that the consultation raised issues needing to be clarified and it was the American hierarchy, not Vatican authorities, that clarified them.

A major issue of concern was the application of moral principles to concrete situations. The Vatican raised the question of how morally binding the pastoral letter of the American hierarchy was on individual members of the church. The American bishops resolved this in the opening page of The Challenge of Peace when they claimed that the letter was "an exercise of our teaching ministry" and "that not all statements in this letter have the same moral authority. At times we state universally binding moral principles found in the teaching of the Church; at other times the pastoral letter makes specific applications, observations and recommendations which allow for diversity of opinion on the part of those who assess the factual data of situations differently."[112] The implications of this resolution were clearly assessed by Jim Castelli in his book *The Bishops and the Bomb: Waging Peace in a Nuclear Age*, when he commented on the unprecedented, almost dramatic, emphasis on the role of individual conscience and the right to dissent on matters of contingent, prudential judgment:

> If people may legitimately disagree over whether or not it is moral to start a nuclear war and still remain Catholics in good standing, the mind boggles at the implications for less cosmic issues like contraception, sterilization, abortion, divorce. The church will, no doubt, try to draw a line between issues like those and issues of war and peace; but many American Catholics, including many bishops, won't accept that. A conscience, once awakened, doesn't easily go back to sleep.[113]

The Challenge of Peace called for a critical examination of nuclear war, its strategies, the concept of first use, and deterrence. The pastoral emphasized the qualitative difference between nuclear and conventional weapons and emphasized the destructive power of nuclear weapons which "threatens the human person, the civilization we have slowly constructed, and even the created order itself."[114] The bishops also became convinced of the "overwhelming probability" that a major nuclear exchange would be unlimited and stated explicitly that "under no circumstances may nuclear weapons or other instruments of mass slaughter be used for the purpose of destroying population centers or other predominantly civilian targets."[115] This condemnation applied to retaliatory second strikes as well. The bishops concluded that "this condemnation, in our judgment, applies even to the retaliatory use of weapons striking enemy cities after our own have already been struck. No Christian can rightfully carry out orders or policies aimed at killing noncombatants."[116] In their argument the hierarchy invoked the just war principles of noncombatant immunity and proportionality first applied by John C. Ford, S.J., to World War II. The bishops also opposed any preemptive first strike when they declared that they did "not perceive any situation in which the deliberate initiation of nuclear warfare, on however restricted a scale, can be morally justified." The bishops again repeated their "extreme skepticism" that a nuclear exchange could be controlled, no matter how limited first use might have been and thus the bishops supported a "no first use" policy.[117] The bishops then concluded that the "first imperative" was to prevent any use of nuclear weapons.

On the issue of deterrence, the bishops accepted Pope John Paul II's formula for deterrence that Casaroli announced at the UN Special Session on Disarmament on 11 June 1982. According to Casaroli deterrence was not as an end in itself, but a temporary transition to true disarmament.[118] The significance of the Vatican consultation became most evident on this issue. By accepting the pope's position, the bishops had to keep their argument for deterrence within those limits. As Bryan Hehir has stated, the only opening left by the bishops on which to accept the pope's position was that the bishops did not explicitly reject the possible retaliatory use of small-yield nuclear weapons against clearly definable military targets. On this "centimeter of ambiguity," the positive support of deterrence rested.[119]

Even though they accepted deterrence, the bishops tried to stop the arms buildup by endorsing several arms control treaties and plans backed by the Nuclear Freeze Movement.[120] They also called for international controls on arms and the arms race, the substitution of conventional weapons for nuclear forces as a means of disarmament, and cast doubt on the validity of civil defense as a defensive option.[121] It was clear that the bishops were saying no to the use of nuclear weapons at a time when new technological possibilities and the Reagan administration's rhetoric had convinced millions of people that the use of nuclear weapons was not only possible but inevitable. The bishops never proclaimed a nuclear-pacifist position because like Bryan Hehir they maintained a "centimeter of ambiguity," in order to support Pope John Paul II's position on deterrence and follow the directive of Bernardin not to support unilateral disarmament and to keep on "center." As a result, the bishops, despite their intense criticisms, never unequivocally condemned nuclear warfare and the possession and use of nuclear weapons. Thus, it was not the bishops but the small community of resisters at Jonah House and Pax Christi–USA who remained the prophets in the church and stood at the cutting edge of the national conscience on nuclear issues.

The most significant factor in determining the ultimate outcome of the bishop's pastoral was the "traditionally" Catholic position taken by the Bernardin committee by using the just war doctrine as the mediating language of the document. Though the bishops proclaimed the qualitative difference between nuclear and conventional warfare, they were unable to address nuclear issues with an ethic that was qualitatively different from that of the just war. The staff at USCC believed that only the just war doctrine spoke to both Christian witness and public policy. They clung to the dominant just war doctrine and Hehir finely crafted its arguments. At best, the just war ethic as presented in *The Challenge of Peace* stressed the new weight given to the protection of the rights of conscience. At worst, the just war ethic could not provide the bishops with an ethic that would unequivocally condemn what they had proclaimed as the supreme crisis of nuclear warfare: "The whole human race faces a moment of supreme crisis in its advance toward maturity. We agree with the [Second Vatican] Council's assessment; the crisis of the moment is embodied in the threat which nuclear weapons pose for the world and much that we hold dear."[122] It was not the failure of the moral norms presented in the just war ethic, but as John Courtney Murray contended, the failure of those who do not make the just war tradition relevant. Merton had used the just war ethic to reach a position of nuclear pacifism; Pope John Paul II, Bernardin, and the staff at the USCC had not.

Indeed, the pastoral did question and criticize the legality and morality of the national-security policies of the U.S. government in relation to nuclear issues, but it left the burden of peacemaking to the individual. *The Challenge of Peace* stated that peacemaking was no longer an option for the Christian, but it failed to deliver the same message to the U.S. government.[123] Though the pastoral rejected pacifism, even nuclear pacifism, as a viable position for the government, it affirmed pacifism and nonviolence as a viable option for the Christian peacemaker.[124] As a result, the pastoral did establish pacifism as well as the just war as valid positions within the Catholic tradition but relegated pacifism and nonviolence to the individual and the more prophetic Parts I and IV of the pastoral. Whenever pacifism or nonviolence was mentioned, it was tied to conscience, individual conversion, suffering, and even martyrdom. The pastoral's message for the individual peacemaker who embraced pacifism and nonviolence was that peacemaking was hard, indeed harder than war. But there is little acknowledgment of the capacity of pacifism and nonviolence to address public-policy issues. At best, the tactics of nonviolence were affirmed as a means of national defense against enemies.

A significant part of the pastoral was the call for a new world order which the bishops described in accordance with the traditional lines of Catholic internationalism. This was the same idea that CAIP and John A. Ryan endorsed in the 1920s. Then, according to the church's approach since Pope John XXIII and Vatican II, the bishops stressed the pressing reality of world interdependence and development in the Third World. The pastoral broke new ground when it called for a new world order based not on the American-Soviet conflict nor on world government, but on the obligations of the United States to share its wealth and resources with the rest of the world. An emphasis was also placed on the moral question raised by the "massive distortion of resources" for armaments when so much of the world remained poor and helpless.[125] The absence of Cold War rhetoric in the document and the emphasis on the link between arms production and the poor of the world was also present in the 1980 pastoral letter on Marxism and would also be present in the economic pastoral issued in 1986. The emphasis on the new world order section acquired a new validity with the dismantling of the Berlin Wall.

What The Challenge of Peace did for the American Catholic peace movement was to validate its existence. The message to Catholics was that peacemaking was not a virtue limited to a few "saints," but an essential commandment to be followed by all. The need to "build a new theology of peace" was acknowledged, but the course of action to be followed was now no longer limited to the just war tradition, but pointed to pacifism and Gospel nonviolence as the base upon which individual conscience and conversion to peacemaking rested. Though many have heralded the pastoral as a revolution in peacemaking marked by the reconciliation of opposing views and the synthesis of a new theology of peace, no such revolution occurred. The just war ethic still dominated the message of the church in its attempt to address public policy; pacifism and Gospel nonviolence dominated its message when the church attempted to defend individual conscience and promote human rights. Though the pastoral recognized opposing views within the Roman Catholic tradition of peacemaking, a new synthesis was not achieved. Nuclear pacifism based on the just war ethic was not the "middle road" toward a new theology of peace. The just war ethic reached its apotheosis when the institutional church would not proclaim nuclear pacifism. Although the just war ethic did not fail when it was applied to the individual in the matter of SCO, it did fail when applied to the state on nuclear issues. At best, the just war ethic did condemn the use of nuclear weapons (and conventional weapons) of indiscriminate effect even in self-defense, but it did not condemn the production and possession of nuclear weapons even with the realization that the use of such weapons could result in the annihilation of humankind.

Though *The Challenge of Peace* received more press coverage than any other Catholic pastoral in American history, many American Catholics remained completely unaware of its message. The bishops provided very little follow-up on the pastoral. Members of the hierarchy, church leaders, journalists, and intellectuals continued to cling to the just war doctrine as the dominant ethic in the church on issues of war and peace. Some just war adherents, as Murray had advised, were applying the principles of the just war in their peacemaking attempts and in conscience arriving at the conclusion that the extent of damage wrought by both conventional and nuclear weaponry all but ends the prospect that any war could be deemed just. Many Catholics, however, continued to believe that a just war was possible.

The bishops wrote their next pastoral (1986) on capitalism and focused their energies almost exclusively on the abortion issue for the rest of the 1980s. Though the peace movement linked both abortion and nuclear issues to their pro-life position, the efforts on the part of the institutional church consistently to make the same link has been limited mainly to the efforts of Bernardin, who has repeatedly emphasized the consistent ethic in his speeches on abortion.[126] Again, it was the work of the American Catholic peace movement, especially Pax Christi–USA that attempted to continue to educate the mainline Catholic on their responsibility of following Jesus's call to peacemaking, "Peace I leave with you; my peace I give to you."

Since the publication of *The Challenge of Peace*, the American Catholic peace movement has continued its religious witness and quest for a new theology of peace. Since 1983, members of the peace movement have worked within a church that recognizes the legitimacy of their positions. Pacifists, nuclear pacifists, practitioners of Gospel nonviolence and resistance, conscientious objectors and selective conscientious objectors are now at home in the church. The American Catholic peace movement also continues to attempt to change the public policies of the U.S. government from the direction of militarism and war toward a policy based on peace and the affirmation of life. But the government has not embraced the peacemakers. Instead it has closed the door to their message as well as to the bishops' "preferential option for peace," offered by the pastoral. In 1990, the greatest obstacle confronting the American Catholic peace movement is not the church but the U.S. government. Thus, the challenge of peacemaking still remains harder than war.

Note on the Sources

In an attempt to locate the origins of the American Catholic peace movement I was able to identify two possible antecedents: the Catholic Association for International Peace (CAIP) and the Catholic Worker movement. Though the latter proved to be the leaven within American Catholicism that fostered the phenomena to emerge in force during the Vietnam era and continue to the present day, both groups had to be presented in order to provide a full understanding of the various approaches to peacemaking.

The Catholic Worker Movement

The principal sources used in the preparation of this study were Dorothy Day's published writings about her life in the Catholic Worker Movement: *From Union Square to Rome* (Maryland: Presentation of the Faith Press, 1939), *Houses of Hospitality* (New York: Sheed & Ward, 1939), *The Long Loneliness* (New York: Curtis Books, 1952), and *Loaves and Fishes* (New York: Harper & Row, 1963). Ammon Hennacy's *The Autobiography of a Catholic Anarchist* (New Jersey: Libertarian Press, 1952), was also very helpful. The latest edition of the book appears under the title, *The Book of Ammon* (Salt Lake City: n.p. 1965). Most essential to any study pertaining to the Catholic Worker is its newspaper, the *Catholic Worker*. I first used the copies of the newspaper located at St. Charles Borromeo Seminary Archives in Philadelphia. Significantly, issues published during World War II were missing. The complete newspaper is available on microfilm at the University of Notre Dame. The manuscript collection of Catholic Worker papers, correspondence, and so on, is in the archives at Marquette University. Dorothy Day named William D. Miller her official biographer. His two books, *A Harsh and Dreadful Love: Dorothy Day and the Catholic Worker Movement* (New York: Liveright, 1973) and *Dorothy Day: A Biography* (San Francisco: Harper & Row, 1982) have been a valuable aid. It must be pointed out that when asked, Day and Miller both contended that there is no pertinent information on peace in the collection at Marquette University.

The Catholic Association for International Peace

The principal source for a study of this group is the CAIP collection located in the archives at Marquette University. Although these papers are open to the public, the material has rarely been consulted. The Catholic University of America possesses the John A. Ryan papers, a limited portion of which were pertinent to this study.

Conscientious Objection

The newspaper, *Catholic CO*, published during World War II by the Association of Catholic Conscientious Objectors (ACCO) is available on microfilm from the University of San Francisco. The Peace Collection at Swarthmore College contains material related to the ACCO, the CAIP, the Catholic Worker; it also has the complete files of the National Service Board for Religious Objectors (NSBRO) as well as the U.S. Selective Service System report published in 1950 as *Conscientious Objection*, Vols. I and II. A copy of Gordon Zahn's unpublished Ph.D. dissertation from Catholic University in 1953, *A Descriptive Study of the Sociological Backgrounds of CO's during World War II*, is also there. The writings of John Courtney Murray on Selective Conscientious Objection (SCO) are located in the archives of Woodstock College at Georgetown University. Arthur Sheehan, director of the ACCO, and Gordon Zahn, a Catholic CO during World War II, provided significant information through interviews and correspondence.

Thomas Merton

For the Thomas Merton section of this study the main sources were Merton's writings on peace and these are found in the endnotes of Chapter V. There is also correspondence between James Forest and Thomas Merton during the last ten years of Merton's life which Forest gave me permission to use; the letters are located at Regina Laudis Monastery in Bethlehem, Connecticut. Also contained in the collection are some of Merton's unpublished writings on peace that he mimeographed and circulated among friends. The definitive biographer of Thomas Merton is Michael Mott, *The Seven Mountains of Thomas Merton* (Boston: Hougton Mifflin, 1984). Mott had access to all of Merton's writings, even his restricted journals. Merton's materials are located at the Thomas Merton Studies Center at Bellarmine College in Louisville, Kentucky.

The Second Vatican Council

The most valuable sources for this section were the writings and correspondence of James Douglass during his intervention at the Second Vatican Council. Douglass lent this collection to me and it proved to be very helpful. I have referred to this correspondence and writings as the "JD Collection" in the endnotes.

PAX

There is much valuable material, especially correspondence, in the possession of Eileen Egan, cofounder and codirector of PAX and Pax Christi–USA. In November 1990 she decided to send her papers on these two organizations to the archives of the University of Notre Dame. Gordon Zahn's papers are also in the archives at the University of Notre Dame.

The Berrigan Brothers

The main sources for Chapter VII were the published writings of the Berrigan brothers and their conversations and writings to me. Jerome and Carol Berrigan provided me with hospitality and access to their personal archives on Daniel and Philip Berrigan. The Berrigan Collection is located in Special Collections, Olin Library, Cornell University. Both Daniel and Philip have placed their writings and documents in the collection.

Catholic Peace Fellowship (CPF)

The CPF Collection is located in the archives at the University of Notre Dame. Thomas Cornell and most recently Bill Ofenloch have submitted material for the collection.

Pax Christi—USA

The Pax Christi Collection is located in the archives at the University of Notre Dame. Mary Lou Kownacki, the national coordinator, has collected and submitted the material. It is very extensive. There are many limitations in the first years of the organization, but the unpublished history of that period, *Pax Christi USA: the Early Years, 1972–78*, written by Gerard A. Vanderhaar in 1988 completes the story for those years. Vanderhaar's papers and material are located in the archives at the University of Notre Dames as well as the "unofficial" papers of Bishop Thomas Gumbleton. His official papers are located in the archives of the Archdiocesse of Detroit.

Oral Interviews

My first interview for this study took place almost twenty years ago when I approached Dorothy Day after she had spoken at a rally at St. Ignatius Hall in Baltimore in support of the Catonsville Nine. I still vividly remember my enthusiasm as I rushed up to her and asked her about the relationship of Daniel Berrigan to the Catholic Worker. Her reply was sharp. "Dan isn't a Catholic Worker, he came to us and stole our young men away into the peace movement." I was shocked and confused. Fortunately I was able to talk to her several other times before she died. Since I was privileged to interview many of the people mentioned in this study, I will just name the few whom I found to be most helpful: Daniel and Philip Berrigan, Henry Browne, Thomas Cornell, James Forest, Gordon Zahn, Paul Hanley Furfey, John Peter Grady, Patrick McDermott, James Jennings, George Shuster, Archbishop Thomas Roberts, Monsignor George Higgins, and Bishop Thomas Gumbleton.

Secondary sources of relevance to this study have been cited in the endnotes.

Notes

Preface

1. National Conference of Catholic Bishops, *The Challenge of Peace* (Washington, D.C.: United States Catholic Conference, 1983), par. 121.
2. William D. Miller, *A Harsh and Dreadful Love: Dorothy Day and the Catholic Worker Movement* (New York: Liveright, 1973), 3.

1: Origins of the Catholic Peace Movement

1. John Tracy Ellis, "American Catholics and Peace: A Historical Sketch " (Washington, D.C.: United States Catholic Conference, 1970), 25, reprint from James S. Rausch, ed., *The Family of Nations* (Huntington, Ind.: Our Sunday Visitor, Inc., 1970).
2. Henry J. Browne, "Catholicism in the United States," in James Ward Smith and A. Leland Jamison, eds., *The Shaping of American Religion* (Princeton, N.J.: Princeton University Press, 1961), 77.
3. John Higham, *Strangers in the Land: Patterns of American Nativism, 1860–1915* (New Brunswick, N.J.: Rutgers University Press, 1966), 218.
4. Browne, "Catholicism in the United States," 77.
5. Richard P. McBrien, *Catholicism*, vol. 2 (Minneapolis, Minn.: Winston Press, 1980), 938.
6. Ibid.
7. Ronald G. Musto, *The Catholic Peace Tradition* (New York: Orbis Books, 1986), 169.
8. Ronald E. Powaski, *Thomas Merton on Nuclear Weapons* (Chicago: Loyola University Press, 1988), 8.
9. John Tracy Ellis, *American Catholicism*, 2d ed., rev. (Chicago: University of Chicago Press, 1969), 141.
10. Musto, *Catholic Peace Tradition*, 240.
11. Ellis, *American Catholicism*, 144.
12. Jay P. Dolan, *The American Catholic Experience: A History from Colonial Time to the Present* (New York: Doubleday, 1985), 342.
13. Joseph M. McShane, *Sufficiently Radical: Catholicism, Progressivism and the*

263

Bishops' Program of 1919 (Washington, D.C.: Catholic University of America Press, 1986), 27.

14. Dolan, *American Catholic Experience*, 343.
15. Ibid., 346–369.
16. David J. O'Brien, *American Catholicism and Social Reform: The New Deal Years* (New York: Oxford University Press, 1968), 42.
17. John A. Ryan, *Social Doctrine in Action, a Personal History* (New York: Harper & Brothers, 1941), 137.
18. McShane, *Sufficiently Radical*, 41.
19. Musto, *Catholic Peace Tradition*, 171.
20. Harry W. Flannery, "CAIP Fights for International Peace," *U.S. Catholic* (September 1963): 25 and 26. See also John A. Ryan's autobiography, *Social Doctrine*, 140, 141, 145.
21. Francis L. Broderick, *Right Reverend New Dealer John A. Ryan* (New York: Macmillan, 1963), 104.
22. Flannery, "CAIP Fights," 25. The correspondence received by Flannery while researching CAIP is located in the CAIP Collection in the archives at Marquette University, hereafter referred to as AMU.
23. Ibid., 25, 26.
24. Broderick, *Right Reverend New Dealer*, 135.
25. Ibid., 160.
26. Ibid., 136.
27. Ibid., 77.
28. Ibid., 138.
29. AMU, CAIP Collection, "Notes on CAIP" by Raymond McGowan, 4 August 1958.
30. Ibid.
31. Ibid.
32. Broderick, *Right Reverend New Dealer*, 138.
33. AMU, CAIP Collection, "CAIP Constitution," Section 2.
34. O'Brien, *American Catholicism and Social Reform*, 121.
35. AMU, CAIP Collection, letter dated 1 March 1963, Mrs. R. M. Patterson to Harry W. Flannery.
36. Dennis Robb, "Specialized Catholic Action in the United States, 1936–1949: Ideology, Leadership, and Organization," Ph.D. diss., University of Minnesota, 1972, 32.
37. Flannery, "CAIP Fights," 27.
38. This point about type of membership is similar to the thesis of Sondra R. Herman, *Eleven Against War: Studies in American International Thought, 1898–1921* (Stanford, Calif.: Hoover Institution Press, 1969), ix.
39. AMU, CAIP Collection, letter dated 2 February 1963, George Shuster to Harry W. Flannery.
40. Flannery, "CAIP Fights," 27.
41. AMU, CAIP Collection, "Summary of CAIP Committee Work," Section 1, 6.

42. AMU, CAIP Collection, "A History of the Catholic Association for International Peace 1927–1953," by Clarence L. Hohl, Jr., 22; see John A. Ryan's *International Ethics* (Washington, D.C.: Paulist Press, 1928).
43. AMU, CAIP Collection, letters to Ms. Elizabeth Sweeney.
44. AMU, CAIP Collection, letters during 1930s, Anna Dill Gamble to Elizabeth Sweeney.
45. AMU, CAIP Collection, letters during 1930s, Mary Workman to Elizabeth Sweeney.
46. AMU, CAIP Collection, "Minutes of the Executive Committee," 27 December 1928, and 22 April 1930.
47. AMU, CAIP Collection, letter dated 5 April 1935, Sister Rose de Lima to Elizabeth Sweeney.
48. AMU, CAIP Collection, letters dated 9 May 1935 and 28 October 1936, Sister Rose de Lima to Elizabeth Sweeney. Also a typed page announcing the two meetings on November 20 at St. Elizabeth College in New Jersey and at Rosary College in River Forest, Illinois.
49. *Congressional Record*, 71st Cong., 3rd Sess., 1931, 74: 2263–2267.
50. Norman Krause Herzfeld, "Working for Peace," *Voice of St. Jude* (December 1954), n.p.
51. AMU, CAIP Collection, letter dated 19 April 1933, Patrick J. Ward to Elizabeth Sweeney.
52. George Q. Flynn, *American Catholics and the Roosevelt Presidency 1932–1936* (Lexington, Ky.: University of Kentucky Press, 1968), 150.
53. Ryan, *Social Doctrine*, 214, 215. Broderick in his biography of Ryan, *Right Reverend New Dealer*, states that Ryan resigned from NCPW because it was too pacifist.
54. Ryan, *Social Doctrine*.
55. AMU, CAIP Collection, letter dated 26 June 1929, Franziskus Stratmann, O.P., to Elizabeth Sweeney.
56. AMU, CAIP Collection, "Summary of CAIP Work 1927 to 1952," 7.
57. Ibid.
58. Broderick, *Right Reverend New Dealer*, 233, 234.
59. *New York Times*, 16 October 1939, cited in Charles J. Tull, *Father Coughlin and the New Deal* (Syracuse, N.Y.: Syracuse University Press, 1965), 217.
60. Ryan, *Social Doctrine in Action*, 216, 217.
61. George Q. Flynn, *Roosevelt and Romanism: Catholics and American Diplomacy 1937–1945* (Westport, Conn.: Greenwood Press, 1976), 189.
62. AMU, CAIP Collection, Hohl, "A History of the Catholic Association . . . ," 55.
63. In this chapter I have presented a general interpretation of Coughlin's relationship to the Catholic peace movement. To achieve this interpretation I have consulted a number of studies on Coughlin. See O'Brien, *American Catholicism and Social Reform*; Tull, *Father Coughlin*; David H. Bennett, *Demagogues of the Depression: American Radicals and the Union Party, 1932–36* (New Brunswick, N.J.: Rutgers University Press, 1969); Aaron Abell, *American Catholicism and Social Action*

(1960, reprint Notre Dame, Ind.: University of Notre Dame Press, 1963); Sheldon Marcus, *Father Coughlin: The Tumultuous Life of the Priest of the Little Flower* (Boston: Little, Brown, 1973); Alan Brinkley, *Voices of Protest: Huey Long, Father Coughlin, and the Great Depression* (New York: Knopf, 1982); Craig A. Newton, "Father Coughlin and His National Union for Social Justice," *Southwestern Social Science Quarterly*, 41 (December 1960): 341–349; and James P. Shenton, "The Coughlin Movement and the New Deal," *Political Science Quarterly*, 73 (September 1958): 353–373. I have also consulted twenty pamphlets written by Coughlin and his newspaper, *Social Justice*, 1937–1942. Pamphlets and newspaper are located in the archives at the University of Notre Dame.

64. *Catholic Worker*, September 1933, and April 1935, cited in O'Brien, *American Catholics and Social Reform*, 195.

65. Dorothy Day's books are mainly autobiographical: *From Union Square to Rome* (Silver Spring, Md.: Presentation of the Faith Press, 1939); *Houses of Hospitality* (New York: Sheed & Ward, 1939); *The Long Loneliness* (New York: Harper, 1952); and *Loaves and Fishes* (New York: Harper & Row, 1963). There is no autobiography by Peter Maurin. There are two biographies, however, Arthur Sheehan, *Peter Maurin: Gay Believer: The Biography of an Unusual and Saintly Man* (New York: Hanover House, 1959), and Marc H. Ellis, *Peter Maurin: Prophet in the Twentieth Century* (New York: Paulist Press, 1981).

66. Day, *The Long Loneliness*, 166.

67. Herman, *Eleven Against War*, ix.

68. The major influences were Benedictine Virgil Michel, Monsignor Paul Hanley Furfey, Tolstoy, Berdyaev, and Emmanuel Mounier.

69. *Catholic Worker*, October 1939 and June 1940.

70. A complete study of American Catholics' reaction to the Spanish Civil War is found in the works of J. David Valaik: "American Catholic Dissenters and the Spanish Civil War," *Catholic Historical Review* 53 (January 1968): 537–546 and "Catholics, Neutrality, and the Spanish Embargo, 1937–1939," *Journal of American History* 54 (June 1967): 73–85.

71. *Catholic Worker*, May 1935.

72. Interview with Dorothy Day, 24 June 1971: Dorothy stated that there was never any significant cooperation with other peace groups until the 1950s.

73. *Catholic Worker*, April 1934, January 1936, and March 1937.

74. Ibid., July–August 1939.

75. Ibid.

76. Ibid., December 1934, also cited in O'Brien, *American Catholicism and Social Reform*, 202.

77. *Catholic Worker*, May 1934.

78. Ibid., July–August 1935, July 1936, May 1937, and January 1938.

79. Ibid., May 1936.

80. Ibid., January 1938.

81. Ibid., October 1938.

82. Charles Chatfield, *For Peace and Justice: Pacifism in America, 1914–1941* (Knoxville: University of Tennessee Press, 1971), 325.

83. "War," *Catholic Encyclopedia*, vol. 15 (New York: Encyclopedia Press, 1913), gives Charles Mackey's definition of the just war criteria and presents it as normative. "War," *New Catholic Encyclopedia*, vol. 19 (New York: McGraw-Hill, 1967), quotes Paul Ramsey: "It has been observed that according to recent papal teaching (Pius XII and John XXIII) there is no longer any just war theory, because these popes have withdrawn the right of war in the situations to which these tests or conditions had reference, i.e., offensive war. This means that contemporary moral teaching represents both a continuation and a radical adjustment of traditional teaching on just warfare."

84. "Dorothy Day Describes the Launching of the *Catholic Worker* and the Movement Behind It, May 1933," cited in John Tracy Ellis, ed., *Documents of American Catholic History*, 2 (Chicago: H. Regnery, 1967), 629.

2: Dorothy Day

1. Chatfield, *For Peace and Justice*, 7.
2. Dwight Macdonald, "The Foolish Things of the World—II," *New Yorker*, 17 (11 October 1952): 40.
3. Ibid., 38.
4. William D. Miller, *Dorothy Day: A Biography* (New York: Harper and Row, 1982), 1.
5. Dorothy Day as quoted in Eileen Egan, "Dorothy Day: Pilgrim of Peace," in Patrick G. Coy, ed., *A Revolution of the Heart: Essays on the Catholic Worker* (Philadelphia: Temple University Press, 1988), 71.
6. Ibid., 49–50.
7. Mel Piehl, "Politics of Free Obedience," in Coy, *A Revolution of the Heart*, 179.
8. Macdonald, "The Foolish Things," 40.
9. As quoted in Macdonald, "The Foolish Things," 40–41.
10. Quotation in Day, *Long Loneliness*, 149–150.
11. Robert Coles, *Dorothy Day: A Radical Devotion* (Reading, Mass.: Addison-Wesley, 1987), 71.
12. Ibid., 62.
13. Piehl, "Politics of Free Obedience," 199.
14. William D. Miller, *A Harsh and Dreadful Love*, 56
15. Miller, *Dorothy Day*, 247.
16. Egan, "Dorothy Day: Pilgrim," 73.
17. Interview with Eileen Egan, 29 November 1990. Egan stated that Day's use of the term Catholic anarchist always upset her. She asked Day why she did not use the term Catholic personalist and Day's response was that she called herself a Catholic anarchist to wake people up and make them think.
18. Coles, *Dorothy Day: A Radical Devotion*, 96.
19. Miller, *A Harsh and Dreadful Love*, 14.
20. Miller, *Dorothy Day*, 247.
21. Dwight Macdonald, "The Foolish Things of the World—I," *New Yorker* 27 (4 October 1952): 46.
22. Miller, *A Harsh and Dreadful Love*, 3.

23. Mel Piehl, *Breaking Bread: The Catholic Worker and the Origin of Catholic Radicalism in America* (Philadelphia: Temple University Press, 1982), 198.
24. Marc H. Ellis, *Peter Maurin*, 24.
25. John C. Cort, "Dorothy Day at 75," *Commonweal* 97 (23 February 1973): 476.
26. Dorothy Day, *Long Loneliness*, 206 as quoted in Egan, "Dorothy Day: Pilgrim," 77.
27. Piehl, *Breaking Bread*, 191–193.
28. Miller, *A Harsh and Dreadful Love*, 139.
29. *Catholic Worker*, September 1936, as quoted in Nancy L. Roberts, *Dorothy Day and the Catholic Worker* (Albany: State University of New York Press, 1984), 119.
30. Piehl, *Breaking Bread*, 194.
31. Marc H. Ellis, *Peter Maurin*, 89, 90, 91.
32. As quoted in Miller, *A Harsh and Dreadful Love*, 166.
33. Ibid., 168.
34. Ibid., 174.
35. Gordon Zahn, "Leaven of Love and Justice," *America*, 127 (11 November 1972): 383.
36. *Catholic Worker*, April 1938.
37. Swarthmore College Peace Collection (hereafter referred to as SCPC) ACCO Collection, PAX Manifesto.
38. Dorothy Day, *Loaves and Fishes*, 60.
39. *Catholic Worker*, May 1943. Perhaps the reading here is too beneficent toward church authorities.
40. Piehl, *Breaking Bread*, 195.
41. Ibid.
42. U.S. Congress, House Committee on Military Affairs, Report of the Hearings anent H.R. 10132, 30 July 1940, 152–160.
43. Ibid., 299–323.
44. Egan, "Dorothy Day: Pilgrim," 79.
45. Ibid.
46. Leslie S. Rothenberg, *The Draft and You* (Garden City, N.Y.: Anchor Books, 1968), 11.
47. Ibid.
48. Day, *The Long Loneliness*, 304.
49. Ibid.
50. Ibid.
51. Ibid., 305.
52. "Editorial," *Catholic Worker*, January 1942.
53. For more about Day's sabbatical, see Egan, "Dorothy Day: Pilgrim," 85–87.

3: World War II and the Just War Tradition

1. Cardinal Spellman as quoted in Lawrence S. Wittner, *Rebels Against War: The American Peace Movement, 1941–1960* (New York: Columbia University Press, 1969), 36.

2. Musto, *Catholic Peace Tradition*, 175.
3. Ibid., 176.
4. Ibid., 177.
5. Ibid., 185.
6. "Atomic Bomb," excerpt from *l'Observatore Romano*, 10 August 1945, in *Tablet*, 18 August 1945, 78.
7. Earl Boyea, "The National Catholic Welfare Conference: An Experience in Episcopal Leadership, 1935–1945, Ph.D. diss., Catholic University of America, 1987, 179. See pp. 159–179 for his complete coverage of the "Bombing of Rome."
8. George Weigel, *Tranquillitas Ordinis: The Present Failure and Future Promise of American Catholic Thought on War and Peace* (New York: Oxford University Press, 1987), 58.
9. Musto, *Catholic Peace Tradition*, 246.
10. Flynn, *Roosevelt and Romanism*, 77, as quoted in Boyea, *National Catholic Welfare*, 123.
11. Boyea, *National Catholic Welfare*, 123.
12. Ibid., 124.
13. Ibid., 130.
14. Paul Comly French, *We Won't Murder* (New York: Hastings House, 1940), 157.
15. "National Catholic College Poll," *America* 62 (11 November 1939): 116–119, and 62 (18 November 1939): 144–147.
16. Lillian Schlissel, *Conscience in America* (New York: E. P. Dutton, 1968), 219.
17. Ibid.
18. Paul Riley, a graduate student in the Department of Religion at Temple University while doing research for Dr. Elwyn Smith on the subject of American Catholicism and conscientious objection from 1776 to 1924, found only four Catholics who were COs in World War I: John Dunn, Francis X. Hennessy, Christian Lellig, and Benjamin Salmon. Ammon Hennacy, a CO during World War I, later converted to Catholicism.
19. U. S. Selective Service System, *Conscientious Objection*, 1950, vol. I, 53, 60, 105, 117, 263, 320,
20. SCPC, NSBRO Collection, Box G-76. Dorothy Day in an article, "Women and War," *Catholic C.O.*, Fall 1946 (also cited in Egan, "Pilgrim," 85), wrote that there were two Catholic COs during World War I and during World War II, 154 Catholic COs in jail and 200 Catholic COs in CPS.
21. Wittner, *Rebels against War*, 70.
22. Clarence Pickett as quoted in Ibid.
23. Schlissel, *Conscience in America*, 225.
24. SCPC, NSBRO Collection, Box G-76.
25. Arthur Sheehan visited Paul Comly French, director of NSBRO, who told him to observe the American Friends CPS camp at Cooperstown, which had a budget of $50,000 a year. Sheehan believed that the Catholic Worker could run a camp for $15,000 annually. Archbishop John T. McNicholas of Cincinnati gave $300 and the American Civil Liberties Union gave $500. Four other bishops helped

financially: Karl J. Alter, bishop of Toledo; Francis J. Beckman, archbishop of Dubuque; John B. Peterson, bishop of Manchester; and Gerald Shaughnessy, S.M., bishop of Seattle. Other sources of revenue came in small donations of $25 or less.

26. Gordon C. Zahn, *Another Part of the War: The Camp Simon Story* (Amherst: University of Massachusetts Press, 1979), xiii.
27. Ibid., 260.
28. *Catholic Worker*, December 1941.
29. SCPC, ACCO Collection, letter from Dwight Larrowe to Miss E. S. Brenton dated 22 July 1942, for an appeal for funds. Larrowe stated that thirty-nine men were at Stoddard and that he was running the camp at $16 a month per man rather than the prescribed $35. He had spent $5,000 in the past year and needed two to three times that amount for the next year.
30. Day, *Loaves and Fishes*, 64.
31. Zahn, *Another Part of the War*, x.
32. Interview with Richard Leonard of LaSalle College, Philadelphia, a Catholic CO at Stoddard, Warner, and Rosewood, on Tuesday, 4 November 1969.
33. Theodore Pojar, Robert Lindorfer, and Francis Bates were three such Catholic COs. See the *Catholic Worker*, May 1942.
34. Zahn, *Another Part of the War*, ix.
35. Ibid., xi.
36. Ibid., 219.
37. Gordon Zahn, *War, Conscience and Dissent* (New York: Hawthorn Books, 1967), 152.
38. *Catholic Worker*, May 1943.
39. Telephone conversation between Arthur Sheehan and the author on 21 October 1969: Mr. Sheehan indicated that the decision to close the CPS camp at Warner was not simply a matter of finances as Wittner in *Rebels Against War* (54) contends.
40. SCPC, NSBRO Collection, Box A-44.
41. Wittner, *Rebels against War*, 60.
42. SCPC, ACCO Collection, Memorandum.
43. *Catholic CO*, October 1944. This newspaper is available on microfilm at the University of San Francisco.
44. *Catholic Worker*, June, 1948.
45. Mulford Q. Sibley and Philip E. Jacob, *Conscription of Conscience* (Ithaca, N.Y.: Cornell University Press, 1952), 468–475.
46. *Catholic CO*, January–March 1946.
47. J. F. Powers, the noted American author of *Morte D'Urban*, is an example of such a Catholic CO.
48. *Catholic Worker*, April–June 1944, and letter from Arthur Sheehan to author dated 30 October 1969.
49. Zahn, *Another Part of the War*, 251–252.
50. John Courtney Ford, S.J., "Morality of Obliteration Bombing," *Theological Studies* 5 (September, 1944): 267.

51. Ibid.
52. Ibid.
53. Ibid., 305.
54. Ibid., 268–269.
55. Ibid., 271.
56. *Catholic Worker*, October 1944. See also Paul H. Furfey, "Bombing of Non-Combatants Is Murder," *Catholic CO*, July–September 1945, and *The Mystery of Iniquity* (Milwaukee: Bruce, 1944), 165–166.
57. "Atomic Bomb," *Commonweal* 43 (31 August 1945): 468.
58. J. M. Gillis, "Editorial Comment," *Catholic World*, 166 (September, 1945): 449–450.
59. *Catholic Worker*, September 1945.
60. Wittner, *Rebels against War*, 126–28.
61. AMU, CAIP Collection, "Summary of CAIP Committee Work—End of War to 1952," 21.
62. Ibid.
63. Wittner, *Rebels against War*, 128–29.

4: The Birth of Nonviolence

1. Wittner, *Rebels against War*, 213.
2. Joan V. Bondurant, *Conquest of Violence: The Gandhian Philosophy of Conflict* (Berkeley: University of California, 1969), 8 and 9.
3. Ibid., 36.
4. Wittner, *Rebels against War*, 62–96. He gives a detailed account of the acts of nonviolent resistance performed by radical pacifists during the war.
5. Ibid., 156, 157.
6. Ibid., 163.
7. Gordon C. Zahn, "The Future of the Catholic Peace Movement," *Commonweal*, 99 (28 December 1973): 338.
8. AMU, CAIP Collection, Memorandum entitled "Organizations to be Represented at Paris," dated 9 July 1948. Other peace groups that held observer status within the United Nations were the Carnegie Endowment for International Peace, Women's Action Committee for Lasting Peace, and the pacifist group, Women's International League for Peace and Freedom.
9. AMU, CAIP Collection. Miss Rita Schaefer represented not only NCWC and CAIP, but also the National Catholic Conference of Women.
10. AMU, CAIP Collection, letter dated 13 April 1948, John Eppstein to Miss Rita Schaefer. John Eppstein, author of *The Catholic Tradition of the Law of Nations*, was director and editor of the British Society for International Understanding.
11. AMU, CAIP Collection, "Summary of the CAIP Committee Work, 1927 to 1952," 25.
12. AMU, "CAIP Collection," Annual Report, 30 June 1949–30 June 1950, 2.
13. Ibid., 25.

14. Michael O'Neill, "The American Catholic Bishops and Foreign Policy—Vietnam and Latin America," Ph.D. diss., University of Edinburgh, 1974, 84.
15. As quoted in ibid., 85.
16. Anne Klejment, "In the Lion's Den: The Social Catholicism of Daniel and Philip Berrigan, 1955–1965," Ph.D. diss., State University of New York at Binghamton, 1980, 106.
17. Miller, A Harsh and Dreadful Love, 219, 220.
18. John Cogley, "A Harsh and Dreadful Love," America 127 (11 November 1972): 395.
19. Piehl, Breaking Bread, 205.
20. Ibid., 206–208.
21. Miller, A Harsh and Dreadful Love, 225.
22. Piehl, Breaking Bread, 205.
23. As quoted in Roberts, Dorothy Day, 140.
24. Ibid., 141.
25. Ibid.
26. Harrington as quoted in ibid., 146, 147.
27. Catholic Worker as quoted in Miller, A Harsh and Dreadful Love, 229.
28. Ibid., 234.
29. Bruce Cook, "Dorothy Day and the Catholic Worker," U.S. Catholic (March 1966): 29, as quoted in Roberts, Dorothy Day, 143.
30. Roberts, Dorothy Day, 143–145.
31. John Courtney Murray as quoted in Donald E. Pelotte, John Courtney Murray: Theologian in Conflict (New York: Paulist Press, 1975), 28.
32. Ibid., 2.
33. Wittner, Rebels against War, 254.
34. John Courtney Murray, S.J., Morality and Modern War (New York: Council on Religion and International Affairs, 1959), 18.
35. Ibid., 15.
36. Ibid., 17.
37. Ibid.
38. In 1962, George Meany received CAIP's Annual Peace Award.
39. Letter dated 17 August 1972, George N. Shuster to author.
40. AMU, CAIP Collection, untitled typed memorandum by Harry W. Flannery.
41. James Douglass Collection (hereafter referred to as JDC), a copy of CAIP critique and cover letter dated 5 August 1964, William V. O'Brien to Most Rev. John J. Wright, D.D. JDC is all the written material of James Douglass from his lobbying efforts at the Second Vatican Council. The collection is in his possession.
42. William Nagle, ed., Morality and Modern Warfare: The State of the Question (Baltimore: Helicon Press, 1960), 6, 7.
43. Charles S. Thompson, ed., Morals and Missiles: Catholic Essays on the Problem of War Today (London: J. Clarke, 1961). This book includes essays by Canon F. H. Drinkwater, Dom Bede Griffiths, O.S.B., Christopher Hollis, Sir Compton Mackenzie, Archbishop Thomas D. Roberts, S.J., Franziskus Stratmann, O.P., and E. I. Watkin.

44. In July 1961, the Institute of World Polity at Georgetown University published the papers presented at the Second Annual Conference on Christian Political and Social Thought. The topic of the conference was "Christian Ethics and Nuclear Warfare." William V. O'Brien was one of the editors of the compendium. The conference noted that much of what had been accomplished through the centuries by way of the just war doctrine in providing limits to warfare collapsed in the nuclear age and that technically "aggressive" modern war became unjustifiable as Pius XII said in his Christmas address of 1944.

45. John C. Ford in "The Hydrogen Bombing of Cities," in Nagle, *Morality and Modern Warfare*, 98–103, bases his argument against the use of nuclear weapons as he did in his arguments against obliteration bombing on the rights of noncombatants. This position is adopted by the Second Vatican Council.

46. Donald J. Thorman, "The Christian's Conscience and Nuclear Warfare," *New City* (15 November 1962), reprint found in AMU, CAIP Collection. Thorman's article provided Donahue's definitions of the major approaches given in this summary.

47. "The moral or political principles on which our most critical decisions are to be made may, in themselves, be relatively simple, but the assumptions on which they are based are immensely complicated. It is not difficult to appeal to traditional norms of justice and law, and apply them to our present situation in such a way as to come up with logical and plausible conclusions. But the very plausibility of the conclusions tends to be the most dangerous thing about them, if we forget that they may be based on premises which we take to be axiomatic and which, in fact have been invalidated by recent developments of weapons technology. . . . There is a very serious danger that our most critical decisions may turn out to be no decisions at all, but only the end of a vicious circle of conjectures and gratuitous assumptions in which we unconsciously make the argument come out in favor of our own theory, our own favorite policy." Thomas Merton, *Breakthrough to Peace: Twelve Views on the Threat of Thermonuclear Extermination* (New York: New Directions, 1962), 219.

48. Wittner, *Rebels against War*, 244.

49. Ibid., 154–55; 247, 248.

50. Miller, *A Harsh and Dreadful Love*, 279.

51. Ammon Hennacy, *The Autobiography of a Catholic Anarchist* (New Jersey: Libertarian Press, 1952). Edition used by author.

52. Miller, *A Harsh and Dreadful Love*, 279.

53. Archives at University of Notre Dame, hereafter referred to as AUND, CPF Collection, letter dated 30 April 1980, Thomas Cornell to Professor William Miller.

54. Patrick G. Coy, "The One-Person Revolution of Ammon Hennacy," in Patrick G. Coy, ed., *A Revolution of the Heart: Essays on the Catholic Worker* (Philadelphia: Temple University Press, 1988), 134–136.

55. Hennacy as quoted in Coy, "The One-Person Revolution," 139.

56. Coy, "The One-Person Revolution," 141.

57. Ibid., 151.

58. As quoted in Coy, "One-Person Revolution, " 142.
59. Coy, "One-Person Revolution," 161.
60. AUND, CPF Collection, letter dated 30 April 1980, Thomas Cornell to Professor William Miller. Cornell goes on to state in the letter that when Ludlow announced his reevaluation of anarchism at the annual Labor Day weekend Pacifist Conference at Peter Maurin Farm on Staten Island, it caused quite a commotion and that the conference was suspended until 1963 when Cornell revived it. Ludlow published his reevaluation in the *Catholic Worker* in June 1955. Cornell agreed with Ludlow's reevaluation and disliked the use of the term anarchism and believed it should not be used since no one affiliated with the Catholic Worker knew what it meant or how to apply it. Cornell preferred the term personalism.
61. Hennacy, "Why I am a Catholic Anarchist," 3, as quoted in Coy, "One-Person Revolution," 162.
62. A spur to Hennacy's decision was a two-week fast in Glen Gardner, New Jersey, begun by Dave Dellinger and others, against the sending of troops to Korea. Hennacy wrote to Dellinger that he too would fast, but was unsympathetic to Dellinger's World Citizen emphasis. See Hennacy, *Autobiography*, 163.
63. A. J. Muste as quoted in Wittner, *Rebels against War*, 265. Wittner gives a very detailed description of the demonstration.
64. *Catholic Worker*, June 1960. A similar event occurred in London's Trafalgar Square where 75,000 people turned out in support of unilateral disarmament of nuclear weapons.
65. Ibid., April 1960.
66. AUND, CPF Collection, letter dated 30 April 1980, Thomas Cornell to Professor William Miller.
67. *Catholic Worker*, January 1962. Jean Morton, Nelson Barr, Bob Kaye, Charles Butterworth, Elain Paulson, Mark Samara, Carol Kramer, and Jim Forest were Catholic Worker participants. Thomas Merton wrote a letter of support that was published in the same issue.
68. Miller, *A Harsh and Dreadful Love*, 300, 301. Much of Miller's information on why Hennacy left is obtained from Dorothy Day's chapter on Hennacy in *Loaves and Fishes*.
69. Dorothy Day as quoted in Miller, *A Harsh and Dreadful Love*, 266.
70. James H. Forest, "No Longer Alone: The Catholic Peace Movement" in Thomas E. Quigley, ed., *American Catholics and Vietnam* (Grand Rapids, Mich.: Eerdmans Publishing Co., 1968), 144.
71. Address given by Archbishop Thomas D. Roberts, S.J., to a small group at Pendle Hill, Pennsylvania (a Quaker center), in the fall of 1970, attended by author.
72. William J. Gibbons, ed., *Pacem in Terris: Encyclical Letter of His Holiness Pope John XXIII* (New York: Macmillan, 1968), par. 127.
73. Ibid., par. 5.
74. Ibid., par. 48.
75. JDC, letter dated 13 August 1965, Thomas Merton to Archbishop George Flahiff states that Merton sent a copy of the letter to *Commonweal* for publication but it was rejected.

76. Thomas Merton, "In Acceptance of the PAX Medal, 1963" in Gordon C. Zahn, *Thomas Merton on Peace*, (New York: McCall, 1971), 257 and 258.

77. The original text in the first draft read as follows: "Although after all helps to peaceful discussion have been exhausted, it may not be illicit, when one's rights have been unjustly trammeled, to defend those rights against such unjust aggression by violence and force. Nevertheless, the use of arms, especially nuclear weapons whose effects are greater than can be imagined and therefore cannot be reasonably regulated by men, exceeds all just proportion and therefore must be judged most wicked before, God and man." See Floyd Anderson, ed., *The Council Daybook*, Session III (Washington, D.C.: National Catholic Welfare Conference, 1966), 243.

78. AMU, CAIP Collection, letter dated 14 March 1963, Harry W. Flannery to Victor C. Ferkiss.

79. JDC, copy of CAIP critique, p. 2 of alternative text section.

80. AMU, CAIP Collection.

81. Ellis, *American Catholicism*, 120–122.

82. AMU, CAIP Collection, Memorandum, "Morality, Nuclear War, and the Schema on the Church in the Modern World."

83. A text of a leaflet issued to explain the purpose of the fast is found in "Appeal to Rome," *Reconciliation Quarterly* (Fourth Quarter, 1965): 612–614.

84. James Douglass attained an M.A. degree in theology at Bellarmine College, and while at the school he became friends with Thomas Merton. After lobbying at the Council, he wrote *The Non-Violent Cross* (New York: Macmillan, 1966). In 1969, he was co-director of the Program in Non-Violence at the University of Notre Dame. In 1971, he wrote his second book *Resistance and Contemplation*. He has remained committed to a life of nonviolence.

85. James Douglass, *The Non-Violent Cross*, 134.

86. *Pastoral Constitution on the Church in the Modern World* (Huntington, Ind.: Our Sunday Visitor, 1968), 85.

87. JDC, copy of the intervention. The intervention was also signed by Archbishop George Flahiff of Winnepeg and English Bishops Gordon Wheeler and Charles Grant.

88. JDC, letter dated 28 November 1964, James Douglass to Philip Scharper. Douglass based much of the final version of the text on the suggestions of Philip Scharper, another member of PAX. Douglass had also consulted many theologians on the wording of the intervention. Fathers Bernard Haring, Yves Congar, and Gregory Baum expressed virtually complete agreement with the text. Father Karl Rahner was reluctant to condemn the concept of a total war deterrent for mainly political reasons and Father Charles Davis wanted more on the responsibilities of the heads of states rather than the emphasis on conscientious objection.

89. JDC, Intervention of Bishop John Taylor (Stockholm, Sweden).

90. JDC, copy of Challenge dated 2 December 1965.

91. *Pastoral Constitution*, 87, 88.

92. JDC, letter dated, 2 February 1966, Donald Quinn to James Douglass. Donald

Quinn at the time was editor of the *St. Louis Review*, the official newspaper of the Archdiocese of St. Louis.
93. Douglass, *The Non-Violent Cross*, 117.
94. Ibid., 118. For a complete text of Cardinal Ritter's Intervention, see pp. 118 and 119.
95. *Pastoral Constitution*, 87.
96. The accepted compromise is very similar to the arguments developed by the American theologian John Ford, S.J., in response to obliteration bombing and the dropping of the atomic bomb on Hiroshima. See Chapter III.
97. JDC, contains copies of both interventions. In the intervention during the third session, Archbishop Roberts called attention to the fact that Catholics have been denied this right. In the fourth session he devoted his intervention to the case of Franz Jagerstatter. See Gordon Zahn, *In Solitary Witness: The Life and Death of Franz Jagerstatter*, (New York: Holt, Rinehart & Winston, 1964).
98. JDC, letter dated 13 August 1965, Thomas Merton to Archbishop Flahiff.
99. *The Council Daybook*, 37.
100. *Pastoral Constitution*, 86.

5: Thomas Merton at the Crossroads of Peace

1. The original unexpurgated manuscript of *The Seven Storey Mountain* is located in the Boston College library.
2. James Thomas Baker, *Thomas Merton: Social Critic* (Lexington: University Press of Kentucky, 1971), 13.
3. This paragraph is a paraphrasing of a letter, dated 17 June 1968, written by Thomas Merton to a student working on her master's thesis in order to assist her in organizing his writings.
4. Letter from Daniel Berrigan to author, dated 12 June 1969.
5. For the best account of Merton's writings on the Cold War and Marxism, see Baker, *Thomas Merton: Social Critic*, 66–97.
6. For accounts of Merton's use of Gog and Magog, see ibid., 70–89, and Gordon C. Zahn's introduction to *Thomas Merton on Peace*.
7. Thomas Merton, *Peace in the Post-Christian Era* (unpublished, mimeographed copy, 1962), 71, 72. A copy is at the Thomas Merton Studies Center at Bellarmine College in Louisville, Kentucky. The author used James Forest's copy.
8. David W. Givey, *The Social Thought of Thomas Merton: The Way of Nonviolence and Peace for the Future* (Chicago: Franciscan Herald Press, 1983), 54. Merton felt that very little was actually known about what really took place in the thinking of the church as this time, the time when he believed "Christiandom went into business." The author is grateful to James Forest, who provided access to his personal correspondence with Merton over a ten-year period. This correspondence was located at Regina Laudis Monastery, Bethlehem, Connecticut, when the author consulted it.
9. Thomas Merton, *Seeds of Destruction* (New York: Macmillan, 1964), 151.

10. Thomas Merton in Gordon C. Zahn, ed., *The Nonviolent Alternative* (New York: Farrar Strauss & Giroux, 1980), 94, 95.
11. Ibid., 95.
12. Ibid.
13. Merton as quoted in Powaski, *Thomas Merton on Nuclear Weapons*, 15, 16.
14. Merton, *Peace in the Post-Christian Era*.
15. Thomas P. McDonnell, ed., *A Thomas Merton Reader* (New York: Harcourt Brace & World, 1962), 291.
16. Ibid., 295.
17. Merton in Zahn, *The Nonviolent Alternative*, 92.
18. Ibid., 93.
19. Merton, *Breakthrough to Peace*, 108.
20. Merton, *Seeds of Destruction*, 129.
21. Michael Mott, *The Seven Mountains of Thomas Merton* (Boston: Houghton Mifflin, 1984), 375, 376.
22. Merton in his *Restricted Journals* as quoted in Mott, *The Seven Mountains*, 374.
23. *Ibid.*, 400.
24. Givey, *The Social Thought of Thomas Merton* 5, 6.
25. Merton, *Seeds of Destruction*, 91.
26. Thomas Merton, "Peace and Revolution: A Footnote from Ulysses," *Peace*, 4 (Fall/Winter, 1968–1969).
27. Merton, *Seeds of Destruction*, 90.
28. Ibid., 123.
29. Thomas Merton, *Faith and Violence* (Notre Dame, Ind.: University of Notre Dame Press, 1968), 8. It is interesting to note that the Catholic peace activists are often admonished for refusing to criticize the use of violence by "revolutionary" groups or to impose restrictions upon others whose leadership they do not share.
30. L. C. McHugh, S.J., "Ethics at the Shelter Doorway," *America*, 105, no. 27 (30 September 1961): 824–826.
31. Interview with James Forest, 3 December 1972.
32. Ibid.
33. Zahn in his introduction to *Thomas Merton on Peace*, reduces and dismisses Merton's qualifications of pacifism as merely a matter of semantics.
34. Ibid., xxvi.
35. Ibid., xxvii.
36. Baker, *Thomas Merton: Social Critic*, 116.
37. Ibid.
38. Merton as quoted in Powaski, *Thomas Merton on Nuclear Weapons*, 94.
39. Merton, *Seeds of Destruction*, 132.
40. Ibid.
41. *Ibid.*, 140, 141.
42. Ibid., 136.
43. Merton, "Blessed are the Meek: The Christian Roots of Non-Violence," in Zahn, *Thomas Merton on Peace*, 210.
44. Ibid.

45. Merton, "Peace and Revolution: A Footnote from Ulysses," 75.
46. Zahn, Introduction, *Thomas Merton on Peace.*
47. Preface to the Japanese edition of *No Man Is An Island,* quoted in James H. Forest, "Thomas Merton's Struggle with Peacemaking," in Gerald Twomey, ed., *Thomas Merton: Prophet in the Belly of a Paradox* (New York: Paulist Press, 1978), 21.
48. For details on these specific events refer to Zahn, Introduction, *Thomas Merton on Peace.*
49. Merton, *Faith and Violence,* 7.
50. Thomas Merton, "The Christian in World Crisis," in Zahn, *Thomas Merton on Peace,* 25.
51. Thomas Merton, *Life and Holiness* (New York: Herder and Herder, 1963), 114.
52. Merton, *Seeds of Destruction,* 122.
53. Thomas Merton, *Raids on the Unspeakable* (New York: Farrar, Straus and Giroux, 1961).
54. Merton, *Faith and Violence,* 108.
55. Ibid., 110.
56. Copy of statement given to author by James Forest.
57. Merton, "Peace and Revolution," 10.
58. Thomas Merton, Preface to Pierre Regamey, *Non-Violence and the Christian Conscience* (London: Herder and Herder, 1966), 12–14.
59. Merton, *Faith and Violence,* 10.
60. Merton, Preface, in Regamey, *Non-Violence and the Christian Conscience,* 13.
61. *Ibid,* 14.
62. Thomas Merton, *New Seeds of Contemplation* (New York: New Directions, 1961), 115.
63. Thomas Merton, *Disputed Questions* (New York: Farrar, Straus and Cudahy, 1960), 115.
64. Thomas Merton, "Christianity and Mass Movements," *Cross Currents,* 14 (Summer 1969): 203, 204.
65. Givey, *The Social Thought of Thomas Merton,* 107.

6: The Catholic Peace Movement and Vietnam

1. "Address of Pope Paul VI to the General Assembly of the United Nations," *Catholic Mind,* 63 (November 1965): 7.
2. Ibid., 8, 9.
3. Musto, *Catholic Peace Tradition,* 193.
4. David J. O'Brien in "American Catholic Opposition to the Vietnam War: A Preliminary Assessment," in Thomas A. Shannon, ed., *War or Peace?* (Maryknoll, N.Y.: Orbis, 1980), contends that "the Vatican did not succeed in detaching itself completely from the Cold War or from association with the Western powers. . . . In Vietnam, the Pope's desire to play the role of peacemaker, flawed at the start by the diplomatic approach, could only appear hypocritical to those who believed not simply that the war was evil, but that the primary responsibility for that evil lay with the governments of South Vietnam and the United States." 124.

5. Dolan, *American Catholic Experience*, 426.
6. Ibid., 446.
7. Ibid., 447.
8. Henry J. Browne, "Groping for Relevance in an Urban Parish: St Gregory the Great, New York, 1968–70" (unpublished paper), 5 as quoted in Dolan, *American Catholic Experience*, 449.
9. See David J. O'Brien, "Styles of Public Catholicism," in O'Brien, *Public Catholicism* (New York: Macmillan, 1989), in which he delineates three styles: evangelical, immigrant, and republican.
10. James Terence Fisher, *The Catholic Counterculture in America 1933–1962* (Chapel Hill: University of North Carolina Press, 1989), 205–248.
11. Dr. Martin Luther King, Jr., as quoted in Mitchell Kent Hall, "Clergy and Laymen Concerned About Vietnam: A Study of Opposition to the Vietnam War," Ph.D. diss., University of Kentucky, 1987, 79.
12. O'Brien, "Catholic Opposition to the Vietnam War," 120.
13. O'Brien, *Public Catholicism*, 238, 239.
14. Charles DeBenedetti and Charles Chatfield, *An American Ordeal: The Antiwar Movement of the Vietnam Era* (Syracuse, N.Y.: Syracuse University Press, 1990), 86.
15. Ibid., 52.
16. Ibid., 68.
17. Mark Clodfelter, *The Limits of Air Power: The American Bombing of North Vietnam* (New York: Free Press, 1989). The United States dropped 6.3 million tons of bombs and other aerial munitions on Indochina in the seven years beginning in 1965. As Clodfelter points out after the greatest amount of bombing and shelling in the history of warfare, peace without victory was the result.
18. AUND, CPF Collection, letter dated 22 July 1964, Thomas Merton to Jim Forest.
19. Musto, *Catholic Peace Tradition*, 185.
20. "1970: A Year of Concern for all CO's," *The Reporter for Conscience's Sake* 27 (January 1970): 2. This coincides with the report dated 11 May 1970 sent to author from NSBRO which gives the number of Catholic COs as of February 1966 as 17, as of November 1968 as 69, and as of September 1969 as 175.
21. AUND, CPF Collection, Thomas Cornell, "The First 10 Years of the CPF," *CPF Bulletin* (February 1975).
22. Ibid.
23. In my first interview with Dorothy Day, I asked her about Daniel Berrigan and his role in the Catholic Worker movement. Dorothy's immediate response was sharp when she contended that she hardly knew Dan. All she knew was that he dedicated a book to her, invited her to speak at LeMoyne College, and took all her men away from the Catholic Worker into the peace movement. Interview occurred at a rally at St. Ignatius Church in Baltimore two days before the opening of the trial of the Catonsville Nine, 1969. Day was at the rally to speak and support the Catonsville Nine.

24. AUND, CPF Collection, *CPF Bulletin* (June 1965). The first list of sponsors appeared as follows: Baron Antoine Allard, Daniel Berrigan, S.J., Dorothy Day, Leslie Dewart, James W. Douglass, Rev. William H. DuBay, Hermene Evans, Edward T. Gargen, John Howard Griffin, Dom Bede Griffiths, Rev. Robert W. Hovda, Edward M. Keating, Robert Lax, Justus George Lawler, Rev. Robert McDole, Rev. Thomas Merton, Rev. Peter J. Riga, STD, Archbishop Roberts, S.J., Karl Stern, Anton Wallach-Clifford, Gordon Zahn. The co-chairs were listed as James H. Forest, Philip Berrigan, SSJ, and Martin J. Corbin. The education advisor was listed as Thomas Cornell and the field secretary as John Lee.
25. AUND, CPF Collection, The Catholic Peace Fellowship, membership pamphlet.
26. AUND, CPF Collection, Cornell, "The First 10 Years."
27. AUND, CPF Collection, letter dated 4 November 1968, Jim Forest to Tom Cornell.
28. AUND, CPF Collection, letter dated 2 July 1969, Alfred Hassler, executive secretary of FOR, to Tom Cornell. In 1975, Tom Cornell recorded that the $10,000 debt of CPF to FOR was paid in full, AUND, CPF Collection.
29. AUND, CPF Collection, letter dated 22 September 1969, Tom Cornell to Jim Forest.
30. Tom Cornell remained very close to Dorothy Day and visited the Catholic Worker at least once a week until her death. Jim Forest had fallen from Day's good graces in 1967 when he divorced his wife and married Linda Hassler, the daughter of Al Hassler, executive director of FOR.
31. AUND, CPF Collection, letter dated 22 September 1969, Tom Cornell to Jim Forest.
32. AUND, CPF Collection, Cornell, "The First 10 Years." Volunteers were Abraham Bassord, a Presbyterian seminarian; Paul Velde, once of *Commonweal*; Maggie Geddes; Ken Curtain and Joanne Sheehan, members of the Christian Appalachian Project in Kentucky; and many others such as Jack Doyle, Paul Frazier, Janet Gallagher, Beth Gregory, Mary McCarthy, Bob Oliva, Jack Riles, Mike Murphy, Walter Hanns, Mary Sheehan, Rick Gaumer, Bill Ofenloch, Brendan Coyne, Bill Dorfer, Steve Kurzyna, and Lyle Young.
33. Forest, "No longer alone," 146.
34. As quoted in ibid., 147.
35. *Peace and Vietnam*, 18 November 1966, *In the Name of Peace: Collective Statements of the United States Catholic Bishops on War and Peace, 1919–1980* (Washington, D.C.: U.S. Catholic Conference, 1983), 25–29.
36. Forest, "No longer alone," 147.
37. Gordon C. Zahn, "The Scandal of Silence," *Commonweal* 95, no. 5 (22 October, 1971): 81, and Musto, *Catholic Peace Tradition*, 255.
38. Forest, "No longer alone," 147.
39. Interview with James Forest, 3 December 1972.
40. Catherine Swann, "Burning a Draft Card," *Catholic Worker*, November 1965. For this section on burning draft cards, most of the factual data is taken from John L.

LeBrun, "The Role of the Catholic Worker Movement in American Pacifism, 1933–1972," unpublished Ph.D. diss., Case Western Reserve, 1974.

41. Michael Ferber and Staughton Lynd, *The Resistance* (Boston: Beacon Press, 1971), 3, 4, 9, 10; and Dwight Macdonald, "Why Destroy Draft Cards?" *Catholic Worker*, November 1965.

42. Edward Forand, "Christie Street," *Catholic Worker*, December 1964.

43. *New York Times*, 11 August 1965, p. 14 and 1 September 1965, p. 17.

44. Tom Cornell, "Life and Death on the Streets of New York," *Catholic Worker*, November 1965; Cornell, "Not the Smallest Grain," in Ferber and Lynd, *The Resistance*, 39, 40. Cornell's statement printed in full as "Why I am Burning My Draft Card," *Commonweal*, 73 (19 November 1965): 205.

45. Schlissel, *Conscience in America*, reprints United States v. Miller, District and Circuit Court Decisions, 1965–66, 275–84.

46. The complete statement was printed in the *Catholic Worker*, March 1966. See also Jim Wilson, "Chrystie Street," 12 January 1966, and the *New York Times*, 12 January 1966, p.8 and 5 March 1966, p.21.

47. "Draft Card Burners Convicted," *Catholic Worker*, December 1966; "CPF Head Found Guilty in Draft Card Case," *Fellowship* 32 (October, 1966): 1; "CPF Head Appeals Six-Month Sentence," *Fellowship*, 33 (February 1967): 3; and *New York Times*, 25 October 1966, p. 11 and 19 July 1967, p. 42.

48. James H. Forest, "In Time of War," in *Delivered into Resistance*, (New Haven, Conn.: The Catonsville Nine-Milwaukee Fourteen Defense Committee, 1969), 5–7. There is no way to document the exact number of draft board raids by the ultra-resistance.

49. DeBenedetti and Chatfield, *The American Ordeal*, 296, 297.

50. Ibid., 108.

51. As quoted in Thomas J. Schlereth, *The University of Notre Dame: A Portrait of Its History and Campus* (Notre Dame: University of Notre Dame Press, 1976), 215. For this section on student unrest during the Vietnam War, the factual data is taken from Schlereth's book, pp. 215–220.

52. Theodore M. Hesburgh, C.S.C., *God, Country, Notre Dame* (New York: Doubleday, 1990), 118.

53. Ibid., 216.

54. Ibid., 216, 219.

55. Ibid., 219, 220.

56. U.S. v. Seeger, 380 U.S. 163 (1965) is reprinted in Schlissel, *Conscience in America*.

57. For a complete transcript of the report of the 1967 President's Advisory Commission on Selective Service, "In Pursuit of Equity: Who serves when not all serve?" see, the John Courtney Murray, S.J., Collection located in the Woodstock Archives at Georgetown University.

58. John Courtney Murray, *Selective Conscientious Objection* (Huntington,Ind.: Our Sunday Visitor, 1968), 5.

59. John A. Rohr, *Prophets Without Honor: Public Policy and the Selective Conscientious*

Objector (Nashville: Abingdon Press, 1971). Rohr more explicitly than any other writer points out the limitations of the just-unjust war theory. According to him, the SCO cannot base his position on the just war theory since it places all responsiblity for war on the state and the individual bears no responsiblity. Therefore, the individual had no obligation to become a SCO; he is free in conscience to comply with the state since the just war theory has made it the decision maker for all individual consciences. He also considers the three cases which were presented for SCO before the Supreme Court during the 1970–1971 term: Negre v. Larsen, U.S. v. Gillette, and U.S. v. McFadden. None of the cases was successful.

60. Interview with Patrick McDermott, S.J., 21 June 1971.

61. "Catholic Conscience and the Draft," *Peace* 5 (Special Draft Issue with n.d.): 31. (PAX did a brief summary of their activities in the campaign).

62. Ibid.

63. AMU, CAIP Collection, Monsignor Higgins made unsuccessful attempts to secure foundation funding for CAIP from 1963 to 1965. See letter dated 27 September 1963, Richard M. Catalano, assistant to George Higgins, to Howard G. Kurtz of the Ford Foundation; letters dated 16 December 1964, Charles J. McNeill to William E. Moran, Jr., president of CAIP and to George Higgins. There are also letters expressing discontent with the committees, for example, letter dated 15 January 1964, Alba Zizzamia to James L. Vizzard on the defunct Cultural Relations Committee and letters to James L. Vizzard dated 15 November 1963 from William Glade, 11 November 1963 from T. J. McDonagh, and (n.d.) from Charles F. Johnson on dissatisfaction with the Economic Life Committee.

64. William V. O'Brien, *War and/or Survival* (Garden City, N.Y.: Doubleday, 1969), 42.

65. Interview with Patrick McDermott, 21 June 1971.

66. Interview with George Higgins, 8 May 1990 at the Catholic University of America.

67. Musto, *Catholic Peace Tradition*, 255.

68. *Human Life in Our Day* (Washington, D.C., U.S. Catholic Conference, 1968), pars. 98 and 99 and as quoted in Musto, *Catholic Peace Tradition*, 255.

69. Ibid., par. 105.

70. Ibid., pars. 106–113.

71. Jim Castelli, *The Bishops and the Bomb: Waging Peace in a Nuclear Age* (Garden City, N.Y.: Doubleday, 1983), 79. Also according to Castelli, Ed Doherty, who was working in the State Department at the time, wrote the draft for Part II at the request of Bordelon. Bordelon used most of the draft verbatim.

72. *Human Life in Our Day*, pars. 144–145, 15–51.

73. Interview with Patrick McDermott, 21 June 1971.

74. *Human Life in Our Day*, pars. 142 and 153.

75. Interview with Thomas J. Gumbleton, bishop of Detroit, at the University of Notre Dame, 26 April 1990.

76. Interview with James Jennings, 8 May 1990.

77. Hall, "Clergy and Laymen," 154.

78. "Declaration on Conscientious Objection and Selective Conscientious Objection" (Washington, D. C.: U.S. Catholic Conference, October, 1971), par. 11. Copy of set of quotes from document given to author by James Jennings, 8 May 1990.

79. AUND, CPF Collection, Doug Lavine, "Interview with Dorothy Day," (n.d. and unpublished).

80. Interview with James Jennings, NCCB/USCC Headquarters on 8 May 1990.

81. Michael True, *Justice Seekers Peace Makers: 32 Portraits in Courage* (Mystic, Conn.: Twenty-Third, 1985), 3–7, 14–18.

82. Hall, "Clergy and Laymen," 16, 17.

83. Ibid., 76.

84. Ibid., 65.

85. Thomas J. Shelley, *Paul J. Hallinan: First Archbishop of Atlanta* (Wilmington, Del.: Michael Glazier, 1989), 275.

86. Ibid.

87. Ibid., 122.

88. Ibid., 219.

89. Ibid., 224.

90. Taped interview with Bishop Gumbleton dated 1 July 1990. The author has placed the tape in the AUND, Pax Christi Collection.

91. "A Declaration on the Threat of Bombardment of Civilian Centers," dated 13 July 1965, *Continuum* (Summer 1965). Copy at AUND, CPF Collection.

92. *New York Times*, 15 February 1966.

93. *National Catholic Reporter,* 30 March 1966.

94. Zahn, "The Scandal of Silence," 8, 9.

95. Ibid.

96. Ibid. The CPF had immediately issued a reprint of the text for sale at 5 cents per copy before the clarification had been added.

97. Paul J. Hallinan and Joseph L. Bernardin, *War and Peace: A Pastoral Letter to the Archdiocese of Atlanta*, October 1966, as quoted in Shelley, *Paul J. Hallinan*, 274.

98. DeBenedetti and Chatfield, *An American Ordeal*, 186.

99. Shelley, *Paul J. Hallinan*, 276, 277.

100. Ibid., 253.

101. Bishop Shannon's name is never mentioned in the memorandum issued by the USCC.

102. O'Brien, "American Catholic Opposition to the Vietnam War," 129.

103. Taped interview with Bishop Gumbleton dated 1 July 1990.

104. Castelli, *The Bishops and the Bomb*, 69.

105. "Getting Out," *Commonweal* 85 (23 December 1966): 335.

106. John G. Deedy, Jr., "The Catholic Press and Vietnam," in Quigley, *American Catholics and Vietnam*, 130, 131.

107. Musto, *Catholic Peace Tradition*, 256.

108. Deedy, "The Catholic Press and Vietnam," 121–132.

109. O'Brien, "Catholic Opposition to the Vietnam War," 136.

110. As quoted in ibid.
111. George Gallup, Jr., and Jim Castelli, *The American Catholic People: Their Beliefs, Practices, and Values* (New York: Doubleday, 1987), 82.
112. Ibid., 78.
113. Ibid., 79.
114. "Resolution on Southeast Asia," Paragraph 13 as quoted in Marvin Bordelon, "The Bishops and Just War," *America* (8 January 1972): 17.
115. Ibid.
116. AUND, CPF Collection, Cornell, "The First 10 Years."
117. Benedetti and Chatfield, *An American Ordeal*, 68.

7: The Berrigan Brothers and the Catholic Resistance

1. Klejment, *In the Lion's Den*, 35, states that "Although I have not conducted an exhaustive search of the origin of the word [New Catholic Left], William O'Rourke, a writer covering the Harrisburg trial was one of the first to use the term. William O'Rourke, *The Harrisburg 7 and the New Catholic Left* (New York: Thomas Y. Crowell, Apollo, 1973), 263.
2. Jack Nelson and Ronald J. Ostrow, *The FBI and the Berrigans: The Making of a Conspiracy* (New York: Coward, McCann & Geoghegan, 1972), 14.
3. It was not the Berrigans who launched the first draft board raid, but a nineteen-year-old Minnesotan named Barry Bondhaus. His eleven brothers and machinist father helped him prepare for the 1966 action by collecting material he would use. Bondhaus dumped two buckets of human feces into a Selective Service filing cabinet. Although the protest, known as The Big Lake One, drew little press notice, it was credited as "the movement that started the movement." See Nelson and Ostrow, *FBI and the Berrigans*.
4. Interview with Robert A. Ludwig, 28 July 1972. At that time Ludwig was a doctoral candidate at the Aquinas Institute of Theology and was completing his dissertation on the theology of Daniel Berrigan. He was most helpful in systematizing the influences on and development of Daniel Berrigan's "political theology."
5. Philip Berrigan, letter to author dated 21 October 1968.
6. All three brothers, Phil, Jerry, and Dan, when asked by the author in 1973 why Dan did not participate responded the same way: "He (I) did not feel free to do it."
7. Daniel Berrigan, *To Dwell in Peace: An Autobiography* (New York: Harper & Row, 1987), 200, 201.
8. For the best account of the Customs House action, see Philip Berrigan, "Blood, War and Witness" in John O'Connor, ed., *American Catholic Exodus* (Washington, D.C.: Corpus Books, 1968).
9. In a letter to Representative William R. Anderson of Tennessee, Daniel Berrigan cited Dorothy Day and the late Thomas Merton as having shaped his nonviolence. Recalling that he and Philip had attended a 1964 retreat conducted by Merton on the "spiritual roots of protest," Daniel Berrigan said: "I wrote him once that I could still remember the article of his in the *Catholic Worker* that turned me

from damp straw to combustible man. . . . He got us started, after Dorothy Day. The consequences are not theirs, but ours."

10. The best-known biography of the Berrigan brothers is that of Francine du Plessix Gray, *Divine Disobedience: Profiles in Catholic Radicalism* (New York: Knopf, 1970). See pp.130–210; The chapter entitled "Berrigans" was reprinted from the *New Yorker*, 14 March 1970.

11. Jay P. Dolan, *The Immigrant Church: New York's Irish and German Catholics, 1815–1865* (Baltimore: Johns Hopkins University Press, 1975).

12. Daniel Berrigan, *To Dwell in Peace*, 42.

13. Ibid., 43.

14. Ibid., 43, 44.

15. Interview with Mrs. Frida Berrigan, 2 November 1968 in Syracuse, New York. Interviews with Mr. and Mrs. Jerome Berrigan on the family were also conducted.

16. Daniel Berrigan, *To Dwell in Peace*, 43.

17. Philip Berrigan and Elizabeth McAlister, *The Time's Discipline: The Beatitudes and Nuclear Resistance* (Baltimore: Fortkamp, 1989), 7.

18. Ibid., 6.

19. Daniel Berrigan, "Reflections on the Priest as Peacemaker," *Jubilee* 12 (February 1966): 25.

20. Interview with Robert A. Ludwig, 18 July 1972.

21. Daniel Berrigan, *The World Showed Me Its Heart* (St. Louis, Mo.: National Sodality Service Center, 1966), 11; an interview with Jerome Berrigan on 2 November 1968, and visit to International House on LeMoyne campus, 2 November 1968.

22. Interview with Matthew O'Rourke, S.S.J. and use of the file on Philip Berrigan, in the archives of the Josephite Provincialate in Baltimore, Maryland, on 5 October 1968. The quotation is cited in Nelson and Ostrow, *The FBI and the Berrigans*, 40.

23. From 1968 to 1972, the author was personally involved in the Catholic Resistance. Many statements and motivations attributed to Philip Berrigan came from conversations and correspondence with him through the years. The author's relationship with Daniel Berrigan was limited to two interviews, three letters of correspondence, and a proofreading by him of the author's M.A. thesis on Daniel Berrigan entitled "The Evolution of a Conscience."

24. Interview with Richard Wagner, S.S.J., on 6 October 1968.

25. Philip Berrigan, "The Challenge of Segregation" *Worship* 35 (November, 1960): 597–603.

26. Interview with Robert A. Ludwig, 28 July 1972.

27. Cornell University, Special Collections, Olin Library, Berrigan Collection, a copy of Letter dated 14 October 1968 from John Heidbrink to author.

28. Ibid.

29. Cornell University, Special Collections, Olin Library, Berrigan Collection, letter from Daniel Berrigan to his family from Eastern European trip in 1964.

30. Interview with Tony Walsh on 31 October 1968.
31. Interview with Daniel Berrigan, on 17 November 1968. The author read many letters of correspondence between Daniel and his religious superiors in the Society of Jesus. Upon Daniel's request these are not quoted directly and are paraphrased.
32. Nelson and Ostrow, *The FBI and the Berrigans*, 45.
33. Interview with John P. Grady on 6 October 1968. Grady, a Catholic layman and father of five children had spent much of his time since the mid-1950s working with Daniel and Philip in their many projects and very closely with Philip in developing the Catholic Resistance.
34. Interview with Beverly Bell, S.N.D., on 8 April 1973. Philip Berrigan had told her this when they were discussing the viability of religious life.
35. Daniel Berrigan, *The World Showed Me*, 25, 26.
36. Cornell University, Special Collections, Olin Library, Berrigan Collection, letter from Daniel Berrigan to his family from Eastern European trip in 1964.
37. Many of Daniel's essays during this time reflect this attitude.
38. Later Thomas Cornell also became a co-chair.
39. Cornell University, Special Collections, Olin Library, Berrigan Collection, a copy of letter dated Monday, 21 October 1968 from Philip Berrigan, at the Baltimore County Jail to author.
40. Interview with Thomas Cornell in summer of 1968.
41. Reverend Richard J. Neuhaus, letter to author dated 21 October 1968.
42. Daniel Berrigan, *To Dwell in Peace*, 182.
43. Interview with Francis Keating, S.J., and Daniel Kilfoyle, S.J., on 6 October 1968. These men along with Daniel Berrigan agreed that the best reporting was done by John Leo from the *National Catholic Reporter*. James Hennesey, S.J., who was the executive assistant to the provincial superior of the New York Province of the Society of Jesus at the time of Berrigan's transfer, said that the Archdiocese of New York and Cardinal Spellman as the press contended had nothing to do with it. It was the Jesuits who initiated the action. James Hennesey, *American Catholics: A History of the Roman Catholic Community in the United States* (New York: Oxford University Press, 1981), 374.
44. " 'Peace' Priest Muzzled," *Christian Century* 82 (8 December 1965): 1500 and 1501, as quoted in Hall, *Clergy and Layman*, 26.
45. Daniel Berrigan, "Berrigan at Cornell," *Jubilee* 15 (February 1968): 29.
46. Daniel Berrigan, *To Dwell in Peace*, 186–214. The chapter, "Cornell: Poison in the Ivy," provides his reflections on the period.
47. Daniel Berrigan, *Night Flight From Hanoi: War Diary With 11 Poems* (New York: Macmillan, 1968).
48. Daniel Berrigan, "My Brother, the Witness," *Commonweal* 88 (26 April 1968): 181.
49. Philip Berrigan, letter to author dated 21 October 1968.
50. Interview with Paul Mayer, 4 October 1968.
51. Daniel Berrigan, *Trial of the Catonsville Nine* (Boston: Beacon Press, 1970).
52. Interview with Neil McLaughlin, 10 April 1973.

53. Interview with Theodore Glick, 3 February 1969. Estimates of the number of draft board raids that actually occurred varied with different members of the Catholic Resistance. Glick gave the highest estimate.

54. Anne Klejment, "The Berrigans: Revolutionary Christian Nonviolence," in Charles DeBenedettii, ed., *Peace Heroes in Twentieth Century America* (Bloomington: Indiana University Press, 1988), 246.

55. William Hardy, the informer of the Camden Twenty-eight draft board raid, told the FBI that John P. Grady had confessed to him that he had engineered the raid at Media. *Philadelphia Inquirer*, 16 March 1972, p. 1.

56. Nelson and Ostrow, The *FBI and the Berrigans*, 188.

57. These were the author's impressions after attending several such retreats.

58. Nelson and Ostrow, *The FBI and the Berrigans*, 60, and author's eyewitness account.

59. Interview with Jay P. Dolan on 8 January 1972; at the time of the search he was in residence at St. Gregory the Great rectory.

60. Observations of the author, who attended the rally.

61. Interview with John P. Grady on 21 April 1970. Grady stayed with Philip much of the time that he was underground.

62. Robert Coles and Daniel Berrigan, *Geography of Faith* (Boston: Beacon Press, 1971). The Introduction provides Coles's analysis.

63. Nelson and Ostrow, *The FBI and the Berrigans*, 56.

64. No one knew exactly how the FBI found out about Daniel's existence at Block Island. After the letters were released by the prosecution at the Harrisburg Seven Trial, it was assumed that the letters provided the FBI with the knowledge.

65. Daniel Berrigan, "Notes From the Underground; or I was a Fugitive from the FBI," *Commonweal* 92 (29 May 1970): 263–265.

66. Nelson and Ostrow, *The FBI and the Berrigans*, 17, 18.

67. Interview with Jack Levine on 22 April 1971.

68. Nelson and Ostrow, *The FBI and the Berrigans*, 303.

69. The process of selection of lawyers was tedious. For example, the Berrigan brothers met with Ramsey Clark who offered his services in the case. Personal and political motivations between them were discussed and not found to be in conflict. Interview with Neil McLaughlin at the University of Notre Dame, 15 October 1971.

70. Nelson and Ostrow, *The FBI and the Berrigans*, 111–128, presents lengthy excerpts from the letters. Nelson also treats Boyd Douglas on the witness stand in great detail, pp. 237–281. His book contains great detail, more factual material, and more political analysis of the trial than does the more impressionistic character portrayals of the book by William O'Rourke.

71. Interview with Neil McLaughlin and Joseph Wenderoth on 17 February 1973.

72. Nelson and Ostrow, *The FBI and the Berrigans*, 303–306.

73. Ibid., 302, 303.

74. See John C. Raines, ed., *Conspiracy* (New York: Harper & Row, 1974). The various contributors attempt to evaluate the significance of the Harrisburg trial.

75. Nelson and Ostrow, *The FBI and the Berrigans*, 215.
76. DeBenedetti and Chatfield, *An American Ordeal*, 3, 278–280.
77. Interviews with Neil McLaughlin and Joseph Wenderoth and Anthony and Mary Scoblic, 17 February 1973.
78. Daniel Berrigan, *To Dwell in Peace*, 215. First two lines of his poem, "Catonsville: The Fires of Pentecost."
79. Interview with Dorothy Day at St. Ignatius Hall in Baltimore at a rally in support of the Catonsville Nine, 1968.

8: Catholic Peacemaking

1. Castelli, *The Bishops and the Bomb*, 182.
2. *The Challenge of Peace: God's Promise and Our Response*, (Washington, D.C.: USCC, 1983), par. 333.
3. Philip Berrigan and McAlister, *The Time's Discipline*, 13.
4. Ibid., 226–232. Appendix B, The Chronicle of Hope, lists the actions.
5. Daniel Berrigan, "Swords into Plowshares," in Arthur J. Laffin and Anne Montgomery, eds., *Swords into Plowshares: Nonviolent Direct Action for Disarmament* (New York: Harper & Row, 1987), 60.
6. *New York Times*, Wednesday, 11 April 1990, p. A10.
7. Laffin and Montgomery, *Swords into Plowshares*, 3. A description of each action and each person involved in the actions is given in the book.
8. *New York Times*, Wednesday, 11 April 1990, p. A10.
9. Daniel Berrigan, "Swords into Plowshares," 61.
10. Philip Berrigan and McAlister, *The Time's Discipline*, 16.
11. Ibid., 17.
12. Daniel Berrigan, *To Dwell in Peace*, 300.
13. Ibid., 17.
14. AUND, CPF Collection, letter dated 21 May 1974 from Jim Forest to Kathleen Keating.
15. Ibid.
16. Daniel Berrigan, *To Dwell in Peace*, 284.
17. Ibid., 285.
18. AUND, CPF Collection, letter dated 15 September 1972, Daniel Berrigan to Jim Forest.
19. AUND, CPF Collection, letter dated 21 September 1972, Jim Forest to Al Hassler.
20. For the full text of the Berrigans' letter and Hanoi's reply, see *Win*, (6 September 1973): 16.
21. Guenter Lewy, *Peace & Revolution: The Moral Crisis of American Pacifism* (Grand Rapids, Mich.: Eerdmans, 1988). Lewy covers the issue of political prisoners and human rights in great detail.
22. Daniel and Philip Berrigan, "On the Torture of Prisoners," *Fellowship*, 35 (September 1973): 4.

23. AUND, CPF Collection, letter dated 23 December 1973, Daniel Berrigan to Jim Forest.
24. James H. Forest, "Solzhenitsyn and American Pacifists," *Fellowship*, 35 (August 1973): 2.
25. AUND, CPF Collection, Memo on Appeal had been signed by Dorothy Day, Jim and Shelly Douglass, Arthur W. Clarke, and Bishop John J. Dougherty.
26. AUND, CPF Collection, letter dated 24 August 1977, Jim Forest to Daniel Berrigan.
27. AUND, CPF Collection, letter dated April 1975, Daniel Berrigan to Jim Forest.
28. Daniel Berrigan, *To Dwell in Peace*, 303.
29. Ibid., 305.
30. Ibid.
31. Ibid., 318.
32. Ibid., 281.
33. *New York Times*, Wednesday, 11 April 1990, p. A10.
34. AUND, CPF Collection, letter dated 23 June 1977, Jim Forest to Tom Cornell.
35. AUND, CPF Collection, Hermene Evans sent $10,000. Zahn continued his pledge of $1,000 a year to CPF, and the Goss-Mayrs sent enough to purchase a woodburning stove.
36. AUND, CPF Collection, letter dated 15 January 1980, Tom Cornell to Hildegard Goss-Mayr.
37. Telephone conversation with Tom Cornell, Tuesday, 22 July 1990.
38. For Gumbleton's own story of how he became involved in the peace issue, see "The Bishop as Social Activist," *Origins* 12, no. 18 (30 September 1982): 249–256.
39. AUND, Pax Christi Collection, Gerard A. Vanderhaar, "Pax Christi USA: the Early Years, 1972–78,"(unpublished history, 21 June 1988), 1–5. Direct quote from p. 6. There is also a collection of the letters and writings of Gerard A. Vanderhaar at the AUND.
40. Carroll T. Dozier, Bishop of Memphis, *Peace: Gift and Task—Pastoral Letter to the People of the Diocese of Memphis*, December 1971. Pamphlet reprint from the diocese of Memphis.
41. AUND, Pax Christi Collection, letter dated 5 September 1973, from Eileen Egan to Ed Guinan; also quoted in Vanderhaar, "Pax Christi," 15.
42. AUND, Pax Christi Collection, Vanderhaar, "Pax Christi," 15.
43. Ibid., 15 and 16.
44. AUND, Pax Christi Collection. In the third *Pax Christi Thirdly* twelve local peace groups were identified in Boston, Erie, Washington, Pittsburgh, Richmond, Norfolk, Kansas City, Milwaukee, Dubuque, Davenport, New Orleans, and Portland.
45. AUND, Pax Christi Collection, Bishop Dozier's Files, letter dated 7 August 1974, Ed Guinan to Bishops Dozier and Gumbleton, Eileen Egan and Gordon Zahn as quoted in Vanderhaar, "Pax Christi," 18.
46. AUND, Pax Christi Collection, Vanderhaar, "Pax Christi," 18–20.

47. AUND, Pax Christi Collection. The first members of the executive committee were Bishop Carroll Dozier, Memphis; Bishop Thomas Gumbleton, Detroit; Alden Brown, Queens College, Flushing, New York; Clare Danielsson, Beacon, New York; Edward Cripps, S.J., *America* magazine, New York; Dorothy Dohen, Fordham University, New York; Jean Eckstein, National Council of Catholic Laity, Iowa City; Eileen Egan, New York; Joseph Fahey, Manhattan College, New York; Mary Evelyn Jegen, S.N.D., Catholic Relief Service, New York; Paul McLaughlin, Regis College, Boston; Gerard Vanderhaar, Christian Brothers College, Memphis; Mary Rae Waller, O.P., Network, Washington, D.C.; Gordon Zahn, Boston. List of people taken from Vanderhaar, "Pax Christi," 28.

48. "Current Comment," *America* 131 (14 December 1974).

49. Ibid., 30.

50. AUND, Pax Christi Collection. The membership file for 1973 to 1977 lists the following bishops as members of Pax Christi in March 1976: Joseph J. Donnelly, John J. Dougherty, Daniel Hart, James Rausch, Kenneth J. Povish, Marion Forst, Walter Schoenker, Walter F. Sullivan, William Johnson, Carroll T. Dozier, Thomas Gumbleton, Joseph L. Howze, Daniel E. Sheehan, J. Francis Stafford, and Ernest L. Unterkoefler.

51. AUND, Pax Christi Collection, Financial Records, Budget 3/31/77 to 1/15/78.

52. AUND, Pax Christi Collection, Membership and Financial files.

53. See M. Evelyn Jegen, S.N.D., "The Pacifist Vision," *Fellowship* 42 (10 May 1980).

54. The irony of the differences between the two agendas was that Reagan had appointed many Catholics to key positions in his administration: Alexander Haig, John Lehmann, and William Clark. The military services included Catholics in the highest ranks of command, Admiral James Watkins and General Paul X. Kelley. Edward Hickey had major responsibilities in the Secret Service detail. And General Vernon Walters, a State Department appointee later became ambassador to the United Nations. See Eugene Kennedy, *Cardinal Bernardin: Easing Conflicts—and Battling for the Soul of American Catholicism* (Chicago: Baners Books, 1989), 201, 202.

55. AUND, CPF Collection, letter dated 27 September 1980, Tom Cornell to Daniel J. Corcoran, Winona State University.

56. *In the Name of Peace*, 83–86.

57. AUND, Pax Christi Collection, Minutes of National Council meetings.

58. *Reporter for Conscience Sake*, 30, no. 6 *(June 1983): 27, as referred to in Musto, The Catholic Peace Tradition*, 325.

59. This is a summary of Pax Christi–USA activities described in Vanderhaar, "Pax Christi," 30–36, and a reading of the *Pax Christi Newsletter* published by Vanderhaar during this time period. Copies of the newsletter are in the AUND, Pax Christi Collection.

60. AUND, Pax Christi Collection, *Pax Christi–USA Newsletter*, December 1979.

61. Ibid.

62. *Statement on Central America* dated 10 November 1981, published Washington, D.C., as cited in Musto, *The Catholic Peace Tradition*, 325.
63. AUND, Pax Christi Collection, *Pax Christi–USA Newsletter*, January 1982.
64. AUND, Pax Christi Collection, *Pax Christi–USA Newsletter*, January 1983.
65. AUND, Pax Christi Collection, Correspondence of M. Evelyn Jegen, S.N.D.
66. Frances B. McCrea and Gerald E. Markle, *Minutes to Midnight: Nuclear Weapons Protest in America* (Newbury Park, Calif.: Sage Publications, 1989), 15, 16.
67. AUND, Pax Christi Collection, *Pax Christi Newsletter*, May 1978.
68. Vanderhaar, "Pax Christi," 37.
69. The debate among Catholics on the ratification of SALT II is presented in *Commonweal* (2 March 1978) in an article by Bishop Thomas Gumbleton against ratification and in another article by J. Bryan Hehir supporting the treaty. Joseph Fahey in *America* (24 February 1978) wrote an article advocating a third position between active support and opposition of SALT II.
70. Castelli, *The Bishops and the Bomb*, 23
71. John J. Cardinal Krol, "SALT II: A Statement of Support," testimony before the Senate Foreign Relations Committee on 6 September 1970, reprinted in *Origins* 9, no. 14 (20 September 1979): 197.
72. AUND, Pax Christi Collection, *Pax Christi–USA Newsletter*, September 1979.
73. AUND, Pax Christi Collection, *Pax Christi–USA Bulletin*, April 1979.
74. AUND, Pax Christi Collection, *Pax Christi–USA Newsletter*, March 1980.
75. AUND, Pax Christi Collection, "New Abolitionist Covenant" pamphlet.
76. Castelli, *The Bishops and the Bomb*, 60.
77. AUND, Pax Christi Collection, *Pax Christi–USA*, May 1982.
78. AUND, Pax Christi Collection, *Pax Christi–USA*, December 1981.
79. Castelli, *The Bishops and the Bomb*, 95.
80. The PAX Center was run by Benedictine nuns who were the first to make a corporate witness to peace by giving $100 a month and 10 percent of their profits from fundraisers to Pax Christi–USA. In 1985, Pax Christi–USA would name Mary Lou Kownacki, a Benedictine nun, its national coordinator and locate its headquarters in Erie.
81. Castelli, *The Bishops and the Bomb*, 95.
82. Eugene Kennedy, *Cardinal Bernardin: Easing Conflicts*, 255.
83. See Weigel, *Tranquillitas Ordinis*, 314–324 for a comprehensive analysis of Hehir's thought. In conversation with Bryan Hehir in the summer of 1989, Hehir stated that Weigel is the first author to attempt an analysis of his thought and that basically it is an accurate assessment, but Weigel's point of view must be taken into account.
84. This was true of Hehir's position in the early years of the formation of Pax Christi–USA. The author directly questioned Hehir on his just war position in relation to nuclear warfare. Hehir responded that he was a nuclear pacifist. Annual Pax Christi–USA conference, University of Dayton, 1976. Hehir explains his nuclear pacifist position in J. Bryan Hehir, "The New Nuclear Debate: Political and

Ethical Considerations," in Robert A. Gessert and J. Bryan Hehir, *The New Nuclear Debate* (New York: Council on Religion and International Affairs, 1976), 35–76.

85. Letter to author from J. Bryan Hehir dated 12 April 1991. For clarification of Hehir's new position, see J. Bryan Hehir, "Moral Issues in Deterrence Policy," in Douglas MacLean, ed., *The Security Gamble Deterrence Dilemmas in the Nuclear Age* (Totowa, N.J.: Rowman & Allanheld, 1984), 53–71.

86. Ed Doherty, who was on Hehir's staff, was responsible for many of the initial drafts on the nuclear issue. Castelli, *The Bishops and the Bomb*, 22, 23.

87. *To Live in Christ Jesus: A Pastoral Reflection on the Moral Life*, as quoted in Castelli, *The Bishops and the Bomb*, 22.

88. Castelli, *The Bishops and the Bomb*, 23. Castelli also contends that "Doherty argued in the conference—without much reaction—that the statement meant Catholics could not serve in the nuclear branch of the military."

89. *In the Name of Peace*, 63.

90. In Robert Heyer, ed., *Nuclear Disarmament: Key Statements of Popes, Bishops, Councils and Churches* (Ramsey, N.J.: Paulist Press, 1982). This book also contains the statements of eighteen North American Catholic bishops who spoke out against nuclear disarmament.

91. Castelli, *The Bishops and the Bomb*, 39. Castelli contends that "Reporters ask the local bishops, 'And what do you think?' and another statement is made."

92. Weigel, *Tranquillitas Ordinis,*, 170–173, presents a distorted view of James Douglass's influence on Archbishop Hunthausen. Certainly Douglass was an influence, but insufficient credit is given to the archbishop himself and his own conversion experience and the influence on him caused by the actions of other bishops on the issue.

93. Castelli, *The Bishops and the Bomb*, 27.

94. Archbishop Raymond G. Hunthausen, Pastoral Letter to the Archdiocese of Seattle, 28 January 1972.

95. AUND, "Pax Christi Collection," *Pax Christi–USA*, March 1983.

96. The subsequent investigation of Hunthausen by the Vatican was not related to his position and action on the nuclear issue. Interview with Bishop Thomas Gumbleton, 26 April 1990 at the University of Notre Dame. Gumbleton stated that he had never been under investigation because of his position on peace. For a complete account of the investigation, see Kennedy, *Cardinal Bernardin: Easing Conflicts*.

97. Archbishop John Quinn, "Remarks as President of NCCB, on President Carter's decision to defer production of neutron warheads," 14 April 1978, in Heyer, *Nuclear Disarmament*, 95, 96.

98. Castelli, *The Bishops and the Bomb*, 28, 29.

99. AUND, Pax Christi Collection, *Pax Christi–USA*, January 1982.

100. Castelli, *The Bishops and the Bomb*, chaps. 1, 5. Also see Weigel, *Tanquillitas Ordinis*, 267.

101. Weigel, *Tranquillitas Ordinis*, 267, 268.

102. Castelli, *The Bishops and the Bomb*, 81.
103. Ibid., 79.
104. Ibid., 135.
105. Interview with Bishop Thomas Gumbleton, 26 April 1990 at the University of Notre Dame.
106. Ibid.
107. AUND, Pax Christi Collection, letter dated 20 July 1981 from Mary Evelyn Jegen, S.N.D., to Dr. Gordon Zahn.
108. *Wall Street Journal*, Wednesday, 9 June 1982.
109. "A Vatican Synthesis," *Origins* 12, no.43 (7 April 1983): 691, 692.
110. As quoted in Weigel, *Tranquillitas Ordinis*, 275, 276.
111. Weigel, *Tranquillitas Ordinis*, 275–280. Weigel places too much emphasis on Vatican intervention. In terms of the NCCB's challenging the authority of the pope as Hehir points out in his article, "From the Pastoral Constitution of Vatican II to *The Challenge of Peace*," in Philip J. Murnion, ed., *Catholics and Nuclear War: A Commentary on "The Challenge of Peace" The U.S. Catholic Bishops' Pastoral Letter on War and Peace* (New York: Crossroad, 1983), 71, the pastoral does go beyond the moral teaching of the pastoral constitution.
112. *The Challenge of Peace*, "Summary," par. 3.
113. Castelli, *The Bishops and the Bomb*, 181.
114. *The Challenge of Peace*, par. 123.
115. Ibid., par. 147.
116. Ibid., par. 148.
117. Ibid., par. 153.
118. Ibid., pars. 172–177.
119. As quoted in Weigel, *Tranquillitas Ordinis*, 271.
120. *The Challenge of Peace*, pars. 188–191
121. Ibid., pars. 221–225.
122. Ibid., "Summary."
123. *The Challenge of Peace*, pars. 332 and 333.
124. All the sections of the pastoral pertaining to pacifism and nonviolence were the results of the labor of Bishop Thomas Gumbleton.
125. *The Challenge of Peace*, pars. 234–279.
126. Interview with Monsignor George Higgins, 8 May 1990, at the Catholic University of America,

Index

abortion issue: and antinuclear issue, 244–245; and Daniel Berrigan, 223; as focus of American Catholic hierarchy in 1980s, 157
Afghanistan, Soviet invasion of, and draft, 237, 329
African Americans: advice from consulting firm to Josephites on, 187; and Berrigan brothers, 181–182; and Black Panthers, 206; and militancy and separatism in civil rights movement, 187; priests, appointed to Catholic hierarchy, 133
Age of Constantine, and pacifism of primitive Christian church, x, 29
Ahmad, Eqbal, 199, 201, 204; and draft, 237; and Harrisburg Seven trial, 205, 208; and human rights issue, 220. See also Harrisburg Eight case
air raid test demonstrations, 91–92, 122
Alfrink, Bernard, 230
Alinsky, Saul, 133
America, 32, 54, 116, 191; attitude toward obliteration and atomic bombing, 67, 68
American Catholic bishops: aid to Civilian Public Service camps, 269n25; and Catholic Peace Fellowship ad, 145; conflict with Reagan administration, 237; joining Pax Christi—USA, 235, 236; and Jonah House demonstrations, 213; and League of Nations, 7; and nuclear freeze, 243; reorganization after Second Vatican Council, 156–157; Statement on Registration and Conscription for Military Service, 238; support for Franco, 17–18; and Vietnam War, 142, 145, 157–160. See also American Catholic hierarchy; National Conference of Catholic Bishops
American Catholic hierarchy: and abortion issue, 244–245, 257; annual meeting of 1939, 53; and anti-communist crusade, 74;

appointment of black priests to, 133; attitude toward Catholic peacemakers, xiii, 146; attitude toward obliteration and atomic bombing, 68; attitude toward United Nations, 52; and bombing of Rome during World War II, 51; and CAIP, xi, 98; and CALCAV, 162; and Catholic immigrants, 1–2; and Catholic participation in civil rights movement, 133; and Catholic Worker call for draft resistance during World War II, 43; and Catholic Worker movement, 22; on causes of World War II, 40; and Central America, 239–240; and Challenge of Peace, 211, 212, 249–258; and Cold War, 51–52; Committee on Reconstruction, 6; and conscientious objectors, 43, 46, 52–54, 138, 159–160, 165, 166; and conscription during World War II, 45, 65; and debate on ratification of SALT II, 241–242; and draft legislation during World War II, 53–54; focus on domestic concerns, 1–2; as focus of PAX during Vietnam War, 139, 140; and formation of National Catholic War Council, 4; and Harrisburg Seven trial, 207; impact of American Catholic peace movement on, 172; influence of anti-communism on foreign policy positions of, 135–136; influence of Catholic peacemakers on, xiii; influence of Hehir on, 246–247; influence of PAX on, xii, 160; involvement in urban affairs, 133–134; and isolationism, 51–52; and just war doctrine, x, 69–70; and National Catholic Welfare Council, 4–6; and nuclear weapons freeze campaign, 240; and obliteration bombing, 65; pastoral letter after World War I, 4; pastoral letters on social problems in 1983, ix; and Pax Christi—USA, 230, 234–235; and PAX lobbying at Second

Merton, Thomas, x–xi, 98, 99–100, 105–
130, 170, 183, 232, 240, 246; background,
105–106; and Catholic Resistance, 210;
and conscientious objection, 102–103; conversion to catholicism, 106; criticism of "realists," 111; Day and, 115–116; on early
Christian church, 276n; enters Trappist Abbey of Gethsemani, 106; and Forest, 141,
260; influence on American Catholic peace
movement, 105; influence on Berrigans,
176, 248n9; influence at Second Vatican
Council, 104; and just war doctrine, 255;
and new theology of peace, 119–130; on
nonviolence, 113; nonviolent activities in
peace movement, 122; Open Letter to hierarchy at Second Vatican Council, 96–97;
and organization of Catholic Peace Fellowship, 189; and PAX, 94; retreat on the
"Spiritual Roots of Protest," 129; and socialism and communism, 105; sources for
study of, 260; and World War II draft, 106;
writings of (see Merton, Thomas, writings)
Merton, Thomas, writings, 106–120; first period, 106–107; on Gandhian nonviolence,
117–118, 121–122; on individual and
state, 123–125, 127–129; influence of,
129–130; on just war doctrine, 108–110,
112–113; on King's nonviolent movement,
117–118; letter to Forest, 125–126; on limited warfare, 116–119; on mass movements, 128–129; on nonviolent resistance,
114–116, 121–130; on nuclear deterrence,
110–111; on nuclear war, 107–109; and
Original Child Bomb, 113–114; on pacifism, 115–116; on peace, 107–113; on political action, 119–120, 121–122; on right
or duty to bear arms, 118–119; on role of
Christian monasticism, 122; second period,
107; on spiritual base for nonviolent resistance, 125–127; transition from focus on
nuclear pacifism to nonviolence, 137; on
war, silenced by superiors, 114
Meyer, Karl, 89, 92, 93, 148, 185
Military Draft Bill (1940), 53–54
Miller, David, xii, 169, 190; and test case of
draft card burning law, 146–148
Milwaukee Fourteen, 149
Mische, George, 193
Mobilization for Survival, 228
Mobilization to End the War in Vietnam,
142
modern warfare: and CAIP after World War
II, 81–86; popes on, 112. See also nuclear
war; obliteration bombing

Moriarity, John E., 83, 84, 97
Mott, Michael, 112–113
Muldoon, Peter J., 4, 9–10
Murphy, P. Francis, 249–250
Murray, John Courtney, 71, 74, 80–81, 246,
255; and CAIP's position on nuclear issues,
81–82; and Catholic case for selective conscientious objection, 154–155; on just war
doctrine and modern warfare, 81–82; and
"limited" nuclear warfare, 110, 111; writings of, compared with Merton's writings,
107
Muste, A. J., 89, 125, 147; on civil defense,
91; Merton's influence on, 129

Nagasaki. See atomic bombing of Hiroshima
and Nagasaki
Nagle, William J., 83–84, 97
napalm: and symbolism of Catonsville action,
193; and symbolism of draft card burning,
146–147
National Catholic Reporter, 146, 191, 218,
233; on Daniel Berrigan's transfer, 286n43;
and first draft of Challenge of Peace, 251;
questionnaire to bishops on Vietnam War,
164; on Vietnam War, 167
National Catholic War Council, 4. See also
National Catholic Welfare Council
National Catholic Welfare Council (NCWC):
and CAIP, 12, 19–20, 73, 156; Catholic
CO on, 63; and Catholic Worker movement, 24–25; organization of, 4, 14; reorganization into United States Catholic Conference, 156; and Second Vatican Council,
101; Social Action Department, 4–6, 8,
11; support for Franco in Spain, 17–18.
See also Ryan, John A.
National Committee for a Sane Nuclear Policy (SANE): cooperation with rest of peace
movement, 92; origins of, 86
National Conference of Catholic Bishops
(NCCB): and Challenge of Peace, 211, 212;
criticized for lack of support for conscientious objectors and selective conscientious
objectors, 159; establishment of, 156–157;
Merton's influence on, 130; on pacifism,
nonviolence, nuclear pacifism, and just
war doctrine, x; pastoral letter on birth control and Vietnam War, 157–158; Pro-Life
committee of, 245; resolution condemning
Vietnam War, 168–169; and SALT II, 241;
and selective conscientious objection, 165.
See also American Catholic bishops; American Catholic hierarchy